INTERNET HOW-TO

The worldwide data superhighway of the '90s is open and waiting for you...learn how to access people, news, databases, and a wealth of software from your PC with this problem solver

HARRY HENDERSON

WAITE GROUP PRESS™

Corte Madera, California

Publisher: **Mitchell Waite**
Editor-in-Chief: **Scott Calamar**
Editorial Director: **Joel Fugazzotto**
Managing Editor: **Joanne Miller**
Production Director: **Julianne Ososke**
Content Editor: **Heidi Brumbaugh**
Technical Reviewer: **John H. Maurer**
Copy Editor: **Judith Brown**
Design: **Karen Johnston**
Production: **Gracie Artemis**
Illustrations: **Pat Rogondino**
Cover Design: **Michael Rogondino**

© 1994 by The Waite Group, Inc.®
Published by Waite Group Press™, 200 Tamal Plaza, Corte Madera, CA 94925.

Waite Group Press is distributed to bookstores and book wholesalers by Publishers Group West, Box 8843, Emeryville, CA 94662, 1-800-788-3123 (in California 1-510-658-3453).

All rights reserved. No part of this manual shall be reproduced, stored in a retrieval system, or transmitted by any means, electronic, mechanical, photocopying, desktop publishing, recording, or otherwise, without permission from the publisher. No patent liability is assumed with respect to the use of the information contained herein. While every precaution has been taken in the preparation of this book, the publisher and author assume no responsibility for errors or omissions. Neither is any liability assumed for damages resulting from the use of the information contained herein.

All terms mentioned in this book that are known to be registered trademarks, trademarks, or service marks are listed below. In addition, terms suspected of being trademarks, registered trademarks, or service marks have been appropriately capitalized. Waite Group Press cannot attest to the accuracy of this information. Use of a term in this book should not be regarded as affecting the validity of any registered trademark, trademark, or service mark.

The Waite Group is a registered trademark of The Waite Group, Inc.
Waite Group Press and the Waite Group logo are trademarks of The Waite Group, Inc.
America Online is a trademark of America Online, Inc.
Apple and Macintosh are registered trademarks of Apple Computer, Inc.
Bix is a trademark of Delphi Internet Services, Inc.
CompuServe is a registered trademark of CompuServe Incorporated, an H&R Block Company
Delphi is a trademark of Delphi Internet Services, Inc.
GEnie is a registered trademark of General Electric
IBM is a registered trademark and Power PC is a trademark of International Business Machines Corporation
Lotus is a registered trademark of the Lotus Development Corporation
Microsoft Word and Microsoft Windows are registered trademarks of Microsoft Corp.
Pentium is a trademark of Intel, Inc.
Prodigy is a registered servicemark and trademark of Prodigy Services Company
TRS-80 is a trademark of Tandy, Inc.
Unix is a registered trademark of AT&T

Henderson, Harry, 1951-
    The Waite Group Internet how-to/ Harry Henderson.
       p.   cm.
    Includes Index
    ISBN 1-878739-68-9 $34.95
    1. Internet (Computer network)   I. Waite Group. II. Title.
  III. Title: Internet how-to.
TK5105.875.I57H46 1994
384.3'3--dc20

94-19086
CIP

DEDICATION

This book is dedicated to my brother, Bruce Henderson. It all started back in 1978 when he brought his Apple II over. I saw the world inside the box and have been hooked ever since.

ABOUT THE AUTHOR

Harry Henderson has edited and written for The Waite Group for more than ten years. He is co-author of the successful title *Unix Communications* that has introduced Unix mail, news, and other services to many first-time users. He has been enjoying and using the Internet since 1986.

TABLE OF CONTENTS

Introduction *XIII*

Chapter 1   **An Internet Sampler** *1*

Chapter 2   **Getting Started** *11*

Chapter 3   **Using Internet Mail** *39*

Chapter 4   **Reading the Usenet News** *103*

Chapter 5   **Talking to Other Users** *155*

Chapter 6   **Basic File Management** *187*

Chapter 7   **Getting Files with ftp** *223*

Chapter 8   **Advanced File Techniques** *249*

Chapter 9   **Transferring Files Between Your PC and the Internet** *275*

Chapter 10   **Working on Remote Systems with telnet and rlogin** *303*

Chapter 11   **Finding Software with archie** *325*

Chapter 12   **Finding Resources with Gopher** *349*

Chapter 13   **Looking Up Information with WAIS** *383*

Chapter 14   **Navigating the Information Highway with the World Wide Web** *411*

Chapter 15   **Choosing Tools and Using Resources** *439*

                      Index *461*

CONTENTS

Introduction *XIII*

Chapter 1 An Internet Sampler *1*

Chapter 2 Getting Started *11*
- 2.1 Connect my PC to the net *17*
- 2.2 Set up terminal emulation *20*
- 2.3 Get help when starting to use the system *22*
- 2.4 Use windows to manage the Internet session *25*
- 2.5 Get help while using an Internet program *26*
- 2.6 Get answers to frequently asked questions *29*
- 2.7 Use the Internet responsibly *32*
- 2.8 Use the Internet safely and protect my privacy *35*

Chapter 3 Using Internet Mail *39*
- 3.1 Read my mail *43*
- 3.2 Get help while using Elm *48*
- 3.3 Reply to a mail message *49*
- 3.4 Search for messages by sender or subject *52*
- 3.5 Print out a copy of all my mail *53*
- 3.6 Send an original e-mail message *54*
- 3.7 Send mail without bothering with menus *55*
- 3.8 Send someone a file *57*
- 3.9 Figure out what an Internet address means *58*
- 3.10 Find someone's Internet address *60*
- 3.11 Fix and resend returned mail *65*
- 3.12 Forward a message to someone *66*
- 3.13 Get information about incoming mail *68*
- 3.14 Set up an address book *69*
- 3.15 File mail for future reference *73*
- 3.16 Read my mail folders *74*
- 3.17 File mail automatically by sender or subject *76*
- 3.18 Automatically forward my mail to another address *78*
- 3.19 Work with several messages at once *79*
- 3.20 Change Elm's default behavior *80*
- 3.21 Tell people about myself *85*
- 3.22 Add a personal "signature" to my messages *87*
- 3.23 Edit message headers *88*
- 3.24 Run a system command from Elm *89*
- 3.25 Encrypt mail for added security *91*
- 3.26 Exchange mail between the Internet and other networks *92*
- 3.27 Join a mailing list *93*
- 3.28 Learn more about Elm *96*

Chapter 4 Reading the Usenet News *103*
- 4.1 Select and read news articles *108*
- 4.2 Get help while using nn *112*

CONTENTS

  4.3 Use nn's online manual *113*
  4.4 Select consecutive articles *115*
  4.5 Select articles by subject *116*
  4.6 Arrange the menu by conversation "threads" *117*
  4.7 Reply to an article by mail *119*
  4.8 Post a follow-up to an article *121*
  4.9 Post an original news article *122*
  4.10 Subscribe or unsubscribe to a newsgroup *126*
  4.11 Move to a particular newsgroup *128*
  4.12 Move between newsgroups *129*
  4.13 Specify the order in which to see newsgroups *130*
  4.14 Search for newsgroups *132*
  4.15 Save news to a file *134*
  4.16 Save news to a folder *135*
  4.17 Read a news folder *136*
  4.18 Read encrypted articles *137*
  4.19 Save an article with a program or graphic image *138*
  4.20 Save a shell archive *140*
  4.21 Filter out unwanted articles *141*
  4.22 Select articles automatically *143*
  4.23 Catch up with unread news *144*
  4.24 Specify nn's features and behavior *145*
  4.25 Execute system commands from nn *147*
  4.26 Collect news by subject *148*
  4.27 Change nn's key commands *149*
  4.28 Use macros to create shortcut commands *150*
  4.29 Learn more about nn *152*

Chapter 5 Talking to Other Users *155*
  5.1 Send someone a message *159*
  5.2 Reply to a message *161*
  5.3 Recall old messages *162*
  5.4 Carry on an interactive conversation *163*
  5.5 Set up a multiparty conversation *165*
  5.6 Screen out unwanted messages *167*
  5.7 Connect to Internet Relay Chat (IRC) *169*
  5.8 Enter IRC commands *170*
  5.9 Get help while using IRC *171*
  5.10 Give myself an online nickname *173*
  5.11 Find a conversation *174*
  5.12 Carry on a conversation *175*
  5.13 Send private messages *177*
  5.14 Get information about people *178*
  5.15 Keep track of comings and goings *180*
  5.16 Invite someone to join a conversation *181*
  5.17 Start my own channel *181*
  5.18 Deal with harassment *183*
  5.19 Change IRC settings *184*
  5.20 Learn more about IRC *185*

INTERNET HOW-TO

Chapter 6 Basic File Management *187*
    6.1   Enter a Unix command *190*
    6.2   Get help for a Unix command *193*
    6.3   List a directory *195*
    6.4   Change the current directory *199*
    6.5   Read a text file *200*
    6.6   Edit a text file *202*
    6.7   Specify user settings *207*
    6.8   Copy a file *209*
    6.9   Move or rename a file *210*
    6.10 Compare two files *211*
    6.11 Delete a file *212*
    6.12 Make or remove a directory *213*
    6.13 Work with a group of files using wildcards *214*
    6.14 Find a particular file *215*
    6.15 Find text in a file *216*
    6.16 Check my disk space *218*
    6.17 Keep my files private *219*
    6.18 Learn more about Unix *222*

Chapter 7 Getting Files with ftp *223*
    7.1   Connect to an ftp server *227*
    7.2   Get help on ftp commands *229*
    7.3   List directories and files on the remote system *231*
    7.4   Get a file with ftp *233*
    7.5   Read a text file on the remote system *234*
    7.6   Get a binary file *236*
    7.7   Get a group of files *237*
    7.8   Send a file to the remote system *239*
    7.9   Set ftp options *240*
    7.10 Work with the local system while connected to ftp *242*
    7.11 Simplify the connection process *243*
    7.12 Use ftp by mail *245*

Chapter 8 Advanced File Techniques *249*
    8.1   Figure out what to do with a file *256*
    8.2   Prepare a binary file for mailing *257*
    8.3   Restore an encoded binary file *258*
    8.4   Use btoa with binary files *259*
    8.5   Compress a file to save space and time *260*
    8.6   Restore a compressed file *262*
    8.7   Read a compressed text file without uncompressing it *263*
    8.8   Compress and uncompress files for my PC *264*
    8.9   Compress and uncompress files for my Macintosh *267*
    8.10 Package files with tar *269*
    8.11 Unpack a tar file archive *270*
    8.12 Mail or receive a compressed tar archive *271*
    8.13 Create a shell archive *271*
    8.14 Unpack a shell archive *272*

CONTENTS

Chapter 9   Transferring Files Between Your PC and the Internet   *275*

- 9.1   Capture a text file to my PC's hard disk   *281*
- 9.2   Paste text from my PC to the Internet host   *282*
- 9.3   Choose a file transfer protocol   *283*
- 9.4   Download files with Xmodem, Ymodem, or Zmodem   *287*
- 9.5   Upload files with Xmodem, Ymodem, or Zmodem   *289*
- 9.6   Use Kermit to connect to the net   *291*
- 9.7   Download files with Kermit   *293*
- 9.8   Upload files with Kermit   *294*
- 9.9   Get help with Kermit commands   *295*
- 9.10   Use a session file to save communications settings   *298*
- 9.11   Use a login script to simplify connection   *299*
- 9.12   Learn more about telecommunications   *301*

Chapter 10   Working on Remote Systems with telnet and rlogin   *303*

- 10.1   Connect to a service or program   *308*
- 10.2   Log on a remote system   *310*
- 10.3   Get help while using telnet   *311*
- 10.4   Change connections within telnet   *313*
- 10.5   Control a remote program   *314*
- 10.6   Change telnet settings   *316*
- 10.7   Suspend telnet and run local commands   *318*
- 10.8   Make an rlogin connection   *320*
- 10.9   Automate an rlogin connection   *321*
- 10.10   Copy files between systems with rcp   *322*

Chapter 11   Finding Software with archie   *325*

- 11.1   Use an archie client   *328*
- 11.2   Use an interactive archie server   *330*
- 11.3   Get help with archie   *334*
- 11.4   Select archie features   *337*
- 11.5   Specify the type of search   *339*
- 11.6   Control how archie displays information   *341*
- 11.7   Sort the search results   *342*
- 11.8   Have archie mail me the results   *344*
- 11.9   Search by keyword   *345*
- 11.10   Use archie's output with a Unix command   *346*
- 11.11   Use archie by mail   *347*

Chapter 12   Finding Resources with Gopher   *349*

- 12.1   Connect to a Gopher server   *356*
- 12.2   Navigate the Gopher menus   *357*
- 12.3   Get help while using Gopher   *358*
- 12.4   Connect to other Gopher servers   *360*
- 12.5   Use bookmarks to create my own menu   *362*
- 12.6   Identify Gopher item types   *363*
- 12.7   Read a text file   *365*
- 12.8   Get a file by mail   *367*
- 12.9   Save a file   *367*
- 12.10   Download a file   *368*

IX

12.11 Access ftp sites from Gopher *369*
12.12 Use a subject tree *371*
12.13 Use telnet from Gopher *373*
12.14 Find a person in an online directory *374*
12.15 Search a database *376*
12.16 Use Veronica to find Gopher items *376*
12.17 Combine keywords to refine a search *378*
12.18 Use Jughead to search a particular Gopher *380*

Chapter 13 Looking Up Information with WAIS *383*

13.1 Use a WAIS client *387*
13.2 Select a database *390*
13.3 Use the list of servers *393*
13.4 Get help with WAIS *395*
13.5 Perform a WAIS search *396*
13.6 Set WAIS options *399*
13.7 Look at a retrieved document *400*
13.8 Get a copy of a WAIS document *401*
13.9 Refine my search *402*
13.10 Use WAIS through Gopher *405*
13.11 Do a streamlined WAIS search *408*
13.12 Learn more about WAIS *409*

Chapter 14 Navigating the Information Highway with the World Wide Web *411*

14.1 Connect to the World Wide Web with Lynx *415*
14.2 View a document *416*
14.3 Follow a hypertext link *418*
14.4 Get help with Lynx *420*
14.5 Search for text in a document *422*
14.6 Get a copy of a document *424*
14.7 Send a comment to a document's author *425*
14.8 Recall a previously seen document *427*
14.9 Use bookmarks for fast navigation *428*
14.10 Use URLs for direct access to services *429*
14.11 Perform a database or index search *431*
14.12 Read Usenet news from the Web *432*
14.13 Look at an ftp site through the Web *435*
14.14 Search Gopher menus from the Web *437*

Chapter 15 Choosing Tools and Using Resources *439*

15.1 Approach the Internet with a question or problem *441*
15.2 Choose the right communication tool *443*
15.3 Choose the right data retrieval tool *444*
15.4 Choose the right navigation tool *446*
15.5 Use The Desktop Internet Reference *447*
15.6 Find services with Hytelnet *453*
15.7 Create my own resource guide *456*
15.8 Find out more about the Internet *458*

Index *461*

ACKNOWLEDGMENTS

A book like this can't be done without the collaboration of many talented and creative individuals in its conception, execution, and production. I would particularly like to thank:

Mitch Waite, for creating the unique Waite Group approach to technical writing and the presentation of information and for encouraging me to apply it to the new frontier of the Internet.

Scott Calamar and Joel Fugazzotto, for creating the concept for this book and helping me turn the proposal into detailed structure.

Joanne Miller, for firm but patient management of the writing, editing, and production process.

Heidi Brumbaugh, for perceptive and helpful editing and for fixing all my parentheses. (I think I know where the period goes now.)

John H. Maurer, for helpful technical comments on the manuscript.

Judith Brown, for careful copy editing.

Dear Reader,

What is a book? Is it perpetually fated to be inky words on a paper page? Or can a book simply be something that inspires—feeding your head with ideas and creativity regardless of the medium? The latter, I believe. That's why I'm always pushing our books to a higher plane; using new technology to reinvent the medium.

I wrote my first book in 1973, *Projects in Sights, Sounds, and Sensations*. I like to think of it as our first multimedia book. In the years since then, I've learned that people want to *experience* information, not just passively absorb it—they want interactive MTV in a book. With this in mind, I started my own publishing company and published *Master C*, a book/disk package that turned the PC into a C language instructor. Then we branched out to computer graphics with *Fractal Creations*, which included a color poster, 3D glasses, and a totally rad fractal generator. Ever since, we've included disks and other goodies with most of our books. *Virtual Reality Creations* is bundled with 3D Fresnel viewing goggles and *Walkthroughs and Flybys CD* comes with a multimedia CD-ROM. We've made complex multimedia accessible for any PC user with *Ray Tracing Creations, Multimedia Creations, Making Movies on your PC, Image Lab*, and three books on Fractals.

The Waite Group continues to publish innovative multimedia books on cutting-edge topics, and of course the programming books that make up our heritage. Being a programmer myself, I appreciate clear guidance through a tricky OS, so our books come bundled with disks and CDs loaded with code, utilities, and custom controls.

By 1995, The Waite Group will have published 150 books. Our next step is to develop a new type of book, an interactive, multimedia experience involving the reader on many levels.

With this new book, you'll be trained by a computer-based instructor with infinite patience, run a simulation to visualize the topic, play a game that shows you different aspects of the subject, interact with others on-line, and have instant access to a large database on the subject. For traditionalists, there will be a full-color, paper-based book.

In the meantime, they've wired the White House for hi-tech; the information super-highway has been proposed; and computers, communication, entertainment, and information are becoming inseparable. To travel in this Digital Age you'll need guidebooks. The Waite Group offers such guidance for the most important software—your mind.

We hope you enjoy this book. For a color catalog, just fill out and send in the Satisfaction Report Card at the back of the book.

Sincerely,

Mitchell Waite

Mitchell Waite
Publisher

WAITE
GROUP
PRESS™

Introduction

> "The technology that makes virtual communities possible has the potential to bring enormous leverage to ordinary citizens at relatively little cost—intellectual leverage, social leverage, commercial leverage, and most important, political leverage. But the technology will not in itself fulfill that potential; the latent technological potential must be used intelligently and deliberately by an informed population."
>
> Howard Rheingold, *The Virtual Community*

WHY I WROTE THIS BOOK

The 1990s are turning out to be the decade of the Internet. Pundits and science fiction writers speak of "the matrix" or "cyberspace," an electronic world in which we will carry on an increasing part of our social and professional lives—job hunting, sharing opinions and personal experiences, collaborating on projects, researching databases, playing games, and even falling in love. The Clinton administration talks about "data superhighways" that will revolutionize every aspect of communications, and even the comic strip *Doonesbury*, an infallible trend-spotter, has chronicled the rise and fall of a cyberspace romance.

Depending on how you look at it, the Internet is either the next great revolution, akin to Gutenberg's invention of movable type, or "a set of interconnected networks using the TCP/IP protocol." The first definition, the cocktail party one, is inspiring and thought-provoking. As Howard Rheingold suggests, there's no better time than now to start thinking about how being part of a global communications and data-sharing community will change our lives. The latter definition, dry, technical (and somewhat obsolete) is useful if you want to develop software for use on the Internet, or if you've been entrusted with the job of managing an Internet site. But somewhere between punditry and wiring diagrams you need the practical steps that will unlock all of the resources and turn you into an effective Internet user.

The Waite Group Internet How-To, like all of the books in the How-To series, emphasizes a step-by-step, problem-solving approach to using the Internet. For our purposes the Internet (also referred to simply as the net) can be defined as "a widespread and inexpensive set of facilities and services that lets you connect your PC so you can communicate with people, keep up with news, and tap into data and program files." My goal in writing this book is to show you how to quickly use the most important, exciting, and useful services the Internet makes available. I will include a bit of philosophy or technical detail only when it helps illuminate your hands-on learning.

GETTING STARTED

As the word implies, the Internet is a connected "web" of computer networks, each of which may have hundreds or even thousands of computers participating. Using the

INTERNET HOW-TO

Internet begins with connecting to a computer called an *Internet site*, as described in Chapter 2. The Internet site serves as your *host* and provides you with services such as mail, news, or file access. Once you're connected to that host computer, you run a variety of programs that provide the services you want to access. You use one program to send or receive electronic mail, another program to read or post news messages, and yet another program to download programs and data files for your PC from *archive sites*. You also have at your disposal a facility that lets you run programs on other computers by "remote control," whether you're in New York or New Zealand, Minneapolis or Minsk. In effect, you tap into computing power all over the world. And if you're not sure where to find the program or data file you need, yet another assortment of programs stands ready to skim over the net and root them out for you.

Learning to use the Internet is somewhat different from mastering commercial software packages such as Microsoft Word or Lotus 1-2-3. While quite complex, commercial products are self-contained: you buy the box, open it, install the software on your computer, and follow the on screen instructions (or read the manual).

With the Internet, however, you can't go down to your local Egghead or Software, Etc. and say "I want to buy Internet 6.0." There's no box, no disks, and the friendly salesperson probably won't be much help.

Working with the Internet is also different from being online with commercial information services (such as Prodigy or CompuServe) or dialing up your local computer bulletin board (BBS). While they vary in size and complexity, these information services house all their computing power and services under one roof, giving you menu-driven access to whatever facilities they choose to provide.

The Internet, on the other hand, is a vast cooperative effort that includes educational institutions, businesses, government, and individual users, involving (at this writing) at least a couple million computers and 20 million people (and growing by leaps and bounds). If Microsoft Word is like an office and CompuServe is like a library, then the Internet is like a whole city in its complexity and diversity. No one "owns" the Internet, any more than someone "owns" the city of New York. The individual organizations and networks that make up the Internet have evolved practices, customs, and local rules to manage this burgeoning resource, but there is no single Policy Manual or User's Guide.

Fortunately, the fact that "the Internet software" is really a constantly expanding set of individual programs has a plus side. You don't have to commit yourself to buying a $500 package or paying $12 an hour for online access, and you don't have to learn everything at once. For a dollar or two an hour you can start with electronic mail (nowadays you can reach just about anyone who is connected to *anything*, including the high-priced commercial spreads). Once you're comfortable with that, you can have a look at Usenet, the Internet's news service, and pick a few of the hundreds of available forums (*newsgroups*) to read. A bit later, you can learn how to use a program called ftp to fetch programs and data files that your new friends and acquaintances on the net have recommended. Next, you can learn how another program called telnet gives you "remote control" of any one of hundreds of computers that provide their electronic visitors with facilities at no additional charge.

And after that, well, the possibilities are limitless. You can choose from a variety of services and obtain whatever information is vital, useful, or just intriguing in some way: weather reports and earthquake predictions, Supreme Court decisions, White House press releases, scientific papers, dozens of classics of world literature, jokes, job openings, dating services, car repair tips, movie reviews, software bug reports...you name it. (And did I mention that you can play games, from chess to elaborate dungeon-delving adventures, with your fellow cyberspace denizens?)

WHAT YOU NEED

To get started learning the Internet with *Internet How-To* you need only the following: a PC and a modem, some communications software, a little money, and a couple hours a week to try things out.

Unlike that $500 box of software, the hardware requirements for using the Internet are truly minimal. Any IBM PC-compatible or Macintosh will work fine. You don't need the latest Pentium or Power PC processor, heaps of memory, or a big hard disk. For that matter, just about any old microcomputer or terminal will do (even a dated and battered TRS-80, Commodore 64, or Apple II), as long as it has communications software that lets it connect to other computers via a phone line.

Unless you're directly connected to an Internet host (perhaps on a local area network), you'll need a modem and a phone line to make the connection. Today, 2400 baud modems are cheaper than many movies at the local video emporium, but you really should consider paying a little more and getting a modem that runs at 9600 baud or faster—it will save you time when you start transferring big programs or other files between the Internet site and your PC.

A variety of communications programs work with the Internet. You can use fancy software if you want, but the examples in this book use the no-frills Terminal program that comes free with Microsoft Windows. The main requirement is that your software be able to mimic, or *emulate*, one of the standard terminals recognized by Internet systems. (Just about any software sold today can emulate the VT-100 terminal, and that's pretty much the lingua franca of the Internet now.)

Once you have the hardware and software in hand, how do you find an Internet site to connect to? Well, if you aren't a student or professional who is already connected to the Internet through your school or business, you'll need to obtain Internet access through one of a growing list of commercial Internet sites. Pricing plans vary, but many are surprisingly inexpensive; see Chapter 2 for some tips.

WHAT YOU'LL LEARN

Before you start using the individual programs that open up the Internet for you, it's a good idea to get an overview of the variety of services and resources the net offers.

Chapter 1, *An Internet Sampler*, surveys the major Internet facilities that are discussed in this book: mail, news, file transfer, remote access, and a variety of programs that search for and retrieve information. Some example screens will give you an idea of what the Internet looks like and how it works when you're interacting with it.

Chapter 2, *Getting Started*, covers the basic things you must do to use the Internet at all: finding an Internet site, getting online, and knowing where to go for help when you need it. The rest of the chapters each deal with a particular aspect of the Internet.

Chapter 3, *Using Internet Mail*, gets you started with probably the single most useful Internet service: electronic mail. Our program of choice for this chapter is Elm, a mail program that is very easy to use, yet supports advanced features. You'll also learn how to work with Internet addresses and solve returned mail problems.

Chapter 4, *Reading the Usenet News*, introduces the second most popular Internet application: the Usenet newsgroups. The program I've picked for this chapter is nn, a news reading program that does for news what Elm does for mail. You'll find easy menu-driven access to messages on hundreds of topics.

Chapter 5, *Talking to Other Users*, shows you how to access the real time part of the net. While certainly not the most important Internet application, programs such as send/reply, talk, and IRC can provide an enjoyable social outlet.

Chapter 6, *Basic File Management*, might be subtitled "the bit of Unix you need to get by." Once you're receiving mail and saving news messages, you're going to have to cope with the files that pile up in your home directory at the Internet site. Fortunately the commands and file management techniques you need are simple. (If you already know Unix or even DOS, you can give this chapter a quick review and move on.)

Chapter 7, *Getting Files with ftp*, is about a favorite activity of netters: grabbing software, graphics files, articles, databases, or whatever from archive sites that are packed to the virtual rafters with goodies of all kinds. ftp is like a super "file copy" command that lets you reach out and get copies of these publicly available files for your own use.

Chapter 8, *Advanced File Techniques*, deals with some of the complications that come with certain kinds of files, such as files that have been compressed to save space. You'll see step-by-step how to "unpack" such files so they're ready to use.

Chapter 9, *Transferring Files Between Your PC and the Internet*, has more details about managing the dial-up connection of your PC to the net. In particular, you'll learn how to download files from your Internet account to your PC, and upload files from your PC to the Internet site. Programs featured in this chapter include Kermit and Xmodem.

Chapter 10, *Working on Remote Systems with telnet and rlogin*, shows you how to run programs on computers all over the Internet. By running such programs with the telnet command you can get weather reports, library catalog records, and a host of other services.

Chapter 11, *Finding Software with archie*, begins the transition from the basic Internet access tools to the services that help you find the information and files you want. This chapter introduces archie, a program that finds out for you where a given file can be obtained on the net.

Chapter 12, *Finding Resources with Gopher*, deals with the problem of how you can find resources by topic when you don't know specific file names. Gopher presents a series of menus that let you select services and files, browse directories, and otherwise access the resources of an Internet site. (There's even a kind of "super Gopher" called Veronica. She specializes in finding the right Gopher menus for you to use!)

Chapter 13, *Looking Up Information with WAIS*, shows you how to use WAIS (Wide Area Information Service) databases to look up information ranging from library books and periodicals to weather data. There are hundreds of WAIS databases to choose from, and the vast majority of them are available free of charge.

Chapter 14, *Navigating the Information Highway with the World Wide Web*, introduces an alternative approach to managing information: *hypertext*. With the Web and a program called a *browser*, you read documents and click on *links* that take you to other documents and services. The result is a kind of living, interconnected, interactive encyclopedia.

Chapter 15, *Choosing Tools and Using Resources*, sums things up by taking a broad view of the different strategies for using the Internet. With the aid of tables and lists of guidelines, you will learn how to choose the appropriate tool for a given task. The chapter also introduces you to directories of Internet services that you can have at hand on your PC as you connect to the net.

A NOTE ABOUT KEYS

Most how-tos in this book will include steps where you type a keystroke or command. When you are to press a single key (or sometimes two keys in succession), the keys are shown in keycaps, like this (KEYCAPS). You often do not have to press (ENTER) after these keys, but this varies with the program.

Sometimes you need to press the Control (CTRL) along with another key. For example, (CTRL)-(D) Means to press the (CONTROL) key together with the (D) key. While the (D) key is shown in uppercase, you can actually press either the uppercase or lowercase letter while holding down the (CONTROL) key.

When you are to type a command consisting of a word or phrase, the command is shown in a monospace listing font, like this: `pwd` or `xmrb`. After you type a command like this, you need to press (ENTER) to send the command to the computer.

A NOTE ABOUT SCREEN DISPLAYS

The Internet is constantly changing. During the month or so between the time the final draft of this book was written and the time it came back from the editors, several screen displays had changed. This is inevitable. Just keep in mind that the basic commands used with the programs we discuss should not change, although a new version of a program might include some new commands. The menus and displays used by the services illustrated in Chapters 10 through 14 (sites accessed through telnet, Gopher, WAIS, and the Web) will no doubt be somewhat different by the time you see them. I believe my recipes are trustworthy, but keep in mind that you may be working with a slightly different set of ingredients.

HOW TO USE THIS BOOK

Starting with Chapter 2, each chapter in this book is organized into a series of "how-tos" (Figure I-1). These entries break down a general subject (such as Internet mail) into its various aspects, starting with the most basic and working toward the more advanced and esoteric. For example, the discussion of mail starts with such basics as reading a mail message, replying to a message, and finding someone's mail address. Eventually it proceeds to such things as keeping messages neatly arranged in "folders" or sending mail to users on other networks such as CompuServe.

To help you access the information you need, each chapter begins with an overview of its subject. This is followed by a list of the how-tos in the chapter, with a sentence or two describing how each is used. A "Related Topics" table refers you to other chapters where you may find useful information in connection with the material being discussed.

Each how-to begins with a statement of the *problem:* what do you want to accomplish here, and why is it important? The next section, *technique,* explains the general approach to getting the job done. This is followed by a series of *steps:* the decisions you make, the commands or keystrokes you enter, and so on. When appropriate, a *how it works* section then explains in greater detail what you've done, so you can better apply the knowledge to similar situations. Often a *comment* concludes the how-to by pointing out things you should watch for or describing a resource that might help you learn more.

INTERNET HOW-TO

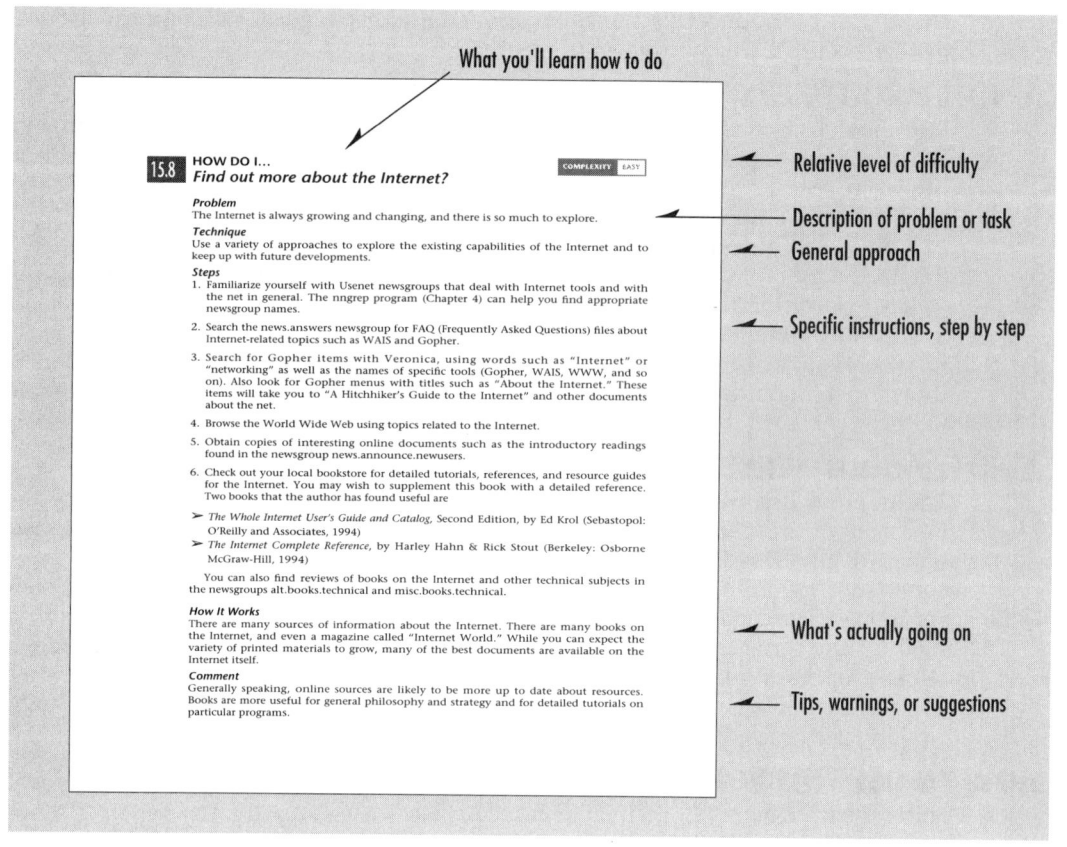

Figure I-1 A sample how do I

    This how-to approach combines the learning process of a tutorial with the utility of a reference. By reading through a chapter's how-tos you learn how to use programs step-by-step. But if you already know the basics of how to use a program such as Elm or ftp, and just want to find out how to go about doing something, all you have to do is to skim the how-to summaries at the beginning of the chapter until you find the section you need.

    The Internet is vast and complex, but it need not be intimidating if you take the step-by-step approach presented here. I cannot claim to teach you everything you might need to know in one book. No one can, really. When you're dealing with such a vast sea of information, the essential thing is to know how to fish.

    Let's begin!

XVIII

An Internet Sampler

Just reading the table of contents can't give you a real feeling for what this book covers, or for how you will interact with the diverse services that are waiting for you on the Internet. In order to give you a better idea of what's in store, this chapter previews the basic tools you will be learning about in the coming chapters. As you read what follows, keep in mind that this is intended to be an overview: savor the flavor but don't worry about the details.

Getting Connected

Chapter 2 deals with the necessary preliminaries for Internet access: how to find an Internet site, how to connect your PC to the Internet computer, and how to get oriented in general. You'll also learn that there are a variety of forms of online help that can assist you with particular programs and environments. While Internet help usually isn't as easy to use as the help supplied with a Windows or Macintosh program, some Internet sites have created menus of files that can be helpful to you as you start your Internet career. Figure 1-1 shows one such menu provided by The WELL (The Whole Earth 'Lectronic Link of Sausalito, California, a system much beloved by your author). Menus like this are just one way to get help while you're using the Internet. Later, I'll outline a strategy for getting help with any Internet program or service.

Chapter 2 also contains some guidelines to follow if you want to be considered a responsible member of the online community. A few of these are legal guidelines (with some exceptions, you can't use the net to advertise products or send out invoices, for example). Most of the guidelines are a mixture of common sense and the same courtesy that is appropriate in face-to-face meetings. This will get you off on the right foot.

Gonna Sit Right Down and Write Myself a Letter

Chances are pretty good that you already have some familiarity with the concept of electronic mail or e-mail. Many companies and college campuses provide their own in-house e-mail systems. National information services such as CompuServe, GEnie, America Online, and Prodigy provide ways for subscribers to send each other messages.

Internet provides a variety of mail programs (such as the ubiquitous Unix mail and mailx programs) and lets you send mail not only to millions of other Internet users, but

INTERNET HOW-TO

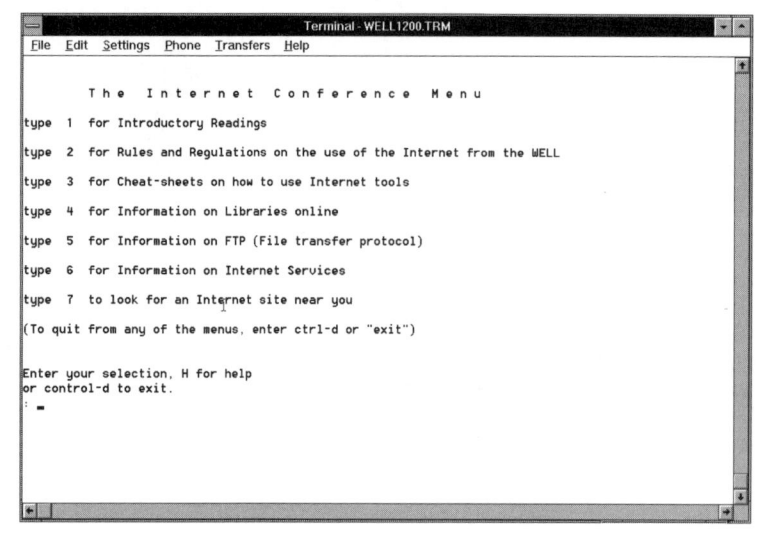

```
                  Terminal - WELL1200.TRM
 File  Edit  Settings  Phone  Transfers  Help

         T h e   I n t e r n e t   C o n f e r e n c e   M e n u
 type  1  for Introductory Readings
 type  2  for Rules and Regulations on the use of the Internet from the WELL
 type  3  for Cheat-sheets on how to use Internet tools
 type  4  for Information on Libraries online
 type  5  for Information on FTP (File transfer protocol)
 type  6  for Information on Internet Services
 type  7  to look for an Internet site near you
 (To quit from any of the menus, enter ctrl-d or "exit")

 Enter your selection, H for help
 or control-d to exit.
 :
```

Figure 1-1 An Internet help menu

to the users of all those other information services as well. This book concentrates on Elm, a mail program that combines the simplicity of menu-driven access with a good assortment of optional features. Figure 1-2 shows the screen you'll see when you read your mail with Elm. Reading a message is as easy as typing its number and pressing (ENTER). As you'll see when you read Chapter 3, it's equally easy to reply to a mail message or file the message away in a folder for future reference.

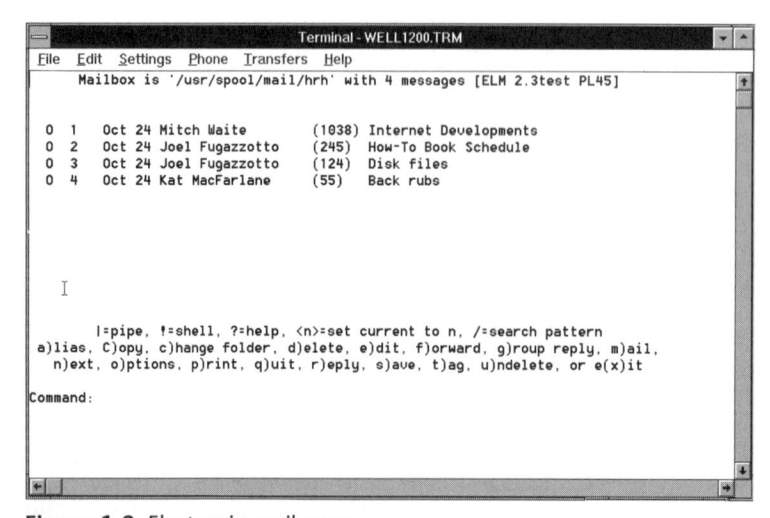

```
                  Terminal - WELL1200.TRM
 File  Edit  Settings  Phone  Transfers  Help
         Mailbox is '/usr/spool/mail/hrh' with 4 messages [ELM 2.3test PL45]

 O  1   Oct 24  Mitch Waite        (1038)  Internet Developments
 O  2   Oct 24  Joel Fugazzotto    (245)   How-To Book Schedule
 O  3   Oct 24  Joel Fugazzotto    (124)   Disk files
 O  4   Oct 24  Kat MacFarlane     (55)    Back rubs




         |=pipe, !=shell, ?=help, <n>=set current to n, /=search pattern
 a)lias, C)opy, c)hange folder, d)elete, e)dit, f)orward, g)roup reply, m)ail,
     n)ext, o)ptions, p)rint, q)uit, r)eply, s)ave, t)ag, u)ndelete, or e(x)it

 Command:
```

Figure 1-2 Electronic mail menu

I Read the News Today Oh Boy

After you've mastered mail, the Internet's extensive news service is the next logical step. News messages look very much like mail messages: one big difference is that a news message is read by thousands of people at once. What sort of news might this be? Just about everything, but the most important kinds of news for many people involve technical discussions about operating systems, programming languages, and software. If you're not primarily a computer person, however, there is also a wide variety of news on political and social events, recreational activities, and the arts.

The other important thing about Internet news is that it isn't a one-way street. Most of us can't talk back to Tom Brokaw or Connie Chung if we don't agree with something we see on the tube. (Well, we can talk, but they won't hear us.) On the Internet, however, you can post a follow-up to a news message and give your own take on the matter under discussion. Your follow-up message will appear on the screen of everyone who reads this news "thread." Indeed, although it's called "news," Internet's Usenet news is more like a large collection of mini bulletin boards devoted to a wide variety of topics. You can *lurk* (read without replying) or join the conversation.

Figure 1-3 shows the news program described in Chapter 4, called nn. As Elm does for mail, nn arranges the news messages in each topic (newsgroup) in menu form, so you can easily select what you want to read. The newsgroup shown here, news.announce.newusers, is particularly valuable to the beginner because it includes a number of documents that have been designed to help you understand and use the news facilities. Chapter 4 gives you the scoop on how to read and write news.

Yakkety-Yak: You Can Talk Back

As we move to Chapter 5, things get a little wilder. In this chapter, we show you how you can talk to people on the net in real time as fast as you can type. You can use a pair of simple programs called send and reply to exchange messages with another user

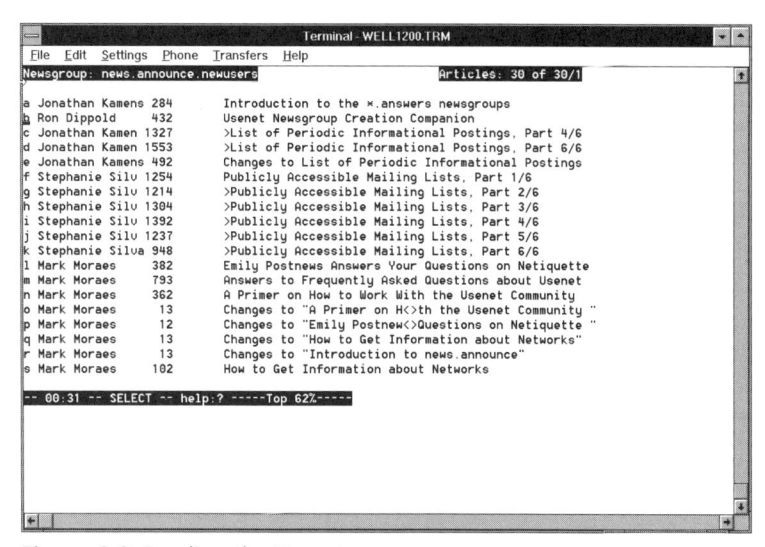

Figure 1-3 Reading the Usenet news

INTERNET HOW-TO

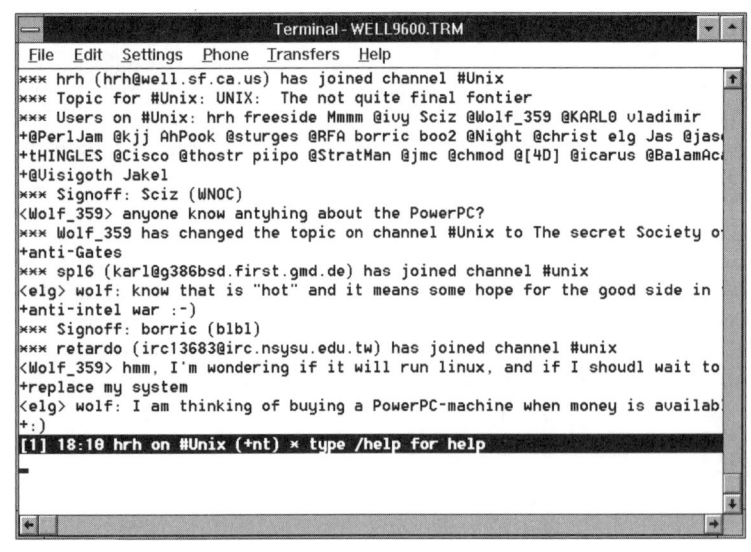

Figure 1-4 Talking on IRC

online. The "talk" program lets you make a continuous connection and type messages back and forth (some versions let more than two people talk together). Finally, the Internet Relay Chat (IRC) program is the Internet's answer to CB radio. Every hour of every day, on hundreds of separate "channels," users are talking in real time about every topic imaginable. Figure 1-4 shows an IRC session in progress.

Rank and File Maneuvers

You don't have to be a power user to enjoy the Internet, but there *are* some commands you'll want to know. Chapter 6 reviews the basic commands that you'll type at the system prompt to work with files on the Internet machine. Since most sites on the Internet use Unix, that's the operating system you'll learn about. Unix has a reputation for being as easy to use as an underwater bicycle. Actually, though, you're only going to need a handful of commands to be able to view, copy, move, and edit files—and you'll see that they're really quite simple after all. Figure 1-5 shows the author's home directory on The WELL and the use of the Unix "more" command to get a look at the contents of a file. When you're done with Chapter 6, you'll be able to keep your own Internet "home away from home" clean and well-organized.

All You Can Eat (and Then Some)

Now that you've learned how to keep your room clean, it's time to go back to the fun stuff. Chapter 7 shows you how you can get files from hundreds of sites on the Internet. What kind of files? Thousands of programs for your PC, Macintosh, or other computer. (Many are free, some are *shareware* requiring a modest payment if you find the program to be useful.) Figure 1-6 shows how easy it is to get a copy of a file from an Internet archive site.

1 🌐 **AN INTERNET SAMPLER**

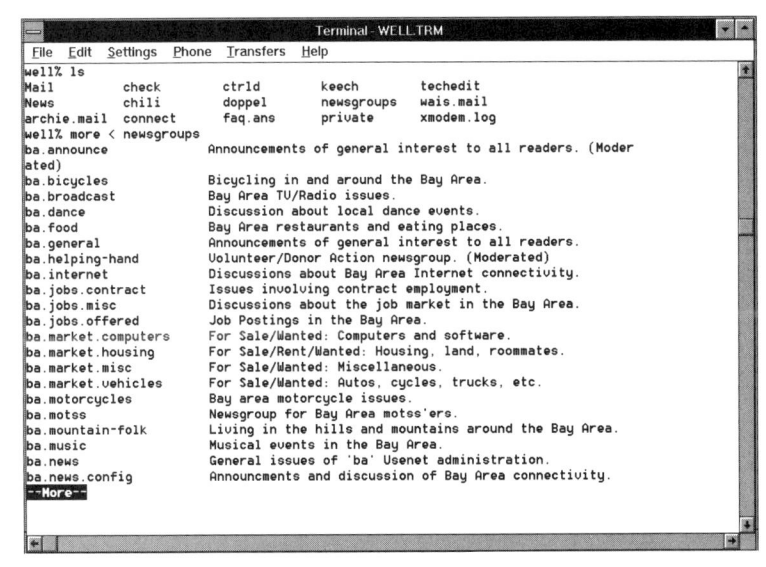

```
                          Terminal - WELL.TRM
 File  Edit  Settings  Phone  Transfers  Help
well% ls
Mail         check        ctrld        keech        techedit
News         chili        doppel       newsgroups   wais.mail
archie.mail  connect      faq.ans      private      xmodem.log
well% more < newsgroups
ba.announce              Announcements of general interest to all readers. (Moder
ated)
ba.bicycles              Bicycling in and around the Bay Area.
ba.broadcast             Bay Area TV/Radio issues.
ba.dance                 Discussion about local dance events.
ba.food                  Bay Area restaurants and eating places.
ba.general               Announcements of general interest to all readers.
ba.helping-hand          Volunteer/Donor Action newsgroup. (Moderated)
ba.internet              Discussions about Bay Area Internet connectivity.
ba.jobs.contract         Issues involving contract employment.
ba.jobs.misc             Discussions about the job market in the Bay Area.
ba.jobs.offered          Job Postings in the Bay Area.
ba.market.computers      For Sale/Wanted: Computers and software.
ba.market.housing        For Sale/Rent/Wanted: Housing, land, roommates.
ba.market.misc           For Sale/Wanted: Miscellaneous.
ba.market.vehicles       For Sale/Wanted: Autos, cycles, trucks, etc.
ba.motorcycles           Bay area motorcycle issues.
ba.motss                 Newsgroup for Bay Area motss'ers.
ba.mountain-folk         Living in the hills and mountains around the Bay Area.
ba.music                 Musical events in the Bay Area.
ba.news                  General issues of 'ba' Usenet administration.
ba.news.config           Announcments and discussion of Bay Area connectivity.
--More--
```

Figure 1-5 Working with your home directory

Chapter 8 shows you how to deal with some of the special kinds of files you may encounter, (for example, files that have been compressed to save disk space and transmission time).

Once the file has been moved to your Internet site, you'll need to get it home to your PC. Chapter 9 delves into the details of managing the dial-up connection between your PC and the Internet site. There are a number of alternatives that you can use to

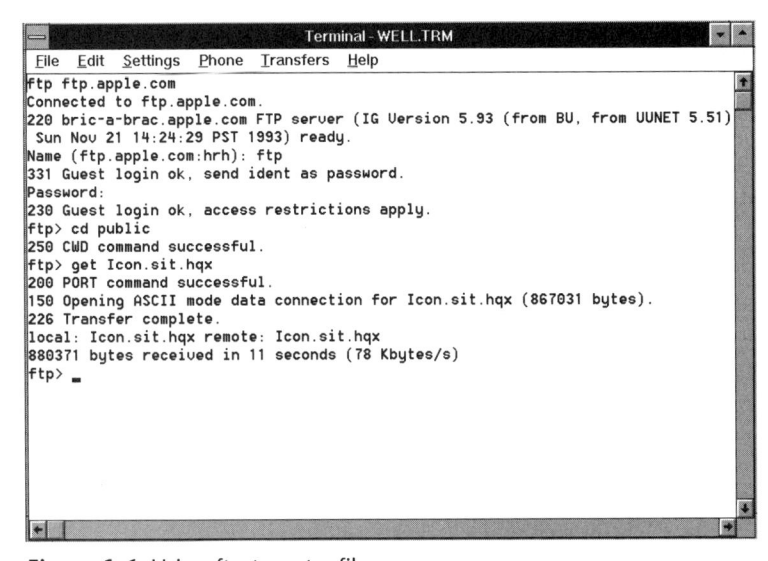

```
                          Terminal - WELL.TRM
 File  Edit  Settings  Phone  Transfers  Help
ftp ftp.apple.com
Connected to ftp.apple.com.
220 bric-a-brac.apple.com FTP server (IG Version 5.93 (from BU, from UUNET 5.51)
 Sun Nov 21 14:24:29 PST 1993) ready.
Name (ftp.apple.com:hrh): ftp
331 Guest login ok, send ident as password.
Password:
230 Guest login ok, access restrictions apply.
ftp> cd public
250 CWD command successful.
ftp> get Icon.sit.hqx
200 PORT command successful.
150 Opening ASCII mode data connection for Icon.sit.hqx (867031 bytes).
226 Transfer complete.
local: Icon.sit.hqx remote: Icon.sit.hqx
880371 bytes received in 11 seconds (78 Kbytes/s)
ftp>
```

Figure 1-6 Using ftp to get a file

INTERNET HOW-TO

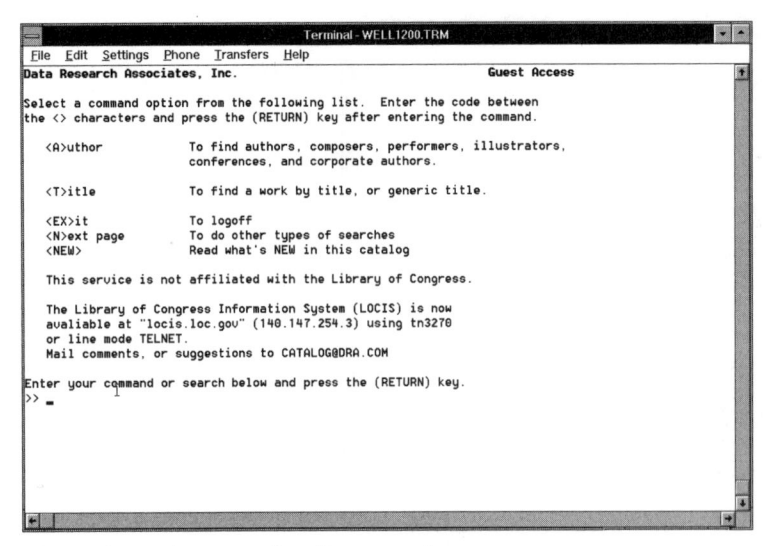

```
Data Research Associates, Inc.                          Guest Access

Select a command option from the following list.  Enter the code between
the <> characters and press the (RETURN) key after entering the command.

    <A>uthor           To find authors, composers, performers, illustrators,
                       conferences, and corporate authors.

    <T>itle            To find a work by title, or generic title.

    <EX>it             To logoff
    <N>ext page        To do other types of searches
    <NEW>              Read what's NEW in this catalog

This service is not affiliated with the Library of Congress.

The Library of Congress Information System (LOCIS) is now
available at "locis.loc.gov" (140.147.254.3) using tn3270
or line mode TELNET.
Mail comments, or suggestions to CATALOG@DRA.COM

Enter your command or search below and press the (RETURN) key.
>> _
```

Figure 1-7 Using an online library catalog

move data back and forth: the chapter looks at Kermit and Xmodem, as well as variations such as Ymodem and Zmodem.

Remote Control

One more fundamental tool you need to access the Internet is the telnet program. Once you're connected to your local Internet site, telnet lets you connect to any other site on the net. Once connected, you log on and can run a variety of publicly accessible programs. Figure 1-7 shows a site that provides Library of Congress catalog records for bibliographic searching.

Another service available through telnet is current weather forecasts for hundreds of locations across the United States. Figure 1-8 shows a connection to a service called the Weather Underground. A simple menu lets you search for kinds of forecasts or find a forecast for a particular community or region.

These are only two examples of programs you can run with telnet. As you explore the net, you'll find hundreds more.

archie Finds the Goods

It's one thing to be told "here's a neat file I found at such and such a site." You just fire up ftp and get it. But suppose you know a program or other file exists, but you don't know who on the net might have it? Chapter 11 presents archie, a program that keeps a database of available files. Once you've used telnet to connect to an archie server, you can search for files using complete or partial file names. Figure 1-9 shows a typical archie display after asking archie to find files related to the Xmodem file-transfer program (discussed in Chapter 9).

The Electronic "Yellow Pages"

The Internet provides a variety of powerful tools that you can use to find the information you need. One of the most ubiquitous is called Gopher. Gopher is a kind of

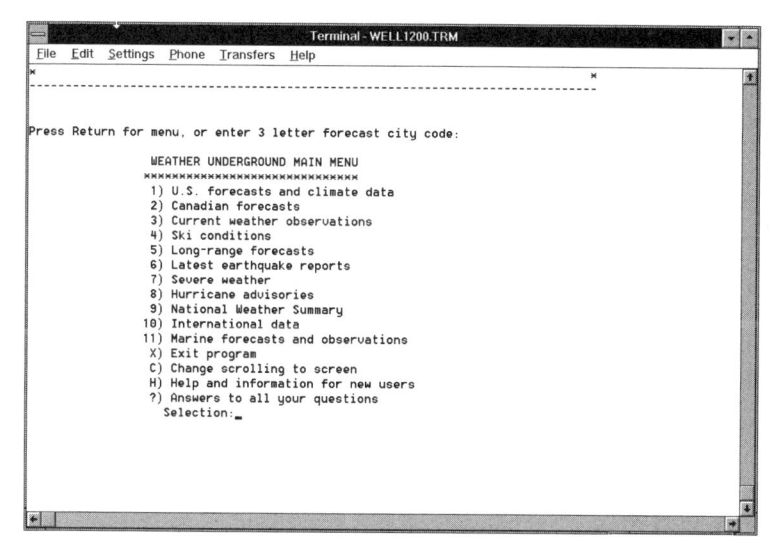

Figure 1-8 Getting the latest weather

intermediary between you and the providers of Internet services and resources. A program called the *Gopher client* presents menus representing different kinds of information it gets from *Gopher servers*. As you choose from the menus (some of which lead to other menus), the Gopher connects to the service providers and automatically sends the requested information to the Internet site to which you're connected. The big plus is that you don't have to know filenames, addresses, or other details. Figure 1-10 shows The WELL's Gopher.

There are thousands of Gophers out there on the net, and many are specialized to suit the needs of the people who are most likely to use them. (A Gopher for a university

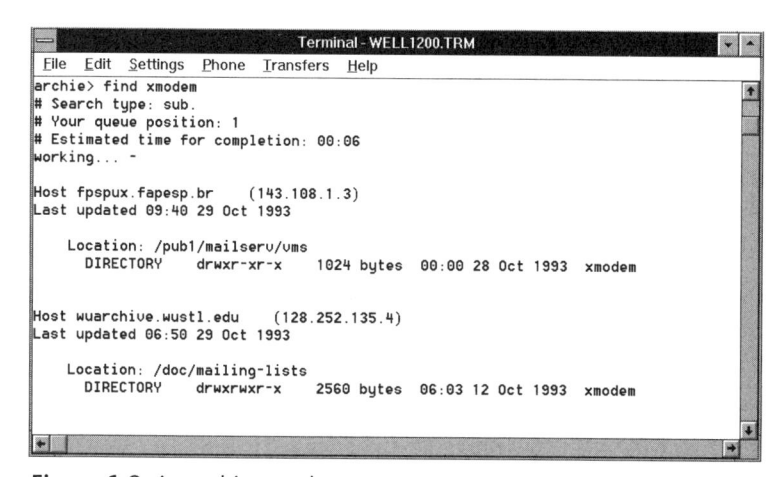

Figure 1-9 An archie search

INTERNET HOW-TO

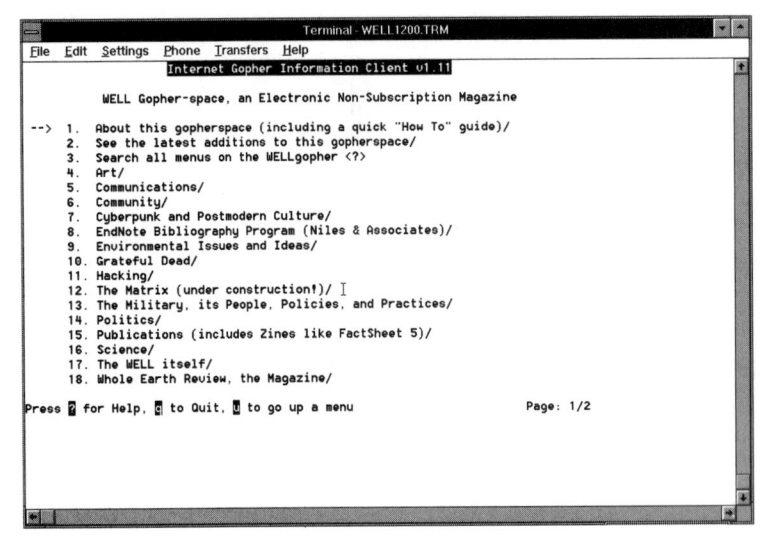

Figure 1-10 A Gopher menu

computer is likely to have quite different menus from those of a Gopher for a software company, though there will likely be *some* overlap.)

So how do you find the Gopher you need? With a "super Gopher" called Veronica. Think of Veronica as a Gopher that knows about the contents of all the other Gophers. With Veronica, you can input some keywords and get a list of all the Gopher menus whose descriptions include those words.

The Library of the Future—Today

Gophers and their ilk aren't the only tools that will help you make sense of the Internet and zero in on the parts that most interest you. While Gopher is oriented toward finding files, WAIS (Wide Area Information Service) finds data in databases around the world, drawing from hundreds of data sources to answer your query. You pick one or more sources and then specify keywords that describe what you're searching for. As with many other skills, database searching requires practice. Chapter 13 will get you started with some simple but effective strategies.

Suppose, for example, that you are doing a research paper on earthquakes and you want to find scientific papers, weekly summaries of seismic data, earthquake predictions from various sources, and tips to help you prepare your family for the Big One. Figure 1-11 shows the beginning of a WAIS search.

WAIS first presents a menu of information sources (databases). You pick the databases whose descriptions most closely match the kind of information you are seeking. (Figure 1-11 shows an earth sciences database.) If you type in the keyword "San Andreas," you receive 40 possible items of which a selection is shown. (This search will need to be refined, perhaps by an additional search on the keyword "earthquake.")

A different approach to organizing information on the net is called World Wide Web (WWW). This program uses a hypertext approach that lets you use a program called a browser to move through a "web" of keywords and related topics until you find the

1 AN INTERNET SAMPLER

Figure 1-11 A WAIS search screen

information you seek. Again, the process of actually retrieving information and transferring it to your local Internet site is automatic and transparent. Figure 1-12 shows an initial WWW screen. In keeping with its powerful features, the Web takes some time to master. Chapter 14 covers the WWW in detail, using a browser called Lynx that is well-suited to dial-up use.

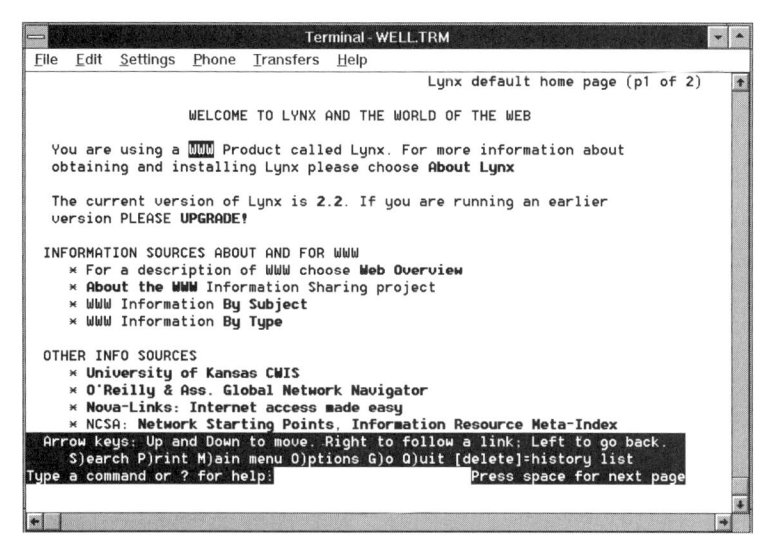

Figure 1-12 Main screen for World Wide Web

Moving On

As you have seen, mastering the Internet starts with learning how to use basic tools such as mail programs, news readers, ftp, and telnet. Once you're comfortable with these tools, you can use them to access the more powerful and sophisticated facilities such as information services and databases. Chapter 15 concludes the book by looking at some strategies for choosing tools for communication, data retrieval, and information browsing.

From this brief tour of the Internet and its features you should have a better idea of the services available and the tools you'll use to access them. Now let's get down to business. The next chapter shows you how to establish an Internet connection and orient yourself to the online environment.

Getting Started

How do I...

2.1   Connect my PC to the net
2.2   Set up terminal emulation
2.3   Get help when starting to use the system
2.4   Use windows to manage the Internet session
2.5   Get help while using an Internet program
2.6   Get answers to frequently asked questions
2.7   Use the Internet responsibly
2.8   Use the Internet safely and protect my privacy

To get started using the Internet, you must obtain access to the network and then make a connection to the machine that will be providing you with the services discussed in this book (mail, news, file transfer, and so on).

This chapter looks at some common ways people can get connected to the Internet and makes some suggestions about choosing a service provider. It also contains some general guidelines you can follow to get help, be a good network citizen, and protect yourself from risks.

Connections, Clients, and Servers

Generally speaking, Internet services use a *client-server* model for connections. This means that large computers running server programs at locations on the net around the world provide services such as mail, news, files, and other information services. When you connect your computer to the Internet you run a matching client program that lets you access the resources provided by the server through a user interface.

There are basically two types of connections to the Internet. With a *direct* connection, your computer is actually part of the Internet and runs the client programs that get services from the server. With an *indirect* connection, you use your PC, communications software, and a modem to log on to a computer that is connected to the Internet

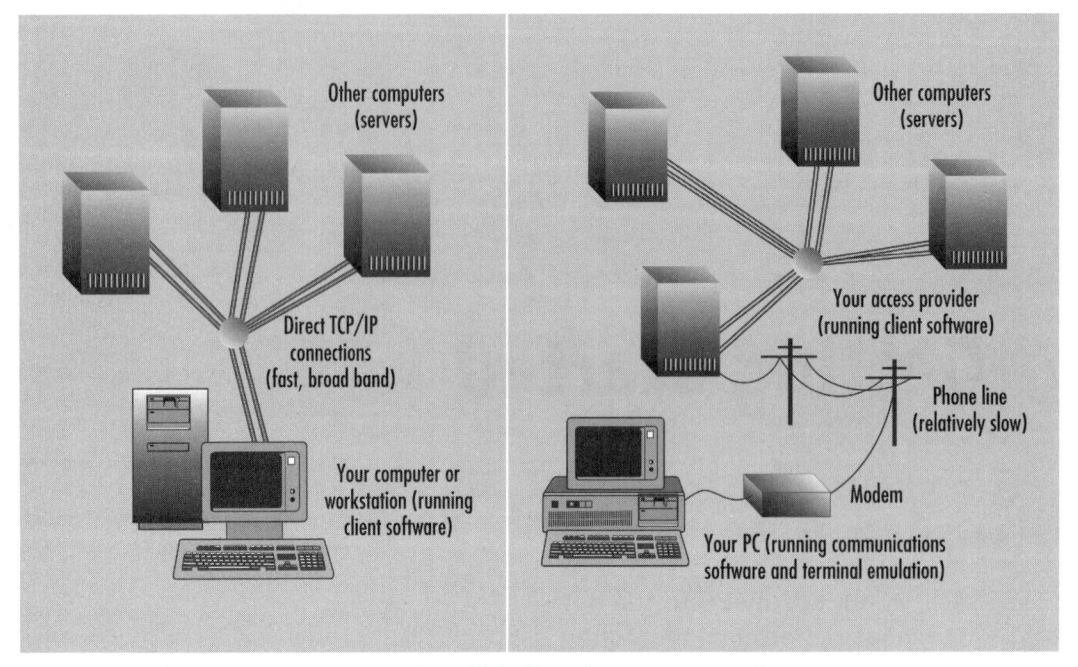

Figure 2-1 (A) Direct Internet connection; (B) indirect Internet connection

and that runs the client programs. Figure 2-1 compares the direct and dial-up methods of connection to the Internet.

Direct Connection to the Internet

In a direct connection, your PC or workstation is physically part of the network. Your machine sends and receives data packets using a specially formatted transmission called the Internet Protocol (IP) as managed by the Transmission Control Protocol (TCP). Collectively this is called a *TCP/IP connection*. Your machine has an IP address, and mail and files can be sent directly between your machine and other machines on the Internet.

Having a direct connection has two main advantages. First, it tends to be faster than an indirect connection (though this is actually because faster phone lines and modems or hardwired network connections are used). Second, the Internet is easier to use when you are directly connected. For example, you can get files directly from another site to your PC's hard disk, without going through an intermediary as you must do when you have indirect access. Also, having a direct connection is necessary for running most of the client programs that provide an easy-to-use GUI (graphical user interface) by means of Microsoft Windows, the Macintosh System, or X-Windows for Unix.

If you have a direct Internet connection at work or school, you should by all means take advantage of it and the easier-to-use client programs it provides.

Direct Connection with SLIP or PPP
Direct connections are available to dial-up users through two protocols called SLIP (Serial Line Internet Protocol) and PPP (Point-to-Point Protocol). These schemes, provided by the appropriate software on the server and your PC, let your PC, modem, and ordinary phone line function as a direct connection to the Internet, by allowing the transmission of data using TCP/IP. The result is that you get most of the advantages of having a machine that is actually part of the Internet. (The technical differences between SLIP and PPP aren't important here, but PPP is more efficient and is the better choice if available.)

The big advantage of dial-up with SLIP or PPP is that you are free to obtain and run the client programs of your choice, which can include graphical user interfaces. (Your service provider will probably offer you a basic set of client programs with which to start.) On the other hand, SLIP and PPP tend to cost more than simple dial-up connections (although the price gap is narrowing). SLIP and PPP can also be difficult to configure for your Windows PC or Mac, so you want to make sure the provider offers good technical support and assistance. Finally, if you are using SLIP or PPP over a slow speed modem and phone line (say 9600 baud or less), clients with graphical user interfaces may run unacceptably slowly because of the increased data needed to provide the graphics.

Connection with Ordinary Dial-up Access
Finally, you have ordinary dial-up access. This is the simplest, most popular, and usually least expensive way to get on the Internet if you don't already have access through work or school. For a modest fee (typically about $20 a month flat fee and/or $1 or $2 an hour, plus your phone charges), you dial up and connect to a machine that provides client programs that you use to access Internet services.

The main drawback of ordinary dial-up access is that you're stuck with whatever client programs the provider offers. These client programs will typically be text-only terminal emulation: you won't get a graphical user interface, you won't be able to view graphic images or play sound files directly, and you will be faced with learning commands and wading through menus. (Fortunately, this book makes it easy to learn your way around the net.) When you transfer or save a file, it will end up in the directory for your account on the dial-up machine, and you'll need to perform an additional step to download files to your PC.

What Do You Need to Access the Internet?
The bottom line is that either direct access or dial-up access with SLIP or PPP can make the Internet easier to use and more enjoyable, but simple dial-up access will get you all the services talked about in this book. By the end of the decade, everyone will probably have graphical, multimedia-aware, full-spectrum access to the Internet. Meanwhile, however, this book presents the text-based client programs that just about anyone can obtain and use. If you have (or move up to) a fuller Internet connection, you'll find that the principles and techniques for finding and obtaining information on the Internet that you learn here will still be relevant and useful.

Obtaining Internet Access
Nowadays it isn't unusual for an individual to use computers in several different contexts. You may use a PC, Mac, or a terminal in a computer lab or workstation at school,

have a PC on your desk at work, and use a different PC at home. It's even possible that you're already connected to the Internet and don't know it!

Do You Already Have Access to the Internet?
The first thing to do is to take a survey of the computing resources you already have available at school, work, or home. If you are a university student, your school is probably already connected to the Internet. If you already have an account on the university computer, you can find out if you have Internet access by asking teachers, fellow students, or personnel at the computer center. Basically, if you are told you can read mail and news *and* transfer files with ftp and log in to other systems through telnet, you have Internet access.

If your school computer appears not to be on the Internet, or if you don't have an account on that computer, contact your school's Computer Science Department, Computing Center, or similarly named department. Ask them if you can get Internet access through your school.

If you're not in school but you are a professional or businessperson, there's an increasing chance that you, too, already have Internet access. If you're not sure, ask whoever is in charge of your company's computer services (often they're called MIS, or Management Information Services). Companies involved with the computer business or with scientific research are particularly likely to have Internet access.

Dial-up Access to the Internet from Your PC
Those of you who don't have an affiliation that provides Internet access, but do use a PC at home, can obtain a connection through a growing number of public access Internet sites. There are a few sites called Freenets sponsored by libraries or other nonprofit institutions. You may be able to get free Internet access through one of these sites (though the waiting list may be long and it may be hard to get an open phone line).

Most likely you'll have to obtain service by paying for it. When considering a commercial public access Internet site, there are a number of things that will affect your ultimate cost.

What are the Base and Connect Charges?
Some sites have a base or flat rate charge; for example, $25 for the first 20 hours of access each month. Other sites charge by the hour. Some sites combine these charges; for example, The WELL charges $15 per month plus $2 an hour. Since you are likely to be spending a considerable number of hours online as you learn your way around the net, look for a combination of rates that works out to no more than $2 to $3 an hour. For example, if a site charges a base rate of $20 plus $2 an hour, and you think you'll be online about 20 hours per month; that works out to 20 + (20 * 2) = $60 divided by 20 hours, or an effective rate of $3 per hour. Watch out for charges that vary with the time of day or day of the week (peak versus off-peak hours).

What About Phone Charges?
Connect charges for Internet service may include access through an 800 number (whose cost is included in the hourly connect charge). Otherwise, you have to figure in the phone charges for reaching the site. Try to find a site in your local calling area. A site that charges only $2 an hour for its services but requires $0.20 per minute charges for long distance (or its 800 number) works out to $14 an hour. This is no bargain.

If you can't find an Internet site in your local calling area, consider using a *public data network*. For example, CPN (CompuServe Packet Network) provides local numbers you can call to access remote computers. The charges typically work out to $2 to $6 per hour but can vary with the site you're connecting to and the time of day. Call 1-800-848-8199 (voice) for information about CPN rates and local access numbers.

Will I Get Full Internet Service?

Some sites, particularly local computer bulletin boards, may advertise "Internet access" but provide only mail and Usenet news. While you *can* get files and a surprising number of other services from the Internet using mail alone, such indirect use of the net is more difficult and more limiting than using a client program. If a site tells you they have mail, news, ftp, and telnet, then you can probably access all the other programs discussed in this book.

The growing popularity of the Internet has led a number of commercial information services to begin providing Internet access to their members. For example, CompuServe announced in March 1994 that it was in the process of implementing access to Internet news, ftp, telnet, and perhaps other services. While this is convenient if you already belong to CompuServe, we'll have to wait to see whether the pricing is competitive with that of other Internet providers.

Finding a Provider

Once you decide what kind of access you want or need, it's time to look for an Internet service provider. There are several resources you can use to find the service with the best combination of cost and features for you.

The NixPub and PDIAL Lists

There are two frequently updated lists of Internet access providers. NixPub (which stands for Unix public access) lists sites that run the Unix operating system and offer public dial-up accounts. While *most* of these sites offer the full set of Internet services (mail, news, ftp, telnet, and so on), some may offer only news and mail. If you already have (or can borrow) Internet access, you can obtain this list from the newsgroups comp.misc or alt.bbs (see Chapter 4 for more on Usenet news). Look for the article subject "NixPub Long List...".

If you at least have access to Internet e-mail, you can get the list by sending a message to mail-server@bts.com. In the message body type the phrase `get PUB nixpub.long` to get the latest version of the list. You can use the command `subscribe nixpub-list` followed by your name. This way you receive an updated list regularly. (For more information on subscribing to mailing lists, see Chapter 3.)

The PDIAL list, compiled by Peter Kaminski, describes providers who offer the full set of Internet services. You can obtain the PDIAL list from Usenet newsgroups including alt.internet.access.wanted and news.answers. You can also send a message to info-deli-server@netcom.com. Type the phrase `send pdial` in the subject of your message if you want the latest copy, or `subscribe pdial`, if you want to receive regular updates.

Other Information Sources

InterNIC is an organization dedicated to providing information about Internet resources. It distributes a document called the "Internet Starter Kit" that introduces the Internet and its services and includes information about service providers. To quote this document:

INTERNET HOW-TO

InterNIC Information Services provides contact information for Network Service Providers in all areas of the country, and some international locations. To request a copy of the Network Service Providers list, call, FAX, or send postal or electronic mail to us at the following addresses.

Telephone:	1-800-444-4345 [Select option #1]
Direct Phone:	1-619-455-4600
FAX:	1-619-455-4640
E-mail:	info@is.internic.net
Postal mail:	InterNIC Information Services
	P.O. Box 85608
	San Diego, CA 92186-9784

We can send it by e-mail, postal mail, and FAX. When requesting the Network Service Providers list, please include your Name, Address, Telephone number, FAX number, and/or e-mail addresses.

You can also obtain a document called "How to Get Information About Networks" from the newsgroup news.answers (see Chapter 4). This file gives information about InterNIC and other information services.

CompuServe and other online services are starting to provide a good selection of documents relating to the Internet (including the NixPub and PDIAL lists and the "Internet Starter Kit"). In March 1994 CompuServe opened a forum dedicated to the Internet. The WELL includes a conference on the Internet (and many other conferences) in addition to providing Internet access.

Related Topics

To Learn How to...	See Chapter
Subscribe to a mailing list	3
Read a Usenet newsgroup	4
Get files by ftp	7
Evaluate Internet services for information retrieval and navigation	15

How-Tos in this Chapter

2.1 Connect my PC to the net
To connect to a dial-up Internet site you run your communications program on your PC with appropriate settings. You have the program dial the remote machine, and you go through a registration process the first time you log in.

2.2 Set up terminal emulation
Your PC communications program and the remote site must agree on what terminal control commands to use to display text. You make a setting (such as VT-100) on both your PC and your account at the Internet site.

2.3 Get help when starting to use the system
Some Internet sites are friendlier than others. Most offer some introductory help in the form of menus or commands.

2.4 Use windows to manage the Internet session

2 GETTING STARTED

Most PC users today use some form of graphical user interface, such as Microsoft Windows or the Macintosh System. Opening several file windows in addition to your communications session lets you look up commands and save or transfer information between the Internet site and your PC.

2.5 Get help while using an Internet program
Internet utilities and client programs offer help in various ways. This how-to acquaints you with the most common forms of online help.

2.6 Get answers to frequently asked questions
FAQ (Frequently Asked Questions) files have been compiled by volunteers to help beginners get answers to their most common questions or problems when using Internet software. These files are a valuable resource for the new user.

2.7 Use the Internet responsibly
Following basic rules of courtesy and using computer resources wisely helps everyone get the most out of the information highway. This how-to introduces you to a few simple "rules of the road."

2.8 Use the Internet safely and protect my privacy
Every new frontier has its outlaws. It's important to safeguard your password and protect your valuable information. While this can be a complex subject, we will offer a few basic safety tips.

2.1 HOW DO I... Connect my PC to the net?

COMPLEXITY: INTERMEDIATE

Problem
Having decided which Internet site to connect to, you must now establish a connection between your PC and the remote computer. (Some people who are accessing the net at a college campus or business may have a permanent connection between their terminal, workstation, or PC and the net via a local area network (LAN). If this is true of you, you can skip this how-to and just type in the login name and password given to you by the appropriate support person.)

Technique
You configure your communications software, make a phone call to the site's computer, connect, and then go through the login procedure at the remote computer. There is a wide variety of communications software for PCs, Macintoshes, and other computers. The example used here is the simple Terminal program that comes with Microsoft Windows. The basic steps should be very similar to what you do with your own software, but you may have to check the manual for your communications program for some details.

Steps
1. Configure your communications software. The software usually has menus that you use to specify the phone number to dial, the modem speed (for example, 2400 baud), and the settings that determine how information is interpreted by the local and remote computers (number of data bits, parity, and stop bits).

   The main thing about these settings is that they must match between your PC and the remote computer. The information listing for the service to which you're

INTERNET HOW-TO

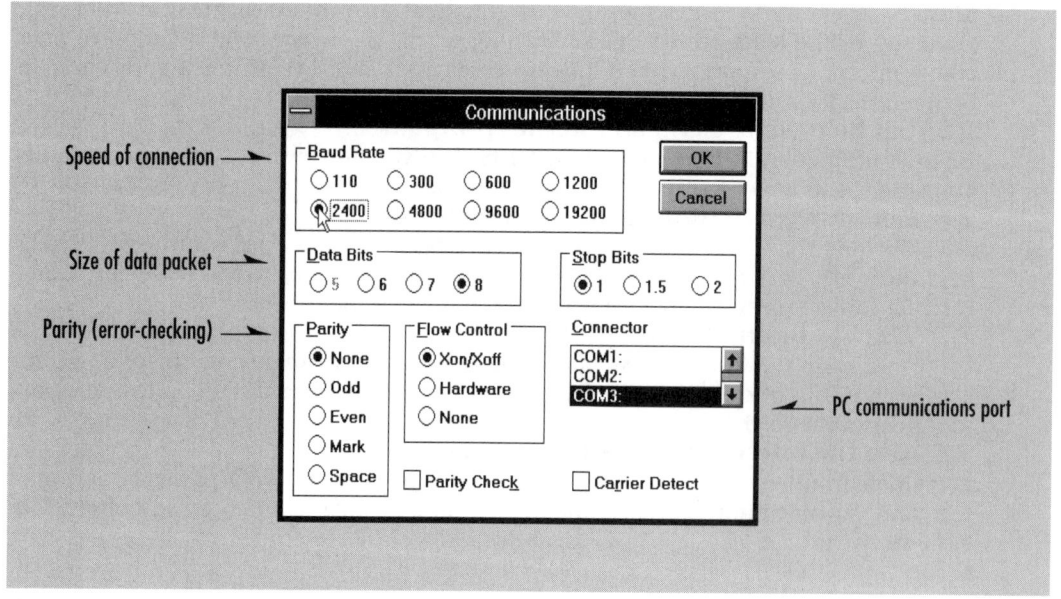

Figure 2-2 Terminal communications settings

connecting should specify the settings. The two most common combinations are 8-N-1 (8 data bits, no parity, 1 stop bit) and 7-E-1 (7 data bits, even parity, 1 stop bit). Figure 2-2 shows the Communications settings dialog box for the Windows Terminal program.

2. Select the appropriate terminal emulation in your communications software. (Terminal emulation is necessary so that programs on the Internet can properly display data on your PC's screen.) Unless you have special needs, the VT-100 setting is probably the best choice: just about all communications software has it, and nearly all Internet sites support it.

3. Choose the menu item or command that tells your communications software to dial the access number for your Internet site (for Windows Terminal, choose Dial from the Phone menu). If all goes well, a connection will be made (you will hear a hissing or whistling sound).

Next, you'll be presented with a login prompt. For example, if you call The WELL you'll see

```
This is The WELL.

Type    newuser   to sign up.
Type    trouble   if you are having trouble logging in.
Type    guest     to learn about The WELL.

If you already have a WELL account, type your username.
```

18

2 GETTING STARTED

```
well.sf.ca.us login:
```

(The cursor will be waiting after the colon for you to enter the text.)

4. You must now log in to the Internet computer. Some systems require that you arrange to set up your account *before* you call with your modem. If you've done this, just type the login name and password that you've arranged. On other systems, such as The WELL, you can call the system with your modem and make all the arrangements online as you log in for the first time.

   Here, since you're a "newuser," you would type `newuser` and press (ENTER). (Some systems, including The WELL, accept a login of "guest" rather than "newuser." If you're a guest you'll receive information about the system and possibly a demo of some kind, but you won't be able to actually use the Internet until you've registered as an official user.)

5. The system then takes you through the setup procedure for new users. On The WELL, it looks like this:

```
newuser
Last login: Wed Nov  3 19:06:59 from dialup-2.well.sf



WELCOME TO THE WELL

    Welcome to The WELL newuser registration program!  This is where you
    sign up for a WELL account.  Basic charges for using The WELL are as
    follows (all prices are in U.S. Dollars):

      Monthly service charge:  $15.00

                 Connect time:  $ 2.00/hour (figured by the minute)

         High-speed modem use:  $ 1.00/hour extra (by the minute)

                   Disk space:  Up to 512K at no additional charge.  Disk
                                space over 512K is charged at the rate of
                                $20/megabyte per month, pro-rated on a
                                daily basis.

    From the time your account is activated, your WELL account will
    remain active and will incur monthly service charges until you
    tell us to close your account.

Press [Return] to continue...
```

   Continue to press (ENTER) (sometimes referred to as Return), and you'll see more screens of information about The WELL and its terms for access.

6. Complete the user registration by supplying the required information, such as a credit card number. Be sure to note the charges and any regulations, and make sure

INTERNET HOW-TO

they are agreeable to you. (Some systems offer other billing options, such as being billed by mail.)

7. As part of the registration process you'll acquire a permanent login name and a password. The login name is usually a variant of your real name (such as first initial and last name, initials, or some combination). For example, the author's login name on various systems might be hhenderson, or hrh. You will also be asked to choose a password. The password should *not* be your name (or part of your name): it should be something that's hard for unscrupulous people to guess. For more about passwords, see How-To 2.8.

Once you've completed registration, you should have Internet access. (You may be asked to agree to a set of rules for use of the Internet. These rules are discussed in How-To 2.7).

8. When you're finished using the Internet system, log out properly. Usually you type `logout` at a system prompt. If that doesn't work, try typing `bye`, or press CTRL-D a couple of times. You want to log out properly so that the accounting system at the Internet site doesn't continue to charge you for online time when you've hung up.

Comment

If you try to dial an access number and you get an assortment of garbage characters, your communications settings are probably wrong for that site. If you're using 8-N-1, switch to 7-E-1, or vice versa. If the connection "hangs" without giving you a login prompt, there may be a problem on the remote system. Make a voice call to get help.

2.2 HOW DO I...
Set up terminal emulation?

COMPLEXITY: INTERMEDIATE

Problem

In order to display properly formatted information, the remote computer and your PC must agree on what set of terminal control commands to use. As noted in How-To 2.1, you should start by setting your communications software so that it emulates a VT-100 (or similar) terminal.

Suppose you've done this but your display is misaligned and shot through with gibberish such as "[HJ333"? In this case you'll need to set your terminal type on the *remote* system so that it matches what you have on your PC.

Technique

You want to specify the same terminal type on both remote and local systems. The remote system may prompt you for a terminal type, or you may have to put settings in a special file that the remote system can read.

Steps

1. You may be prompted for a terminal type like this:

TERM = (vt100)

Since the default shown is VT-100, just press ENTER if that's the terminal type you are using. You should be all set.

2 GETTING STARTED

2. An increasing number of systems offer you a menu-driven program that helps you make proper configuration settings, including terminal emulation.

   For example, on The WELL, you can type `help terminal` at any prompt and get an explanation of terminal emulation. You can then run a program called "custom" that lets you specify what terminal your communications software will use. Type `custom` at any WELL prompt and press (ENTER).

```
well% custom

This menu allows you to make a number of changes to your WELL account.

You select an item by typing the number associated with that choice, and
then typing <return>

Press [Return] to continue...
```

   After you press (ENTER), you see the menu:

```
                        CUSTOM MENU

                  1 - Change Your Password
                  2 - Conference List
                  3 - Privacy and Security
                  4 - Change Editor
                  5 - Change Terminal Emulation
                  6 - Change Pager
                  7 - Forwarding Your Mail
                  8 - Miscellaneous

                  h=get Help from a real person
q=Quit menus                                          p=turn Pager OFF
```

```
Select one of the above items (1-8 or a letter) ==>
```

   Read the information presented, then press 5 to change your terminal emulation. Finally, press the number of the appropriate terminal (for example, press 1 for VT-100).

   Of course the facilities offered by other providers will be different from those provided by The WELL.

3. If you aren't offered a prompt for the terminal type, observe the command prompt that the system is showing you. If the prompt is the $ character, then the system is running a command processor called the Bourne shell or one called the Korn shell. If the prompt contains the % character, the system is running the C shell. If it is none of these, the system may not be running Unix at all. While most Internet systems run Unix, some run other operating systems such as VMS. You'll need to get help from the system operator in that case. Some systems run a customized shell "on top" of Unix. Again, if you can't figure out what's going on, ask for help.

INTERNET HOW-TO

4. If you are using the Bourne or Korn shells (**$** prompt), look for a file called .profile in your current working directory. (You can type `ls-al` to list the files in your home directory. See Chapter 6 for more on working with files.) Add the following line to the file (or create a new file with that line):

```
set TERM = vt100; export TERM
```

5. If you are using the C shell, look for a file called .cshrc and add this line:

```
setenve TERM vt100
```

Once you have edited the appropriate file, log out, redial, and log in again, and your programs should give you properly formatted text.

How It Works
In simple terms, the Unix system provides support for a variety of terminals (some of which are quite obscure). Your PC's communications software supports a few of these terminals by providing an *emulator* that interprets and responds to the terminal control commands in the same way an actual hardwired terminal would do.

Most of the programs you will be using in this book use the full screen to show information and thus require that you be set up with a proper terminal emulation. (A few programs, such as ftp, work line by line and don't require any terminal setting. There are also line-oriented mail and news programs, but since these are harder to use than their full screen, menu-driven competitors, this book features the latter.)

Comment
If you're prompted for a terminal, don't use such settings as ASCII, dumb, or ANSI. These won't work with Elm, nn, or most of the other software in this book. (Remember, when in doubt, use VT-100.)

2.3 HOW DO I...
Get help when starting to use the system?

COMPLEXITY EASY

Problem
Once you're connected to an Internet system, what do you do next? Many systems just leave you staring at a Unix prompt. While you probably aren't going to get the copious and easy-to-use help that's familiar to Windows or Macintosh users, many Internet systems *have* created some menus with help and tips for beginners. How do you find this help?

Technique
The actual help available will vary with the site. Often a message following your successful login will tell you what to do to get help. Examples from The WELL are used here.

Steps
1. Look for a special area that is set up to provide help for new users. Some Internet sites, such as The WELL, are also conferencing systems. This means that in addition to all the Internet facilities (mail, news, and so on), these sites have their own discussion groups (usually called *forums* or *conferences*).

2 GETTING STARTED

2. Activate the help menu if available. On The WELL, you type

```
g internet
```

to go to the Internet conference and then type

```
netmenu
```

The following menu of selections to help learn more about the Internet appears:

```
       T h e    I n t e r n e t    C o n f e r e n c e    M e n u

type  1  for Introductory Readings

type  2  for Rules and Regulations on the use of the Internet from The WELL

type  3  for Cheat-sheets on how to use Internet tools

type  4  for Information on Libraries online

type  5  for Information on FTP (File transfer protocol)

type  6  for Information on Internet Services

type  7  to look for an Internet site near you

(To quit from any of the menus, enter ctrl-d or "exit")

Enter your selection, H for help
or control-d to exit.
: 1
```

3. Explore the menu. Note that this menu system is crude but serviceable. To make choices you type the number of the item you want or press (CTRL)-(D) to exit. (CTRL)-(D) is commonly used on Unix systems to exit from programs. Since the shell that is processing your Unix commands is itself a program, pressing (CTRL)-(D) at the shell prompt ($ or %) is one way to log off the system. Sometimes you'll press (CTRL)-(D) one too many times and log yourself off by mistake.

4. Press (1) (and (ENTER)) in response to the preceding menu, and get a list of introductory readings about the Internet:

```
Introductory Readings Menu

(Add an "a" to any item number to view without pagination (e.g. 1a))

type  1  to read the Hitchhiker's Guide to the Internet online (62Kb)
type  2  to read Zen and the Art of the Internet online (191Kb)
type  3  to get information on finding email addresses (25Kb)
type  4  to get The Internet Companion (Intro sample) (167Kb)
type  5  to get excerpts from the Krol Internet book (26Kb)

type  m  to go back to the Main menu

(To quit from any of the menus, enter ctrl-d or "exit")
```

INTERNET HOW-TO

When you get text from this type of menu, it is usually sent to you through a program called a *pager*. You can tell you're using a pager because text will be presented to you one screen at a time, and at the bottom of each screen you'll see a prompt like this:

```
—More—(1%)
```

(The prompt may vary a bit depending on which pager is in use.) Press `SPACEBAR` to continue to the next page, press `B` to go back one page or `Q` to stop reading the file.

Notice that this menu also offers you the option of reading a continuous stream of text by appending the letter *a* to the number of your selection. Thus, specifying **1a** will get you "The Hitchhiker's Guide to the Internet" without any pauses. Before you do this, tell your communications software "receive a text file" or "file capture on" or "log file." (The exact term will vary: in Windows Terminal, you select Receive Text File from the Transfers menu.) This will cause all the text being displayed on your terminal screen to be saved for you in a file on your PC's hard disk.

5. The helpful folks at The WELL have also provided cheat sheets to help you use some of the main Internet programs. Press `3` on the Conference menu to get a list of these:

```
Cheat-sheets to jog your memory...

(Add an "a" to any item number to view without pagination (e.g. 1a))

type  1   to get a cheat sheet on using FTP (File Transfer Protocol) (9Kb)
type  2   to get a cheat sheet on using Telnet (network terminal emulation)(4Kb)
type  3   to get a cheat sheet on using "ping" (2Kb)
type  4   to get a cheat sheet on using "whois" (3Kb)

type  m   to go back to the Main menu.

(To quit from any of the menus, enter ctrl-d or "exit")


Enter your selection, H for help
or control-d to exit.
:
```

Comment

The help available varies greatly with the Internet site and the front-end software it uses, if any. Reading large amounts of text online can be awkward: it's a good idea to capture the text for later use. When you learn to use ftp in Chapter 7 you'll have a quicker and easier way to get these helpful files.

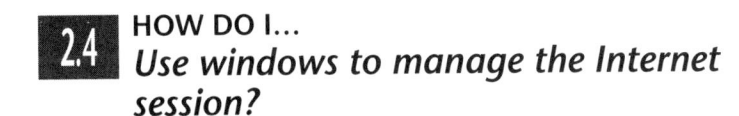

2.4 HOW DO I...
Use windows to manage the Internet session?

COMPLEXITY INTERMEDIATE

Problem
While using the Internet, you'll often find yourself in one of the following situations:
- You want to make a note of something you've just read (perhaps someone's net address or the name of a newsgroup that discusses a particular topic).
- You have something on your PC that you'd like to include in a mail or news message (for example, information about a book you read recently).
- You'd like to be able to see both a program and its help file at the same time.

If you have a windowing environment (Windows, Macintosh, X-Windows, or something similar), there are some simple but powerful techniques that can help you keep track of information in several files at once.

Technique
The general approach is to take advantage of the fact that in a windowing system you can have several files open at once, in addition to your communications program (see Figure 2-3). Windowing systems also let you cut, copy, or paste text from one window into another.

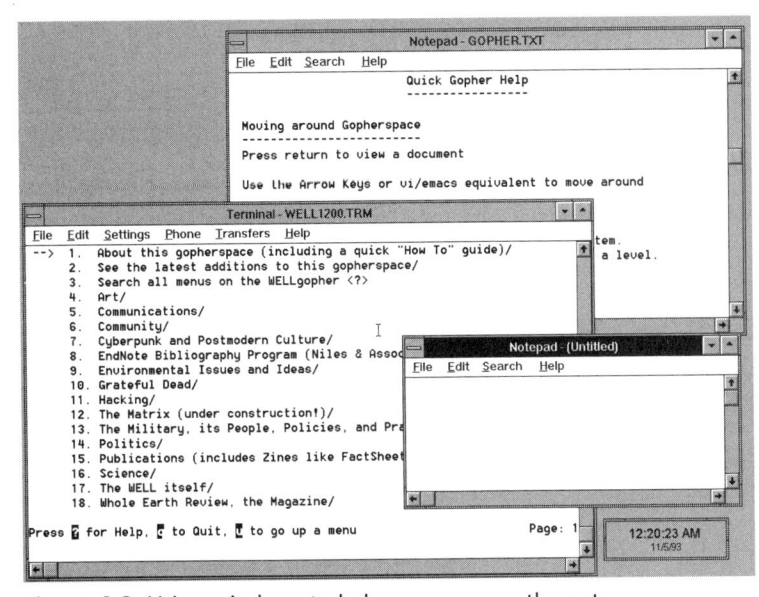

Figure 2-3 Using windows to help you manage the net

Steps

1. Run your communications program as usual and log on the Internet. If you're learning how to use a program, load its help file into a notepad window. (Notepad is the simple text editor that comes with Windows.) When you're stuck, click on that window and view the help file, then click on the Internet window to continue working with the Internet system.

2. Open a blank notepad or text editor window that you can use for saving text that you copy from the Internet screen.

3. When you want to make a note of something, just type it into the blank notepad window. If you want to save something you've seen in the Internet communications window, just use your copy and paste facilities to transfer a copy of the text from the Internet window into your blank notepad window.

4. If you want to include text from your PC in a mail or news message (or any other text file you are creating at the Internet site), copy the text from a notepad window into the Internet window at the cursor position.

Comment

The techniques discussed in this how-to are designed for working with small amounts of text (up to a few paragraphs). If you want to transfer longer text files (or any sort of binary or graphics file) between your PC and the Internet, you'll want to use the file transfer techniques discussed in Chapter 9.

2.5 HOW DO I...
Get help while using an Internet program?

COMPLEXITY: EASY

Problem

Using the Internet effectively means mastering a group of separate client programs or tools that manage different aspects of communications, information retrieval, and file transfer. As with most Unix programs, these Internet tools were written by different people, have different kinds of interfaces, and exemplify different styles or approaches to the task at hand. Since the programs are constructed differently, they also vary in the way they provide help to you, the user. The uniform, consistent help conventions used in Windows or Macintosh systems are absent on the net, so you must develop a different strategy to get help with your Internet applications.

Technique

The bywords to follow are "observe" and "experiment." Observe the screen to see what kinds of help options you are offered, and experiment with some of the different kinds of help described below.

Steps

1. Determine whether the program you are using works screen by screen or line by line. Most programs, such as Elm and nn, use the full screen to present menus and information. For such programs the menu usually includes the keystroke that brings up help: usually [H] or [?]. (The [F1] key favored by DOS programs will seldom work.)

2 🌐 GETTING STARTED

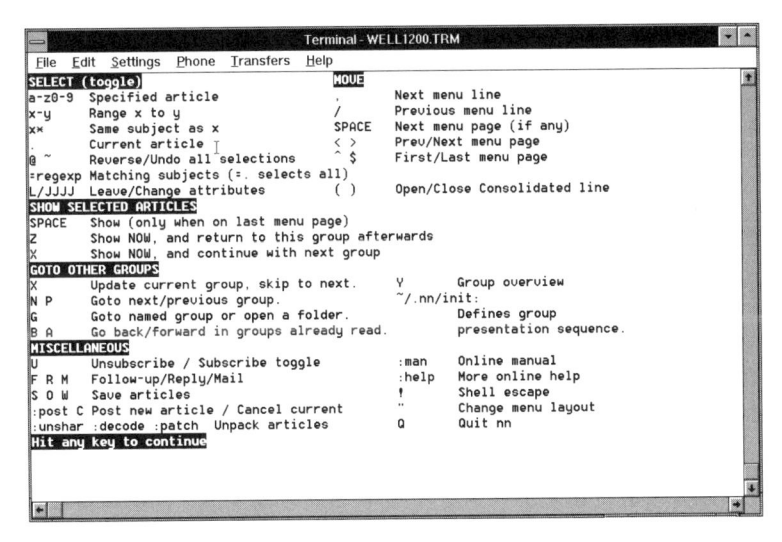

```
                    Terminal - WELL1200.TRM
 File  Edit  Settings  Phone  Transfers  Help
SELECT (toggle)                      MOVE
a-z0-9   Specified article           ,        Next menu line
x-y      Range x to y                /        Previous menu line
x*       Same subject as x           SPACE    Next menu page (if any)
         Current article             < >      Prev/Next menu page
@ ~      Reverse/Undo all selections ^ $      First/Last menu page
=regexp  Matching subjects (=. selects all)
L/JJJJ   Leave/Change attributes     ( )      Open/Close Consolidated line
SHOW SELECTED ARTICLES
SPACE    Show (only when on last menu page)
Z        Show NOW, and return to this group afterwards
X        Show NOW, and continue with next group
GOTO OTHER GROUPS
X        Update current group, skip to next.    Y       Group overview
N P      Goto next/previous group.              ~/.nn/init:
G        Goto named group or open a folder.             Defines group
B A      Go back/forward in groups already read.        presentation sequence.
MISCELLANEOUS
U        Unsubscribe / Subscribe toggle        :man     Online manual
F R M    Follow-up/Reply/Mail                  :help    More online help
S O W    Save articles                         !        Shell escape
:post C  Post new article / Cancel current     "        Change menu layout
:unshar :decode :patch  Unpack articles        Q        Quit nn
Hit any key to continue
```

Figure 2-4 nn help screen

For example, suppose you are running the nn news reading program. With this program you can press the ⑦ key at any time to get help. The help screen is shown in Figure 2-4. (As mentioned in How-To 2.4, Windows users can cut this help screen and paste it into a text editor window for convenient reference.) Note that the bottom of the help screen tells you to press any key to leave the help screen and return to nn.

2. Look for any special help features that your program may offer. With nn, for example, you can type `:man` at the main command prompt, and an online manual will come up, as shown in Figure 2-5. The author of nn cleverly designed the online manual to look like an ordinary newsgroup, with the "articles" as help topics. You can select and view help topics just as you would news articles (the use of nn is discussed in detail in Chapter 4).

3. A few programs, such as ftp, are line-oriented rather than screen-oriented. This means that the program accepts and displays information only one line at a time. With such programs, typing `help` (and pressing ENTER) is likely to provide some assistance. Here is the help you get with ftp:

```
% ftp
ftp> help
Commands may be abbreviated.  Commands are:

!          cr          macdef     proxy      send
$          delete      mdelete    sendport   status
account    debug       mdir       put        struct
append     dir         mget       pwd        sunique
ascii      disconnect  mkdir      quit       tenex
bell       form        mls        quote      trace
binary     get         mode       recv       type
```

Continued on next page

27

INTERNET HOW-TO

Continued from previous page

```
bye       glob      mput      remotehelp  user
case      hash      nmap      rename      verbose
cd        help      ntrans    reset       ?
cdup      lcd       open      rmdir
close     ls        prompt    runique
```

Now repeat the help command with the name of a specific keyword that you want help with, for example:

```
ftp> help binary
binary          set binary transfer type
ftp>
```

As you can see, this sort of help is usually pretty minimal.

4. For more detailed help on a program you can take advantage of the Unix "man" command ("man" stands for manual). You type `man` followed by the name of the program you want help on. For example,

```
% man ftp
```

to read about the ftp (file transfer program) discussed in Chapter 7.

The Unix reference manual entry for ftp is shown in Figure 2-6. You can page through this entry a screen at a time by pressing (SPACEBAR).

5. You can also enter a command like this at the system prompt:

```
% man ftp > ftp.man
```

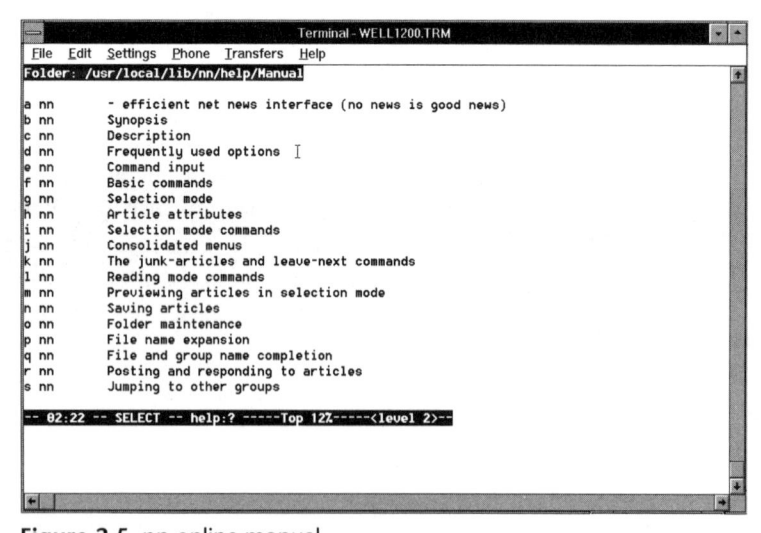

Figure 2-5 nn online manual

2 GETTING STARTED

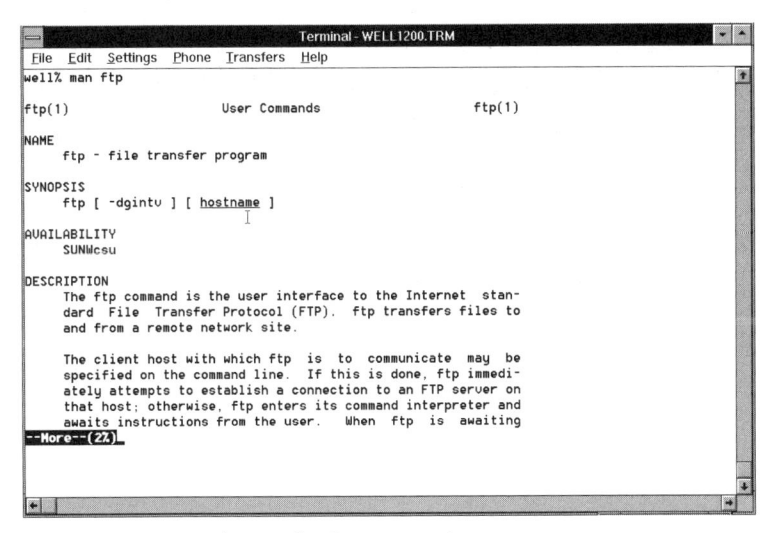

Figure 2-6 Manual entry for ftp

This Unix command tells the man program to store the manual for the ftp program in the file ftp.man in your home directory. Chapter 6 will show you how to look at this file, and Chapter 9 will explain how you can download this file to your PC (where, for example, you can print it out). Note that some locally written programs may not have entries in the online Unix manual.

Comment
Not all the help strategies outlined here will work with every program, but at least one of them probably will. As the Internet grows ever more popular, additional user-friendly, Windows-style help systems are likely to become available. (Chapter 15 shows an example of a Windows Help-based system for Internet resources.)

2.6 HOW DO I...
Get answers to frequently asked questions?

COMPLEXITY   INTERMEDIATE

Problem
Online help tends to be pretty brief. The Unix manual may be cryptic in places. Even books like this one can't cover everything you might need to know. What do you do when you can't find an answer to your question about one of the Internet programs?

Technique
You use the Internet itself to get more help! You can find FAQ (Frequently Asked Questions) files on many topics, including Internet programs and resources, computing in general, and other activities. These files list questions beginners frequently ask about a given topic, give brief answers, and usually provide suggestions for further reading. You can also find Usenet newsgroups devoted to discussion of the more popular programs.

INTERNET HOW-TO

Steps

1. Get a list of active Usenet newsgroups. Two lists posted regularly are the List of Active Newsgroups and Alternative Newsgroup Hierarchies. You can find these lists in the newsgroups news.lists, news.groups, news.announce.newusers, or news.answers. (See Chapter 4 to learn how to read the newsgroups.)

2. Once you have a list, look for a newsgroup that is likely to discuss the topic you are interested in. (For example, if you have questions about the Unix operating system, the group comp.unix.questions is likely to be helpful to you.)

3. On many systems you can also type `nngrep` at the system prompt, followed by a keyword. For example,

```
% nngrep unix
```

will list newsgroups that have something to do with Unix in their names or descriptions. (See Chapter 4 for more information about the nngrep program.)

4. Once you have a newsgroup name, type `nn` followed by the name, and nn will put you in that newsgroup. The available articles will be shown in a menu format. For example, a listing of the group comp.unix.questions might look like this:

```
Newsgroup: comp.unix.questions     Articles: 380 of 157/1 NEW READ *NO*UPDATE*

a.G W Woodbury       1166  UNIX BBS Software FAQ with Answers
b.B.N.Blackmore       305  UNIX shell differences an<>e your shell (Monthly Posting)
c.Sander-Beuermann     20  >>Help on e-mail encryption needed
d.Wojtek Swiatek       21  >>
e.Hobbes Tiger         17  >
f.DDCA                 31  >>>
g.Sander-Beuermann     16  >logfinger
h.Wojtek Swiatek       27  >>>
i.Sander-Beuermann      7  >Tar Question
j.Volkmar Grote        33  >
k.Ted M A Timar       390  >Unix - Frequently Asked Q<>ions (1/7) [Frequent posting]
l.Ted M A Timar       977  >Unix - Frequently Asked Q<>ions (2/7) [Frequent posting]
m.Ted M A Timar       740  >Unix - Frequently Asked Q<>ions (3/7) [Frequent posting]
n.Ted M A Timar       635  >Unix - Frequently Asked Q<>ions (4/7) [Frequent posting]
o.Ted M A Timar       277  >Unix - Frequently Asked Q<>ions (5/7) [Frequent posting]
p.Ted M A Timar       868  >Unix - Frequently Asked Q<>ions (6/7) [Frequent posting]
q.Ted M A Timar       348  >Unix - Frequently Asked Q<>ions (7/7) [Frequent posting]
r.Ted M A Timar       165  Unix - Frequently Asked Q<> (Contents) [Frequent posting]
s.Ted M A Timar       205  Welcome to comp.unix.questions [Frequent posting]
```

Each article is preceded by a menu letter (a, b, c, and so on). Press the menu letters of any articles you would like to read. Press [SPACEBAR] to go to the next screen. After you've finished looking at the last menu screen, the articles you've selected will be presented to you. (See Chapter 4 for more details on how to read news and how you can save news articles for future reference.)

5. While reading newsgroups, look for articles in which the subject (the descriptive phrase in the right half of each line) mentions "FAQ" or "Frequently Asked Questions." In the preceding listing, article "a" has the subject "UNIX BBS Software

2 GETTING STARTED

FAQ with Answers." This article contains a series of common questions about software for Unix bulletin boards, with answers to each question. Here's an example question and answer from this file:

```
From: news@wolves.durham.nc.us (G. Wolfe Woodbury)
Subject: 1. What is a BBS?
Date: Wed Aug 11 19:29:48 EDT 1993

BBS is an acronym for Bulletin Board System.  This is software that allows
a computer to be used as a message posting and reading system that has
some similarities to a bulletin board you might find in an office
or in a grocery store.  Users of the system can post messages and read
messages posted by others.  Many computer BBSes also allow the users to
send private messages to other users, andor to "download" files that are
stored on the computer.  Some BBSes also allow users to run other
programs (such as games) in addition to the BBS program.

Some BBS programs allow the individual BBS systems to share messages by
using a communications medium to exchange the messages via a standard
protocol which the BBSes understand.  Such systems are "networked"
BBSes.  There are several BBS Networks around the world. Among them are
FIDOnet, WWIVnet, RIMEnet, VNET and Usenet.
```

Note that the question is asked in the Subject field and answered in the body of the message.

6. Another way to find FAQ files is to go to the newsgroup news.answers. This newsgroup consists mainly of FAQ files. As you can see in the following listing, the subjects covered vary considerably:

```
Newsgroup: news.answers                              Articles: 157 of 157/1

 a David Mar         502  ADMIN: Amethyst Coffeehouse Frequently Asked Questions
 b pete              897  Project Management Progra<>equently asked Questions (FAQ)
 c Paul Johnson     3280  sci.skeptic FAQ: The Frequently Questioned Answers
 d Rich Thomson      892  (28mar94) Welcome to comp.windows.x.pex! (FAQ)
 e Jeff Warringto   1894  AIX Frequently Asked Questions (Part 1 of 3)
 f Jeff Warringto   1610  AIX Frequently Asked Questions (Part 2 of 3)
 g Jeff Warringto   1570  AIX Frequently Asked Questions (Part 3 of 3)
 h Laura Burchard    975  rec.arts.sf.written FAQ
 i rec Moderator     206  rec.radio.info Submission Guidelines
 j rec Moderator     227  Welcome to rec.radio.info!
 k Bill Fenner      1060  Waffle Frequently Asked Questions (FAQ)
 l Nick C. Fotis    1524  (31 Mar 94) Computer Grap<> Listing : BIWEEKLY [part 1/4]
 m Nick C. Fotis    1229  (31 Mar 94) Computer Grap<> Listing : BIWEEKLY [part 2/4]
 n Nick C. Fotis    1636  (31 Mar 94) Computer Grap<> Listing : BIWEEKLY [part 3/4]
 o Nick C. Fotis    1378  (31 Mar 94) Computer Grap<> Listing : BIWEEKLY [part 4/4]
 p Nick C. Fotis     890  (31 Mar 94) Soc.Culture.Greek FAQ - Culture
 q Nick C. Fotis    1013  (31 Mar 94) Soc.Culture.Greek FAQ - Linguistics
 r Nick C. Fotis    1584  (31 Mar 94) Soc.Culture.Greek FAQ - Technical Information
 s Nick C. Fotis     830  (31 Mar 94) Soc.Culture.Greek FAQ - Tourist Information
```

INTERNET HOW-TO

How It Works
FAQ files are written by dedicated volunteers who have moderated or helped with newsgroups. After observing the kinds of questions people ask about their group's topic, they compose a list of the most frequently asked questions and provide an answer to each question. Often the FAQ file is circulated among participants in the newsgroup so that corrections and additions can be made. Most FAQ files are revised regularly.

Comment
When you learn how to use the ftp program in Chapter 7 you'll be able to get FAQ files directly from archive sites, and you won't have to search through newsgroups for them. Of course if the FAQ file doesn't answer your particular question, the next step is probably to post a news article asking for help (see Chapter 4 to learn how to post news).

2.7 HOW DO I...
Use the Internet responsibly?

COMPLEXITY | INTERMEDIATE

Problem
The situation with the Internet today is something like the advent of the automobile in the early 1900s, before such things as stop signs or traffic lights existed. When there were only a few cars on the road, signs and lights weren't really necessary. As traffic grew, so did the need to regulate it and to encourage people to drive in a responsible way. Similarly, as the Internet grows by leaps and bounds, the need for each user to use the net responsibly, courteously, and efficiently grows. We must each do our part.

Technique
As you use the net, review your actions in the light of the following three criteria:

➢ Am I fulfilling legal requirements?
➢ Am I treating people with the same courtesy I'd expect in a face-to-face encounter?
➢ Am I using the Internet's resources as efficiently as possible?

Steps
1. When you first sign up with an Internet site you may be asked to read and agree to a set of standards for "acceptable use" of the net. The most common set of standards comes from the NSFNET, (NSF is the government-run National Science Foundation) the source of the government funding that originally built the Internet's ancestor (ARPANET) and that still plays an important part today:

```
THE NSFNET BACKBONE SERVICES ACCEPTABLE USE POLICY

                    June 1992

GENERAL PRINCIPLE:

(1) NSFNET Backbone services are provided to support open research and
    education in and among US research and instructional institutions,
    plus research arms of for-profit firms when engaged in open
    scholarly communication and research.  Use for other purposes is
    not acceptable.
```

SPECIFICALLY ACCEPTABLE USES:

(2) Communication with foreign researchers and educators in connection with research or instruction, as long as any network that the foreign user employs for such communication provides reciprocal access to US researchers and educators.

(3) Communication and exchange for professional development, to maintain currency, or to debate issues in a field or subfield of knowledge.

(4) Use for disciplinary-society, university-association, government-advisory, or standards activities related to the user's research and instructional activities.

(5) Use in applying for or administering grants or contracts for research or instruction, but not for other fundraising or public relations activities.

(6) Any other administrative communications or activities in direct support of research and instruction.

(7) Announcements of new products or services for use in research or instruction, but not advertising of any kind.

(8) Any traffic originating from a network of another member agency of the Federal Networking Council if the traffic meets the acceptable use policy of that agency.

(9) Communication incidental to otherwise acceptable use, except for illegal or specifically unacceptable use.

UNACCEPTABLE USES:

(10) Use for for-profit activities, unless covered by the General Principle or as a specifically acceptable use.

(11) Extensive use for private or personal business.

This statement applies to use of the NSFNET Backbone only. NSF expects that connecting networks will formulate their own use policies. The NSF Division of Networking and Communications Research and Infrastructure will resolve any questions about this Policy or its interpretation.

> The most important part of this statement is the last part, under "Unacceptable Uses." The *general* rule is that you can use the Internet for reasonable personal use and for communication on matters of research or professional interest. These guidelines prohibit "commercial use," a somewhat hazily defined area: it's usually not OK to advertise products or solicit or process orders, but it is OK to announce the availability of a new product or service, or to post job offers.

INTERNET HOW-TO

What makes "acceptable use" more complicated is that a number of Internet sites and even entire networks have been set up for explicitly commercial purposes. Indeed, as more of the business world discovers the utility of the net, commercial use is likely to increase. A commercial site can do one of two things to operate legally: it can avoid the use of the government-sponsored sites for transmitting information (that is, work out alternate routes) or it can arrange to compensate such sites for the use of their resources.

As a user, however, you usually need not worry too much about these matters. If your Internet site allows uses that would go beyond what the NSFNET statement allows, the site will spell them out in its own acceptable use agreement. (If there's no explicit agreement, it's safest to go by the stricter NSFNET rules.) If in doubt, send mail to the site's system operator (sysop). Usually an address of "sysop" or "support" will work.

In addition to acceptable use guidelines, there are many other laws that apply to the net just as they do in the "real world." In general, assume that if you shouldn't do it offline, you shouldn't do it online. This includes things like posting passwords or credit card numbers, distributing pirated copies of software, or violating some other law. While some areas of computer law are still hazy, be aware that such things as libelous or slanderous attacks might expose both you and the operators of the Internet site to legal liability.

2. The next part of responsible net use is not codified in legalese. The general rule of courtesy remains "treat others as you would like them to treat you." The fact that we are communicating using words on a screen instead of faces or voices should not blind us to the reality that there are real human beings like ourselves at the other end of the data stream. Here are a few additional guidelines for courteous use of the Internet:

- In discussing issues, keep personal attacks *(flames)* out of the discussion.
- If the forum (newsgroup, mailing list, or whatever) is moderated, follow the moderator's guidelines.
- Be patient with beginners—we were all beginners once.
- As a beginner, make an effort to find the right place to ask your questions, and take advantage of the helpful resources discussed in this chapter before you ask a question on the net.
- In general, be aware of *context*. A posting in a newsgroup discussing Unix may be quite inappropriate in a group discussing religion (or vice versa). Try not to disrupt the flow of conversation. If you think of an interesting spin-off, it's usually better to start a new topic or discussion thread.

3. Finally, *efficient* use of the Internet is part of being a responsible member of the online community. Generally speaking, the growth in the number of users is outstripping the capacity of many of the existing sites where you can get files or other information. The result is often the equivalent of a busy signal: a message saying that there are too many people trying to get in, please call later. There are some general things you can do to help keep traffic flowing smoothly on the net:

2 GETTING STARTED

- If possible, call during off-peak hours. You'll not only be smoothing out the traffic flow, you'll also probably be rewarded with faster response time.
- If possible, plan your strategy before you get online. For example, if you're going to use ftp to get some files, have the appropriate directory and file names handy before you make the connection. (There are times when you're going to have to browse online, and browsing can be a good way to widen your horizons. But when you *do* know what you want, try to get it in the most efficient way possible.)
- Be aware that mail, news, and other files can eat up large amounts of disk space. Periodically review your home directory on the Internet system and download or delete unneeded files. (Many systems charge for disk space beyond some specified minimum, so keeping too many files around can be costly as well as inconsiderate.) Don't arrange to receive more material than you can keep up with. (Chapters 6, 8, and 9 will show you efficient ways to deal with files.)

Comment
Wise and efficient use of the Internet is something you must develop from experience. Sometimes all you have to do is pause and think a minute about the implications of what you are doing. On the other hand, there's no need to spend all your time worrying. The net is a robust and forgiving place. If someone flames you, don't take it personally: just learn what you can from the experience and move on.

2.8 HOW DO I...
Use the Internet safely and protect my privacy?

COMPLEXITY | INTERMEDIATE

Problem
The Internet gives you access to the world. That's power. The flip side is that once you're connected, the Internet also gives the world access to *you*. That can be vulnerability. The system administrators who run your Internet site have primary responsibility for security against intrusion or misuse of the system, but there are some steps you can take to help prevent abuses.

Technique
The main ways to improve your security as an Internet user are to use a good password, watch for suspicious activity online, and check the files you download for possible computer virus infection.

Steps
1. When you sign up on an Internet system you are asked to create a password. Give some thought to making your password difficult for intruders to guess. Some systems display specific guidelines or rules for passwords, and you should follow them. Here are some general rules:

- Use at least six characters.
- Include both upper and lowercase letters (passwords are case-sensitive).

- ➤ Include a number and/or punctuation mark.
- ➤ Don't use real English (or even foreign) words, proper names, initials, or common phrases.

Some examples of relatively secure passwords might be:

- ➤ Mitch5346
- ➤ Hope666
- ➤ MØnster
- ➤ PLatyPUS94

The general idea is to increase the number of possibilities for your password, thus making it harder for intruders to guess it. Intruders can use *cracking* programs that check common words, phrases, and names in an attempt to learn your password. Passwords that use the above rules are hard for such programs to guess.

2. At the same time, *you* want to be able to remember your password. But how can a password be both hard for others to guess and easy for you to remember? A common solution to this problem is to pick a phrase that means something to you but is not likely to mean anything to other people. (Some examples might be a bit of a nursery rhyme, the first words your baby said, or a passage from a favorite book.) Take the first letter from each word in the phrase, capitalize one, throw in a number or punctuation mark, and you're all set. For example, you might use "I get my kicks on Route 66" to create the password "Igmkor66."

3. Some systems require that passwords be changed at regular intervals. Even if there isn't such a requirement, it's a good idea to change your password every few months or so. On Unix systems you can run the "password" command to change your password. (Some systems make other provisions.)

4. Once you've got a secure password, keep your eyes open online. Watch out for suspicious or unusual behavior. For example:

- ➤ In the middle of a session you're suddenly prompted again for your login ID and password. This *could* be a system glitch, but don't take chances. Log out (press (CTRL)-(D) if necessary) and dial up again. Someone could be running a program that mimics the real login sequence and stores the password you enter.
- ➤ Someone claiming to be the system operator asks you for your password. Don't give it! Call or send e-mail to the operator (usually the address "sysop," "admin," or "support" will do) and describe what has happened. System operators seldom if ever need to know your password.
- ➤ When you log in, the system usually tells you the date and time when you *last* logged in. Check that date and time. If you don't think you were online, be suspicious. Someone may have cracked your account.
- ➤ You see evidence of suspicious behavior or warnings are posted about the system having possibly been cracked (compromised).

If any of these things happen, do two things: contact your system administrator, and *change your password immediately.*

5. Be aware that system administrators, privileged users, or intruders can read e-mail. It's best not to put sensitive information in e-mail (such as what you really think about your boss, or your credit card number). Chapter 3 will show you how you can *encrypt* mail to make it harder for other people to read. It's also a good idea to download a copy of your e-mail (see Chapter 9) to your PC and delete it from the Internet system.

6. Finally, when you download a program from the Internet for personal use, run a virus-checking utility on it just to be safe. Antivirus programs are available for PCs, Macs, and most other types of computers. Viruses aren't as prevalent on the Internet as the media might lead you to believe, but it's better to be safe than sorry.

Comment

As with securing your neighborhood against crime, there's no way to be 100 percent safe. Common sense, general awareness (cyber-street-smarts), and basic safety precautions on the part of every user will reduce the incidence of abuses considerably.

Using Internet Mail

How do I...

3.1 Read my mail
3.2 Get help while using Elm
3.3 Reply to a mail message
3.4 Search for messages by sender or subject
3.5 Print out a copy of all my mail
3.6 Send an original e-mail message
3.7 Send mail without bothering with menus
3.8 Send someone a file
3.9 Figure out what an Internet address means
3.10 Find someone's Internet address
3.11 Fix and resend returned mail
3.12 Forward a message to someone
3.13 Get information about incoming mail
3.14 Set up an address book
3.15 File mail for future reference
3.16 Read my mail folders
3.17 File mail automatically by sender or subject
3.18 Automatically forward my mail to another address
3.19 Work with several messages at once
3.20 Change Elm's default behavior
3.21 Tell people about myself
3.22 Add a personal "signature" to my messages
3.23 Edit message headers

Continued on next page

INTERNET HOW-TO

Continued from previous page

  3.24 Run a system command from Elm
  3.25 Encrypt mail for added security
  3.26 Exchange mail between the Internet and other networks
  3.27 Join a mailing list
  3.28 Learn more about Elm

When you move to a new residence, you know you're settled in when you start receiving mail. When you start using the Internet, it won't be long before you're getting electronic mail. This chapter will show you how to feel at home with the mail system. You'll learn how to read, reply to, send, and otherwise manage your e-mail.

Mail Programs

Most Internet sites use a program called *sendmail* to send and deliver mail to and from the system's users. As a user, you generally don't need to know anything about this low-level software. Instead of working with the mail system directly, you use a program called a *user agent* to manage your mail. The user agent presents your mail messages and lets you read them, make replies, file messages away for later use, and perform other useful functions related to electronic mail. You can think of the user agent as a kind of electronic secretary.

  A number of user agents are available in the Internet world. A common one is the standard Unix mail program (called mail, mailx, or binmail depending on the version of Unix in use). While these basic programs certainly let you handle your mail, they were designed back in the days of teletype-style, line-by-line computer displays. It's hard to keep track of what you're doing when using such primitive programs because there is no menu, and information about your current activity is always disappearing from the screen.

Elm's Features

The need for a more user-friendly mail program has led to the development of a variety of new approaches. While there are more advanced or specialized programs available, a program called Elm is described in this book. Elm is a good choice because it is easy to use yet sufficiently powerful and flexible for the needs of experienced users.

  Elm has the following key features:

➢ Menu-driven selections with online help
➢ An uncluttered display that avoids showing you unnecessary information
➢ The ability to file mail in folders that you can work with later
➢ Easy ways to customize the way the program presents and disposes of your mail
➢ An easy-to-manage alias system that works like an electronic address book and avoids the need to keep track of the Internet addresses of your correspondents
➢ A variety of utility programs that can help you automate your mail processing

  In this chapter you'll learn how to use the most important and useful features of Elm.

3 USING INTERNET MAIL

Related Topics

To Learn How to...	See Chapter
Connect to the Internet with your PC	2
Get files by ftp	7
Read a Usenet newsgroup	4
Transfer files between your PC and the Internet machine	9

How-Tos in this Chapter

3.1 Read my mail
The most basic skill in handling mail is the ability to display and read your incoming messages. Elm makes it easy to select and work with messages.

3.2 Get help while using Elm
Elm offers online help that summarizes what the command keys do.

3.3 Reply to a mail message
After you've read a mail message, you can send a reply. Elm hooks up to your favorite text editor, which you use to create the message.

3.4 Search for messages by sender or subject
If you get lots of mail, you may have several screens full of messages. Elm lets you search for particular messages according to words in their subject or by the name of the sender.

3.5 Print out a copy of all my mail
Sometimes it's necessary to have hard copy of your mail messages. You'll learn how to use a simple utility program to save all the messages to a file that you can then print.

3.6 Send an original e-mail message
Besides replying to messages, you'll probably want to send your own messages to people on the net. This is easy to do, provided you have the correct e-mail address.

3.7 Send mail without bothering with menus
Elm's menu-driven system makes it easy to use. But if you just want to send a quick message to someone, you can use Elm to send a message (or a prepared text file) from the system prompt.

3.8 Send someone a file
Once you're replying to a message (or creating a new message), Elm puts you in the text editor. You can use an editor command to insert a previously uploaded file into the message you are preparing.

3.9 Figure out what an Internet address means
Besides identifying a person or organization, an Internet address often contains useful information about location and affiliation. Understanding how addresses are constructed will help you determine the correct address to use.

3.10 Find someone's Internet address
While there's no single white pages that covers the whole Internet, there are a number of services that can help you find someone's mail address. This how-to shows you some useful techniques to try.

3.11 Fix and resend returned mail
"Return to sender...address unknown": the e-mail system has its equivalent messages, and can return mail to you for various reasons. This how-to looks at the most likely causes of mail problems and ways to fix them.

INTERNET HOW-TO

3.12 Forward a message to someone
If you get a message that you think someone else should handle, you can have Elm forward the mail to that person. (Pass the buck...electronically!)

3.13 Get information about incoming mail
Your Internet site will probably display a "You have mail" message when mail is pending. You can set things up so that you are given more detailed information about mail as it arrives.

3.14 Set up an address book
You probably don't want to have to memorize (and type) complicated mail addresses. Instead, you can use your Elm address book to store the mail addresses of frequent correspondents. You can then just type an *alias* (nickname or abbreviation), and Elm will supply the address automatically.

3.15 File mail for future reference
Elm lets you organize messages by sender or topic into handy *folders*. This makes it easy to keep track of your correspondence.

3.16 Read my mail folders
Once you have a mail folder set up, you can read it and work with it in the same way you do with your incoming messages.

3.17 File mail automatically by sender or subject
You can use an advanced Elm feature called *filters* to have Elm sort and save your mail automatically, based on sender or subject.

3.18 Automatically forward my mail to another address
If you have more than one Internet account, you may find it handy to have mail that arrives for you on one system sent automatically to your account on another system. You can do this by setting up a .forward file with the appropriate forwarding address.

3.19 Work with several messages at once
Sometimes it's convenient to work with several messages at once (for example, to save a group of messages to a file). You can *tag* messages in Elm and then have them operated on all at once.

3.20 Change Elm's default behavior
You will find that most of Elm's features work the way you would want or expect them to. Nevertheless, there are a number of options or settings that you can specify to control how Elm works and to configure your environment. You'll learn two different ways to specify these settings.

3.21 Tell people about myself
Unix has a program called *finger* that can display information about a user, including a person's interests or goals. To make this information available to the public, you put it in a file called .plan.

3.22 Add a personal "signature" to my messages
You can also create a signature that identifies you and can include a favorite slogan or aphorism. Elm will then automatically add this signature file to your outgoing messages.

3.23 Edit message headers
Sometimes you may need to add information to the header of a message, such as the names of additional recipients who will get "carbon copies."

3.24 Run a system command from Elm
You're running Elm and you want to include a file in a message. Uh-oh, you've forgotten the name of the file. Don't worry: you can *shell out* from Elm, get a command prompt, and run other programs or commands (such as "ls" to list your files).

3.25 Encrypt mail for added security
Encryption can help protect confidential or sensitive information from prying eyes. You can include instructions in a message that tells Elm to encrypt it. Your recipient then uses the secret "key" you provide to decrypt the message.

3.26 Exchange mail between the Internet and other networks
In addition to the Internet, there are a variety of other networks and information services (such as CompuServe) that provide their own e-mail systems. Thanks to e-mail *gateways* you can send mail from the Internet to just about any other network (and they can send mail to you), provided you know how to address the message properly.

3.27 Join a mailing list
There are hundreds of mailing lists that regularly distribute messages on a variety of topics, including technical news and hobby interests. This how-to shows you how mailing lists work and how to subscribe to them.

3.28 Learn more about Elm
This chapter covers Elm's basic features plus a number of interesting bells and whistles, but there is much more. We'll look at some of the documents and other sources that can help you learn more about Elm.

3.1 HOW DO I...
Read my mail?

COMPLEXITY: EASY

Problem
When you're logged in, you may see messages from the system that read "you have mail" or possibly "you have new mail." As you exchange addresses with more people (and perhaps participate in mailing lists and newsgroups), you'll get even more mail. Once you know there's something in your electronic mailbox, how do you read the mail messages?

Technique
You read your mail by running Elm and then choosing mail messages from the list shown on the screen.

Steps
1. Type `elm` at the system prompt and press (ENTER). The first time you run Elm, the program will ask you if it is OK to set up a special directory (called .elm) to hold files relating to the mail system. Press (Y) and then (ENTER).

```
% elm
Notice:
This version of ELM requires the use of a .elm directory in your home
directory to store your elmrc and alias files. Shall I create the
directory .elm for you and set it up (y/n/q)? Yes.
Great! I'll do it now.
```

Elm also asks you for permission to create a directory to store mail folders (groups of messages that you save):

INTERNET HOW-TO

Notice:
Elm requires the use of a folders directory to store your mail folders in.
Shall I create the directory /home/h/hrh/Mail for you (y/n/q)?

(The path location for the directory will be different when you do this, of course.) Press Y and Elm will set up your directories.

2. Elm then presents you with an "index" or list of the messages in your mailbox. This is the main screen from which you'll perform most Elm commands. Figure 3-1 shows the Elm Index screen. There are two other screens you'll see later: the Options Editor screen is used to change options (configuration settings) for Elm, and the Alias Mode screen is used to access or set aliases (shortcut addresses for your correspondents).

3. As you look at the figure, note that one mail message is listed on each line. (By default, up to ten messages will be listed on one screen. If you have more than ten messages, you will be able to see them on subsequent "pages" as explained later.)

Each message line contains the following information:

➢ One or more letters indicating the status of the message. The status is usually either N (a new, unread message) or D (a message that has been marked for deletion). A status of O ("old") means the message has been presented to you in an earlier session but you haven't read it yet. There are other possible status types, but they aren't important.

➢ The message number. You can use this for selecting a message to work with.

➢ The date the message was sent.

➢ The person who sent the message. If the mail system knows the person's full name (that is, it is in the message or in an alias file), it will be listed, for example, Joe Smith. Otherwise, the person's net address will be given, such as jsmith@netcom.com.

➢ The total number of lines in the message.

➢ The first few words of the subject of the message.

4. Note that the first message will be highlighted in some way. On most terminals, the highlight is in reverse video (light letters on a dark background), as in Figure 3-1. In the regular listings in this book, boldface is used to simulate this highlight. The highlight indicates the *current* message—that is, the message that will be acted on by your next command.

The easiest way to read your messages is to press (SPACEBAR). The first message will be listed on your screen. Pressing (SPACEBAR) to read message 1 gives you:

```
Return-Path: james@uclink.berkeley.edu
Date: Mon, 22 Nov 1993 16:33:06 -0800
Subject: Do you know a good book on C++?

Hi
I'm trying to find a list of good beginner's books on C++
that I could recommend for my upcoming class at UCB
this Spring. Any suggestions?
thanks
James P.
```

3 🌐 USING INTERNET MAIL

Command ('i' to return to index):

Pressing (SPACEBAR) at the end of a message lists the next message. You can thus read through all your mail by repeatedly pressing (SPACEBAR) until no messages are left. Note that you can press (ENTER) instead of (SPACEBAR) and get the same result, except that (ENTER) won't take you to the next message from within a message. Press (i) to return to the Index screen rather than continuing to read.

5. Sometimes you may want to read a particular message first, or read only a few messages that look important and save the remainder for a later session. To read a particular message, press the message number and then (ENTER).

Command: New Current Message   Set current message to : 5

Elm always displays the command name as soon as it recognizes what you're trying to do. As soon as you press (5), it changes the command to "New Current Message." You then press (ENTER) to set the current message to 5. The highlight now moves to message 5, and the Index screen looks like this:

```
        Mailbox is '~/.inbox' with 6 messages [ELM 2.4 PL22]


     1   Nov 22 james@uclink.berke (18)   Do you know a good book on C++?
  N  2   Nov 22 Joel S. Fugazzotto  (12)   Your chapter's late
  N  3   Nov 22 BIGWAR-list         (19)   Results of turn 19
  N  4   Nov 22 james@newsoft.rese  (16)   Friday appointment
  N  5   Nov 22 sarah@bigu.edu      (36)   Welcome to the World
  N  6   Nov 22 Dorothy J Heydt     (18)   Re: Need correspondent's address
```

Press (SPACEBAR) (or (ENTER)) to read message 5:

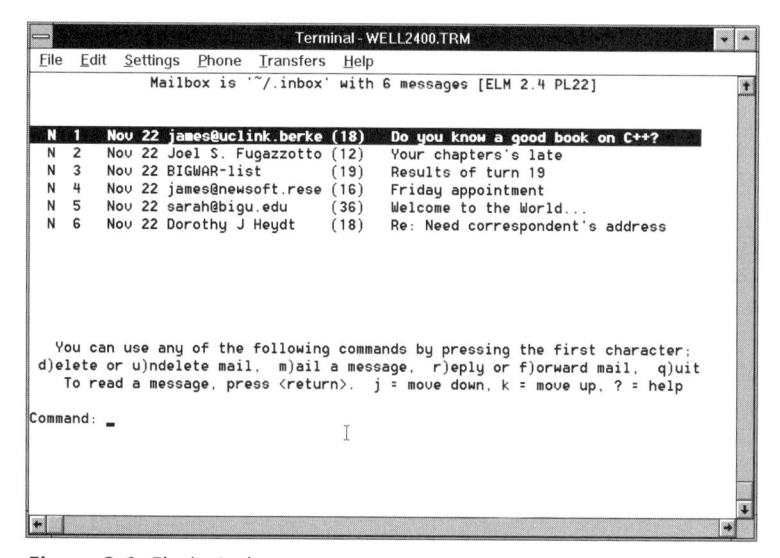

Figure 3-1 Elm's Index screen

INTERNET HOW-TO

```
Return-Path: sarah@bigu.edu
Date: Mon, 22 Nov 1993 16:23:34 -0800
Subject: Welcome to the World

Hey, I hear you've finally gotten with the 90s and gotten on the net!
I'm sure you'll be getting the hang of it in no time. I've sent you
this mail message so you can see how email works.

Personally, I recommend Elm. It's easy to get started (what with the
menus and all). Elm also does a good job of helping you file away your
mail into folders and letting you review it periodically. Anyway,
when I get a reply from you I'll know you've started learning your way
around...You might want to pick up a copy of the "Internet How-To" book
from the Waite Group folks along with a beginner's Unix manual. A little
light reading for your next business trip (heh)...

Don't forget about the Usenet news, either. Hundreds of groups on
every imaginable topic (and some I bet you didn't imagine..) I'm
always getting into arguments about what's the best C++ compiler, so
I spend too much time in some of those "techie" groups. Your mileage
   There are 11 lines left (69%). Press <space> for more, or 'i' to return.
```

> Since this message is too long to fit on one screen, a pager prompt appears at the bottom of the listing. (This prompt may look a bit diffrent on your system.) Press (SPACEBAR) to continue reading the message:

```
may vary...

There's so much else to do on the net. Just the other day I found
a Gopher menu that listed ways to arrange low-cost trips to the Amazon
rain forest with environmental groups. You get to see what they're
really trying to save there, and part of the money goes to their
research and advocacy efforts.

You never know what will turn up on the net next. Let me know if you
find something interesting!

Command ('i' to return to index):
```

> 6. Alternatively, you can press (J) or (↓) to advance the highlight to the next unread message, or press (K) or (↑) to move back one message. (You don't press (ENTER) after single letter commands like these.) Once you've moved the highlight to the message you want, press (SPACEBAR) (or (ENTER)) to read the message.
>
> 7. You may find it convenient to press (i) after each message to return to the Index screen, rather than pressing (SPACEBAR) or (ENTER) to read the next message. If you press (i) you can then press (D) to mark the message you just read for deletion, and then press (SPACEBAR) to continue to the next message.
>
> 8. If there are more than ten messages, you can continue to press (SPACEBAR) to automatically advance to the remaining screens of message listings. You can also press (.) or (→) to go immediately to the next screen, and then select a message to

read. If you want to return to a previous Index screen, press ⊟ (the minus key) or the ⬅ key.

9. For any messages that you don't need to keep and that haven't already been marked for deletion, select the message and press Ⓓ. The status letter for that message will change to D, indicating that it is marked for deletion. This means the message will be removed from your current mail folder at the end of your current Elm session.

10. To end your Elm session, press Ⓠ. If you've marked any messages for deletion, you'll be asked:

```
Command: Quit                                    Delete messages? (y/n) n
```

Press Ⓨ unless you decide you'd rather keep the messages.

If you've read some messages but *haven't* marked them for deletion, you'll then be asked:

```
Move read messages to "received" folder? (y/n) n
```

If you'd like to get the messages out of your mailbox but still be able to retrieve them later, answer Ⓨ. Otherwise press ENTER to accept the n (no) prompt, and your messages will be left in the mailbox. You'll see them again next time you run Elm, along with any new messages that come in. (The messages that were left over from a previous session will have a status of O. Later you'll learn how to save specific messages to folders of your choice.)

11. Finally, Elm tells you what it has done with the contents of your mailbox. For example:

```
[Storing 1 message and deleting 2.]
```

Table 3-1 summarizes the keys used for selecting and reading messages, and for exiting Elm.

How It Works
Each mail message is actually a standard text file that begins with fields called *headers*. The mail system uses some of these headers (such as To: and Return:) to route the mail. Other headers, such as Subject, are for the user's benefit. One of Elm's many good features is that it avoids cluttering your screen with headers that contain information meaningful only to the electronic post office.

The mechanism for sending message files from a user on one machine to a recipient on another is normally transparent: you don't have to worry about it any more than you have to worry about how the phone company connects your phone to someone else's. There *can* be a few problems that arise when trying to send mail, and you'll see how to cope with them in How-To 3.11.

Comment
If you haven't received any mail yet, you can still try out the mail reading commands. Go to How-To 3.6 and use the instructions there to send yourself some mail messages.

INTERNET HOW-TO

TO DO THIS...	PRESS OR TYPE THIS
Read messages	[SPACEBAR] or [ENTER]
Select a particular message	message number [ENTER]
Select next unread message	[J] or [↓]
Select previous unread message	[K] or [↑]
Select next message (read or not)	[J]
Select previous message (read or not)	[K]
Go to next index page	[+] or [→]
Go to previous index page	[-] or [←]
Quit Elm (prompts for deleting or saving)	[q]
Quit Elm (no prompts)	[Q]
Note: The arrow keys on a PC keyboard may not work if your terminal emulation doesn't support them.	

Table 3-1 Keys for reading and selecting messages

3.2 HOW DO I... Get help while using Elm?

COMPLEXITY EASY

Problem
When you're learning Elm you may need to refresh your memory about the various Elm command keys and their functions. If you just need a quick reminder, Elm's online help may be faster and easier than looking things up in a book.

Technique
Getting help is a simple matter of pressing the [?] key and following the prompts.

Steps
1. Press the [?] key. You will enter the Elm help system:

```
ELM Help System
    Press the key you want help for, '?' for a key list, or '.' to exit help
Help for key:
```

2. To find out what a particular key command does, press that key. Elm will display a brief message describing the purpose of that key. For example, if you press [j] you'll see the following message:

```
j = Go to the next undeleted message. This is the same as the DOWN arrow.
```

3. If you want a summary of what all the available key commands do, press [?] a second time. The summary you see will depend on what part of the Elm system you're using (Index, Options Editor, or Alias Mode screen). All three of these summary screens are printed at the end of this chapter.

4. You can continue pressing keys for which you want to see help, or press [.] (period) to exit the help system and return to regular command processing.

3 🌐 USING INTERNET MAIL

How It Works
Elm has several text files that it uses for retrieving the help messages it shows you. You don't have to worry about this unless your help request is met by an error message (of the "Cannot find...file" variety). In that case contact your system operator.

3.3 HOW DO I...
Reply to a mail message?

COMPLEXITY: EASY

Problem
Often you will want to type in your reply to a mail message and send it to the person who sent you the mail. Fortunately, Elm makes this easy to do.

Technique
Once you've selected the message to which you want to reply, you compose your reply and send it to your correspondent. You write your reply using one of the commonly available text editors. One of the most popular is called *vi*. vi is a screen-oriented text editor that is no substitute for a word processor, but works fine for typing in a few paragraphs. vi is used for the example below, but you can use any available editor.

Steps
1. Select the message to which you wish to reply by pressing the message numbers or using the (J), (K), (↑), or (↓) key or typing the message number. For example, to select message 4 in Figure 3-1, press (4) and (ENTER). The message will be highlighted to show that it is the current message.

2. Press (R). Elm will prompt you as follows:

```
Command: Reply to message         To: james@newsoft.research.com
Subject of message: Re: Friday meeting
```

   Elm fills in the address from the current message.

3. If the message you are replying to was sent to more than one person and you want your reply to be seen by everyone who received the message, press (G) (group reply) instead of (R). The g and r commands are otherwise identical. Note that you can tell that a message was sent to more than one person if it has additional addresses in the CC: (carbon copies) header.

4. The cursor will be on the subject line. Normally you'll accept the subject by pressing (ENTER), but you could change the subject by pressing your *line kill* character (usually (CTRL)-(X)) and then typing a new subject.

5. After you press (ENTER), you will be prompted as to whether to send copies of your message to anyone:

```
Copies to:
```

   If you wish someone else to get a copy of your reply, type that person's address. Separate multiple addresses with commas.

6. The next prompt is:

49

INTERNET HOW-TO

Copy message (y/n)?

    Press Ⓨ if you want a copy of the mail message to be included in the text you will be editing. By default, the text will be preceded with the prefix character, >, to indicate that it is from the original message:

```
>Are you going to the project update meeting this afternoon?
>It looks like management is getting real anxious to see some results.
>Jerry
```

    7. You'll now be in a text editor. The editor used will depend on the program specified when the system manager set up Elm. vi is the most common choice. If you wish, you can specify that a different editor be used when you write mail (see How-To 3.20).

    Use the editor to write your reply. The commands available will vary with the editor in use. See Chapter 6 for a brief guide to vi, or see Table 3-2 for a list of basic vi editing key commands. You begin by positioning the cursor and pressing Ⓐ or Ⓘ to enter text entry mode. Here's what it looks like when you're writing a reply using vi:

```
I'll be there. I'm not going to be able to have lunch first,
so can you save me a sandwich?
thanks
Jerry
~
~
~
~
~
~
~
~
~
~
~
~
~
"/tmp/snd.14415" 0 lines, 0 characters
```

    8. Exit the editor with its "write and quit" command. For vi, you press (ESC) to get back into command mode, and then type :wq.

    9. When you return to Elm, you will be prompted as to what to do with your message:

```
Please choose one of the following options by parenthesized letter: s
        e)dit message, edit h)eaders, s)end it, or f)orget it.
```

    ➤ Press Ⓢ to send the message to the person who sent you the mail.

    ➤ Press Ⓔ to edit (revise) the message.

➤ Press Ⓗ to edit the message headers (this is usually not necessary, but see How-To 3.23).

➤ Press Ⓕ to forget (discard) your reply without sending it.

10. Elm will send your reply and return you to the Index screen:

```
Mail sent!
```

How It Works

Like many larger Unix programs, Elm is designed to let you "plug in" your favorite tools (editor, screen pager, and so on). When you reply to a message, Elm hands over control to the specified editor. The editor creates a temporary file, which is then accessed by Elm to send the message.

Comment

If your reply addresses some specific material in the message, you may wish to respond yes to the "Copy message (y/n)?" prompt. The entire message will be put in the editor buffer, ready for you to work with. You can then delete unnecessary parts of the original message and intersperse the key parts with your reply. For example:

```
In answer to your questions:
> I'd like to know whether you'll be free next month for a special project
I could be. What do you have in mind?
> Do you have any experience with large Unix networks?
I worked last summer at NSF helping monitor their network connections.
I guess that counts as "some experience."
```

Here the lines that begin with > are from the original message.

TO DO THIS...	PRESS OR TYPE THIS
Begin adding text	Ⓐ
Insert text before cursor	Ⓘ
Change from text entry to cursor movement or command mode	ⒺⓈⒸ
Move cursor up one line	Ⓙ
Move cursor down one line	Ⓚ
Move cursor one character left	Ⓗ
Move cursor one character right	Ⓛ
Move to beginning of next word	Ⓦ
Write text to file and exit	:wq
Exit editor without saving text	:q!

Table 3-2 Some basic vi editing keys

3.4 HOW DO I... Search for messages by sender or subject?

COMPLEXITY: INTERMEDIATE

Problem
If you have a lot of mail, it may be hard to find a message from a particular person or about a certain subject. Elm can help you find the right message.

Technique
You provide Elm with the text to search for. If Elm finds a message with the matching text, that message becomes the current message.

Steps
1. Make sure that the current message is set to the message from which you want to search. Usually you'll want to search from the beginning of the list:

```
Mailbox is '~/.inbox' with 6 messages [ELM 2.4 PL22]


    1   Nov 22 james@uclink.berke  (18)   Do you know a good book on C++?
N   2   Nov 22 Joel S. Fugazzotto  (12)   Your chapter's late
N   3   Nov 22 BIGWAR-list         (19)   Results of turn 19
N   4   Nov 22 james@newsoft.rese  (16)   Friday appointment
N   5   Nov 22 sarah@bigu.edu      (36)   Welcome to the World...
N   6   Nov 22 Dorothy J Heydt     (18)   Re: Need correspondent's address
```

Here, since message 5 is highlighted, you would press ⓘ to set the current message back to the first message.

2. Press ⁄ . You'll see the following prompt:

```
Command:                          / = Match anywhere in messages.

Match pattern: appointment
```

Type the text that you want Elm to search for in the From: or Subject: lines of the messages. This way you can search for messages either from a particular individual or about a particular subject. Here, typing **appointment** causes message 4 to be highlighted, since that message has the word "appointment" in its subject.

3. If you want Elm to look for your specified text anywhere in the messages (not just in the From: or Subject: headers), press a second ⁄ before typing your text, and the prompt will change to:

```
Command:                          / = Match anywhere in messages.

Match pattern (in entire message): royalties
```

4. Elm will highlight the first message that matches your search phrase. In this case message 6 will be highlighted if it's the first message to have the word "royalties" somewhere in the headers or message body.

3 USING INTERNET MAIL

How It Works
All the messages you see on the Index screen are actually in a single text file called a folder. Elm simply searches through this file. Without the second /, Elm looks for lines that begin with From: or Subject:. When you type the second slash and then the text, Elm looks through every line in the folder.

Comment
Elm's searches are not case-sensitive.

3.5 HOW DO I...
Print out a copy of all my mail?

COMPLEXITY: INTERMEDIATE

Problem
People have been saying for at least 20 years that we're entering a "paperless society." Sometimes, though, it's still necessary to have things down on paper for times when a computer isn't handy.

Technique
Since your mail messages make up a text file called a folder, this text file can be formatted and printed like any other file. A utility program called *printmail* does this simple job.

Steps
1. From the system prompt (or from a shell escape from Elm, as described in How-To 3.24), type `printmail >` followed by the name of the file you want to contain the formatted messages. Press (ENTER). For example:

```
%printmail > temp.txt
```

2. Elm separates the messages in the file with a line of dashes, like this:

```
well% cat tmp
Date: Mon, 22 Nov 1993 16:30:27 -0800
From: "Joel S. Fugazzotto" <fugie>
Subject: Your chapter's late

I hope it's coming along. Please let me know when it's ready.
—Your anxious editor

------------------------------------------

Date: Mon, 22 Nov 1993 16:33:06 -0800
From: james@uclink.berkeley.edu
Subject: Do you know a good book on C++?

Hi
I'm trying to find a list of good beginner's books on C++
that I could recommend for my upcoming class at UCB
this Spring. Any suggestions?

thanks
James P.
```

INTERNET HOW-TO

You can also add the -p option to printmail, to get a formfeed after each message (thus usually printing one message per page).

3. By default, printmail prints the *inbox* folder (your current mailbox contents). To print from a different folder, add the name of the folder to the printmail command. For example:

```
% printmail Mail/important > tmp
```

This puts a formatted version of the "important" folder in the file "tmp." (Note that folders are normally subdirectories of your Mail directory; for more on using folders see How-Tos 3.15 and 3-16.)

4. Download the formatted message file to your PC. (You can use a program such as Xmodem or Kermit for this purpose; see Chapter 9 for details.)

5. Print the file at your PC using your favorite word processor or text editor.

How It Works
Printmail takes the inbox or the specified folder and formats it so that the messages are easy to read. The > character in the command directs the output of the printmail program to the filename you specify. You then download the formatted file and print it at your PC.

Comment
Elm has a P (for print) command on the main menu, but this command is designed to print on the system printer, which will normally be attached to a remote computer. This isn't very useful for most users.

3.6 HOW DO I...
Send an original e-mail message?

COMPLEXITY: EASY

Problem
It's easy to just reply to mail, but sometimes you'll want to send an original mail message. Elm lets you do this without leaving the Index screen.

Technique
Send an original e-mail message when your message is not directly related to any message you've read. (That is, the message is not a reply to someone.) Sending an original message is like starting a new conversation.

For example, let's say you want to send a message to Sarah (the author of message 5 in Figure 3-1). Rather than just replying to her message, you want to start a new topic by asking her a question.

Steps
1. Press [M] at the main Elm menu. You will see the following prompt:

```
Command: Mail                    Send the message To: sarah@bigu.edu
```

When you see the To: prompt, you type in the net address of the person to whom you're sending the message. (Later you'll see how you can avoid having to remember addresses.) Here the address is sarah@bigu.edu.

3 USING INTERNET MAIL

2. You are now prompted for the subject of the message. Type in the subject and press `ENTER`:

```
Subject of message: Are there any social clubs for Internet users?
```

3. The remaining steps are like those used when replying to a message (see How-To 3.3). You're given the opportunity to specify other people to receive a copy of your message.

4. Elm puts you in the text editor. Write the message and exit the text editor as you do when writing a reply.

5. You will then see the same message disposition menu that you see when replying to a message:

```
Please choose one of the following options by parenthesized letter: s
     e)dit message, edit h)eaders, s)end it, or f)orget it.
```

➢ Press `S` to send the message.
➢ Press `E` to edit (revise) the message.
➢ Press `H` to edit the message headers (this is usually not necessary, but see How-To 3.23).
➢ Press `F` to forget (discard) your message without sending it.

6. Elm will send your message and return you to the Index screen.

How It Works
The mechanism for sending new mail is just like that for mailing a reply, except that you must provide the address of the recipient. Elm hands the message over to the local *mail transport agent* (usually the sendmail program).

Comment
Electronic mail is less formal than paper mail, and easier to create. Nevertheless, it is subject to the same considerations as paper letters: brevity, clarity of style, courtesy, and other aspects of effective letter writing.

You should *not* assume that e-mail is safe from all prying eyes. It's best not to put sensitive information or valuable items such as credit card numbers in e-mail. If you want to make certain messages more secure, you can encrypt them (see How-To 3.25).

3.7 HOW DO I...
Send mail without bothering with menus?

COMPLEXITY | **INTERMEDIATE**

Problem
Sometimes you just want to send a quick note to someone. You don't need all those menus and help screens and other stuff. Also, you might want to send a file that you've already prepared rather than write the message online.

Technique
Elm lets you send mail from the system command line without using the normal menu system. (This behavior is similar to that of the traditional Unix mail program.)

55

INTERNET HOW-TO

You run Elm by specifying the address to which you're writing mail. Elm prompts you for the rest of the necessary information.

Steps

1. At the system prompt, type `elm` followed by the address of the recipient of the letter. For example, suppose we want to send mail to the system billing department to check on our usage charges:

```
%elm accounts
            Send only mode [ELM 2.4 PL22]

To: WELL Billing Dept.
```

Something interesting happened here. We typed `accounts` as the address for our message. But Elm filled in the To: prompt as "WELL Billing Dept." Elm got this name from the *system alias file*, which matches full names with login IDs (*usernames*) of accounts on the system. Elm always shows you the full name if possible. In How-To 3.14 you'll learn how to create your own personal alias file.

2. Elm prompts you for the subject of the message. Type in the subject and press (ENTER).

```
Subject of message: Questions about my July bill
```

3. Elm now asks you whether you want to send copies of the message to other recipients. If you do, type in the address(es) of the other recipients, separated by a comma and space. If you don't want to send copies, just press (ENTER).

```
Copies to:
```

4. You are placed in your text editor, as usual. Write the message, save it, and exit the editor.

5. Elm sends the mail and you are returned to the system prompt.

How It Works

Running Elm from the command line puts it in "Send only mode". This is a useful shortcut if you just want to send a quick message and aren't interested in using other Elm features.

You can specify additional information on the command line and avoid the corresponding prompts. For example, if you type `-s` followed by the subject, as in

```
%elm -s "Meeting minutes" jwoodward
```

you won't be prompted for a subject. If you specify a filename (using <, the Unix "redirect-from" character), as follows,

```
elm -s "To-Do List" john < list.txt
```

you won't go to the text editor: the file "list.txt" will simply be mailed to John.

Comment

If you know how to write Unix shell scripts you can use these Elm features to send mail automatically. (To learn how to write shell scripts, consult an intermediate-level Unix text.)

3.8 HOW DO I... *Send someone a file?*

COMPLEXITY: INTERMEDIATE

Problem
It isn't always convenient to write mail messages with the text editor on the Internet system. You may want to write longer messages using a fuller-featured or easier-to-use program on your PC, and then upload the file to your Internet site (see Chapter 9). You might also want to mail an already existing text file to someone.

Technique
There are two ways to send someone a file with Elm. The first, using Elm in command mode with a filename, was shown at the end of the preceding how-to. The second method is to go through the usual message sending procedure but, when you are placed in the text editor, to read an already existing file into the edit buffer. The latter technique is explained here.

Steps
1. Run Elm, and press (M) as usual to mail a new message.

2. When Elm puts you in the editor, use the editor's "read in a file" command to place a copy of the file in your message. In vi, you would press (ESC) (to go to command mode) and then type

```
:r form_letter
```

   to read the text file "form_letter" into the edit buffer.

3. After making any desired changes or additions to the text, exit the editor (with vi, type `:wq`) and mail the message as usual.

How It Works
As far as Elm is concerned, a file is a file. Elm doesn't really care how or where you created a text file. This makes it easy to share files that you've gotten on the net. Most text editors let you read in a file, though some very simple ones may not.

Comment
The advantage of the "read in a file" technique over the command line technique is that when you work with the file in a text editor you can make additions or changes (such as adding comments or filling in information for a form letter or document template).

The techniques discussed here work with any text file. See Chapter 8 for information on handling binary files such as programs, graphic images, or files formatted in a word processor.

INTERNET HOW-TO

3.9 HOW DO I...
Figure out what an Internet address means?

COMPLEXITY | INTERMEDIATE

Problem
Each person accessible through the Internet has a unique address that tells the mail system where to send messages for that person. Basically an address consists of a name that describes the site to which that person connects and his or her user ID. Of course it's a bit more complicated than that. While you can normally reply to a mail message without paying attention to the user's address, you need the correct address if you want to send an original message.

Internet addresses use what's called the *domain name system*. A domain address consists of two parts:

➢ The user name (that is, login ID)
➢ A domain name (usually consisting of several parts)

The user ID is easy to understand: it's the name (or initials) you type when the system gives you the login prompt.

A domain name is a way to describe a computer site and its nature and relationship to other sites. A domain name can consist of several parts (called *subdomains*) separated by periods. For example, the domain microsoft.com has two parts: "microsoft" (the name of the organization) and "com" (a description of the purpose of the organization). "Com" means "commercial," indicating a business concern rather than a government agency or university.

There are several *functional* subdomains: the most common are given in Table 3-3.

The functional subdomains given in Table 3-3 generally apply only within the United States. Sites in other countries use a *geographical* subdomain system.

Watching for geographical subdomains is a good way of identifying sites that are outside the country. (Given a choice, it's better to transfer large files from a site within the country because it uses less communications resources.) Table 3-4 shows some examples of geographical subdomains.

Thus the name "barrowdowns.uk" would refer to a site called Barrow Downs in the United Kingdom. Geographical subdomains are also sometimes used within the United

DOMAIN	PURPOSE
com	Commercial organization (business)
edu	Educational institution (college or university)
gov	Government agency
int	International organization
mil	Military installation
net	Organization related to networking
org	Nonprofit organization

Table 3-3 Functional subdomains

3 ⊕ USING INTERNET MAIL

DOMAIN	LOCATION
au	Australia
ca	Canada
ch	Switzerland ("cantons of Helvetia")
de	Germany ("Deutschland")
fr	France
jp	Japan
uk	United Kingdom
us	United States
ca	California
mi	Michigan

Table 3-4 Geographical subdomains

States. For example, The WELL's full domain name is well.sf.ca.us, which means: The WELL, San Francisco, California, United States. Notice that when several geographical subdomains are used together, moving from left to right takes you from the most local (San Francisco) to the most general (United States). (Actually, The WELL has informed us that it can also be addressed as well.com.)

The name of the organization can itself be divided into subdomains. For example, "newsoft.research.com" might mean the research and development department of the Newsoft company.

Technique
Reading net addresses involves learning to recognize the types of domain names and using them to understand the location and purpose of the organization.

Steps
1. Look at the first part of the address (up to the @ or "at sign"). This is the user's ID.

2. Look at the last part of the address (following a period). If it is one of the subdomains in Table 3-3 (such as .com or .edu), note the type of organization (business, university, government, and so on).

3. If the last part of the address indicates a geographical area, as in Table 3-4, note where the site is located (for example, uk for United Kingdom).

4. Now look at the middle of the address. This will be the organization name (for example, Microsoft). If there is more than one part here, then the site is a department or other subdivision of the organization.

5. If the address doesn't follow these rules, it may be formatted for a network other than the Internet. See How-To 3.26 for details on how to send messages to non-Internet networks.

How It Works
The domain name system works on the assumption that computers, not people, should figure out how to get messages from one site to another. A program called a *name server*

INTERNET HOW-TO

translates a domain name address to a numerical routing address that specifies the location of the destination on the network, and a router selects machines through which the message must pass to reach the destination. Unlike the older UUCP system, the Internet is quite robust: many messages can take a variety of routes to get to their destination.

Comment

Don't worry about understanding everything about Internet addresses. You don't usually need to know the details to communicate successfully.

3.10 HOW DO I... *Find someone's Internet address?*

COMPLEXITY: ADVANCED

Problem

It's not always easy to find someone's Internet address. You can't just dial Information. However, there are some commands and services you can use to search for more information about people on the net.

Technique

The technique is "if this doesn't work, try that." The techniques presented here start out easy and get more complicated. One of them should give you the address you need.

Steps

1. One way to find someone's Internet address is to look at any mail that person has sent you, or a news article he or she has posted. Elm lets you automatically "grab" an address from the current mail message and store it for later use under an alias (see How-To 3.14).

2. If the person hasn't communicated with you electronically, you might need to use conventional means (phone or paper mail) to ask for the e-mail address.

3. If you know the person's login ID and site, but you want to make sure you have the right person (or you just want to know more about him or her), try the *finger* command. Type `finger` followed by the address. For example, suppose you knew Sarah was at Big U, and you wanted to know more about what she did there. You could type

```
% finger sarah@bigu.edu
[bigu.edu]
Login name: sarah                In real life: Sarah Goodson
Directory: /home/sarah           Shell: /bin/csh
Last login Tue Nov 23 17:53 on ttymc from dialup-c
Plan:
I want to finish my master's degree in Computer Science and then get a job with an exciting startup company in the computer graphics field.
```

The finger command looks up the person's .plan file. (See How-To 3.21 for information on how to set up your own .plan file.)

4. If you think you know what site the person is connected to, but don't know the user ID, you can try the *whois* command if it's available on your system. In its simplest

form, you can use whois to find out more about a domain of the Internet. For example, to find out about the "uk" domain, type:

```
% whois uk
Silverman, Michael (MS55)          uk@PORTMAN.COM         +44 (0)71 437 4402
UK Academic Joint Network Team (NET-JANET-IP) JANET-IP         146.97.0.0
UK TeX Archive (NET-TEX-NET)       TEX-NET                     193.63.78.0
United Kingdom of Great Britain top-level domain (UK-DOM)              UK
```

You'll get a description of the domain and some key people or organizations involved with it.

5. Type `whois -h` followed by the name of the *whois server* for the person's site, and then the person's last name, or complete name in single quotes. A widely used whois server is whois.internic.net.

For example, to see if James Kirk has an e-mail address, you can try one of the following commands:

```
% whois -h whois.internic.net kirk
% whois -h whois.internic.net 'james t kirk'
% whois kirk
```

The first two commands use the whois.internic.net whois server. The first finds all Kirks known to that server. The second looks specifically for James T. Kirk. (The search is not case-sensitive; leave out periods after initials when typing in the command.) The last search uses whatever whois server is the default for your system. This may be a server *on* your system, or perhaps an outside one such as whois.internic.com.

6. Another technique that will retrieve many (though not all) e-mail addresses is to mail a message to mail-server@rtfm.mit.edu. Leave the subject of the message blank. Put a single line in the message body, with the form,

send usenet-addresses/*name*

where *name* is all or part of the name of the person you're looking for. The mail-server site automatically records the addresses and names from the thousands of Usenet news articles that pass through the wires every week. The addresses of persons who have posted news during the past year or so and that match your search name will be sent back to you by mail.

For example, to find the addresses of my friends Wilson (Hal) and Dorothy Heydt, I sent this message:

```
% elm mail-server@rtfm.mit.edu
Subject:
send usenet-addresses/heydt
```

An hour or so later, I received the following reply (unnecessary lines deleted):

```
dorothy.j.heydt@cld9.sccsi.com (Dorothy J Heydt)       (Aug 31 93)
whheydt@PacBell.COM (Wilson Heydt)         (Jun 30 93)
whheydt@pbhya.PacBell.COM (Wilson Heydt)        (Jun 30 93)
```

Continued on next page

INTERNET HOW-TO

Continued from previous page

```
whheydt@pbhya.pacbell.com (Wilson H. Heydt Jr). (Mar 11 93)
whheydt@pbhya.pacbell.com (Wilson Heydt)       (May 11 93)
djheydt@uclink.berkeley.edu (Dorothy J Heydt)  (Nov 22 93)
heydt@eniac.seas.upenn.edu (Dr. Seuss)  (Sep 29 93)
```

You may have to use some common sense to determine which entry is likely to be the person you seek.

7. A final technique involves a program called *netfind*. Netfind takes a name and a location description and tries to figure out whether the person you named is connected to a machine on that part of the net. A simple way to use this program is to type `netfind` followed by the last name of the person you seek and the name of an organization where you suspect that person works. For example, to see whether Bill Gates works at Microsoft, you could try

```
netfind gates microsoft
```

You can also use subdomains that you know relate to the person in question. For example,

```
netfind fugazzotto sf ca us
```

would restrict the search to the San Francisco Bay Area.

8. If you don't have netfind on your Internet system, you can use the telnet program (covered in Chapter 10) to connect to a netfind server (login as "netfind"). For example, let's connect to the server at bruno.cs.colorado.edu:

```
well% telnet bruno.cs.colorado.edu
Trying 128.138.243.150...
Connected to bruno.cs.colorado.edu.
Escape character is '^]'.

SunOS UNIX (bruno)

Login as `netfind' to access netfind server

login: netfind
nsh: Too many Netfind sessions are active.  Please try again later.
Or, please try one of the Alternate Netfind servers:
        archie.au (AARNet, Melbourne, Australia)
        bruno.cs.colorado.edu (University of Colorado, Boulder)
        dino.conicit.ve (Nat. Council for Techn. & Scien. Research, Venezuela)
        ds.internic.net (InterNIC Directory and DB Services, S. Plainfield, NJ)
        eis.calstate.edu (California State University, Fullerton, CA)
        hto-e.usc.edu (University of Southern California, Los Angeles)
        krnic.net (Korea Network Information Center, Taejon, Korea)
        lincoln.technet.sg (Technet Unit, Singapore)
        malloco.ing.puc.cl (Catholic University of Chile, Santiago)
        monolith.cc.ic.ac.uk (Imperial College, London, England)
        mudhoney.micro.umn.edu (University of Minnesota, Minneapolis)
        netfind.anu.edu.au (Australian National University, Canberra)
```

```
        netfind.ee.mcgill.ca (McGill University, Montreal, Quebec, Canada)
        netfind.if.usp.br (University of Sao Paulo, Sao Paulo, Brazil)
        netfind.oc.com (OpenConnect Systems, Dallas, Texas)
        netfind.sjsu.edu (San Jose State University, San Jose, California)
        netfind.vslib.cz (Liberec University of Technology, Czech Republic)
        nic.uakom.sk (Academy of Sciences, Banska Bystrica, Slovakia)
        redmont.cis.uab.edu (University of Alabama at Birmingham)
```

Well, we *tried*. There were too many people connected, so we got bounced off, but with a helpful list of other servers to try. Let's try eis.calstate.edu:

```
well% telnet eis.calstate.edu
Trying 130.150.102.33...
Connected to eis.calstate.edu.
Escape character is '^]'.


SunOS UNIX (eis.calstate.edu)

login: netfind


===============================================================
Welcome to the California Online Resources for Education Netfind server.
===============================================================


I think that your terminal can display 24 lines.  If this is wrong,
please enter the "Options" menu and set the correct number of lines.

Top level choices:
        1. Help
        2. Search
        3. Seed database lookup
        4. Options
        5. Quit (exit server)
 > 2
```

We're in. Note the menu, which you can use to get help (selection 1) and learn more about the netfind program. Or we can press ② and specify a search with the person's name and likely location. Let's try the author, hrh, who hangs out on The WELL:

```
Enter person and keys (blank to exit)  > hrh well
Please select at most 3 of the following domains to search:
        0. well.com (whole earth 'lectronic link, sausalito, california)
        1. well.fi (datawell oy, finland)
        2. well.sf.ca.us (the whole earth 'lectronic link, sausalito, california
)
```

Netfind finds several possible matches in its database. Let's select the first one:

```
Enter selection (e.g., 2 0 1)  > 0
( 1) SMTP_Finger_Search: checking domain well.com
SYSTEM: well.com
```

Continued on next page

INTERNET HOW-TO

Continued from previous page

```
Login: hrh                          Name: Harry Henderson
Directory: /home/h/r/hrh            Shell: /usr/bin/csh
On since Tue Apr  5 16:30 (PDT) on pts/13 from ts-tty136-slow
Plan:
I'm a freelance technical writer/editor.  I work with books on all
sorts of microcomputer applications, but am especially involved in
languages and operating systems (DOS and UNIX). Also interested in
educational software.  I often work with my wife Lisa, who is an
educational writer/editor.  I'm always interested in new projects (what
freelancer isn't?), so send mail if you've got a project you think we
could help you with.  I'm also interested in cognitive studies, F&SF,
military stuff, computer games, and the promotion of individual liberty.


              Mail Address: hrh                 Registered: Thu Sep 12 01:54:37
      1985
```

Notice that netfind traces the connections and runs the finger command to get information about the person. It then provides some additional technical information, which may or may not be useful:

```
( 1) SMTP_Finger_Search: well.com leads us to 19 other machines
( 2) SMTP_Finger_Search: checking host ts-tty135-slow.well.com
( 3) SMTP_Finger_Search: checking host ts-tty130-slow.well.com
( 4) SMTP_Finger_Search: checking host netcom10.netcom.com
( 5) SMTP_Finger_Search: checking host ayesha.well.com
( 3) get_host_addr: gethostbyname for ts-tty130-slow.well.com failed - no such host
( 2) get_host_addr: gethostbyname for ts-tty135-slow.well.com failed - no such host

FINGER SUMMARY:
- "hrh" is currently logged in from
  ts-tty136-slow.well.com, since Tue Apr  5 16:30 (PDT).
- The most promising email address for "hrh"
  based on the above finger search is
  hrh@ts-tty136-slow.well.com.

Continue the search ([n]/y) ?  >
```

Well, the "most promising e-mail address" should be taken with a grain of salt (evidently netfind is confused by the fact that The WELL actually connects users to a "terminal server" that in turn connects them to the main machine).

How It Works

Before the 1990s are over, there will probably be one giant white pages that you can use to easily retrieve the electronic address for anyone who belongs to any network anywhere on planet Earth. Actually tons of addresses are already out there somewhere in cyberspace: what we're seeing now is a series of increasingly sophisticated tools that record and store names and addresses. Unfortunately, each of these services works differently and many aren't easy to use or very reliable.

Comment
Not all programs and commands discussed here will be available on all systems. The behavior of the finger program may vary on different systems. One version requires that you begin the address with an @ to tell finger that you're looking at a remote system (for example, finger `@hrh.well.com`.). If you leave out the @, this finger will look for the user on your own system.

3.11 HOW DO I...
Fix and resend returned mail?

COMPLEXITY: INTERMEDIATE

Problem
Most of the time your mail will go where you send it. Sometimes, however, mail will be *bounced* (returned to sender) with a message from MAILER-DAEMON. A *daemon,* or demon, is a program that runs continuously "in background" and performs some routine task. In this case MAILER-DAEMON is our old friend sendmail in disguise.

Technique
A MAILER-DAEMON message includes a lot of extraneous text. What you're looking for is the actual error message that describes what the daemon thinks is wrong with your message. Use the following steps to identify the message and correct the problem.

Steps
1. Ignore the message headers from the daemon message and read down to where it says something like this:

```
—Transcript of session follows—
```

   This is where the actual interactions of the mail system involving your message took place. Now supposing you sent a message to jeffrey@bigu.edu. You might see a line that ends like this:

```
jeffrey@bigu.edu  User unknown
```

   This means one of two things: either you don't have the right username for Jeffrey, or Jeffrey isn't on the system bigu.edu. Try the steps in How-To 3.10 and see if you can determine Jeffrey's correct address.

2. If the message says "host unknown" rather than "user unknown," it means that there is no such host (site) accessible on the net. Make sure you typed the site's name (including all subdomains) correctly. If you're not sure, try using netfind as in How-To 3.10. You may be able to come up with the correct host name (and subdomains) that way.

3. Sometimes a "host unknown" or "host inaccessible" message means that the computer in question is temporarily unavailable, or that there's some problem in the addressing system such that sendmail or another program can't find that machine. It may help to type `host` followed by the site name. Assuming the site is registered in the name database, host will reply with a series of numbers that represent the site's *IP address* (the internal address used by the protocol that transports files). For example:

INTERNET HOW-TO

```
% host well.sf.ca.us
well.sf.ca.us has address 198.93.4.10
well.sf.ca.us mail is handled by well.sf.ca.us
well.sf.ca.us mail is handled by nkosi.well.com
```

This gives you The WELL's IP number. Using the host command with the IP number gives you the host name:

```
% host 198.93.4.10
Name: well.sf.ca.us
Address: 198.93.4.10
Aliases:
```

You can try sending your mail by substituting the IP address for the domain address, for example,

hrh@198.93.4.10

instead of

hrh@well.sf.ca.us

If the IP address is valid but there was some problem interpreting the domain address, this technique may get your mail through. This situation is uncommon, however. Also note that IP addresses may change without notice.

How It Works

Put simply, the MAILER-DAEMON sends you a kind of audit trail that tracks your mail as it moves from one machine to another. (Some messages may pass through as many as half a dozen sites on their way to the destination.) If your mail gets bounced, this means that somewhere along the line the message could not be delivered as specified. Your job is to isolate where the breakdown occurred.

Comment

You can avoid many address problems by creating aliases (see How-To 3.14) rather than typing in addresses by hand, which is prone to errors. Besides, it's much easier.

Occasionally, mail will simply seem to vanish rather than being returned to you by MAILER-DAEMON. Possibly your recipient inadvertently (or purposely!) failed to respond. Another possibility is that a system crash at the destination site (or one of the intermediary sites) destroyed the message file. Try again, and if you keep running into problems, consult your system administrator.

3.12 HOW DO I...
Forward a message to someone?

COMPLEXITY INTERMEDIATE

Problem

You may receive a message that contains a question or request for help. If you cannot help directly, but you know someone who can, you'll want to forward the message to that person.

Technique

You tell Elm to forward the message, and supply the address of the person to whom the mail will be forwarded. Let's say you've received a message from Richard Hutchinson

3 ⊕ USING INTERNET MAIL

asking for advice in choosing a Windows database. You don't work with databases much yourself, but you think your colleague Mary Garrett, who is a database expert, might be able to help Richard.

Steps

1. Select (highlight) the message you wish to forward. (See How-To 3-1.)

2. Press (F). You'll be asked whether you want to edit the forwarded message. Press (Y) to be placed in the editor with the text of the current message. Often you'll want to do this so you can include an explanation of why you're forwarding the message.

```
Command: Forward                          Edit outgoing message? (y/n) y
```

3. Elm then asks you for the forwarding address:

```
Send message to: maryg@pbhya.com
```

4. You are prompted with the subject of the original message, followed by the word "(fwd)". You usually won't need to change this subject. You're then asked, as usual, if you want to send copies of the message to anyone else:

```
Command: Forward                       To: maryg@pbhya.com
Subject of message: Re: Want recommendation for Windows databases (fwd)
Copies to:
```

5. Now, assuming you responded yes to the "Edit outgoing message?" prompt earlier, you are placed in the text editor with the body of the original message:

```
> From rhutchinson@uclink.berkeley.edu Mon Nov 22 18:30:41 1993
> Date: Mon, 22 Nov 93 15:35:52 -0800
> From: rhutchinson@uclink.berkeley.edu (Richard Hutchinson)
> Message-Id: <9311222335.AA07529@uclink.berkeley.edu>
> To: hrh@well.sf.ca.us
> Subject: Re: Want recommendation for Windows databases
>
> I've just installed Windows. I used to use the PC-File database
> under DOS to keep track of my CD and video collection. Can you
> recommend an easy to use database program for Windows that will
> read my old files?
```

As with a message reply, you see the original message lines prefixed with the > character. You can now add your own comments to the beginning of the message so that it looks like this:

```
Hi Mary. As you know, I'm a Mac user, so I can't help this guy.
He's a good friend, and I'd appreciate it if you could give him a
few tips.

> From rhutchinson@uclink.berkeley.edu Mon Nov 22 18:30:41 1993
> Date: Mon, 22 Nov 93 15:35:52 -0800
> From: rhutchinson@uclink.berkeley.edu (Richard Hutchinson)
> Message-Id: <9311222335.AA07529@uclink.berkeley.edu>
> To: hrh@well.sf.ca.us
> Subject: Re: Want recommendation for Windows databases
>
```

Continued on next page

INTERNET HOW-TO

Continued from previous page

```
> I've just installed Windows. I used to use the PC-File database
> under DOS to keep track of my CD and video collection. Can you
> recommend an easy to use database program for Windows that will
> read my old files?
```

6. You exit the editor as usual, and see the standard prompts that you've seen in sending or replying to messages:

   ➤ Press (S) to send the message to the person to whom you're forwarding it.
   ➤ Press (E) to edit (revise) the message.
   ➤ Press (H) to edit the message headers (this is usually not necessary, but see How-To 3.23).
   ➤ Press (F) to forget (abandon) the operation.

How It Works
Forwarding is much like replying to a message. The difference is that the message is sent on to someone else. This facility can be very useful for cases such as a "help desk" where requests for help can be forwarded by a coordinator to the appropriate specialist.

Comment
The forward command shows the message as having come through you, and the message will contain your return address (so if that person replies, the reply would come back to you). If you want to forward mail to someone else *without* letting them know you did so, use the b (bounce) command instead of forward. This is also handy because the recipient of the message can then reply directly to the original author (rather than to you). Otherwise forward and bounce work identically.

3.13 HOW DO I... *Get information about incoming mail?*

COMPLEXITY: INTERMEDIATE

Problem
Most Internet hosts are set up so that when you log in you are told whether there's any mail waiting for you. If mail arrives later in your session, you are told that you have more mail. Unfortunately, these messages simply say "You have mail" or "You have more mail" without telling you anything about who sent you the mail or what the mail is about. You can have Elm provide more complete information so that you can decide whether you need to interrupt what you're doing and deal with mail immediately.

Technique
There are several mail notification utilities that work with Elm. Running a program such as frm in your startup command file (.login or .profile) will give you details about your mail after you log in. A utility called newmail will monitor your mailbox continually while you're online, and notify you if any new mail arrives.

Steps
1. To get details of mail that's waiting when you log in, add the frm command to your .login or .profile file. (These files, which are in your home directory, contain a list of commands that are run when you log in.) You use the .login file if you run the C

shell (% prompt) or .profile if you run the Bourne or Korn shell ($ prompt). See Chapter 6 for more information on editing files.

2. If there is mail in your mailbox, frm will display information about the messages, giving the sender and subject for each:

```
sarah@bigu.edu            Welcome to the World
james@newsoft.research.com  Friday appointment
BIGWAR-list               Results of turn 19
Joel S. Fugazzotto        Your chapter's late
james@uclink.berkeley.edu  Do you know a good book on C++?
Dorothy J Heydt           Re: Need correspondent's address
```

3. If you want to check on any mail that has come in during your session, you can re-type frm at the system prompt.

4. You can be continually notified of details of newly arrived mail by running the newmail program. Add a line with newmail to your .login or .profile file. Whenever mail comes in you'll see a notice like this:

```
New mail from james@newsoft.research.com  - Friday appointment
```

How It Works
Programs such as frm simply check the mailbox file in your home directory to see if any mail is there, and read and format the From: and Subject: headers. Continuously running programs such as newmail do essentially the same thing, except they run "in background" and check at specified intervals of time. (By default, newmail checks your mailbox every 60 seconds.)

Comment
The frm and newmail programs have several additional options and capabilities. See documentation files for these programs and similar programs such as wfrm and wnewmail (for windowed systems). See How-To 3.28 for more information on Elm's documentation files.

3.14 HOW DO I...
Set up an address book?

COMPLEXITY: INTERMEDIATE

Problem
When you reply to a message, Elm knows the recipient's address, so there's no problem. But if you're sending an original message, you have to tell Elm the address. Remembering mail addresses is hard, so Elm lets you set up a system of aliases. When you've set up an alias, you can type `jim`, for example, and Elm will know it means jimr@well.sf.ca.us.

Technique
You use the Elm Alias Mode screen shown in Figure 3-2 to create and manage aliases. You can create aliases for addresses you already know, or you can alias an address in an incoming message for future use.

Steps
1. From the Index screen, press (A) to go into Alias mode.

INTERNET HOW-TO

```
┌─────────────────────── Terminal - WELL2400.TRM ───────────────── ▼ ▲ ┐
│ File  Edit  Settings  Phone  Transfers  Help                         │
│                  Alias mode: 0 aliases [ELM 2.4 PL22]              ↑ │
│                                                                      │
│                                                                      │
│                                                                      │
│                                                                      │
│                                                                      │
│                                                                      │
│                                                                      │
│   You can use any of the following commands by pressing the first character:│
│       a)lias current message, n)ew alias, d)elete or u)ndelete an alias,    │
│    m)ail to alias, or r)eturn to main menu.  To view an alias, press <return>.│
│                    j = move down, k = move up, ? = help              │
│  Alias: _                                                            │
│                                                                    ↓ │
└──────────────────────────────────────────────────────────────────────┘
```

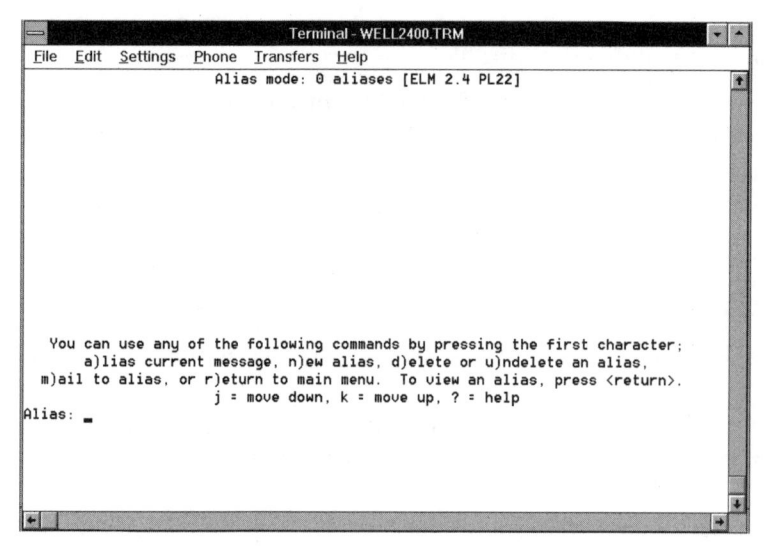

Figure 3-2 Elm's Alias Mode screen

    2. To create a new alias, press (N). You will be prompted for the name to use for the alias. For example, if you send a lot of e-mail to the president of the United States, you might use the alias "prez".

```
Alias: Add a new alias to database
Enter alias name:  prez
```

    3. Next you are prompted for the last and first names of the person you are aliasing. You can also enter an optional comment that can help you remember why you have this person's address:

```
Enter last name for prez: clinton
Enter first name for prez: bill
Enter optional comment for prez: he's the guy
```

    4. Finally, you'll be asked for the net address of the person you're aliasing. You may have found this address in a news article, mail message, book, business card, or whatever:

```
Enter address for prez: president@whitehouse.gov
```

(That's a real address, by the way, in case you want to send e-mail to the White House. Or you can reach the second in command at vice.president@whitehouse.gov.)

Elm lets you review the information you've entered. If everything's OK, press (Y) to add the new alias to the system:

```
Alias: Add a new alias to database...             Accept new alias? (y/n) y
New alias: prez is 'bill clinton, he's the guy'.
Messages addressed as: president@whitehouse.gov (bill clinton)
```

3 🌐 USING INTERNET MAIL

5. Once you've added an alias, it will appear in a list on the Alias Mode screen next time you run Elm. (To make it appear right away, you need to "resynchronize" Elm by pressing (S).)

   Aliases are listed much as messages are on the Index screen. The order of information for an alias is alias number, first name, last name, comment, type of alias (Person or Group), and alias name.

```
Alias mode: 1 alias [ELM 2.4 PL22]


1    bill clinton, he's the guy                  Person    prez




You can use any of the following commands by pressing the first character;
   a)lias current message, n)ew alias, d)elete or u)ndelete an alias,
m)ail to alias, or r)eturn to main menu.  To view an alias, press <return>.
                   j = move down, k = move up, ? = help
Alias:
```

   Note that the menu says that you can select aliases with the (J) and (K) keys, just as you do mail messages. Pressing (ENTER) displays the address for the current alias:

```
Aliased address: president@whitehouse.gov
```

6. If you want to mail a message to anyone on the alias list, just select that alias and press (M). You will go through the same sequence of prompts as you do to mail a message from the Index screen. Indeed, you may find it easier to work from the Alias Mode screen when sending new messages, since you won't have to remember the address, or even alias name, for anyone you've aliased.

   In other parts of the Elm system, once you've aliased a name, you need only type that alias name when asked for an address to send, reply to, or forward mail.

7. As with mail messages, you can delete an alias by selecting it and pressing (D).

8. An especially nice feature of the alias system is the ability to automatically capture the address from a message on the Index screen and create an alias for it. Here are the steps to follow:

   ➤ Select the desired message on the Index screen.
   ➤ Press (A) to go to the Alias Mode screen.
   ➤ Press (A) for "alias current message." You will be prompted for the necessary information:

```
Alias: Add address from current message...
Current message address aliased to: sarah
Enter last name for sarah: byers
Enter optional comment: advisor at BigU
```

Continued on next page

INTERNET HOW-TO

Continued from previous page

```
Alias: Add address from current message        Accept new alias? (y/n) y
New alias: sarah is 'sarah byers, advisor at BigU'.
Messages addressed as: sarah@bigu.edu (sarah byers)
```

9. So far we've made aliases for single individuals (Person aliases). You can also make an alias for a group of people, such as a team working on a project. Follow the same procedure as for a Person alias, except you give a list of addresses separated by commas:

```
Enter alias name:  editors
Enter last name for editors: Editors
Enter first name for editors:  Waite Group
Enter optional comment for editors: WGP editorial staff
Enter address for editors: scalamar, fugie, jcrudo
```

(Since these persons are on our local system, we just used their user IDs rather than complete addresses.) Now a message to "editors" will automatically go to all the editors on the list.

How It Works

Elm uses two separate alias files. The first, the system alias file, is set up by the system administrator. This file contains aliases that consist of the user IDs for people on the system. If your system is set up this way, you can send mail to anyone on your system simply by using their user ID. What's nice is that you'll see the full name that goes with the user ID, so you can make sure you have the right person!

The aliases you create in Alias mode go in your personal alias files. These actually consist of a number of separate files, of which the only one you might use directly is aliases.text. This has a list of your aliases in the form:

alias = Last; First, comment = address

For example:

prez = Clinton; Bill, he's the guy = president@whitehouse.gov

If you wish, you can add aliases directly to this file with a text editor. After entering the text and saving the file, type `newalias`, and Elm will create the complete aliases from the data in the file.

Comment

Using aliases is strongly recommended if you correspond with more than a very few people. They prevent typing errors, which are particularly easy to make with addresses that include numbers (such as CompuServe addresses). Note that you may have to re-enter aliases if people's electronic addresses change. You can either edit the data in the aliases.text file (and run newalias) or delete the alias from the Alias Mode screen and then reenter it with the correct information.

3.15 HOW DO I...
File mail for future reference?

COMPLEXITY: INTERMEDIATE

Problem
Once you're "well-connected" on the Internet you may receive a couple dozen e-mail messages a day—more if you've subscribed to some mailing lists (see How-To 3.27). You can read and delete some messages, but others will need to be filed away for future reference. How can you organize your mail filing system so that you can keep a history of your correspondence and retrieve messages as needed?

Technique
Elm provides a system of folders that you can use to store your electronic correspondence. Like the folder that Elm uses to store all of your messages, these folders are files where you can store all the mail to or from a particular person, or all the messages about a particular subject.

The simplest strategy is to let Elm create a separate folder for each person you correspond with. For example, suppose you want to save the message from Dorothy Heydt; that is, message 6 in Figure 3-1:

```
Mailbox is '~/.inbox' with 6 messages [ELM 2.4 PL22]


     1   Nov 22 james@uclink.berke  (18)   Do you know a good book on C++?
N    2   Nov 22 Joel S. Fugazzotto  (12)   Your chapter's late
N    3   Nov 22 BIGWAR-list         (19)   Results of turn 19
N    4   Nov 22 james@newsoft.rese  (16)   Friday appointment
N    5   Nov 22 sarah@bigu.edu      (36)   Welcome to the World
N    6   Nov 22 Dorothy J Heydt     (18)   Re: Need correspondent's address
```

Steps
1. Make the message you want to save the current message (if it isn't already), then press (S). Elm will prompt you for a folder in which to save the message:

```
[save to folder]
Command: Save to folder              (Use '?' for help)
Save message to:  =djheydt
```

2. By default, Elm suggests a folder with the same name as the user who sent you the message. Note that the = (equal sign) before a folder name means that the folder will be created in the Mail subdirectory of your home directory (the usual default).

```
Message 1 saved to folder /home/h/r/hrh/Mail/djheydt.
```

The folder is created the first time you save a message to it. If you see the message,

```
Message 6 appended to folder /home/h/r/hrh/Mail/djheydt.
```

it means that the folder already exists, so the message is appended to it.

3. If you want to use a folder name other than what Elm suggests (or want to name your folders by subject rather than by person), respond to the folder prompt by pressing line kill, (CTRL)-(X), and typing in the desired name. For example, at the prompt

INTERNET HOW-TO

```
Save message to: =djheydt
```

Press CTRL-X. Then at the prompt type

```
=business
```

How It Works
Elm extracts the username from the message and suggests it as a folder name. As you save messages, they are added (appended) to the folder. Although you might think that an Elm folder is a subdirectory of your Mail directory, a folder is actually just an ordinary Unix text file. If you want, you can use your favorite utilities (such as grep) to search for information directly in a folder. (See Chapter 6 for more on Unix commands and files.)

Comment
Folders can grow quite large if you don't "prune" your mail periodically. You can use the Unix rm command to remove unwanted folders. Remember that folders are usually in the Mail directory. For example,

```
%rm Mail/dheydt
```

removes the dheydt folder from the Mail directory.

3.16 HOW DO I...
Read my mail folders?

COMPLEXITY: EASY

Problem
Now that you've filed mail away in folders, how do you read or otherwise dispose of the stored messages?

Technique
The important thing to remember is that Elm is always reading *some* folder. When you start up Elm, it is reading the .inbox folder, which is your mailbox with newly arrived mail (or old mail that you haven't disposed of). You use the c (change folder) command to switch to a different folder. Once you're reading another folder, you can do everything with the messages in the folder that you can with the mail in your mailbox.

Steps
1. On the Elm Index screen, press c (for change folders). You will see the following prompt:

```
Command: Change folder              (Use '?' for help)
Change to which folder:
```

2. Decide what folder you want to switch to. If you're not sure how your folders are named (or how to specify a folder), press ? and Elm will give you a bit of help:

```
You must specify a file or folder to change to.  Several options
are available:

    '!' will use your incoming mailbox (/home/h/r/hrh/.inbox)
    '>' will use your "received" folder (=received)
```

```
'<'  will use your "sent" folder (=sent)
'@alias' will use the default folder for "alias"
```

> If you enter a filename Elm will use that file. If the file name begins with a '=', Elm will look for the file in your folder directory (your folder directory is /home/h/r/hrh/Mail).
>
> You may use wildcards in the name, exactly as you do in the shell. If you do this, a list of all matching files or folders will be printed and you will be prompted for another name. Thus typing '=a*' will print the names of all folders in your folder directory starting with 'a'. Typing 'b*.c' will print all files in your local directory starting with 'b' and ending in '.c'. A star (*) will usually list everything. See your local shell manual for more information on wildcards.
>
> Sometimes Elm will help you out by suggesting a name. If you want to use the suggested name, simply hit return. If you don't like it, hit your erase or line erase keys.

3. Note the special shortcuts that Elm recognizes for referring to your inbox, received, or sent folder. (You learned about inbox in How-To 3.5. The *received* folder gets a copy of each incoming message you've read if, when you exit Elm, you accept the prompt to store messages there. The *sent* mail folder gets a copy of each outgoing message if you set the copy option variable to on. (See How-To 3.20 for information on setting Elm options.)

   If you want a list of your folders, type =* at the folder prompt:

```
[Change to which folder: =*]
Folders which match `*':

art     djheydt    gnn-list    gnnlist    hrh
```

> The = means "look in the Mail directory," and the * means "match any filenames you find." This gives you a list of all the files in the Mail directory, most of which should be Elm folders.

4. Once you've looked around, if necessary, type the name of the folder you want to change to. In this case we'll change to the djheydt folder, which contains messages from Dorothy Heydt:

```
[Change to which folder:  =djheydt
```

> Elm responds by changing the Index screen display to reflect the contents of the new folder:
>
> ```
> Folder is '=djheydt' with 2 messages [ELM 2.4 PL22]
> ```

```
  0  1   Nov 22  Dorothy J Heydt     (19)    Re: Need correspondent's address
     2   Nov 22  Dorothy J Heydt     (19)    Re: your mail

  You can use any of the following commands by pressing the first character;
  d)elete or u)ndelete mail,  m)ail a message,  r)eply or f)orward mail,  q)uit
```

Continued on next page

INTERNET HOW-TO

Continued from previous page

```
    To read a message, press <return>.  j = move down, k = move up, ? = help
Command:
```

5. You're now ready to do whatever you want with the messages in the folder—read them again, forward them, delete them, or otherwise dispose of them (or keep them).

   If you want to return to your inbox, just repeat the c command with a folder name of ! (exclamation point).

How It Works
Elm reads the folder file and uses the message headers to break the file into separate messages that it displays on the Index screen.

Comment
See How-To 3.20 for some options that you can set to change the way Elm handles folders.

3.17 HOW DO I...
File mail automatically by sender or subject?

COMPLEXITY: ADVANCED

Problem
If you have many correspondents or belong to several mailing lists, you can receive an overwhelming amount of e-mail. If you get, for example, 30 to 50 messages per day, it could take more time than you can afford to examine, save, or otherwise dispose of all those messages.

Technique
Elm works together with a program called *filter* to automatically process mail that fits certain criteria that you specify. You provide a file with a set of *rules* (if-then statements that specify which messages are to have what done with them). You then have mail forwarded to the filter program, which examines your incoming mail and disposes of it according to the rules you've specified.

Steps
1. Use a text editor to create a file called filter-rules in your .elm directory (see Chapter 6 for more on creating files). This file has one or more rules in the form:

   if (*condition*) then *action*

   Condition can be a variety of tests. In general, the rules test the subject, sender, from, or to lines for a particular value. For example:

   ➤ subject = "monthly meeting"
   ➤ sender = "sarah@bigu.edu"

   The "action" can include:

➢ delete the message(s)
➢ save the message(s) in a specified folder
➢ save a copy of the message(s) in the folder (but keep the original in the mailbox)
➢ execute a system command
➢ forward the message(s) to another address
➢ leave the message(s) alone

Note that the filter rules file must be "world readable" to work. See Chapter 6 for more on setting file permissions.

The example rule used here is very simple. Let's suppose you get a considerable amount of mail about a book you're writing. You can specify a rule like this:

```
if (subject = "book") then savecopy "/home/h/r/hrh/Mail/writing"
```

This rule says "if the subject header of the message contains the word 'book,' save a copy of that message in the 'writing' folder in my Mail directory."

2. Use your editor to create a .forward file in your home directory. (See How-To 3.18 for more on .forward files.) The .forward file normally has an address to which mail arriving in your mailbox is automatically forwarded (should you desire to do so). In this case, however, you will be forwarding mail to the filter program. Put a command such as this in the .forward file:

```
"|/usr/local/bin/filter -o /home/h/r/hrh/filter-errors"
```

This command forwards messages to the filter program via a Unix "pipe" (|). The filter program checks the messages against the rules and reports any errors in processing to a filter-errors file.

3. When mail arrives the filter leaves a record of its processing in a file called *filterlog* in your .elm directory:

```
Mail from test-sender about contract for new book
    SAVED in file "writing" AND PUT in mailbox by rule #1
```

4. You can also ask filter for more details of its last processing by typing `filter -S` at the system prompt:

```
%filter -S

                A Summary of Filter Activity
                _____


A total of 1 message was filtered:

Rule #1: (left in mailbox and saved in "writing")
        applied 1 time (100%)

Explicit log of each action;

Mail from test-sender about contract for new book
        SAVED in file "writing" AND PUT in mailbox by rule #1
```

INTERNET HOW-TO

How It Works
The mail system is actually a burgeoning group of separate programs and utilities. Because Unix lets you hook programs together easily so that they can work on each other's output, filter is able to process mail and use other parts of the mail system to dispose of it automatically. If Elm is your secretary, then filter is the clerk on the graveyard shift.

Comment
The conditions specified by filter rules and the processing of messages can be much more complex than shown here. For a full discussion, see the "Elm Filter System Guide" in the Elm documentation directory.

3.18 HOW DO I...
Automatically forward my mail to another address?

COMPLEXITY | INTERMEDIATE

Problem
You may have accounts on more than one machine. There may be accounts that you log onto only occasionally. Mail sent to you at seldom-used accounts may not be answered in a timely fashion. You can set up a forwarding system so that mail sent to one account is automatically forwarded to another.

Technique
You set up a .forward file on the machine from which you wish to forward mail. The file contains the address to which you wish to forward the mail.

Steps
1. Log into the account from which you wish to forward mail.

2. Create a file called .forward in the home directory of this account. (See Chapter 6 for more on creating files.)

3. Put a single line in this file that contains the Internet address to which you wish to forward mail (for example, sarah@bigu.edu).

4. Save the file (with the vi editor, you would us the :wq command).

How It Works
The mail transport system notices that you have a .forward file, and finds the forwarding address in it. As mail arrives, it is automatically forwarded to the specified address.

Comment
Forwarding requires some configuration on the part of the system operator. If forwarding doesn't appear to work on your system, ask a support person for help.

3.19 HOW DO I... *Work with several messages at once?*

COMPLEXITY: INTERMEDIATE

Problem
Sometimes it is convenient to work with several messages as a group. For example, you might want to mark and then save all the messages from a particular person.

Technique
You highlight and tag each message that you want to be part of the group. You can then give a command (such as save, copy, or delete) that will operate on all the tagged messages.

Steps
1. To tag a message for later processing, select that message using the keys described in How-To 3.1, and press `T`. Alternatively, you can press `T` to tag the current message and move to the next undeleted message. This can be useful for tagging several messages in a row.

   Tagged messages will be indicated with a + symbol in front of the message number, like this:

```
Folder is '=important' with 4 messages [ELM 2.4 PL22]

    +1   Nov 22  jean@uclink.berke  (19)    Notes for Friday's meeting
     2   Nov 22  Joel S. Fugazzotto (13)    Your chapter's late
    +3   Nov 22  james@newsoft.rese (17)    Friday meeting agenda
     4   Nov 22  Dorothy J Heydt    (19)    Re: Need correspondent's address
```

   Here we've tagged messages 1 and 3 (which both have to do with our Friday meeting).

2. You can also tag messages that match text in the From: or Subject: fields. To do this, press `CTRL`-`T`, enter the word or phrase you want to match, and press `ENTER`:

```
Command: Tag messages that match pattern
Enter pattern: Friday

Tagged 2 messages.
```

   This example will also result in messages 1 and 3 being tagged, since both these messages have "Friday" as part of their Subject: fields. Tagging like this is a good way to work with all messages from a particular sender or all messages on a particular subject.

3. Once you've tagged messages, you can work with them as a batch. For example, if you press `S` (the save messages command) and have tagged messages, you'll be asked for a folder in which to save all the tagged messages.

4. To tag and delete a group of messages, press `CTRL`-`D` and enter text to be matched in the From: or Subject: field. Matching messages will be marked for deletion. (You can also use `CTRL`-`U` to specify a pattern for messages that are to be *undeleted*.)

INTERNET HOW-TO

Note that with pattern matching (the `CTRL`-`T` and `CTRL`-`D` commands), if you have already tagged one or more messages, you'll first be asked whether you want to remove the existing tags.

How It Works
Tagging lets a group of messages be treated as a batch for use with certain commands (such as save or delete). The `CTRL`-`D` and `CTRL`-`T` commands let you use pattern matching for finding messages that should be worked on together.

Comment
Tagging and pattern matching can be useful for saving messages in groups by sender or subject. You can also press `CTRL`-`T` and then `S` to tag and save a group of messages, and then press `CTRL`-`D` to mark them for deletion from the mailbox.

3.20 HOW DO I...
Change Elm's default behavior?

COMPLEXITY | INTERMEDIATE

Problem
Since it uses sensible defaults, Elm satisfies most user needs "right out of the box." But because people's needs and preferences differ, Elm includes a variety of options (sometimes called variables) that can be specified in order to change the way the program behaves.

Technique
There are two ways to change Elm's options. You can change some options interactively on the Options Editor screen. You can also change options by specifying them in a file called elmrc that Elm puts in your .elm directory.

Steps
1. To change options interactively, press `O` at Elm's Index screen prompt.

2. You will see the Elm Options Editor screen shown in Figure 3-3. From that screen, press the letter of the option you want to change and supply the correct value when prompted. There are actually three kinds of options, and they are prompted for in different ways.

3. The simplest kind of option is *Boolean*, which simply means a toggle that can be on or off. For example, you can have the arrow cursor on or off. If it's on, you'll see an arrow in front of the current message or alias, rather than that item being highlighted in reverse video. (This can be useful if you have a weird terminal that doesn't support highlighting.)

   If you press `A` for "Arrow cursor" on the Options Editor screen, you get a prompt like this:

   A)rrow cursor   : OFF   (use <space> to toggle, any other key to leave)

   (Note that you can use upper or lowercase on the Options and Alias menus.) If you now press `SPACEBAR`, the option switches from off (the default) to on:

   A)rrow cursor   : ON   (use <space> to toggle, any other key to leave)

3 🌐 USING INTERNET MAIL

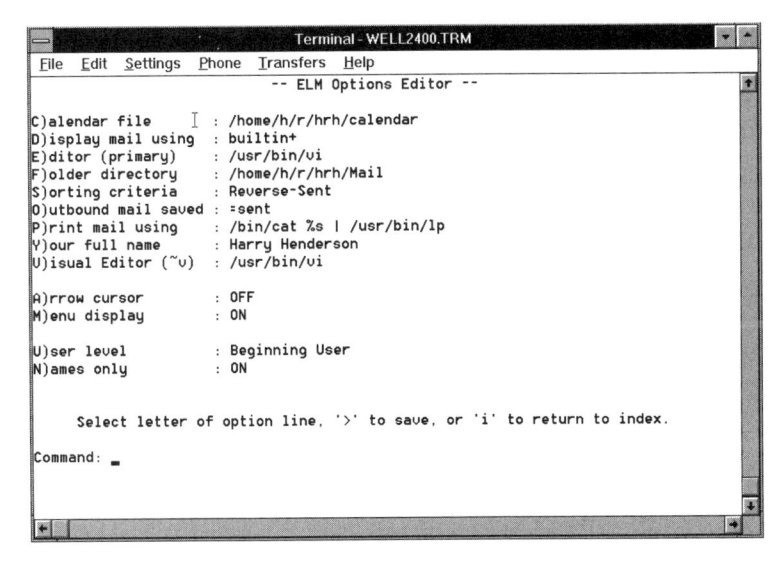

```
┌─────────────────────────────────────────────────────────────┐
│                    Terminal - WELL2400.TRM              ▼ ▲ │
│ File  Edit  Settings  Phone  Transfers  Help                │
│                    -- ELM Options Editor --                 │
│ C)alendar file    I : /home/h/r/hrh/calendar               │
│ D)isplay mail using : builtin+                              │
│ E)ditor (primary)   : /usr/bin/vi                           │
│ F)older directory   : /home/h/r/hrh/Mail                    │
│ S)orting criteria   : Reverse-Sent                          │
│ O)utbound mail saved: =sent                                 │
│ P)rint mail using   : /bin/cat %s | /usr/bin/lp             │
│ Y)our full name     : Harry Henderson                       │
│ U)isual Editor (~v) : /usr/bin/vi                           │
│                                                             │
│ A)rrow cursor       : OFF                                   │
│ M)enu display       : ON                                    │
│                                                             │
│ U)ser level         : Beginning User                        │
│ N)ames only         : ON                                    │
│                                                             │
│     Select letter of option line, '>' to save, or 'i' to return to index. │
│ Command: _                                                  │
└─────────────────────────────────────────────────────────────┘
```

Figure 3-3 Elm's Options Editor screen

4. A multivalue option works similarly, except that each time you press (SPACEBAR) the value is set to the next possible value. A good example is the "U)ser level" option. You can use this to set the user menu level to beginner, intermediate, or expert. The default beginner menu on the Index screen looks like this:

```
You can use any of the following commands by pressing the first character;
  d)elete or u)ndelete mail,  m)ail a message,  r)eply or f)orward mail,  q)uit
     To read a message, press <return>.   j = move down, k = move up, ? = help

Command:
```

For a menu that includes more advanced commands, you can select the intermediate or expert level. At these levels the menu looks like this:

```
  |=pipe, !=shell, ?=help, <n>=set current to n, /=search pattern
a)lias, C)opy, c)hange folder, d)elete, e)dit, f)orward, g)roup reply, m)ail,
  n)ext, o)ptions, p)rint, q)uit, r)eply, s)ave, t)ag, u)ndelete, or e(x)it

Command:
```

To set the user level, type >u on the Options Editor screen. The current user level "cycles" to the next level each time you press the (SPACEBAR):

```
U)ser level         : Beginning User      <space> to change

U)ser level         : Intermediate User   <space> to change

U)ser level         : Expert User         <space> to change
```

5. The last kind of option requires that you type in some text. This is frequently the case for options that specify a directory or program name. For example:

```
F)older directory    : /home/h/r/hrh/Mail
```

81

INTERNET HOW-TO

Here the cursor will be at the end of the current folder directory name (/home/h/r/hrh/Mail), and you can press line kill, CTRL-X, and then type in the name of a new directory that you want to use for your folders. There are also a few options (such as "builtinlines") that require that you type an appropriate number.

6. Once you've set the options you want, be sure to press > to save the changed options to the .elmrc file.

7. Options not listed on the Options Editor screen (or those the Elm reference manual says can be added to it) must be changed directly in the elmrc file. To do this, run your favorite text editor (such as vi) with the filename elmrc. Here's what the beginning of the default elmrc file on my system looks like:

```
#
# .elm/elmrc - options file for the ELM mail system
#
# Saved automatically by ELM 2.4 PL22 for Harry Henderson
#
# For yes/no settings with ?, ON means yes, OFF means no

### aliassortby = Name
### alteditor = /usr/bin/vi
### alwaysdelete = OFF
### alwayskeep = ON
### alwaysstore = OFF
### arrow = OFF
### ask = ON
### askcc = ON
### autocopy = OFF
### bounceback = 0
### builtinlines = -3
### calendar = /home/h/r/hrh/calendar
### configoptions = ^_cdefsopyv_am_un
### confirmappend = OFF
### confirmcreate = OFF
```

8. Table 3-5 lists some important ways in which you can change Elm's behavior, broken down into categories. Find the required option(s) and change them as indicated in the table. (Note: This table includes some of the most generally useful Elm options. For a complete list, see the Elm reference guide.)

3 USING INTERNET MAIL

TO SPECIFY...	CHANGE THESE OPTIONS	NOTES:
Folders and Files		
Directory to contain mail folders	maildir = *directory path*	Default is Mail
Folder to contain copies of mail you have read	receivedmail = *directory path*	Default is received
Folder for copies of mail you send	sentmail = *directory path* copy = ON	Default is sent
How to sort your messages in folders	sortby = *field*	Field can be: from, lines, received, sent, status, subject, or mailbox (to keep in mailbox order)
Prompt before adding message to file or folder	confirmappend = ON	Default is OFF
Prompt before creating new file or folder	confirmcreate = ON	Default is OFF
Confirm before any operation that would add messages to a nonfolder file	confirmfiles = ON	Defaut is OFF
Copies will be made of all outgoing mail	copy = ON	Default is OFF
Automatically set up folders for outbound mail by name of recipient	forcename = ON	Default is OFF
Save all mail in folders by recipient name	savename = ON	Default is ON

Note: To save all messages by recipient, set both forcename and savename to ON. To save only messages for recipients for whom you've set up folders, set forcename OFF and savename ON (this is the default.)

Get a copy of mail you send to a mailing list you're on	metoo = ON	default is OFF
Prompts		
Make yes the default for "Delete messages" exit prompt	alwaysdelete = ON	Default is OFF
Make yes the default for "Keep unread mail in incoming mailbox" exit prompt	alwayskeep = ON	Default is OFF
Make yes the default for "Store read mail in received folder" exit prompt	alwaysstore = ON	Default is OFF
Don't give the "delete messages" prompt when you exit, change folders, and so on (just delete as specified)	ask = OFF	Default is ON
Don't prompt for carbon copy recipients when sending mail	askcc = OFF	Default is ON

Note: You can still specify carbon copies by editing the headers. See How-To 3.23.

Continued on next page

INTERNET HOW-TO

Continued from previous page

Mail Replies

Tell Elm about other addresses where you get mail, so you won't get duplicate copies of group replies	alternatives = *address*,...	Default is none
Specify how you refer to author of original message in reply or forward Example: %s says: in message from hrh becomes hrh says:	attribution = *text*	default is none
Specify character that begins lines quoted from original message	prefix = *character* (use underscore to specify space)	Default is >_
Automatically copy original message into edit buffer when replying	autocopy = ON	Default is OFF

Addresses, Signatures, and Aliases

Your name as it will appear in mail you send	fullname = *name*	Default is from system password file or .fullname file
Signature to use for messages to local users	localsignature = *filename*	Default is no signature
Signature to use for messages to remote users	remotesignature = *filename*	
Signature to use for all messages	signature = *filename*	
Note: Specify either local=, remote=, or just signature= for both.		
How to sort aliases on Alias Mode screen	aliassortby = *field*	Alias, name, or text prefix by reverse- to reverse order Default is name order

Editors and Other Tools

Editor to use when typing new mail	editor = *pathname*	Default is value of variable $EDITOR in user environment; otherwise set by system
Program for displaying message text	pager = *pathname*	Default is $PAGER; otherwise set by system
How to print messages Note: Not usually used by off-site users.	print = *command*	Default is set by system
Shell for running system commands with shell escape (!)	shell = *pathname*	Default is $SHELL or set by system

3 USING INTERNET MAIL

Miscellaneous Features

Options to appear on Options Editor screen	configoptions = *letters*	See Elm Reference Manual
Completeness of Index screen menu	menulevel = *number*	0 = beginner 1 = intermediate 2 = expert
Remove menus from Elm screens	menu = OFF	Default is ON
Note: Removing menus can make more room for messages, aliases, and so forth.		
Highlight current message with arrow instead of reverse video	arrow = ON	Default is OFF
Note: May be needed on old terminals.		

Table 3-5 Possible customizations for Elm

How It Works

Elm's configuration values act as "flags" that the program checks in order to decide how to interact with the user. When the system administrator installs Elm, certain defaults may be set for all users in a systemwide version of the elmrc file. Each user then has his or her own elmrc file in which the options can be customized to suit the user's preferences.

Comment

Depending on how Elm has been set up, you may not have an elmrc file when you first run Elm. In that case, just go to the Options Editor screen, press >, and an elmrc file with default options (and useful comments preceded by a # character) will be created for you.

It's a good idea to make a backup of your elmrc file before tinkering with it. You can do this by executing a command such as the following system prompt.

```
%cp .elm/elmrc .elm/elmrc.bak
```

3.21 HOW DO I... *Tell people about myself?*

COMPLEXITY: INTERMEDIATE

Problem

As an Internet user, you are constantly meeting new people through electronic mail and other forms of electronic communication. It's helpful to have a way to tell interested people a bit about yourself automatically, and to advertise your occupation and interests in the hope of finding like-minded people (or perhaps job offers).

Technique

A file called .plan can be used to contain a statement of your background, interests, and other information that you'd like to make publicly available. Other people can see your .plan file by running the finger command with your user ID or Internet address.

Steps

1. Using your favorite editor, create a file called .plan in your home directory. This file should say something about your background and interests (see Chapter 6 for more information on creating and editing files). As an example, here's the author's .plan file:

```
I'm a freelance technical writer/editor.  I work with books on all
sorts of microcomputer applications, but am especially involved in
languages and operating systems (DOS and UNIX). Also interested in
educational software.  I often work with my wife Lisa, who is an
educational writer/editor.  I'm always interested in new projects (what
freelancer isn't?), so send mail if you've got a project you think we
could help you with.  I'm also interested in cognitive studies, F&SF,
military stuff, computer games, and the promotion of individual liberty.
```

Your .plan file (and some other identifying information about you culled by your system) will be shown to other users who use the finger command with your user ID:

```
well% finger hrh
Login: hrh                       Name: Harry Henderson
Directory: /home/h/r/hrh         Shell: /usr/bin/csh
On since Mon Nov 22 21:07 (PDT) on pts/7 (messages off)
     from dialup-2.well.sf.ca.us
Plan:
I'm a freelance technical writer/editor.  I work with books on all
sorts of microcomputer applications, but am especially involved in
languages and operating systems (DOS and UNIX). Also interested in
educational software.  I often work with my wife Lisa, who is an
educational writer/editor.  I'm always interested in new projects (what
freelancer isn't?), so send mail if you've got a project you think we
could help you with.  I'm also interested in cognitive studies, F&SF,
military stuff, computer games, and the promotion of individual liberty.

Mail Address: hrh                    Registered: Thu Sep 12 01:54:37 1985
```

In addition to the .plan file, other information may be provided as above, depending on how the system is set up. Usually you can get more information about local users than about remote users.

How It Works

For local users, finger can look up information directly from the user's accounting and .plan files. For remote users, an information protocol is used to query about the user. Some users may choose not to give out finger information to remote users.

Comment

There are a number of different versions of finger. See How-To 3.10 for more on using finger to verify addresses.

3.22 HOW DO I...
Add a personal "signature" to my messages?

COMPLEXITY: INTERMEDIATE

Problem
Electronic mail can look pretty impersonal. Many users add signatures to their messages that contain useful information (job title, other addresses, and so on) and sometimes a colorful phrase or aphorism.

Technique
You simply create a file with your signature information, and then tell your mail, news, or other programs to use it. (Some may use it automatically.) Here we'll limit ourselves to using signatures with Elm.

Steps
1. Use your favorite text editor to create a file called .signature in your home directory. Add a few lines (no more than 4 or 5) containing some phrase or saying that you'd like people to remember you by. Caution: Jokes grow old fast. The author's signature file looks like this:

```
"Life, liberty, and the pursuit of happiness"
The opinions expressed are my own, but you're welcome to share them.
Harry Henderson (freelance technical editor/writer).
hrh@well.sf.ca.us
```

2. Some programs need to be told to use your .signature file. Elm is one such program. Edit the elmrc file in your .elm directory, and change the line `signature = off` to `signature = on`.

3. Elm will now automatically add the signature lines to the end of each mail message you send.

How It Works
Signature files are recognized and used by a variety of mail and news programs. The ability to use material in files you've created separately is an example of the flexibility of Elm and other Unix programs.

Comment
If you wish, you can have separate signatures for messages sent to your local system and those sent to remote systems. Simply create the files .localsignature and .remotesignature with the appropriate text, and change your elmrc file to read

```
localsignature = ON
remotesignature = ON
```

INTERNET HOW-TO

3.23 HOW DO I...
Edit message headers?

COMPLEXITY: INTERMEDIATE

Problem
By default, Elm prompts you for the necessary information for your mail messages, including the To:, Cc:, and Subject: headers. However, you may decide while editing your message that you'd like to go back and change one or more of these headers. There are also some headers (such as Bcc: for "blind carbon copy") that aren't prompted for by Elm when you start to prepare a message.

Technique
You exit the text editor, activate the header editing screen, and add or revise the message headers as needed. You can then send your message as usual.

Steps
1. After you have finished composing a reply or an original mail message (see How-Tos 3.1 and 3.6), you will see the following menu:

```
Please choose one of the following options by parenthesized letter: s
        e)dit message, edit h)eaders, s)end it, or f)orget it.h
```

2. Press **H** to edit the message headers. You will be placed in the Message Header Edit screen:

```
                    Message Header Edit Screen

T)o: dheydt


C)c:


B)cc:

S)ubject: Here's your bibliography

R)eply-to:
A)ction:                          E)xpires:
P)riority:                        Precede(n)ce:
I)n-reply-to:




        Choose header, u)ser defined header, d)omainize, !)shell, or <return>.
Choice:c
```

3. Select the header you wish to edit. Here are some things you might do:

➤ Press **T** to change the To: header (the name or complete address of the person you're writing to).

88

3 USING INTERNET MAIL

➤ Press Ⓒ to edit the Cc: header and add one or more recipients for copies of this message.
➤ Press Ⓑ to edit the Bcc: header and add one or more recipients of blind carbon copies of this message. A *blind* carbon copy differs from a regular carbon copy in that the recipient is not told the names of any other persons receiving copies of the message.
➤ Press Ⓢ to revise the subject of the message.

The Header Edit Screen lists other headers, but these are seldom needed. See the Elm reference manual for details.

4. You will be prompted for the new or revised value for the selected header. For example, if you press Ⓒ (for the Cc: header) you'll get this prompt:

```
Enter value for the header.
```

Cc:

Type in the new value and press (ENTER). (Remember to separate multiple addresses with commas.)

5. You may select and edit additional headers, or press (ENTER) to return to message creation mode. You'll then see the usual message prompt:

```
Please choose one of the following options by parenthesized letter: s
       e)dit message, edit h)eaders, s)end it, or f)orget it
```

6. You can then send, reedit, or otherwise work with your message.

How It Works
Elm presents a minimum number of necessary headers (To:, Cc:, and Subject:) to you when you are replying to a message or sending a new message. The headers editing facility lets you correct these headers or add new ones without being prompted for them unnecessarily.

Comment
Take a moment to check your changed header(s) on the Header Edit screen before returning to the message sending process.

3.24 HOW DO I...
Run a system command from Elm?

COMPLEXITY INTERMEDIATE

Problem
Suppose you're in the middle of using Elm and you realize that you need to get some information about your directories or files, or perhaps run a program? It's inconvenient to exit Elm, perform your commands, and then go back and try to take up where you left off. Fortunately Elm, like most major Unix programs, lets you run system commands without leaving the program.

INTERNET HOW-TO

Technique
You run a single system command, or run a *shell* (command processor) that lets you run a succession of commands. When you're done, you're back in Elm exactly where you left off.

Steps
1. Press ! at the main prompt on the Index, Alias Mode, or Options Editor screen. You will get a prompt to enter your command:

```
Command: !                          (Use the shell name for a shell).
Shell command:
```

2. Enter your system command. For example, if you need to check the files in your home directory, type `ls` and press ENTER. You'll get a directory listing, as usual. (See Chapter 6 for a discussion of basic Unix file management commands.)

```
Mail              ctrld                       m
News              doppel                      private
check             elm.monthly                 test
crypt.test        internetwork-mail-guide


Press any key to return to ELM:
```

Press any key to return to Elm.

3. If you need to enter more than one command, it may be helpful to run a shell session. To do this, use the name of your shell as the command. For example, to run the C shell:

```
Command: !                          (Use the shell name for a shell).
Shell command: csh

%
```

4. Enter commands normally at the shell prompt. When you're done, press CTRL-D to exit the shell and return to Elm.

How It Works
Unix programs have the ability to "spawn" other programs, run them, and then resume. Since one of the commands you can run is "run the shell," this means that you can leave Elm and perform all your normal housekeeping tasks.

Comment
Some systems may disable shell access for security reasons.

3 USING INTERNET MAIL

3.25 HOW DO I...
Encrypt mail for added security?

COMPLEXITY: INTERMEDIATE

Problem
Sometimes you may need to include secret or sensitive information in a mail message, such as business plans, salaries, and so on. Since mail files can be read by certain people who have system access privileges (or by unauthorized hackers), it may be a good idea to encrypt sensitive information before mailing it.

Technique
You simply embed in the message instructions that tell Elm when to start encoding it and when to return to "plain text." Elm does the rest.

Steps
1. Start writing your message normally. When you reach the part you want encrypted, type [encode] at the beginning of a line by itself.

2. Write the secret part of your message.

3. Type [clear] on a line by itself.

4. When you press (s) to send the message, Elm will prompt you for a code key to use for this message. (Obviously, the code must be something that your recipient will know.)

```
Enter encryption key: silverbird
Please enter it again: silverbird
```

> The second prompt is to ensure that you don't type the key incorrectly and make the message unreadable by your recipient. The message is then sent normally.

5. When the recipient tries to read the coded part of the message, he or she is prompted for the key:

```
Enter decryption key: silverbird
```

> If the correct key isn't entered, the recipient won't be able to read the encoded part of the message (it will be gibberish).

6. If the correct key is entered, the message can be read normally. The recipient will be asked for the key each time the message is read.

How It Works
Elm uses the standard Unix encryption program called crypt to perform the coding and decoding. This encryption is reasonably secure, especially if you choose a hard-to-guess password.

Comment
Due to licensing restrictions, the encryption facility will probably not be available at sites outside the United States.

Encryption is provided by the Unix crypt program, which is not considered secure against determined code-breakers.

3.26 HOW DO I...
Exchange mail between the Internet and other networks?

COMPLEXITY: INTERMEDIATE

Problem
There are many computer networks out there, some very large, some small. Each network has its own way to address and transport mail. You'd like to be able to communicate electronically with anyone who has access to any of the major networks or commercial information services.

Technique
You identify which network your non-Internet correspondent is using, and then put the person's username or user number into the appropriate format needed to address that network from Internet, as shown in Table 3-6.

Steps
1. Obtain your correspondent's username (or user number) on the non-Internet network.

2. If the non-Internet network is listed in Table 3-6, change the format of the non-Internet username to an Internet domain name, as shown in the table. For example, if a CompuServe user has a user number 74459,3017, you'd address that user via

NETWORK	ADDRESS FROM INTERNET	ADDRESS TO INTERNET
America Online	username@aol.com	Internet-address
Applelink	user@applelink.apple.com	Internet-address
Bitnet	user%site.bitnet@gateway	Internet-address
	(where "gateway" is a gateway host such as cunyvm.cuny.edu or mitvma.mit.edu)	
BIX	username@bix.com	Internet-address
CompuServe	usernumber@compuserve.com	>INTERNET:Internet-address
	Note: When sending, replace comma in CompuServe address with a period.	
Delphi	username@delphi.com	Internet-address
Fidonet	user@p4.f3.n2.z1.fidonet.org	Internet-address ON 1:1/31
	(where the numbers represent a Fidonet address in the original form of user at 1:2/3.4)	
GEnie	username@genie.geis.com	Internet-address
MCI Mail	username@mcimail.com or user number @mcimail.com	name(EMS) INTERNET (at EMS prompt)
	Note: Remove spaces from name or hyphen from number.	Internet-address (at Mbx prompt)
Prodigy	username@prodigy.com	Internet-address

Table 3-6 Sending mail between the Internet and other networks

Internet as 74459.3017@compuserve.com. (As shown in the table, the comma in a CompuServe user number gets changed to a period in the Internet address.) Note that most networks have an Internet domain name that consists of the network name (or the network operator's name) followed by .com, for example, compuserve.com or aol.com.

3. Use the domain version of the address to send mail to the non-Internet user.

4. The non-Internet user should be able to send mail back to you using your Internet address in the form given in the table. If there is a problem, have the non-Internet user check with his or her system administrator or support person for information on how to send mail from the non-Internet network to you and other Internet users. Note that in the table "Internet-address" means a standard domain address in the form user@site.

Note that many commercial services are now connecting themselves directly to the Internet rather than using a "gateway" site. When a service is connected directly, you can send mail to the user of that service using the address user@service.com, where "service.com" is the service's name on the Internet. In turn, you can send mail from the service to the Internet by using the person's standard Internet address.

How It Works
The need to provide mail exchange between major networks has led to the creation of a number of gateways. A gateway is a machine connected to two or more networks which has software that can route messages from one network to another. In this case we're concerned with gateways between the Internet and other major networks.

Comment
New gateways between the Internet and other networks are constantly being developed. An up-to-date list of internetwork connections can be found in the "Inter-Network Mail Guide" by John Chew. This is in the file internetwork-mail-guide and can be found via anonymous ftp (see Chapter 7) to ftp.mmstate.edu in the /pub/docs directory.

3.27 HOW DO I...
Join a mailing list?

COMPLEXITY: INTERMEDIATE

Problem
Mail is great for exchanging messages between two people. With the aid of carbon copies, mail can be used by several people to discuss a project. When you get to topics of broader interest in which dozens or hundreds of people want to participate, having everyone mail everything to everyone else isn't practical.

Technique
One solution to this problem is called a *mailing list*. The basic idea of a mailing list is that one person maintains an address to which everyone sends their contributions. A mechanism at that address then sends each message to everyone else on the list. This can be done by a person who manually maintains a list of the addresses of participants, or by a program called Listserv that manages the list automatically. There are hundreds of mailing lists on the Internet today.

INTERNET HOW-TO

Listserv lists can usually be identified by the name "listserv" in their address, or by references to "bitnet." You communicate with a Listserv list by sending it special messages containing commands that you use to subscribe or unsubscribe to the list.

Most lists on the Internet (rather than Bitnet) are administered by a person rather than by the listserv program.

Steps

1. Identify the type of mailing list (Listserv or human-administered).

2. If it is a Listserv list, send a message to the Listserv address with no subject. In the body of the message put a line like this,

    subscribe *listname yourname*

    where *listname* is the name of the list and *yourname* is your first and last name (not your net address). You may receive an acknowledgement, or you may just start getting a lot of mail from the list!

3. To unsubscribe from a Listserv list, repeat the process in step 2, but simply put the line,

    unsubscribe *listname*

    in the message body.

4. If the list is run by a person, send a mail message to the list address. Add a hyphen followed by the word "request" to the username portion of the address. For example, if the list is named developers@newsoft.com, you would send the message to developers-request@newsoft.com. Put your request to subscribe or unsubscribe in the message (you can include a subject, and you use your own words—no special format).

5. Once you have joined the list, you send a response to a message from the list in the same way as you respond to other mail. Your response is automatically distributed to everyone on the list. To send an *original* message to a Listserv list, simply mail the message to the Listserv address. If it is a human-run list, however, you send the message to the address *without* the -request part. (Remember: The -request version is for administrative requests; the regular version is for actual contributions to the list.)

How It Works

While the Listserv and human-run lists are administered differently, the idea is basically the same. Everyone sends mail to one address and the mail is distributed to everyone else automatically. Listserv lists are easy to maintain because commands are processed automatically, but users have to use a precise syntax to subscribe or unsubscribe. (Every such list gets periodically flooded by someone requesting to unsubscribe without using the command given above.)

Some human-run lists are *moderated*. This means that the person running the list reviews messages for suitability before distributing them to the list. This can cut down on the amount of less than useful mail generated.

Comment

There are many mailing lists on Bitnet that have parallel Usenet newsgroups whose names begin with "bit." As an alternative to mailing to the Listserv, Internet users can participate in these lists by reading and posting to the newsgroups. See Chapter 4 for instructions on how to participate in newsgroups.

If you're interested in seeing what mailing lists are available, there are a number of "lists of lists" available. One of the easiest to obtain is called "Publicly Accessible Mailing Lists" and is posted as a series of news articles in the news.announce.newusers newsgroup (and in other places). Here's what the beginning of this list looks like:

```
Archive-name: mail/mailing-lists/part1
   Original-author: chuq@apple.com (Chuq Von Rospach)
   Previous-maintainer: spaf@purdue.edu (Gene Spafford)
   Last-change: 19 November 1993 by arielle@taronga.com (Stephanie da Silva)

[This is the first of six articles on mailing lists.]

Quick Summary of Changes

   Added since last list:
     Boston Bruins            Cyber-Sleaze            Dallas Stars
     Deborah Harry/Blondie    dragnet                 Everton
     france-foot              Friends of Ohio State   Fringeware
     GOTHIC-TALES             LDS-Net                 Los Angeles Kings
     Maria McKee/Lone Justice middlesex               Mighty Ducks of Anaheim
     Milieu                   New York Islanders      NHL Goalie Stats
     nissan                   NORWEAVE                obed-l
     PAGEMAKR                 pd-games                PHOTO-CD
     pro-rkba-democrats       reader                  Rocky Horror
     Saints-Best              se-r                    ssi_mail
     St. Louis Blues          Supercomputing Sites    TheWho
     Vancouver Canucks        Western Hockey League
```

It goes on for hundreds of lines, giving list names and summaries, such as:

```
         Specific Information on Groups

12step
      Contact: suhre@trwrb.dsd.trw.com  (Maurice Suhre)

   Purpose: To discuss/share experiences about 12 step programs
   such as Alcoholics Anonymous, Overeaters Anonymous, Alanon,
   ACA, etc.  Questions will also be answered.  Please include a
   phone number in case of trouble establishing an e-mail path.

30something
      Contact: 30something-request@fuggles.acc.virginia.edu (Marc Rouleau)

   Purpose:  Discussion of the TV show by the same name, including
   actors, episodes, plots, characters, etc.

386users
      Contact: 386users-request@udel.edu (William Davidsen, Jr.)

   Purpose:  Topics are 80386 based computers, and all hardware and
   software which is either 386-specific or which has special interest
   on the 386.
```

INTERNET HOW-TO

You can get a summary of Listserv lists by mailing a message to any Listserv mailing list. In the body of the message put the command "list global."

Subscribing to mailing lists is a good way to fill your mailbox with mail. You may have to spend extra time with mail processing (but see How-To 3.17 for a possible solution). You may have to prune this mail periodically to avoid charges for excess disk usage; check with your system administrator if you're not sure if such charges are made.

3.28 HOW DO I...
Learn more about Elm?

COMPLEXITY | **INTERMEDIATE**

Problem
There are many more features of Elm and nuances of usage than can be covered in this chapter. You can find Elm documentation in a variety of places and formats, but some items may be harder to find than others.

Technique
The basic Elm documents should be found at your Internet site—but where? Use the whereis command to find the directories that store Elm and its related files on your system.

Steps

1. Type `whereis elm` at the system prompt:

```
% whereis elm
elm: /usr/src/elm2.4 /usr/local/bin/elm
```

2. If more than one directory path is shown (as in this case), it probably means that one directory is for the source files (program code and documentation) and the other for the executable program. A directory such as /usr/local/bin/elm usually contains the program. A directory such as /usr/src/elm2.4 contains the source files. Use the cd (change directory) command to change to that directory:

```
%cd /usr/src/elm2.4
```

3. See if this directory has a subdirectory called doc (for documents). Look in there with the ls command to see what Elm documentation is available:

```
% cd doc
% ls
Alias.guide   Makefile.SH   chkalias.1   elmalias.1   listalias.1   tmac.n
Config.guid   Ref.guide     elm-help.0   elmrc-info   messages.1    wnewmail.1
Elm.cover     Users.guide   elm-help.1   elmrc.samp   newalias.1
Filter.guid   answer.1      elm-help.2   fastmail.1   newmail.1
Form.guide    autoreply.1   elm-help.3   filter.1     printmail.1
Makefile      catman        elm.1        frm.1        readmsg.1
```

The files with extensions of .guide or .guid are reference manuals. The most important of these are Users.guide (pretty much for beginners) and Ref.guide (which covers commands exhaustively).

4. Identify the file type and download the desired files. The .guide, .guid, and .1 files are in nroff or troff format and will have to be formatted. (Nroff and troff are Unix text-

formatting programs.) Try to find files with the words "text" or "plain" in their names; these should be printable as is. For more information on navigating in the Internet site's file system, see Chapter 6. For information on handling files in compressed formats, see Chapter 8. Files in PostScript format should be directly printable on a PostScript printer.

5. An alternative way to get these files is via ftp (see Chapter 7). This may be useful for getting plain text versions of the files. Try ftp to ftp.mcs.com in subdirectories of ftp/mcsnet.users/dattier/elmguides. archie (covered in Chapter 11) may also help you find them.

How It Works
Elm comes with a variety of well-written documentation. Use the Elm reference guide to look up configuration options, command switches, and key commands. The "Alias Guide" and "Filter Guide" discuss the alias system and filter utility, respectively. Small utilities, such as frm or autoreply, each have their own documentation file.

Comment
The newsgroup comp.mail.elm is devoted to the Elm mailer and associated programs. This is a good source for news about Elm, periodic updates, and a FAQ (Frequently Asked Questions) file about Elm.

Key Command Help Screens in Elm

For your convenience, the help screens that Elm displays for each of its modes of operation are printed here. The first group consists of commands that you use while viewing the Index screen (or reading mail). The second group deals with the Options Editor screen, and the third group deals with the Alias Mode screen.

Elm's Index Help Screen

Command	Elm 2.4 Action
<RETURN>	Display the current message, or (builtin pager only) scroll current message forward one line
<SPACE>	Display the next screen of the current message (builtin pager only), or if at the end of a message, the first screen of the next message
|	Pipe current message or tagged messages to a system command
!	Shell escape
?	This screen of information
>	Save current message or tagged messagesto a folder
<	Scan current message for calendar entries
b	Bounce (re-mail) current message
c	Copy current message or tagged messages to a folder
d	Delete current message
f	Forward current message

Continued on next page

INTERNET HOW-TO

Continued from previous page

Command	Elm 2.4 Action
g	Group (all recipients) reply to current message
h	Headers displayed with message
i	Return to index screen
J	Increment current message by one
j, <DOWN>	Advance to next undeleted message
K	Decrement current message by one
k, <UP>	Advance to previous undeleted message
m	Mail a message
n	Display next message
p	Print current message or tagged messages
q	Quit pager mode and return to index screen
r	Reply to current message
s	Save current message or tagged messages to a folder
t	Tag current message for further operations
T	Tag current message and go to next message
u	Undelete current message
x	Exit leaving folder untouched, ask permission if folder changed
X	Exit leaving folder untouched, unconditionally

Elm's Options Editor Help Screen

Commands available from the Options Menu in Elm 2.4

Key	Meaning
>	Save current options to elmrc file.
a	Arrow cursor. Changes from "->" to inverse bar and back for indicating the current message. Change with <space>.
b	Border on copy. Sets the prefix for copied lines of forward and reply.
c	Calendar file. See '<' at top level menu for more information on this.
d	Display pager. "builtin" and "builtin+" will use the built-in pager, or enter the name of an external pager, like "more".
e	Editor to use when composing messages.
f	Folder directory. This is what '=', '+', or '%' on the front of a folder name expands to.

3 USING INTERNET MAIL

h	Hold sent message. This enables automatically saving a copy of outgoing messages.
i,q	Return to the index screen.
j	Reply editor. Replacement for builtin editor when replying.
k	Pause after pager or always return to index screen.
^L	Redraw screen.
l	Alias sorting criteria. Step through with <space>, <return> selects.
m	Mini-menu displayed on index screen or not. Change with <space>.
n	Names only or names and address displayed. Change with <space>.
o	Outbound mail file. Where to save copies of outbound mail when not saved by the recipient's name.
p	Print messages with this command. '%s' can be used in the command as a filename holder.
r	Reply copies message. Automatically copy message into reply.
s	Sorting criteria. Step through with <space>, <return> selects.
t	Text editor. Editor selected by '~e' builtin editor command.
u	User's expertise level. Change with <space>.
v	Visual editor. Editor selected by '~v' builtin editor command.
w	Want Cc: prompt. Ask for Cc: recipients when mailing and replying.
x	Exit leaving folder untouched unconditionally.
y	Your full name to be used in outbound mail.
z	Insert dashes before signature.

Elm's Alias Mode Help Screen

Commands available from the Alias Menu in Elm 2.4

Key	Meaning
?	Help on a specific key, or this summary of commands.
$	Resynchronize the alias display, processing deletions and additions to the alias database.
/	Search for specified name or alias in list.
<SPACE>, <RETURN>, v	View the address of the current alias.
a	Add the return address of current message to alias database, (or the regular address if current message is copy of a message sent).
c	Change (modify) the current alias. Changes are effective upon the next alias resync. (Changed aliases are marked with 'N'.)
d	Delete current user alias.
^D	Delete user aliases with a specified search pattern.
e	Edit the alias text file directly and rebuild database when done.
f	Display fully expanded alias for the current selection.
^L	Redraw screen.
l	Limit alias list by specified criteria.
m	Mail a message to the address of the current alias or the currently tagged aliases.
n	Make a new user alias. It is added to alias database upon the next alias resync.
r,q,i	Return to index screen, possibly prompting concerning deletions.
R,Q,I	Return to index screen immediately, no prompting.
t	Tag current alias for further operations.
T	Tag current alias and go to next alias.
^T	Tag aliases with a specified search pattern.

3 USING INTERNET MAIL

u	Undelete current user alias.
^U	Undelete user aliases with a specified search pattern.
x	Exit from the alias system without updating the alias database.

Display Navigation Commands

Key	Meaning
+, <RIGHT>	Display next index page.
-, <LEFT>	Display previous index page.
=	Set current alias to first alias.
*	Set current alias to last alias.
<NUMBER><RETURN>	Set current alias to <NUMBER>.
J	Increment current alias by one.
j, <DOWN>	Advance to next undeleted alias.
K	Decrement current alias by one.
k, <UP>	Advance to previous undeleted alias.

Reading the Usenet News

How do I...

4.1	Select and read news articles
4.2	Get help while using nn
4.3	Use nn's online manual
4.4	Select consecutive articles
4.5	Select articles by subject
4.6	Arrange the menu by conversation "threads"
4.7	Reply to an article by mail
4.8	Post a follow-up to an article
4.9	Post an original news article
4.10	Subscribe or unsubscribe to a newsgroup
4.11	Move to a particular newsgroup
4.12	Move between newsgroups
4.13	Specify the order in which to see newsgroups
4.14	Search for newsgroups
4.15	Save news to a file
4.16	Save news to a folder
4.17	Read a news folder
4.18	Read encrypted articles
4.19	Save an article with a program or graphic image
4.20	Save a shell archive
4.21	Filter out unwanted articles
4.22	Select articles automatically
4.23	Catch up with unread news

Continued on next page

INTERNET HOW-TO

Continued from previous page

4.24 Specify nn's features and behavior
4.25 Execute system commands from nn
4.26 Collect news by subject
4.27 Change nn's key commands
4.28 Use macros to create shortcut commands
4.29 Learn more about nn

What do sex, the Unix operating system, Ren and Stimpy, and about 4,997 other subjects have in common? The answer is that you can read and discuss all of them in the Internet news. Whether your interests are professional, technical, social, or recreational, you can surely find the news topic (newsgroup) for you.

From its humble beginnings less than 15 years ago, the Usenet news system (now commonly thought of as "Internet news") has grown to encompass thousands of topics, tens of thousands of articles, and tens of millions of bytes zipping across the phone lines of America and much of the world each day.

Of course the sheer volume and variety of the Internet news can be daunting. One way to get a handle on it is to survey the news *hierarchy*, or organization of newsgroups into categories. This will help you figure out what a name like "comp.unix.questions" means.

The first part of a newsgroup name is a very broad category, such as one of those listed in Table 4-1.

In addition to the broad topical categories that make up the mainstream of the news there are also alternative categories, such as "alt," which indicates groups that are informally distributed; geographical categories for local news, such as "ba" for the San Francisco Bay Area; and others.

The second part of a newsgroup name indicates a more specific topic. For example, there are many aspects of computers discussed in the "comp" category, and Table 4-2 shows some example subcategories.

Some newsgroups have two-part names; for example, comp.risks is a group discussing risks involved with computer systems and related technology. Most groups have three or more names, however. For example, comp.sources.mac breaks down to

CATEGORY	SUBJECTS
comp	Computers (hardware, software, theory)
misc	Topics that don't fit in another category
news	The news network and software itself
rec	Arts, hobbies, crafts, recreational activities
sci	The sciences
soc	Social issues and social interaction
talk	Discussion and debate (unstructured and sometimes endless)

Table 4-1 The main news categories

SUBCATEGORY	MEANING
ai	Artificial intelligence
answers	Regularly posted articles (such as Frequently Asked Questions)
arch	Hardware architecture
binaries	Programs (broken down by machine type)
bugs	Discussion of software bugs (broken down by system)
databases	Databases in general and particular products
dcom	Data communications
graphics	Computer graphics (broken down by aspect)
lang	Computer languages (C, Lisp, and many others)
mail	Mailing programs (Elm, for example)
org	Professional organizations related to computing
os	Operating systems
risks	Potential risks or problems with computers or other technology
society	Social issues relating to computing
software	Aspects of software development
sources	Program source code (by system)

Table 4-2 Subcategories of the comp category

"computers, program source code, for Macintosh." You'll occasionally run into inconsistencies. For example, most operating systems are subcategories of comp.os, as in comp.os.mswindows (which in turn is broken down into newsgroups to discuss various aspects), but groups related to the Unix operating system are in the comp.unix family of groups.

In this chapter you will learn how to explore the fascinating world of newsgroups by using a program called nn. Just as there are many mail programs, there are also many "news readers." The nn program for reading and posting news was chosen for the same reason that Elm was chosen for mail: like Elm, nn combines an easy-to-use menu interface with many powerful commands and options that you can master as you go along.

The philosophy of nn is perhaps best described by the program's author in the "greeting" screen you see when you run the program for the first time, as shown in Figure 4-1. The idea behind this bit of whimsy is that nn strives to avoid cluttering your screen with unnecessary information. It shows you what's new and helps you do something about it. If there's no news, it quietly exits and leaves you at the system prompt.

The use of nn breaks down into three parts or phases: *article selection mode*, where you choose news articles from the menu for the current newsgroup; *reading mode*, where you read the selected articles and possibly reply to them in some way; and *newsgroup navigation*, where you choose another newsgroup to look at. The key to organizing the wealth of nn commands is to remember what you are doing at a given time: selecting articles, reading or replying to articles, or deciding which newsgroup to read.

INTERNET HOW-TO

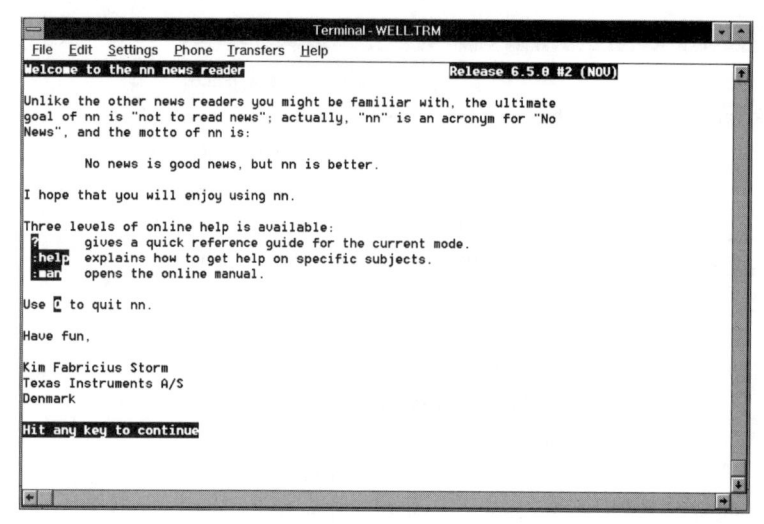

```
┌─────────────────────── Terminal - WELL.TRM ───────────────────┬─▲─┐
│  File  Edit  Settings  Phone  Transfers  Help                 │   │
│ Welcome to the nn news reader         Release 6.5.0 #2 (NOV)  │ ▲ │
│                                                                │   │
│ Unlike the other news readers you might be familiar with, the ultimate
│ goal of nn is "not to read news"; actually, "nn" is an acronym for "No
│ News", and the motto of nn is:
│
│        No news is good news, but nn is better.
│
│ I hope that you will enjoy using nn.
│
│ Three levels of online help is available:
│  ?     gives a quick reference guide for the current mode.
│  :help explains how to get help on specific subjects.
│  :man  opens the online manual.
│
│ Use Q to quit nn.
│
│ Have fun,
│
│ Kim Fabricius Storm
│ Texas Instruments A/S
│ Denmark
│
│ Hit any key to continue
│                                                                │ ▼ │
│ ◄                                                            ► │   │
└────────────────────────────────────────────────────────────────┴───┘
```

Figure 4-1 The nn greeting screen

Related Topics

To Learn How to...	See Chapter
Read or write mail messages	3
Use the Internet responsibly	2
Transfer files between the Internet and your PC	9
Get files by ftp	7

How-Tos in this Chapter

4.1 Select and read news articles
You'll begin by looking at the article menu for a newsgroup. You'll learn how to select and read the articles that interest you.

4.2 Get help while using nn
nn provides a variety of ways to get help while you're using each phase of the program. Pressing ⑦ gets you a summary of the most important commands that you can use while selecting or reading articles.

4.3 Use nn's online manual
nn also includes a complete online manual. It's presented to you just like a newsgroup so you can read and save the parts you need.

4.4 Select consecutive articles
It's easy to select a group of related articles or an article that comes in more than one part.

4.5 Select articles by subject
Tell nn what subject you're interested in, and nn will find and select the articles for you!

4.6 Arrange the menu by conversation "threads"
Some people find it easier if the menu groups an article and all of its responses or *follow-ups* into one menu entry. You can try it out for yourself.

4.7 Reply to an article by mail
When you have something to say to an article's author that's not for the world at large, you can use nn to mail a response. This is handy if your information is personal, business-related, or likely to be duplicated if everyone posts it in public.

4.8 Post a follow-up to an article
When you have something to contribute to a public discussion, you use follow-ups to give the world your thoughts on the matter.

4.9 Post an original news article
This is how you start a brand new topic of your own. It may be a request, an announcement, or just an invitation to your fellow beings to discuss something of interest.

4.10 Subscribe or unsubscribe to a newsgroup
No, you don't pay by the group. You subscribe to start being shown a particular group, and you unsubscribe if you want to stop seeing that group when you run nn.

4.11 Move to a particular newsgroup
Sometimes you just want to "jump" to a particular group and start reading it. The jump command is versatile and has many options.

4.12 Move between newsgroups
You can step forward or backward through the list of newsgroups that your Internet site subscribes to.

4.13 Specify the order in which to see newsgroups
You'll probably want to use specifications in the "init" file to pare down the list of groups to a manageable size. Most of us don't have time to read all 5000 of them! You can also decide which groups you want to see first.

4.14 Search for newsgroups
You can get a list of all the newsgroups that may be out there. You'll also see how to use the "nngrep" utility to list the groups related to a particular topic.

4.15 Save news to a file
The easiest way to save a news article for future reference is to save it to a file. You can then view, print, or download it at your leisure.

4.16 Save news to a folder
If you're accumulating a lot of news on a particular subject, it may be more convenient to create a folder in which you can later review the articles individually.

4.17 Read a news folder
Once you've created a folder and saved some articles, you can read the folder just as you would read a newsgroup. Without learning any new commands, you can read, save, or otherwise deal with your accumulated news.

4.18 Read encrypted articles
If an article contains humor that might be offensive, or perhaps the solution to a tricky part in an adventure game, the author can encrypt it using a simple cipher. nn lets you decode these articles so the gibberish on your screen turns back into readable text.

4.19 Save an article with a program or graphic image
Executable programs and graphics are examples of *binary* files. Because of the special characters in them, binary files require special handling, so nn provides facilities for saving an article into a binary file.

4.20 Save a shell archive
The shell archive is a somewhat clunky but serviceable mechanism that Unix systems sometimes use to combine a bunch of small files into one big file. nn knows how to "unpack" one of these "shar" files into its individual components.

4.21 Filter out unwanted articles
Are you tired of reading that argument about the IBM PC versus the Mac? Does Joe Bozo insist on posting irritating, useless articles day after day? You can tell nn to "kill" or filter out unwanted news for 30 days or forever.

4.22 Select articles automatically
The converse of killing unwanted news is automatically selecting news related to subjects of interest. This can be a real time-saver, and it helps make sure you don't miss anything.

4.23 Catch up with unread news
You take a long-awaited three week vacation, and your significant other makes you leave the laptop and modem at home. Now you're back, and thousands of news articles are waiting for you. Here's how to toss them in the wastebasket and get a clean start.

4.24 Specify nn's features or behavior
nn has more options you can set than the Ginsu knife has blades. There isn't enough space in this book to cover them all, but this how-to shows you the settings, and it points out a few of particular interest.

4.25 Execute system commands from nn
As with Elm and many other programs, you can jump from nn to Unix and take care of some housekeeping business or run a utility program on a news article. You can then jump back into nn where you left off.

4.26 Collect news by subject
Here's something for you batch-processing fans: a utility called "nngrab" that can search through all the newsgroups for a word or phrase in the subject and assemble all the articles for your perusal.

4.27 Change nn's key commands
Do you ever wish nn used a different key for a particular command? Well, you can change the key map so that the key of *your* choice performs a particular function.

4.28 Use macros to create shortcut commands
nn includes a powerful macro programming language that you can use to simplify complex commands or to have nn perform certain actions automatically at certain times (such as upon entering a newsgroup). This how-to gives you a couple of examples and hints about what you can do with this feature.

4.29 Learn more about nn
All right, then, how *do* you learn more about options and macros and of the advanced features of nn? This how-to shows you where to find more documentation and help.

4.1 HOW DO I...
Select and read news articles?

COMPLEXITY: EASY

Problem
Usenet is a cooperative venture where articles posted by users on hundreds of newsgroups are distributed to many sites on the Internet (and elsewhere). The volume of material distributed is quite substantial (a site can receive 80MB or more worth of text per day). No one has time to read all the news posted in even a few large newsgroups. You must therefore choose which articles you wish to read.

Technique
You use selection commands to select the articles that interest you. When you have finished selecting articles nn presents them to you for reading. Let's give nn a tryout with one of the more interesting newsgroups so you can see how this is done.

Steps
1. The best way to start practicing nn is to go to the system prompt and type nn followed by the name of an interesting newsgroup. If you don't know about an interesting group yet, try news.answers. This group is full of FAQ (Frequently Asked Questions) files and other resources related to hundreds of newsgroups. It's a fun browse.

% nn news.answers

2. The first time you run nn you'll see the greetings screen in Figure 4-1. The program may take a few moments to set up the special file called .newsrc that is used to keep track of your news reading. In a few moments you'll see a screen that lists the first 20 or so news articles in the news.answers newsgroup. Figure 4-2 shows the nn article selection screen.

   The top line of the screen gives the name of the current newsgroup, the number of articles available in the group (this is a big group!), and the total number of articles and subscribed groups available. (Since we specifically told nn to get the news.answers group, it only displays statistics for that one group.)

   Each menu entry consists of a letter, the author of the article, the number of lines in the article, and the subject.

3. If the subject of a particular article interests you and you'd like to read it, press the menu letter for that article. For example, press (J) if you are interested in answers to

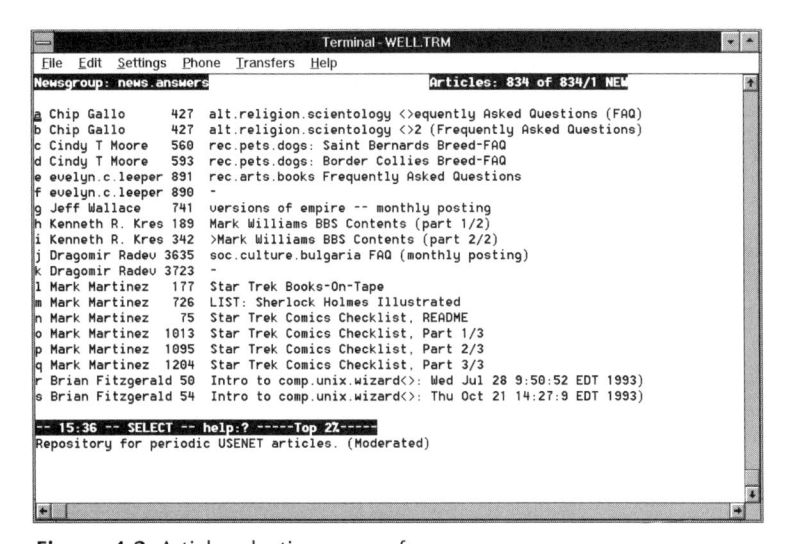

Figure 4-2 Article selection screen for nn

INTERNET HOW-TO

TO DO THIS...	PRESS OR TYPE THIS
Select an article	Article's letter or number
Read an article immediately	% *article-letter*
Move cursor down	↓
Move cursor up	↑
Select article at cursor	.
Move to next page	>
Move to previous page	<
Move to first page	^
Move to last page	$

Table 4-3 Basic article selection commands

frequently asked questions about Bulgarian culture. You can select as many articles as you like.

The current article is indicated by a small blinking underline cursor under the article's letter. You can select articles by moving the cursor with the ↑ or ↓ keys. Once the cursor is on the article you want, press . (period) to select the article at the cursor and move the cursor down to the next article.

4. Most newsgroups have too many articles to fit on one screen page. Press > (the greater than symbol) to go to the next page. You can press < (less than) to go back a page. Table 4-3 shows the basic article selection commands.

5. Once you have made your selections, you begin the reading process by pressing (SPACEBAR) (while looking at the last page for a newsgroup), or pressing Z or X. (The difference between these two keys is that Z returns you to the current group after reading, while X takes you to the next group on your list.)

Figure 4-3 shows what the screen looks like while you're reading an article. The article is presented using a pager program that lets you scroll back and forth through the article if you wish. The basic commands for reading articles are shown in Table 4-4.

How It Works

nn creates a menu for each screen page of articles in the newsgroup. Depending on how many lines fit on your terminal, the menu can have up to 36 articles per page, indicated by the letters a through z and numerals 0 through 9.

When you select an article, it is highlighted (shown in reverse video or, if your terminal doesn't support this feature, indicated with an asterisk next to the article's letter).

Once you've made your selections and indicated that you want to start reading, nn presents the articles you've selected one at a time. If you just want to read everything in order, you can keep pressing (SPACEBAR) until there are no articles left. You can also use the commands in Table 4-4 to skip forward or backward within an article or between articles.

4 READING THE USENET NEWS

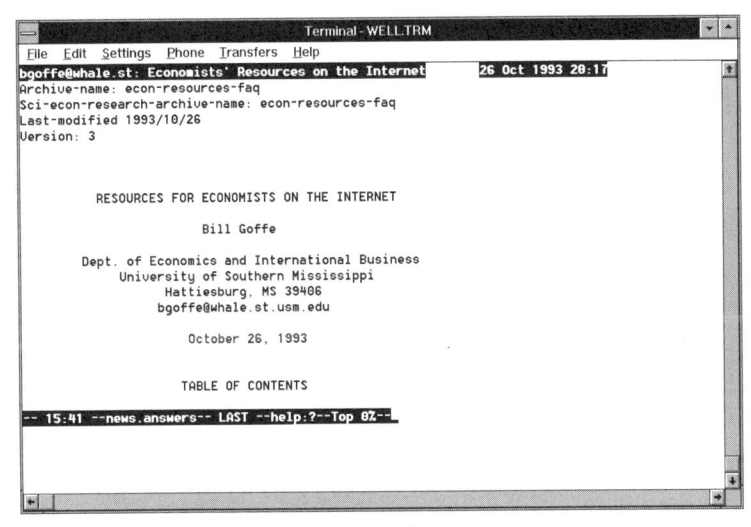

Figure 4-3 Beginning to read an article

Comment

Article selection commands are *toggles*. That is, to deselect an article, simply repeat the selection command. For example, pressing Ⓑ selects article b, but pressing Ⓑ a second time deselects the article (and removes the reverse video).

The % or "preview" command is very useful. It lets you select and read an article immediately without waiting to complete the selection process for the whole newsgroup. Simply move the cursor to the desired article and press Ⓟ.

TO DO THIS...	PRESS OR TYPE THIS
Read next page of article	SPACEBAR
Read previous page	DEL
Go to beginning of article	^
Go to end of article	$
Find word or phrase in text	/ word
Skip to next article	Ⓝ
Look at previous article	Ⓟ

Table 4-4 Basic article reading commands

111

INTERNET HOW-TO

4.2 HOW DO I...
Get help while using nn?

COMPLEXITY: EASY

Problem
As mentioned earlier, nn has three phases of use (newsgroup selection, article selection, and article reading and disposition). Each of these phases has many relevant nn commands. While it's not hard to pick up the basics, it is useful to have access to help while you're online in case you get stuck.

Technique
As shown in Figure 4-1, nn provides three kinds of online help: a quick reference guide, a more detailed description of specific subjects, and a complete online manual. The first two are covered in this how-to.

Steps
1. You can press (?) at any nn prompt. The help you see will be appropriate for the mode you are currently using (article selection or reading an article). The article selection and reading help screens are shown at the end of the chapter for your convenience.

2. You can also type `:help` followed by the name of one of the topics listed in Table 4-5.

   For example, typing `:commands` gets you a list of all the nn key commands. Each entry gives you the command name, the key used to invoke this command at the article menu, the key used at the More prompt (that is, while reading articles), and a brief description of the function of the command. Figure 4-4 shows the beginning of this list.

HELP CATEGORY	DESCRIPTION
commands	Brief description of nn command keys
extended	Special commands that begin with : (colon)
help	Ways to get help
helpfiles	Available help files
map	How to assign keys to commands
menu	How to select articles from the menu
more	How to read articles
read	Same as more
set	How to set/unset option variables
show	Commands that show status of nn
sort	Use of the sort-mode variable to sort article menus
variables	Options that can be set by command line switches

Table 4-5 Categories of information with the help command

4 🌐 READING THE USENET NEWS

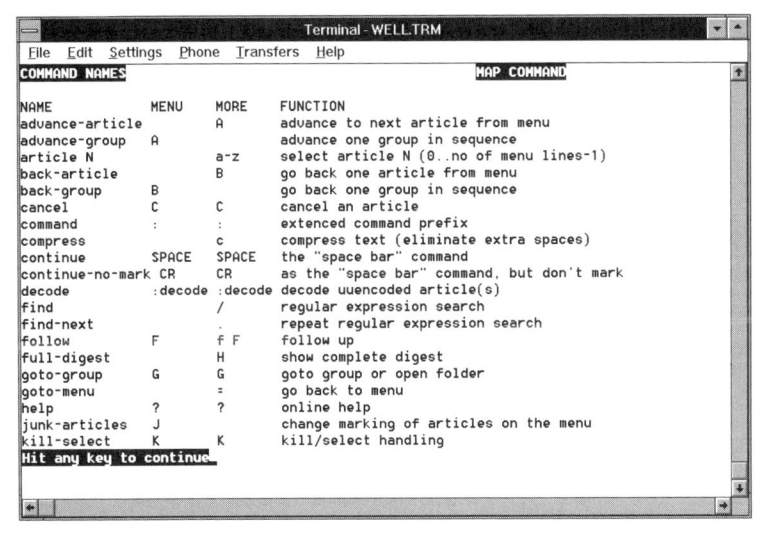

```
┌─────────────────────── Terminal - WELL.TRM ──────────────────── ▼ ▲ ┐
 File  Edit  Settings  Phone  Transfers  Help
 COMMAND NAMES                                         MAP COMMAND
 
 NAME            MENU    MORE    FUNCTION
 advance-article          A      advance to next article from menu
 advance-group    A              advance one group in sequence
 article N                a-z    select article N (0..no of menu lines-1)
 back-article             B      go back one article from menu
 back-group       B              go back one group in sequence
 cancel           C       C      cancel an article
 command          :       :      extenced command prefix
 compress                 c      compress text (eliminate extra spaces)
 continue         SPACE   SPACE  the "space bar" command
 continue-no-mark CR      CR     as the "space bar" command, but don't mark
 decode           :decode :decode decode uuencoded article(s)
 find                     /      regular expression search
 find-next                .      repeat regular expression search
 follow           F       f F    follow up
 full-digest              H      show complete digest
 goto-group       G       G      goto group or open folder
 goto-menu                =      go back to menu
 help             ?       ?      online help
 junk-articles    J              change marking of articles on the menu
 kill-select      K       K      kill/select handling
 Hit any key to continue
```

Figure 4-4 Help with nn commands

How It Works
nn keeps its various kinds of help in a directory that usually has a path like /usr/local/lib/nn/help. You may find it convenient to go into this directory and download the files to your PC and print them.

Comment
If you ask for help and you get a message that says the help file was not found, ask your system administrator for assistance.

4.3 HOW DO I...
Use nn's online manual?

COMPLEXITY: EASY

Problem
Sometimes you may need more extensive help while using nn. Books like this one can be very useful, but it's not possible to cover all of the commands and features available.

Technique
You can display an online version of the nn user's manual and then select and read the topic(s) you need.

Steps
1. Type `:man` at any nn prompt and press (ENTER).

2. You'll see a list of entries excerpted from the nn manual. Figure 4-5 shows the nn manual screen.

113

INTERNET HOW-TO

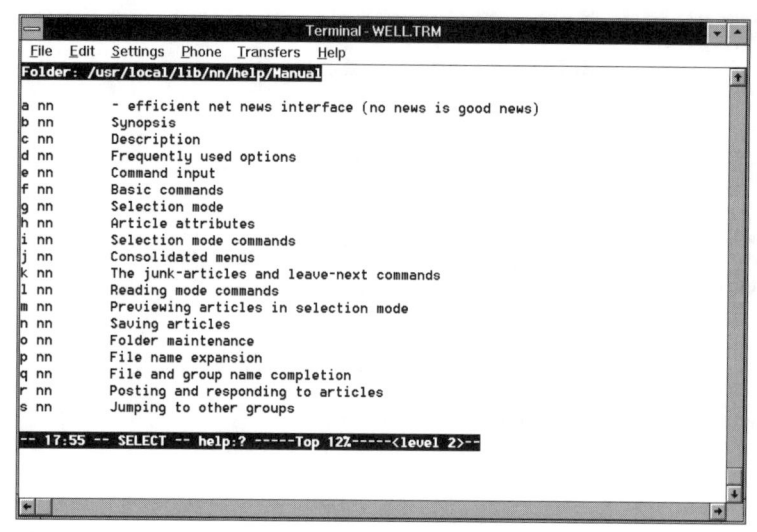

```
                        Terminal - WELL.TRM
 File  Edit  Settings  Phone  Transfers  Help
Folder: /usr/local/lib/nn/help/Manual
a nn       - efficient net news interface (no news is good news)
b nn       Synopsis
c nn       Description
d nn       Frequently used options
e nn       Command input
f nn       Basic commands
g nn       Selection mode
h nn       Article attributes
i nn       Selection mode commands
j nn       Consolidated menus
k nn       The junk-articles and leave-next commands
l nn       Reading mode commands
m nn       Previewing articles in selection mode
n nn       Saving articles
o nn       Folder maintenance
p nn       File name expansion
q nn       File and group name completion
r nn       Posting and responding to articles
s nn       Jumping to other groups
-- 17:55 -- SELECT -- help:? -----Top 12%-----<level 2>--
```

Figure 4-5 nn's online manual

As you can see, the manual entries are listed just like news articles. You can read them or save them to a file, just as you can with news articles. For example, if you select and read item g in Figure 4-5, "Selection mode," you'll see the following:

```
nn: Selection mode
In selection mode, the screen is divided into four parts: the header line
showing the name of the news group and the number of articles, the menu lines
which show the collected articles - one article per line, the prompt line
where you enter commands, and the message line where nn prints various
messages to you.

Each menu line begins with an article id which is a unique letter (or digit if
your screen can show more than 26 menu lines). To select an article for
reading, you simply enter the corresponding id, and the menu line will be
high-lighted to indicate that the article is selected. When you have selected
all the interesting articles on the present menu, you simply hit space.

If there are more articles collected for the current group than could be
presented on one screenful of text, you will be presented with the next
portion of articles to select from. When you have had the opportunity to
select among all the articles in the group, hitting space will enter reading
mode.

If no articles have been selected in the current group, hitting space will
enter selection mode on the next news group, or exit nn if the current group
was the last news group with unread articles. It is thus possible to go
— 18:06 —nn/help/Manual— PREVIEW+next —help:?—Top 27%—
```

3. When you're finished using the manual, press Q and you'll be returned to the newsgroup you were reading.

114

How It Works
The author of nn has formatted a version of the user's manual into a series of news articles. This way nn can show the manual entries just like news articles, and it lets you select, read, and print them using commands that you probably already know. The article format also breaks the lengthy manual down into convenient "bite-sized" pieces.

Comment
The most convenient way to use the manual is to press % (preview) and then the letter of the entry you wish to view.

You can also get a printed version of the online manual by saving all the entries to a file and then downloading the file. See How-Tos 4.15 and 4.16 to learn how to select and save multiple articles.

4.4 HOW DO I...
Select consecutive articles?

COMPLEXITY EASY

Problem
Long articles often come in several parts. These parts are usually listed consecutively in nn's menu. Normally you'll want to select all the parts of an article before reading or saving it.

Technique
You simply specify a range of article letters from the first article to the last. For example, the "Star Trek Comics Checklist" in the following listing consists of articles n through q.

Steps
1. To select several consecutive articles on the article selection screen, press the menu letter for the first article and then a hyphen. In this case press (N) and then (-). You'll be prompted as follows:

```
Select range n-
```

2. Press the letter of the last article in the set ((Q) in this case). As shown below, articles n through q are selected (highlighted).

```
Newsgroup: news.answers              Articles: 834 of 1864541/2615
a.Chip Gallo          427  alt.religion.scientology <>equently Asked Questions (FAQ)
b.Chip Gallo          427  alt.religion.scientology <>2 (Frequently Asked Questions)
c.Cindy T Moore       560  rec.pets.dogs: Saint Bernards Breed-FAQ
d.Cindy T Moore       593  rec.pets.dogs: Border Collies Breed-FAQ
e.evelyn.c.leeper     891  rec.arts.books Frequently Asked Questions
f.evelyn.c.leeper     890  -
g.Jeff Wallace        741  versions of empire — monthly posting
h.Kenneth R. Kres     189  Mark Williams BBS Contents (part 1/2)
i.Kenneth R. Kres     342  >Mark Williams BBS Contents (part 2/2)
j.Dragomir Radev     3635  soc.culture.bulgaria FAQ (monthly posting)
k.Dragomir Radev     3723  -
l.Mark Martinez       177  Star Trek Books-On-Tape
m.Mark Martinez       726  LIST: Sherlock Holmes Illustrated
```

Continued on next page

INTERNET HOW-TO

Continued previous from page

```
n Mark Martinez      75   Star Trek Comics Checklist, README
o Mark Martinez    1013   Star Trek Comics Checklist, Part 1/3
p Mark Martinez    1095   Star Trek Comics Checklist, Part 2/3
q.Mark Martinez    1204   Star Trek Comics Checklist, Part 3/3
r.Brian Fitzgerald   50   Intro to comp.unix.wizard<>: Wed Jul 28 9:50:52 EDT 1993)
s.Brian Fitzgerald   54   Intro to comp.unix.wizard<>: Thu Oct 21 14:27:9 EDT 1993)

— 15:58 — SELECT — help:? ——Top 2%——<level 2>—
```

3. As a shortcut, if you want to select all the articles from the current article to a subsequent article, press (-) (hyphen) followed by the letter for the last article to be selected.

How It Works

This is an example of nn's interactive prompting technique. As soon as nn figures out what you want to do, it changes the prompt accordingly. Thus when you press just (N), nn assumes that you are just selecting article n, and highlights it. When you press the (-), nn knows that you are selecting a range of articles and prompts you for the letter of the last article.

Comment

As with regular selections, you can undo a multiple article selection simply by repeating it.

4.5 HOW DO I...
Select articles by subject?

COMPLEXITY: EASY

Problem

It can be tedious to go through the many pages of a large newsgroup and scan for interesting subjects. nn gives you a way to scan for a subject automatically and select any articles that match your request.

Technique

You specify the subject you want to search for, and nn does the rest.

Steps

1. Press (=) at the article selection menu. You will see the following prompt:

```
Select regexp
```

2. Type the subject you wish to search for and press (ENTER). For example, type `unix` to find articles with the word "unix" in their subject.

3. Articles throughout the newsgroup whose subjects contain the words you typed will be selected and highlighted. For example, if you search for the word "unix" on the screen shown back in Figure 4-2, the following articles will be selected automatically:

```
r Brian Fitzgerald  50   Intro to comp.unix.wizard<>: Wed Jul 28 9:50:52 EDT 1993)
s Brian Fitzgerald  54   Intro to comp.unix.wizard<>: Thu Oct 21 14:27:9 EDT 1993)

— 16:17 — SELECT — help:? ——Top 2%——
Selected 32 articles
```

4 READING THE USENET NEWS

Note that nn displays a message saying how many articles it selected in response to your query. Here, 32 articles were selected. Although only two articles were found on the current page, nn automatically searches through the entire newsgroup.

4. Another way to select articles is to find an article whose subject interests you, make it the current article (by moving the cursor there with the arrow keys and pressing (.)), and then press (*). This selects all articles with the same subject as the current article. nn will automatically select articles on subsequent screen pages.

How It Works
nn matches your search word or phrase against the subjects of the articles in the newsgroup. All matching articles are selected for reading. (Matching is not case-sensitive.) You can also use "regular expressions" to match variations in a subject. For example, typing `hack*` will match hack, hackers, and hacking. See Chapter 6 for more details about regular expressions.

Comment
You can select *every* article in the newsgroup by pressing (=) and then (SPACEBAR)-(.) (a space and a period).

You can search by sender instead of subject by first typing `:set select-on-sender on` and then pressing (=) and entering your search word. Don't forget to set select-on-sender off before doing a subject search during the same session. See the nn reference manual for more details.

4.6 HOW DO I...
Arrange the menu by conversation "threads"?

COMPLEXITY | INTERMEDIATE

Problem
If a lot of people have posted follow-ups to certain articles, the menu screen can be cluttered with only a few different subjects but numerous articles under each subject. This makes selecting articles more difficult.

Technique
You can tell nn to list just the original articles on the menu, and hide the follow-up articles. You can then select an article and its follow-ups together by selecting just the original article.

Steps
1. Type `:set consolidated-menu` and press (ENTER).

2. All the articles that have the same subject will be presented as a single entry on the menu. This means that you can select (and read) all articles on a given subject at once. To see the difference, compare this regular menu listing,

```
Newsgroup: news.answers                    Articles: 827 of 827/1

a Brian Fitzgerald 54  Intro to comp.unix.wizard<>: Thu Oct 21 14:27:9 EDT 1993)
b Brian Fitzgerald 54  -
c Brian Fitzgerald 54  -
```

Continued on next page

117

INTERNET HOW-TO

Continued from previous page

```
d Brian Fitzgerald  54    -
e Brian Fitzgerald  54    -
f bgoffe@whale.s  1251    Economists' Resources on the Internet
g bgoffe@whale.s  1467    -
h Randy Bush        498   comp.lang.modula2: Answer<>mmon Questions - v1.7 93.10.29
i Nick Simicich     684   [rec.scuba] FAQ: Frequent<>s about Scuba, Monthly Posting
j Nick Simicich     684   -
k Nick Simicich     684   -
l Nick Simicich     684   -
m Nick Simicich     342   [alt.fan.howard-stern] FA<> Howard Stern, Monthly Posting
n Nick Simicich     342   -
o Nick Simicich     223   [rec.sport.pro-wrestling] FAQ: Wrestling Relations
p Nick Simicich     223   -
q John Gregory      944   Linear Programming FAQ
r John Gregory      930   -
s John Gregory      287   Nonlinear Programming FAQ

— 13:01 — SELECT — help:? ———4%———
```

with the consolidated version:

```
Newsgroup: news.answers                              Articles: 827 of 827/1

a Brian Fitzgerald  54   [6]  Intro to comp.unix.wizard<>Oct 21 14:27:9 EDT 1993)
b.bgoffe@whale.s  1251   [2]  Economists' Resources on the Internet
c,Randy Bush       498        comp.lang.modula2: Answer<>Questions - v1.7 93.10.29
d.Nick Simicich    684   [4]  [rec.scuba] FAQ: Frequent<>ut Scuba, Monthly Posting
e.Nick Simicich    342   [2]  [alt.fan.howard-stern] FA<>rd Stern, Monthly Posting
f.Nick Simicich    223   [2]  [rec.sport.pro-wrestling] FAQ: Wrestling Relations
g.John Gregory     944   [2]  Linear Programming FAQ
h John Gregory     287   [2]  Nonlinear Programming FAQ
i Alf the Poet     123        >alt.buddha.short.fat.guy <> Questions (FAQ), 1 of 2
j Alf the Poet     158        >alt.buddha.short.fat.guy <> Questions (FAQ), 2 of 2
k Murray Chapman  1696        BLADE RUNNER Frequently Asked Questions (FAQ)
l Cindy T Moore    375        rec.pets.dogs: Nova Scoti<>lling Retriever Breed-FAQ
m Aydin Edguer     353        comp.infosystems.wais Fre<>ions [FAQ] (with answers)
n Cindy T Moore    619        rec.pets.dogs: Alaskan Malamutes Breed-FAQ
o Cindy T Moore    249        rec.pets.dogs: Bloodhounds Breed-FAQ
p Cindy T Moore    264        rec.pets.dogs: Chesapeake Bay Retrievers Breed-FAQ
q Cindy T Moore    381        rec.pets.dogs: Chow Chow Breed-FAQ
r Cindy T Moore    359        rec.pets.dogs: Collies Breed-FAQ
s Cindy T Moore    178        rec.pets.dogs: Greyhounds Breed-FAQ

— 13:02 — SELECT — help:? ———5%———
```

In the consolidated version, nn precedes each subject with the number (in brackets) of articles dealing with that subject. For example, line a groups six articles on the subject "Intro to comp.unix.wizards."

Notice that with one different subject on each line nn can show 5 percent rather than 4 percent of the group, as shown in the prompt at the bottom of the screen.

4. Normally you'll treat these consolidated subjects as single articles for purposes of selection and reading. When you read a consolidated subject, the individual articles will still be presented to you one at a time. You can, however, "open up" a consolidated subject by pressing Ⓣ and then the menu letter, or press Ⓣ Ⓣ twice for the current article. The subject will again be displayed with each article as a separate menu item. To close a subject again, press Ⓣ Ⓣ followed by the subject letter, or Ⓣ Ⓣ twice for the current subject.

How It Works
This facility lets you view article selections similar to the way you view directories and files in many file management programs. You can consolidate the menu for ease of viewing and selection, and then open up the parts you want to examine more closely.

The preceding listing also illustrates a shortcoming of the consolidated menu facility: many multipart articles have the same subject except for a part that reads "part 1 of 5," "part 2 of 5," and so on, or, as in the listing, a subject like "rec.pet.dogs" followed by the breed of dog. nn doesn't consider such multipart articles to have the *same* subject, so it doesn't consolidate them.

Comment
The default is open menus, but many users prefer consolidated menus. To set the consolidated-menu option in your init file permanently, see How-To 4.24.

4.7 HOW DO I...
Reply to an article by mail?

COMPLEXITY INTERMEDIATE

Problem
You may wish to reply privately to something asked or offered in an article. In such cases, nn lets you reply to the article's author by mail.

Technique
First, you decide whether to reply by mail or post a follow-up article, as discussed in the next how-to. For example, suppose you are reading the following article:

```
Michael Turner: How do I post an article from nn?        Wed, 8 Dec 1993 14:22
Hi, can anyone tell me how to post a new, original article with nn?
I can't find any key that I can press that will do the job.
Thanks!

mturner@ucsd.edy - "The Brash Beginner"
```

You happen to know the answer to Michael's question (maybe you've read How-To 4.9). Do you reply by mail or post a follow-up?

The general rule is to use mail if your reply should be private, is of little interest to the general community, or is likely to be sent in by many people and thus clutter up the newsgroup. Examples of things that should be private include responses to business offers or "help wanted" messages. Besides being private, such matters are also of little interest to the general community. (You probably don't want to read an article about how much Joe Smith is offering for Betty Brown's old VW bus.) Finally, when someone asks a question like "how do you post in nn" chances are thousands of people will

INTERNET HOW-TO

know the answer. If everyone posts a follow-up article with the answer, everyone's menus will be filled with these essentially uninteresting articles. So you decide to send Michael the answer by mail.

Steps

1. Make the article you are replying to the current article and then press (R). If you're already reading the article, just press (R) (or (r)).

   You'll see the following prompt:

```
Include original article?
```

2. It's often a good idea to include a bit of the original article so that the author knows exactly what you are responding to. To do that, press (Y) at this prompt. nn will then load the original article into the edit buffer and run your editor:

```
To: mturner@ucsd.edu.
Orig-To: mturner@ucsd.edu. (Michael Turner)
Subject: Re: How do I post an article from nn?
Newsgroups: news.software.nn
References: <mturner.755360546@ucsd.edu>


>Hi, can anyone tell me how to post a new, original article with nn?
>I can't find any key that I can press that will do the job.
>Thanks!

>mturner@ucsd.edy - "The Brash Beginner"




~
~
~~
~
~


"/usr/tmp/nn.a00656" 7 lines, 168 characters
```

3. If you did choose to include the original article, edit out the unnecessary parts such as the signature of the sender. In lengthy articles edit out the parts that you aren't responding to. The basic idea is to give your reader only what's necessary to understand what you are saying.

4. Type your response into the editor. Note that nn has already provided the appropriate address and subject headings for your mail.

5. Save and quit the editor as usual. nn will prompt you as follows:

```
a)bort e)dit h)old m)ail r)eedit s)end v)iew w)rite
Action: (send letter)
```

   You can press (V) to view your message before sending it. If you're happy with your reply, simply press (ENTER), and it will be mailed to the article's author. If you want to edit the message again, press (E). If you want to throw out your reply and start over, press (R). To just forget the whole thing, press (A).

How It Works

nn constructs a mail message with appropriate headers and includes the text of the original article if you ask it to. Once you tell nn to mail the letter, it is sent via the system's normal lower-level mail facilities (usually the sendmail program).

Comment

You can also mail an article to anyone you wish by pressing (M) at the selection menu. You will be prompted for the article to mail (type the article's menu letter) and the address of the recipient. Alternatively, if you press (M) while reading an article, nn will default to mailing that article.

4.8 HOW DO I...
Post a follow-up to an article?

COMPLEXITY: INTERMEDIATE

Problem

The rule of thumb is to reply by mail unless you have something to say that is likely to be of public interest. If a discussion is underway and you want to join it publicly, you post a follow-up to a news article. The follow-up is added as a new article to the newsgroup.

Technique

You tell nn you want to post a follow-up to the current article, and nn prompts you for the necessary information.

Steps

1. Make the article you are responding to current and press (F). (You can also press (F) or (f) while reading an article.) nn prompts you:

```
Include original article?
```

2. Press (Y) if you want to include the original article in the edit buffer, or press (ENTER) if you do not want to not include it. The considerations for including the original article are similar to those involved with mail in the previous how-to. However, because many people may read your follow-up days after they saw the original article, it becomes more important to include a few lines from the original article that identify what you are responding to. On the other hand, since your article is sent all over the Internet it is also more important not to waste machine resources (or readers' time) with unnecessary verbiage.

3. Your text editor is started with the article headers already filled in (and the text of the original article if you asked for it). Edit to remove unwanted text and to add your own words in response to the article. For example, if you are posting a response to Jennifer Johnson's article asking for recommendations for books on C++, your editor buffer will look something like this:

```
Newsgroups: comp.lang.c++
Subject: Re: Want book recommendations
Keywords: C++ book recommendations wanted
References: <jjohnson.755360546@well.com>
```

Continued on next page

INTERNET HOW-TO

Continued from previous page

```
jjohnson@well.com. (Jennifer Johnson) writes:

>Can anyone recommend some good beginner's books on the
> C++ Language?

When I was learning C++ I found the books by Robert LaFore with Waite Group Press to be good,
especially for system considerations for PCs. I also went through the interactive disk tutorial
*Master C++* and learned the basics from it. Do you have any particular operating systems or
platforms in mind?

>--
"/usr/tmp/nn.a000xV" 27 lines, 1289 characters
```

4. After you've finished your reply, save it and quit the editor. You'll see the same set of prompts as with mailing a reply:

```
a)bort c)c e)dit h)old m)ail p)ost r)eedit v)iew w)rite
Action: (post article)
```

Press (V) to view and check your article before sending it. If you're happy with what you've written, simply press (ENTER), and it will be posted to the newsgroup. If you want to edit the article again, press (E). If you want to throw out your writing and start over press (R). To forget the whole thing, press (A).

How It Works

Instead of constructing a mail message, as with the previous how-to, nn constructs a new news article that is linked to the original by subject but contains your own contributions to the matter under discussion. nn then uses a news posting utility to send the article to the Internet nodes to which your system is connected.

Some newsgroups are moderated, as indicated by their description in newsgroup lists and at the bottom of the screen upon entry to the group. In a *moderated* group, a person will review your posting for appropriateness and may reject articles that are deemed inappropriate.

Comment

Posting a few thoughtful follow-ups is a good way to "get your feet wet" before posting original news messages.

4.9 HOW DO I...
Post an original news article?

COMPLEXITY: INTERMEDIATE

Problem

Sometimes you might want to start a new topic rather than join an existing discussion.

Technique

First make sure that your topic is appropriate for the newsgroup. A joke that might fit well in rec.humor would probably stick out like a sore thumb in comp.unix.questions.

More subtly, a beginning question about Unix will receive a much more sympathetic and useful reply in comp.unix.questions than it will in comp.unix.wizards, which is designed for advanced questions and discussions. The "list of active newsgroups" posted regularly in news.answers and the blurb that appears at the bottom of the screen when you enter a newsgroup will give you a rough idea of what is appropriate for the group in question. Before you post, read the group for a few days to get a better sense of what people like to talk about. Before asking questions about a technical matter, look for an appropriate FAQ article on the subject and read it first. Your question may well be answered, and you may save yourself some rude comments.

Once you've decided that posting is appropriate, you tell nn you want to post an original article. nn prompts you for information such as the group to post to, the subject, and so on.

Steps

1. Type `:post` and press (ENTER). You'll be prompted for the name of the newsgroup you want to post to.

`POST to group`

> Suppose you have a new carpooling idea and want to try it out in your local newsgroup, ba.transportation:

`POST to group ba.transportation`

2. You'll be asked for the subject of your article. Take a moment to think of something that will clearly describe what your article is about, and that will help it stand out among the others on readers' menus:

`Subject: Carpooling: let's put networks to work!`

3. Next you'll be asked for keywords that might help people find your article:

`Keywords: carpooling automation computer networks`

4. Write a one or two-line summary of your article:

`Summary: Let's create software that knows how to connect people and rides`

5. The next prompt asks how widely you want your article to be distributed:

`Distribution: (default 'world')`

> If the newsgroup (such as ba.transportation) is already local, or if you want the article distributed everywhere, just press (ENTER). But it's often useful to limit requests for information or help to a local area even if the newsgroup is itself netwide. For example, limiting a request for help with a basic Unix command to the local area (such as your own state or country) will help cut down on the number of responses you'll have to wade through, while probably still getting you the answer you need. The geographical areas supported depend on your site, but "na" (North America), "usa," and sometimes two-letter state abbreviations (like "ca") will work.

INTERNET HOW-TO

6. You will now enter your text editor. The article headers will be at the top of the editor buffer:

```
Newsgroups: ba.transportation
Distribution: world
Subject: Carpooling: let's put networks to work!
Summary: Let's create software that knows how to connect people and rides
Keywords: carpooling automation computer networks



~
~
~
~
~

"/usr/tmp/nn.a004GO" 7 lines, 222 characters
```

Take a moment to review the headers and refine them if necessary. You can also add newsgroups to which the article will be posted. This is called *cross-posting* and should be done only if the subject of your article is likely to be genuinely interesting to readers in more than one group. Excessive cross-posting will get you flamed (vehemently criticized by other users).

7. Finish writing your article, save it, and quit your editor as usual:

```
Newsgroups: ba.transportation
Distribution: world
Subject: Carpooling: let's put networks to work!
Summary: Let's create software that knows how to connect people and rides
Keywords: carpooling automation computer networks

Since we live in the networking age and our computers know more
and more about how to find us, why can't we put some of this power
to use for matching up people and rides? We could start by setting up
a regional newsgroup that lists people who need and want rides
(and when and where they want to go), as well as people who can
offer rides (and where and when they're going). If we use a
standard format we can then write software that will match rides
and riders up and automatically send them email notifying them
of their match!
```

8. You'll see the (now familiar) prompt:

```
a)bort e)dit h)old m)ail p)ost r)eedit v)iew w)rite
Action: (post article)
```

It's a good idea to press (V) and view your article to make sure everything looks right. Press (E) to edit the article if necessary. Press (ENTER) to send (post) the article.

9. nn responds:

```
Be patient! your article will not show up immediately
```

This is because it takes time for the computers on the net to make their regularly scheduled data transfers and for the article to be distributed. This time lag can sometimes be useful: if, a few minutes or hours after posting, you decide you made a horrible mistake, you can try the C (cancel) command. Go to the newsgroup to which you posted the article, and press ⓒ. If the article has arrived there, you can respond to the prompt with the article letter and cancel distribution of the article. (Of course some people may have already seen it.)

How It Works

When your article gets to regional *backbones* or distribution sites, it is then quickly propagated to backbones in other regions (or nations) and in turn distributed throughout those regions. As a result, your follow-up or original posting is seen by thousands to millions of other people on the Internet in a matter of hours to a few days. (The amount of propagation is dependent on whether the newsgroup is netwide or regional, and on the popularity of the newsgroup.)

In a moderated newsgroup, a person will review your posting for appropriateness and may reject articles that are deemed inappropriate.

Comment

Before you start posting news, it's a good idea to read the news.announce.newusers newsgroup, which has a number of articles that introduce the procedures and customs followed by Usenet participants. Here's a sample listing of the beginning of this newsgroup:

```
Newsgroup: news.announce.newusers              Articles: 45 of 45/1 NEW

 a Jonathan Kamens 314   Introduction to the *.answers newsgroups
 b Jonathan Kamens 313   -
 c Mark Moraes      60   Changes to "Emily Postnew<> Your Questions on Netiquette"
 d Mark Moraes      20   Changes to "What is Usenet?"
 e Ron Dippold     470   Usenet Newsgroup Creation Companion
 f Stephanie Silv 1132   Publicly Accessible Mailing Lists, Part 1/8
 g Stephanie Silv 1284   >Publicly Accessible Mailing Lists, Part 2/8
 h Stephanie Silv 1245   >Publicly Accessible Mailing Lists, Part 3/8
 i Stephanie Silv 1219   >Publicly Accessible Mailing Lists, Part 4/8
 j Stephanie Silv 1208   >Publicly Accessible Mailing Lists, Part 5/8
 k Stephanie Silv 1275   >Publicly Accessible Mailing Lists, Part 6/8
 l Stephanie Silv 1183   >Publicly Accessible Mailing Lists, Part 7/8
 m Stephanie Silv 1213   >Publicly Accessible Mailing Lists, Part 8/8
 n taylor          241   A Guide to Social Newsgroups and Mailing Lists
 o Mark Moraes     816   Answers to Frequently Asked Questions about Usenet
 p Mark Moraes     388   A Primer on How to Work With the Usenet Community
 q Mark Moraes      83   Changes to "Answers to Fr<> Asked Questions about Usenet"
 r Mark Moraes      34   Changes to "A Primer on H<>ork With the Usenet Community"
 s Mark Moraes      39   Changes to "Hints on writing style for Usenet"

— 02:48 — SELECT — help:? ——Top 40%——
Explanatory postings for new users. (Moderated)
```

The most important articles in this group are "A Primer on How to Work with the Usenet Community" and "Answers to Frequently Asked Questions about Usenet." Other useful articles include "Emily Postnews Answers Your Questions on Netiquette," "Hints on Writing Style for Usenet," and "Rules for Posting to Usenet."

INTERNET HOW-TO

4.10 HOW DO I...
Subscribe or unsubscribe to a newsgroup?

COMPLEXITY EASY

Problem
There are thousands of newsgroups. Even the most voracious reader can't keep up with more than a few dozen of them. By default, most systems start you out with subscriptions to a large number of groups, many of which probably won't interest you.

While you can use newsgroup names on the nn command line (or the G command discussed in How-To 4.11) to go to specific groups, you will soon want to pare down your .newsrc list so that you are subscribed only to the groups you want to see. That way you can use the (A), (B), and other navigation keys to step through a short sequence of interesting groups.

Technique
You can subscribe (or unsubscribe) to a group while you're reading it, but the most effective technique involves editing your .newsrc file so that you are subscribed only to the groups you want to read.

Steps
1. If you haven't already done so, run nn by typing nn at the system prompt. nn will create the .newsrc file for you in your home directory. The groups listed in your .newsrc will vary with how nn is configured at your site. A typical .newsrc might begin like this:

```
news.announce.important:
news.announce.newusers:
well.general:
news.announce.conferences:
news.announce.newgroups:
news.answers:
news.config:
news.future:
news.groups:
news.lists:
```

2. Make a backup copy of your .newsrc by typing the following at the system prompt:

```
% cp .newsrc .oldnewsrc
```

Now, if you make any mistakes in the following steps, you can use the command `cp .oldnewsrc .newsrc` to restore your original .newsrc.

3. Use a text editor such as vi to examine your .newsrc. For example, type

```
vi .newsrc
```

4. Use your editor to globally change the : at the end of all the newsgroup entries to !. For example, you can do this in vi by typing

```
:s/:/!/
```

The above .newsrc file will now look like this:

```
news.announce.important!
```

126

```
news.announce.newusers!
well.general!
news.announce.conferences!
news.announce.newgroups!
news.answers!
news.config!
news.future:!news.groups!
news.lists!
```

5. You will be "unsubscribed" to all newsgroups. You can now go through the list and manually change the ! back to a : for each group that you would like to subscribe to.

6. Save your new .newsrc file and quit the editor (for vi, use the :wq command). Next time you run nn with no newsgroup on the command line you will be shown the first of your subscribed groups that has unread news.

   Note that the order in which newsgroups in your .newsrc is presented is controlled by a file called init, which is initially set up globally by your system administrator. This means that when you run nn you may see groups in an order different from that found in your .newsrc. See How-To 4.13 for information on how to specify your own order for newsgroup presentation.

7. While using nn, you can unsubscribe to a group that you've read by pressing Ⓤ. You will be ask to confirm your intention:

Unsubscribe to comp.sys.ibm.pc.digest ?

Press Ⓨ to unsubscribe, or any other key to cancel. The U command is a toggle: pressing Ⓤ at an unsubscribed group resubscribes you to the group. You will get a prompt like this:

Already unsubscribed. **Resubscribe** to comp.sys.ibm.pc.digest ?

Press Ⓨ to resubscribe. Remember that you can still get to an unsubscribed group via the G (jump) command and then resubscribe.

How It Works
The .newsrc file puts a : after the names of all groups to which you are subscribed. Unsubscribed groups are indicated by an ! instead of a colon. By using your editor to globally change all colons to exclamation points you unsubscribe to all the groups. You can then browse through the list and selectively change exclamations back to colons to resubscribe to the groups you actually want to see.

Comment
You can use your editor's search functions to help you find interesting newsgroups to subscribe to. For example, with vi you can type `:/comp.` to get to the beginning of the listings for the comp groups.

INTERNET HOW-TO

4.11 HOW DO I...
Move to a particular newsgroup?

COMPLEXITY: EASY

Problem
Someone tells you about a neat newsgroup. How do you get there without wading through all the other newsgroups on your list?

Technique
You use the versatile goto command to tell nn where you want to go next. Here you'll learn how to jump to a particular newsgroup. (The goto command can also jump to files or news folders. See How-To 4.17.)

Steps
1. Press (G) (go to). You will be prompted for a folder, file, or group to go to.

```
Group or Folder (+./~ %=sneNgG)
```

2. Type the name of the newsgroup to which you want to go. For example, let's go to the group rec.humor.funny, which contains a variety of jokes:

```
Group or Folder (+./~ %=sneNgG) rec.humor.funny
```

3. You will see the following menu.

```
Number of articles (juasne) (j)
Use: j)ump u)nread a)ll @)archive s)ubject n)ame e)ither or number
```

Press (U) if you wish to see only articles you haven't read before. Press (A) if you want to see all articles in the group, regardless of whether you read them before.

4. You can also ask to be shown only articles that match certain criteria:

➤ Press (S) followed by a word if you want to see articles with that word in the subject.

➤ Press (N) followed by a word if you want to see articles with that name as their sender.

➤ If you want to use a regular expression (wildcards), type `</>` before the word. For example, (S)/run* will match articles with run, runner, and running in the subject.

How It Works
The goto command is your gateway to the newsgroup of your choice. If you accept the defaults, you just see articles you haven't read before. But by choosing "all articles" you can reread material or reselect material that you've decided to save to a file or folder.

Comment
The s option at the G prompt is similar to pressing (=) while selecting articles (as shown in How-To 4.5), except that rather than highlighting the matching articles in the menu, it presents a menu consisting only of the matching articles.

4.12 HOW DO I...
Move between newsgroups?

COMPLEXITY: EASY

Problem
So far we've asked nn to read a particular newsgroup (news.answers). Often, though, you'll want to just type nn at the system prompt:

```
% nn
```

In this case nn puts you in the first group on its list (How-To 4.10 explains how nn constructs its list of newsgroups that are "subscribed" to.) You might see something like this:

```
Newsgroup: alt.1d                    Articles: 799 of 1881528/2633

a  M J WOODFORD       19  >>My Friend Ben.
b  TOM                11  >>>
c  Harry Baldwin      12  >>>
d  TOM                26  >>>>
e  welshc0754         58  >>>
f  Robert Whitton     17  >>>
g  Naz Bedrossian      0  >
h  Grace Sauser       18  >>>
i  Blanka             23  >jokes any one?
j  Phil               16  >>>>
k  M Shouldice        22  >>>>>>
l  Kara Drew          66  >>>
m  Lost in space      24  >>>>>
n  Lost in space      32  >>>>>>>
o  Malcolm Cowe       18  >>new comer
p  Lost in space      29  >>>
q  Golebiowski M T    33  >>>
r  Malcolm Cowe       33  >>>>
s  M Shouldice        41  >>>>

-- 16:17 -- SELECT -- help:? -------Top 2%------
```

Technique
One way to read news is to browse through the list of newsgroups, moving back and forth as desired. This is a good way to find interesting newsgroups that you didn't know about. Also, if you've "pruned" your .newsrc as described in How-To 4.10, and set up your init file (How-To 4.13), the browsing commands take you efficiently through the list of groups you've chosen to subscribe to.

Steps
1. After you have read the last article in a newsgroup (or gone to the last page without selecting any articles to read), pressing (SPACEBAR) automatically moves you to the next group in your presentation sequence.

INTERNET HOW-TO

2. You can also press Ⓐ to go immediately to the next group without finishing your selections or reading in the current group. Pressing Ⓐ repeatedly steps you through the groups in your list.

3. Similarly, you can press Ⓑ to go back to the preceding group in your list. Pressing Ⓑ repeatedly steps you back toward the beginning of your list.

4. Press Ⓝ to go forward to the next group with unread articles (this differs from A, which takes you to the next group regardless of whether it has any articles).

5. Press Ⓟ to go back to the preceding group with unread articles.

How It Works

nn keeps a list called .newsrc in your home directory. This lists all of the groups available at your site and keeps track of whether you subscribe to each group, as well as the numbers of the articles you've read in each group. The beginning of a .newsrc file might look like this:

```
news.announce.conferences:
news.announce.important: 1-14
news.announce.newgroups: 1-12,15-47
alt.3d:
alt.activism: 1-38
alt.activism.d:
alt.aeffle.und.pferdle:
alt.alien.visitors:
alt.angst:
alt.aquaria: 1-10,13,18
```

By default, nn presents newsgroups to you in the order that they appear in the .newsrc file. Many sites arrange it so that a few key groups containing important announcements appear first in the .newsrc so that everyone sees them.

Comment

In general the most efficient procedure for setting up nn is to use a text editor to specify subscriptions in your .newsrc (see How-To 4.10) and then use the commands in this how-to to navigate among the groups to which you have subscribed. You can also specify the order in which subscribed newsgroups will be presented to you (see How-To 4.13).

4.13 HOW DO I...
Specify the order in which to see newsgroups?

COMPLEXITY: INTERMEDIATE

Problem

It's pretty tedious going through your whole .newsrc and finding and subscribing to newsgroups. Many users find they can get more control with less effort by using their init file to control how groups are presented by nn.

Technique

In addition to .newsrc, nn uses a file called init in the .nn directory to control the presentation of news. Besides letting you specify options (see How-To 4.24), the init file also lets you specify what newsgroups will be shown and in what order. The order in the init file overrides the default order in .newsrc, and if you wish you can specify that only the listed articles be presented, rather than everything in your .newsrc.

Steps

1. Check to see if you already have an init file. Remember that it's in your .nn directory, so the following command should find it.

```
% ls .nn/init
```

2. If you already have an init file, back it up by typing:

```
% cd .nn
% cp init init.bak
```

3. Use a text editor (such as vi) to create or edit the init file:

```
% vi init
```

This assumes you've changed to the .nn directory. If not, either type `cd .nn` or use .nn in your path (.nn/init).

4. Type the word `sequence` on a line by itself in the init file. (If the file has other stuff in it, make sure you put sequence *below* the last line.)

Follow "sequence" with the list of groups to which you want to subscribe, one group per line. For example:

```
sequence
news.announce.newusers
news.answers
comp.sys.ibm-pc
comp.lang.c++
rec.org.sca
```

You can also specify whole sets of groups. For example,

```
sequence
news.
comp.lang
```

presents *all* the newsgroups that begin with news. and then all the newsgroups that begin with comp.lang.

5. You can also automatically *exclude* groups from subscription. You will usually do this by preceding the group name with ! (exclamation point). For example, `!alt*` will keep all of the "alt" groups out of the presentation sequence.

There are a number of special symbols that you can use to control exclusion or inclusion of groups. Some useful ones are given in Table 4-6. (Note that *groupspec* means part or all of a newsgroup name, such as comp or comp.lang.c++.)

INTERNET HOW-TO

TO DO THIS...	PUT THIS ON A LINE IN THE INIT FILE
Ignore groups that are unsubscribed but see newly created groups	!:U *groupspec*
Ignore unsubscribed groups and not be bothered with new groups	!:X *groupspec*
Ignore all groups except new ones that turn up	!:O *groupspec*
Show all newly created groups here	NEW
Show this group first	< *groupspec*
Show this group last	> *groupspec*

Table 4-6 Controlling newsgroup presentation

How It Works

The newsgroups that you see and the order in which you see them is the result of a process involving several stages:

➢ nn looks at the systemwide init file.
➢ nn then looks to see if you have an init file. If so, the sequence (and inclusions or exclusions) you specify override those in the system init file.
➢ If you don't have an init file, nn just uses your .newsrc.

Note that it is the .newsrc that specifies whether you are subscribed to a group or not. The init file, if it exists, determines whether (and when) you will *see* that group.

Comment

One handy strategy is to list just the groups (or families of groups, such as comp or comp.sys) that you wish to see, in the order in which you want to see them. You then put !! (two exclamation points) on the last line of your init file. The !! instruction tells nn to show only what has been specified in the sequence section of the init file, rather than following your specified sequence and then showing the rest of the newsgroups in your .newsrc.

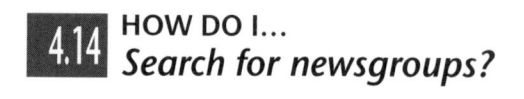

4.14 HOW DO I...
Search for newsgroups?

COMPLEXITY: INTERMEDIATE

Problem

The list of active newsgroups that you can obtain from the news.answers newsgroup is very long. It may be hard to find particular groups (or families of related groups) by looking at the list.

Technique

There are two ways you can zero in on groups that are likely to be of interest. One is to use the G (goto) command with wildcards that let you browse interactively through part of the newsgroup hierarchy. The other way is to use a stand-alone utility called nngrep.

4 READING THE USENET NEWS

Steps

1. After running nn, press ⒢ at the article selection prompt. You will see this prompt:

```
Group or Folder (+./~ %=sneNgG)
```

2. When prompted for a file or folder, type in the first part of a newsgroup name, followed by the * (asterisk). For example, type `comp.sys.*` to begin browsing at the start of the comp.sys newsgroups.

3. nn will ask you whether you want to read each group, starting with the first:

```
Goto comp.sys.3b1 ?
```

Press ⓨ to jump to that group, or press ⓝ to continue browsing.

4. To use the second method, type `nngrep` at the system prompt (or at a shell you've run from nn; see How-To 4.25). Follow nngrep with a word or pattern you want to search for, and nngrep will list the names of all entries in the list of newsgroups to which you can subscribe that match. Here are some examples:

➤ Find all the comp.sys groups relating to the Macintosh:

```
% nngrep comp.sys.mac*
comp.sys.mac.announce
comp.sys.mac.apps
comp.sys.mac.comm
comp.sys.mac.databases
comp.sys.mac.digest
comp.sys.mac.games
comp.sys.mac.hardware
comp.sys.mac.hypercard
comp.sys.mac.misc
comp.sys.mac.programmer
comp.sys.mac.system
comp.sys.mac.wanted
```

➤ Find out whether there is a newsgroup about chess:

```
% nngrep chess
alt.chess.bdg
alt.chess.ics
gnu.chess
rec.games.chess
rec.games.chinese-chess
well% nngrep "chess"
alt.chess.bdg
alt.chess.ics
gnu.chess
rec.games.chess
rec.games.chinese-chess
```

➤ Add the -l option to get more information about the groups:

```
% nngrep chess -l
SUBSCR IN_RC NEW UNREAD SEQUENCE GROUP
```

Continued on next page

INTERNET HOW-TO

Continued from previous page

```
yes    yes    yes           173    alt.chess.bdg
yes    yes    yes    14     174    alt.chess.ics
yes    yes    yes    18    2350    gnu.chess
yes    yes    yes   339    2695    rec.games.chess
yes    yes    yes    20    2696    rec.games.chinese-chess
```

When used with the -l (long) option, nngrep tells you whether you currently subscribe to the group, whether the group is listed in your .newsrc, whether the group is new (you haven't read it before), and the number of unread articles. Note that by default, nngrep finds only groups that are subscribed to in your .newsrc.

➢ Use the -a option to look for all groups, subscribed or unsubscribed.

➢ Use the -n option to look for only new groups. You can combine these options as appropriate.

4.15 HOW DO I... *Save news to a file?*

COMPLEXITY **INTERMEDIATE**

Problem
A news article may contain information that you'll want to refer to again. Since news articles automatically expire after a few days or weeks, you'll need to save them in a permanent location.

Technique
The simplest way to save an article for later reference is to tell nn to save the article to a file.

Steps
1. Run nn and go to the appropriate newsgroup. Select the article or articles that you wish to save, then press (S). This command works in both article selection and reading modes.

2. You will be prompted for the place to save the article. The default is a folder named after the current newsgroup (folders are discussed starting in the next how-to).

```
Save on (+~|) +comp/sys/3b1
```

3. If you don't want to use the prompted name, press (CTRL)-(W) until the suggested name is removed, and then type in the desired filename, for example,

```
Save on (+~|) ~/unixinfo
```

and press (ENTER).

4. If the file doesn't already exist, nn will prompt you whether to create it:

```
Create /home/h/r/hrh/"unixinfo" ?
```

(If the file *does* exist, nn will simply append the articles to it.)

5. Next, nn asks you whether to save the selected articles on this page, or save all selected articles in the newsgroup:

```
Save /home/h/r/hrh/unixinfo Article (* +):
* selected articles on this page, + all selected articles
```

6. Press (*) to save just the selected articles on this page, or (+) to save all selected articles in the newsgroup.

The article will be saved to the indicated file. nn confirms that the file was created:

```
/home/h/r/hrh/unixinfo created: 25 lines written
```

How It Works

nn groups the selected articles (on a page or in a whole newsgroup) and lets you send them to a file. The articles will appear in the file in the order they did in the newsgroup, with adjacent articles separated by a blank line.

You can use the shortcut pathname ~/ to refer to your home directory: thus ~/research/report would save the file as "report" in the research directory of your home directory.

Comment

To save the article with just a brief header (author, subject, posting date), use (o) instead of (s). To save the article's text without any header, use (w).

A very useful technique is to make selections by subject (using the (=) key), and then save all the articles with that subject to a file or folder. Don't forget to deselect the current selections (by pressing the (~) key) before repeating the process with a new subject.

To save all articles in a newsgroup to a file or folder, select with (=), and then save with the + option for "all pages."

4.16 HOW DO I... *Save news to a folder?*

COMPLEXITY INTERMEDIATE

Problem

While saving an occasional article to a file is easy, if you are accumulating large numbers of articles from a particular newsgroup (or on a particular subject within a newsgroup), you'll need a better way to organize the articles for later retrieval.

Technique

nn's solution to the problem of filing articles is the same as Elm's for filing mail: it uses folders. You can save a selected article or group of articles to a folder where they will accumulate and await future retrieval.

Steps

1. Select the article or articles that you wish to save, then press (s). This command works in both article selection and reading modes. For example, assume that you've selected article h in comp.unix.questions and now wish to save it to a folder.

2. You will be prompted for the place to save the article. The default is a folder named after the current newsgroup, using a directory hierarchy that reflects the group's name.

INTERNET HOW-TO

Save on (+~|) +comp/unix/questions

In this case, nn is proposing to save the article to a folder named "questions" in a subdirectory called "unix" in a directory called "comp" in your News directory. While these pathnames can get pretty long, they do have the virtue of organizing your news folders logically. Press (ENTER) to accept the suggested folder name:

Create /home/h/r/hrh/"News/comp/unix/questions" ?

Press (Y) to confirm creation of the new folder.

3. You can also press (CTRL)-(U) to remove the suggested name, and then type in the desired folder name. For example, type

Save on (+~|) ~/+unix

and press (ENTER). (The result here is that a folder called unix will be created in your home directory rather than several layers down below the News directory.) Again, nn will prompt you to confirm creation of the new folder.

4. Next, nn asks you whether to save the selected articles on this page, or save all selected articles in the newsgroup:

Save /home/h/r/hrh/~News/comp/unix/questions Article (* +):
 * selected articles on this page, + all selected articles

5. Press (*) to save just the selected articles on this page, or (+) to save all selected articles in the newsgroup.

The article will be saved to the indicated folder, and nn confirms that the file was created:

/home/h/r/hrh/News/comp/unix/questions created: 18 lines written

How It Works
If you follow nn's defaults, it will create a directory hierarchy based on your News directory. The subdirectory paths will reflect the newsgroup organization scheme: thus you will have main subdirectories for comp, sci, news, and so forth, and then further subdirectories for the subtopics. At the bottom of the hierarchy will be the actual folders, which are files, not directories (as they would be in DOS).

Comment
While the long paths take getting used to, the default folder organization works well with other Unix programs. You will learn more about working with pathnames and directories in Chapter 6.

4.17 HOW DO I...
Read a news folder?

COMPLEXITY EASY

Problem
Once you've saved some news in folders, you need to periodically review and dispose of the saved material.

Technique
The procedure is very simple. You use the goto command (G) with the name of the folder you wish to examine.

Steps
1. Press (G) and then (ENTER). You will see the usual prompt for the jump command:

```
Group or Folder (+./~ %=sneNgG)
```

2. When prompted for the name of a folder or file, press (.). The prompt will change to ask you for a folder name. Type in the name of the folder you want to select. Since nn normally uses your News directory as the current directory, you can start your path from there:

```
Folder + comp.unix.questions
```

3. The contents of the folder will be displayed using the same format as for a newsgroup, and you use the same selection and reading commands as you would with a newsgroup.

4. When you're finished, press (Q) to exit nn, or press (G) and give the name of the next folder or group you wish to see.

How It Works
Since nn formats its folders like a newsgroup, it is very convenient to work with the saved articles. You can read them, save them elsewhere, and even reply to them by mail or follow-up.

Comment
Experiment by using folders for a couple of the newsgroups or subjects that are most important to you or for which you read the most articles.

4.18 HOW DO I...
Read encrypted articles?

COMPLEXITY   EASY

Problem
Authors can use the "rot13" facility to encrypt articles that some people may not want to see; for example, potentially offensive jokes, game hints ("spoilers"), and movie or book endings. Such postings appear as gibberish until decrypted by the reader.

Technique
nn provides a command that decrypts and redisplays encrypted articles so that you can read them.

Steps
1. While reading an article encrypted by the Caesar cipher (rot13), press (D). The article will be reshown in normal (clear) text. For example, a line that reads

```
WtkGpupGftqGotuowq GodaeeGftqGda p?
```

      will come out as:

```
Why did the chicken cross the road?
```

INTERNET HOW-TO

2. To create your own rot13 message, first write the message in plain text in a text file using any editor. Then type the following command at the system prompt,

```
tr '[a-m] [n-z] [A-M] [N-Z]' ' [n-z] [a-m] {N-Z] [A-M]' <file > rotfile
```

where *file* is your original filename, and *rotfile* is the name of the file containing the rot13 version of the text.

3. Now, when you compose your posting, simply use your text editor to insert the rot13 text in the appropriate place.

How It Works

The rot13 or Caesar cipher is a simple scheme where each letter in the original message is replaced by a letter 13 places farther down the alphabet, with Z wrapping around to A. This is not intended to be a secure cipher; it simply to allows readers to skip over something they may not want to read.

nn decrypts the encoded text on-the-fly and displays it as clear text. The actual text in the article is not affected.

Comment

The use of rot13 for potentially offensive jokes seems to be declining. It is more common to exile such jokes to certain newsgroups such as alt.tasteless.jokes. In this case the newsgroup name is deemed to be sufficient warning about the content.

4.19 HOW DO I...
Save an article with a program or graphic image?

COMPLEXITY: INTERMEDIATE

Problem

Binary files such as executable programs or graphic images cannot generally be mailed or posted "as is" on the net. This is because many programs strip the eighth bit from characters; if the "character" is really a byte of binary data, doing so changes the meaning of the data and renders the file unusable.

Technique

You select the article(s) that make up the binary data and tell nn to decode them.

Steps

1. Select the article or articles that contain the program, picture, or other binary data. For example, here's an article menu listing for a 21-part image of the Space Shuttle:

```
g news@ast.saic   913  shuttle.gif (Part 1/21) Space Shuttle
h news@ast.saic   912  shuttle.gif (Part 2/21) Space Shuttle
i news@ast.saic   912  shuttle.gif (Part 3/21) Space Shuttle
j news@ast.saic   912  shuttle.gif (Part 4/21) Space Shuttle
k news@ast.saic   912  shuttle.gif (Part 5/21) Space Shuttle
l news@ast.saic   912  shuttle.gif (Part 6/21) Space Shuttle
m news@ast.saic   912  shuttle.gif (Part 7/21) Space Shuttle
```

```
n news@ast.saic    912  shuttle.gif (Part 8/21)  Space Shuttle
o news@ast.saic    912  shuttle.gif (Part 9/21)  Space Shuttle
p news@ast.saic    912  shuttle.gif (Part 10/21) Space Shuttle
q news@ast.saic    912  shuttle.gif (Part 11/21) Space Shuttle
r news@ast.saic    912  shuttle.gif (Part 12/21) Space Shuttle
s news@ast.saic    912  shuttle.gif (Part 13/21) Space Shuttle
```

(Remember that you can select a group of consecutive articles by using the first and last article letters when all articles are on the same page, or press ⌐=⌐ and select all articles with same words in the subject.)

Make sure you select *all* the parts of the program or image, or the decoding won't work. Also make sure that nothing other than the desired files is selected on the current page or, if the files extend between pages, that nothing else in the newsgroup has been selected.

2. Type `:decode` and press (ENTER). You will be asked for the name of a directory to contain the decoded file (~/temp is a good choice).

```
Decode Directory: ~/temp
```

3. Next you'll be asked whether to decode selected articles on the current page or in the whole newsgroup. Since the shuttle image extends to the next page, you press ⌐·⌐. nn will give a series of messages as the various files are processed:

```
Decode /home/h/r/hrh/temp/ Article (* +):
 * selected articles on this page, + all selected articles

processing 'shuttle.gif (Part 1/21)
Decoding: shuttle.gif (Part 1/21)

<messages for remaining 20 files>
shuttle.gif complete
```

The decoded file is placed in the directory you specify, along with the file Decode.Headers, containing the original message header.

```
Decode.Headers    shuttle.gif
```

4. You can now download the file to your PC using a program such as Xmodem. Be sure to specify that you are transmitting a binary file! See Chapter 9 for more information on downloading files.

How It Works

Binary data files are usually processed with the "uuencode" program before posting. This program replaces the binary data with pairs of ASCII characters that can survive transmission unchanged. When you tell nn to decode the selected files, nn runs the "uudecode" utility to turn the ASCII characters back into binary data, and combines the result into a single file for the graphic image or executable program.

INTERNET HOW-TO

Comment
See Chapter 8 for more information on encoding and decoding binary files. There are tons of neat pictures in popular formats such as GIF available on the net.

4.20 HOW DO I...
Save a shell archive?

COMPLEXITY: INTERMEDIATE

Problem
It can be tedious to mail or send a large number of separate files from one site to another. The "shar" (shell archive) can be used to package a group of files and post it to the news. When you read an article that contains a shell archive, you must break the archive into its parts before you can read (or otherwise use) the article.

Technique
You select the file(s) that make up the shell archive and then tell nn to unpack them to a directory of your choice.

Steps
1. Select the article or articles that contain the shell archive. (The subject should mention that the article is a shell archive.) For example, here is part of a listing showing a three-part article that is a .shar file. This file contains the C language source code files needed to compile a game:

```
q CBIP Moderator 1505   v24inf07: briksrc1.shar, brik source (part 01/01)
r CBIP Moderator 1290   v24inf08: briksrc2.shar, brik source (part 01/01)
s CBIP Moderator 1400   v24inf09: briksrc3.shar, brik source (part 01/01)

— 23:55 — SELECT — help:? ——Bot——<level 4>—
Selected 3 articles
```

2. Type :unshar and press ENTER.

3. You will be prompted for the name of a directory where the archive will be unpacked. A good choice would be ~/temp, which creates a temporary subdirectory in your home directory.

```
Unshar Directory: ~/temp
Create /home/h/r/hrh/"temp/" ? y
```

4. nn uses a copy of the Bourne shell to unpack the archive. You will see various messages relating to the unpacking process:

```
UNPACKING v24inf07: briksrc1.shar, brik source (part 01/01)
x - extracting brik.c (Text)
x - extracting turboc.c (Text)
x - extracting brik.h (Text)
x - extracting turboc.cfg (Text)
UNPACKING v24inf08: briksrc2.shar, brik source (part 01/01)
x - extracting brik.doc (Text)
x - extracting initcrc.c (Text)
x - extracting install (Text)
x - extracting vms.c (Text)
```

4 READING THE USENET NEWS

```
x - extracting getopt.c (Text)
x - extracting makefile.nix (Text)

UNPACKING v24inf09: briksrc3.shar, brik source (part 01/01)
x - extracting brik.1 (Text)
x - extracting addbfcrc.asm (Text)
x - extracting Makefile (Text)
x - extracting options.opt (Text)
x - extracting makefile.tcc (Text)
x - extracting makefile.msc (Text)
x - extracting makebrik.com (Text)
x - extracting descrip.mms (Text)
x - extracting crc.lst (Text)
x - extracting brik.prj (Text)
x - extracting assert.h (Text)
x - extracting addbfcrc.c (Text)

Output is saved in /home/h/r/hrh/temp//Unshar.Result
```

The unpacked material will be placed in a file called Unshar.Result in the specified directory. The article's original headers will be found in Unshar.Headers. The file Unshar.Result will contain a copy of the status messages output by the shar program. Thus a listing of your temp directory following the unpacking looks like this:

```
!ls ../temp
Makefile         assert.h      brik.prj      install         options.opt
Unshar.Headers   brik.1        crc.lst       makebrik.com    turboc.c
Unshar.Result    brik.c        descrip.mms   makefile.msc    turboc.cfg
addbfcrc.asm     brik.doc      getopt.c      makefile.nix    vms.c
addbfcrc.c       brik.h        initcrc.c     makefile.tcc
```

How It Works
nn essentially hands the .shar file over to a shell and tells the shell to execute the instructions in the file. The .shar file contains instructions in shell scripting language that cause the appropriate parts of the file to be saved under specified filenames.

Comment
See Chapter 8 for more information on shell archives.

4.21 HOW DO I...
Filter out unwanted articles?

COMPLEXITY INTERMEDIATE

Problem
Heated arguments called flames often break out in newsgroups. You may wish to automatically exclude such articles from the menu presented to you, or simply exclude subjects that don't interest you.

Technique
nn has a powerful kill/select facility that creates rules for deciding which articles will be excluded or selected from the article menus. While reviewing menus, you can tell nn to exclude certain subjects or articles from certain senders in the future.

INTERNET HOW-TO

Steps
1. When you see an article with a subject or author that you wish to filter out, select the article and then press Ⓚ. (You can also use this command with an article that you're currently reading.) You will see this prompt:

```
AUTO (k)ill or (s)elect (CR => Kill subject 30 days)
```

Since the default is to kill (exclude) the subject for 30 days, simply press ENTER if that's what you want to do.

2. If you want to kill the subject for a different length of time, or you want to kill by author rather than by subject, press Ⓚ. You will see this prompt:

```
AUTO KILL on (s)ubject or (n)ame  (s)
```

Press Ⓢ to kill by subject or Ⓝ to kill by name.

3. You will then be asked for the subject or name to kill:

```
KILL Subject: (=/)
```

or

```
KILL Name: (=/)
```

Type in the name of the person or subject you wish to exclude.

4. Next nn asks you whether the exclusion should take place only in the current newsgroup or in all newsgroups:

```
KILL in (g)roup 'rec.org.sca' or in (a)ll groups  (g)
```

The default is to kill only in the current group. Press ENTER to accept this default, or Ⓐ to kill in all groups.

5. You are prompted for the length of time the exclusion is to be in effect. You can enter the number of days, press ENTER for 30 days, or press Ⓟ to make the exclusion permanent.

```
Lifetime of entry in days (p)ermanent  (30)
```

6. The exclusion you have requested will be summarized, and you'll be asked to confirm it:

```
CONFIRM KILL Subject 30 days: rubber ducks
```

Press Ⓨ to confirm your kill setting. The appropriate entry will be added to the kill file in your .nn directory.

How It Works
nn checks the kill file each time you enter a newsgroup and applies the rules found there. For example, if you have told nn to exclude articles about Star Trek Books-On-Tape (maybe you're not a Trekkie), the following statement will be placed in your kill file:

```
758622876:news.answers:!s=:Star Trek Books-On-Tape
```

4 ♦ READING THE USENET NEWS

Comment
If you change your mind about an exclusion you can simply use an editor to remove the appropriate line from your kill file.

The matching of subjects or names is not case-sensitive.

4.22 HOW DO I...
Select articles automatically?

COMPLEXITY | INTERMEDIATE

Problem
Sometimes you want to make sure that you don't miss any news on a certain subject. Since many newsgroups have hundreds of articles, it can be tedious to go through them "by hand," or even to remember to do a subject search.

Technique
Just as nn can exclude articles from menus automatically, it can also select articles automatically when you enter a newsgroup. You go through a dialog similar to that used for the exclusion (kill) procedure in the preceding how-to.

Steps
1. Make current the article whose subject or author you want to select automatically and press [K]. (You can also use an article that you are currently reading.) You will see this prompt:

```
AUTO (k)ill or (s)elect (CR => Kill subject 30 days)
```

2. Press [S] to tell nn that you want to select rather than kill. nn then asks you what to select on:

```
AUTO SELECT on (s)ubject or (n)ame  (s)
```

3. Press [S] or [N] as appropriate. For example, let's assume you want to select for the subject "Xmodem":

```
SELECT Subject: (=/) Xmodem
```

4. Next nn asks you whether to make the selection only in the current newsgroup or in all groups:

```
SELECT in (g)roup 'comp.unix.questions' or in (a)ll groups  (g)
```

5. You are then asked how long the selection is to last. Press [ENTER] for 30 days or type the number of days:

```
Lifetime of entry in days (p)ermanent  (30)
```

6. nn asks you to confirm your selection entry:

```
CONFIRM SELECT Subject 30 days: Xmodem     y
```

How It Works
nn creates an entry in the select file in your .nn directory based upon your responses in the selection dialog. The preceding example would result in the following select file entry:

143

INTERNET HOW-TO

```
758623188:comp.unix.questions:+s:Xmodem
```

nn reads the select file (along with the kill file) before entering each newsgroup.

Comment
You can use your editor to delete unwanted selections from the select file. The matching of names or subjects is not case-sensitive.

4.23 HOW DO I...
Catch up with unread news?

COMPLEXITY: EASY

Problem
If you go on vacation for a couple of weeks a lot of unread news will accumulate. You may not want to take the time to look at everything.

Technique
You can "catch up" by telling nn to automatically mark as "read" all unread news. Then you can simply read new news as it comes in.

Steps
1. Start nn by typing

```
% nn -a0
```

at the command prompt. (That's a letter *a* with a zero after it.)

2. nn will ask you whether you want to catch up interactively or automatically:

```
Release 6.5.0 #2 (NOV), Kim F. Storm, 1991

Catch-up on 572396 unread articles ? (auto)matically (i)nteractive
```

3. Type `auto` and press `ENTER` to have nn catch up in all newsgroups automatically. nn will respond:

```
UPDATING .newsrc FILE....DONE
```

4. To catch up interactively, press `i`. nn prompts you to take an action for each subscribed group that has unread news:

```
y - mark all articles as read in current group
n - do not update group
r - read the group now
U - unsubscribe to current group
? - this message
q - quit

Update alt.1d (718)? (ynrU?q) n
```

➢ Press `Y` to mark all articles in the group as read. This means that you won't see them again.

➢ Press `R` to enter normal reading mode for the group (where you can make selections and read articles as usual).

➤ Press (N) to leave the group so that you'll see the articles next time.
➤ Press (U) to unsubscribe to the group.
➤ You can also press (Q) to leave the updating process at any time. nn will then ask if you want to update the rest of the newsgroups automatically.

How It Works
nn marks the .newsrc file according to your instructions. Since .newsrc keeps track of the articles that have been read, marking it to show that the full range of article numbers has been read means that nn won't present any news to you from that group until new news comes in.

Comment
If you don't particularly care about missing anything, use the automatic update on all groups. If there are some groups where you *do* want to read your article backlog, select interactive update and enter reading mode (press (R)) for those groups.

4.24 HOW DO I...
Specify nn's features and behavior?

COMPLEXITY: INTERMEDIATE

Problem
People differ in their preferences for handling news. Since "one size doesn't fit all," nn comes with a cornucopia of options that can be set to control the program's behavior.

Technique
There are several ways you can specify options for nn:
➤ You can specify switches in the command line when you run nn.
➤ You can use the :set and :unset commands while nn is running.
➤ You can set or unset options in the init file.

Options are also sometimes called *variables* since they can hold different values.

Steps
1. To use command switches, simply type them on the command line following nn, and then press (ENTER). The nn -a0 command line in the preceding how-to is an example of a command line option. Table 4-7 lists a few of the more popular command line options. See the nn user's manual for more details.

2. To set command options while running nn, type `:set` or `:unset` at the article selection menu, followed by the option name. If the variable is a Boolean (yes/no) variable, you need only press (ENTER). The consolidated-menu variable discussed in How-To 4.6 is an example:

```
:set consolidated-menu
```

This consolidates the menus, while

```
:unset consolidated-menu
```

makes the menus open again.

INTERNET HOW-TO

OPTION	EFFECT
-a0	Catch up with unread news
-g	Have nn prompt for newsgroup or folder when started
-r	Repeat the prompting after each group or folder
-s*word*	Have nn collect only articles with *word* in the subject
-s*regep*	Have nn collect only articles with *regular expression* in the subject
-n*word* -n*regexp*	Like -s, but searches for sender's name rather than subject
-m	Merge all articles into one "metagroup"—usually used with -s or -x
-x*number*	Include last *number* of unread articles
-X	Include unsubscribed groups

Table 4-7 Some useful nn command line options

You can also use the :toggle command to switch a variable to its opposite setting.

Thus,

```
:set consolidated-menu
```

followed by

```
:toggle consolidated-menu
```

also reopens the menus.

3. Some options require a numeric value (such as a number of lines) or a string value (such as a directory path). With these variables you must include the specified information. For example,

```
:set stop 15
```

specifies that only the first 15 lines of an article will be shown before you are prompted to continue. The specification,

```
:set news-record ~/corres
```

tells nn to save copies of your follow-ups and postings in the "corres" subdirectory of your home directory.

4. You set variables in the init file by inserting lines with your text editor. The lines begin with set, unset, or toggle. The only difference from setting variables interactively is that no colon precedes the command (set, not :set). For example:

```
set consolidated-menu
set news-record ~/my.articles
```

How It Works

Each option variable has a default value or condition. When you set or change a variable's value interactively or in the init file, nn changes its behavior accordingly. Settings in the init file take effect for every session, while interactive settings are lost (reset to default) when the session ends.

4 READING THE USENET NEWS

TO SPECIFY...	OPTIONS	VALUE
Where articles you post will be distributed (by default)	default-distribution	Geographical prefix (for example, ba.)
Terse menus for advanced users	expert	set*
Directory in which to create news folders	folder	Directory pathname
Layout of article menu	layout	0, 1, 2, or 3 (1 is default)
File to be used for copies of outgoing replies or mail	mail-record	Pathname and filename
File to be used for copies of outgoing follow-up articles and postings	news-record	Pathname and filename
Save articles automatically into a file without prompting for filename	quick-save	Pathname and filename

*A Boolean option that you set to turn on or unset to turn off.

Note: See Chapter 6 for more about pathnames, directory names, and filenames.

Table 4-8 Some possible customizations for nn

Table 4-8 gives some common ways in which you might want to change nn's default behavior. The table gives the option to change in each case, and possible values.

Comment
See the nn user's manual for a lengthy listing of option variables and their effects. It is best to become familiar with the basic operation of the program before experimenting with variable settings.

4.25 HOW DO I...
Execute system commands from nn?

COMPLEXITY EASY

Problem
Sometimes you need to execute a system command without ending your nn session. For example, you may want to get a listing of files in your home directory.

Technique
You "escape" to a shell, execute one or more system commands, and then return to nn.

Steps
1. Press (!) at the article selection or reading prompt. You will be prompted for a system command.

2. Type the system command you wish to run and press (ENTER). Here we enter ls to get a listing of our current directory:

```
! ls
Mail          doppel        private
News          faq.ans       spr08.mov
archie.mail   joke          strategy
```

Continued on next page

INTERNET HOW-TO

Continued from previous page

```
check                joke13                strategy2
connect              lynx_bookmarks.html   wais.mail
ctrld                nn.faq                xmodem.log
```

3. After your command is executed, you will see the ! prompt again. Continue to enter commands (as you would at the normal system prompt), or press (ENTER) to return to where you left off in nn. Note that some commands (such as cd) won't work in this temporary shell.

How It Works
nn runs a copy of the Bourne shell (a Unix command processor), which interprets your command(s).

Comment
The nn reference manual lists several special variables that you can refer to while entering shell commands. For example, if you entered the shell from reading mode, you can use $A to refer to the full pathname of the file that contains the current news article. This means that if you want, for example, to download the article you were reading to your PC via Xmodem (see Chapter 9), you can type `xm st $A` at the shell prompt and then tell your software to receive the Xmodem download.

4.26 HOW DO I...
Collect news by subject?

COMPLEXITY | **INTERMEDIATE**

Problem
It's not always easy to know which newsgroups might contain news on a given subject. Nor is it easy to search through all those newsgroups and gather the news.

Technique
You can use the nngrab utility to find all articles with a particular word or phrase in their subject. The articles found will be presented to you in one big newsgroup.

Steps
1. Type `nngrab` at the system prompt. Follow it with the word or phrase you are searching for. (If it is more than one word, enclose it in quotes, for example, `Russia` or `"Internet access."`)

2. nngrab will show you a running display of the groups it's checking. For example:

```
nngrab Russia
810s rec.arts.sf
```

   The number is the number of the newsgroup in the list of active newsgroups.

3. When nn is done it will present the merged newsgroup. In this example the group contains all articles that have Russia in their subject:

```
MERGED NEWS GROUPS:   671 ARTICLES

a Peter Kovacs      10  Help w/ russian research.
```

148

```
b A Gruntsev        293  CFP First Conference on D<>tion in RUSSIA (July 5-8,1994)
c Mikhail Zeleny     32  >>>Mr. Bil and other Russian homophobes
d Mikhail Zeleny     32  >>>
e Mikhail Zeleny     32  >>>
f Keith Instone     218  CFP (2nd): East-West Huma<>mputer Interaction 94 (Russia)
g Mike Kelly         23  my last and the russian echo
h Marcus Endicott    69  Expedition Tour Agency for Russia
i pav0sh             51  "INFO",Moscow-marketing r<>ies of the CIS market of goods
j B Patrick         175  CFP: East-West Human-Computer Interaction 94 (Russia)
k S Baldassarra       9  >UN: Russian Aircraft Copy
l S Baldassarra      16  >
m T Hietaniemi       29  >>Russian rapid deployment force
n Pyotr Shmelev      28  -
o Pyotr Shmelev      28  -
p Egils Kaljo        29  >
q Terry Chan         11  >>Russian and German Body Parts
r Andrew Bulhak      17  >>>
s Kim Greer           9  >>

— 11:39 — SELECT — help:? ——Top 2%——
Read 430781 articles in 788 seconds (0 kbyte/s)
```

4. You can read or otherwise dispose of the news in the merged group using the usual commands.

How It Works
nngrab scans all the newsgroups and checks the subject of each article against the keyword or phrase you supplied. Matching articles are gathered and presented like a news folder.

Comment
Since there are so many groups and articles nowadays, it can take nngrab 15 minutes or longer to run.

4.27 HOW DO I...
Change nn's key commands?

COMPLEXITY ADVANCED

Problem
You find some of nn's key commands aren't hard to remember. You've seen which key to press for each command, but you can tell nn to use a different key for a given command. For example, you might decide to use (CTRL)-(N) key rather than (N) to move to the next newsgroup.

Technique
You put *key map entries* in your init file. These entries tell nn what key to associate with a given command.

Steps
1. Use a text editor to edit your init file.

2. On a new line type the word `map`.

INTERNET HOW-TO

3. If the key is to be redefined for article selection mode, add the word `menu`.
4. If the key is to be redefined for reading mode, add the word `show`. (You cannot redefine for both selection and reading mode in the same command.)
5. Type the letter of the key to be redefined. Use ^ before the letter to indicate a control key.
6. Type the name of the command the key is to execute.

Here are two examples:

```
map menu ^N advance-group
map menu ^B back-group
```

The (CTRL)-(N) and (CTRL)-(B) keys will now move you ahead one newsgroup or back one newsgroup, respectively, when typed in menu (article selection) mode.

How It Works
nn keeps a set of internal tables that associate keys and commands. The map commands in the init file redefine these tables.

Comment
See the nn user's manual for more details, including ways to specify certain special keys and the names of the commands.

4.28 HOW DO I...
Use macros to create shortcut commands?

COMPLEXITY: ADVANCED

Problem
Some expert users might want even more control over nn than is provided by option variables.

Technique
nn includes what amounts to a macro programming language. Among other things, you can define a combination of keystrokes and/or commands, and you can bind your definition to a key so it will be executed when that key is pressed.

The general procedure is to place a statement in your init file that has the following form,

> define *macro-number*
> *body*
> end

where *macro-number* is from 0 to 100. *Body* is a sequence that can contain:

➤ Comments (beginning with #), for example, `# new macro to test`
➤ Command names (see the key mapping section of the nn user's manual for valid command names)
➤ Extended commands (the ones you execute beginning with a colon), such as `:show`

➤ Keystrokes (letters or special symbols representing keys). For example, regular keys are placed in single quotes, as in 'a'; special keys have their own names (such as left); and control keys are preceded by the ^ symbol, as in ^B.
➤ Shell commands (commands to be passed to the operating system for execution). Precede the command with ! if it requires input or output, or !! if it doesn't use the terminal in any way; for example, ! save > tempfile.
➤ Conditional (tells nn when or under what circumstances to execute the macro). For example: ?menu in menu mode or ?show in reading mode.
➤ A variety of other commands that can ask for user input, display a prompt, execute another macro, and so on.

Here's a simple example of a macro. It selects all articles in the current newsgroup that have the word "unix" in their subject, regardless of case:

```
define 1
# this macro is invoked as number 1
?menu find "{Uu}{Nn}{Ii}{Xx}" # in menu mode
                    # select articles with unix in subject
end
```

Steps

1. If possible, first try out your series of commands interactively to make sure that they work as expected.

2. Open your init file with a text editor.

3. Write your macro. (Don't put macros or anything else at the *end* of your init file if there is a presentation sequence there.)

4. Use the map command (discussed in the previous how-to) to bind your macro to a key so that you can execute it with a keystroke. A binding command for our example macro might be:

```
map menu ^U macro 1
```

Now pressing (CTRL)-(U) will execute macro number 1.

5. Save your init file and exit the editor. The macro will become available the next time you run nn.

How It Works

nn reads the init file on startup and sets up the macros found there. Macros take effect in menu (selection), reading, or other mode as specified in their definitions. (You can also set up commands in your init file that take effect under specified conditions, such as upon entry to a newsgroup or when the connection is slow or fast.)

Comment

See the nn user's manual for more information on macros and key bindings.

INTERNET HOW-TO

4.29 HOW DO I...
Learn more about nn?

COMPLEXITY: INTERMEDIATE

Problem
This chapter covers the most important and useful features of nn, but a whole book could be written about this one program.

Technique
There are several things you can do to learn more about nn.

Steps
1. Get a copy of the nn user's manual. To find it, use the command

```
%whereis nn
```

   at the system prompt, and search the paths shown for the documentation files. (The path may be something like /usr/local/lib/nn.) Ask your system support person for help if you can't find the manual. You can also get the regular Unix manual for nn by typing `man nn> filename` where "filename" is the name of the file in which you want to save your copy of the manual.

2. Run the :man command, select all the articles (with s = .), then save them all to a file with the S command. The resulting file will be a somewhat more terse version of the nn manual.

3. Read the newsgroups devoted to the news system. Two important ones are news.announce.newusers and news.lists.

4. Read the news.software.nn newsgroup. If you have questions about nn you can ask for help from the "wizards" there.

How It Works
There's actually quite a lot of documentation and help for nn, but it's scattered in different places and presented in different ways. Someday someone will write "The Complete nn Encyclopedia."

Comment
If at first you don't succeed...try an alternate route!

Help Screens for nn

Finally, here are the main help screens for nn. The first screen is presented when you press ⑦ while looking at a newsgroup's menu of articles; the second screen pops up when you press ⑦ while reading an article. Note that some commands are available in both modes.

Help screen for selecting articles

```
SELECT (toggle)                              MOVE
a-z0-9    Specified article              ,      Next menu line
x-y       Range x to y                   /      Previous menu line
x*        Same subject as x              SPACE  Next menu page (if any)
.         Current article                < >    Prev/Next menu page
@ ~       Reverse/Undo all selections    ^ $    First/Last menu page
=regexp   Matching subjects (=. selects all)
L/JJJJ    Leave/Change attributes        ( )    Open/Close Consolidated line
SHOW SELECTED ARTICLES
SPACE     Show (only when on last menu page)
Z         Show NOW, and return to this group afterwards
X         Show NOW, and continue with next group
GOTO OTHER GROUPS
X         Update current group, skip to next.    Y         Group overview
N P       Goto next/previous group.              ~/.nn/init:
G         Goto named group or open a folder.               Defines group
B A       Go back/forward in groups already read.          presentation sequence.
MISCELLANEOUS
U         Unsubscribe / Subscribe toggle         :man      Online manual
F R M     Follow-up/Reply/Mail                   :help     More online help
S O W     Save articles                          !         Shell escape
:post C   Post new article / Cancel current      "         Change menu layout
:unshar :decode :patch  Unpack articles          Q         Quit nn
```

Help screen for reading articles

```
SCROLLING              ABSOLUTE LINE         SEARCHING
SP     1 page forw     ^      top            /RE     find regular expr.
d      1/2 page forw   gNUM   line NUM       . //    repeat last search
CR     1 line forw     $      last line
DEL    1 page back     h      header         TEXT CONVERSIONS
u      1/2 page back   H      full digest    D       decrypt article (rot13)
TAB    skip section                          c       compress spaces
GOTO ANOTHER ARTICLE
SP     next (at end of current article)      CANCEL, SUBSCRIBE, KILL
n, p   next/previous article                 C       cancel article
l      mark article for later action         U       (un)subscribe to group
k      kill subject (not permanently)        K       kill/select handling
*      select subject
                                             QUIT / ESCAPE
SAVE                                         =       back to menu
s, o, w   save with full/short/no header     N       goto next group
:unshar :decode :patch   unpack article      X       as N, mark as read
                                             !, ^Z   Shell escape, suspend
REPLY, POST                                  Q       quit nn
r      mail reply to author of article
m      mail (or forward article)             REDRAW
f      post follow-up to article             ^P      Repeat last message
:post  post new article                      ^L, ^R  Redraw screen
```

Talking to Other Users

How do I....

5.1   Send someone a message
5.2   Reply to a message
5.3   Recall old messages
5.4   Carry on an interactive conversation
5.5   Set up a multiparty conversation
5.6   Screen out unwanted messages
5.7   Connect to Internet Relay Chat (IRC)
5.8   Enter IRC commands
5.9   Get help while using IRC
5.10   Give myself an online nickname
5.11   Find a conversation
5.12   Carry on a conversation
5.13   Send private messages
5.14   Get information about people
5.15   Keep track of comings and goings
5.16   Invite someone to join a conversation
5.17   Start my own channel
5.18   Deal with harassment
5.19   Change IRC settings
5.20   Learn more about IRC

Internet mail and news messages are examples of delayed communications—you post something, and sometime later you get a response. But the Internet also has the equivalent of a telephone, where you can communicate in real time with another user. That other person can be connected to the same site as you, or he or she can be typing words from the other side of the world. You each type your thoughts and read what the other person has to say right away. There are even facilities for "party line" conversations, where several people talk to each other electronically.

The Internet even has its version of CB radio, where users can (and do) log in by the thousands and discuss hundreds of topics on separate "channels." Like CB, the reasonableness of the participants varies widely, and there's a pretty high "noise to signal ratio." Nonetheless, this form of communication can be exciting and rewarding.

In this chapter you will learn how to use the major Internet facilities for interactive communication: one on one, a few at a time, or many to many. Chances are you will find that one or more of the programs discussed meet your daily communications needs.

Sending Messages

The simplest communication facility is send/reply. One person sends another person a message. Assuming the other person is logged on, the message shows up on his or her screen, and a reply can be sent. It's like mail in that each person takes turns sending messages and making replies, but it's like the phone in that the communication is in more or less real time. Send/reply is most often used for simple requests, such as asking for technical help from a more experienced user.

Simple Talk Programs

The next step up in interactivity is the simple "talk" program. Instead of sending messages back and forth one at a time, two (or several) users are continuously connected and can type whatever words they want the other user(s) to see. Talk programs are ideal for lengthier conversations or small online meetings.

Internet Relay Chat

Internet Relay Chat (IRC) is the CB radio of the net. As Figure 5-1 shows, each user runs a client program at his or her Internet site. The client program in turn connects the users at the site to an IRC server. The servers coordinate all the messages coming from the users.

As a user, you have hundreds of channels to choose from. Each channel is created by a user and can be run by one or more users. It's a kind of floating crap game of conversation, where users come and go. Some channels have definite topics, while others are just places to hang out.

As you might expect, sex talk of one sort or another seems to be the most popular activity on IRC. But there are many other topics discussed on IRC channels, from technical subjects to news and gossip of the day. (When a major world crisis breaks out, you can be sure IRC channels will be humming!)

IRC is a complicated program with many features that are beyond the scope of this book, such as the ability to create *bots*, a kind of automated alterego that can interact with other users (or other bots). But this chapter will get you started so you can find and participate in the conversations of your choice.

5 TALKING TO OTHER USERS

Related Topics

To Learn How to...	See Chapter
Find information about other users	3
Join a mailing list	3
Read and post news articles	4
Read and send electronic mail	3

How-Tos in this Chapter

5.1 Send someone a message
Are you stuck trying to get some program to work? Well, if you notice that a more experienced user is online, you can send that person a message asking for help. The message will show up right on his or her screen.

5.2 Reply to a message
Replying to a message is even simpler than sending one. You can usually read and reply to a message without leaving whatever program you're running.

5.3 Recall old messages
Of course if you exchange a lot of messages with several different people, it's easy to forget what someone said or who sent you the last message. You'll learn how to use a simple utility called "huh" to keep track of your messages.

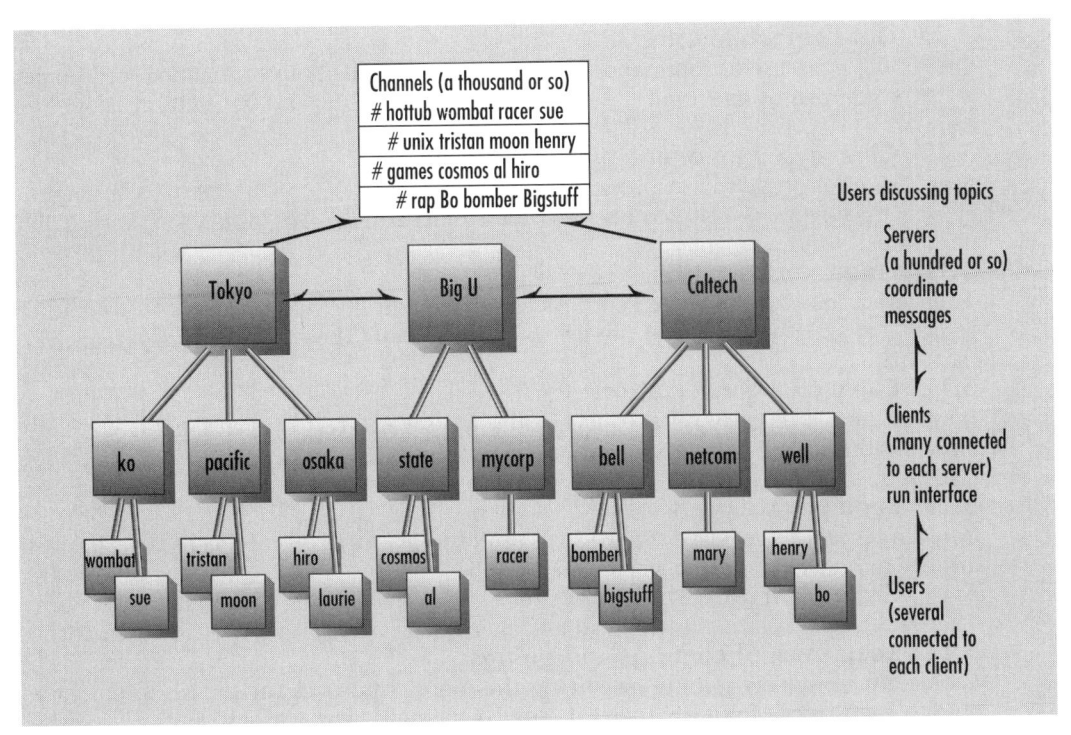

Figure 5-1 How IRC works

INTERNET HOW-TO

5.4 Carry on an interactive conversation
Talk programs let you connect to someone for direct conversation. Each of your screens gets divided into two parts, and each person can type messages while reading messages from the other person. It's easy to get used to "talking" in this way.

5.5 Set up a multiparty conversation
There's also a version of the talk program (called ytalk), that lets more than two people connect at the same time. This is ideal for meetings between members of work groups that might be physically scattered around the country (or the world). You'll see how to set up and manage such a party line conversation.

5.6 Screen out unwanted messages
For every advance in technology, there is the potential for new kinds of distraction or annoyance. Sometimes you may want to "take your phone off the hook" and not be interrupted by messages. There is a way to turn messages off as well as selectively block messages from annoying individuals.

5.7 Connect to Internet Relay Chat (IRC)
Now it's time to get a little wild. Internet Relay Chat is a vast, sprawling, entertaining, infuriating, and occasionally informative facility for real-time conversation with whomever decides to drop in. The first step is to run the IRC client at your Internet site and connect to the service.

5.8 Enter IRC commands
There are many IRC commands, but most are needed only by experts. You'll need to learn just a dozen or so to get around.

5.9 Get help while using IRC
One of the more useful commands is, not surprisingly, the help command. You can get a list of commands and topics for which help is available, and get help on a specific item.

5.10 Give myself an online nickname
Most IRC users prefer to use a nickname (like the "handles" on CB radio), for anonymity or self-expression. You can also register a nickname so that other people (usually) won't use it for their own.

5.11 Find a conversation
There are a thousand or more channels established on IRC, with perhaps a hundred or so active at any one time. You can list the channels and then join the one you want to participate in.

5.12 Carry on a conversation
It's very simple to carry on a conversation. Messages typed by participants gradually crawl up the screen. When you want to say something, you just type it and everyone else on the channel sees it.

5.13 Send private messages
You can also post a message that will be seen just by a particular recipient. This lets you arrange to find a quiet place where you can talk.

5.14 Get information about people
There are several commands that will tell you a bit about your fellow IRC participants.

5.15 Keep track of comings and goings
People are constantly joining or leaving the more popular channels. It's useful to be able to keep track of who is there at a given moment. You can also notify the other folks that you'll be back as soon as you've attended to a call of nature...

5 TALKING TO OTHER USERS

5.16 Invite someone to join a conversation
If you're participating in an interesting conversation and you "see" someone you know logged in, you can send that person a message inviting him or her to join your current channel.

5.17 Start my own channel
It's very easy to start your own channel. You can make it a private channel for people at your business or school, or start a new public channel on a topic that you're dying to talk about.

5.18 Deal with harassment
Unfortunately there *are* some bozos on this bus—people who want to hassle, harass, or make unwanted advances. You'll learn a few basic tools for dealing with such occurrences.

5.19 Change IRC settings
Like most complicated programs, IRC has a number of settings that you can change. In case you wish to do so, this how-to shows you how.

5.20 Learn more about IRC
Finally, you'll look at some documents and sources for more information on IRC.

5.1 HOW DO I...
Send someone a message?

COMPLEXITY: EASY

Problem
You'd like to send a message to someone else who is online. Perhaps you need a quick bit of help about how to use that text editor you've been trying out.

Technique
You use the send command to send a message to the other person. This is pretty much a standard command on Unix systems nowadays.

Steps
1. Make sure the person to whom you wish to send a message is currently online. You can do this by prior agreement, or by using the finger command with the person's address, as in:

```
% finger helen@bigu.edu
```

   If the person is online, the third line of the output of the finger command will say something like this:

```
On since Thu Apr  7 16:40 (PDT) on pts/15
```

   If instead it says something like this,

```
Last login Tue Apr  5 23:19 (PDT) on pts/15
```

   it means the person isn't currently logged in, and you can't send a message to that person—you can send mail, of course.

2. At the system prompt, type `send` followed by the name of the recipient. (If the recipient isn't on the same machine, be sure to include the full Internet address.) If Helen is connected to the same machine as you are, type

INTERNET HOW-TO

```
% send helen
```

If Helen is at Big U and you're connected somewhere else, type

```
% send helen@Bigu.edu
```

3. Type the message you want to send. Note that send doesn't use a text editor, so you can't go back and correct things. You also need to press (ENTER) at the end of each line. Remember, send is mainly used to send short messages—from a couple of sentences to a few paragraphs—so the lack of editing capability is tolerable.

```
Hi Helen
I heard from a colleague that they're having a conference on business use of the Internet at Big
U next month. Can you give me any info about it?
```

4. To send your message, press (CTRL)-(D) or type a single period on a line by itself. The recipient will get your message and can reply to it (see the next how-to for details).

How It Works

Send uses an automatic program (daemon) to display your text on the other user's terminal.

If the person you've sent the message to is not online (or logged off before your message could be sent), you will get the following system message,

```
<user> is not online. Mailing message instead ...
```

where "user" is the person's user ID. Your message will be sent as mail with the subject header:

```
Subject: this was a failing send
```

Similarly, if the recipient is blocking messages (see How-To 5.6), you will get this message:

```
<user> has turned incoming messages off.
can't open terminal (/dev/pts/55); sending mail instead.
```

In either case, if you *don't* want the message to be sent as mail, press (CTRL)-(C) and the send will be aborted.

Comment

There is a bug in many versions of send that can cause a message to be misrouted if the recipient is logging off at the time the message is sent. Sometimes the message will go to whomever has just logged into the vacated terminal connection; at other times the message will simply disappear (this is known as "dropped into the bit bucket"). Therefore you should not use send for confidential information or if you need to be absolutely sure your message will be received. Use e-mail instead.

Some systems may have a program called "write" instead of send. It works similarly.

5.2 HOW DO I...
Reply to a message?

COMPLEXITY: INTERMEDIATE

Problem
A message from someone has just appeared on your screen. How do you keep track of what you *were* doing and still reply to the message?

Technique
You can read the message, redisplay your program's screen to get rid of the message, and then reply to the message.

Steps
1. When someone sends you a message you'll see something like this appear on your screen:

```
[barbara@well (ttyb4 12:11):
Hi, Joe!
Can you help me with a communications problem?
```

   The message begins with the address of the user who sent it (barbara@well in this case). The message will simply appear in the middle of whatever text you are working with (such as a mail or news message listing or text you're editing in a text editor). While this can be disconcerting, the incoming text doesn't alter the text on your screen in any way.

2. Read the message. If you want to finish what you're doing before replying, press [CTRL]-[l]. For most programs, this will refresh the screen and redisplay the original text without the message in the middle of it.

3. If you want to reply, type `reply` at the system prompt.

   If you are running a program such as mail, news, or an editor, you'll either have to finish what you're doing and exit the program to get to the system prompt, or "shell out" to the system prompt without exiting the program. You can shell out in vi by entering :!. In Elm and nn you can use !. (In fact, ! works for many, though not all, programs. Consult your program documentation under "shell escape.")

4. A line like this will now appear:

```
To: barbara@well
```

5. Type your reply:

```
Sure, I've got a few minutes. What's the problem?
```

6. When you're done, press [CTRL]-[D] or type a period on a line by itself and press [ENTER]. Your reply will be sent.

How It Works
Reply is simply the counterpart of send. It sends your text to the person who last sent you a message, or an earlier correspondent if you so specify.

INTERNET HOW-TO

Comment
It's a good idea to make sure the original message was for you before you reply. Sometimes, if someone has just logged off, you "inherit" their terminal connection when you log on, and you can receive a send that was intended for that person (this is a pretty rare occurrence). In that case it's polite to reply and explain what happened.

5.3 HOW DO I...
Recall old messages?

COMPLEXITY EASY

Problem
By default the reply command sends the reply to the last person who sent you a message. But suppose you don't remember what was in the last message, or you want to reply to a different person who sent you a message earlier?

Technique
You use the "huh" command to redisplay the last message you received. You can then read and reply to it.

Steps
1. Type huh at the system prompt to see the last message you've received:

```
% huh
        [joe@well (Xty/a 18:22):
Can you help me with this #$%^^ text editor?
```

2. To see earlier messages, put the number of messages you want to see after your huh command:

```
huh 3
        [joe@well (Xty/a 18:22):
Can you help me with this #$%^^ text editor?

        [mary@BigU.Edu  pts44 15:18:
Are you going to the game Saturday?

        [thursday@well (Xty/f 10:21):
The system sure seems slow now. I've tried to read some news and I
couldn't even tell whether the program was broken or the system was just too slow...
```

3. By default, messages are listed starting with the most recently received. To see messages in reverse order (with the oldest first), add -r to your huh command:

```
% huh 3 -r
        [thursday@well (Xty/f 10:21):
The system sure seems slow now. I've tried to read some news and I
couldn't even tell whether the program was broken or the system was just too slow...

        [mary@BigU.Edu  pts44 15:18:
Are you going to the game Saturday?

        [joe@well (Xty/a 18:22):
Can you help me with this #$%^^ text editor?
```

5 TALKING TO OTHER USERS

4. To see messages from a particular sender, add that person's user ID or address. For example,

`%huh joe`

lists all messages from Joe.

5. To see messages that contain a particular word anywhere in the text, add the word. For example,

`%huh terminal`

lists all messages that contain the word "terminal."

How It Works
The send/reply facilities maintain a buffer of recent messages. huh taps into that buffer to display your recent messages.

Comment
You can also keep a permanent record of messages you've received. Just type `huh` followed by `>` and the name of the file where you want to save the messages. For example,

`% huh 10 > messages`

puts the contents of the last ten messages in the messages file, using the Unix output redirection character (>).

5.4 HOW DO I...
Carry on an interactive conversation?

COMPLEXITY EASY

Problem
You'd like to carry on a longer conversation with someone. Sending separate sends and replies is awkward.

Technique
You can use the talk program to set up a connection so that you and another user can type messages to each other interactively.

Steps
1. Make sure the person you want to talk to is currently online. You can do this by prearrangement, or type `finger`:

```
% finger hrh
Login: hrh                          Name: Harry Henderson
Directory: /home/h/r/hrh            Shell: /usr/bin/csh
On since Tue Feb 22 13:53 (PDT) on pts/124, idle 0:03,
    from dialup-2.well.sf.ca.us
```

This is just the first part of the finger output. Notice the "On since..." line that indicates that the user is currently online. If this line says something like "Last login..." it means the person isn't online. Don't forget to use the complete address if you're "fingering" a user on a different system.

INTERNET HOW-TO

2. Type `talk` followed by the user ID of the person to whom you wish to talk. Don't forget to specify the complete Internet address if the person is not on the same machine as you are.

3. The person to whom you're trying to talk will get a message like this:

```
Message from Talk_Daemon@BigU.edu at 15:35...
talk: connection requested by joe@BigU.edu
talk: respond with: talk joe@BigU.edu
```

4. As the message says, that person should type `talk` followed by your user ID:

```
talk joe@BigU.edu
```

Assuming you're both still online, you'll both see the message:

```
[connection established]
```

The screen will split into two parts, as shown in Figure 5-2.

5. Simply type whatever you want to say, and your partner can do the same. Each person's typing will appear on their side of the screen. Depending on your preferences, you can either take turns typing (ending your typing with -o- meaning "over" or `ga` meaning "go ahead"), or just type when you want and read what your partner has to say.

6. When you want to end the conversation, say good-bye (or -oo- for "over and out") and then press (CTRL)-(C), which is the equivalent of hanging up the phone. You'll be returned to the system prompt.

How It Works
The talk program takes over the screens of the two participants and connects their terminal input (typing) to each other's terminals so that each sees what the other types.

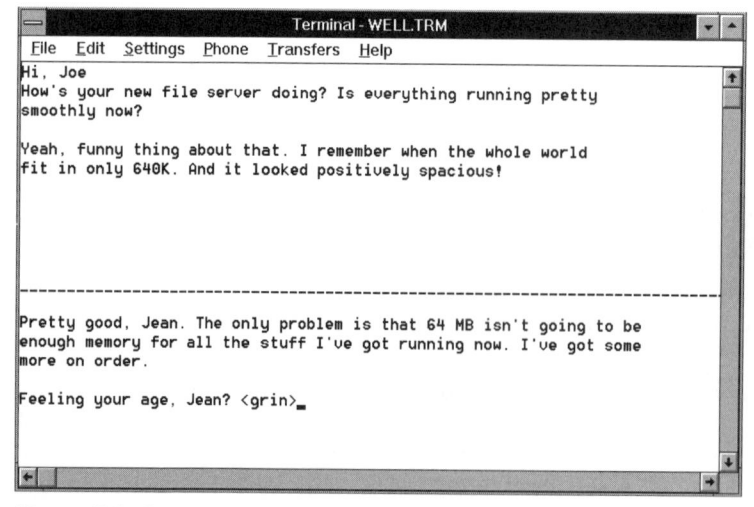

```
Terminal - WELL.TRM
File  Edit  Settings  Phone  Transfers  Help
Hi, Joe
How's your new file server doing? Is everything running pretty
smoothly now?

Yeah, funny thing about that. I remember when the whole world
fit in only 640K. And it looked positively spacious!

-------------------------------------------------------------
Pretty good, Jean. The only problem is that 64 MB isn't going to be
enough memory for all the stuff I've got running now. I've got some
more on order.

Feeling your age, Jean? <grin>_
```

Figure 5-2 Conversation with the talk program

164

The split screen makes it easy for both people to see what they're typing as well as what's being said to them.

Comment

Since talk uses a full-screen display, you and your conversation partner must have terminal emulation set up (see Chapter 3).

Occasionally two systems may have incompatible versions of the talk program, and your attempts to establish a connection won't work. The best bet in that case is for you and your conversation partner to use ytalk instead of talk (see the next how-to).

Some systems have an older program called "chat" that works similarly to talk.

5.5 HOW DO I...
Set up a multiparty conversation?

COMPLEXITY INTERMEDIATE

Problem

Sometimes it's useful to have more than two people talking to one another. You can set up a conference call using the ytalk program.

Technique

Each person runs the ytalk program. Everyone can type and see what everyone else is typing. Each person's output is displayed in a separate portion of the screen, as shown in Figure 5-3. You can also invite people to join a conversation in progress.

Steps

1. Make sure the person or persons to whom you want to talk are online. (You may wish to prearrange a time or use the finger command as described in How-To 5.4.)

2. At the system prompt, type `ytalk` followed by the person's user ID (use the complete address if the person is on a different system). For example:

```
% ytalk gerry@microsoft.com
```

3. To set up a conversation with more than one person, simply type all the user IDs (or addresses) of the parties involved:

```
% ytalk charlene@newsoft.com joe@bigu.edu richard@consultant.com
```

4. Each person you're trying to reach will receive a message like this:

```
Message from Talk_Daemon@well at 14:33 ...
talk: connection requested by ben@newsoft.com
talk: respond with:   ytalk ben@newsoft.com
```

To join the conversation, each person types `ytalk` followed by your user ID or address. (In this example you're Ben.)

After the connection is established, ytalk will divide the screen into as many parts as there are people involved in the conversation. Figure 5-3 shows a three-part conversation.

5. You can add more people to a conversation in progress. The new person just types `ytalk` with your user ID or address. You'll get a message like this:

165

INTERNET HOW-TO

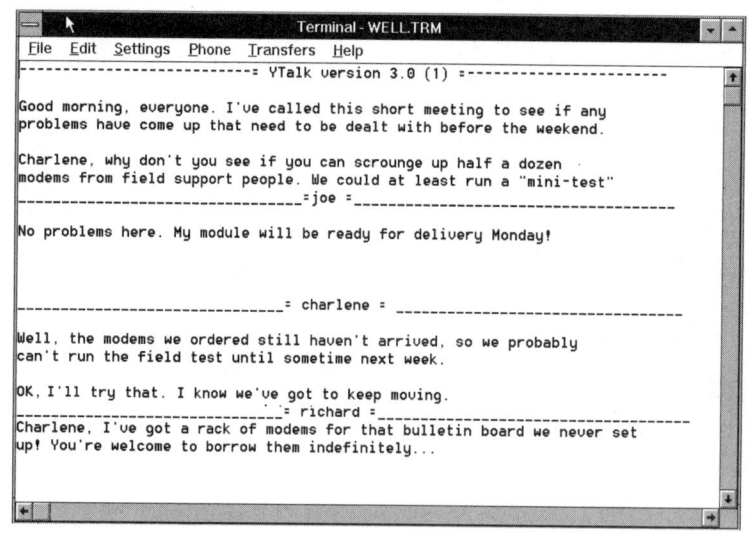

```
┌─────────────────────── Terminal - WELL.TRM ──────────────────┬─┬─┐
│ File  Edit  Settings  Phone  Transfers  Help                 │ │ │
├─────────────────────: YTalk version 3.0 (1) :────────────────┤▲│ │
│Good morning, everyone. I've called this short meeting to see if any│
│problems have come up that need to be dealt with before the weekend.│
│                                                                    │
│Charlene, why don't you see if you can scrounge up half a dozen     │
│modems from field support people. We could at least run a "mini-test"│
│──────────────────────────────: joe :───────────────────────────────│
│                                                                    │
│No problems here. My module will be ready for delivery Monday!      │
│                                                                    │
│                                                                    │
│──────────────────────────: charlene :──────────────────────────────│
│Well, the modems we ordered still haven't arrived, so we probably   │
│can't run the field test until sometime next week.                  │
│                                                                    │
│OK, I'll try that. I know we've got to keep moving.                 │
│──────────────────────────: richard :───────────────────────────────│
│Charlene, I've got a rack of modems for that bulletin board we never set│
│up! You're welcome to borrow them indefinitely...                   │▼│
└────────────────────────────────────────────────────────────────────┘
```

Figure 5-3 A multiparty conversation with the ytalk program

```
###############################
# talk with len@newsoft.com? #
###############################
```

       If you press (Y), your screen is redrawn to include a portion for the additional person. The other participants will also be prompted to add the new person to *their* screens:

```
###########################
# Import len@newsoft.com #
###########################
```

       If they press (Y), their screens will be reapportioned.

     6. You can also call up a menu to perform other housekeeping with your ytalk session. Press (ESC) and you'll see a menu like this:

```
###########################
#       Main Menu         #
#                         #
# a: add a user           #
# d: delete a user        #
# o: options              #
# s: shell                #
# u: user list            #
# w: output user to file  #
# q: quit                 #
###########################
```

       To add a new user, press (A) and enter the user ID or address of the person to be invited to the conversation. The person will receive a message, and if the person presses (Y), he or she will be added to the conversation.

5 TALKING TO OTHER USERS

To remove a user from the session, press Ⓑ and enter the person's user ID as shown on the screen. The connection to that person will be terminated.

Finally, to save everything that one of your conversation partners types to a file, press Ⓦ and enter the user ID and the name of a file. From now on, everything that person types will be saved to that file. By repeating this option for each user (including yourself), you can create a complete "log" of the conversation. (It's polite to let people know you're doing this!)

How It Works
ytalk is similar to talk, except that it can hook up more than two people, and it lets you change the number of people in the conversation on-the-fly.

Comment
Someone using the plain old talk program can talk to you while you're using ytalk. That person will appear in a portion of your screen, and you can talk with him or her. This will be a two-way conversation only (the person won't be able to talk with the other participants in your ytalk conversation).

ytalk may not be available at your Internet site. If it isn't, why not ask your system administrator to obtain the program (via ftp) and install it?

5.6 HOW DO I...
Screen out unwanted messages?

COMPLEXITY INTERMEDIATE

Problem
You may be doing something complicated and not wish to be interrupted by a message or you may not wish to receive messages from a particular person.

Technique
You use the mesg command to control whether you will receive messages in general. You can also use a file called .sendrc to specify people who are either authorized to send you messages, or from whom you don't wish to receive messages.

Steps
1. To block *all* messages, type `mesg n`.

2. If you have been blocking messages temporarily but you're now ready to see them again, restore other people's access to you by typing `mesg y`.

3. To specify the only people from which you wish to receive messages, create a file called .sendrc in your home directory. (See Chapter 6 for information on editing files.) For each person, enter a line that begins with `only`, followed by the person's user ID:

```
only joe
only helen
only support
```

Save the file. Now only Joe, Helen, and "support" (a shared account used by support personnel) will be able to send you messages. Anyone else will be told that you aren't accepting messages.

4. To specify people from whom you don't wish to receive messages, create a .sendrc file, and for each person enter a line with `ignore` followed by the user ID:

```
ignore larry
ignore bozo
```

Now you'll be able to receive messages from anyone *except* Larry and Bozo. When they try to send you something, they'll see the message "Ignored." You can add a message to the .sendrc file that elaborates on this; for example, if .sendrc has the line,

```
ignore larry Sorry, I'm only doing business-related things here!
```

when Larry sends you something he'll see:

```
Ignored.  Reason: I'm only doing business-related things here!
```

If you want to reject messages from a sender without any notification whatsoever, type `stonewall` instead of ignore in the .sendrc file:

```
stonewall bozo
```

Now Bozo will think he's sent you a message, but nothing will happen. Obviously this isn't very polite, but might be appropriate in dealing with certain people.

Note that the approaches in steps 3 and 4 are mutually exclusive. That is, you either specify *only* the people you want to be able to send you messages or *just* the people who shouldn't be allowed to send you messages. If you use *only*, you automatically exclude all people not specified. On the other hand, if you use *ignore*, you allow all people *except* those listed to send you messages.

How It Works
The mesg command sets a flag (yes or no) that determines whether the send or reply commands can send text to your terminal. The send daemon also consults the .sendrc file to see if you've specified people who should (or shouldn't be) allowed to communicate with you.

Comment
If you've set up a .sendrc file, you can still turn *all* messages off with mesg n. This is useful, since there may be times when you don't want to receive messages at all, and other times when messages are OK as long as they're from certain people (or not from certain people).

The finger program will sometimes tell you whether someone is refusing messages (it depends on the configuration of finger at a particular site).

5 TALKING TO OTHER USERS

5.7 HOW DO I...
Connect to Internet Relay Chat (IRC)?

COMPLEXITY EASY

Problem
You would like to connect to the Internet Relay Chat so you can explore this interactive communications medium.

Technique
Usually, all you have to do is type `irc` to run the IRC client at your site. If there isn't a client, you can use telnet to connect to an IRC server. (See Chapter 10 for more on telnet.)

Steps
1. Type `irc` at the system prompt. After a few moments, you should see a message saying that IRC is connecting to a server. (The server used is determined by the people who set up IRC at your site.)

```
% irc
```

2. Once you are connected, you'll see a screen like the one in Figure 5-4 which is from the IRC server at irc.caltech.edu.

   The messages you see will vary with the server. The messages in Figure 5-4 give you some idea of the scope and extent of the IRC services—several thousand users, about a thousand channels, with about a hundred of them active.

   The messages about "bots" and "floodbots" refer to automated response mechanisms created by advanced IRC users. Since these can generate a lot of message traffic of dubious value, most servers frown on their use.

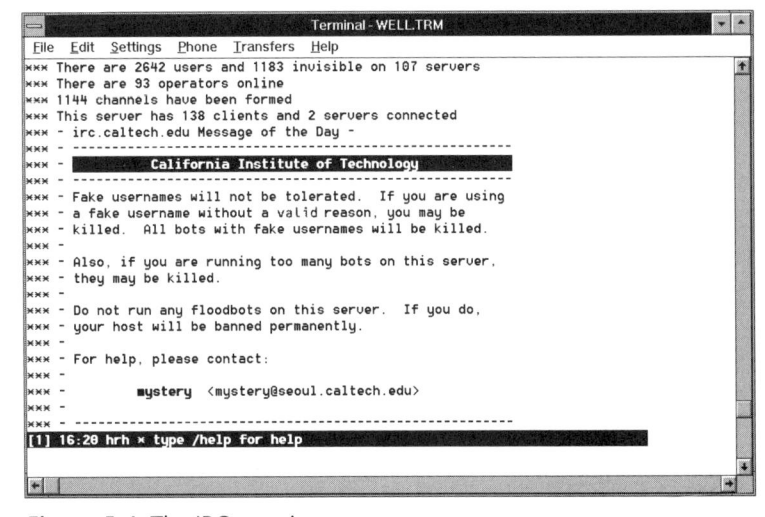

Figure 5-4 The IRC opening screen

INTERNET HOW-TO

How It Works
As Figure 5-1 illustrated, you, the user, run a client program at your site that sets up your terminal display and accepts and displays messages. The client program in turn connects to a server that handles the messages. The servers in turn connect to each other to maintain a pool of users and messages.

Comment
If you type `irc` and get "command not found" (or the equivalent), it probably means that your site doesn't have an IRC client. You can urge your system administrator to install a client. Some administrators may resist that suggestion because they view IRC as a frivolous waste of time, machine resources, and worker productivity.

Even if you don't have an IRC client, however, you can still use IRC by using telnet (see Chapter 10) to connect to an IRC server. To find a site that is accessible to telnet, look for lists of clients in the newsgroup alt.irc.answers. (In the United States, you can try the servers at csa.bu.edu, irc.colorado.edu, or irc.uiuc.edu.) Running a client at your site is preferable because telnet access tends to be slow or unavailable during busy times of the day.

5.8 HOW DO I...
Enter IRC commands?

COMPLEXITY: EASY

Problem
Once you're connected to IRC (see How-To 5.7), you need to enter commands to get help, find out about people, or change various settings.

Technique
You enter your command text by beginning it with a slash (/) and pressing (ENTER) at the end of the command line.

Steps
1. Figure 5-4 shows what the screen looks like when you start IRC. Note that it is divided into two parts by a wide highlighted line showing the time, your user ID, and a message about how to get help. You enter your commands and messages at the prompt below this line. The output from your commands (or the text of your message and messages from other people) appears in the main part of the screen above the line.

2. To enter a command, press (/) followed by the command name. For example, to get a list of channels and their topics, you would type

```
/list
```

   (You must press (ENTER) after each command or message.)

3. Anything you type that doesn't begin with a slash (/) is considered to be a message and is "broadcast" over IRC so everyone can see it. Thus if you type

```
Hi, everyone!
```

   the words "Hi, everyone!" will appear on the screens of everyone who is on IRC and connected to the same channel as you are.

5 TALKING TO OTHER USERS

4. To quit IRC, type /quit (you can also use /bye, /signoff, or /exit).

How It Works
IRC looks at the text you are typing. If it sees a line that starts with a slash (/), it interprets it as a command. Otherwise it assumes that you're typing a message to be displayed to other users.

Comment
Beginners commonly forget to put the slash before a command, and the command then becomes a message that is seen by everyone. Polite people will ignore this when it happens. Rude people may hassle you about it. Don't worry, you'll get used to entering the slash soon enough.

5.9 HOW DO I...
Get help while using IRC?

COMPLEXITY: EASY

Problem
It takes awhile to learn the basic IRC commands. You may want to get help to remind you what a command does, or to explore a more advanced command.

Technique
You enter the help command and then ask for help on a particular topic.

Steps
1. Type /help at the IRC prompt.

2. You'll see a help screen like the one in Figure 5-5, listing the commands available, as well as a few general topics in lowercase (such as "intro" and "newuser").

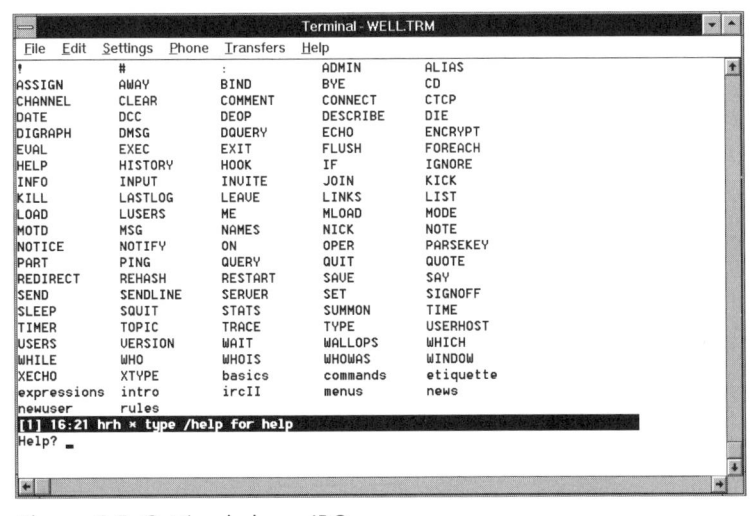

```
                        Terminal - WELL.TRM
File  Edit  Settings  Phone  Transfers  Help
!            #              :              ADMIN        ALIAS
ASSIGN       AWAY           BIND           BYE          CD
CHANNEL      CLEAR          COMMENT        CONNECT      CTCP
DATE         DCC            DEOP           DESCRIBE     DIE
DIGRAPH      DMSG           DQUERY         ECHO         ENCRYPT
EVAL         EXEC           EXIT           FLUSH        FOREACH
HELP         HISTORY        HOOK           IF           IGNORE
INFO         INPUT          INVITE         JOIN         KICK
KILL         LASTLOG        LEAVE          LINKS        LIST
LOAD         LUSERS         ME             MLOAD        MODE
MOTD         MSG            NAMES          NICK         NOTE
NOTICE       NOTIFY         ON             OPER         PARSEKEY
PART         PING           QUERY          QUIT         QUOTE
REDIRECT     REHASH         RESTART        SAVE         SAY
SEND         SENDLINE       SERVER         SET          SIGNOFF
SLEEP        SQUIT          STATS          SUMMON       TIME
TIMER        TOPIC          TRACE          TYPE         USERHOST
USERS        VERSION        WAIT           WALLOPS      WHICH
WHILE        WHO            WHOIS          WHOWAS       WINDOW
XECHO        XTYPE          basics         commands     etiquette
expressions  intro          ircII          menus        news
newuser      rules
[1] 16:21 hrh * type /help for help
Help?
```

Figure 5-5 Getting help on IRC

INTERNET HOW-TO

The prompt will now read:

Help?

3. Enter the command or topic for which you want help. Press (ENTER), and you will be given a summary of the command or topic. For example, to find out what the list command does:

```
list
*** Help on LIST
Usage: LIST [<flag> [<arg>]] [<channel>]
   LIST gives you a listing of channels which includes channel name,
   number of users, and a topic (if one is set).  If no channel
   is specified, all channels are shown, otherwise only channels
   that match are displayed (the channel may contain wildcards)
   If the channel given is the character "*" LIST only returns the
   information for the current channel.
   The displayed list may also be limited by using one or more of
   the following flags:
         -MIN n          When n the minimum number of user.  Channels
                         with less than n users are not shown.
         -MAX n          When n the maximum number of user.  Channels
                         with more than n users are not shown.
         -PUBLIC         Only shows Public channels
         -PRIVATE        Only shows Private (*) channels
         -ALL            Overrides previous -PUBLIC and/or -PRIVATE
         -TOPIC          Show channels with topic set
         -WIDE           Shows channel names and sizes in as little
                         space as possible. Listing can be sorted using:
                  -NAME   Sort by name of the channel
                  -USERS  Sort by number of users in the channel

[1] 16:26 hrh * type /help for help
*** Hit any key for more, 'q' to quit ***
```

4. Many help listings (such as the one above) are too long to fit on one screen. Press (q) to quit the display, or any other key to display the rest of the text.

5. To finish asking for help, just press (ENTER) at the Help? prompt.

How It Works

IRC provides a help facility that is reminiscent of those used on some mainframes. While it isn't as easy to use as it could be, it does work. IRC help is divided into numerous commands (and some general topics). When you type /help, you get a list of commands and topics. Specifying the command or topic then gives you more specific help on that subject.

Comment

The display of the help command (and other commands) may become interspersed with messages being posted by other users. You will soon learn how to sort things out, however.

5.10 HOW DO I...
Give myself an online nickname?

COMPLEXITY INTERMEDIATE

Problem
You'd like a more colorful identity than you're usually allowed in the mundane world. Perhaps you'd like a bit of anonymity (though people can still find out who you really are if they want to).

Technique
You use the nick command to set your nickname on-the-fly. There are also various ways to set up permanent nicknames.

Steps
1. By default, your nickname is your user ID. To change your nickname to something else, type /nick at the IRC prompt followed by the nickname. For example, to change your nickname to wombat, type

```
/nick wombat
```

2. IRC will acknowledge the change in your nickname:

```
*** hrh is now known as wombat
```

3. To automatically set your nickname when you enter IRC, define the variable IRCNICK in your .profile file at your local site (if you're using the Bourne or Korn shells), or in the .login file (if you're using the C shell). For example, type

```
IRCNICK = wombat; export IRCNICK
```

for Bourne shell or,

```
setenv IRCNICK wombat
```

for C shell.

(See Chapter 6 for more information on editing files.)

4. IRC requires that nicknames in active use be unique. If you try to change your nickname to one that someone online is already using (either with the nick command or through the IRCNICK variable), you will be asked to enter a different nickname.

5. IRC provides something called NickServ (nickname service), with which you can register a nickname for your indefinite use. Someone else who tries to use that nickname will be informed that it is already in use, even if you're not online at the time. (The software doesn't *prevent* someone from using a nickname that belongs to someone else, but it's considered very impolite to do so.)

To get more information on NickServ, issue the command

```
/msg NickServ@service.de help
```

and follow the instructions provided.

INTERNET HOW-TO

How It Works
IRC uses your chosen nickname as a kind of handle or alternate identity. In using many IRC commands you can refer to users by their nicknames rather than their complete addresses. The NickServ is an automated service that lets people register nicknames and access them by providing passwords.

Comment
Nicknames are currently limited to a maximum of nine characters.

5.11 HOW DO I...
Find a conversation?

COMPLEXITY: INTERMEDIATE

Problem
There are a thousand or so channels on IRC at any given time. How do you find a conversation that interests you, or one on a particular topic?

Technique
You use the list command to get a list of channels. You can use switches to limit the list to popular channels (many users) or to channels with just a few users. You can also use the names command to find channels that have people you know on them.

Steps
1. Type /list at the IRC prompt to see a list of channels. Figure 5-6 shows part of such a list, showing the channel name, the number of users currently connected to the channel, and (where provided) the channel's topic.

2. Since there can be hundreds of channels, you may want to limit the number of channels you see. You do this by adding options to your list command.

   To see only channels with a minimum number of participants, add -min followed by the number. Use -max to specify channels that have no more than the specified number of users.

   In Figure 5-6 we entered the command

/list -min 35

   to show only channels with at least 35 participants. Similarly, the command

/list -max 5

   would show only channels that have 5 or fewer users.

3. If you know the nicknames of some friends on IRC, you can check to see whether they're on any IRC channel. Type /names and you'll get a listing like this:

```
Pub: #aussies      rick wombat @kangaroo
Pub: #wildbunch    carey turtle dragon sparks
Pub: #unix         prof wizard kruger nixbot
```

   Channel names always begin with the # character. "Pub:" means that the channel is public (to find out how to set up private channels, see How-To 5.17). This is followed by the name of the channel and a list of the nicknames of the users on that channel. Names prefixed with @, such as @kangaroo, are *channel operators* who manage and control the channel.

5 🌐 TALKING TO OTHER USERS

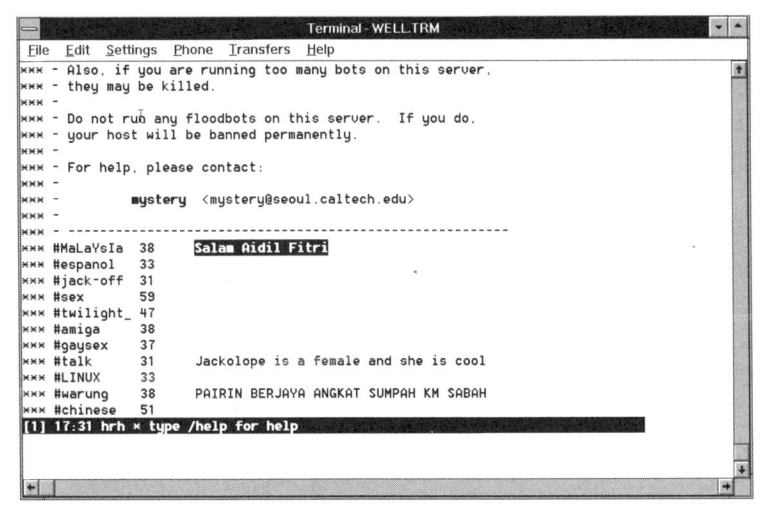

```
┌─────────────────── Terminal - WELL.TRM ───────────────────┐
│ File  Edit  Settings  Phone  Transfers  Help              │
│ *** - Also, if you are running too many bots on this server,│
│ *** - they may be killed.                                  │
│ *** -                                                      │
│ *** - Do not run any floodbots on this server.  If you do, │
│ *** - your host will be banned permanently.                │
│ *** -                                                      │
│ *** - For help, please contact:                            │
│ *** -                                                      │
│ *** -          mystery   <mystery@seoul.caltech.edu>       │
│ *** -                                                      │
│ *** ------------------------------------------------------ │
│ *** #MaLaYsIa    38    Salam Aidil Fitri                   │
│ *** #espanol     33                                        │
│ *** #jack-off    31                                        │
│ *** #sex         59                                        │
│ *** #twilight_   47                                        │
│ *** #amiga       38                                        │
│ *** #gaysex      37                                        │
│ *** #talk        31    Jackolope is a female and she is cool│
│ *** #LINUX       33                                        │
│ *** #warung      38    PAIRIN BERJAYA ANGKAT SUMPAH KM SABAH│
│ *** #chinese     51                                        │
│ [1] 17:31 hrh * type /help for help                        │
└────────────────────────────────────────────────────────────┘
```

Figure 5-6 Listing IRC channels

As with the list command, you should use -min or -max to limit your names command so that the list isn't too long.

How It Works
IRC maintains lists of channels, users, and users on each channel. The list and names commands access these lists and help you find interesting conversations by channel name, topic, or people involved.

Comment
The channel list facility is pretty unwieldy, due to the number of channels and people involved. It would be nice to have a command that searched for channels on a particular topic.

5.12 HOW DO I...
Carry on a conversation?

COMPLEXITY: INTERMEDIATE

Problem
Now that you've found an interesting channel, how do you join in? And how do you make sense of all the different kinds of messages that keep scrolling up the screen?

Technique
You use the join command to join a channel. Once on the channel, you read the messages as they come in, and when so moved, type some messages of your own. The main thing to be aware of is the special symbols that IRC uses to distinguish between different kinds of messages.

Steps
1. After giving a list or names command, find a channel whose name or topic interests you. If you're not sure what channel you want, try #hottub (as the name suggests, a friendly place for introductions).

INTERNET HOW-TO

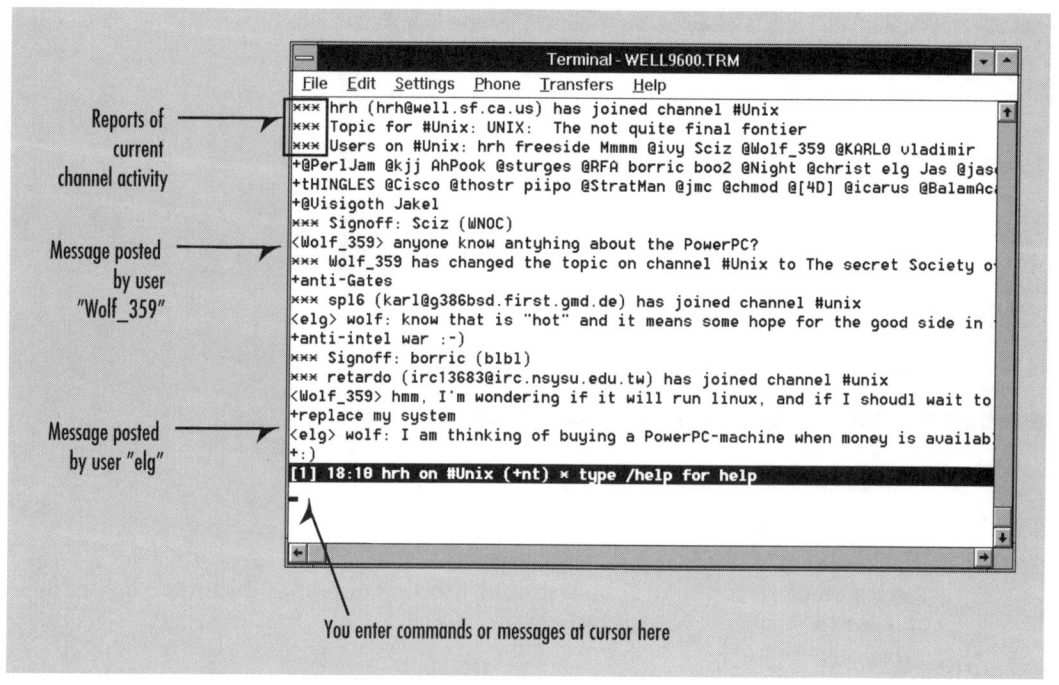

Figure 5-7 Conversation on an IRC channel

(Annotations on figure:)
- Reports of current channel activity
- Message posted by user "Wolf_359"
- Message posted by user "elg"
- You enter commands or messages at cursor here

2. At the IRC prompt, type /join followed by the channel name. (Remember that channel names begin with the # character.) For example, to join the #Unix channel, you would type

```
/join #Unix
```

3. The result of our visit to #Unix is shown in Figure 5-7. Note that the screen records a continuous flow of events. You can identify what is going on by noting the characters that each line begins with:

***	Reports on comings or goings, someone joined or left (signed off) the channel, or changed their nickname.
\<user\>	Means a message posted by the indicated username or nickname.
user	Means a *private* message from that user. You see it, but others won't. See How-To 5.13 to learn how to send private messages.
->	Is a message that *you* have typed (it will be seen by others with your nickname in brackets).

4. To type a public message, simply type the text. (Unlike commands, you *don't* precede the text with a slash.) For example, if your nickname is wowza and you type

```
Has anyone played the new game Dungeon Blaster yet?
```

176

5 TALKING TO OTHER USERS

you will see your message on the screen like this,

```
-> Has anyone played the new game Dungeon Blaster yet?
```

while *others* will see it on their screen like this:

```
<wowza> Has anyone played the new game Dungeon Blaster yet?
```

5. Many IRC users have a theatrical bent and like to have "virtual body language" accompany their actions. You can do this by typing the command /me followed by a description of the action of your virtual self. For example, the command

```
/me rolls on the floor laughing
```

results in people seeing the following:

```
* wowza rolls on the floor laughing
```

6. When you no longer wish to participate in a channel, type /leave.

How It Works
IRC distinguishes on your screen between public and private messages from others, and messages you've typed yourself. By learning these distinctions you can more easily follow the flow of conversation. On many channels the proper mood is that of a kind of play, where your persona is acting in the presence of other people's personas. (Of course there are also plenty of channels for conventional conversation—use the channel name and the "flavor" of the messages to cue you to appropriate responses.)

Comment
It's a good idea to mostly listen the first time you visit a channel. Get a feel for the channel and then start contributing (or perhaps, decide that the channel is not for you).

5.13 HOW DO I...
Send private messages?

COMPLEXITY EASY

Problem
You'd like to discuss something privately on IRC without other users seeing your messages.

Technique
You use the msg command to send a single private message, or the query command to set up a private connection that you can use for a while.

Steps
1. Type /msg followed by the nickname of the person to whom the private message is to be sent, and the text of the message. For example,

```
/msg calliope Are you free for dinner tonight?
```

results in calliope seeing the following on her screen

```
*wowza* Are you free for dinner tonight?
```

177

INTERNET HOW-TO

(assuming, of course, that your nickname is wowza.)

2. To send the same private message to more than one person, simply include all the people's nicknames, separated by commas with no spaces in between:

`/msg rick,happy,moon Let's go meet on #crash and hang out there`

The users with the nicknames rick, happy, and moon will all get your private message.

3. If someone sends *you* a private message, an easy way to reply is to type `/msg ,` followed by your message. The comma stands for "the last person who sent you a private message," so you don't have to type the nickname.

4. If you want to exchange several private remarks with someone, it's awkward to have to type /msg before each message. (It's also easy to forget to do so, which might prove embarrassing...) Instead, you can use the query command. Type `/query` followed by the nickname of the recipient:

`/query bobcat`

5. Now everything you type (other than commands) goes as a private message to bobcat. You no longer need to begin each message with /msg. This means that if you and another person both execute this command, you can "talk" to each other simply by typing. Each person's messages will appear on the other person's screen as private messages.

6. To cancel this private conversation, enter `/query` again without the nickname.

How It Works

IRC keeps track of several attributes about each message. One of them is whether the message is public (to be displayed to everyone) or private (to be seen only by the sender and recipient). The /msg command marks a particular message as private, while the query command automatically marks all of your subsequent input (and that of your partner) as private messages.

Comment

Remember that privacy and security are relative. While it isn't easy for someone to find a particular private message, it is possible for skilled intruders to intercept just about any text that passes from one system to another, and IRC doesn't encrypt text.

5.14 HOW DO I...
Get information about people?

COMPLEXITY: EASY

Problem

You'd like to find out about the person behind the nickname.

Technique

You can look at lists of nicknames matched with their "real" Internet addresses, or get more information about a specific person whose nickname you know.

5 TALKING TO OTHER USERS

Steps

1. To get a list of people who are connected to IRC, type /who followed by the name of a channel (or use * to stand for the current channel). For example:

```
/who #games
Channel  Nickname      S    User@Host         (Name)
#games   wombat             H*   hrh@well.com
   (a plump marsupial)
#games   moondog       H    jgreen@BigU.edu (John Green)
#games   rover         H*@  marcus@surenet.com
#games   mark          G    markj@well.com
```

From left to right, the columns give the channel name, nickname, status (H for "here" G for "gone," @ for a channel operator), the user's actual Internet address, and an optional comment (as in the case of "wombat").

2. You can use the whois command to get more information about a specific person. Type /whois followed by the person's nickname. For example:

```
/whois wombat
*** wombat is hrh@well.com
*** on channels: #hottub #games
*** on via server irc.caltech.edu
```

3. If the person you're interested in is no longer connected to IRC (or has changed his or her nickname), the whois command will simply report something like this:

```
/whois wombat
*** wombat: no such nickname
```

4. If the person has disconnected from IRC, you can try the whowas command. Type /whowas followed by the nickname:

```
/whowas wombat
```

whowas will report on the last person who used the specified nickname, giving information similar to that provided by whois.

How It Works
IRC keeps a kind of database of nicknames, addresses, and other information about participants.

Comment
Note that people can and do change nicknames, or a nickname that had been used by one person might be taken over by another person. This means that the personal information attached to a given nickname might not be the same today as it was yesterday. If it's important, try to confirm information by e-mail.

INTERNET HOW-TO

5.15 HOW DO I...
Keep track of comings and goings?

COMPLEXITY | **INTERMEDIATE**

Problem
You'd like to know whether a particular individual is currently connected to IRC. Also, you might need to go somewhere for a few minutes, and wish to notify the people on the channel that you'll be gone.

Technique
You can use the notify command to build a list of people whose comings and goings will be reported to you. You can use the away command to let people on your channel know that you're taking a break.

Steps
1. If you want to know when a particular person or persons enters or leaves IRC, type /notify followed by the nickname of the person you want to watch for. For example,

/notify Jupiter

   sets things up so you'll be notified when the user with the nickname Jupiter either connects to IRC or leaves the system.

2. Each time you use the notify command, the nickname you specify is added to a list of users. Thus if you enter /notify BigStar, you'll be notified about the comings or goings of either Jupiter or BigStar.

3. To remove a person from your notification list (so you no longer track them), type /notify followed by a hyphen and the nickname. Thus,

/notify - Jupiter

   removes Jupiter from your notification list.

4. If you need to leave the channel for a while, type /away followed by the reason for your departure (optional):

/away Nature calls! Back in a moment!

   People will see a message like this:

<wombat> is away: Nature calls! Back in a moment!

5. When you're back, just type /away and press (ENTER), and you will be listed as having returned to the channel.

How It Works
When someone connects to IRC (or leaves the system), IRC checks the notification lists and notifies users on whose lists the arriving or departing user appears.

The away command simply lets people know that you're going to be away for a while.

5 TALKING TO OTHER USERS

Comment
If you're not directly involved in the conversation, it isn't particularly useful to tell people you'll be away for a while.

5.16 HOW DO I... Invite someone to join a conversation?

COMPLEXITY EASY

Problem
You find that a friend or colleague is on IRC, and you'd like to invite the person to join your current conversation.

Technique
First you make sure the person is online. Then you invite him or her to join your current channel.

Steps
1. Check to see if the person you want to invite is connected to IRC, using the whois or names command (see How-Tos 5.11 and 5.14).

2. If the person is connected, type `/invite` followed by the person's nickname and the channel to which you want to invite the person. (Leaving out the channel means that you're inviting the person to your current channel.) For example,

```
/invite wombat #games
```

   invites wombat to the #games channel.

3. The person being invited sees a message like this:

```
*** BigStar invites you to channel #games
```

   Wombat can join you on the channel by typing either `/join -invite` (to join the last channel invited to), or `/join` followed by the channel name.

How It Works
In addition to conversations on channels, IRC has various facilities that can pass messages or notifications to users. The invite command finds the user you specify (if connected) and invites him or her to join your current channel (or the channel you specify).

Comment
If the person doesn't show up, you can assume they chose not to join your channel.

5.17 HOW DO I... Start my own channel?

COMPLEXITY INTERMEDIATE

Problem
You'd like to discuss a topic you haven't found elsewhere on IRC. Or perhaps you just want to set up a meeting place for your class, group, or company.

Technique
You simply use the join command with the name of a nonexistent channel. You then become channel operator and can specify characteristics of the channel and control its visibility and access.

Steps
1. To start your own channel, type /join followed by the name of a channel that doesn't currently exist. For example,

/join #round_table

> creates a new channel called round_table. You become the channel operator, the person who controls a number of characteristics about the channel and who has certain powers over other users.

2. It's a good idea to set a *topic* for the channel. The topic will appear in listings with the list command, and will give browsers a better idea of what's happening on your channel. To set a topic, type /topic followed by the topic description. For example,

/topic Talking about Arthurian Legends

> sets the topic for your round_table channel.

3. By default, a new channel is *public*. That is, anyone can list the channel or join it. On a *private* channel, people can tell that you're online, but the channel is simply listed as "priv:"—they can't join the channel unless they know the name, or you invite them.

   Finally, a *secret* channel is "invisible:" you don't appear in any listings of users (such as with the names command). Again, to join the channel, people must know the channel name (or you may invite them to join).

4. To set the channel mode, type /mode followed by the channel name and +p for private or +s for secret. (Use - instead of + if you want to *remove* a mode.) For example,

/mode #round_table +p

> makes #round_table a private channel.

How It Works
IRC keeps track of a number of modes for each user and each channel. User modes control the kinds of messages a user will receive, as well as other characteristics. Channel modes determine whether the channel's name will be shown in listings (and thus whether people can find out about the channel and join it).

Comment
There are a variety of other modes you can set, both for your channel and for yourself as a user. Type /help mode for more information and see the IRC documentation for more examples.

5.18 HOW DO I... *Deal with harassment?*

COMPLEXITY INTERMEDIATE

Problem
Unfortunately there are always people who like to hassle other people in one way or another. IRC and other computer communications facilities aren't immune to this problem, of course.

Technique
A combination of cooperation by the channel operator and your use of the ignore command can help minimize harassing, annoying, or abusive communications.

Steps
1. If possible, complain to the channel operator (you can tell who this person is because there's an @ before the nickname in listings). The channel operator can use the kick command to remove an obnoxious person from a particular channel.

2. You can also block all output from a particular person from your screen. To do this, type /ignore followed by the person's nickname or Internet address (the latter is more effective, since it's easy for people to change their nickname). For example,

```
/ignore scumbag@BigU.edu
```

   will block any messages (public, private, or whatever) from scumbag from appearing on your screen.

3. As with the notify command, the ignore command builds a list of users. Each time you use the command, the user you specify is added to the list of people to be ignored. To remove a person from the list (and thus be able to see his or her messages again), type /ignore followed by the person's nickname or address and none. The following lets you see messages from scumbag again.

```
/ignore scumbag@BigU.edu none
```

How It Works
The channel operator has the ultimate power to eject or bar people from his or her channel. As a user, however, you have the ability to block out messages from a particular person.

Comment
People need to keep in mind that things they say at their keyboard can be subject to legal constraints, and *should* be subject to basic rules of courtesy.

Note that if you are using IRC via telnet, your "ignore" list isn't saved between sessions, so you have to re-create it each time.

5.19 HOW DO I...
Change IRC settings?

COMPLEXITY: INTERMEDIATE

Problem
You may want (or need) to change a setting that determines how IRC works.

Technique
You can use three techniques to make IRC settings: set variables in your shell, use the set command to change settings interactively, or put settings in an initialization file called .ircrc.

Steps
1. You can set some characteristics by specifying a variable in your shell. (See Chapter 6 for more information on environmental variables and how to set them, as well as How-To 5.10 for an example using the IRCNAME variable.) As another example, if the IRC screen is getting jumbled, you can set the TERM variable to your terminal type so that IRC will recognize it. See the IRC documentation (or type `/help set`) for more information on variables you can set.

2. You can also set variables in a file called .ircrc in your home directory. Simply create this file with a text editor (see Chapter 6), and enter the appropriate statements. This file can contain any IRC commands. For example:

```
/nick wombat
/set auto_whowas on
/join #marsupials
/ignore scumbag@bigu.edu none
```

Now, when you enter IRC, your nickname will be automatically set to "wombat" (assuming no one else is using that name). You will automatically run a whowas command when you type /whois and the person is no longer there. You will automatically join the #marsupials channel after you connect to IRC. Finally, you won't see any messages from scumbag.

3. To see your current settings, type `/set`.

4. To change a setting interactively, type `/set` followed by the variable name and its value. Variables can be Boolean (on/off), numeric, limited to a small set of values, or defined as strings. For example,

```
/set beep on
```

means you'll hear any "beeps" that are sent to you in messages. This command,

```
/set beep_max 1
```

means that you'll only hear one beep, even if many are sent.

How It Works
Like most Unix programs, IRC responds to shell variables (see Chapter 6), and also provides its own internal variables and an initialization file (.ircrc).

5 TALKING TO OTHER USERS

Comment
Beginners shouldn't have to set or change anything except perhaps their terminal type, if the screen display isn't working right. For more information on IRC variables, see the document "IRC tutorial" by Ronald van Loon, in four parts and available at most IRC sites.

5.20 HOW DO I...
Learn more about IRC?

COMPLEXITY | INTERMEDIATE

Problem
IRC has many more features that aren't covered here. How do you find out more?

Technique
You can explore the usual sources: online help, documents (tutorials and reference manuals), and interactive help (such as newsgroups or mailing lists).

Steps
1. Try out the help system by using the help command with different topics. The following topics are particularly useful for beginners: newuser, rules, intro, etiquette, menus, and commands.

2. Get a copy of a document called "The IRC primer" and the IRC tutorials. They are available by ftp from cs.bu.edu in the /irc/support directory. (See Chapter 7 for information on how to use ftp.)

3. Subscribe to the alt.irc.answers newsgroup. This group also distributes a FAQ file on IRC.

4. Use the above sources to find out about resources for more advanced users (such as mailing lists).

5. Cruise IRC and look for channels that discuss IRC itself.

How It Works
As with many other programs, a variety of helpful individuals have compiled information and tutorials for IRC.

Comment
Take your time. IRC takes some getting used to.

Basic File Management

How do I....

6.1   Enter a Unix command
6.2   Get help for a Unix command
6.3   List a directory
6.4   Change the current directory
6.5   Read a text file
6.6   Edit a text file
6.7   Specify user settings
6.8   Copy a file
6.9   Move or rename a file
6.10 Compare two files
6.11 Delete a file
6.12 Make or remove a directory
6.13 Work with a group of files using wildcards
6.14 Find a particular file
6.15 Find text in a file
6.16 Check my disk space
6.17 Keep my files private
6.18 Learn more about Unix

Many people enticed by the promise of the Internet are reluctant to take the plunge because they've heard that most machines on the net run the Unix operating system. The media (including the computer trade press) tends to stress the user-*un*friendly nature of Unix, the obscurity of many of its commands, and the often unforgiving syn-

INTERNET HOW-TO

tax. Fortunately you only have to know a little bit about Unix to manage your Internet session, and that little bit isn't that hard to learn, as you'll see in this chapter.

If you're one of the small (but growing) number of people lucky enough to be accessing the Internet through a GUI (graphical user interface), you may have little or no need to deal with the underlying Unix operating system at your Internet site. Your GUI may be a Windows or Mac front end to Internet, or it could be a version of Unix using Xwindows or an operating environment like that on Sun workstations.

If you can copy, list, move, and delete files on the Internet system without leaving the GUI, you probably don't *have* to learn Unix. If, on the other hand, the GUI provides some functions (such as mail and news reading) but doesn't let you manage files, you'll probably still want to learn Unix so you can do some housekeeping in your home directory. Why? For one thing, many systems charge you for disk storage above a certain minimal amount, so you'll have to prune, discard, or download the files that accumulate as you save mail or news articles or get files from elsewhere on the Internet with the ftp program.

Your learning curve for Unix will vary with your experience. If you're an experienced MS-DOS user, for example, the only thing you must do to learn enough Unix to get by is to start using forward slashes (/) instead of backslashes (\) in pathnames; use - instead of / in front of command switches; and learn the Unix equivalents to your bread-and-butter DOS commands (use ls instead of DIR, cat instead of TYPE, and so on). That's about it.

If you're a Mac or Windows user accustomed to doing everything with menus, icons, and mouse, things will be a bit more difficult at first. You will be confronted with a command prompt where you will have to type a command followed (usually) by a filename or two and maybe an option. Unix will perform the command, display the results on your screen, and wait patiently for your next command. While this isn't as easy as pulling down a menu and clicking on something, it isn't hard once you get the hang of it.

Before going on, you should know that there are two major versions of the Unix operating system. Basically these are the Berkeley BSD-based systems and the AT&T System V-based systems. You need to know this only because you may run into systems that have some commands not found on other systems. All of the commands discussed in this chapter work with both kinds of Unix. The two Unix versions are gradually being blended together.

Table 6-1 lists the Unix commands that will be covered in this chapter, along with their DOS equivalents for the benefit of PC users.

How-Tos in this Chapter

6.1 Enter a Unix command
Unix uses a program called a shell to process your commands. You'll learn how to enter a command at the Unix prompt and how to deal with some common error messages.

6.2 Get help for a Unix command
Some Unix commands have many options or switches that can be useful in certain circumstances. It's not easy to remember exactly how to enter each command. Fortunately, you can read a summary of any command or consult a more detailed entry in the online Unix manual.

UNIX COMMAND	DOS EQUIVALENT	PURPOSE
cat	TYPE	Display a file (continuous scrolling)
cd	CD	Change directory
chmod	ATTRIB	Set access permissions for a file
cmp	FC	Compare two files
cp	COPY	Copy a file
du	CHKDSK	Check disk space
head	<none>	Read first few lines of a file
ls	DIR	List a directory
man	HELP	Get description of a command
mkdir, rmdir	MD, RD	Create or remove a directory
more	MORE	Read file a screenful at a time
mv	MOVE, REN	Move or rename a file
rm	DEL	Delete a file
vi	EDIT	Edit a text file

Table 6-1 Unix commands covered in this chapter

6.3 List a directory
Like many other operating systems, Unix organizes files into directories. You'll learn how to list the files in a directory and master the simple rules for naming files and directories.

6.4 Change the current directory
By default, many Unix commands work with your current directory. For example, it is convenient to change to the directory to which you will be copying files, and then make the copies.

6.5 Read a text file
Text files are probably the most common kind of file you'll encounter when working with the Internet. You'll learn how to read a whole file a piece at a time, all at once, or just take a quick look at the beginning.

6.6 Edit a text file
You've already learned a bit about editing some kinds of text files (mail messages and news articles). Here you'll take a more general look at editing files with the vi text editor.

6.7 Specify user settings
There are a number of variables and settings that can specify what type of terminal you're using, which programs you'd like to use for editing or displaying text, or the location of certain directories. You can put commands in a special "login" or "profile" file so that your settings take effect automatically each session.

6.8 Copy a file
Sometimes it's important to make a backup copy of a file. Other times it's handy to have your own copy of a file found elsewhere in the system.

INTERNET HOW-TO

6.9 Move or rename a file
As you organize your system of directories you may want to move a file from one place to another, or change the name of a file to something that's easier to remember. You'll need to work out the best file organization for your needs, but this how-to will show you the basic tools.

6.10 Compare two files
Sometimes you'll need to know whether a file and its backup are identical, or whether a file in one directory is the same as a file in another directory. You'll learn how to quickly compare any two files.

6.11 Delete a file
Getting rid of unwanted files will keep your home directory neat and well-organized, and may save you money in disk usage charges.

6.12 Make or remove a directory
You'll learn how to create or remove directories as your organizational needs change.

6.13 Work with a group of files using wildcards
You don't have to copy, move, or delete files one at a time. You can use wildcards to specify a group of files.

6.14 Find a particular file
There can be tens of thousands of files on a large Unix system. You'll learn how to find the location of the one you want.

6.15 Find text in a file
Suppose you have a list of names or addresses that's 300K long, and you want to find a particular person? Unix includes a command that will find the desired information for you.

6.16 Check my disk space
After you've been using mail, news, and particularly ftp for a while, you can accumulate several megabytes of files in your home directory. Many systems will charge you for file storage beyond a minimal amount, so it's a good idea to check periodically and make sure you don't have too much stuff.

6.17 Keep my files private
Most Internet users respect other users' privacy, but there are the inevitable exceptions. You'll see how to "lock out" your files from unauthorized access.

6.18 Learn more about Unix
This chapter closes with a few suggested books, both tutorial and reference, that can give you a more comprehensive knowledge of the Unix operating system.

6.1 HOW DO I...
Enter a Unix command?

COMPLEXITY: EASY

Problem
There are a variety of housekeeping functions that you will need to perform from time to time while connected to a machine on the Internet. These functions can be broken down into such categories as:

➤ Directory organization (creating and rearranging your organization of files as your needs change)

6 BASIC FILE MANAGEMENT

➤ File disposition (deleting, moving, or renaming files as appropriate)
➤ Accounting (keeping track of your disk usage)

Unless you have some menu-driven front end to perform these functions, you will be using about a dozen or so Unix commands for the purpose. You will need to become familiar with what each command does and with its typical and appropriate use.

Technique
When you log onto your Internet account you will be presented with either a set of menus (if there's a GUI front end or a text-based command system like PicoSpan) or with a Unix command prompt. If you have a GUI with menu options that deal with the functions discussed above, you can go ahead and use the menus together with whatever online help is provided. You may still want to read this chapter in order to get an idea of how the underlying operating system works, and because some operations can be performed more quickly at the command line than through menus.

If you have a GUI but the menus do not cover all these functions (for example, they let you deal with mail and news but not with files you transfer into your home directory), you will need to tell the system to give you a Unix prompt so you can use the commands discussed in this chapter. Look for a menu option such as "Unix," or "Shell," or an equivalent text command. (Systems vary so much that it is difficult to be more specific. Pressing ! or typing the word `unix` and pressing (ENTER) might do the trick; otherwise consult your online help.)

Once you get to a Unix prompt, it may be a single character (either % or $) or some variation, such as the name of the system (Well%). This prompt is actually presented by the Unix shell, a program that interprets and executes your commands, just as the program COMMAND.COM does for MS-DOS users. The $ prompt is from a shell called the Bourne shell or a newer one called the Korn shell, while the % prompt indicates the C shell. For purposes of this chapter, all these shells perform identically. The only time you'll need to pay attention to which shell you are using is when you are dealing with user settings (How-To 6.7).

Steps
1. If you don't see a $ or % prompt (or some variation that includes the system name), it probably means that some sort of menu system has been set up at the site. Examine the menus to see if they let you work with your files. If not, find out how to exit from the front end program and run a shell.

2. Once you see the shell prompt, you can type any Unix command.

3. Following the name of the command, give the name of one or more files or paths, as appropriate (see How-To 6.3 for a brief explanation of paths and filenames). For example, if you're copying a file from one place to another, you'd give the pathname for the file to be copied followed by the pathname for the directory to which the file is to be copied:

`%cp temp News/notes`

4. If the command has option switches, include them as appropriate. Note that Unix command options begin with a hyphen (-) rather than the forward slash (/) used with DOS. Table 6-2 lists some sample Unix commands.

INTERNET HOW-TO

COMMAND	PATHNAME(S)	OPTION(S)	COMPLETE COMMAND	PURPOSE
cat	mytext		cat mytext	Displays the "mytext" file in home directory
cp	/usr/lib/news/active temp		cp /usr/lib/news/active/temp	Copies "active" file in /usr/lib/news directory to the name "temp" in home directory
ls	Mail	-l	ls -l Mail	Lists files in Mail directory in home directory, showing length and other information
ls	.nn	-a	ls -a .nn	Lists all files in .nn subdirectory of the home directory (including hidden files)
man	cat		man cat	Shows the online manual for the cat command

Table 6-2 Some sample Unix commands

5. Once you've typed your complete command, press (ENTER) and the system will process the command.

How It Works

The Unix shell *parses* your command, breaking it down to the component bits of information. Each command is actually a separate little program (either built into the shell or existing as a separate file on disk). When you press (ENTER) the shell runs the program and sends it your file or pathnames and option switches as "command line parameters."

Comment

There are basically two kinds of error messages you can get after entering a command. The first kind is a syntax error (for example, you needed to have a pathname and didn't supply one, or you used an invalid command switch). The second is an error that occurs when the command tries to execute and finds a problem, such as the file you specified not being found on the disk. Table 6-3 lists some of the common error messages and what they mean.

6 BASIC FILE MANAGEMENT

ERROR MESSAGE	MEANING
Cannot open <filename>	You specified a file that doesn't exist, or typed the filename incorrectly.
Directory not empty	You tried to remove a directory that has files in it. You have to remove the files before you can remove the directory.
Illegal option	You used a command switch that doesn't exist for this command. This will be followed by a syntax statement showing which options are valid.
No such file or directory	You specified a file or directory that does not exist. Check to make sure you've used the correct path.
Permission denied	You've tried to do something that you don't have permission to do, such as deleting a system file or perhaps working with a file in another user's directory.
Target temp must be a directory	You tried to copy several files. You specified a file for the destination, but the destination has to be a directory.

Table 6-3 Some common Unix error messages

6.2 HOW DO I...
Get help for a Unix command?

COMPLEXITY: EASY

Problem
Unix commands can have a variety of command options. If you're having trouble using a command, or are looking for a way to apply a command to solving a particular problem, you may want to read the online manual entry for that command.

Technique
You can use the man command to display the online Unix manual entry for a particular command. You can also save the manual entry in a file for later reading or printing.

Steps
1. Type `man`, followed by the command name, and press (ENTER):

```
% man cat
```

You will see the first page of the manual entry for the command:

```
cat(1)                      User Commands                      cat(1)

NAME
     cat - concatenate and display files

SYNOPSIS
     cat [ -bnsuvet ] filename...

AVAILABILITY
     SUNWcsu
```

Continued on next page

INTERNET HOW-TO

Continued from previous page

```
DESCRIPTION
     cat reads each filename in sequence and  writes  it  on  the
     standard output.  Thus:

          example% cat filename

     prints filename on your terminal, and:

          example% cat filename1 filename2 >filename3

--More--(11%)
```

The main things to look at in the manual entry are the "synopsis," which lists the switches and parameters (filenames, and so on) that you can use with the command, and the "description," which summarizes what the command does, and usually includes an example or two.

2. To save a manual entry to a file, type `man`, the command name, `>`, and a filename. For example:

```
% man cat > cat.man
```

This command takes the manual entry and redirects it to the file whose name you gave. (The > symbol in Unix, as in DOS, means to put the output of the preceding command or program in the specified file.)

3. You can also search for commands by keyword. An easy way to do this is to type `apropos` followed by the keyword. For example, to find all commands that have something to do with terminals, type

```
%apropos terminal
resize          resize (1)       - utility to set TERMCAP and terminal settings t
o current window size
5A(189)         C-Kermit (1)     - communications software for serial and network
 connections: file transfer, terminal connection, character-set translation, and
 script programming
C-Kermit        C-Kermit (1)     - communications software for serial and network
 connections: file transfer, terminal connection, character-set translation, and
 script programming
terminal        terminal (1)     - specify the terminal emulation you would like
 to use
xbin            xbin (1)         - convert BinHex file to binary before downloadi
ng to MacTerminal
cbreak          curs_inopts (3x) - curses terminal input option control routi
nes
```

The display isn't well formatted, and it will probably list a number of commands that are mainly of interest to programmers. But if you browse the descriptions and find a command that you think might do the job, use the man command to get the documentation, and try it out!

How It Works
Unix comes with an online manual that has an entry for each command, giving a description, summary of syntax, listing of command options, and miscellaneous notes. The man command fetches the manual entry for the command you specify.

Comment
Don't neglect other possible sources of help on your system. Sometimes typing `help` will give you a list of commands or other topics, and you can select an item from that list to get more information. The availability and nature of such help systems varies.

6.3 HOW DO I...
List a directory?

COMPLEXITY EASY

Problem
Often you'll need to know what files are stored in a particular directory, or want to find out whether a particular file is there. For example, after transferring files to your home directory via ftp (see Chapter 7), you may need to check the filenames before downloading the files.

Technique
You use the ls (list) command to list the files in a directory. Conceptually, this command works much like DIR in DOS. Before you can use ls and many other commands successfully, you need to know how directories work in a Unix system. As with DOS and other operating systems, a Unix system has many directories containing files that the system or its users are using to store programs or data.

Figure 6-1 shows an example "file tree" of directories on a typical Unix system. The top, or highest part of the tree, is called the *root* (for obscure reasons computer trees are upside down). The root directory contains a number of main directories such as "bin" and "lib" that hold programs and files needed by the system. The "usr" directory usually contains programs and other files that have been added on to those distributed with Unix itself.

As the tree diagram shows, the usr directory in turn has three subdirectories: games, mail, and news. The news directory has several individual files (active, newsgroups, and subscriptions). Note that any directory can contain more directories, files, or both. Obviously the actual directories on your system are likely to be different (your system may not have any games, for example).

When you specify the location of a directory or file in the Unix file system you use a *pathname* (sometimes just called a *path*). Figure 6-2 shows a typical path. Note that forward slashes (/) separate the levels of the file tree: the first slash represents the root, followed by the usr directory, another slash separator, then the lib directory, and so on down to newsgroups, which is a file. By comparing the tree diagram in Figure 6-1 with the pathname in Figure 6-2, you can quickly see how the pathname shows the relationship between directories and the location of the newsgroups file.

One important thing to remember is that Unix, unlike DOS, is *case-sensitive*. This means that the names "Mail" and "mail" do not refer to the same directory or file.

INTERNET HOW-TO

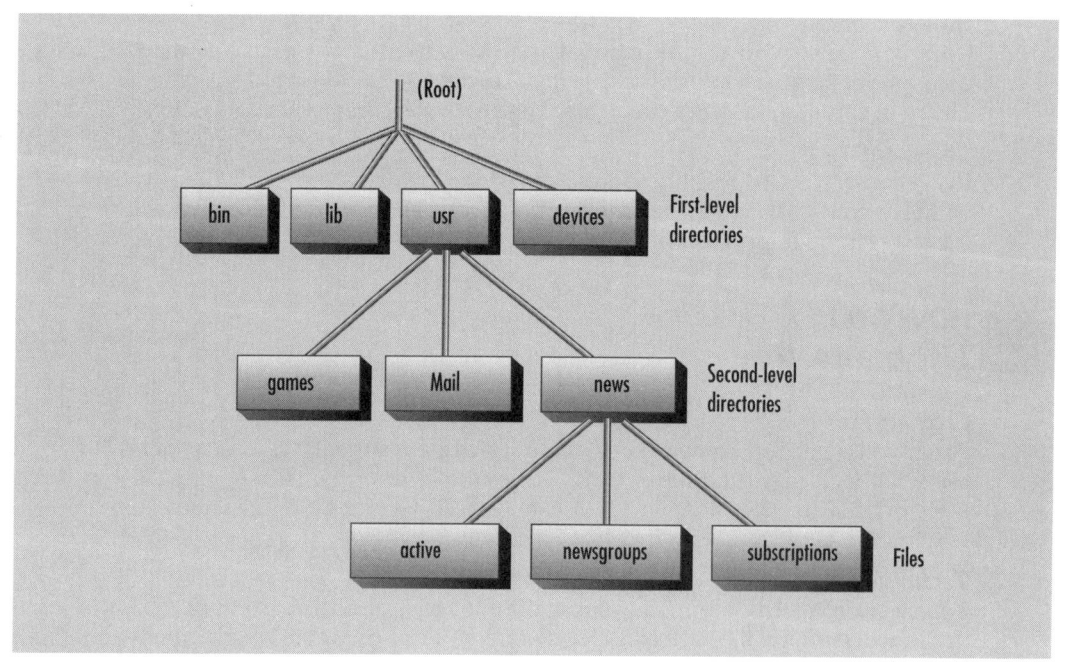

Figure 6-1 File system tree

Steps

1. Type `ls` followed by the name of the directory you want to see. If you want to see the current directory, just type ls alone. If you want to see a directory that is *not* a subdirectory of the current directory, type the complete pathname. For example

`% ls`

shows the current directory (which will be your home directory unless you've changed directories). This command,

`%ls Mail`

shows the Mail subdirectory of the current directory, and

`%ls /usr/news`

shows the news subdirectory of the usr directory, using a path that starts with the root.

2. You will see a list of files in the directory. For example, here is the contents of the Mail directory on the author's system:

```
%ls Mail
art         fugie       hudu            matisse     rlo
cloclo      gnn-list    important       mitch       scalamar
dao         gnnlist     jerod23         mrw         test
djheydt     heidib      mail-server     received    tmi
dvb         hrh         mailer-daemon   reply
```

6 🌐 BASIC FILE MANAGEMENT

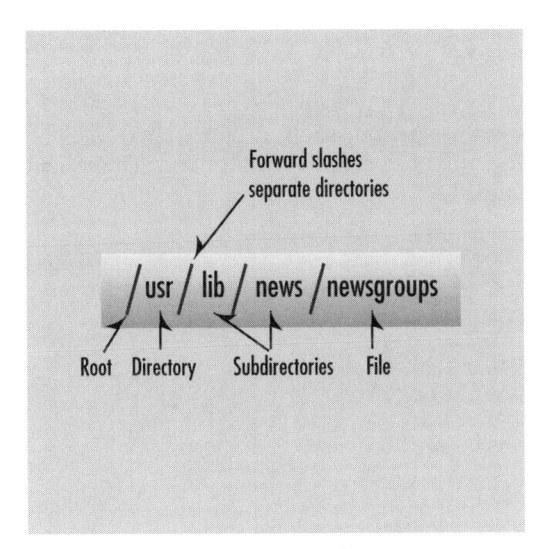

Figure 6-2 Constructing a pathname

3. One drawback of this compact format is that you can't tell whether a given item is a file or a subdirectory. You can get more information in the listing by adding the -l switch to your ls command:

```
%ls -l
drwxr-xr-x   2 hrh    well    512 Jan  3 10:25 Mail
drwxr-xr-x   3 hrh    well    512 Dec 16 00:11 News
drwxr-xr-x   2 hrh    well    512 Dec  6 10:55 corres
drwxr-xr-x   2 hrh    well    512 Jan  2 13:57 docs
-rw-------   1 hrh    well    176 Jan  5 10:43 fal01.mov
drwxr-xr-x   2 hrh    well    512 Jan  2 13:58 games
drwxr-xr-x   2 hrh    well    512 Jan  5 11:26 misc
-rw-r--r--   1 hrh    well    642 Jan  4 00:58 predict
-rw-r--r--   1 hrh    well    434 Jan  1 16:14 xmodem.log
```

Here, since we didn't specify a directory, the listing is of the current directory. The -l switch changes the format so that each entry begins with a series of symbols. When the first symbol is a d, it means that this entry is a directory rather than a file. (The other entries relate to who has permission to do what with the file, as you will see in How-To 6.17.)

In addition to these special symbols, you get the following information in the -l format listing:

➤ The number of "links" to the file (not important for beginning users).
➤ The person and group who "own" the file. This can affect who has permission to delete or change the file.
➤ The size of the file in bytes. This can help you prioritize files for removal or downloading to save disk space.

INTERNET HOW-TO

➤ The date the file was created or last changed.
➤ The name of the file.

4. Some programs create files that begin with a period, such as .elm. These files are called *hidden* files because they aren't shown by the default ls command. To see such files, add the -a option to your ls command:

```
well% ls -al
total 226
drwx--x--x  10 hrh     well     2560 Jan  5 12:33 .
drwxr-sr-x   7 root    sys       512 Oct 27 12:17 ..
-rw-r--r--   1 hrh     well      577 Dec 16 23:34 .article
-rw-r--r--   1 hrh     well      282 Oct 25 23:24 .cflist
-rw-r--r--   1 hrh     well       28 Jun 15  1989 .cfonce
-rw-r--r--   1 hrh     well        9 Oct 22  1992 .cfrc
-rw-r--r--   1 hrh     well       41 Nov 18 11:15 .cshrc
drwx------   2 hrh     well      512 Dec 23 10:20 .elm
-rw-r--r--   1 hrh     well       19 Nov 20  1986 .exrc
-rw-r--r--   1 hrh     well        0 Jul 17 11:34 .gopherrc
-rw-r--r--   1 hrh     well       12 Oct 26 10:26 .hushlogin
-rw-------   1 hrh     well        0 Jan  5 10:45 .inbox
-rw-r--r--   1 hrh     well       85 Mar 16  1990 .lib
-rw-r--r--   1 hrh     well      195 Dec  4 11:07 .login
-rw-r--r--   1 hrh     well      229 Nov  2 01:19 .login.bak
-rw-r--r--   1 hrh     well       45 Nov  3 19:12 .login.publicbak
-rw-r--r--   1 hrh     well     4120 Aug  6  1990 .mailrc
-rw-r--r--   1 hrh     well      610 Nov 29 15:29 .netplan
-rw-r--r--   1 hrh     well        0 Dec 22 21:20 .news_time
-rw-r--r--   1 hrh     well    69644 Jan  1 11:32 .newsrc
drwxr-xr-x   2 hrh     well      512 Jan  1 11:32 .nn
-rw-r--r--   1 hrh     well      167 Jul 10  1990 .oldlogin
-rwxr-xr-x   1 hrh     well      185 Jul 10  1990 .oldprofile
-rw-r--r--   1 hrh     well      610 Nov 28  1989 .plan
-rw-r--r--   1 hrh     well      609 Nov 28  1989 .planak
-rw-r--r--   1 hrh     well        0 Jan 19  1987 .pnewsexpert
-rwxr-xr-x   1 hrh     well      210 Dec  4 11:06 .profile
wxr-xr-x     2 hrh     well      512 Jan  3 10:25 Mail
drwxr-xr-x   3 hrh     well      512 Dec 16 00:11 News
drwxr-xr-x   2 hrh     well      512 Dec  6 10:55 corres
drwxr-xr-x   2 hrh     well      512 Jan  2 13:57 docs
-rw-------   1 hrh     well      176 Jan  5 10:43 fal01.mov
drwxr-xr-x   2 hrh     well      512 Jan  2 13:58 games
drwxr-xr-x   2 hrh     well      512 Jan  5 11:26 misc
-rw-r--r--   1 hrh     well      642 Jan  4 00:58 predict
-rw-r--r--   1 hrh     well      434 Jan  1 16:14 xmodem.log
```

Since the period comes before the letter *a* in the sort sequence, all the hidden files are listed first. Most of these files are used for keeping track of user settings for various programs. The .profile, .login, and .cshrc files establish settings when your shell first runs. See How-To 6.7 for more details.

6 BASIC FILE MANAGEMENT

How It Works
Each directory has a list of the files that it contains. The ls command goes through this list and displays the filenames.

Comment
You can restrict your listing to a subset of the files in the directory by using wildcards. For example, the command

```
ls *.Z
```

will list only files with the extension Z (which happen to be compressed files).

6.4 HOW DO I...
Change the current directory?

COMPLEXITY EASY

Problem
When you log onto your Internet site you will be in your home directory. Sometimes it will be more convenient to work from the vantage point of a different directory. For example, if you are copying several files from a different directory such as /usr/lib/news to your home directory, it may be easier to change to that directory so you don't have to type all those long pathnames.

Technique
You use the cd command followed by the name of the directory to change to. This directory becomes the new current directory, and subsequent commands will default to that directory.

Steps
1. Type `cd` followed by the name of the directory you want to change to. If the directory isn't in your current directory you'll need to use a pathname:

```
%cd /usr/lib/news
```

2. The directory you've changed to becomes your new current directory. You can verify the current directory by typing `pwd` ("print working directory") and pressing ENTER:

```
% pwd
/usr/lib/news
```

3. You can now type the name of any file in the new directory without using pathnames, and refer to any subdirectory with just the directory name. You would now have to type the full pathname to refer to your home directory, except that there's a shortcut. You can use $HOME in place of the path of your home directory. Thus to copy the "groups" file to your home directory when your current directory is /usr/lib/news, you can type,

```
%cp groups $HOME
```

and the shell will substitute the actual path of your home directory for $HOME.

How It Works
As with DOS, Unix always has a *pointer* to a current directory. This directory is the default and can be referred to without adding pathnames to your filenames.

INTERNET HOW-TO

Comment
Get in the habit of checking your current location before issuing commands to copy, delete, or move files.

6.5 HOW DO I... Read a text file?

COMPLEXITY EASY

Problem
It's easy to end up with a large number of text files such as news articles, mail messages, instructions for running programs, manual entries, and so on. Sometimes you may want to read enough of a file to identify its contents. Other times, you might want to read a short text file and dispose of it without having to download it to your PC.

Technique
The command you choose depends on your purpose. You can read a file one screen at a time, or you can have the file scroll continuously on your terminal while you stop or start the display when desired. You can also get a quick look at the first few lines of a file in order to identify its contents.

Steps

1. Type `more` followed by `<`, a space, and the name of the file you wish to view:

```
%more < /usr/lib/news/newsgroups
```

2. You will see the first screen of text:

```
ba.announce            Announcements of general interest to all readers. (Moder
ated)
ba.bicycles            Bicycling in and around the Bay Area.
ba.broadcast           Bay Area TV/Radio issues.
ba.dance               Discussion about local dance events.
ba.food                Bay Area restaurants and eating places.
ba.general             Announcements of general interest to all readers.
ba.helping-hand        Volunteer/Donor Action newsgroup. (Moderated)
ba.internet            Discussions about Bay Area Internet connectivity.
ba.jobs.contract       Issues involving contract employment.
ba.jobs.misc           Discussions about the job market in the Bay Area.
ba.jobs.offered        Job Postings in the Bay Area.
ba.market.computers    For Sale/Wanted: Computers and software.
ba.market.housing      For Sale/Rent/Wanted: Housing, Land, roommates.
ba.market.misc         For Sale/Wanted: Miscellaneous.
ba.market.vehicles     For Sale/Wanted: Autos, cycles, trucks, etc.
ba.motorcycles         Bay area motorcycle issues.
ba.motss               Newsgroup for Bay Area motss'ers.
ba.mountain-folk       Living in the hills and mountains around the Bay Area.
ba.music               Musical events in the Bay Area.
ba.news                General issues of 'ba' Usenet administration.
ba.news.config         Announcements and discussion of Bay Area connectivity.
--More--
```

Press (SPACEBAR) to see the next screen of text. You can also go back to a previous screen or search for particular text. Table 6-4 shows commands you can use at the More prompt.

Note that many commands can be preceded by a number for the times they are to be repeated. For example, pressing (3) and then (SPACEBAR) will move you forward by three screens of text.

Sometimes a command will queue up several files for you to view with more. The "forward a file" and "backward a file" commands can be useful for switching between several files.

3. If you wish to have the text scroll continuously rather than a screen at a time, type c a t followed by the filename. For example, to see the "message of the day" on many systems you can type

```
% cat /etc/motd
Sun Microsystems Inc.    SunOS 5.3     Generic September 1993

You own your own words. This means that you are responsible for the words
that you post on the WELL and that reproduction of those words without
your permission in any medium outside of the WELL's conferencing system
may be challenged by you, the author.

# The WELL was down from approx. 1:45pm Jan 4th until 6am Jan 5th due to a
# serious disk crash.  We have replaced the disk that failed. No user files
# were lost.   Some systems (notably USENET) are still being worked on.
```

The text will scroll continuously. On most systems you can stop the flow of text by pressing (CTRL)-(S) and resume it by pressing (CTRL)-(Q).

4. The cat command is particularly handy for capturing a text file without having to formally download it. Simply turn on your communication software's file log or file capture facility, enter the cat command, and then close your log or capture file. Note

TO DO THIS...	PRESS OR TYPE THIS
Display current filename and line number	:f
Display the next page of text	(SPACEBAR)
End the file display	(q) or (Q)
Find next line containing specified text	(/)<text>
Get a help screen of commands used with more	(?)
Go back to the previous page of text	(B)
Go to next file	:n
Go to previous file	:p
Repeat previous text search	(n)
Skip forward a specified number of lines	<number>s

Table 6-4 Some commands at the More prompt

INTERNET HOW-TO

that no error checking is done on the text, so a wrong character or two might creep in if you have a bad connection.

5. Finally, you can ask for just the first few lines of a file by using the head command. Type `head` followed by the filename. This is handy when you just want to identify the contents of a file. For example:

```
% head /usr/lib/news/newsgroups
ba.announce          Announcements of general interest to all readers. (Moder
ated)
ba.bicycles          Bicycling in and around the Bay Area.
ba.broadcast         Bay Area TV/Radio issues.
ba.dance             Discussion about local dance events.
ba.food              Bay Area restaurants and eating places.
ba.general           Announcements of general interest to all readers.
ba.helping-hand      Volunteer/Donor Action newsgroup. (Moderated)
ba.internet          Discussions about Bay Area Internet connectivity.
ba.jobs.contract     Issues involving contract employment.
ba.jobs.misc         Discussions about the job market in the Bay Area.
```

How It Works

The cat, more, and head commands are actually very similar in their practical effects: they all take a file and start displaying it. Since no other destination is specified for the data, it goes to your terminal screen.

You can, however, send files to another destination, such as another file. This lets you combine two files. For example, the command

```
%cat article1 article2 > articles
```

combines the files article1 and article2 and sends the result to the articles file. The name "cat" is short for "concatenate" or combine. The earlier example actually "concatenates" a file with your terminal (which Unix also considers to be a file), thus displaying the text.

Comment

Some systems store outgoing text in a memory area called a buffer. In this case, you may not be able to interrupt the flow of text until the entire file is displayed. In such cases you are better off using the more or head command rather than cat, unless you are capturing the whole file to your PC's disk.

6.6 HOW DO I...
Edit a text file?

COMPLEXITY INTERMEDIATE

Problem

You probably already have experience editing short files on the Internet system. It is often easier to edit a short mail message or news article while sending mail or posting news, rather than preparing the material on your PC with a word processor or text editor and then pasting or uploading it.

There are several text editors in common use on Unix systems. As with Elm and nn, one had to be chosen for coverage because of space limitations—the vi editor. While vi isn't as intuitive as a modern mouse-driven editor, such as the MS-DOS Edit program or a word processor, it isn't hard to learn the basic commands for creating and editing text. Indeed, you've already seen how to use vi with mail messages (Chapter 3) and news articles (Chapter 4). This how-to takes a more systematic approach to using vi commands.

Technique

The vi editor is always in one of two modes, insert mode or command mode. In insert mode, whatever characters you type are added to the text file you are creating or editing. In command mode, whatever character you type is interpreted as a command to the editor. You press either (I) (insert text) or (A) (append text) to change from command mode to insert mode. While in insert mode, press (ESC) to go into command mode.

Steps

1. Type vi followed by the name of an existing file or the name of the file you wish to create. You start out in command mode. For example:

```
%vi jm.letter1
~
~
~
~
~
~
~
~
~
~
~
~jim.letter1" [New file]
```

(Some of the blank lines on the screen have been left out to save space.)

2. Press (A) and begin typing in your text. For example, the following might be the body of a mail message:

```
Jim, in answer to your last message:
I don't think it's a good idea to split the team up when we're just
starting to see some tangible results. At any rate, don't you think we
should ask the people for feedback first?
~
~
~
~
~
~
~
~
"jim.letter1" [New file]
```

3. To make corrections to existing text, enter command mode (by pressing (ESC)) and move the cursor to the point where you wish to change the text. Figure 6-3 shows

203

INTERNET HOW-TO

the keys you can use to move the cursor. Touch typists will probably find the (h), (j), (k), and (l) keys to be most handy, while others may prefer the arrow keys. (Note that the arrow keys may not work properly if you've specified the wrong terminal type or if your terminal emulation software is incomplete.)

4. If you are inserting text, press (i) and type the text. If you are adding text to the end of the file, press (A). You can also use the (o) or (O) keys to start entering text on a new blank line (see Figure 6-4).

5. Sometimes you'll need to delete or change existing text. Figure 6-5 shows the basic commands for deleting a character, word, line, sentence, or paragraph. You will find these commands to be very handy.

While cutting and pasting isn't as easy with vi as it is with a word processor, you can cut text by using one of the deletion commands, moving the cursor to the insertion point, and pressing (p) to paste the text. You can also copy text by pressing (y) (y) preceded by the number of lines to copy. Then move the cursor where you want the lines copied and press (p). Note that many vi commands can be preceded with the number of times you want the command to operate. For example, pressing (5) and then (d) (d) deletes five lines starting at the cursor position.

6. You can browse through text a screen (or a half screen) at a time. Figure 6-6 shows the keys for paging through text.

7. You can search for text by pressing (/), followed by the text to search for, and (ENTER). Use (?) instead of (/) to search backward (toward the beginning of the file). If the word or phrase you specify is found, the cursor will move to it.

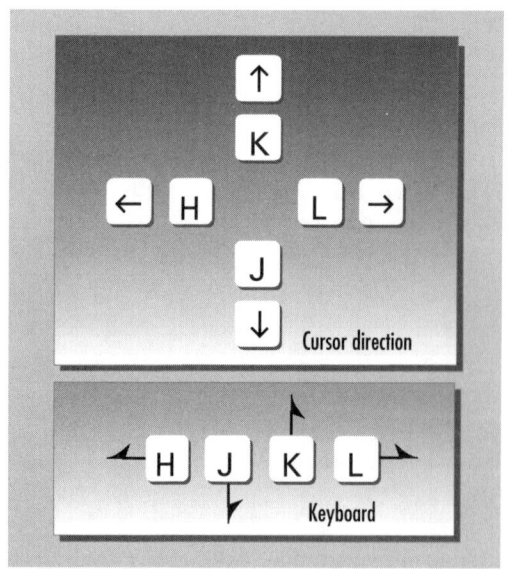

Figure 6-3 Moving the cursor in vi

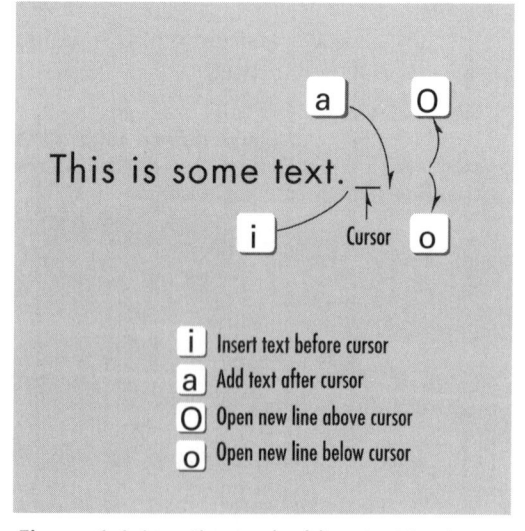

Figure 6-4 Inserting and adding text in vi

204

6 ⊕ BASIC FILE MANAGEMENT

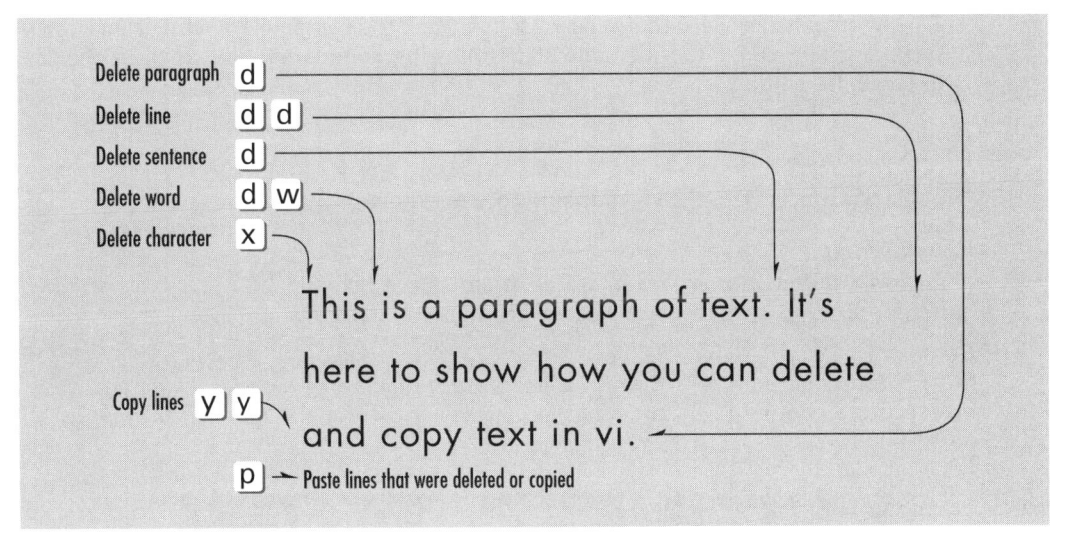

```
Delete paragraph   [d]
Delete line        [d][d]
Delete sentence    [d]
Delete word        [d][w]
Delete character   [x]

                   This is a paragraph of text. It's
                   here to show how you can delete
Copy lines [y][y]  and copy text in vi.
           [p] → Paste lines that were deleted or copied
```

Figure 6-5 Deleting text in vi

8. When you've finished working with your text file, type `:wq` to write the file to disk and quit vi. vi will display a message showing the name and length of the file saved:

`"jim.letter1" 5 lines, 219 characters`

If you want to throw away your changes and not save the file, type `:q!` instead.

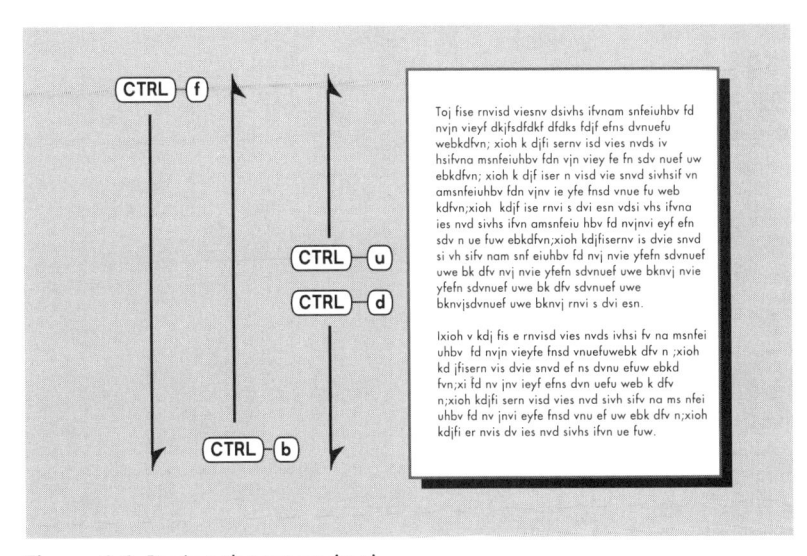

Figure 6-6 Paging the screen in vi

205

INTERNET HOW-TO

9. To edit an existing file, either type `vi` followed by the filename, or, while running vi, type `:r` followed by the filename. The following commands both load in the file letter.txt for editing.

```
vi letter.txt
:r letter.txt
```

Table 6-5 summarizes the vi commands discussed here.

How It Works

vi creates a buffer in memory in which it stores the text file, and it creates another buffer for text you have recently deleted. This lets you cut, copy, or paste text.

Comment

Most PC and Mac editors or word processors are "modeless"—you can always enter text or execute a command by pressing special keys or using the mouse and menus or

TO DO THIS...	PRESS OR TYPE THIS
Add text after cursor	`a`
Begin inserting text	`i`
Copy current line to buffer	`v` `v`
Delete character	`x`
Delete line	`d` `d`
Delete paragraph	`d` `}`
Delete sentence	`d` `)`
Delete word	`d` `w`
Move cursor down one line	`j` or `↓`
Move cursor left one space	`h` or `←`
Move cursor right one space	`l` or `→`
Move cursor up one line	`k` or `↑`
Open new line above cursor	`O`
Open new line below cursor	`o`
Paste line from buffer	`p`
Quit without saving file	`:q!`
Read in a file for editing	`:r`
Save file and quit	`:wq`
Scroll back a page	`CTRL`-`b`
Scroll back half a page	`CTRL`-`u`
Scroll forward a page	`CTRL`-`f`
Scroll forward half a page	`CTRL`-`d`

Note: Control-key commands can be entered in lower or upper case.

Table 6-5 Basic editing commands in vi

button bars. Thus, moving between command and insert modes in vi takes a little getting used to.

Sometimes an error (or system crash) may interrupt your work. The system will often manage to save the file into a temporary buffer file with a name such as "cbf1004". To recover and edit this file, start vi with the -r option and the name of the text file:

```
%vi -r cbf1004
```

6.7 HOW DO I...
Specify user settings?

COMPLEXITY: INTERMEDIATE

Problem
As you have seen in previous chapters, there are a number of system settings or variables that specify such things as what program you want to use for a text editor or pager. You may also want to have certain commands or programs run automatically each time you start your shell.

Technique
You use one of two special files to tell the system what settings or programs you want to use. (DOS users will recognize the similarity of this idea to the use of AUTOEXEC.BAT and CONFIG.SYS files.)

Steps
1. Determine which shell you are using. If your prompt is $, you are using the Bourne or Korn shell and will use the .profile file to establish your settings. If your prompt is %, you are running the C shell and you will use the .login file. (If your prompt has neither of these symbols in it you may be dealing with a front end program or with an exotic shell—contact your system support person for help.)

2. Run an editor such as vi and enter the name of the appropriate file (.profile or .login.) For example:

```
% vi .login
```

(Note that this file probably already exists. If it doesn't, vi will create it when you save your edits.)

3. Add the appropriate lines to define variables or run programs. Here's an example:

```
% vi .profile
PATH=/usr/public/bin:$PATH ; export PATH
MANPATH=/usr/public/man:$MANPATH ; export MANPATH
TERM=vt100 ; export TERM
EDITOR=/usr/ucb/vi ; export EDITOR
stty erase '^h'
stty kill
umask 022
mesg y
```

Note the variety of things specified:

INTERNET HOW-TO

- ➤ The search path is used by the system to find programs (another concept that's very familiar to DOS users). The path here includes the /usr/public directory (containing user-written software). The MANPATH variable works similarly, except it specifies that the man command should also check the additional directory for manual entries.
- ➤ The next lines specify the terminal emulation (which you learned about in Chapter 2) and the preferred text editor.
- ➤ You can also specify some commands that are to be run automatically at startup. The stty command sets certain terminal characteristics. Unless you have trouble with the defaults, you should leave such commands alone; the stty command is beyond the scope of this chapter. The umask command sets default file permissions (see How-To 6.17). The mesg y command says that you're willing to accept interactive talk-type messages from other users (see Chapter 5).

4. When you've made your changes, write the file to disk and exit the editor (:wq command in vi).

How It Works

When the shell starts up it sets the variables you've specified. Many programs (including mailers and news readers) check these variables to determine which pager you want to use to display text (most people use "more," but there are others, including one called "less"), and which editor you want to use to create new messages or articles.

The shell also executes the various commands you've included, such as umask and mesg in the previous example. You can also specify utility programs that do useful things such as notifying you about new mail or news messages; these utilities are covered in the chapters on the appropriate topic.

Comment

The only major difference between the .login file and the .profile file used in the preceding example is in the specification in variables. The line in .profile,

```
TERM=vt100 ; export TERM
```

in .login becomes

```
setenv TERM vt100
```

It's a good idea to use the copy command (see the next how-to) to make a backup copy of the .profile or .login file before you edit the original. Also note that any new settings don't take effect until you restart the shell (which happens automatically next time you log in).

6.8 HOW DO I... Copy a file?

COMPLEXITY: EASY

Problem
There are two main reasons for copying a file on the Internet system. One is the usual need to make a backup of a file (such as your .profile or .login file) before editing it. Another frequent use of the copy command is to make a copy of a text file from elsewhere in the system so you can edit or print it. (For obvious reasons, you usually don't have permission to edit a file that isn't in your home directory or one of its subdirectories. Making a copy gives you a version that you can edit.)

Technique
You specify the file to be copied and the destination to copy it to. The destination can be another filename or the name of a directory.

Steps
1. Type `cp` and the name of the file to be copied. If the file isn't in your home directory, type the appropriate pathname.

2. Type the destination for the copy. If you specify a filename, the file will be copied to that name in your home directory. If you specify a directory, the file will keep its original name but be copied to that directory. Here are a few examples using the cp command. This command,

```
%cp temp Mail/bob.letter1
```

copies the temp file in the current directory to the bob.letter1 file in the Mail subdirectory. The next command,

```
%cp .profile .profile.back
```

makes a backup copy of the .profile file, assuming your current directory is your home directory. Finally,

```
%cp part1 part2 docs
```

copies the files part1 and part2 into the docs directory, where they'll retain the names part1 and part2. Note that if you copy more than one file, the last item on the command line must be the name of a directory.

3. As a shortcut, you can type . (period) to specify your current directory. For example, if your current directory is your home directory, you can type

```
%cp /usr/lib/news/newsgroups .
```

to copy the newsgroups file from the /usr/lib/news directory to your home directory.

4. Normally the cp command won't warn you if you are about to copy a file over an existing file. That is, if you type the command

```
%cp text text.bak
```

any existing text.bak file will be overwritten with the contents of the "text" file. You can have cp warn you about such situations by adding the -i switch:

INTERNET HOW-TO

```
%cp -i text text.bak
cp: overwrite text.bak (y/n)?
```

Press (y) and (ENTER) to go ahead with the copy. Press (n) and (ENTER) to cancel the copy.

5. If you want to copy everything in a directory to another directory, you can use the * (asterisk) wildcard. For example,

```
%cp * /backup
```

copies all the files in the current directory to the backup directory.

If you want to copy all the files in a directory *and all the subdirectories and their files as well*, add the -r option to your cp command:

```
%cp -r misc/* backup
```

This copies all the files and subdirectories in misc into the "backup" directory.

How It Works
The copy command creates an exact copy of the file you specify. You can use wildcards to copy groups of files, or add the -r option to copy whole directories and their contents, including subdirectories.

Comment
Since each additional copy of a file uses up more disk space, it's a good idea to house-clean periodically and get rid of unwanted copies.

Since the default cp command doesn't warn you about writing over existing files, either add the -i option or use ls to determine whether the destination file already exists.

6.9 HOW DO I...
Move or rename a file?

COMPLEXITY: EASY

Problem
As you acquire more kinds of files, you may wish to create a more elaborate structure of directories to keep them in. You may wish to move files to new locations that better reflect their function in your organization.

Technique
You use a simple command called mv that can move and/or rename a file.

Steps
1. Type `mv` followed by the old name of the file and the new name. (As usual, you must use pathnames if the old or new files aren't in the current directory.) For example,

```
%mv letter mary.060595
```

changes the name of the "letter" file to a more descriptive name that includes the recipient and date.

2. You can also move a file from one directory to another. This command

```
%mv letter corres
```

6 BASIC FILE MANAGEMENT

moves the "letter" file to the corres directory, retaining the name "letter."

3. You can combine the move and rename operations like this:

```
%mv letter corres/mary.060595
```

Here the file is both moved to the corres directory and renamed mary.060595.

How It Works
The mv command changes the name (and possibly location) of a file without making a copy of the data. The command simply changes the pointers in the directory entries as appropriate, without physically moving any data.

Comment
Users of recent versions of DOS have come to appreciate the convenience of the mv command, which is faster and more efficient than making a copy of a file and then deleting the original.

6.10 HOW DO I... *Compare two files?*

COMPLEXITY: EASY

Problem
After making copies and backups of your files, you may end up with two files that look like they have similar contents. (They could be two differently named files in the same directory, or two files with the same name in different directories.) The date and size information given in the ls display may help you determine which file is later (or more complete), but there's another way to quickly compare two files.

Technique
You can use the cmp (compare) command to compare two files and find out if they're different.

Steps
1. Type `cmp` followed by the names of the two files you are comparing. For example:

```
%cmp letter letter.bak
```

If the two files have the same contents, you'll see no message and the system prompt will appear. If the two files are different in any way, you'll see a message showing the first place at which the files do not correspond:

```
%cmp letter letter.bak
letter letter.bak differ: char 83, line 9
```

(Normally you won't care *where* the files differ, but only want to know that they are in fact different. In this case you may want to make a new backup with the cp command so that your backup will be up to date.)

How It Works
The cmp command simply reads the two files byte by byte. If it comes to a point where the bytes from the two files don't correspond, it tells you where the discrepancy was found.

INTERNET HOW-TO

Comment
Two text files might be *substantially* the same but differ in some minor way, such as an extra space or two. If the files aren't absolutely identical, cmp will report them as being different. If you add the -l option to the cmp command, cmp will report *each* difference it finds, which may help you see how similar the two files are. (Note however that if all the characters in one file have been displaced in relation to the other file, for example, by adding a space, you'll get screens and screens full of "difference" messages.)

Identifying and deleting unwanted duplicate files is a good way to reduce disk usage charges.

6.11 HOW DO I... *Delete a file?*

COMPLEXITY: EASY

Problem
When you know you aren't going to need a file again (or have downloaded the file to your PC), you'll probably want to delete the file. Eliminating unneeded files makes your file organization less cluttered, and may save disk storage charges.

Technique
Use the rm command and specify the file(s) you want removed. Make sure you are specifying a file that you really want to remove for good. (DOS users have become used to the "undelete" facility that can recover most accidentally deleted files if used quickly enough. While such utilities do exist on some Unix systems, they're still pretty rare. Unless you can persuade someone to restore the file from a backup tape, a file you've deleted from your Internet site's home directory is probably gone for good.)

Steps
1. Type `rm` followed by the name of the file to be removed. For example:

%rm old.letter

2. The file will be removed without any message, unless the file is write-protected (see How-To 6.17). In that case you will be prompted:

rm: test: override protection 444 (y/n)?

If you really did want to remove the file, press (y) and (ENTER); otherwise press (n) and (ENTER), and the file will not be removed.

How It Works
The rm command removes the directory entries for the file so that the data can no longer be accessed.

Comment
You can remove a group of files using wildcards. For example,

%rm *.doc

removes all files in the current directory that have the extension .doc, and

%rm *

6 ⊕ BASIC FILE MANAGEMENT

removes all files in the current directory. You can even add the -r option to remove all files in a directory and all its subdirectories. (Be *very* careful with that one!)

6.12 HOW DO I...
Make or remove a directory?

COMPLEXITY EASY

Problem
You probably already have several directories in your home directory. (For example, mail programs create a Mail directory, news programs a News directory, the nn news reader program creates a hidden .nn directory, and so on.) You may wish to create additional directories, such as an ftp directory to hold files you've received via ftp (see Chapter 7), or a docs directory to hold documents of various kinds. You may also want to remove directories for projects that are no longer active.

Technique
There are a pair of commands for manipulating directories: the mkdir command creates a directory, and the rmdir command removes one.

Steps
1. To create a directory, type `mkdir` followed by the directory name. (If you are creating a directory outside of the current directory, use the appropriate pathname.) For example, to create a docs directory, type

```
%mkdir docs
```

If you wanted to create a misc subdirectory inside the Mail directory, you could type

```
%mkdir Mail/misc
```

If there is no problem, mkdir simply creates the directory without giving any message. Note that a directory cannot have the same name as a file in the same location. For example, you can't make the Mail/misc directory if there's already a *file* called misc in the Mail directory.

2. To remove a directory, first use the ls command to see if there are any files in the directory. If there are, check the files to make sure you want to remove them. (You can use the more or cat command to check the contents of text files.)

```
% ls tempdir
temp1  temp2  temp3
```

3. Use the rm command to remove the existing files:

```
%rm tempdir/*
```

The / and wildcard (*) after the name of the directory tell rm to remove all the files.

4. Once the directory is empty, you can remove it:

```
%rmdir tempdir
```

Note that if your current directory doesn't contain the directory you want to remove, you should use the cd command to change to that directory first and then list and/or remove subdirectories:

INTERNET HOW-TO

```
%cd Mail
% ls corres
letter1  letter2  letter3
% rm corres/*
% rmdir corres
```

Alternatively, you can specify the full pathnames from your current location, like this:

```
% ls Mail/corres
letter1  letter 2  letter 3
% rm Mail/corres/*
% rmdir Mail/corres
```

How It Works
Directories, like files, are removed by deleting the information that the system uses to keep track of them. As with files, removed directories usually can't be restored.

Comment
If you try to remove a directory and keep getting the "Directory not empty" message, use ls with the -a option to see if any hidden files are lurking there. If so, make sure they aren't needed by a program you're using. When in doubt, leave them alone and keep the directory.

6.13 HOW DO I...
Work with a group of files using wildcards?

COMPLEXITY INTERMEDIATE

Problem
It's often faster to work with a group of similar files in one operation. For example, you may want to copy all files with the .txt extension to the docs directory, or delete all files that have a .tmp extension.

Technique
You have already seen some examples using wildcards (as they are known to DOS users). This how-to covers the use of these special characters more systematically.

The basic technique is to specify all files that match a certain pattern (or, if appropriate, simply "all files").

Steps
1. Enter the command name and any options, for example:

```
ls -a
```

2. Type the part of the filename that you want all the files you will be working with to have in common. For example, if you want to list a group of numbered letters (letter1, letter2, and so on), type

```
Letter
```

3. If you want to match all files whose names start with the characters you typed, add * to the end of the name. For example,

```
%ls letter*
```

214

matches all files beginning with "letter," such as letter1, letter2, or letter.to.joe.

4. If you want to match only files that have the specified number of characters (regardless of what those characters might be), use ?. For example,

`%ls letter?`

will match any file beginning with "letter" and having a single additional character, regardless of what that character might be.

The preceding command will match letter1, letter3, or lettera. It won't match "letter" because it lacks the additional character. It also won't match either letter23 or letter.to.joe, because these names have more than one additional character following "letter."

Similarly,

`cp letter??`

will copy all files that begin with "letter" and that have exactly two additional characters.

How It Works
The shell "expands" the name you specify with wildcards, replacing it with a list of all the matching files. The shell then passes this list to the command (such as ls, cat, or cp) for processing.

Comment
Before using a wildcard with an operation that might destroy data, for example a copy (cp) or remove (rm) command, it's a good idea to try it out with ls first. ls will list all the matching files, and you can verify that none of them are files that you don't want to be operated on. You can then repeat the rm or cp command with the same wildcard specification.

6.14 HOW DO I...
Find a particular file?

COMPLEXITY | INTERMEDIATE

Problem
There are tens of thousands of files on the typical Unix system. You may know what's in your home directory, but how do you find the location of a file that's somewhere else in the system?

Technique
There are several commands you can use to search for files. This how-to starts with the simplest (and most specialized) and then moves on to the general-purpose "find" command.

Steps
1. If the file you are looking for is either a program or the manual entry for a program, type `whereis` followed by the program or command name. For example, to find the ftp program, type

INTERNET HOW-TO

```
well% whereis ftp
ftp: /usr/bin/ftp /usr/ucb/ftp /usr/local/bin/ftp /usr/man/man1/ftp.1
```

Sometimes, as in this case, there are several directories listed. These may contain the same program or different versions. The last directory listed gives the file containing the manual for ftp.

2. You can now use cd and ls to explore these directories for files of interest, such as program documentation. The whereis command is also useful for finding the pathname of a program that isn't in your default search path, so you can execute the program.

3. If the file you're looking for isn't a program or manual file, you can use the find command to look for it. Type `find -name` followed by the name of the file you are looking for. (You can use wildcards if you aren't sure of the correct name.) For example,

```
%find -name startup*
```

looks for files beginning with the name "startup." Note that this form of the find command starts with your current directory and works its way down through any subdirectories. It will list the pathnames of any matching files, for example:

```
./startup
./startup2
```

4. Often, you'll want the search to start somewhere other than in the current directory. For example, if you have no idea at all where a file is on the system, you can type a command like this,

```
%find / -name startup
```

which will look for a file called startup anywhere in the system, starting with the root directory. (This might take awhile!)

How It Works

The find command goes through the directory structure looking for matching files. This command has many more powerful features than those shown here: it can find files by date, length, and other variables. It can also automatically operate on the files it finds (such as printing them or removing them). If you're interested in these features, see a Unix manual.

Comment

You may get messages saying that you don't have permission for the find command to examine certain directories. (If you don't have read access to a directory, you can't look in it.)

6.15 HOW DO I...
Find text in a file?

COMPLEXITY INTERMEDIATE

Problem

It can be tedious to search through a long file to see if it has the text you're looking for.

Technique
You can load a file into an editor such as vi and use its search functions to find the text you want. However, it may be more convenient to use a utility command called grep to search for text in a file.

Steps
1. Type `grep` followed by the word you're looking for. (If you're looking for a whole phrase, put it in quotation marks.) For example, type

```
%grep disk
```

   to look for the word "disk", or

```
%grep "disk drive"
```

   to look for the phrase "disk drive".

2. Type the name of the file you want to be searched for the text. You can use wildcards to specify more than one file. For example,

```
%grep disk technotes
```

   or

```
%grep disk notes*
```

   The latter looks for the word "disk" in all files whose name begins with "notes".

3. If grep finds matching lines, they are displayed. For example:

```
well% grep aids /usr/lib/news/newsgroups
hiv.aids.issues        Issues on AIDS.
hiv.aidsweekly         Something weekly on AIDS.
hiv.int-conf-aids.sixth The 6th International Conference on AIDS.
hiv.int-conf-aids.sixth The 6th International Conference on AIDS.
hiv.oz-aids-marc       ? on AIDS.
hiv.oz.aids.marc       ? for HIV.
sci.med.aids           AIDS: treatment, pathology/biology of HIV, prevention. (
Moderated)
```

4. You can use the * character to search for partial words, for example,

```
%grep comput* newsnotes
```

   matches all lines that contain the words computer, computing, or computation.

How It Works
grep actually works with a variety of special patterns called *regular expressions*, which you can read about in any Unix book. The simple examples above are enough to get you started, however.

Comment
You may find it helpful to add the -n option to your grep command. This tells grep to print the number of each matching line. You can use this number with many text editors to take you to that line and let you read the surrounding text. (For example, if grep tells you the matching line is number 238, you can run vi with the file and then type `:/238` to go to that line.)

6.16 HOW DO I... *Check my disk space?*

COMPLEXITY: EASY

Problem
As mentioned before, files tend to pile up on your system. On some systems, you are given a space quota, and the system will simply refuse to let you store any more files when that quota is exceeded. Other systems will let you pile up megabytes of files but send you a bill at the end of the month (ouch!). Therefore, it's a good idea to periodically check the amount of disk space you're using.

Technique
A simple command called du (disk usage) will give you the information you need.

Steps
1. To find out your total disk usage, make sure you're in your home directory (not a subdirectory). You can use the pwd command to verify the current directory:

```
% pwd
/home/h/r/hrh
% du
12      ./.nn
170     ./Mail
52      ./.elm
22      ./misc/backup
2       ./misc/tempdir
46      ./misc
4       ./games
10      ./docs
22      ./backup/misc/backup
44      ./backup/misc
22      ./backup/backup
94      ./backup
22      ./News/comp/unix
24      ./News/comp
46      ./News
6       ./corres
676
```

2. du lists all of your subdirectories, the amount of space used by each, and the total space used (676 in this case). The big question is of course "676 *what?*" The answer depends on what kind of Unix your system is running. If it is running System V (which you can tell from a mention of System V or a blurb about AT&T when you log on), each of these units represents 512 bytes, or half a kilobyte (K). This means that if you have a disk quota of 512K, you can have up to 1024 (512 * 2) of these units worth of files before you're in trouble.

3. BSD Unix systems give the total in 1K rather than in 512-byte blocks. Thus, the same listing given above would say 338 rather than 676. On System V Unix you can add the -k option to your du command to get it to use 1K units:

```
% du -k
```

```
  6    ./.nn
 85    ./Mail
 26    ./.elm
 11    ./misc/backup
  1    ./misc/tempdir
 23    ./misc
  2    ./games
  5    ./docs
 11    ./backup/misc/backup
 22    ./backup/misc
 11    ./backup/backup
 47    ./backup
 11    ./News/comp/unix
 12    ./News/comp
 23    ./News
  3    ./corres
338
```

How It Works
The du command goes through your home directory and its subdirectories and adds up the total bytes used by all the files, as recorded in the individual directory entries.

Comment
If you're not sure what your system's policy is about disk usage, contact a system support person.

6.17 HOW DO I...
Keep my files private?

COMPLEXITY INTERMEDIATE

Problem
You may have private or sensitive information in your home directory, such as personal mail messages or information about work-related projects. You want to make sure that other people can't read or delete those files.

Technique
Unix has something of a reputation for being lax in its security. Actually, most systems today take steps to help you keep information in your personal directory private. Many systems set the default permissions such that all files you create in your home directory or its subdirectories are readable only by yourself. Even systems that don't go this far normally make sure that your waiting mail messages and the contents of your Mail directory are private.

You can't, however, automatically assume that your site has the level of security you need. You therefore have to learn a bit about how Unix handles access permissions for files. You can then set things up so that a particular file (or all files) are protected from reading or deletion by outsiders.

Steps
1. Use the ls command with the -l option to list the files in your home directory. For example:

INTERNET HOW-TO

```
well% ls -l
total 48
drwxr-xr-x   2 hrh      well        512 Jan  5 12:56 Mail
drwxr-xr-x   3 hrh      well        512 Dec 16 00:11 News
drwxr-xr-x   4 hrh      well        512 Jan  5 15:21 backup
drwxr-xr-x   2 hrh      well        512 Dec  6 10:55 corres
drwxr-xr-x   2 hrh      well        512 Jan  2 13:57 docs
-rw-------   1 hrh      well        176 Jan  5 10:43 fal01.mov
drwxr-xr-x   2 hrh      well        512 Jan  2 13:58 games
-rw-r--r--   1 hrh      well      13111 Jan  5 12:55 ls.man
drwxr-xr-x   4 hrh      well        512 Jan  5 15:29 misc
-rw-r--r--   1 hrh      well        642 Jan  4 00:58 predict
-rw-r--r--   1 hrh      well        434 Jan  5 16:17 xmodem.2
-rw-r--r--   1 hrh      well        434 Jan  1 16:14 xmodem.log
```

Notice the first column in the listing. This part of each entry says (in a cryptic way) whether you, members of your group, or users in general can read or write a file or execute a program. For example, note the entry for the Mail directory:

```
drwxr-xr-x   2 hrh      well        512 Jan  5 12:56 Mail
```

The first d says that this is a directory. The next three characters, rwx, mean that you have permission to read, write, or execute this directory. This means you can list or delete the directory, or add files to it. The remaining two sets of three characters each have r-x. This means that members of your group and users in general can read (list) this directory, but they can't write (change) it. This makes sense, since you don't want people deleting your files or directories!

2. Now let's look at the files *in* the Mail directory:

```
well% ls -l Mail
total 168
-rw-------   1 hrh      well       3359 Oct 28 23:53 art
-rw-------   1 hrh      well       5067 Jan  2 13:49 cloclo
-rw-------   1 hrh      well        640 Dec 19 10:53 dao
-rw-------   1 hrh      well       1705 Nov 22 21:46 djheydt
-rw-------   1 hrh      well       1109 Dec 20 10:40 dvb
-rw-------   1 hrh      well       4653 Dec  8 18:25 fugie
```

Notice that these files (which are message folders used by Elm) allow you to read or write, but they don't allow anyone else to do anything at all with these files. Again, this is appropriate, unless you like to have people rummaging in your mailbox!

3. Compare the listings of files in your home and Mail directories with those shown here. If you find that files (in your Mail directory or elsewhere) have a permission entry like this,

```
-rw-rw-rw-  1 hrh      well       3359 Oct 28 23:53 art
```

or anything that indicates that other people can read or write (delete) them, you'll probably want to tighten up your security.

4. The easiest way to lock up your files and directories from prying eyes is to add the umask command to your .profile or .login file, as appropriate. Follow the umask

command with three digits that control the permissions that you, people in your group, or others will have concerning this file. Thus the command

umask 022

means that any files you create will never be writable (able to be deleted or changed) by other users. A umask of 066 is more strict: it ensures that no one can read the files, either. To specify the permissions to be denied, use 1 for execute permission, 2 for write permission, and 4 for read permission. These can be combined; for example, 007 means that users not in your group have no permissions whatsoever with regard to your files.

5. The umask setting affects only newly created files. To set permissions for an already existing file, use the chmod command. Type `chmod` followed by the type of user and the kind of permission you want to grant. For example,

%chmod 0600

means that you have permission to read or write the file, but no one else has any permissions, while chmod 0644 means you can read or write to the file, but others can only read it. Note that chmod and umask are opposite: chmod specifies what permissions are to be granted, while umask specifies permissions that are to be denied.

You can also specify permissions with chmod like this,

%chmod o-w

which means take away write permission from others; or this,

%chmod u+x

which means "give myself permission to execute this file." (Minus means "take away" and plus means "add".)

How It Works

Unix keeps a set of ten "flags" in each directory entry. The first flag says whether the file is really a directory. The other nine flags break down into three groups of three, and refer to the read, write, and execute permissions (r, w, and x). Read permission, as the name implies, is the ability to display the contents of the file. Write permission is the ability to change or delete the file. Execute permission is the ability to run the file (assuming it's a program) or to list it (if it's a directory).

The three groups refer to the user (u), group (g), and others (o). The "user" is the person issuing the commands. The "group" is a group of people who share control of some project (groups are set up by the system administrator). "Others" means all other users.

The umask command "masks out" (removes) specified permissions at the time a file is created. The chmod command changes the permissions for a specific file.

Comment

If you're not sure what the security defaults are on your system, ask the system administrator. Changing permissions incorrectly can cause certain programs to fail because they can't access your files.

INTERNET HOW-TO

6.18 HOW DO I...
Learn more about Unix?

COMPLEXITY: EASY

Problem
You have now learned most of what an average Internet user needs to know about Unix. Suppose you find you need to know more for some particular application, or you're just curious?

Technique
There are numerous classes and books available about Unix. A few suggestions are given here.

Steps
1. Check out your local bookstore. Unix often has its own section in the computer book department, and there are many good titles to choose from. A good beginner's book is *Unix Primer Plus,* by Mitchell Waite, Donald Martin, and Stephen Prata (Indianapolis: H.W. Sams, 1990). If you become interested in some of the more powerful capabilities of Unix, such as writing shell scripts, check out *Advanced Unix: a Programmer's Guide,* by Stephen Prata (H.W. Sams, 1985).

   While you can get sets of official Unix manuals, they are rather unwieldy and often cryptic. A good one-volume reference to Unix commands is *Unix System V Bible: Commands and Utilities,* also by Stephen Prata (H.W. Sams, 1987).

2. Check out your local community college. There are many introductory courses on Unix available.

3. Check to see whether your system has the learn command, which provides brief tutorials on Unix, vi, and other topics.

How It Works
Unix is best approached as a huge toolkit with all sorts of interesting tools and features in it. Take your time learning, and after a while you may grasp the overall philosophy of the system, which is to design small, simple tools that can be combined in a variety of powerful ways.

Comment
Remember that you don't need to be a Unix guru to enjoy the Internet. Don't worry if you don't understand everything about all the commands presented in this chapter.

Getting Files with ftp

How do I...

7.1	Connect to an ftp server
7.2	Get help on ftp commands
7.3	List directories and files on the remote system
7.4	Get a file with ftp
7.5	Read a text file on the remote system
7.6	Get a binary file
7.7	Get a group of files
7.8	Send a file to the remote system
7.9	Set ftp options
7.10	Work with the local system while connected to ftp
7.11	Simplify the connection process
7.12	Use ftp by mail

After mail and news, the most popular facility on the Internet is probably ftp, which stands for *file transfer protocol*. The general function of ftp is to move files from one site on the Internet to another using high-speed connections. This may not sound very exciting until you learn that you, the Internet user, can use ftp to get any of hundreds of thousands of files from about 1500 anonymous ftp sites. An *anonymous ftp site* is a system on the Internet that allows anyone who has Internet access to log in and access a *public directory* containing files that are free for the asking. Here are some of the kinds of files you can find:

- Tutorials or references on using the Internet programs
- FAQ (Frequently Asked Questions) files and other periodically updated references
- Archives of Usenet news articles
- Supreme Court decisions

INTERNET HOW-TO

➤ Text of public domain literature (Shakespeare and the Bible, for example)
➤ Lists of interesting services, sites, mailing lists, and so on
➤ Programs that you can run on your PC, Mac, or other computer, ranging from sophisticated scientific software, to utilities, to games
➤ Graphic images such as stars, galaxies, fractals, and people

...and stuff that doesn't easily fit in any particular category.

Connecting with ftp

In order to make sense of ftp you need to learn a few terms. Figure 7-1 shows the elements of an ftp connection. The *remote system* is the site from which you will be obtaining files. The *local system* is the site through which you are connected to the Internet. The *user* is you, sitting at your PC, which is connected by modem to the local system. (This assumes that you are connecting to the Internet with a PC and modem. If you are directly connected to a system on the Internet, the user and the local system are the same.)

The program you run when you type `ftp` at the system prompt is called an ftp *client*. It connects to the address you specify, where it hooks up with an ftp *server*. If these terms confuse you, just remember that the server provides services (access to files) that the client (you, on your local system) use—just as an attorney provides legal services to her clients.

The ftp client provides a prompt at which you type commands to perform the required tasks. Table 7-1 lists the ftp commands covered in this chapter (there are additional commands that you can read about in the online Unix manual). A typical ftp command sequence might be `dir` (to list a directory on the remote system) followed by `get` (to get a file from that directory).

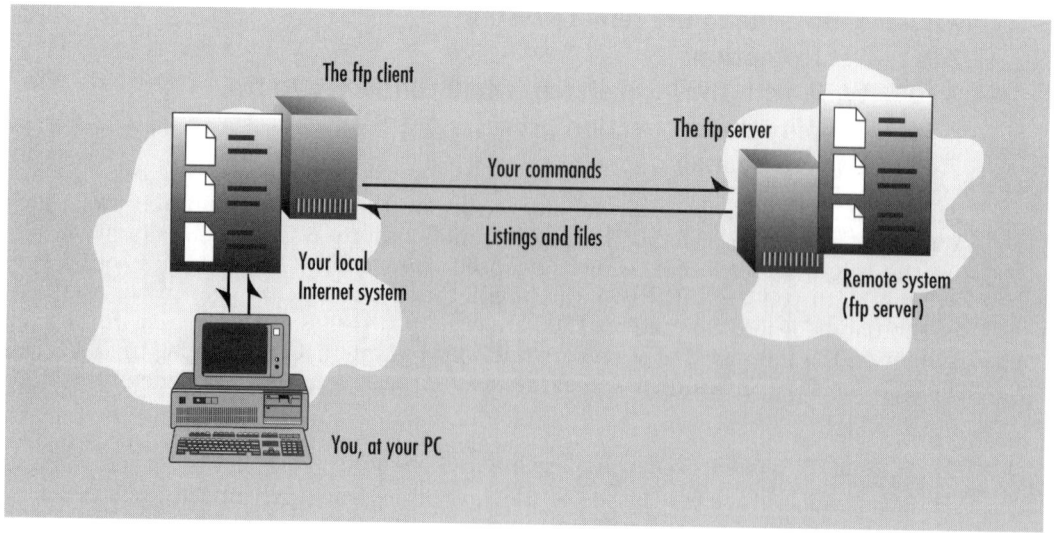

Figure 7-1 Parts of an ftp connection

COMMAND	PURPOSE
!	Run a command or shell on local system
? or help	Get a list of commands or help on a particular command
ascii	Specify that you will be working with text files
binary	Specify that you will be working with binary files
cd	Change directory on remote system
cdup	Change directory to parent directory (remote system)
close	End connection to remote site but remain in ftp
dir	Display a detailed directory listing (remote system)
get	Get a file from remote system (puts a copy of the file on local system)
hash	Display hash marks on terminal as blocks of data are transferred
lcd	Change directory (local system)
ls	Display short directory listing (similar to standard Unix ls command)
mget	Get a batch of files from remote system
open	Connect to a remote ftp site
prompt	Toggle prompting for multiple file transfers
put (or send)	Copy a file to the remote system
pwd	Display current directory path (remote system)
quit	Exit ftp and return to local system prompt
status	Display current status of ftp options
user	Specify your username for remote system

Table 7-1 ftp commands covered in this chapter

Before moving on to the details of each how-to, it is useful to take an overall look at the steps involved in a typical ftp session. When you use ftp, you will usually do the following:

➢ Dial up and log on your local Internet site.
➢ Run the ftp program at the system prompt.
➢ Have ftp connect your local site to the remote site that has the files you want.
➢ If necessary, get directory listings and search for the file(s) you want.
➢ Change to the directory containing the file or files you want.
➢ Tell ftp to get the files for you. The files will be copied into your current directory on the local system.
➢ End the connection to the remote system and exit the ftp program.
➢ Download the files from your local site to your PC.
➢ Log off your local system.

You should know how to do steps 1 and 9 already (if not, see Chapter 2). Step 8 will be covered in detail in Chapter 9; for now all you need to know is that you can use a file transfer protocol such as Kermit or Xmodem to get the files from your local site

225

INTERNET HOW-TO

onto your PC's hard disk. The remaining steps, which involve the use of the ftp program itself, are described in the how-tos in this chapter.

Related Topics

To Learn How to...	See Chapter
Deal with compressed and binary files	8
Download files from your local site to your PC	9
Find out which sites have the files you want	11
List and manage files and directories on your local system	6
Run programs on a remote system	10

How-Tos in this Chapter

7.1 Connect to an ftp server
There are hundreds of sites that make files available via ftp. The site to which your local site connects is called the ftp server. Once you learn about some interesting ftp servers in this book or elsewhere, you use the ftp program at your local site to connect to the server and request listings and files.

7.2 Get help on ftp commands
ftp has a simple help facility that lists the available commands or reminds you of the purpose of a particular command. You can also obtain the usual entry from the online Unix manual.

7.3 List directories and files on the remote system
Unless you know the exact path location for a file at the ftp site, you'll need to list and examine the available directories. ftp provides two commands that list files that are on the remote system. One is ls, which works very much like the regular Unix ls command discussed in Chapter 6. Another command, dir, provides a more detailed listing.

7.4 Get a file with ftp
To get a file, all you have to do is change to the directory containing the file and then type get followed by the filename. A copy of the file will be transferred (usually in only a few seconds) from the remote system to your local site.

7.5 Read a text file on the remote system
Most ftp sites have README files or indexes that can help you find files. You can have the contents of such files displayed on your terminal screen without having to store a copy of the file on your local system.

7.6 Get a binary file
Since binary files store data differently than text files, you have to tell ftp that you're going to be getting (or sending) a binary file. You'll learn which files are likely to be text (ASCII) and which binary.

7.7 Get a group of files
As with many Unix commands, you can use wildcards to work with more than one file at a time. You use a multiple file version of the get command called mget.

7.8 Send a file to the remote system
Most readers of this book will probably just be getting files *from* remote sites, but some sites accept files contributed by users. You use the put command to place a copy of your file on the remote system. Also, if you have accounts on more than one system on the Internet, you can use ftp to move your own files back and forth between the systems.

226

7.9 Set ftp options
ftp has a few options that change the way it works. You can change the file type (text or binary), the kind of prompting used, and the information displayed during file transfers.

7.10 Work with the local system while connected to ftp
As you've probably learned by now, you sometimes need to check something (such as the location of a file) without exiting the program you're running. ftp provides the standard shell escape feature, which you activate by pressing !.

7.11 Simplify the connection process
If you find you are frequently connecting to a particular ftp site, you can store the address, username, and password on your local system so that ftp can connect to that system automatically when you ask for it.

7.12 Use ftp by mail
If you don't have access to the ftp program at your current site but you *do* have mail access to the Internet, you can use a special service to request files from ftp sites by mail.

7.1 HOW DO I... *Connect to an ftp server?*

COMPLEXITY: EASY

Problem
As you read the Usenet news and become familiar with the Internet, you'll often run into recommendations of programs or other files that are interesting, useful, neat, or otherwise desirable to have. The person recommending the file will say something like this: "You can get (this file) by anonymous ftp from (site name)." The first step in getting the file is to run the ftp program and use it to connect to the ftp site, or server.

Technique
You run ftp and tell it what site you want it to connect to. If the connection is successful, the ftp server at the remote site asks you for a username and a password. Unless you have an actual account at that site you use the special "anonymous" username to log on the ftp server.

Steps
1. One way to make an ftp connection is to type `ftp` at the command prompt on your local system. Follow it with the complete net address for the site to which you wish to connect. For example, to connect to the site ftp.sura.net, you can type

```
% ftp ftp.sura.net
```

Assuming the connection is successful, you are prompted for a username:

```
Connected to ftp.sura.net.
220 nic.sura.net FTP server (Version 2.0WU(10) Fri Apr 9 15:43:49 EDT 1993) read
y.
Name (ftp.sura.net:hrh): anonymous
```

2. Type `anonymous` and press ENTER. The system responds with a password prompt:

```
331 Guest login ok, send your complete e-mail address as password.
Password:
```

INTERNET HOW-TO

3. As instructed, you send your complete e-mail address (for example, hrh@well.com) as the password. While not all systems check whether your entry looks like a valid address, it is a good idea to give your real address. Since the ftp site is providing a free public service, the people there are entitled to accurate information that they can use to analyze their connections.

After you enter the password, you will probably see a series of messages describing the status of the ftp site and perhaps its policies and guidelines for use:

```
230-    SURAnet ftp server running wuarchive experimental ftpd
230-
230-Welcome to the SURAnet ftp server.  If you have any problems with
230-the server please mail to the systems@sura.net. If you do have problems,
230-please try using a dash (-) as the first character of your password
230-    — this will turn off the continuation messages that may be confusing
230-your ftp client.
230-
230-Nifty feature:
230-
230-    Compressed files may be uncompressed by attempting to get the
230-name without the .Z. Example: to get zen-1.0.tar.Z uncompressed one
230-would get zen-1.0.tar.
230-
230-    Entire hierarchies may also be tarred and optionally compressed.
230-To get, for example, the sendmail hierarchy tarred & compressed, one would
230-get sendmail.tar.Z.
230-
230-
230 Guest login ok, access restrictions apply.
ftp>
```

4. It's a good idea to read these instructions before proceeding to explore the system.

5. An alternate way to make an ftp connection is to type `ftp` alone at your local system's command prompt. When you get the ftp command prompt, type `open` followed by the address of the site to which you wish to connect:

```
ftp> open ftp.sura.net
Connected to ftp.sura.net.
220 nic.sura.net FTP server (Version 2.0WU(10) Fri Apr 9 15:43:49 EDT 1993) read
y.
Name (ftp.sura.net:hrh): anonymous
331 Guest login ok, send your complete e-mail address as password.
Password:
```

Again, you will be asked for a username and password, and should reply with `anonymous` and your e-mail address. (Some systems accept the username "ftp" instead of "anonymous.")

6. You now enter ftp commands as described in the following how-tos. When you are finished entering commands, exit ftp by typing `bye` at the ftp prompt:

```
ftp> bye
221 Goodbye.
```

7 GETTING FILES WITH FTP

How It Works
The ftp client at your local site attempts to connect to the remote ftp site (the server) via high-speed phone lines. If the connection is successful, the ftp server program running at the remote site gets a username and password from you, the ftp user. You can now use ftp commands to list directories and get files.

Anonymous ftp normally restricts access to a special "public area" at the ftp site. For reasons of security, certain commands (such as the ability to run a shell on the remote system) are usually disabled.

If you have actual accounts on more than one system, you can make an ftp connection from one of your systems to another. The login procedure is the same, except that you use the username and password for your account on the remote system rather than "anonymous." When the login process is complete you have the full access your account entitles you to, not the limited access of the anonymous ftp user. The commands you use will be very similar to those used by the anonymous user, except that you will be able to upload, rename or delete files, make directories, and perform other tasks not available in anonymous ftp. (However, since most readers are likely to have only one Internet account, this chapter deals primarily with anonymous ftp.)

Comment
Many (but not all) anonymous ftp sites have names that begin with "ftp". If you try to ftp to such a site using the name without the ftp prefix, it will be assumed you have an account there, and you'll be asked for a (non-anonymous) password.

Your attempt at an ftp connection can fail for various reasons. Some sites restrict access to off-peak hours and will give you a message to that effect. (Remember that an ftp site may be anywhere in the world, so be aware of time differences.) The message "host not found" may mean that you have mistyped the address for the ftp site. The message "host unavailable" or "connection refused" may mean that the remote site is having problems or is not accepting ftp connections at this time.

The archie program discussed in Chapter 11 offers a more systematic way to find files available through ftp. Running archie will help you determine which ftp sites are the most frequently mentioned, making them good candidates for browsing.

7.2 HOW DO I...
Get help on ftp commands?

COMPLEXITY EASY

Problem
As with most programs, you'll want to get some help while you're learning to use ftp. The online help provided by ftp is rudimentary, but useful as a reminder about what each command does.

Technique
You can get brief interactive help at the ftp prompt, or use the online Unix manual to get a more detailed description of ftp's features and commands.

Steps
1. Once you're running ftp, you can either type `help` or press `?` at the ftp prompt:

```
ftp> help
Commands may be abbreviated.  Commands are:
```

Continued on next page

INTERNET HOW-TO

Continued from previous page

!	cr	macdef	proxy	send
$	delete	mdelete	sendport	status
account	debug	mdir	put	struct
append	dir	mget	pwd	sunique
ascii	disconnect	mkdir	quit	tenex
bell	form	mls	quote	trace
binary	get	mode	recv	type
bye	glob	mput	remotehelp	user
case	hash	nmap	rename	verbose
cd	help	ntrans	reset	?
cdup	lcd	open	rmdir	
close	ls	prompt	runique	

2. ftp replies with a list of available commands. To get a description of what a particular command does, type `help` followed by the command name:

```
ftp> help pwd
pwd             print working directory on remote machine
```

3. You can also look at the online manual entry for ftp by typing `man ftp` at your regular system prompt. The first screen looks like this:

```
ftp(1)                    User Commands                    ftp(1)

NAME
     ftp - file transfer program

SYNOPSIS
     ftp [ -dgintv ] [ hostname ]

AVAILABILITY
     SUNWcsu

DESCRIPTION
     The ftp command is the user interface to the Internet stan-
     dard  File  Transfer Protocol (FTP). ftp transfers files to
     and from a remote network site.

     The client host with which ftp is to communicate may be
     specified on the command line.  If this is done, ftp immedi-
     ately attempts to establish a connection to an FTP server on
     that host; otherwise, ftp enters its command interpreter and
     awaits instructions from the user.  When ftp is awaiting
--More--(2%)
```

How It Works

As you can see, ftp is a rather bare-bones program that provides only brief reminders about what the various commands do. Fortunately most of the commands are easy to use, and many are very similar to regular Unix commands that you already know.

7 GETTING FILES WITH FTP

Comment
After you have read this chapter, you may wish to read the online manual entry for ftp and learn about the more esoteric commands. Remember that you can save a copy of the manual in a file by typing a command such as:

```
%man ftp > ftp.man
```

7.3 HOW DO I...
List directories and files on the remote system?

COMPLEXITY: EASY

Problem
While some people who recommend files will give you the name of the exact directory location where they can be found at the ftp site, this will not always be the case. You may need to get directory listings and check them for the name of the file you want. You may also wish to browse the directories at an ftp site in search of files that look interesting.

Technique
You can use the dir or ls command to list a directory. You use the cd and cdup commands to change directories. Another command, pwd, tells you the name of your current directory. These navigation techniques are very similar to those discussed in Chapter 6 for standard Unix systems.

Steps
1. Once you're connected to an ftp server, you can type `dir` at the ftp prompt to get a listing of files (or subdirectories) in the current directory. (DOS users won't have any trouble remembering this one!)

   When you first connect to an ftp site you will probably be at the top level in the "public" directory. For example, a typical top-level directory listing for an ftp site might be:

```
ftp> dir
200 PORT command successful.
150 Opening ASCII mode data connection for /bin/ls.
total 24
drwxrwx—x    3 0      0            512 Jun 22  1993 bin
drwxr–xr–x   2 0      1            512 Dec  7 04:12 etc
drwxrwx—x    9 0      10           512 Oct 27 19:00 incoming
drwxr–xr–x   2 0      0           8192 Feb 15  1992 lost+found
drwxrwxr–x  21 0      100          512 Dec  1 18:36 pub
226 Transfer complete.
322 bytes received in 0.0083 seconds (38 Kbytes/s)
```

   Notice the last two lines of the listing. Since the listing is being done on the remote system, the information in the listing must be transferred over the phone line to your local system. Depending on the location of the remote system relative to your local system, you may experience a delay of a few seconds before seeing the listing.

2. As an alternative, you can type `ls` to list the current directory:

231

INTERNET HOW-TO

```
ftp> ls
200 PORT command successful.
150 Opening ASCII mode data connection for file list.
lost+found
pub
etc
bin
incoming
226 Transfer complete.
37 bytes received in 0.0083 seconds (4.3 Kbytes/s)
```

    3. To get a longer form of this listing, type `ls -l`:

```
ftp> ls -l
200 PORT command successful.
150 Opening ASCII mode data connection for /bin/ls.
total 24
drwxrwx—x   3 0    0      512 Jun 22  1993 bin
drwxr-xr-x   2 0    1      512 Dec  7 04:12 etc
drwxrwx—x   9 0    10     512 Oct 27 19:00 incoming
drwxr-xr-x   2 0    0      8192 Feb 15  1992 lost+found
drwxrwxr-x  21 0    100    512 Dec  1 18:36 pub
226 Transfer complete.
remote: -l
322 bytes received in 0.0089 seconds (35 Kbytes/s)
```

    4. One nice feature of both the dir and ls commands is that you can specify the name of a file to store the listing *on your local system* for future reference. Simply add the filename after the name of the directory you are listing:

```
ftp> ls pub filelist
200 PORT command successful.
150 Opening ASCII mode data connection for file list.
226 Transfer complete.
local: filelist remote: pub
245 bytes received in 0.0049 seconds (49 Kbytes/s)
```

    Now the listing is in the file named "filelist" in the current directory at your local site. You can examine this file at your leisure, using the cat or more commands, or download the listing to your PC:

```
% cat filelist
pub/security
pub/archie
pub/sendmail
pub/loads
pub/nic
pub/news
pub/maps
pub/networking
pub/articles
pub/README
pub/meetings
pub/dns
```

```
pub/jobs
pub/SURAnet
pub/new.sites.info
pub/databases
pub/mbone
pub/forms
pub/misc
pub/ripe
```

How It Works
The ftp server receives your listing command (ls or dir), generates the desired listing, and sends it to your local system (the ftp client).

Comment
You can use the usual wildcards (* or ?) to get a listing of files whose names match a particular specification. See Chapter 6 for more details on wildcard use.

7.4 HOW DO I...
Get a file with ftp?

COMPLEXITY EASY

Problem
Once you've found a file you want, you need to get a copy of it transferred from the ftp server to your local Internet site.

Technique
There are basically two steps to getting a file: change to the directory that contains the file, and then issue the get command.

Steps
1. If the file is not in the current directory at the remote site, use the cd command to change to that directory. (This command works just like the cd command in Unix, as discussed in Chapter 6.) For example, if you have just connected to ftp.sura.net and you know that the file containing the "Hitchhiker's Guide to the Internet" (an excellent introduction and resource, by the way) is located in the /pub/networking directory, you would issue the command:

```
ftp>cd /pub/networking
```

2. Now you're ready to transfer the file. Type **get** followed by the filename:

```
ftp> get hitchhikers.guide
200 PORT command successful.
150 Opening ASCII mode data connection for hitchhikers.guide (49843 bytes).
226 Transfer complete.
local: hitchhikers.guide remote: hitchhikers.guide
51155 bytes received in 1.3 seconds (39 Kbytes/s)
```

Notice the speed of the Internet: a file containing about 51K has been transferred from the SURAnet Network Information Center in College Park, Maryland to your local site (The WELL, near San Francisco, California) in only 1.3 seconds. This is about 50 times faster than the modems and phones lines that most of us use to connect to our local Internet provider!

3. You now have a copy of the file in your current directory (probably your home directory) at your local site. You can read the file there (using cat or more) or download it to your PC (see Chapter 9).

4. Continue changing directories and requesting files as desired. When you're done, type **bye** at the ftp prompt to exit ftp and return to your local system prompt.

How It Works
The ftp server makes a copy of the requested file and sends it over the high-speed lines to your local site.

Comment
The instructions given here work for text (ASCII) files. Binary files, such as programs or graphic images, require an additional step, as shown in How-To 7.6.

If you get lost while changing directories, try the pwd command. As with the standard Unix version discussed in Chapter 6, this command displays the path of your current directory:

```
%pwd

257 "/pub/games" is current directory.
```

(Ignore numbers such as "257" in the above listing. These are simply a sort of transaction number used by the ftp server.)

If you want the requested file to be copied into a specific directory on your local system, issue the lcd (local change directory) command with the name of the local directory *before* you issue the get command. For example:

```
ftp> lcd docs
Local directory now /home/h/r/hrh/docs
```

Any files you request will now be copied into the "docs" subdirectory of your home directory on your local system.

7.5 HOW DO I...
Read a text file on the remote system?

COMPLEXITY: EASY

Problem
Most ftp sites include files with names such as README, readme.txt, INDEX, or something similar. These files contain lists of files to be found in a given directory, and thus can be very useful to the anonymous ftp user. While you can get and transfer such files, as shown in How-To 7.6, it is sometimes more convenient to simply read the README file at your PC, or perhaps to capture its contents using the file capture facility of your communications software.

Technique
The basic idea is to set your PC for file capture (if desired) and then use a special version of the ftp get command to display the file on your screen.

Steps

1. Let's assume you're connected to an ftp site and have done a directory listing (dir or ls command). You notice that there is a file called README in the current directory, and you'd like to read this file.

2. If you would like the contents of the file to be copied to your PC's hard disk, turn on the file capture facility of your communications software.

3. At the ftp prompt, type `get` followed by the name of the file you want to read, a space, and a hyphen:

```
ftp> get README -
```

The contents of the README file will be displayed on your screen:

```
200 PORT command successful.
150 Opening ASCII mode data connection for README (813 bytes).
This Directory contains information on networking principles and concepts
as well as some papers containing practical advice.

        hedrick-ip-intro.txt        *TCP/IP introductory file
        hedrick-net-admin.txt       *TCP/IP network administration
        tcp-ip-intro.ps             * Postscript version of hedrick-ip-intro.txt
        tcp-ip-admin.p              * Postscript version of hedrick-net-admin.txt

        hitchikers.guide            *Explanation of the Internet
        mailing.to.other.networks   *Info on how to get mail to other
                                     networks.
        network-reading-list.ps     *Bibliography of books that are useful
                                     for networking (in Postscript)
        network-reading-list.txt    * same file as above except in ASCII text

226 Transfer complete.
remote: README
828 bytes received in 0.18 seconds (4.6 Kbytes/s)
```

How It Works

The ftp server sends the text from the specified file to your local site. Instead of storing it as a file, however, it arrives as a "stream" of text that your local system sends to your terminal.

Comment

The use of get with a hyphen has two main purposes: 1) to read short text files without the bother of transferring them to your local site and 2) to capture longer text files directly to your PC without having to first transfer and then download them from your local site.

Note that because this version of the get command ultimately uses your PC, it depends on the speed of your connection to your local site, which is much slower than the connection used between the remote ftp site and your local site. For longer text files it is more efficient to simply get them and then download them from your local site to your PC.

INTERNET HOW-TO

There is no paging of the text, so it just scrolls up your screen. On some systems you can, however, use CTRL-S to stop the text scrolling and CTRL-Q to resume it.

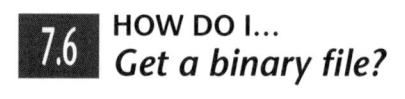

7.6 HOW DO I...
Get a binary file?

COMPLEXITY | **INTERMEDIATE**

Problem
Many files you will be receiving by ftp are binary files rather than text files. Binary files, such as programs, graphic images, and compressed files, require special handling.

Technique
Fortunately, you can simply tell ftp that you will be dealing with a binary file, and ftp will make sure the file is transmitted exactly byte-for-byte without any changes or additions. Let's say for example that you are browsing at an ftp site. You're not sure where you've ended up, so you type `pwd` to display the current directory:

```
ftp> pwd
257 "/pub/pc-blue/util" is current directory.
```

You then type `ls` to get a listing of the directory:

```
ftp> ls
200 PORT command successful.
150 Opening ASCII mode data connection for file list.
blue.bat
browse.scr
cat.exe
cpyright.txt
logo.dat
pcbd.txt
pkunzip.exe
pcb_info.txt
vols.exe
summary.txt
use.me
226 Transfer complete.
123 bytes received in 0.0073 seconds (17 Kbytes/s)
```

Scanning down the list, you come across a directory that has a copy of the popular DOS file compression utility pkunzip.exe—something you know you're going to need to uncompress those .zip files that you're getting for your PC. But since this is an .exe (program) file, you know you can't just have ftp transfer it as a text file, because the transmission procedure is likely to render it unusable.

Steps
1. Once you've decided to get a binary file, type `binary` at the ftp prompt:

```
ftp> binary
200 Type set to I.
```

ftp replies that it has set the current file type to I, which means "image" and is the same thing as "binary."

7 GETTING FILES WITH FTP

2. You can now use the get command followed by the filename, as usual:

```
ftp> get pkunzip.exe
200 PORT command successful.
150 Opening BINARY mode data connection for pkunzip.exe (21440 bytes).
226 Transfer complete.
local: pkunzip.exe remote: pkunzip.exe
21440 bytes received in 0.38 seconds (56 Kbytes/s)
```

How It Works

ftp must know whether the file it will be transferring is text or binary. For text files, ftp may need to change the values of the individual bytes to conform to the text codes used on the requesting system. Binary files, on the other hand, are never changed during transmission.

Comment

Here are a few rough-and-ready guidelines for telling whether a file is text or binary:

- If the file has no extension or an extension indicating program source code (.c, .cpp, for example) it's probably text.
- A file named some variant of readme is almost certainly text.
- Files that are executable programs are binary. (DOS programs will usually have an .exe extension.)
- Files that have been compressed are binary. Example extensions include .Z, .zip, and .zoo. Chapter 8 discusses compressed files in more detail.
- Graphics files (with extensions like .gif or .lbm) are binary.
- Text that has been formatted for a word processor or printer is binary.

When in doubt, try specifying binary. Most text files will still come through unscathed.

Compressed files need further processing after you've downloaded them to your PC (see Chapters 8 and 9).

Note that ftp is set to ASCII text mode by default. Once you've typed `binary`, ftp will remain in binary mode until you type `ascii` at the ftp prompt (or exit ftp).

7.7 HOW DO I...
Get a group of files?

COMPLEXITY INTERMEDIATE

Problem

It can be tedious to issue a separate get command for each file you want to get from the ftp server.

Technique

ftp provides the mget (multiple get) command for requesting a group of files. You can use mget with wildcards (* or ?) to match and retrieve a set of related files.

Let's say we're looking for artificial life simulation programs. We do a little directory browsing and find:

```
ftp> pwd
257 "/pub/msdos/simulatn" is current directory.
```

Continued on next page

237

INTERNET HOW-TO

Continued from previous page

```
ftp> ls
200 PORT command successful.
150 Opening ASCII mode data connection for file list.
divecomp.zip
aalife.zip
00_index.txt
dr-life.zip
process1.zip
statp101.zip
tutsim.zip
aaalife.zip
clife.zip
226 Transfer complete.
117 bytes received in 0.0047 seconds (24 Kbytes/s)
```

Looks like some cool stuff! Let's get all the "life" simulations and a copy of "tutsim" as well.

Steps

1. At the ftp prompt, type `mget` followed by a filename using wildcards. In this example, you might start by asking for all files that have the .zip extension (these are compressed MS-DOS files):

```
ftp> mget *.zip
```

2. By default, mget presents you with the names of matching files, one at a time. For each file, you are asked whether you want to get that file:

```
mget aaalife.zip? y
```

Press y if you want to get the file; n if you don't. In our example, we respond to the prompts for the rest of the matching files as follows:

```
200 PORT command successful.
150 Opening BINARY mode data connection for aaalife.zip (40934 bytes).
226 Transfer complete.
local: aaalife.zip remote: aaalife.zip
40934 bytes received in 0.63 seconds (64 Kbytes/s)
mget aalife.zip? y
200 PORT command successful.
150 Opening BINARY mode data connection for aalife.zip (3171 bytes).
226 Transfer complete.
local: aalife.zip remote: aalife.zip
3171 bytes received in 0.28 seconds (11 Kbytes/s)
mget clife.zip? y
200 PORT command successful.
150 Opening BINARY mode data connection for clife.zip (32286 bytes).
226 Transfer complete.
local: clife.zip remote: clife.zip
32286 bytes received in 0.8 seconds (40 Kbytes/s)
mget divecomp.zip? n
mget dr-life.zip? y
```

```
200 PORT command successful.
150 Opening BINARY mode data connection for dr-life.zip (27293 bytes).
226 Transfer complete.
local: dr-life.zip remote: dr-life.zip
27293 bytes received in 0.5 seconds (54 Kbytes/s)
mget process1.zip? n
mget statp101.zip? n
mget tutsim.zip? y
```

3. Once you have dealt with all the files presented, you are returned to the ftp prompt.

How It Works
The mget command uses the wildcard characters (discussed in Chapter 6) to match filenames in the current directory. It then asks you whether you want to receive each file.

Comment
Remember that the * wildcard matches any number of characters, while each ? character matches any single character.

Note that in the example we could have used `mget *life.zip` if we were sure that all we wanted was the "life" files.

7.8 HOW DO I...
Send a file to the remote system?

COMPLEXITY: INTERMEDIATE

Problem
With anonymous ftp you usually can't copy a file to the remote system. If, however, you have made special arrangements or have actual (non-anonymous) accounts on two systems, you can use ftp to move files back and forth between the two systems.

Technique
You establish an ftp connection and then use the send command to send a file to the remote system. For example, let's assume you have a school account at bigu.edu as well as an account on The WELL. You have a file, "faq.ans," that you want to copy from your bigu account to your directory on The WELL.

Steps
1. Log on the system *from which* you will be copying the file(s). (In this example, that's bigu.edu.)

2. Establish an ftp connection to the system *to which* you will be copying the files, as in How-To 7.1. (In this case, you are using ftp to connect to your account on The WELL.)

3. If necessary, use the cd command to change to the directory on the remote system to which you wish to copy the file. Here you'll just use your home directory, so no cd is necessary.

4. At the ftp prompt, type `put` followed by the name of the file you want to send to the remote system. For example, suppose we want to copy the file faq.ans from our account on bigu.edu to The WELL:

INTERNET HOW-TO

```
ftp> put faq.ans
200 PORT command successful.
150 ASCII data connection for test (198.93.4.10,53272).
226 Transfer complete.
local: faq.ans remote: faq.ans
35098 bytes sent in 0.081 seconds (4.2e+02 Kbytes/s)
```

5. If you want to give the file a different name on the system to which you're copying it, add the filename to your put command. For example, if you want to copy faq.ans as "answers.txt," your put command would read:

```
ftp> put faq.ans answers.txt
```

How It Works
The put command does the same thing as "get" except that it is sending a file from the local system (the client) to the remote system (the server).

Comment
Don't forget to first use the binary command if you will be sending binary files.

You can use the word "send" as a synonym for put.

If you try using this command with an anonymous ftp connection you will probably get the message "permission denied."

You can use the msend (or mput) command to send a batch of files that match wildcards. This is similar to the mget command discussed in How-To 7.7.

7.9 HOW DO I...
Set ftp options?

COMPLEXITY: INTERMEDIATE

Problem
ftp is meant to be a simple program, but it has a few options that you can set to suit special circumstances.

Technique
Each option is a toggle. To set an option, type its name at the ftp prompt and press (ENTER). Specifying an option that is on turns it off, while specifying an option that is off turns it on. You can use the status command to view the current status of your ftp connection and options.

Steps
1. As you have already seen, you should turn on the binary option before transferring binary files. By default, ftp is in ASCII mode, so you will need to specify binary the first time you need it in an ftp session:

```
ftp> binary
200 Type set to I.
```

2. When you go back to working with text files, set the ASCII (text) option:

```
ftp> ascii
200 Type set to A.
```

7 GETTING FILES WITH FTP

3. As you saw in How-To 7.7, ftp by default prompts you for each file in a batch when you are using the mget command. You can turn this prompting off by specifying the prompt option:

```
ftp> prompt
Interactive mode off.
```

Specifying prompt again will turn the interactive mode (prompting) back on.

4. If you will be transferring large files (a megabyte or more), you may wish to have a visual indication of the progress of the file transfer. You can turn the hash option on so that hash marks will be printed after each block of 8192 bytes is transferred:

```
ftp> hash
Hash mark printing on (8192 bytes/hash mark).
```

Once hash is on, file transfers with the get or mget command will look like this:

```
ftp> get Index-byname
200 PORT command successful.
150 Opening ASCII mode data connection for Index-byname (1236099 bytes).
###############################################################################
##########################################################################
226 Transfer complete.
local: Index-byname remote: Index-byname
1249601 bytes received in 25 seconds (48 Kbytes/s)
```

5. After you've become a more experienced ftp user, you can specify the verbose option to reduce the extraneous messages you get from ftp:

```
ftp> verbose
Verbose mode off.
```

(By default, verbose mode is on.)

6. Finally, you can type **status** at the ftp prompt to get a report on ftp's current status and settings:

```
ftp> status
Connected to docs.
No proxy connection.
Mode: stream; Type: ascii; Form: non-print; Structure: file
Verbose: on; Bell: off; Prompting: on; Globbing: on
Store unique: off; Receive unique: off
Case: off; CR stripping: on
Ntrans: off
Nmap: off
Hash mark printing: off; Use of PORT cmds: on
```

(Most of the items listed here are pretty esoteric and of interest mainly to gurus.)

How It Works

The ftp program keeps a set of "flags" that it uses to turn certain behaviors on and off. By specifying a particular status, you switch it from the current setting to the opposite setting. (This is called toggling.)

Comment
Most users will probably need to use only the binary and ASCII settings.

7.10 HOW DO I...
Work with the local system while connected to ftp?

COMPLEXITY: ADVANCED

Problem
While connected to a remote ftp site, you may wish to work with your home directory on the local system—perhaps to check whether a file exists. You can use a "shell escape" to execute commands on your local system while you remain connected to the remote ftp site.

Technique
You press ! to get a shell on your local system. You then execute whatever commands you need (ls, more, and so on) and then return to your ftp connection.

Steps
1. Press ! and (ENTER) at the ftp prompt:

```
ftp>!
```

2. A shell prompt that you can use as you normally would to enter Unix commands appears (see Chapter 6). For example, you can type `ls` to get a listing of the current directory *on your local system*:

```
% ls
FAQslist        cmds        doppel       gnnlist
Mail            corres      filelist     hitchhikers.guide
News            ctrld       ftpmail      xmodem.log
check           docs        ftpmail2
```

3. When you are finished entering local commands, press (CTRL)-(D). You are returned to the ftp prompt.

How It Works
Most Unix programs, including ftp, have a provision for executing a shell without leaving the program. This is something like switching between two windows in Microsoft Windows or on a Mac, though not as convenient.

Comment
The bad news is that many sites disable the shell facility for security reasons. If you try the ! command and get the message "Csh: permission denied," that means you can't use the shell escape from ftp at that site.

7.11 HOW DO I...
Simplify the connection process?

COMPLEXITY: ADVANCED

Problem
It may be hard to remember and type the net addresses of your favorite ftp sites every time you want to make an ftp connection.

Technique
There are two basic techniques that simplify the procedure of logging on ftp sites. The first technique stores the username and password in a special file that ftp can use to carry out the login dialog automatically. The second technique involves creating an alias, or nickname, for the ftp site. (This is similar to the use of mail aliases, as discussed in Chapter 3.)

Steps
1. To have ftp obtain the username and password automatically during login, use a text editor such as vi to create a file called .netrc in your home directory.

2. In the .netrc file, place an entry like this for each ftp site that you frequently connect to:

```
machine rtfm.mit.edu
login anonymous
password hrh@well.com
```

   Note that the word "machine" is followed by the site's full net address, the word "login" is followed by the word "anonymous," and "password" is followed by your address on your local system (*not* the password for your regular account there).

3. ftp requires that the .netrc file be readable only by you, the user. (This makes sense, since you *could* put "real" passwords in there.) At your system prompt, use the chmod command to make the .netrc file unreadable by others:

```
% chmod 600 .netrc
```

   You can check the results of the chmod command with the ls -l command:

```
% ls -l .netrc
-rw-------   1 hrh      well          60 Jan 15 09:34 .netrc
```

   As you can see, only you can read and write this file. (If you're not familiar with the chmod command, see Chapter 6.)

4. Now, when you type `ftp rtfm.mit.edu` to log on that ftp site, the username and password will be supplied automatically during login:

```
% ftp rtfm.mit.edu
Connected to rtfm.mit.edu.
220 rtfm ftpd (wu-2.1c(17) with built-in ls); bugs to ftp-bugs@rtfm.mit.edu
331 Guest login ok, send your complete e-mail address as password.
230 Guest login ok, access restrictions apply.
ftp>
```

INTERNET HOW-TO

5. The only problem is that you *still* have to type the full net address of the ftp site when you run ftp. You can, however, create an alias that associates an easy-to-remember name with the hard-to-remember address. First, use your editor to create a file called .hostaliases in your home directory.

6. In the .hostaliases file, insert a line for each ftp site that contains the alias name followed by the site's complete address. For example, our .hostaliases file might begin with:

```
docs rtfm.mit.edu
```

7. Save this file. Now you have to tell ftp to use the .hostaliases file. To do this, add the following line to your .login file if you're a C shell user (% prompt):

```
setenv HOSTALIASES ~/.hostaliases
```

If you use the Bourne or Korn shells ($ prompt), add the following to your .profile file:

```
HOSTALIASES=$HOME/.hostaliases; export HOSTALIASES
```

8. Next time you log on your local site, you can connect ftp to a remote site simply by following the ftp command with your alias name:

```
$ ftp docs
Connected to docs.
220 rtfm ftpd (wu-2.1c(17) with built-in ls); bugs to ftp-bugs@rtfm.mit.edu
Name (docs:hrh): anonymous
331 Guest login ok, send your complete e-mail address as password.
Password:
230 Guest login ok, access restrictions apply.
```

Everything will be done automatically!

How It Works

The .netrc and .hostaliases files are understood by many different Internet programs. Such programs, including ftp, are able to retrieve the information they need from these files and use them to establish the desired connection with a minimum of typing on your part.

Comment

Although you *can* use passwords for non-anonymous accounts in your .netrc file, it is recommended that you do not. While ftp will warn you when the .netrc file is not restricted to user-only permissions, it is too easy to accidentally change the permissions (such as after copying the file). The "anonymous" user ID and address password, on the other hand, don't tell snoopers more than they already know.

7.12 HOW DO I...
Use ftp by mail?

COMPLEXITY: INTERMEDIATE

Problem
It is generally assumed that readers of this book have full Internet access. However, if you don't have full access for some reason, but you *do* have access to mail, you can obtain ftp services through one of several "ftp mail servers." (For example, if you have a CompuServe account but no Internet access, you can send mail from CompuServe to the ftp mail server and get files from the Internet that way—though CompuServe may have provided direct ftp access by the time you read this.)

Technique
You send a mail message to the ftp mail server. The message consists of a series of ftp commands (typically, change directory and file transfer) that the server executes. The results of the commands (including any files requested) are sent to you by e-mail.

Steps
1. Use your favorite mailer (such as Elm, discussed in Chapter 3) to compose a message to the ftpmail site. For example, here we'll ask the ftpmail site at decwrl.dec.com to give us a listing of available commands:

```
$ mail ftpmail@decwrl.dec.com
Subject: get help
help
quit
Mail sent
```

For convenience we used the standard Unix "mail" program. The subject is simply to remind you what you asked the server to do; it is ignored by the server. What the server sees is the ftp help command and then the quit command, which lets ftp know you're finished.

2. You will get a mail message from the server with the desired information. (Some extraneous headers and material has been left out to save space:)

```
From: "ftpmail service on ftp-gw-1.pa.dec.com" <nobody@pa.dec.com>
To: hrh@well.sf.ca.us
Subject: your ftpmail request has been received [get help]

   — Help —
>>> $Id: help-text,v 1.7 1993/05/05 00:49:43 vixie Exp $
>>>
>>> ftpmail is not a supported service. From time to time it stops working;
>>> we will tend to it when we get the time. Outages of a week or more are not
>>> abnormal.

>>> commands are:

        reply <MAILADDR>        set reply addr, since headers are usually wrong
        connect [HOST [USER [PASS [ACCT]]]]
                                defaults to gatekeeper.dec.com, anonymous
```

Continued on next page

INTERNET HOW-TO

Continued from previous page

```
ascii                     files grabbed are printable ascii
binary                    files grabbed are compressed or tar or both
chdir PLACE               "get" and "ls" commands are relative to PLACE
                                (only one CHDIR per ftpmail session,
                                and it executes before any LS/DIR/GETs)
compress                  compress binaries using Lempel-Ziv encoding
compact                   compress binaries using Huffman encoding
uuencode                  binary files will be mailed in uuencode format
btoa                      binary files will be mailed in btoa format
chunksize SIZE            split files into SIZE-byte chunks (def: 64000)
ls (or dir) PLACE         short (long) directory listing
index THING               search for THING in ftp server's index
get FILE                  get a file and have it mailed to you
                                (max 10 GET's per ftpmail session)
quit                      terminate script, ignore rest of mail message
                                (use if you have a .signature or
                                are a VMSMAIL user)
```

3. To get a file from an ftp mail server, you create a mail message whose body looks like this:

```
connect rtfm.mit.edu
chdir /pub/networking
get hitchhikers.guide
quit
```

The first line tells the ftp mail server to make an ftp connection to rtfm.mit.edu. The second line tells it to change to the /pub/networking directory. The third line tells it to get the hitchhikers.guide file, and the last line tells it to end the ftp session.

4. The ftp mail server will mail you back a report on the processing of your message:

```
Date: Sat, 15 Jan 94 10:01:13 -0800
Message-Id: <9401151801.AA16448@ftp-gw-1.pa.dec.com>
From: "ftpmail service on ftp-gw-1.pa.dec.com" <nobody@pa.dec.com>
To: hrh@well.sf.ca.us
Subject: your ftpmail request has been received [Get Hitchhiker's Guide to Internet]
Precedence: bulk
Reply-To: <nobody@ftp-gw-1.pa.dec.com>
Status: RO
ftpmail is not a supported service. When it works, it is useful to us and to
you. When it does not work, you must be patient. All support of ftpmail is by
volunteers working on their own time. Mostly it runs unattended. Delays of a
week or more are not unknown.

We processed the following input from your mail message:

    connect ftp.sura.net
    chdir /pub/networking
    get hitchhikers.guide
```

```
We have entered the following request into our job queue
as job number 758656872.16436:

    connect ftp.sura.net anonymous -ftpmail/hrh@well.sf.ca.us
    reply hrh@well.sf.ca.us
    chdir /pub/networking
    get hitchhikers.guide ascii

There are 0 jobs ahead of this one in our queue.

You should expect the results to be mailed to you within a day or so.
We try to drain the request queue every 30 minutes, but sometimes it
fills up with enough junk that it takes until midnight (Pacific time)
to clear.  Note, however, that since ftpmail sends its files out with
"Precedence: bulk", they receive low priority at mail relay nodes.
```

5. The actual file you requested ("Hitchhiker's Guide to the Internet" in this example) will arrive as a separate mail message.

How It Works

The ftp mail server looks in the body of your mail message and executes the ftp commands found there. You need to specify every command needed in the correct order, since the process is not interactive. The ftp mail server then mails the report and the requested files to you.

Comment

If you're getting a binary file, don't forget to include the binary command before the get command.

Depending on mail connections, you may get your results in an hour or two, or perhaps as much as a couple of days.

For more information on ftpmail, send the "help" request as described in the example here and read the additional reports provided in the reply.

Advanced File Techniques

How do I...

8.1	Figure out what to do with a file
8.2	Prepare a binary file for mailing
8.3	Restore an encoded binary file
8.4	Use btoa with binary files
8.5	Compress a file to save space and time
8.6	Restore a compressed file
8.7	Read a compressed text file without uncompressing it
8.8	Compress and uncompress files for my PC
8.9	Compress and uncompress files for my Macintosh
8.10	Package files with tar
8.11	Unpack a tar file archive
8.12	Mail or receive a compressed tar archive
8.13	Create a shell archive
8.14	Unpack a shell archive

Files, files, files...Whether you get them by mail, save them from newsgroups, or reach out and grab them with ftp or another program, you will no doubt soon acquire dozens or even hundreds of files from the Internet.

When you go to use the riches you have found, however, you discover that not all files are created equal. Some files can be used right away, either at your Internet site or after being downloaded to your PC or Mac. Other files must be processed in one or more ways before they can be used successfully.

This chapter helps you identify the common types of files that you will encounter on the Internet, and provides the step-by-step procedures that you use to convert each type of file to a usable format. But first, let's go over the basic types of files and look at the reasons why some files are processed or "packaged" before being made available on the Internet.

Text Files

As you probably know, one of the most basic distinctions among files is whether the file is a text file or a binary file. To review briefly, a text file contains readable text characters, sometimes called ASCII text because of the system of character codes that is usually used. You can read a text file right away (using the more or cat commands discussed in Chapter 6). Once you've downloaded a text file to your PC (see Chapter 9), you can print the text file or import it into your favorite word processing program.

Text files can be arranged in a variety of ways. Mail messages and news articles have a series of headers at the beginning that provide information, such as the sender's address, the route by which the file was sent, what the file is about, or a summary or keywords that might help you retrieve the file.

If you're not sure whether a file is a text file, try typing `more` followed by the filename at the system prompt. If the result is readable text, the file is probably a text file. If the result is a jumble of meaningless characters, the file is probably a binary file.

Binary Files

The individual bytes in a binary file don't represent characters. Rather, they represent program instructions, pixels, sound waves, or some other kind of information.

There are two important practical differences between binary files and text files. Unlike a text file, a binary file either *is* a program you can run, or must be interpreted by a specialized program of some kind (for example, a picture file encoded in the popular GIF format). Also, a text file can suffer a certain amount of damage in transmission or processing (due to line noise or interference by other programs) and still be legible. A binary file must generally be transmitted 100 percent perfectly to be useful.

Table 8-1 lists some common types of binary files found on the Internet.

Note that some types of "binary" files may actually contain text (for example, PostScript files), but because of the need to keep the file contents intact, it is better to think of them as binary files.

Encoded Binary Files

The standard Internet mail and news programs are designed to work with text files. One service they provide is to guarantee that a text file can be moved between machines

TYPE OF FILE	FORM OF CONTENTS
Archive	A group of files packaged together
Compressed	File(s) with redundant information removed to save space
Executable	Program in machine language, ready to run
Graphics	Pixel data, colors, and so on
PostScript	Text and printer commands
Sound	Sound wave, patch, MIDI commands, and so on

Table 8-1 Types of binary files

with different character coding systems (for example, the ASCII codes used on Unix systems and PCs and the EBCDIC codes used on many IBM mainframes). This means that mail and news transmissions will frequently modify text files during transmission. Also, many programs consider only the first six or seven bits of each byte to be valid text, while binary files use all eight bits of each byte. As a consequence, trying to process a binary file with most mail or news programs results in the file becoming corrupted (and useless), though some mail programs have special provisions for handling binary files.

A common solution to this problem is to *encode* a binary file so that the binary bytes are replaced by characters that represent their value. The encoded file is in effect a text file, so it can be posted, mailed, or otherwise processed like regular mail or news. When the file reaches its destination, it can be *decoded*: in this process the text characters are replaced with the corresponding binary values. Figure 8-1 shows in simplified form how the encoding/decoding process works.

The most common programs used for encoding files are called uuencode and uudecode. Another program, btoa ("binary to ASCII") is also sometimes used.

Compressed Files

Many text or binary files that people want to make available on the Internet are large (from hundreds of kilobytes to several megabytes in length). Graphics files are particularly prone to be gigantic: a PC VGA screen that is 640 pixels high by 480 pixels wide,

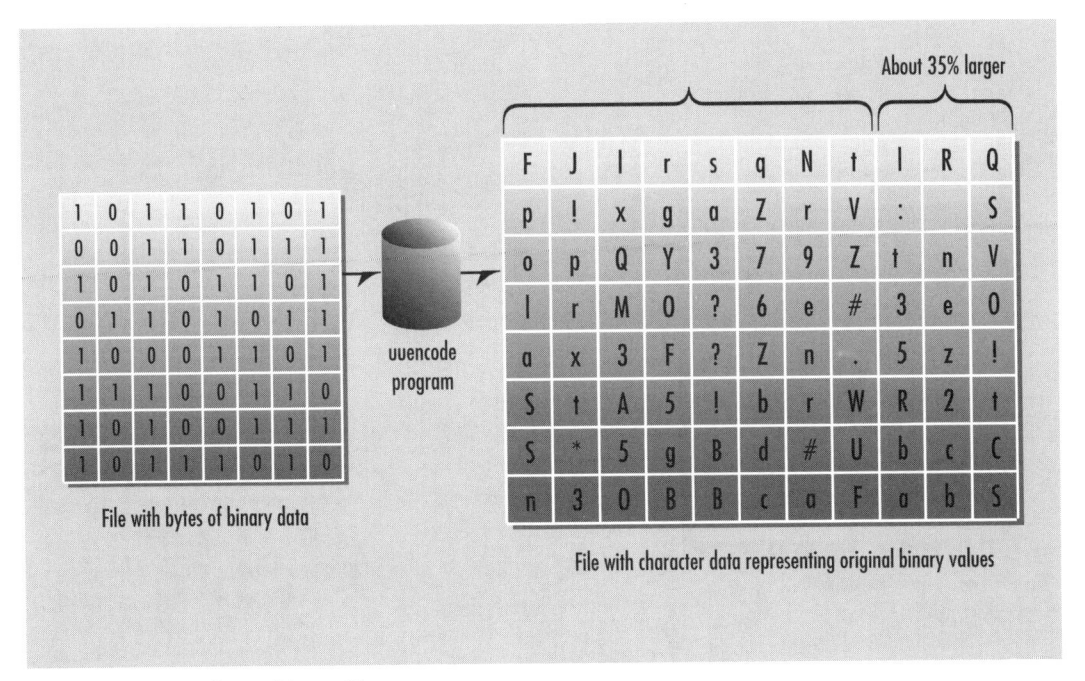

Figure 8-1 Encoding a binary file

INTERNET HOW-TO

with each pixel capable of having one of 256 different colors, might require 640 x 480 x 256 = 78,643,200 bits (or 9,830,400 bytes). While graphics can be coded in ways that reduce the actual number of bits that must be stored, clearly a picture like that can be worth a thousand words or more, at least in terms of real estate on the disk.

Reducing file size has two obvious benefits: the smaller the file, the less disk space is needed, either on the Internet host or on your PC. Equally important, the smaller the file, the more quickly it can be transmitted over the phone lines.

The result of the need to make files as small as possible has been the development of methods for *compressing* files. While the actual algorithms used are beyond the scope of this book, the effect of compression is to replace the large amount of redundant information in a file with a smaller amount of information that can be used to recreate the "missing" material. Examples of redundant information include the many pixels in a graphic image that have the same color, or are blank, and the spaces between characters in a text file. Thus, instead of storing 2480 blue pixels making up the "sky" in a graphics image, just the number 2480 and a single number representing the "blue" value can be stored. The process is later reversed, to *expand* the file back to its original form after it has been received. Figure 8-2 gives a conceptual depiction of how a text file might be compressed.

A variety of compression programs are available on the Internet. Unix files are usually managed with the compress and uncompress programs, the pkzip and pkunzip programs are popular for PCs, and the StuffIt program is a favorite of Mac users.

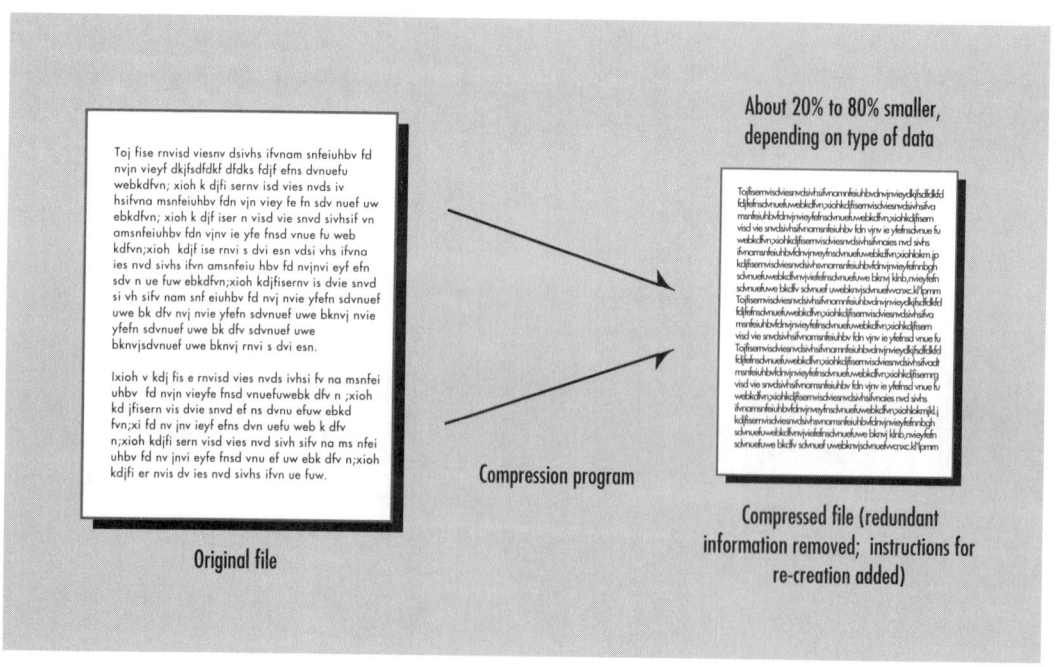

Figure 8-2 Compressing and uncompressing a file

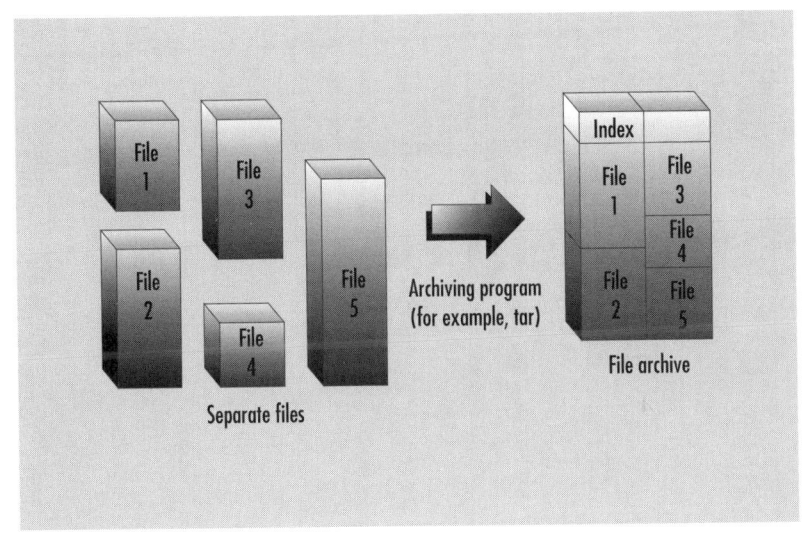

Figure 8-3 Archiving files

Packaging Files in Archives

Many software packages distributed via the Internet consist of several separate files: program files, initialization files, overlays, documentation files, and so on. It would be tedious to transmit and store the dozens of files in a software package individually. Instead, *archive programs* are used to group files into a single large file that can be transmitted as a unit and then *unpacked*, or broken into its component parts by the recipient. Figure 8-3 depicts the concept of file archiving.

There are two main programs used for archiving Unix files: tar and shar. tar (tape archive) packages files with a header that gives the necessary information for extracting the files later. shar (shell archive) uses a shell *script* (a set of instructions in the Unix shell programming language) which, when executed, stores the designated files in a package that can be broken apart by other commands later.

In addition, popular PC programs, such as pkzip and arc, and the Unix gzip and gunzip programs have the capability of both compressing and archiving files for maximum efficiency.

Combined Processing

Many software packages are first archived (to get all the files into one package) and then compressed (to make the package as small as possible). The file extensions reflect the order in which the processing was done. For example, a file named book.tar.Z results from the file named book first being archived with the tar program (thus the .tar extension) and then compressed (adding the .Z extension).

To prepare such a package for use you undo the steps in reverse order. First, you use the uncompress program to restore the full contents of the archive. (This results in the .Z extension being removed, leaving the filename book.tar.) Next, you run the tar pro-

253

INTERNET HOW-TO

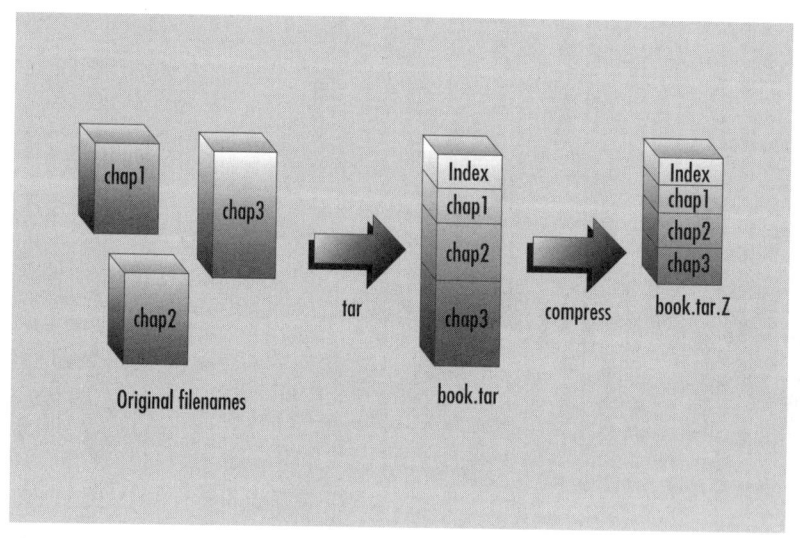

Figure 8-4 Combined file processing

gram, which extracts the files from the archive, and they are ready for use. Figure 8-4 shows the sequence of steps involved in creating and unpacking the book.tar.Z file.

Utilities on Multiple Platforms

Part of adjusting to the Internet means getting used to the diversity of systems that people use. Text files that you'd like to read might have originated on a PC, Mac, Amiga, Sun, IBM mainframe, or perhaps something more exotic. Fortunately, many of the utilities discussed in this chapter are available on a variety of platforms. For example, there is a version of the Unix tar program for IBM PCs, and the Macintosh StuffIt program can deal with files created on other systems by compress, tar, and other utilities.

How to Get File Utilities

Most if not all of the programs discussed in this chapter should be available at your Internet site. If a program isn't available, you can get it with ftp. There are two useful documents that you should obtain for more information about the operation and availability of the encoding, compression, and archiving programs. One is the Frequently Asked Questions (FAQ) file on compression, which is available in the newsgroup news.answers and at archive sites for this newsgroup. (This file comes in three parts: parts 2 and 3 are rather technical, but part 1 surveys the various file compression and archiving programs and gives addresses where you can obtain them by ftp.)

If you decide to become an expert on Internet file formats, you'll want to look at the file with the title "Compression" that can be obtained by ftp from ftp.cso.uiuc.edu (128.174.5.61) in the directory /doc/pcnet (or you can use archie to find a copy of this file; see Chapter 11).

Versions of the common Internet file utilities for PCs and Macs can also be found on many commercial information services and local bulletin boards.

254

Related Topics

To Learn How to...	See Chapter
Copy, move, or delete files	6
Create directories	6
Download files to your PC	9
Get file utilities by ftp	7
Get graphics files from newsgroups	4
Mail a file	3
Read or edit text files	6

How-Tos in this Chapter

8.1 Figure out what to do with a file
A file's extension (or extensions) usually indicates what type of processing the file has undergone. You will be directed to the right how-to for coping with each file type.

8.2 Prepare a binary file for mailing
Before you can mail (or post) a binary file, you need to encode it into a text file with the uuencode program.

8.3 Restore an encoded binary file
At the other end, when you receive a binary file by mail (or find one in a news article), the file will probably be encoded as text. You use the uudecode program to turn the text file back into a binary file.

8.4 Use btoa with binary files
btoa (binary to ASCII) is an alternative method for encoding or decoding binary files.

8.5 Compress a file to save space and time
Before mailing or ftping a file, you may want to save space and time by compressing the file first. The compress program does this job quickly and easily.

8.6 Restore a compressed file
A compressed file can be identified by the .Z extension. You use the uncompress program to restore a compressed file to its original form.

8.7 Read a compressed text file without uncompressing it
If you find several interesting compressed text files and ftp them to your Internet site, you can take a quick look at them without going through the compression process. The zcat program displays the text that is in a compressed file.

8.8 Compress and uncompress files for my PC
Many files of interest to PC users on the Internet are found in compressed form. A number of programs are available for compressing and uncompressing files for IBM PC-compatible systems. You will learn how to use the pkzip and pkunzip programs to compress and uncompress files, as well as two other popular programs (lharc and arc).

8.9 Compress and uncompress files for my Macintosh
The StuffIt program is a popular compression utility for Macintosh users. The BinHex program encodes Mac programs much the way uuencode does for Unix programs.

8.10 Package files with tar
tar, the "tape archive" program is widely used for packaging sets of Unix files. While this program has many options, there are only a few that you really need to know.

8.11 Unpack a tar file archive
Unpacking a tar file is even easier than creating one.

INTERNET HOW-TO

8.12 Mail or receive a compressed tar archive
Often files are both compressed and archived with tar. While you can perform the compression, archiving, and encoding steps separately, there is a handy utility called tarmail that lets you easily send and receive such tar files in a single step.

8.13 Create a shell archive
Many Unix users find the shar (shell archive) program a handy way to package files for mail transmission, news posting, or ftp.

8.14 Unpack a shell archive
The unshar program breaks a shell archive into its component files.

8.1 HOW DO I...
Figure out what to do with a file?

COMPLEXITY: INTERMEDIATE

Problem
It isn't always obvious that a given file needs further processing before it can be used. Fortunately, many file processing programs use standard filename extensions to indicate that they have worked on a file.

Technique
You can use the file's extension (or extensions) as an indication of what programs have been used to process the file. By learning which programs work with which extensions, you can determine which sequence of commands is appropriate for processing the file.

Steps
1. Look at the name of the file you want to work with. If the name has an extension (a part that follows a period, such as .Z or .tar), look for the extension in Table 8-2.

2. If you find the extension in Table 8-2, note the program that the table says should be used for files with this extension. You will use this program to process the file.

3. Process the file using the indicated program. If you don't know how to use this program, turn to the how-to indicated in the table.

4. If the file has two extensions, process the file first for the last extension in the filename. After processing, you will have a file with that extension removed. Repeat the procedure for the remaining extension. For example, a file named picture.tar.Z would be processed first for the .Z extension (using uncompress) and then for the .tar extension (using the tar program).

5. If the filename has no extensions, or has an extension not listed in Table 8-2, look for any instructions accompanying the file for an indication of what program was used to process the file. You can type `more <` followed by the filename at the system prompt to see whether the file is a regular text file. If you think the file is an executable program, you can move it to the appropriate kind of machine, try to run it, and see what happens.

8 ADVANCED FILE TECHNIQUES

EXTENSION	PROCESS BY RUNNING	HOW-TO
arc	arc (PC)	8.8
arj	arj (PC)	8.8
exe	Filename at DOS command line (may be self-extracting)	Note[1]
gz	gzip (Unix, PC)	8.6
hqx	BinHex (Mac)	8.9
lhz	lharc (PC)	8.8
sea	Run on Mac (self-extracting)	Note[2]
shar	unshar or sh	8.14
sit	StuffIt (probably for Mac)	8.9
tar	tar	8.11
uue	uudecode	8.3
Z	uncompress	8.6
zip	pkunzip (PC)	8.8
zoo	zoo (may be PC)	8.8

[1] Run at DOS prompt. Program will either run or self-extract into its component files.

[2] Run with Macintosh Finder. Program will self-extract into its component files.

Table 8-2 File extensions and what to do with them

8.2 HOW DO I...
Prepare a binary file for mailing?

COMPLEXITY: EASY

Problem
Binary files cannot be mailed "as is" because the mail program adds headers for the sender, routing, and other information to the file. These headers will make the binary file unusable.

Technique
Use the uuencode program to turn the binary file into a text file. The mail program will add headers as usual, but the uudecode program can be used later by the recipient to remove the headers and restore the original binary file.

Steps
1. At the system prompt for the Internet site, type `uuencode` followed by the name of the binary file to be encoded. Follow this with the name that the file is to have when decoded (usually the same as the original name of the binary file). Add `>` and the name of the encoded file (by convention, this is the same as the name of the original binary file with the .uue extension added). For example, consider a utility program called fileutil. Its listing looks like this:

```
% ls -l fileutil
-rwxr-xr-x   1 hrh      well          9004 Jan 25 02:20 fileutil
```

INTERNET HOW-TO

You can turn the fileutil program, which is a binary file, into an encoded file using the following command:

```
% uuencode fileutil fileutil > fileutil.uue
```

This command says to take the fileutil file, encode it as the same name (fileutil), and name the encoded file fileutil.uue. (The .uue extension reminds anyone who sees this name that the file is an encoded binary file that must be decoded with the uudecode program.)

2. You can run the ls command to see the following:

```
% ls -l fileutil*
-rwxr-xr-x   1 hrh     well      9004 Jan 25 02:20 fileutil
-rw-r--r--   1 hrh     well     12433 Jan 25 02:35 fileutil.uue
```

Notice that the encoded fileutil.uue is larger than the original fileutil file, because the text information takes up more room than the equivalent binary values. Also note that your original file is intact. (You may wish to delete the original if you aren't going to need it.)

3. Once the file has been encoded, you can mail it with any mailer. A convenient way to combine the encoding and mailing operation is to use a Unix pipe. For example, to encode and mail a game called rogue to your friend George, type the following at the command prompt:

```
%uuencode rogue rogue | mail george
```

The *pipe* (indicated by the | symbol) sends the encoded rogue file directly to the mail program, which sends it to the recipient, George.

How It Works
The uuencode command converts the binary bytes of the file to characters that represent their values. The result is an ASCII text file (though the text doesn't make any sense when read, of course). Since every three bytes of the original binary file are replaced with four bytes of ASCII characters plus some control information, encoding a file replaces it with a file that is about 35 percent longer.

Comment
It is a good idea to check the permissions on the file before encoding (see Chapter 6 for an explanation of file permissions and the use of the chmod command). To successfully decode the file (with uudecode), the recipient must have write permission for the original file. You can add that permission by typing `chmod o+w` followed by the filename at the system prompt, before running encode.

8.3 HOW DO I...
Restore an encoded binary file?

COMPLEXITY EASY

Problem
A binary file encoded as a text file must be restored to its original binary form before it can be used (that is, before the program can be run, the picture viewed, and so on).

8 ADVANCED FILE TECHNIQUES

Technique
You use the uudecode program to restore a binary file that is encoded with the uuencode program.

Steps
1. At the system prompt, type `uudecode` followed by the `<` symbol and the name of the encoded file. For example, to decode the file fileutil.uue, you would type:

```
% uudecode < fileutil.uue
```

The uudecode program decodes the encoded file and gives it the filename that was specified when the file was originally encoded—fileutil in this case.

2. You can verify this by running the ls command:

```
% ls -l fileutil*
-rw-r--r--   1 hrh     well        9004 Jan 25 02:38 fileutil
-rw-r--r--   1 hrh     well       12433 Jan 25 02:35 fileutil.uue
```

Note that fileutil is the exact same size it was before it was encoded in How-To 8.2. The fileutil.uue file is still there; unless you need it for some reason, you can get rid of it with the rm command.

How It Works
When the uuencode program encodes a binary file, it inserts a "begin" marker to indicate where the actual binary data begins. The uudecode program removes any text that appears before this marker (for example, headers added by the mailer), and then converts the remaining characters back to their original binary values. The result is an identical copy of the original binary file.

8.4 HOW DO I... Use btoa with binary files?

COMPLEXITY: EASY

Problem
Some files on the Internet are binary files that have been encoded as ASCII text using the btoa program. These files must be converted back to binary values before they can be used. You may also wish to use btoa to encode a binary file before mailing it.

Technique
You use the btoa program to convert a binary file to encoded text, or to convert an encoded text file back to its original binary form.

Steps
1. To convert a binary file to encoded text with btoa, type `btoa` followed by the name of the binary file and the name to be given to the encoded text file. For example, to convert the binary image file spaceship.pic to the encoded file spaceship.bto, type

```
% btoa spaceship.pic spaceship.bto
```

The resulting encoded text file can be mailed or posted to news. The purpose of the .bto extension is to alert the recipient that the file needs to be converted back to binary form with btoa.

259

INTERNET HOW-TO

2. To decode a file encoded with btoa, type `btoa -a` followed by the filename:

```
%btoa -a spaceship.bto
```

btoa will convert spaceship.bto back to the binary file spaceship.pic.

3. As with uuencode, you can use btoa with a pipe to encode and mail a file with a single command. Thus to mail spaceship.pic in encoded form to Janet on The WELL, type

```
%btoa spaceship.pic | mail -s 'convert this program with btoa' janet@well.com
```

Since you can't change the extension of the file with this method, you use the subject of the mail message to alert the recipient that this is a btoa file.

How It Works
btoa works like the uuencode program, replacing binary values with ASCII text characters so the file can be safely mailed or posted as news. btoa encodes the original name of the file so that btoa -a can restore it with the correct name. btoa -a also automatically skips over headers introduced by the mail program before decoding the file.

Comment
Using uuencode/uudecode is recommended over btoa since the former programs seem to be more universally available.

8.5 HOW DO I...
Compress a file to save space and time?

COMPLEXITY: EASY

Problem
Big files cause two problems. First, they take up disk space, and many Internet providers impose quotas on disk usage and/or charge for additional space. Second, it takes longer to upload or download large files, and this can lead to increased phone expenses. And while ftp moves even big files very quickly, thousands of newcomers are trying to merge onto the information superhighway every day. Reducing file size helps keep capacity available for other users.

Technique
You can use either the compress program or the gzip program to shrink a file down and save disk space and transmission time.

Steps
1. At the system prompt, type `compress` followed by the name of the file you want to compress. For example, to compress the graphics file palace.gif, you type

```
% compress palace.gif
```

The compressed file will have the same name as the original, with the extension .Z added. In this case, the compressed graphics file will be palace.gif.Z.

2. A listing of the two files shows the extent of the compression:

```
%ls -l palace*
-rw-r--r--   1 hrh      well         207049 Jan 25 02:46 palace.gif
-rw-r--r--   1 hrh      well         185970 Jan 25 02:46 palace.gif.Z
```

3. If you would like a more detailed report on the compression process, add the `-v` switch to your compress command:

```
% compress -v palace.gif
palace.gif: Compression: 10.18% — replaced with palace.gif.Z
```

4. You can use wildcards to compress more than one file at a time. For example, consider the following three files whose names all begin with "gnn". The * wildcard lets you work with all of the files:

```
% ls -l gnn*
-rw-------   1 hrh      well           2655 Jan 21 23:40 gnn2
-rw-------   1 hrh      well           6441 Jan 14 20:27 gnnlist
-rw-------   1 hrh      well           3105 Jan 20 16:59 gnnsub
```

You can compress all these files at once by specifying the filename `gnn*` in the compress command:

```
% compress -v gnn*
gnn2: Compression: 34.04% — replaced with gnn2.Z
gnnlist: Compression: 38.73% — replaced with gnnlist.Z
gnnsub: Compression: 34.62% — replaced with gnnsub.Z
```

5. The gzip program is a widely available alternative to the compress program. You use gzip in the same way as compress. For example, to compress the text file jpeg.txt, type

```
% gzip jpeg.txt
```

gzip adds the .gz extension to the name of the compressed version of the file:

```
% ls -l jpeg.txt*
-rw-r--r--   1 hrh      well          61199 Jan 24 03:40 jpeg.txt
-rw-r--r--   1 hrh      well          23577 Jan 24 03:40 jpeg.txt.gz
```

Notice that this text file was compressed by about 60 percent, considerably more than the graphics file in the earlier example. Often graphics files will compress further than text files, but this example shows how the effectiveness of compression varies considerably with the contents of the file.

How It Works

The compress and gzip programs use an algorithm called Lempel-Ziv to replace all repeating sequences of text (or binary values) with the minimum amount of information needed to re-create the file. (The ftp file named "Compression," mentioned at the beginning of this chapter, has more technical details and a list of readings on compression theory.)

Comment

gzip and its relatives, gunzip and zcat, can be very handy for PC users because versions of these utilities are available for both Unix and DOS systems. This means you can gzip a file on the Internet machine, download the (shrunken) file to your PC, and then use a PC version of gunzip to restore the file, or you could use Unix zip and pkzip (see How-To 8.8).

INTERNET HOW-TO

8.6 HOW DO I...
Restore a compressed file?

COMPLEXITY: EASY

Problem
A compressed file with an extension such as .Z or .gz must be uncompressed before you can use it.

Technique
You use the uncompress program (for .Z files) or the gunzip program (for .gz files). The result is an exact copy of the original file.

Steps
1. For a .Z file, type `uncompress` followed by the name of the compressed file. For example, to uncompress the palace.gif.Z graphics file, type:

```
% uncompress palace.gif.Z
```

   The result is a file without the .Z extension:

```
well% ls -l palace.gif
-rw-r--r--   1 hrh      well       207049 Jan 25 02:46 palace.gif
```

2. For a more detailed report on the decompression, add the `-v` option:

```
well% uncompress -v palace.gif.Z
palace.gif.Z:  -- replaced with palace.gif
```

3. You can uncompress a group of files using wildcards. For example, to uncompress all files whose names begin with gnn, type

```
well% uncompress -v gnn*
gnn2.Z:     -- replaced with gnn2
gnnlist.Z:  -- replaced with gnnlist
gnnsub.Z:   -- replaced with gnnsub
```

   The * wildcard matched all the files beginning with gnn and passed them to the uncompress program.

4. To uncompress a .gz file that was created with gzip, type `gunzip` followed by the filename, for example:

```
well% gunzip jpeg.txt.gz
```

   The result is a file without the .gz extension, namely jpeg.txt. Note that on some systems you may have to use gzcat rather than zcat.

How It Works
The decompression programs (uncompress and gunzip) reverse the processing of their counterparts, compress and gzip. They use the codes and strings of values in the compressed files to re-create the original file contents.

Comment
Unlike compress and uncompress, gzip and gunzip *replace* the file they work on, so the original is no longer on disk.

8.7 HOW DO I...
Read a compressed text file without uncompressing it?

COMPLEXITY: EASY

Problem
Let's say you've grabbed a number of compressed text files from your favorite ftp server or newsgroup. Since downloading files can be time-consuming, you might want to take a quick look at the contents of each file before deciding to uncompress and/or download it.

Technique
You can use the handy zcat program to read a compressed (.Z or .gz) file without performing the full decompression procedure.

Steps
1. Type `zcat` followed by the name of the compressed file you want to read. For example, to read the file gnnlist.Z, type

```
% zcat gnnlist.Z
```

The text in the file will scroll from the beginning, just as it does with the regular Unix cat command (see Chapter 6):

```
From server@ora.com Fri Jan 14 20:26:18 1994
Return-Path: server@ora.com
Received: from amber.ora.com (amber.ora.com [140.186.65.13]) by well.sf.ca.us (8
.6.5/8.6.5) with SMTP id UAA25737; Fri, 14 Jan 1994 20:25:44 -0800
Received: by amber.ora.com (5.65c/Spike-2.1)
        id AA17094; Fri, 14 Jan 1994 16:41:53 -0500
Date: Fri, 14 Jan 1994 16:41:53 -0500
Message-Id: <199401142134.AA10378@rock.west.ora.com>
Errors-To: gnn-list@ora.com
Reply-To: gnnlist@ora.com
Originator: gnn-announce@gnn.com
Sender: gnn-announce@ora.com
Precedence: bulk
From: gnnlist@ora.com (The GNN Subscription Account)
To: Multiple recipients of list <gnn-announce@ora.com>
Subject: 2nd GNN Magazine issue
X-Listprocessor-Version: 6.0a — ListProcessor by Anastasios Kotsikonas
X-Comment: To subscribe, please send mail to info@gnn.com
Status: RO

                THE INTERNET — AN EDUCATION IN ITSELF

Announcing the 2nd Issue of GNN Magazine, January 1994 (ISSN 1072-0413)

The Education issue of GNN Magazine is now available.    See
the Table of Contents below.
```

INTERNET HOW-TO

On many systems you can press CTRL-B to stop the listing when you've seen enough; or use CTRL-S to stop the scrolling and CTRL-Q to resume it.

2. As with the cat command, you can also use a pipe to send the output of the zcat command to another program. Thus, to read the contents of gnnlist.Z a screenful at a time, type

```
% zcat gnnlist.Z | more
```

How It Works
The zcat program decompresses the file on-the-fly and presents it to you line by line.

Comment
Remember that zcat will provide useful results only with regular text files. If the file is an archive (.tar extension), you will have to extract the files from the archive (see How-To 8.11) and then read them with a regular Unix command such as cat or more. Note that zcat will work with text files compressed with either the compress program or the gzip program.

8.8 HOW DO I...
Compress and uncompress files for my PC?

COMPLEXITY: INTERMEDIATE

Problem
PC users can find hundreds of useful files on the Internet, including games, utilities, shareware, graphics, and others. Most of these files will have been compressed using one of the compression programs available for the PC. The most widely used archiving and compression program for PCs today is pkzip, but there are also plenty of files that have been packaged using the arc or lharc programs.

Technique
Once you've downloaded a file to your PC, you use the file extension to identify the compression program used. Files with the .zip extension have been compressed with pkzip; the .arc extension is used by the arc program; and the .lhz extension is used by the lharc program.

Once you have identified the program used, run it to uncompress the file. (If the file is an archive it will be unpacked as well as uncompressed.)

Since archive files can contain many separate files, it is a good idea to move the compressed/archive file to a temporary directory on your hard disk before processing it. That way all the relevant files will stay together and not be intermingled with unrelated files. (The examples here use a program archive called prog, which contains a program and a couple of documentation files.)

Steps
1. Download the file(s) from the Internet site to your PC. (See Chapter 9 for methods you can use to download files.)

2. To process a .zip file with pkunzip, go to the DOS prompt and type `pkunzip` followed by the name of the compressed (.zip) file:

```
C:\TEMP>pkunzip prog.zip
```

pkunzip displays a version screen and information that varies with the version. The main thing to look for is the message indicating success and naming the files that were re-created:

```
PKUNZIP (R)    FAST!    Extract Utility    Version 2.04c   12-28-92
Copr. 1989-1992 PKWARE Inc. All Rights Reserved. Shareware version
PKUNZIP Reg. U.S. Pat. and Tm. Off.


_ 80486 CPU detected.
_ EMS version 4.00 detected.
_ XMS version 2.00 detected.
_ DPMI version 0.90 detected.

Searching ZIP: PROG.ZIP
  Exploding: PROG.DOC
  Exploding: PROG.EXE
  Exploding: READ.ME
```

Here, it turns out that prog.zip has three component files, a program file (prog.exe) and two text files (prog.doc and read.me). Note that unlike the case with the compress program, the original .zip file is not removed or altered in any way.

3. Making your own .zip archive is also easy. Let's say you have the files prog.exe and prog.doc and you want to archive and compress them as prog.zip so you can send them to someone. Type `pkzip -a` followed by the name of the archive file you wish to create, and then the name(s) of the files to be included in the archive:

```
C:\TEMP>pkzip -a prog.zip prog*.*
```

Note the use of a DOS wildcard to tell pkzip to include all files whose names begin with "prog".

pkzip reports the results:

```
      PKZIP (tm)    FAST!   Create/Update Utility   Version 1.02   10-01-89
Copyright 1989 PKWARE Inc.   All Rights Reserved.   PKZIP/h for help

Creating ZIP: PROG.ZIP
  Adding: PROG.DOC     imploding (40%), done.
  Adding: PROG.EXE     imploding (42%), done.
```

("Exploding" and "imploding" are pkzip terminology for uncompression and compression, respectively.)

4. To extract files from an .lzh archive (created with the lharc program), type `lha e` followed by the name of the archive (the .lzh extension is optional). Thus to unpack the archive file myprog.lzh, you simply type

```
C:\TEMP>lha e myprog

Extracting from archive : MYPROG.LZH

Melted     PROG.DOC      o
Melted     PROG.EXE      ooo
Melted     READ.ME       o
```

INTERNET HOW-TO

5. To create an archive with lharc, type `lha a` followed by the archive name and the names of the files to add to the archive:

```
C:\TEMP>lha a myprog *.*

Creating archive : myprog.LZH

==> 52% PROG.DOC      o
==> 57% PROG.EXE      ooo
==> 35% HISTORY.ENG   oo
==> 37% READ.ME       o
```

Here the wildcard *.* specifies that all files in the current directory will be added to the archive. The lharc program automatically adds the .lzh extension to the archive name, so the archive created here will be myprog.lzh.

6. The arc program uses virtually the same syntax as lharc. To extract files from an archive with the .arc extension, type `arc e` followed by the name of the archive (the .arc extension is optional):

```
C:\ARCHWIN\TEMP>arc e myprog
Extracting file: PROG.DOC
Extracting file: PROG.EXE
Extracting file: READ.ME
```

7. To make an archive with arc, type `arc a` followed by the name of the archive to be unpacked:

```
C:\TEMP>arc a myprog *.*
Creating new archive: MYPROG.ARC
Adding file:   PROG.DOC       analyzing, crunching, done.
Adding file:   PROG.EXE       analyzing, squeezing, done.
Adding file:   READ.ME        analyzing, crunching, done.
```

How It Works

While they differ in details, the pkzip/pkunzip, arc, and lharc programs all compress files and (if given multiple files) package them into an archive file. The reverse process uncompresses compressed files and unpacks archives into their component files. (Note that pkzip for PCs will also work with files created with the Unix version of zip.)

Comment

The pkzip, arc, and lharc programs are available via ftp (see the "Compression" file mentioned at the beginning of this chapter). They are also widely available on CompuServe and other services and bulletin boards.

See the documentation file that accompanies each program for further details and options.

8.9 HOW DO I...
Compress and uncompress files for my Macintosh?

COMPLEXITY: INTERMEDIATE

Problem
Like PC users, Mac users can find lots of neat files on the Internet. Most of the files have been packed into archives and/or compressed to save space. The files must be unpacked and uncompressed before they can be used.

Technique
The two most popular file processing programs for the Macintosh are BinHex and StuffIt. BinHex is an encoding program (similar to uuencode and uudecode for Unix). It turns binary files into text files so they can be transmitted over the Internet.

StuffIt is a multipurpose archiving and compression program similar to pkzip for IBM PC systems. It handles files that have been processed by BinHex and a variety of other encoding or compression methods. A version called StuffIt Lite is available as shareware from ftp sites and bulletin boards. This is the program used in the following examples.

Steps
1. Download the StuffIt archive from the Internet site to your Macintosh. (Chapter 9 discusses several methods you can use to download files.)

2. To unstuff the archive, run StuffIt and choose Open Archive from the File menu (or press ⌘-O).

3. From the Open dialog box, choose the archive you want to work with (this will presumably be the one you just downloaded).

4. The screen will look something like Figure 8-5. Specify the filename for the unstuffed file, or click on Unstuff or Unstuff All, as appropriate.

5. To create a StuffIt archive, run StuffIt and choose New Archive from the File menu (or press ⌘-N).

6. You will see a dialog box that asks for the name of the archive you are creating and the place where it is to reside in your file system. Fill in the appropriate information.

7. Once you have created an archive, you can add or remove files from it, using the dialog box shown in Figure 8-6.

How It Works
StuffIt is a multipurpose program that lets you create, work with, or unpack and uncompress files from archives. StuffIt can work with other file types not shown here (such as BinHex).

Comment
For more information, see the StuffIt (or StuffIt Lite) manual and online help.

INTERNET HOW-TO

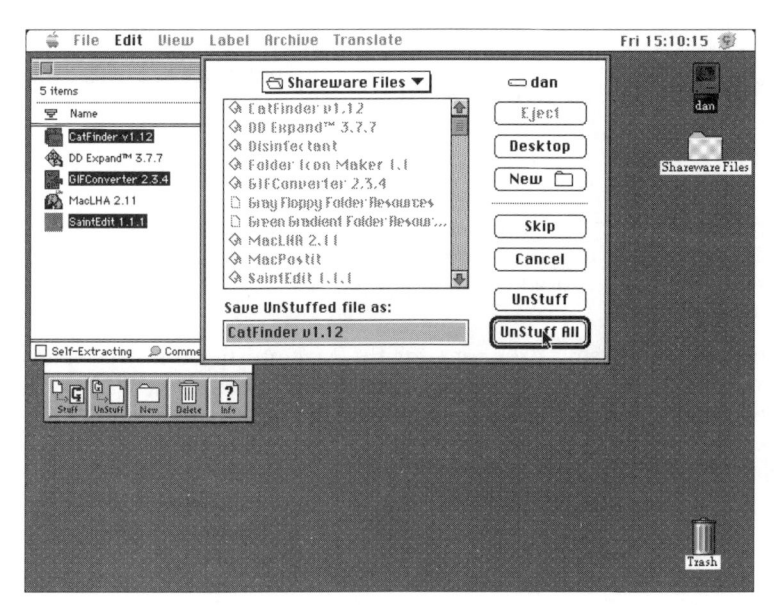

Figure 8-5 Uncompressing with StuffIt

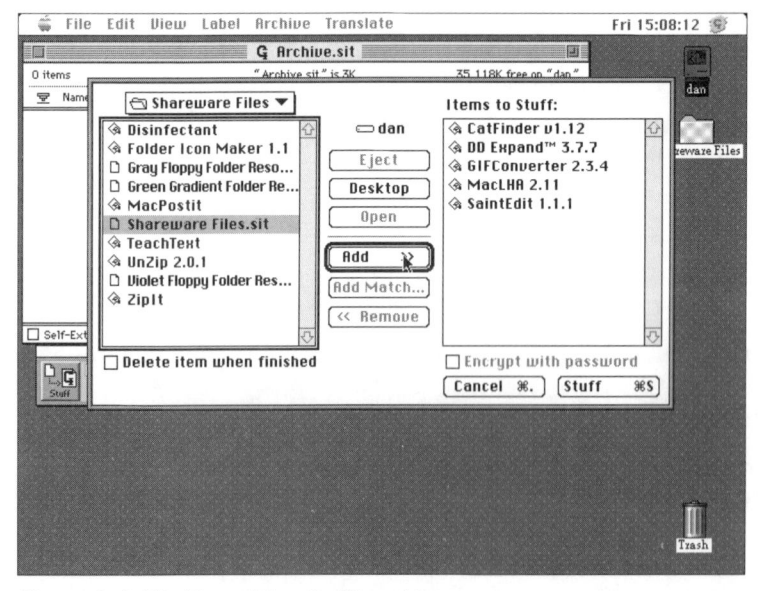

Figure 8-6 Working with a Stuffit archive

8.10 HOW DO I...
Package files with tar?

COMPLEXITY: EASY

Problem
Software packages for Unix systems often consist of dozens of separate files of source code and documentation. Transmission is simpler and more efficient if you package a bunch of small files so they can be sent as a single mail message, news article, or file.

Technique
Use the tar program to create a tar archive from separate files.

Steps
1. To create a tar archive, type `tar -cvf` followed by the name to be used for the archive and the names of the files to be archived. The options used are c (create an archive), v (have the program give a "verbose" explanation of its processing), and f (use the named file for the archive).

   For example, suppose we have the following files:

```
well% ls -l *.txt
-rw-r--r--   1 hrh      well       13111 Jan 25 03:07 chap1.txt
-rw-r--r--   1 hrh      well       13111 Jan 25 03:07 chap2.txt
-rw-r--r--   1 hrh      well       18292 Jan 25 03:07 chap3.txt
-rw-r--r--   1 hrh      well        4128 Jan 25 03:07 chap4.txt
-rw-r--r--   1 hrh      well        3950 Jan 25 03:07 index.txt
```

   To package these in an archive file called book.tar, you can type:

```
well% tar -cvf book.tar *.txt
chap1.txt
chap2.txt
chap3.txt
chap4.txt
index.txt
```

2. You can use the ls command to verify that the tar file was created:

```
well% ls -l book.tar
-rw-r--r--   1 hrh      well       61440 Jan 25 03:20 book.tar
```

How It Works
Like other archiving programs, tar packages the specified files into a single archive file. Unlike zip and similar PC programs, tar does no compression, but Unix users often create the .tar file and then compress it. Thus, you can compress the book.tar file in the example by typing `compress book.tar`, and the result will be a file called book.tar.Z.

The tar program does not remove the original files, but rather places copies of them in the archive.

Comment
The name tar is from "tape archive," reflecting the use of the program for backing up or distributing files on magnetic tape.

INTERNET HOW-TO

8.11 HOW DO I...
Unpack a tar file archive?

COMPLEXITY: EASY

Problem
When you see a file in Unix-land that has the .tar extension, you know you've found an archive created with the tar program. You must unpack the archive into its component files before you can use them.

Technique
You use the tar program to unpack the archive.

Steps
1. Move the .tar file to an empty temporary directory. This will ensure that all (and only) the unpacked files will be together. (See Chapter 6 for information on creating directories.)
2. At the system prompt, type `tar -xvf` followed by the name of the archive. The option switches used are x (extract from archive), v (give a "verbose" report of processing), and f (use the archive given in the filename that follows). For example, to unpack the tar archive book.tar, type:

```
% tar -xvf book.tar
chap1.txt
chap2.txt
chap3.txt
chap4.txt
```

3. Use the ls command to verify that the contents have been unpacked:

```
%ls *.*
-rw-r--r--  hrh/well    13111 Jan 25 03:07 1994 chap1.txt
-rw-r--r--  hrh/well    13111 Jan 25 03:07 1994 chap2.txt
-rw-r--r--  hrh/well    18292 Jan 25 03:07 1994 chap3.txt
-rw-r--r--  hrh/well     4128 Jan 25 03:07 1994 chap4.txt
-rw-r--r--  hrh/well     3950 Jan 25 03:07 1994 index.txt
```

4. If you just want to see what's in a tar archive without actually unpacking the contents, type `tar -tvf` followed by the archive name:

```
% tar -tvf book.tar
-rw-r--r--  hrh/well    13111 Jan 25 03:07 1994 chap1.txt
-rw-r--r--  hrh/well    13111 Jan 25 03:07 1994 chap2.txt
-rw-r--r--  hrh/well    18292 Jan 25 03:07 1994 chap3.txt
-rw-r--r--  hrh/well     4128 Jan 25 03:07 1994 chap4.txt
-rw-r--r--  hrh/well     3950 Jan 25 03:07 1994 index.txt
```

How It Works
Tar uses the header information in the archive to break it up into the original, separate files.

Comment
You can type tar options without the hyphen: `tar -cvf` is the same as `tar cvf`. But since just about all other Unix commands use the hyphen, you might as well get in the habit.

8 ADVANCED FILE TECHNIQUES

If a file has both the .tar and .Z extensions (such as book.tar.Z), you must uncompress the file first (see How-To 8.6.) and then use tar to unpack the archive (book.tar).

The original .tar file is not affected by the extraction process. Use the rm command to remove it if it's no longer needed.

8.12 HOW DO I...
Mail or receive a compressed tar archive?

COMPLEXITY INTERMEDIATE

Problem
A common scenario on Unix systems is that you make a tar archive, compress it, and then mail it to someone. This can be done in three steps using the tar, compress, and mail programs; or the steps can be combined with pipes. Since typing this long series of commands can be tedious, the tarmail utility has been created to let you do everything at once.

Technique
You use the tarmail program to specify the person you want to mail the files to and the names of the files to be packaged.

Steps
1. At the system prompt, type `tarmail` followed by the address of the person you're mailing the files to, an optional subject for the message, and the names of the files you want to be packaged together. For example, to send the files report1, report2, and index to Mary at The WELL, you would type

```
%tarmail mary@well.com 'My report' report1 report2 index
```

2. The recipient will receive a file that has been both archived and compressed. Rather than "manually" uncompressing and unpacking the file, the recipient merely saves the mail message to disk and then types

```
%untarmail myreport
```

(or whatever name the archive was saved under). The untarmail program automatically uncompresses and then unpacks the tar archive.

How It Works
The tarmail utility simply combines and automates three procedures: creating a tar archive, compressing the archive, and mailing the archive to someone. untarmail reverses the procedure by uncompressing and then unpacking the archive.

Comment
The tarmail program may not be available at your Internet site.

8.13 HOW DO I...
Create a shell archive?

COMPLEXITY EASY

Problem
You may wish to package a group of text files into an archive to mail or post them, but you may not be sure what archiving utilities your recipient has available.

271

Technique

You can use the shar (shell archive) program to create an archive that any Unix user can unpack, since shar uses a language understood by the standard Unix shells.

Steps

1. Type `shar`, followed by the names of the files to be archived, the > symbol, and the name for the archive file. For example, to archive the files part1, part2, and part3 into a shell archive called report.shar, type

```
% shar part? > report.shar
```

The wildcard ? matches the names part1, part2, and part3. You can specify the names separately if you wish.

2. Use the ls command to verify that the shell archive named report has been created:

```
well% ls -l report
-rw-r--r--   1 hrh      well       14188 Jan 25 03:32 report.shar
```

3. You can also use the more command to see what a shell archive looks like:

```
well% more < report.shar
#! /bin/sh
# This is a shell archive.  Remove anything before this line, then feed it
# into a shell via "sh file" or similar.  To overwrite existing files,
# type "sh file -c".
# The tool that generated this appeared in the comp.sources.unix newsgroup;
# send mail to comp-sources-unix@uunet.uu.net if you want that tool.
# Contents:  part1 part2 part3
# Wrapped by hrh@well on Tue Jan 25 03:32:16 1994
PATH=/bin:/usr/bin:/usr/ucb ; export PATH
echo If this archive is complete, you will see the following message:
echo '          "shar: End of archive."'
```

How It Works

The shell archive is actually a shell script, or program written in the shell language. This program includes comments (such as those in the preceding listing), commands that tell the shell how to re-create the text files, and the contents of the files themselves.

Comment

shar won't add the .shar extension unless you specify it in the archive name. It's a good idea to use this extension so the recipient will know that the file is a shar archive.

8.14 HOW DO I...
Unpack a shell archive?

COMPLEXITY EASY

Problem

When you see a shell archive file (in a newsgroup, for example), you need to unpack the archive into its component files.

Technique

You use the unshar program to unpack a shell archive.

8 ADVANCED FILE TECHNIQUES

Steps
1. At the system prompt, type `unshar` followed by the name of the .shar file to be unpacked. For example, to unpack the report.shar file you would type

```
well% unshar report.shar
```

unshar will report its progress:

```
unshar:  Sending header to report.shar.hdr.
unshar:  Doing report.shar (with /bin/sh)
If this archive is complete, you will see the following message:
         "shar: End of archive."
shar: Extracting "part1" (2655 characters)
shar: Extracting "part2" (6441 characters)
shar: Extracting "part3" (3105 characters)
shar: End of archive.
```

How It Works
unshar first strips off any extraneous headers (such as those added by the mail system) and saves them in a file named for the .shar file with the .hdr extension added. unshar then unpacks the individual files in the shell archive.

Comment
You can also unpack a shell archive simply by feeding it to a shell, like this:

```
%sh < report.shar
```

It is better to use unshar, however, because unshar can recognize and strip the headers that mail or other programs may have added.

Transferring Files Between Your PC and the Internet

How do I...

9.1	Capture a text file to my PC's hard disk
9.2	Paste text from my PC to the Internet host
9.3	Choose a file transfer protocol
9.4	Download files with Xmodem, Ymodem, or Zmodem
9.5	Upload files with Xmodem, Ymodem, or Zmodem
9.6	Use Kermit to connect to the net
9.7	Download files with Kermit
9.8	Upload files with Kermit
9.9	Get help with Kermit commands
9.10	Use a session file to save communications settings
9.11	Use a login script to simplify connection
9.12	Learn more about telecommunications

Once you've saved mail or news articles or fetched files by ftp, the files will be sitting in your home directory on the Internet system. In many cases, however, you'll want to move the files to your PC where you can use them. (A nifty utility or game for Windows won't do you much good sitting on a Unix system, after all.) You'll also want to transfer files from your Internet account (where they might incur storage charges) to your PC's hard disk (which you've probably already paid for). Of course the file transfer can go in the other direction, too: you may want to transfer files you've created with your word processor or spreadsheet on the PC to the Internet system, where they can be mailed to another user.

INTERNET HOW-TO

This chapter is about methods for transferring files between your PC and the remote computer, which is called the *Internet host*. These methods range from simply capturing or "pasting" text to transferring files using error-correcting protocols. You will also learn the basics of using Kermit, a widely available (and free) package that provides communications, terminal emulation, and file transfer capabilities for just about every computer system imaginable.

It's a fact of life in the telecommunications world that different hosts will have different programs and facilities available. Not all Internet hosts have the same versions of file transfer programs such as Xmodem or Zmodem. On the PC end there is even more variation in the communications programs available and the file transfer facilities they support. This chapter shows examples using Windows Terminal, Windows Kermit, and WinLink (a shareware Windows communications program). On the host side you see how your communications software can be connected to xm (Xmodem), C-Kermit, and a set of Zmodem programs.

You will probably have to generalize the techniques illustrated here and find the exact menu items or commands used to accomplish them in your own communications software. As you read, keep your eye on the basic ideas and techniques and worry about the details later.

File Transfer Protocols

If you capture a text file to your PC or paste some text from a Windows word processor into a text editor at your Internet host, you may notice that some garbage characters (wrong letters or little graphic symbols) creep in from time to time. This is due to bursts of interference on the phone lines, sometimes called *line noise*.

With a text file, getting a few characters wrong is probably no big deal; you can always fix the errors with your editor. But with a binary file, such as an executable program, a single garbage character can render the entire file useless. For this reason techniques have been developed to ensure that no mistranslations or garbage characters can get into a file that is being sent from one computer to another. The general term for such a method of checking and verifying data as it is received is a *communications protocol*, or specifically, an *error-correcting protocol*.

While the technical details of how such protocols work is beyond the scope of this book, Figure 9-1 gives a conceptual view of the process. Data that is being transmitted is broken into *packets* or *blocks* (usually from 128 bytes up to about 4K in length). The sending program examines the data and calculates a value, such as a checksum or a CRC (cyclic redundancy check). The program then sends the packet of data along with a header that includes the calculated value. The receiving program notes this value and performs the same calculation on the data it has just received. If the values match, all is well, and the receiving program says the equivalent of, "OK, send me more data." If there is a discrepancy, however, the receiving program says, "It doesn't match. Try again." Usually, the next time the data is sent it will get through correctly. If not, after a certain number of *retries* (set by the software), the file transfer will fail.

A file transfer can fail for one of several reasons:

➢ The basic communications settings (speed, parity, data bits, stop bits) don't match on both systems. If this is the case, the transfer won't even start—it will appear to "hang," *time out* (not make the connection within the time limit set by the program), or spew garbage characters on the screen.

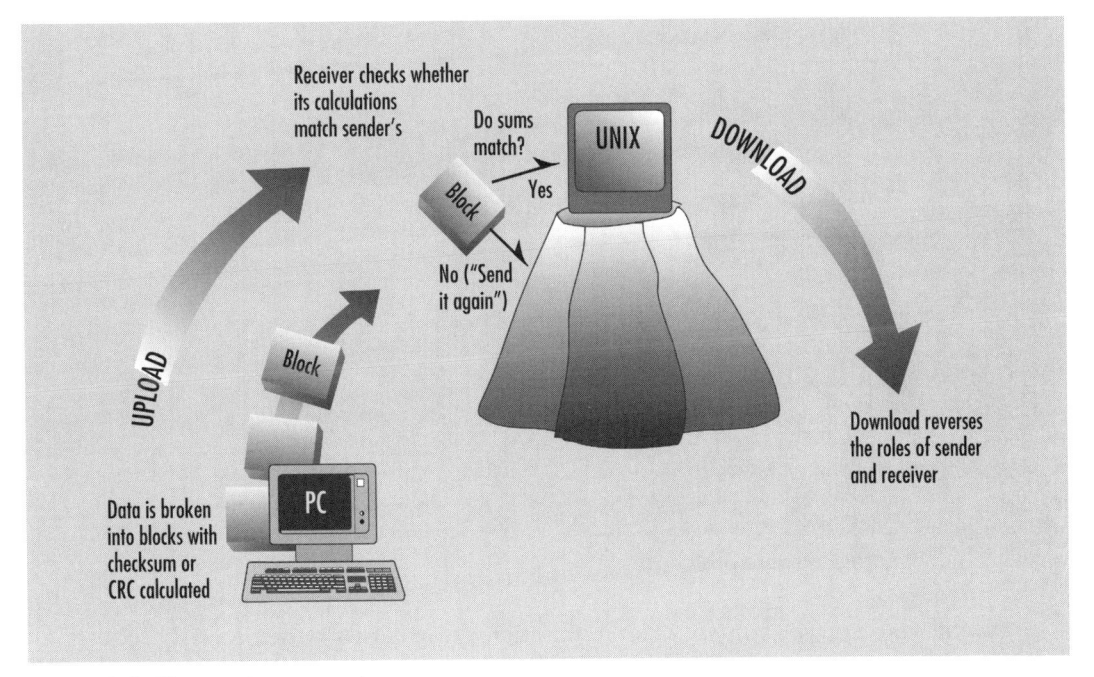

Figure 9-1 File transfer protocol

➤ You specified the wrong type of file (text or binary) on one or both ends of the connection.
➤ You have a noisy phone line. In this case, some communications programs allow a "relaxed modem setting," which gives the software more time to synchronize at the expense of slowing things down a bit. (You can also complain to your friendly local phone company about persistent bad connections, of course.)

Running the Software

You've seen a bit about protocols and why they're needed. Let's now look at the big picture. How do you set up a file transfer between your PC and an Internet host? The general steps you take are given in the following list. While reading them, keep in mind that *uploading* means that you are transferring files from your PC to the Internet host, and *downloading* means that you are transferring files from the Internet host to your PC.

As shown in Figure 9-2, the way communications protocols are implemented differs between PCs and host systems. On PCs, the protocols are usually provided as features of an integrated software package (such as Windows Terminal or Microphone). At the host, however, the protocols are separate utilities with names such as Xmodem (or xm), sz, rz, and so on. The basic communications and terminal emulation are handled by separate software. Therefore, you are matching features of your PC communications program against utility programs available on the host.

INTERNET HOW-TO

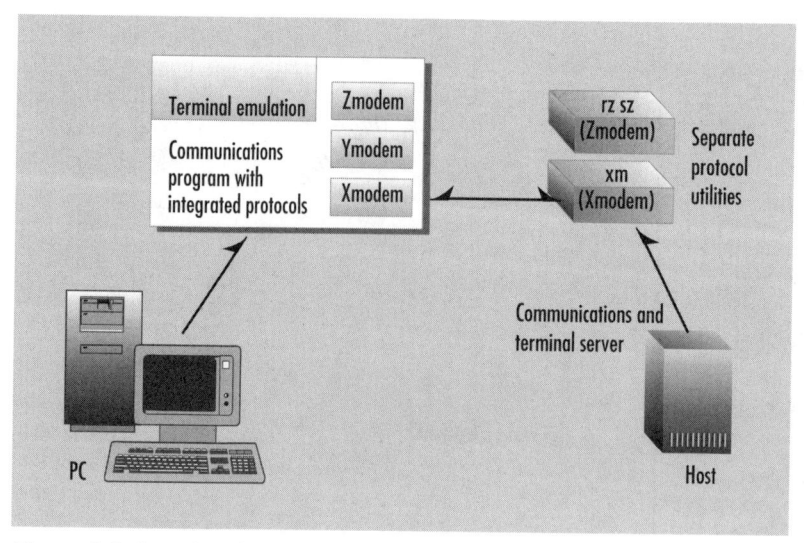

Figure 9-2 Running the software protocol

1. On your PC, you run your communications program with the necessary settings to dial up and connect to the Internet host. (This is covered in Chapter 2.)

2. At the Internet host, you run a file transfer program such as Xmodem, Zmodem, or Kermit. Usually you have to specify settings that determine whether you are downloading a file to your PC (in which case the remote program is *sending* a file) or uploading a file from your PC to the host (in which case the remote program is *receiving* a file). You may also have to specify whether the file is binary or text. (When in doubt, it's safer to specify binary.)

3. If you're downloading, you tell the remote program what file or files it is to send. If you're uploading, you tell the remote program to get ready to receive a file.

4. Now you turn your attention back to your PC. First, make sure you've selected the same protocol you're using on the Internet host. (That is, if the host is running the Xmodem (or xm) program, you tell your software to use Xmodem.)

5. You tell your software whether you're sending a file (if uploading) or receiving a file (if downloading). You may also have to tell it whether you are transferring binary or text files. If you're uploading, tell your software what file or files it is to send.

6. Now you sit back and watch the transfer take place. Usually the software on your PC will show you some kind of running total of blocks sent or received, and perhaps an estimate of the amount of time remaining before the transfer will be complete.

7. Assuming the transfer completes successfully, you can repeat the process to transfer more files, or continue with other activities on the Internet host. (You may have to press (ENTER) a couple of times to get the remote system's attention after a file transfer is completed.)

Some General Tips for File Transfers

While the available software and facilities vary, there are some general guidelines and tips that apply to just about any system.

➤ If you're running a multitasking system (Microsoft Windows, for example), you can do something else on your PC while the files are being transferred. You should switch into the communications window periodically to check on progress, however, in case the transfer "hangs" or aborts.

➤ With Windows-type systems you can avoid the need to transfer small text files by cutting and pasting text between the communications program's window and the window of a text editor, notepad, and so forth. (See How-To 9.2.)

➤ If you have a selection of modem speeds available, you should generally connect at the highest speed before transferring files. Some systems charge more for higher speed connections. In that case, do your mail, news, and ftp at a lower, cheaper speed, then log out, reconnect at a higher speed and do your file transfers. Even at higher hourly cost you usually come out ahead when you transfer files at high speed.

➤ Since file transfers can be time-consuming, try to schedule them for evening or weekend hours when phone rates are lower.

➤ Be aware of the different rules for naming files in different operating systems. Unix and Mac both allow long names, DOS (and Windows) limit filenames to eight characters plus a three-character extension. Many communications programs automatically shorten names when moving files from Unix to DOS.

➤ Many programs let you use wildcards (* and ?) to transfer groups of files (see How-To 9.7).

➤ Don't forget to remove the copies of files on the Internet host after you've transferred them to your PC.

➤ If files have an extension that indicates they've been packaged in an archive (.arc, .zip, .tar, or .shar), you'll need to unpack the files before you can use them (see Chapter 8).

➤ If you're uploading many files and/or big files from your PC to the Internet host, you may want to archive and compress the files first (see Chapter 8). This will save you transmission time and make it easier to mail or post the files later.

➤ If you have trouble transferring files, there's probably someone at the Internet host who can help you. Also, some systems, such as The WELL, have menu-driven utilities that can set up and execute a file transfer for you.

These lists of steps and tips may make file transfer seem tedious and complicated. While it's true that file transfer *is* one of the trickier aspects of using the Internet, it becomes pretty much routine once you've found the software that works best for you. Also, there is a movement toward developing software that takes care of more of the picky details.

INTERNET HOW-TO

Kermit Versions

There are two common versions of Kermit for PCs, 2.X and 3.X. We have used 2.X (2.32 specifically) as the main DOS version of Kermit in this chapter. While older, this version is stable and comes with complete documentation. A later version, 3.X (3.11, etc.) has additional features but doesn't come with complete documentation (instead, you must buy a separate book). Some commands work differently in version 3.X; if you are using that version, see the notes in the how-to text and the online help.

Related Topics

To Learn How to...	See Chapter
Copy, move, or delete files on the Internet host	6
Make a basic connection between your PC and the Internet host	2
Package and compress files for faster uploading	8
Uncompress compressed files (.Z)	8
Unpack file archives (.arc, .zip, .tar, and so on)	8

How-Tos in this Chapter

9.1 Capture a text file to my PC's hard disk
If you have a short text file (mail message, news article, perhaps a README file), you don't have to use an elaborate file transfer protocol. You can set your communications software to "receive" or "log" a file and then have the Internet host display the file with the cat command. The file will be saved to your PC's disk.

9.2 Paste text from my PC to the Internet host
If you're using Windows or a Mac (or some DOS programs), you can use copy and paste commands to transfer small amounts of text (such as a brief mail message) from your PC to the Internet host without doing an actual file transfer.

9.3 Choose a file transfer protocol
Some file transfer facilities are faster, more efficient, or more robust than others. This how-to has some suggestions on which ones are best and how you can check availability.

9.4 Download files with Xmodem, Ymodem, or Zmodem
While the features of these protocols differ a bit, the process for downloading a file from the Internet host to your PC is pretty much the same for all of them.

9.5 Upload files with Xmodem, Ymodem, or Zmodem
Reversing the direction and sending files from your PC to the Internet host is simply a matter of changing a few settings and/or menu selections.

9.6 Use Kermit to connect to the net
While Kermit isn't quite as easy to use as some Windows or Mac communications programs, it provides standard commands and is available for an incredible variety of platforms. Learning about Kermit also helps you learn procedures that can be applied to a wide variety of communications programs.

9.7 Download files with Kermit
Kermit has a built-in file transfer protocol. It's easy to transfer one or many files with Kermit.

9.8 Upload files with Kermit
Since you run one Kermit on your PC and the other on the Internet host, it's easy to make them "change places" and send files in the other direction.

9 TRANSFERRING FILES BETWEEN YOUR PC AND THE INTERNET

9.9   Get help with Kermit commands
Kermit provides useful online help for commands and procedures.

9.10   Use a session file to save communications settings
Kermit and many other Windows and DOS communications programs let you store settings in a file that you can use to connect automatically to a particular host computer.

9.11   Use a login script to simplify connection
An alternate approach to making connection easier is to use a *login script*, or file with a series of commands that are executed automatically to log you on the Internet host. You'll see an example of a generic login script that you can translate into the language used by your particular program.

9.12   Learn more about telecommunications
This how-to suggests some sources for further reading and help, including newsgroups.

9.1 HOW DO I...
Capture a text file to my PC's hard disk?

COMPLEXITY: EASY

Problem
Sometimes you'll have a short text file on the Internet host (such as a mail message, news article, or README file). It can be tedious to have to set up a formal file transfer each time you want to copy such a file to your PC.

Technique
You can tell most PC communications programs to "capture to file" the text that appears on the screen. This provides an easy way to get information from the Internet host to your PC without having to set up a file transfer.

Steps
1. Set your PC's communication software to "log to file," "capture to file," or "receive text file." Give the name of the file in which you wish to store the text. (Check your software's documentation for the exact menu selection to use.)

2. At the Internet host, type `cat` followed by the name of the file you wish to capture. For example:

```
% cat READ.ME
```

   The file will be displayed continuously on the screen. (See Chapter 6 for more information on Unix file display commands.)

3. When the display reaches the end of the file, turn off the file capture feature of your PC communications program. The text from the file on the host will now be stored in the file specified on your PC.

How It Works
The PC communications program simply stores all the incoming characters in a file. Rather than transferring a file as such, the stream of text (from whatever source) is copied to the PC's disk.

Comment
You can use this facility to store the output of just about any command you issue on the Internet host. If you wish, you simply leave the "capture to file" facility on and

INTERNET HOW-TO

record your entire Internet session, though the resulting file might be rather large and awkward to use.

Note that "capture to file" works only with text files. Binary files will be captured, but they'll end up stored as text files, rendering them useless. Also note that capturing the output of a Unix program that uses terminal features (such as many mail and news programs) can be difficult because the special terminal control characters will end up mixed in with the text on the PC's disk. Therefore it's best to use file capture with commands such as cat or head that simply display lines of text.

9.2 HOW DO I...
Paste text from my PC to the Internet host?

COMPLEXITY EASY

Problem
Let's say someone has sent you e-mail asking for an address and phone number. You have that information in a text file (or perhaps a database) on your PC. It would be tedious to have to retype this information (and you might make an error).

Technique
If you have Windows, Macintosh System, or similar software, you can simply copy and paste text between your communications program and other programs running on your PC. Figure 9-3 summarizes the steps involved.

Steps
1. Open one window for your communications program and one for a word processor, text editor, database, or other program.

2. In the other program, open the file that contains the text you wish to send to the Internet site.

3. At the Internet site, run the program that you wish to receive the text (for example, a mail program or text editor). The screen for that program will appear in the window of your communications program.

4. If necessary, put the remote program in a mode where it is ready to receive text (for example, press (a) or (i) while running vi).

5. Use your mouse to mark and cut or copy the selected text in its window on your PC.

6. Move the mouse to the window for your communications program and select Paste from the Edit window. The selected text will be copied into the remote program as though you had entered it from the keyboard.

How It Works
Windowing environments let you use the mouse to mark text in any program's window. You then use the Edit menu for that window to indicate whether you will be cutting or copying the text. You can then click on any other program's window and use the menu to paste the text. The other program receives the pasted text. (The difference between cutting and copying is that cutting and pasting text moves it from the original window to the new window, while copying and pasting simply makes a copy of the text in the new window.)

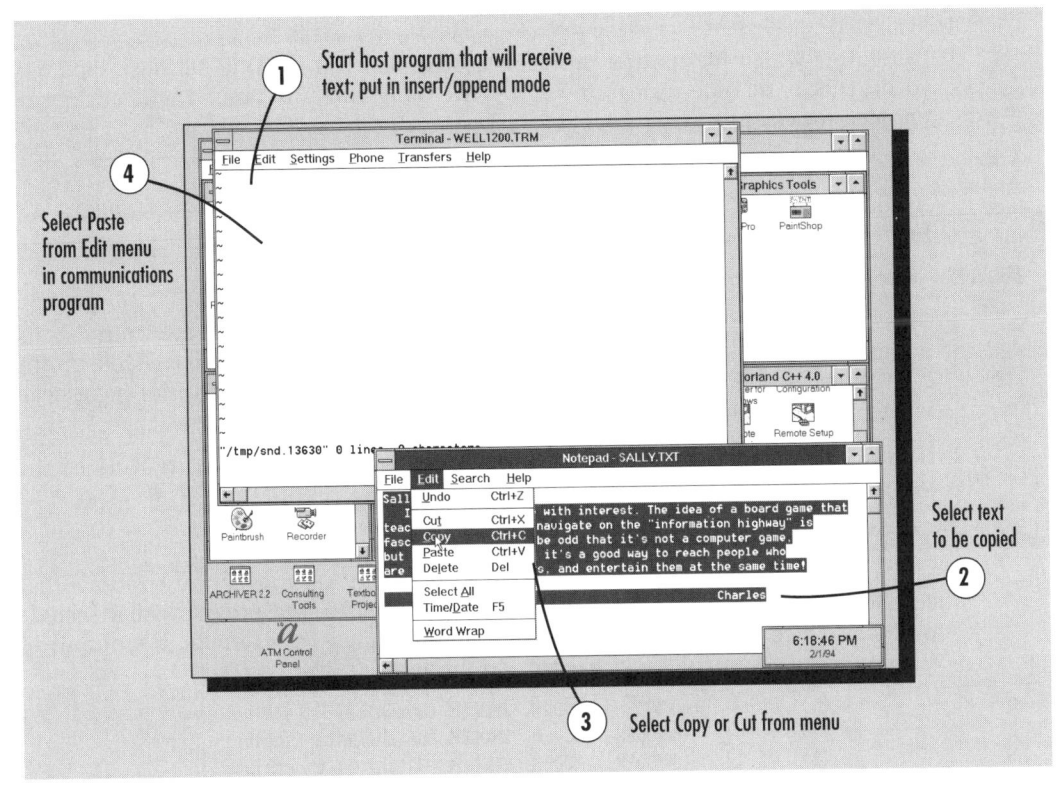

Figure 9-3 Transferring text with copy and paste

Comment
Before you can paste text, you have to make sure the cursor in the receiving program is in the right place and that the program is ready to receive text, that is, in input mode. For a word processor or text editor, this is simply a matter of having the cursor positioned correctly. Other programs, such as databases, may have to be given appropriate commands to set up the data entry process.

9.3 HOW DO I...
Choose a file transfer protocol?

COMPLEXITY INTERMEDIATE

Problem
There are four common file transfer protocols: Xmodem, Ymodem, Zmodem, and Kermit, plus many other lesser-known ones. How do you determine which are available and, of the ones available, which one will work best for you?

Technique
The basic approach is to make a survey of both your Internet host and your PC working environment. You find out which protocols are offered by the available programs, and then decide which is likely to be easiest to use and/or most efficient.

INTERNET HOW-TO

Steps

1. Determine which file transfer protocols are available on the Internet host. One way to do this is to type `man` followed by the names of programs discussed in this chapter, for example

```
% man kermit
```

If you get an online manual entry for the program, it should be available on the host. You may, however, get a response like this:

```
No manual entry for kermit.
```

This means that there is no "official" entry for this program in the online Unix manual. It doesn't necessarily mean that the program you want isn't available on the host, however. That's because most communications protocol utilities have been written by individuals outside of the official Unix distribution process.

2. If you don't find a manual entry, try typing `apropos` followed by one of the program names, as in:

```
% apropos xmodem
```

The apropos program searches the database of manual entries for descriptions that contain the specified keyword. This may enable you to find programs that include protocols (such as Zmodem) but have different names. For example, the output of the preceding command looks like this on the author's host:

```
rb              rx (1)          - XMODEM, YMODEM, ZMODEM (Batch) file receive
rb              rx (1)          - XMODEM, YMODEM, ZMODEM (Batch) file receive
rb              rx (1)          - XMODEM, YMODEM, ZMODEM (Batch) file receive
rx              rx (1)          - XMODEM, YMODEM, ZMODEM (Batch) file receive
rx              rx (1)          - XMODEM, YMODEM, ZMODEM (Batch) file receive
rx              rx (1)          - XMODEM, YMODEM, ZMODEM (Batch) file receive
rz              rx (1)          - XMODEM, YMODEM, ZMODEM (Batch) file receive
rz              rx (1)          - XMODEM, YMODEM, ZMODEM (Batch) file receive
rz              rx (1)          - XMODEM, YMODEM, ZMODEM (Batch) file receive
sb              sx (1)          - XMODEM, YMODEM, ZMODEM file send
sb              sx (1)          - XMODEM, YMODEM, ZMODEM file send
sb              sx (1)          - XMODEM, YMODEM, ZMODEM file send
sx              sx (1)          - XMODEM, YMODEM, ZMODEM file send
sx              sx (1)          - XMODEM, YMODEM, ZMODEM file send
sx              sx (1)          - XMODEM, YMODEM, ZMODEM file send
sz              sx (1)          - XMODEM, YMODEM, ZMODEM file send
sz              sx (1)          - XMODEM, YMODEM, ZMODEM file send
sz              sx (1)          - XMODEM, YMODEM, ZMODEM file send
xmodem          xmodem (1)      - Christensen protocol file transfer utility

% apropos kermit
5A(189)         C-Kermit (1)    - communications software for serial and network
 connections: file transfer, terminal connection, character-set translation, and
 script programming
```

This tells us that there is a program called Xmodem, plus rb, rx, rz, and so on. These refer to protocols that are provided under the umbrella of a few programs such as xm, sz, and rz. Typing `apropos kermit` also reveals that Kermit does appear to be on our system even though it doesn't have a manual entry.

3. You can also type `whereis` followed by a program name, as in:

`% whereis kermit`

If the program exists on the system, whereis will give you the directory path:

`kermit: /usr/src/cmd/kermit /usr/local/bin/kermit`

Often there is one path for the source code and one for the executable program. The former directory is usually where you will find documentation files. Note that on some systems, communications programs may be somewhere separate from the regular Unix commands, since many of these programs are not part of the official Unix distribution. This means that some of these programs may not have regular Unix manual entries.

4. Make a list of what you found. The list might look like this:

PROTOCOL	PROGRAM
Xmodem	xm
Ymodem	xm
Zmodem	rz, sz
Kermit	Kermit

5. Now take inventory of the file transfer protocols available on your PC. Run each available communications program. Check for menu entries under "File" or "Transfers" or similar headings. Look for dialog boxes that let you specify the file transfer protocol and note the options available. (Figure 9-4 shows the relevant dialog box for the WinLink program.) If the program has a manual, check the table of contents and index for such terms as Xmodem, Zmodem, upload, or download. Make a list similar to the one you made in the previous step:

PROTOCOL	PROGRAM
Xmodem	Windows Terminal WinLink ProComm
Zmodem	WinLink
Kermit	Windows Kermit Windows Terminal

6. Finally, match the list of protocols you made for the remote system with the list for your PC. To use a particular protocol, you must have at least one program that uses it at the Internet site, and one that uses it on the PC.

Of the common protocols, Xmodem is the most likely to be available with just about any communications program. Ymodem and Zmodem are a little less common but are widely available. Kermit is both a program *and* a protocol, and you may find it either as a stand-alone program or as one of several protocols offered by a general

INTERNET HOW-TO

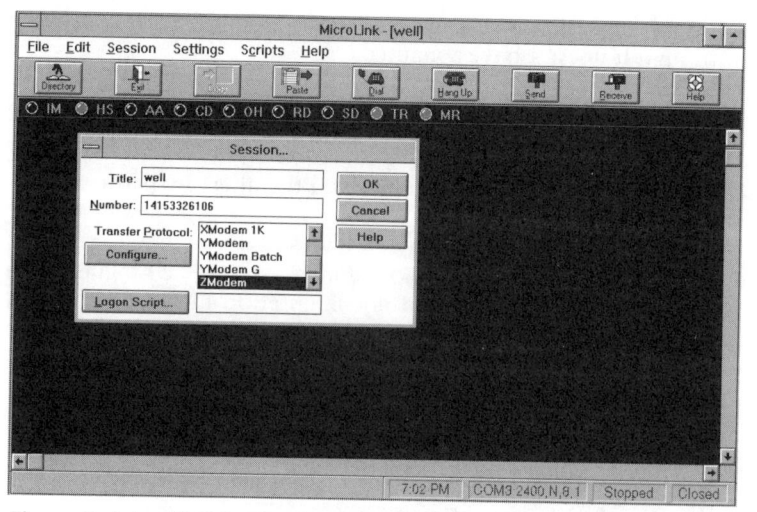

Figure 9-4 Looking for protocols in a communications program

communications program. On the Unix side, it is somewhat more common to have each protocol in a separate program, though the xm version of Xmodem includes Ymodem. PC programs usually provide several different protocols, although the bare-bones Windows Terminal program provides only Xmodem and Kermit.

How It Works

Some programs offer several different communications protocols, while others are simply utilities that perform a single protocol. The object of the game is to find out which protocols are available on *both* your PC and your Internet host, and then to choose the best from that common list.

Comment

So which one is best? Well, if available, Zmodem is generally the fastest protocol, because it sends data continuously rather than waiting for acknowledgments. (If some data doesn't check out on the receiving end, it is then re-requested.) Zmodem has the added capability of letting you resume a file transfer that was interrupted by a problem at either end or with the phone connection.

If Zmodem isn't available, it's pretty much a toss-up between Xmodem and Kermit. Xmodem is available in more PC software packages that are easier to use. Kermit has traditionally relied upon text and key commands rather than windows and menus, but there are versions of Kermit for both Windows and Macintosh.

9.4 HOW DO I...
Download files with Xmodem, Ymodem, or Zmodem?

COMPLEXITY INTERMEDIATE

Problem
You have one or more files on your Internet host that you want to get to your PC.

Technique
You decide which protocol you will be using, and run the appropriate programs on both the PC and the Internet host. You then set some specifications and the file is transferred.

Note: On the host side, this how-to uses the program xm for Xmodem and Ymodem, and the program sz for Zmodem. The programs available on your host may be different (for example, you may need to type `xmodem` rather than `xm`).

Steps
1. To download a file with Xmodem, type `xm` at the host prompt, followed by `sb` (for a binary file) or `st` (for a text file), and the name of the file to be sent to your PC. For example, to send a binary file called neato.zip, you would type

```
% xm sb neato.zip
```

2. To use Ymodem instead of Xmodem, add y to the above commands, specifying `sby` (for a binary file) or `sty` (for a text file). For example, to send the binary file picture.gif using Ymodem, enter the command

```
% xm sby picture.gif
```

3. To use Zmodem for the download, type `sz -b` (for a binary file) or `sz -a` (for a text file, that is, ASCII), followed by the filename. For example, to send the ASCII file news.txt with Zmodem to your PC, you would type

```
% sz -a news.txt
```

4. Whichever protocol you use, you will see a message from the host saying that the file transfer is beginning. At your PC, tell your communications software to receive a file, specifying the same protocol as you used on the host. (Each protocol may have its own menu option, or you may have to select the protocol from a dialog box, as in Figure 9-4.)

For example, with Windows Terminal, to receive (download) a file with Xmodem you would simply choose Receive binary file or Receive text file from the Transfers menu, after making sure that you have selected Xmodem in the Binary Transfers dialog box.

For MicroLink you would choose Session from the Settings menu and then select the protocol from the list presented in the dialog box. Other programs will have different commands, so you may have to experiment a little. Note that with most programs the protocol you select will stay selected until you select another. Your selections can be saved as a "session file" so they will take effect whenever you call a particular host (see How-To 9.10).

INTERNET HOW-TO

Remember: You must specify the same protocol and the same file type as you are sending from the Internet host.

If you discover you've made a mistake or that you're not ready to transfer the file, press `CTRL`-`X` a few times. This will abort the transfer and you'll see a message like this:

```
Reception canceled at user's request
```

5. The file will be transferred from the Internet host to your PC. The process will look something like that shown in Figure 9-5, which is using the xm program at The WELL and the Windows Terminal program on the PC. When the transfer is complete, a copy of the host's file will reside in the current directory of your PC's hard disk.

How It Works

Your PC is set up to receive data using the specified protocol. The host is then told to send a file or files using that same protocol. The two systems undergo a sort of handshaking process where they synchronize, send, receive, and verify the data, which flows in blocks or packets.

Comment

You can download a group of files using the Ymodem or Zmodem protocol. (Xmodem generally doesn't support transfer of multiple files.) Simply add more than one filename to the command, or use a wildcard to specify more than one file. For example,

```
% xm sby picture1.zip picture2.zip
```

downloads both picture files, while

```
% xm sby picture?.zip
```

does the same thing with a wildcard character, and

```
% sz -b picture?.zip
```

uses Zmodem instead of Ymodem.

For multiple file transfers to work, your PC's program must also support multiple file transfers (most do).

Since Unix can have longer filenames than DOS, some programs (such as Kermit) will automatically shorten the names of Unix files so they will fit in the DOS eight-character-three-character format. However, most PC communications programs require that you type in the name to be given to the file you are receiving.

Note that Zmodem has a crash recovery feature. If the host system or your PC fails for some reason, or the phone connection is dropped, you can resume your upload or download where you left off by repeating the Zmodem command with the -r (recover) switch added. For example, to resume the download of the file archive.zip from the host to your PC, you would type

```
% sz -b -r archive.zip
```

You would then tell your PC software to receive the file. If your software says that the file already exists (a partial file), tell it to keep the existing file. You may have to tell

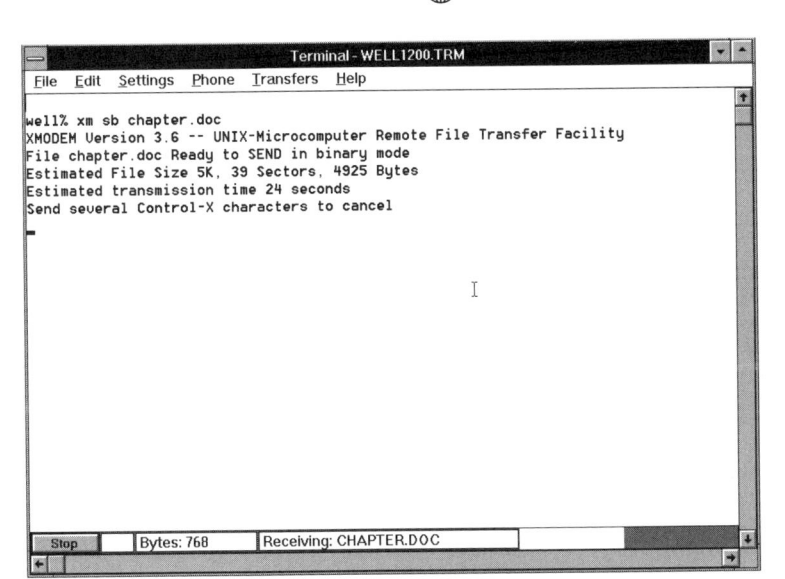

9 TRANSFERRING FILES BETWEEN YOUR PC AND THE INTERNET

Figure 9-5 Downloading a file with Xmodem

your software to always retain partial files before you can do crash recovery—see your PC software's documentation for details.

Some communications programs support variants of Xmodem or Ymodem, such as Xmodem 128, Xmodem 1K, and so on. This refers to the size of the data packets transferred by the program. All else being equal, larger packets mean faster, more efficient data transfer; though if you have a noisy line and there are a lot of retries, larger packets can be *less* efficient because they have a greater chance of including an error. Generally speaking, you should try the largest size packets the program will support (1K or 4K rather than 128 bytes), and if transfers consistently fail with a certain host, try the next smaller packet size.

9.5 HOW DO I...
Upload files with Xmodem, Ymodem, or Zmodem?

COMPLEXITY: INTERMEDIATE

Problem
Uploading is the opposite process to downloading. You have some files on your PC that you need to get to the Internet host, probably so you can mail them to someone.

Technique
As with downloading, you choose a protocol, run programs on both the PC and the host, and make the necessary specifications.

289

Steps

1. To upload a file with Xmodem, type `xm` followed by `rb` (for binary) or `rt` (for text) at the host prompt. For example, to send a binary file called archive.zip from your PC to the Internet system, you would type

```
% xm rb archive.zip
```

The host's xm program will tell you that it's ready to receive a file:

```
XMODEM Version 3.6 — UNIX-Microcomputer Remote File Transfer Facility
Ready to RECEIVE File archive.zip in binary mode
Send several Control-X characters to cancel
```

2. To upload a file with Ymodem, add `y` to the above commands. For example, to upload a file called letter.txt using the xm program and the Ymodem protocol, you would type

```
% xm rty letter.txt
```

If you discover you've made a mistake or that you're not ready yet to transfer the file, press CTRL-X a few times. This will abort the transfer and you'll see a message like this:

```
Reception canceled at user's request
```

3. To upload a file with Zmodem, type `rz` followed by `-a` (for text files) or `-b` (for binary files), and the filename. To upload the binary file manual.doc you would thus type

```
% rz -b manual.doc
```

4. Set your PC communications program to *send* a file and specify the correct protocol and the filename(s). The transfer will begin. When it ends, a copy of the file will now exist in your current directory on the host (probably the home directory).

How It Works

Uploading is the same process as downloading except the sender and receiver are switched around: the data is going from your PC to the Internet host.

Comment

You can upload a group of files using the Ymodem or Zmodem protocol. (Xmodem generally doesn't support transfer of multiple files.) Simply add more than one filename to the command, or use a wildcard to specify more than one file. For example,

```
% xm rty report1.txt report2.txt
```

uploads both report files, while

```
% xm rty report?.zip
```

does the same thing with a wildcard character, and

```
% rz -a report?.zip
```

uses Zmodem instead of Ymodem.

9 TRANSFERRING FILES BETWEEN YOUR PC AND THE INTERNET

Zmodem can be used to resume an upload or download that was halted due to a system crash or phone line problem. See How-To 9.4 for details.

9.6 HOW DO I...
Use Kermit to connect to the net?

COMPLEXITY INTERMEDIATE

Problem
You have a Kermit program for your PC and you've determined that your host has Kermit, too. You want to connect the two Kermits so you can transfer files.

Technique
Use your PC Kermit to dial up and connect to the host. You then run the host Kermit so the two systems can exchange files.

This How-To gives you an example of running a stand-alone Kermit program on the PC. You can also run another PC communications program that includes the Kermit protocol. In that case, you also run the remote Kermit, but on the PC you use your communications program's menus to handle transfers, rather than using Kermit commands.

Steps
1. Run your PC Kermit program.

```
C:\> kermit
```

If it is a traditional text-based Kermit program, it will present a prompt at which you enter commands:

```
C:\>Kermit-MS>
```

2. Type `connect` to get Kermit ready to connect to the host:

```
Kermit-MS>connect
[Connecting to host, type Control-] to return to PC]
```

There are two things to notice here: first, you can type the escape character (CTRL-]) in this case) to switch between issuing *remote* commands that apply to the host and *local* commands that apply to your PC. (The latter are useful housekeeping commands such as dir to list files, copy, delete, and so on.)

The other thing to notice is that although Kermit is "connected," it hasn't actually established contact with the host yet. To do that, you have to dial the phone number.

A Windows or Macintosh version of Kermit works differently. You don't type commands at prompts, you make selections from menus and dialog boxes. For example, you might connect by selecting Connect from the Session menu.

3. If necessary, set the appropriate communications parameters (speed, parity, and so on). Usually the default parameters will work, other than the need to set an appropriate speed for your modem. With a Windows or Mac Kermit, you set these with dialog boxes from the Configure menu, which are self-explanatory. On a text-based Kermit you enter the appropriate commands at the Kermit prompt. Here are some sample commands. This command sets the modem speed to 9600:

INTERNET HOW-TO

`Kermit-MS> set baud 9600`

The next example sets parity to none (space):

`Kermit-MS> set parity space`

Finally, you can turn on VT-100 terminal emulation with:

`Kermit-MS> set vt100 on`

See your Kermit documentation for more commands, and see How-To 9.9 for information on how to get help while using Kermit.

DOS Kermit version 3.X uses a somewhat different syntax. For example, the last example above would be

`Kermit-MS> set terminal vt100`

in version 3.X. If you are using this version of Kermit, see the online help.

4. Once your parameters are properly set, dial the host, either by entering the phone number in a dialog box (for Windows-type Kermits) or by typing the modem dial command at the Kermit prompt:

`Kermit-MS>atdt14153326106`

This calls up The WELL, for example.

5. Once the number has been dialed and a connection made, you will see the usual messages and prompts from the host system. You enter your login name and password as usual. Figure 9-6 shows a typical host connection from Kermit.

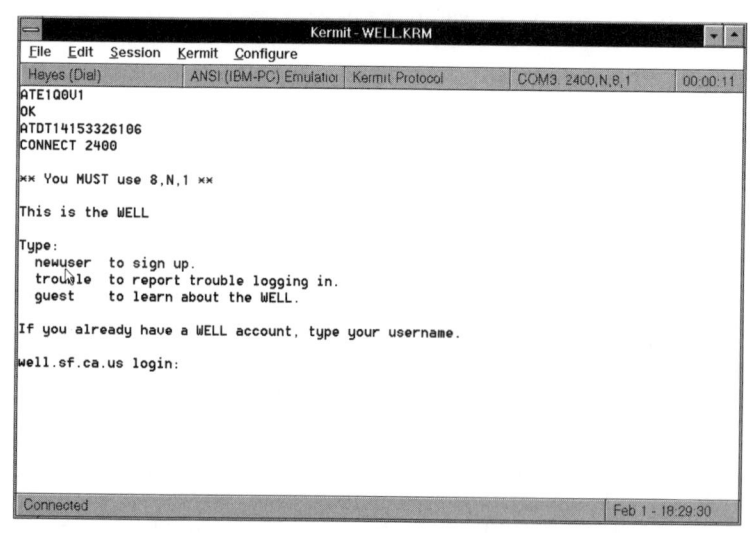

```
                          Kermit - WELL.KRM
 File  Edit  Session  Kermit  Configure
 Hayes (Dial)        ANSI (IBM-PC) Emulatio  Kermit Protocol    COM3  2400,N,8,1    00:00:11
ATE1Q0U1
OK
ATDT14153326106
CONNECT 2400

** You MUST use 8,N,1 **

This is the WELL

Type:
  newuser  to sign up.
  trouble  to report trouble logging in.
  guest    to learn about the WELL.

If you already have a WELL account, type your username.

well.sf.ca.us login:




 Connected                                                Feb 1 - 18:29:30
```

Figure 9-6 Using Kermit to connect to an Internet host

9 ⊕ TRANSFERRING FILES BETWEEN YOUR PC AND THE INTERNET

How It Works
Kermit is basically a stand-alone communications program that does terminal emulation and file transfer using the Kermit protocol. Indeed, once you are connected you can use Kermit just like another communications program, typing text and commands for the remote system and viewing its displays. When you want to transfer files, however, you must run the remote Kermit as well.

Comment
These steps look tedious, particularly the typing of parameters and phone numbers. Don't worry, though, How-Tos 9.10 and 9.11 will show you how to automate these procedures.

9.7 HOW DO I...
Download files with Kermit?

COMPLEXITY: INTERMEDIATE

Problem
You're running Kermit on your PC. You want to download a file from your Internet host.

Technique
You run your PC Kermit, connect to the host, and then run the remote Kermit. You can then exchange files.

Steps
1. Run Kermit and connect to the remote host using the procedure in How-To 9.6, or by means of a session file with Windows or Mac Kermit (How-To 9.10), or a login script (How-To 9.11).

2. Once you've logged in and are at a system prompt, run the remote Kermit:

```
% kermit
C-Kermit 5A(189), 30 June 93, Solaris 2.x
Type ? or HELP for help
C-Kermit>
```

3. At the remote Kermit prompt, type `send` followed by the name of the file you want to download (you can use multiple filenames or wildcards if you wish). For example,

```
C-Kermit>send chapter1
```

sends the file chapter1, and

```
C-Kermit>send chap*
```

sends all files whose names begin with "chap."

The host Kermit will give you a status message, such as that shown in Figure 9-7.

4. Press CTRL-] to return control to your local Kermit. (With Kermit 3.X, use CTRL-C or ALT-X.)

INTERNET HOW-TO

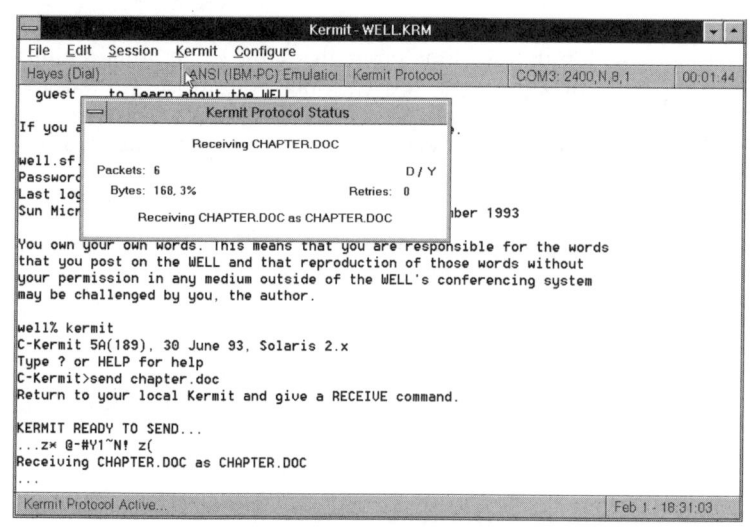

Figure 9-7 Transferring a file with Kermit

5. Type `receive` and the file transfer will begin. Your PC Kermit will keep you informed as to the status of the file transfer (Windows Kermit in Figure 9-7 uses a small window for this purpose).

6. When the transfer is complete, a copy of the host's file will be on your PC's hard disk.

How It Works
The two Kermit programs set up the Kermit file transfer protocol, synchronize, and transmit the data.

Comment
Remember the distinction between giving commands to the *remote* Kermit (which is the default), and escaping back (with CTRL-]) to give commands to your *local* Kermit on the PC.

9.8 HOW DO I...
Upload files with Kermit?

COMPLEXITY: INTERMEDIATE

Problem
You have a file on your PC that you want to upload to the Internet host.

Technique
Run your PC Kermit, connect to the host, and then run the remote Kermit. You can now tell your local Kermit to send a file to the host Kermit.

Steps
1. Run Kermit and connect to the remote host, using the procedure in How-To 9.6, or by means of a session file with Windows or Mac Kermit (How-To 9.10), or a login script (How-To 9.11).

9 TRANSFERRING FILES BETWEEN YOUR PC AND THE INTERNET

2. Once you've logged in and are at a system prompt, run the remote Kermit:

```
% kermit
C-Kermit 5A(189), 30 June 93, Solaris 2.x
Type ? or HELP for help
C-Kermit>
```

3. At the remote Kermit prompt, type `receive`.

   The host Kermit will give you a reminder, such as:

```
Return to your local Kermit and give a SEND command.

KERMIT READY TO RECEIVE..
```

4. Press CTRL-] to return control to your local Kermit. (With version 3.X, use CTRL-C or ALT-X.)

5. Type `send` followed by the name of the file you want to upload (you can use multiple filenames or wildcards if you wish). For example,

```
C-Kermit>send chapter1
```

   prepares to upload the file chapter1, and

```
C-Kermit>send chap*
```

   uploads all files whose names begin with "chap."

   The file transfer begins. Your PC Kermit will keep you informed as to the status of the file transfer.

6. When the transfer is complete, a copy of the file from your PC will be in your current directory on the Internet host.

How It Works
An upload works in the same way as a download, except that the roles of sender and receiver are reversed.

Comment
Remember that when you download you specify on the remote Kermit the files you will be *sending* to your PC, while when you upload you specify on the local Kermit the files you will be *sending* to the host.

9.9 HOW DO I...
Get help with Kermit commands?

COMPLEXITY EASY

Problem
Recent versions of Kermit don't come with much documentation. (Instead, they refer you to a separately published book.) Fortunately, Kermit *does* provide basic online help that should enable you to perform most operations successfully.

Technique
You use Kermit's intro and help commands to get more information.

295

INTERNET HOW-TO

Steps
1. Run Kermit, either on your PC or at the host prompt. (A Unix version, C-Kermit, is shown here.) C-Kermit shows an introductory screen as follows (your version may vary):

```
C-Kermit>help
C-Kermit 5A(189), 30 June 93, Copyright (C) 1985, 1993,
Trustees of Columbia University in the City of New York.

Type INTRO for an introduction to C-Kermit, press ? for a list of commands.
Type HELP followed by a command name for help about a specific command.
Type NEWS for news about new features.
While typing commands, you may use the following special characters:
 DEL, RUBOUT, BACKSPACE, CTRL-H: Delete the most recent character typed.
 CTRL-W:  Delete the most recent word typed.
 CTRL-U:  Delete the current line.
 CTRL-R:  Redisplay the current line.
 ?        (question mark) Display a menu for the current command field.
 ESC      (or TAB) Attempt to complete the current field.
 \        (backslash) include the following character literally
          or introduce a backslash code, variable, or function.
Command words other than filenames can be abbreviated in most contexts.
From system level, type "kermit -h" for help about command-line options.

DOCUMENTATION: "Using C-Kermit" by Frank da Cruz and Christine M. Gianone,
Digital Press.  DP ISBN: 1-55558-108-0; Prentice-Hall ISBN: 0-13-037490-3.
DECdirect: +1-800-344-4825, Order Number EY-J896E-DP, US $34.95.
```

From this screen you learn that you can type the commands intro or help to get more help. You also learn about some basic terminal key functions, such as for deleting text. Finally, you learn about the aforementioned book.

2. Type `intro` to get an introduction or overview of Kermit:

```
C-Kermit>  intro
Welcome to C-Kermit communications software for:
 . Error-free file transfer
 . Terminal connection
 . Script programming
 . International character set conversion

Supporting:
 . Serial connections, direct or dialed.
 . Automatic modem dialing
 . TCP/IP network connections
 . UNIX, VAX/VMS, OS/2, AOS/VS, OS-9, Commodore Amiga, Atari ST.

Basic C-Kermit commands:
  EXIT       exit from C-Kermit
  HELP       request help about a command
  TAKE       execute commands from a file

Commands for file transfer:
```

9 TRANSFERRING FILES BETWEEN YOUR PC AND THE INTERNET

```
  SEND         send files
  RECEIVE      receive files
  SERVER       be a file transfer server
more?
```

3. You are asked if you want to see more text. Press (v):

```
Essential settings:
  SET PARITY   communications parity
  SET FLOW     communications flow control, such as XON/XOFF
  SET FILE     file settings, for example TYPE TEXT or TYPE BINARY

To make a direct serial connection:
  SET LINE     select serial communication device
  SET SPEED    select communication speed
  CONNECT      begin terminal connection

To dial out with a modem:
  SET MODEM    select modem type
  SET LINE     select serial communication device
  SET SPEED    select communication speed
  DIAL         dial
  CONNECT      begin terminal connection

To make a network connection:
  SET NETWORK  select network type
  SET HOST     select network host
  CONNECT      begin terminal connection

more?
```

And still more...

```
  TELNET       select a TCP/IP host and CONNECT to it

To return from a terminal connection to the C-Kermit prompt:
  Type your escape character followed by the letter C.

To display your escape character:
  SHOW ESCAPE

To display other settings:
  SHOW COMMUNICATIONS, SHOW TERMINAL, SHOW FILE, SHOW PROTOCOL, etc.
```

For further information about a particular command, type HELP xxx, where xxx is the name of the command. For documentation, news of new releases, and information about other Kermit software, contact:

```
  Kermit Distribution       E-mail:
  Columbia University       kermit@columbia.edu (Internet)
  612 West 115th Street     KERMIT@CUVMA (BITNET/EARN/CREN)
  New York, NY 10025  USA
  Phone: +1 212 854-3703    Fax: +1 212 662-6442
```

INTERNET HOW-TO

4. To find out about a particular command, type `help` followed by the command name:

```
C-Kermit>help receive

Syntax: RECEIVE (or R) [filespec]

Wait for a file to arrive from the other Kermit, which must be given a
SEND command.  If the optional filespec is given, the (first) incoming
file will be stored under that name, otherwise it will be stored under
the name it arrives with.
```

The combination of intro, help, and whatever documentation files are available should be enough to get you started.

How It Works
The kind of online help (and the amount of detail) varies with the version of Kermit. Windows-based Kermits may include standard Windows or Macintosh help files.

Comment
Here's a tip: The older (2.X) versions of PC Kermit come with lengthy (and still useful) documentation files that have been removed from the later versions.

If you want to study Kermit in depth, see the book, *Using MS-DOS Kermit: Connecting Your PC to the Electronic World*, by Christine M. Gianone (Bedford, MA: Digital Press, 1992).

9.10 HOW DO I...
Use a session file to save communications settings?

COMPLEXITY: EASY

Problem
You don't want to have to set the communications parameters and type the phone number every time you want to connect Kermit or another communications program to a host.

Technique
Nearly all contemporary PC communications programs (including Windows Kermit) let you save a number of settings to a file for future use. You can then simply load that file and tell the program to "do" that connection.

Steps
1. Select the necessary settings as usual. These typically include phone number, modem speed, parity, data and stop bits, handshaking, and terminal emulation. With most programs (including all Windows or Mac programs), you make these settings by choosing menu items under a menu typically called Settings or Configuration. Figure 9-8 shows the Settings menu from Windows Terminal.

2. Choose Save or Save As from the File menu. Give a descriptive name for your settings file (such as "well"). Usually the program will reserve a particular extension for these filenames (.cfg or .ini, for example).

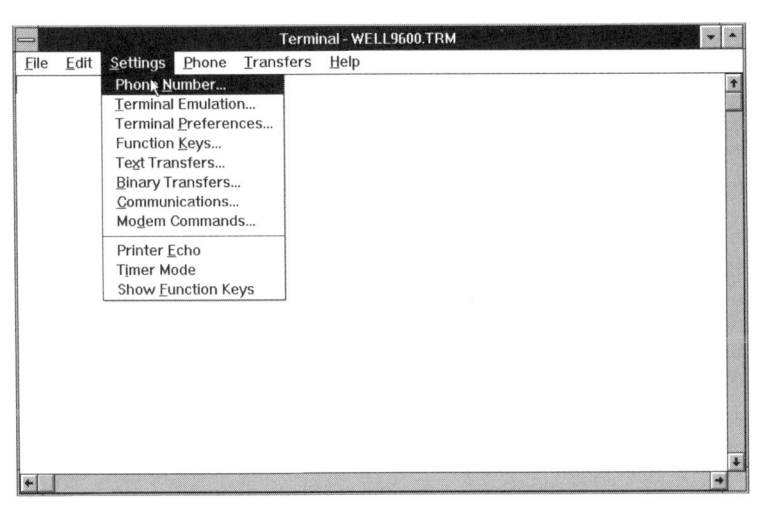

Figure 9-8 Selecting session settings

3. When you want to connect to a particular host, choose its settings file. With Windows or Mac programs, each settings file can have an icon attached. Double-clicking on the icon runs the communications program with those settings. (Depending on the program, the host may be automatically dialed, or you may have to choose a Dial command from the menu.)

How It Works
In most Windows-type systems the specifications for a particular connection are considered to be a kind of document. When you choose that document, the settings in the associated file take effect.

Comment
If you decide to change any settings, simply make the changes and then choose Save from the File menu to save the changed settings.

You may wish to make several settings files for a given host. For example, well2400 and well9600 reflect different modem speeds for settings files for The WELL.

9.11 HOW DO I...
Use a login script to simplify connection?

COMPLEXITY INTERMEDIATE

Problem
You may have trouble remembering settings, IDs, or passwords that you need to connect to a host, or you may simply want to save typing.

Technique
You write a simple login script that contains the commands and input needed to connect to and log on your Internet host.

INTERNET HOW-TO

Steps

1. Check your communications program's documentation for a list of commands that can be used in scripts. (Not all programs support scripting.)

2. Use the provided facility or a text editor to open a script file.

3. Enter the commands you will need. Usually there are three kinds of commands: settings, actions, and conditions. A setting specifies some value such as the modem speed. An action performs an operation such as dialing a phone number. A condition specifies when an action is to be performed. A typical condition takes a form like this: "when the specified text appears, perform this action."

   The following is a simple example of a login script. Note that the actual commands you will use will vary with your software.

```
set speed = 9600
set data = 8
set stop = 1
set parity = none
set handshake = xon
dial 1-415-332-6106
if busy redo
waitfor "login: "
type "kirk"
waitfor "password: "
type "Enterprise"
type "status"
```

   In this script, the first five items establish communications settings. The next command dials the host's phone number. If a busy signal is received, the number is redialed. If a connection is made, the script waits for the prompt "login:" to appear. When it does, the username "kirk" is entered. When the "password:" prompt appears, the password "Enterprise" is supplied. Finally the word "status" is typed at the host prompt. This might be the name of a shell script that reports on things such as the amount of disk space in use or the number of users logged on.

4. Once you've written your script, save it to disk with the appropriate menu item. Test it out: you may have to make some changes before it runs correctly.

How It Works

The script automatically performs commands and actions. The program is able to sense whether a successful connection has been made, and is also able to wait until standard prompts from the host are received, and supply the necessary text in response.

Comment

There are two caveats to using scripts. First, some programs store scripts as plain text files. If your PC is subject to snooping, intruders might be able to get your Internet user ID and password from the script file. (More sophisticated programs encrypt the stored IDs and passwords.)

The other problem is that places in a script that look for particular prompts or other text from the host are vulnerable to "breaking" when the administrators at the host

9 ⊕ **TRANSFERRING FILES BETWEEN YOUR PC AND THE INTERNET**

change their prompts or a new version of a program that the script is interacting with is installed. You will then have to revise the script.

Scripts can also be used to automatically read and download mail, news, and other files. You will have to study your program's documentation to see what is possible. You may find that other users have already written and provided sophisticated scripts for various operations.

9.12 HOW DO I... *Learn more about telecommunications?*

COMPLEXITY: EASY

Problem
Data communications and file transfer is one of the most complicated aspects of using computers.

Technique
There are a number of possible sources for help and further exploration, a few of which are summarized here.

Steps
1. Make sure that you obtain all available manual entries, documentation files, and online help for the communications programs you use.

2. Read the com.dcom newsgroups for announcements and discussion of data communications protocols, modem features, and so on. (There is also a comp.protocols.kermit group.)

3. There are a number of books dealing with data communications at various technical levels. A good introductory book that includes software and information about computer bulletin boards is *Dvorak's Guide to PC Telecommunications,* by John C. Dvorak and Nick Anis (Berkeley, CA: Osborne McGraw-Hill, 1992).

How It Works
Because there are so many programs and protocols that can interact with one another, data communications is rather more an art than a science. Sometimes direct help from a knowledgeable person at your school or business may be necessary.

Comment
The upside is that communications and file transfers are getting easier year by year. More programs offer the ability to perform these functions with the click of a mouse on an icon or menu. Sometimes the proper initial configuration of the program can be difficult, but once it is running, the program may be easy to use.

Working on Remote Systems with telnet and rlogin

How do I...

10.1 Connect to a service or program
10.2 Log on a remote system
10.3 Get help while using telnet
10.4 Change connections within telnet
10.5 Control a remote program
10.6 Change telnet settings
10.7 Suspend telnet and run local commands
10.8 Make an rlogin connection
10.9 Automate an rlogin connection
10.10 Copy files between systems with rcp

A powerful feature of the Internet is the ability to connect to your local host and then log on to hosts located just about anywhere in the world. This gives you access to hundreds of specialized programs and services, ranging from weather forecasts, to library catalogs, to databases, to games. Best of all, while you're running a program in Tokyo, you're still only paying for a call (and connect time) to your local Internet provider! Distance hardly matters on the information highway, except for a bit of sluggishness in response now and then. In this chapter you will learn how to use two commands, telnet and rlogin, that provide remote access to Internet sites. You can even switch back and forth between sending commands to a remote site and doing work on your local site.

If you have personal accounts on two or more machines, you can connect to your favorite (or closest) site and then use telnet or rlogin to log into your accounts at other sites.

INTERNET HOW-TO

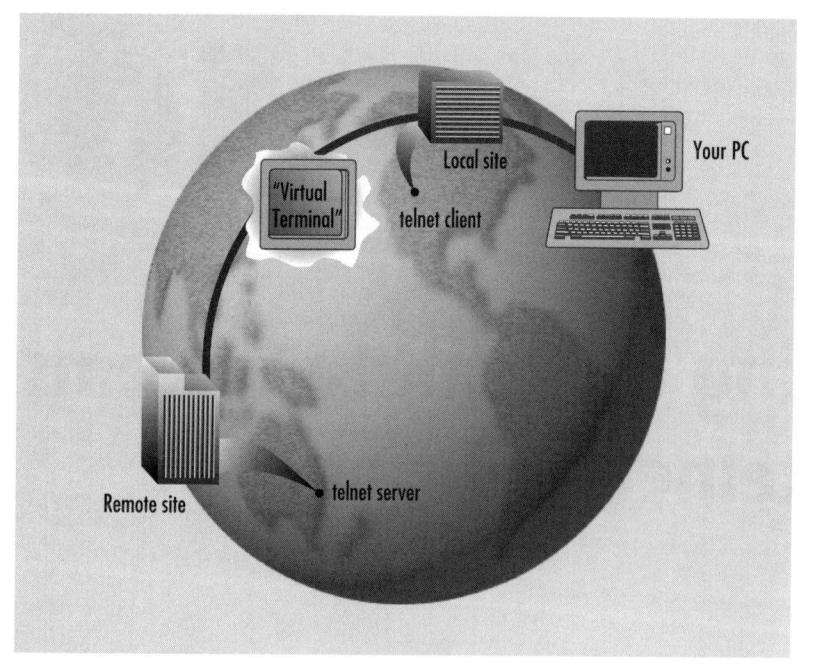

Figure 10-1 Elements of a telnet connection

Logging on Remote Systems

As Figure 10-1 illustrates, using telnet involves several steps. First, you connect your PC to your local site through dial-up or an existing network connection. Once you've logged on your local site, you issue the telnet command with the Internet address of the remote site that you want to log on.

Your telnet program (the telnet *client*) negotiates with the telnet *server* at the remote site. The two programs set up a communications protocol so that characters you type at your PC and send via your modem to your local site get relayed from your local site to the remote site. In turn, the output of the remote program goes to your local site and then travels from there over the phone lines back to your PC. The result is a *virtual terminal* that lets you work in the same way as though you had dialed the remote site directly.

What you see when you make a telnet connection depends on whether you are connecting to a particular service or just logging on the remote machine. If you're connecting to a service, the remote program starts to run and you see its menus and other information, as in Figure 10-2. This figure shows a service called the Weather Underground, which provides weather forecasts. You can now follow the menus to get the information or service you want. As Figure 10-3 shows, you can provide a city code for San Francisco (sfo) and get a current weather report and forecast.

If the address you specify isn't set up to provide a particular service, the remote machine assumes you're trying to log in. Just as though you were dialing it directly, the

10 ⊕ WORKING ON REMOTE SYSTEMS WITH TELNET AND RLOGIN

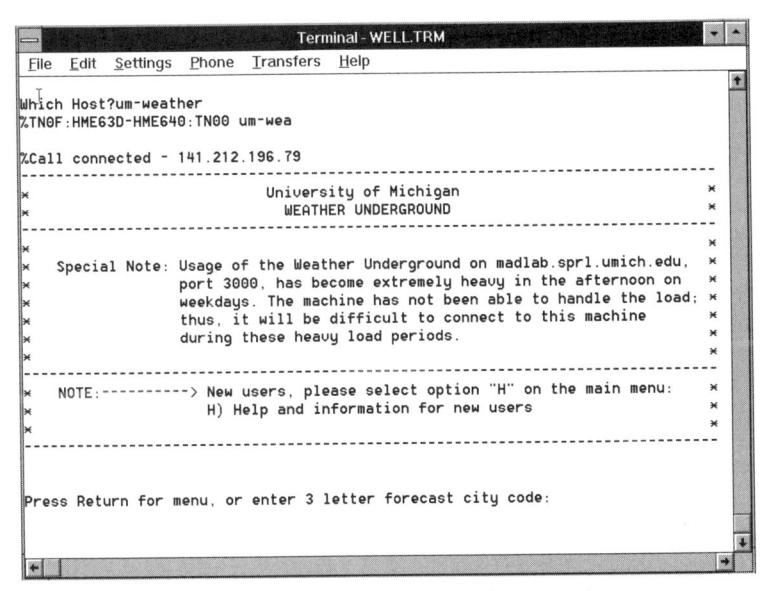

```
Terminal - WELL.TRM
File  Edit  Settings  Phone  Transfers  Help
Which Host?um-weather
%TNOF:HME63D-HME640:TN00 um-wea

%Call connected - 141.212.196.79
------------------------------------------------------------
*                    University of Michigan                *
*                    WEATHER UNDERGROUND                   *
------------------------------------------------------------
*                                                          *
*   Special Note: Usage of the Weather Underground on madlab.sprl.umich.edu, *
*                 port 3000, has become extremely heavy in the afternoon on  *
*                 weekdays. The machine has not been able to handle the load;*
*                 thus, it will be difficult to connect to this machine      *
*                 during these heavy load periods.                           *
*                                                          *
------------------------------------------------------------
*   NOTE:---------> New users, please select option "H" on the main menu:   *
*                   H) Help and information for new users                   *
------------------------------------------------------------

Press Return for menu, or enter 3 letter forecast city code:
```

Figure 10-2 Connecting to the Weather Underground program

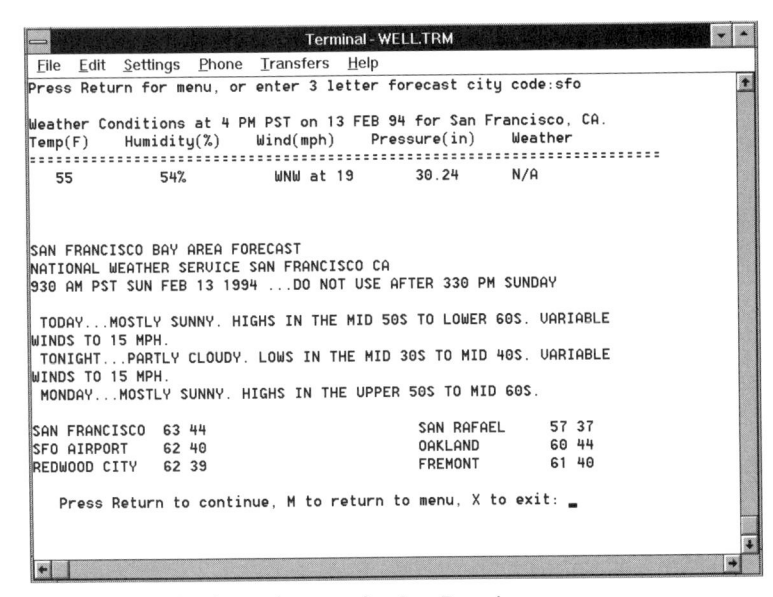

```
Terminal - WELL.TRM
File  Edit  Settings  Phone  Transfers  Help
Press Return for menu, or enter 3 letter forecast city code:sfo

Weather Conditions at 4 PM PST on 13 FEB 94 for San Francisco, CA.
Temp(F)   Humidity(%)    Wind(mph)    Pressure(in)    Weather
===========================================================
  55          54%        WNW at 19       30.24          N/A


SAN FRANCISCO BAY AREA FORECAST
NATIONAL WEATHER SERVICE SAN FRANCISCO CA
930 AM PST SUN FEB 13 1994 ...DO NOT USE AFTER 330 PM SUNDAY

 TODAY...MOSTLY SUNNY. HIGHS IN THE MID 50S TO LOWER 60S. VARIABLE
WINDS TO 15 MPH.
 TONIGHT...PARTLY CLOUDY. LOWS IN THE MID 30S TO MID 40S. VARIABLE
WINDS TO 15 MPH.
 MONDAY...MOSTLY SUNNY. HIGHS IN THE UPPER 50S TO MID 60S.

SAN FRANCISCO   63 44            SAN RAFAEL     57 37
SFO AIRPORT     62 40            OAKLAND        60 44
REDWOOD CITY    62 39            FREMONT        61 40

  Press Return to continue, M to return to menu, X to exit: _
```

Figure 10-3 Getting a forecast for San Francisco

remote machine asks you for your login ID and password. These must match the ones specified for the account you've set up on the remote machine. (How-Tos 10.8 and 10.9 show you how you can use an alternative command, rlogin, to avoid having to type IDs

INTERNET HOW-TO

and passwords for remote systems that already "know" about you.) Figure 10-4 shows a remote login via telnet.

Running Remote Programs

Running a remote program is pretty much like running a local program. You may notice a bit of lag time if you're connected to a program running at a site that is far away or that suffers from congested network connections.

Most menus and commands that you will encounter are simple and self-explanatory. Usually you'll be told how to get help (such as by pressing (?) or (h)). When you're finished with the program, use its exit menu option or command. (How-To 10.5 also has some tips for dealing with problem situations, such as a program that appears to "hang" and no longer responds to your input.)

telnet also lets you run a remote session "in background." This means that you can start a remote command that you expect will take some time, tell telnet to go into the background, and continue to work at your local site. After a few minutes you can bring telnet back into the foreground and check on the progress of your remote session.

Finding Services

So where do you find all those neat remote services that you can telnet to? There are many sources of information about services that are accessible on the Internet. Articles in newsgroups often announce or recommend particular services. There are also compilations of services with sample sessions. One of the best is called The Desktop Internet Reference, and is available as a Windows help file. (You can get this file via ftp after using archie to find a site that has it. See Chapter 11 for more on archie and Chapter 15 for more about The Desktop Internet Reference.) There are also books that catalog

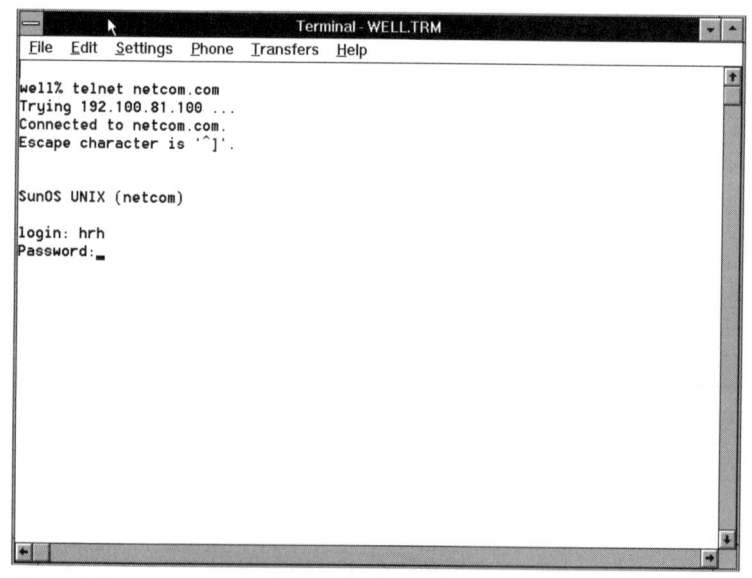

```
well% telnet netcom.com
Trying 192.100.81.100 ...
Connected to netcom.com.
Escape character is '^]'.


SunOS UNIX (netcom)

login: hrh
Password:_
```

Figure 10-4 Logging on a remote system

10   WORKING ON REMOTE SYSTEMS WITH TELNET AND RLOGIN

Internet services, but because the landscape of the net is constantly changing, information in printed books can rapidly go out of date.

The rlogin Alternative

Some Internet sites (usually those running a BSD-based version of Unix) offer the rlogin command. (Most sites today have both telnet and rlogin, thanks to the merger of the two main "flavors" of Unix.)

rlogin is usually used for logging on remote systems, not for connecting to dedicated services. rlogin works in much the same way as telnet, but with two advantages. First, you can use a file called .rhosts in your home directory on one system to allow you to make an rlogin connection to your account on another system without having to supply your ID or password. It's a convenience, but also a potential security risk, and thus not allowed on some systems.

The other advantage of rlogin is that it lets you use the "remote copy" (rcp) command to transfer files back and forth between two machines on which you have accounts.

Related Topics

To Learn How to…	See Chapter
Access database services	13
Find software for your PC	11
Get information and services via menus	12
Talk to users on other systems	5
Transfer files between Internet sites	7
Transfer files between your PC and the Internet site	9
Use hypertext to explore the Internet	14

How-Tos in this Chapter

10.1   Connect to a service or program
Once you've learned the name of an interesting service, you can connect to it by simply typing `telnet` and the appropriate domain or numeric address. The remote program will start running automatically.

10.2   Log on a remote system
If you want to log on a machine rather than use a dedicated service, you can also use the telnet command. In this case, however, you will be prompted for your user ID and password.

10.3   Get help while using telnet
There are only a few telnet commands you need to know. You'll see how to ask for a command list and get help.

10.4   Change connections within telnet
Once you're finished with one system or service, you can close your connection and open another without leaving telnet.

10.5   Control a remote program
Sometimes a program may stop responding, or there may be no obvious way to exit it. You'll see you how to use the telnet send command to send control characters to remote programs.

INTERNET HOW-TO

10.6 Change telnet settings
Usually you don't have to tinker with telnet settings, but there are a few that are worth learning about for special circumstances.

10.7 Suspend telnet and run local commands
You can suspend telnet and carry out any commands or programs you want at your local site. If you're dexterous, you can even run more than one telnet session at a time.

10.8 Make an rlogin connection
rlogin works in much the same way as telnet, though it is normally used for general logins rather than accessing dedicated services.

10.9 Automate an rlogin connection
You can use the .rhosts file and related facilities for an easier rlogin connection.

10.10 Copy files between systems with rcp
The "remote copy" command makes it easy to move files back and forth between two systems on which you have accounts.

10.1 HOW DO I...
Connect to a service or program?

COMPLEXITY EASY

Problem
You are reading an article about the Internet (or a catalog of services) and you see an interesting service, such as the Weather Underground weather information service. You want to access that service with your PC.

Technique
You log on your local site as usual. You then use the telnet command to open a connection to the remote service, and follow the instructions that appear on the screen.

Steps
1. Run your communications program and log on your local Internet host as usual.

2. At your local host's system prompt, type `telnet` followed by the address of the service you wish to access. For example, the Weather Underground can be accessed through the address hermes.merit.edu, so you type

```
% telnet hermes.merit.edu
```

3. telnet attempts to make the connection to the remote service. If it is successful, you will see a message similar to the following:

```
Trying 35.1.48.176 ...
Connected to hermes.merit.edu.
Escape character is '^]'.
```

(The use of the escape character is explained in How-To 10.3.)

Note that some services may require that you connect to a specific port number. For example, if a service were provided at well.com, port 70, you would issue the telnet command as follows:

```
%telnet well.com 70
```

10 WORKING ON REMOTE SYSTEMS WITH TELNET AND RLOGIN

If the connection fails, with a message such as "host unavailable," this probably means that the remote system is down or isn't accepting telnet connections for some reason. Many systems also limit the total number of people who can be connected by telnet at any one time. In this case, try again at a less busy time of day.

4. Following a successful connection, the remote service takes over and displays its greetings screen. It may prompt for further information, such as your terminal type or the name of a particular host (service). For example, hermes.merit.edu provides several services, so let's specify `um-weather` for the Weather Underground:

```
%Merit:Hermes (HME65E:TNOF:VT100:EDIT=MTS)
%You have reached MichNet, operated by Merit Network, Inc.
%Enter a destination, or enter HELP for assistance.

Which Host?um-weather
```

5. Depending on the service, you may have to work through several layers of menus to get the information you want. For the Weather Underground, you can either go through a set of menus or type a city code to get a specific forecast, as shown in Figure 10-3.

6. Once you have finished using the remote service, follow its instructions for terminating the program (this may involve selecting an exit menu option or typing a command such as exit or quit). If you have trouble figuring out how to exit the remote program, see How-To 10.5.

How It Works
When you give the telnet command, the telnet program (which is a client) connects to the telnet server at the site you specified. Assuming the remote site is up and running and accepting telnet requests, a connection is established. In effect, telnet connects your terminal (your communications software) through the local site to the remote site. In turn, output from the remote program is passed back to you. You appear to be interacting directly with the remote program.

Comment
A particular service may be offered through several sites. Some sites may be busier than others, and thus harder to connect to. It is best to make telnet connections in off-peak hours (assuming you live in the United States). Be sure to read any information about alternate addresses or sites provided by the remote program.

If a connection fails, with a message such as "unknown host," check your typing of the address. You can also try using the numeric address instead of the name address, if you know it. For example, the following command also connects to hermes.merit.edu, but uses the numeric form of the address:

```
%telnet 35.1.48.150
```

309

INTERNET HOW-TO

10.2 HOW DO I...
Log on a remote system?

COMPLEXITY: EASY

Problem
You have accounts on more than one system. You're doing work on one system and realize you need some information available from the other system. You want to be able to access that other system without losing your connection to the current system.

Technique
You can use telnet from the system you are currently logged on and connect to another system on which you have an account. You can then work on the other system and return to what you were doing without having to log in again.

Steps
1. At the prompt on the system to which you are currently logged in, type `telnet` followed by the Internet address of the system to which you wish to connect. For example, if you are on The WELL and you want to do something on netcom.com, you would type

```
% telnet netcom.com
```

Assuming the other system is up and running, you will get a "connect" message from telnet:

```
Trying 192.100.81.100 ...
Connected to netcom.com.
Escape character is '^]'.
```

2. This will be followed by the normal sign-on messages and login prompts from the remote system. Enter your login ID and password for that system as prompted:

```
SunOS UNIX (netcom)

login: hrh
Password:platypus

Last login: Mon Feb 14 00:20:16 from 131.247.150.250

SunOS Release 4.1.3 (NETCOM) #1: Wed Sep 23 05:06:55 PDT 1992

NETCOM On-line Communication Services, Inc.

>>>>
>>>>   Users on /u43, /u44, /u45, /u46 and /u48 have been moved to /u1.
>>>>   /u47/ftp has been moved to /u2/ftp.
>>>>
>>>>   PALO ALTO PNC numbers were down Saturday due to a Pac Bell
>>>>   problem.
>>>>
>>>>   AUSTIN, TX POP is now on-line (512) 206-4950
>>>>
```

10 WORKING ON REMOTE SYSTEMS WITH TELNET AND RLOGIN

```
This disk usage summary is for the last 18 days.
Your average usage to date is:     0.01 meg
At this rate your disk charge will be: $  0.00
Your account balance is:           0.00
```

3. You can now go about your business as usual, listing directories, sending or receiving mail, or whatever.

4. When you're finished with the remote system, log out as usual (by pressing CTRL-D for Unix systems, for example). You will be returned to your local system prompt (or possibly to the telnet prompt).

How It Works
When you run telnet on your local system, telnet requests a connection to the specified remote system. This connection is basically treated in the same way as it would be if you had dialed the remote system directly. You are asked for your login ID and password as usual. When you log off the remote system, telnet closes the connection and returns you to the system prompt at your local site.

Comment
If you have accounts on several systems you can often save phone charges by dialing up the closest system and then using telnet to connect to the other systems as needed. The only phone charges you'll pay will be for the call to your local system.

Note however that when you telnet to a remote system on which you have an account, you will pay the normal *connect* charges for that system, just as though you had dialed directly. And since you will be telneting from another system, you will be paying the connect charges for that system as well. Therefore it makes sense to try to telnet from a system that has a fixed monthly charge (no hourly rates), or failing that, the system with the lowest hourly charges.

10.3 HOW DO I... Get help while using telnet?

COMPLEXITY: EASY

Problem
telnet has only a few commands that are important in everyday use, but you might not remember them all.

Technique
You can use variations of the telnet help command to get more information. If you are currently connected to a remote host, you must first type the telnet escape character to let telnet know that you are issuing commands to the local telnet rather than to the remote host.

Steps
1. If you are currently connected to a remote host, press CTRL-]. This (by default) is the telnet escape character. (If you are running telnet but aren't currently connected to a remote host, you will already be at a telnet prompt and can skip this step.)

2. At the telnet prompt, type `help` to get a list of telnet commands:

```
telnet>help
```

Continued on next page

INTERNET HOW-TO

Continued from previous page

```
Commands may be abbreviated.  Commands are:

close      close current connection
display    display operating parameters
mode       try to enter line-by-line or character-at-a-time mode
open       connect to a site
quit       exit telnet
send       transmit special characters ('send ?' for more)
set        set operating parameters ('set ?' for more)
status     print status information
toggle     toggle operating parameters ('toggle ?' for more)
z          suspend telnet
?          print help information
```

3. If you just want to be reminded of the function of a particular command, type help followed by the command name. For example, to get a summary of the set command, type

```
telnet> help set
set operating parameters ('set ?' for more)
```

4. In this case the help message tells you that you can get more details by typing set ?:

```
telnet> set ?
echo       character to toggle local echoing on/off
escape     character to escape back to telnet command mode

           The following need 'localchars' to be toggled true
erase      character to cause an Erase Character
flushoutput     character to cause an Abort Output
interrupt       character to cause an Interrupt Process
kill       character to cause an Erase Line
quit       character to cause a Break
eof        character to cause an EOF
?          display help information
```

Here you get a list of the characters that you can specify, if for some reason the defaults aren't suitable. Usually you won't need to make such settings, but if you do, How-To 10.6 will show you the procedure.

5. When you're finished issuing help commands (or other local telnet commands), you can return to your current remote connection by pressing (ENTER). (You may have to press (ENTER) twice to get the remote system's attention.)

How It Works

Once you've established a telnet connection, telnet assumes by default that all the characters you're typing are intended to be sent to the remote program. The escape character (by default (CTRL)-(])), tells telnet to interpret your subsequent input as telnet commands rather than as input to the remote program. This allows you to request help, change settings, or view status reports. Pressing (ENTER) without giving a telnet command tells telnet that you want your input reconnected to the remote site.

10 WORKING ON REMOTE SYSTEMS WITH TELNET AND RLOGIN

Comment
Depending on how the remote site handles text display (line by line or full-screen terminal), it may be hard for you to see where you left off when you return to your remote connection after issuing local commands. Usually pressing an extra (ENTER) will get the remote program to redisplay the current menu if it is using full-screen menus.

10.4 HOW DO I...
Change connections within telnet?

COMPLEXITY: EASY

Problem
Sometimes it's handy to connect to several different hosts or services during a telnet session without having to restart telnet each time. You may also need to try a connection again after an error message.

Technique
Once telnet is running, you can use the open command to make a connection, and the close command to close it. You can repeat open and close commands to connect to several hosts in succession. Also, if a connection fails and you're left at the telnet prompt, you can use the open command to try the connection again.

Steps
1. Start telnet. At the telnet prompt, type `open` followed by the address of the system or service to which you wish to connect. For example, let's try the Food and Drug Administration's BBS:

```
well% telnet
telnet> open FDABBS.FDA.GOV
Trying 150.148.8.48 ...
Connected to FDABBS.FDA.GOV.
Escape character is '^]'.
```

2. If the connection is successful, the remote program will run. If you are connecting to a whole system rather than a dedicated service, you will be prompted for a login ID and password. In this case we get login and password prompts for the FDA (Food and Drug Administration) BBS:

```
UNIX System V  R.3 (WINS) (FDABBS)

login: guest
Password: <Enter>
Login incorrect
```

Unfortunately, we don't know the password for this system. Sometimes a login of "guest" or "anonymous" will get you limited services (and information about signing up for full service). Unfortunately, that's not true in this case:

```
Login: anonymous
Password: <Enter>
Login incorrect
Login:
```

INTERNET HOW-TO

3. If you can't log in (or the connection fails with an error message), you can type `close` to close the telnet connection:

```
telnet> close
Connection closed.
```

4. You can now use the open command to connect to another site if you wish:

```
telnet> open dra.com
```

How It Works

The open command attempts to make a connection with the specified host, in the same way as typing `telnet` followed by the host name. Remember that you can add a port number if it is mentioned in your documentation, and that you can substitute a numeric address for the domain name, as shown in How-To 10.1.

The close command tells the remote telnet to close the connection. You are returned to the telnet prompt.

Comment

Unfortunately, many dedicated services don't return you to the telnet prompt when you exit them normally. Instead, you are thrown back to your local system prompt and have to run telnet again. This limits the utility of the open and close commands for connecting to several hosts in succession. As shown in the preceding examples, however, it is handy to use open and close to be able to try another connection if a connection fails for some reason. The FDA BBS now tells callers they can login as bbs.

10.5 HOW DO I...
Control a remote program?

COMPLEXITY: INTERMEDIATE

Problem

Sometimes a remote program will appear to lock up or otherwise fail to respond to your keyboard input. You need a way to be able to interrupt or terminate the remote program.

Technique

You can use the telnet send command to send various types of special characters to the remote program. Sometimes one of these characters will break the logjam and enable you to continue running the remote program. Failing that, you'll at least be able to regain control of your local telnet and close the connection.

The telnet status command shows the current status of your connection. For example, suppose we have connected to dra.com (the site that provides Library of Congress catalog records). We press (CTRL)-(]) to escape to local mode, and type `status`:

```
telnet> status
Connected to dra.com.
Operating in character-at-a-time mode.
Escape character is '^]'.
```

The status display shows the site to which you are connected. It also indicates whether telnet is currently operating in character-at-a-time mode or line-by-line mode.

10 WORKING ON REMOTE SYSTEMS WITH TELNET AND RLOGIN

In the latter case, whole lines of text are sent when you press (ENTER), rather than each character being sent immediately as you type it. Line-by-line mode can be more efficient, but many menu-driven programs get confused by it. Character-at-a-time mode is the default.

Finally, the status display indicates the current escape character ((CTRL)-(]) by default). Remember that this is the character you press when you want to switch from your remote connection to your local telnet prompt, for issuing commands.

You can type `display` at the telnet prompt to get more details about the current telnet settings:

```
telnet> display
will flush output when sending interrupt characters.
won't send interrupt characters in urgent mode.
won't map carriage return on output.
won't recognize certain control characters.
won't process ^S/^Q locally.
won't turn on socket level debugging.
won't print hexadecimal representation of network traffic.
won't show option processing.

[^E]     echo.
[^]]     escape.
[^H]     erase.
[^O]     flushoutput.
[^C]     interrupt.
[^U]     kill.
[^\]     quit.
[^D]     eof.
```

The first part of this listing is of interest mainly to expert users and won't be covered here. The second part, however, lists the keys that you can type while using the remote program. Note particularly the escape character, (CTRL)-(]), and the interrupt and quit characters, (CTRL)-(C) and (CTRL)-(\).

Steps

1. Once you've connected to a host (see How-Tos 10.1 and 10.2), you can escape to the telnet prompt and type `send ?`. This gives you a list of characters that you can use to control the current program:

```
telnet> send ?
ao       Send Telnet Abort output
ayt      Send Telnet 'Are You There'
brk      Send Telnet Break
ec       Send Telnet Erase Character
el       Send Telnet Erase Line
escape   Send current escape character
ga       Send Telnet 'Go Ahead' sequence
ip       Send Telnet Interrupt Process
nop      Send Telnet 'No operation'
synch    Perform Telnet 'Synch operation'
?        Display send options
```

INTERNET HOW-TO

Note that you can only type this command when you're actually connected to a host, since the available keys are established by agreement between your telnet client and their telnet server.

2. If your remote program appears to be frozen and not responding, first try typing the interrupt character (`CTRL`-`C` by default). This can also be useful if the program is doing something that you decide is taking too much time (such as a long database search).

3. If `CTRL`-`C` doesn't work, try escaping to your telnet prompt (by pressing `CTRL`-`]`), and then issue one of the following commands:

```
telnet>send brk
telnet> send ip
```

These commands attempt to send a break character (similar to `CTRL`-`C`) or an interrupt signal to the remote system). If one of these works, you may regain control of the program.

4. If you can't gain control of the program, or the program has no obvious way for you to exit or log out, try closing the session by escaping to the local telnet prompt and typing `close`:

```
telnet>close
```

5. If nothing else has worked, you can try the quit character (`CTRL`-`\` by default). This is a more drastic alternative. Sometimes this will throw you completely out of the remote session and even out of telnet, all the way back to your local system prompt. Still, it may be the only way to get out of a recalcitrant program.

How It Works

The telnet client at your local site and the remote telnet server agree on a set of characters that will signal various intentions to the remote program, such as "stop what you're doing and pay attention," "quit right now," and so on. Other characters also supply editing functions, such as erase or delete line, which you can use while entering text in the remote program. The telnet status, display, and set ? commands list the current status of the connection and the applicable keys.

Comment

Always try to find out the proper way to exit a remote program or log off the remote service. This helps ensure that you don't tie up a port or possibly incur additional connect charges because the remote system thinks you are still connected. Use the techniques in this how-to when you can't otherwise break into or quit from the remote service.

10.6 HOW DO I...
Change telnet settings?

COMPLEXITY INTERMEDIATE

Problem

telnet has a number of settings that you can change, including the characters to be used for certain functions such as escaping to the local telnet prompt. Usually you won't have to change any of these settings, but occasionally they conflict with another piece of software.

Technique
You use the set command at the local telnet prompt to change settings. (If you are currently connected to a remote host you must first press your escape character—CTRL-] by default—to get to the local prompt.)

Steps
1. To get a list of settings that can be changed, type `set ?` at the local telnet prompt while connected to a host:

```
telnet> set ?
echo       character to toggle local echoing on/off
escape     character to escape back to telnet command mode

           The following need 'localchars' to be toggled true
erase      character to cause an Erase Character
flushoutput    character to cause an Abort Output
interrupt      character to cause an Interrupt Process
kill       character to cause an Erase Line
quit       character to cause a Break
eof        character to cause an EOF
?          display help information
```

2. To view a summary of telnet's current settings, type `display` at the telnet prompt:

```
telnet> display
will flush output when sending interrupt characters.
won't send interrupt characters in urgent mode.
won't map carriage return on output.
won't recognize certain control characters.
won't process ^S/^Q locally.
won't turn on socket level debugging.
won't print hexadecimal representation of network traffic.
won't show option processing.

[^E]    echo.
[^]]    escape.
[^H]    erase.
[^O]    flushoutput.
[^C]    interrupt.
[^U]    kill.
[^\]    quit.
[^D]    eof.
```

(It's the second part of the listing—the list of keys, that's usually important.)

3. To change a setting, type `set` followed by the setting name and the character you want to assign to that setting. For example, suppose that the program you are connected to uses CTRL-] for some special purpose. Since this character is, by default, the telnet escape character, this character will be intercepted by telnet and never seen by the remote program. To get around this, you can change the escape character for the current session to a character not needed by the remote program, for example, CTRL-E:

INTERNET HOW-TO

```
telnet> set escape ^E

escape character is '^E'.
```

4. Your new setting(s) will take effect immediately. Note that settings aren't saved between sessions, so you'll have to repeat them as necessary. Fortunately, settings changes are seldom needed.

How It Works

telnet keeps an internal table that assigns particular characters to each function. The set command changes settings so you can use a different character to perform a particular function.

Comment

Don't change a setting to a character that you need for some other purpose. For example, you'd never want to change the escape character to (ENTER)!

10.7 HOW DO I... Suspend telnet and run local commands?

COMPLEXITY: INTERMEDIATE

Problem

A remote program that you are running in a telnet session may be doing something that requires a long wait on your part. You'd like to be able to do something else on your local system while you're waiting.

Technique

You use the telnet z command to put your telnet session "in the background" and return you to your local shell. You can then perform other activities, such as edit a file, read mail, check a directory listing, and so on. When you want to check on your telnet session, you type fg at the shell prompt.

Steps

1. Run telnet and connect to the desired host. In this example, we are connected to dra.com to look at Library of Congress records:

```
Data Research Associates, Inc.                          Guest Access

Select a command option from the following list.  Enter the code between
the  characters and press the (RETURN) key after entering the command.

    <A>uthor          To find authors, composers, performers, illustrators,
                      conferences, and corporate authors.

    <T>itle           To find a work by title, or generic title.

    <EX>it            To logoff
    <N>ext page       To do other types of searches
    <NEW>             Read what's NEW in this catalog

This service is not affiliated with the Library of Congress.
```

10 ⊕ WORKING ON REMOTE SYSTEMS WITH TELNET AND RLOGIN

```
The Library of Congress Information System (LOCIS) is now
available at "locis.loc.gov" (140.147.254.3) using tn3270
or line mode TELNET.
Mail comments, or suggestions to CATALOG@DRA.COM

Enter your command or search below and press the (RETURN) key.
>>
```

    Now suppose you've entered a bibliographic search and have been informed that the search will take a long time (probably because it consists of common words). The best thing to do is to try a more specific search (to conserve computing resources), but if you can't, you can let the search run while you do something else at your local system prompt.

2. When you want to switch from your telnet session to your local system prompt, type CTRL-] to escape to the telnet prompt. Then type z to put the telnet session in the background:

```
^]
telnet>z
```

    You will see the following message and get your regular shell prompt from the local system:

```
Stopped (user)
%
```

3. You can now enter Unix commands on the local system. For example, we can use the finger command to check on a friend:

```
% finger rturney
Login: rturney                      Name: Raymond D Turney
Directory: /home/r/t/rturney        Shell: /usr/local/shell/picospan
On since Sun Feb 13 20:45 (PDT) on pts/8,  idle 83 days 23:00,
    from dialup-2.well.sf.ca.us
Last login Sun Feb 13 21:11 (PDT) on pts/68 from dialup-2.well.sf
Plan:
Registered: Thu Dec 23 08:57:38 1993
Computers: 386 PC Clone
Where I Live: Bay Area

I am not sure what I want to say, so for the moment I am saying nothing.
Feel free to send email to me if you want more information.  Thank you for
reading this file.  Yours Truly, Raymond Turney
```

4. When you want to return to the telnet session, type fg at the shell prompt:

```
% fg
telnet dra.com
```

    You may have to press ENTER once or twice to get the attention of the remote program.

How It Works

Some Unix shells have a feature called job control, which allows jobs (programs or processes) to be run in background if they don't require any input from the user. At the same time, one program can be run in foreground, receiving whatever the user types. Putting telnet in background means that the telnet session can be left to its own devices for lengthy operations while you do other useful work in foreground at your local shell prompt.

Comment

There are a few things to be careful about. First, not all Unix shells support job control: in particular, the Bourne shell does not, while the Korn shell and C shell do. You cannot suspend telnet if the current shell doesn't support job control.

Also, a remote program that is waiting for input from you will do just that—wait—while it is in background. Therefore, you should periodically check on a background telnet session to make sure it isn't waiting for your next input. Also, many remote programs will time out if they don't receive input within a specified time (perhaps 10 to 15 minutes).

10.8 HOW DO I... *Make an rlogin connection?*

COMPLEXITY: EASY

Problem

You're already connected to your local Internet site. You'd like to connect to another site without losing your current connection, or you'd like to take advantage of the lack of phone charges between your local site and the remote site.

Technique

You can use the rlogin command to log into another system while connected to your local Internet site. The procedure is quite straightforward.

Steps

1. If you haven't already done so, connect to your local site and log in as usual.

2. At your local system prompt, type `rlogin` followed by the Internet address of the site to which you wish to connect. For example, let's say we're on The WELL and want to connect to netcom.com:

```
% rlogin netcom.com
Password:
```

3. By default, rlogin assumes that your user ID on the remote site is the same as on the site from which you're logging in. Thus you are asked only for the password. If you have a different user ID on the remote site, you add -l followed by the user ID to your rlogin command, for example:

```
% rlogin netcom.com -l hhenderson
```

4. Supply your password for the remote site, and you're logged in, just as though you'd dialed the remote site directly. Log out when you're done at the remote site, and you'll be returned to the system prompt at your local site.

10 WORKING ON REMOTE SYSTEMS WITH TELNET AND RLOGIN

How It Works
rlogin sends a login request to the specified system as though you'd dialed it directly. Once you're connected to the remote system you can do anything there that you could do from a direct dial-in.

Comment
Remember that your session on the system from which you issued the rlogin command continues to run along with the new session to which you've connected. This may increase connect charges. Don't forget to log off your local system after you've logged off the remote system.

As with telnet, you can suspend an rlogin session and work at your local system prompt. To suspend an rlogin session, press CTRL-Z. To return to the rlogin session, type `fg` at the shell prompt. The considerations described in How-To 10.7 also apply to suspended rlogin sessions.

10.9 HOW DO I...
Automate an rlogin connection?

COMPLEXITY: ADVANCED

Problem
If you have accounts on several systems, it may be difficult to remember all of the login IDs and passwords.

Technique
There are two ways that you can simplify your login to a remote system. One, the /etc/hosts.equiv file, is set up by the administrator of the remote system. The other method, using the .rhosts file, may be available to you, the user. Both methods involve telling the remote system "who you are" so you can be allowed to log in without having to supply login IDs or passwords.

Steps
1. To use the first method, the administrator at the remote system must put the name of your local system in a file called /etc/hosts.equiv on the remote system. Once this is set up, any user of your local system can simply type `rlogin` followed by the name of the remote system, and be logged in automatically without having to supply his or her own login ID or password.

2. If such an arrangement is not available to you (and it usually won't be, for security reasons), you can use an .rhosts file. First, log on the system to which you want to have automated access.

3. On the remote system, use a text editor (such as vi) to create a file called .rhosts. In that file, put a line containing the address of the computer from which you want to access this system, followed by a space and your login ID on that computer. For example, if you want to access the computer at bigu.edu from your account "george" on The Well, you'd add a line reading,

```
well.com george
```

to the .rhosts file in your home directory at bigu.edu. Here well.com is the Internet address of the computer that you will be using to log on the bigu.edu site. Note that

321

unlike the case with the hosts.equiv file, your user ID can be different on the local and remote systems. Make sure that this file isn't readable or writable by other users. (See Chapter 6 for information on setting file access permissions.)

4. Once the .rhosts file is properly set up on the remote system, you can log on the remote system simply by typing rlogin followed by the remote address. You won't be asked for a login ID or password.

How It Works
rlogin, and similar commands such as rcp, use the /etc/hosts.equiv or .rhosts file to check for the names of "trusted" users who are allowed to log in without IDs or passwords.

Comment
While these automatic login facilities can be convenient, they represent a potential security problem. With /etc/hosts.equiv, compromising *any* account on one machine gives the intruder access to the other machine. The .rhosts method is a bit more secure, but still, if your account is compromised, the intruder has access to your account on the other machine. Some system administrators thus forbid the use of these techniques, and you shouldn't try to work behind the administrator's back.

10.10 HOW DO I...
Copy files between systems with rcp?

COMPLEXITY: INTERMEDIATE

Problem
You have set up automated login between two or more systems (as shown in How-To 10.9), and you'd like to copy files to or from the remote system.

Technique
You can use the rcp (remote copy) command to copy files between systems on which you have accounts.

Steps
1. Log on a system that is set up to access one or more remote systems through /etc/hosts.equiv or .rhosts files.

2. If necessary, use rlogin to log on a remote system and list or examine files, and so on.

3. To copy a file between a remote system and your local system, type `rcp` followed by the source and destination filenames. The filename on the remote system must be preceded by the address of that computer. For example, to copy the file report94 from the remote system bigu.edu to your local system, you would enter this command:

```
%rcp bigu.edu:report94 myreport
```

This command, issued from your local system, copies the file report94 from your account on the machine at bigu.edu and gives it the name myreport.

Similarly, the command

```
%rcp posting.txt bigu.edu:posting.txt
```

10 WORKING ON REMOTE SYSTEMS WITH TELNET AND RLOGIN

copies the local file posting.txt to your account at bigu.edu, giving it the same name.

Note that the computer name (bigu.edu) is separated from the filename by a colon (:).

How It Works

rcp checks to make sure you have set up remote access correctly through /etc/hosts.equiv or .rhosts, as shown in How-To 10.9. If things are set up correctly, rcp copies the files as indicated without requiring any login procedure at the remote site.

Comment

Remember, rcp won't work if your /etc/hosts.equiv or .rhosts files aren't set up correctly (or are not allowed).

Finding Software with archie

How do I...

- 11.1 Use an archie client
- 11.2 Use an interactive archie server
- 11.3 Get help with archie
- 11.4 Select archie features
- 11.5 Specify the type of search
- 11.6 Control how archie displays information
- 11.7 Sort the search results
- 11.8 Have archie mail me the results
- 11.9 Search by keyword
- 11.10 Use archie's output with a Unix command
- 11.11 Use archie by mail

The ftp program gives you the ability to get copies of thousands of different files from sites all over the Internet. In many cases, someone will recommend a program or document and give the name of a site where you can obtain a copy. In that case, it's a simple matter to use ftp to get the file from that site, as explained in Chapter 7.

But things aren't always that simple. Someone may mention a file that's available by ftp, but not mention a specific site, let alone the proper directory location. Sometimes, the exact filename may not be clear (Which version number is it? What's the extension—.exe, .arc, .zip, or something else?). And suppose you want to look not for a specific program but for a *kind* of program, such as a Windows screen saver? You could ftp to one of the large archive sites and browse around in the directories. You might

INTERNET HOW-TO

even be able to figure out which directory is likely to have the files you seek, and find the right file by trial and error. But such a search is likely to be both inefficient and frustrating.

What's needed is an index to the vast collection of software that's available by ftp. To meet this need, a program called archie was developed by a talented and public-spirited group of programmers at McGill University, Montreal, Canada. The name archie is derived from the word "archive," and it is usually spelled in lowercase, presumably in honor of the cockroach of literary fame.

In this chapter, you'll learn how to use archie to find sites and directory locations from which you can obtain the programs or documents you seek. You will also learn how to use the growing "whatis" database to find resources by keyword.

How archie Works

archie is a database that tracks the contents of over 800 anonymous ftp sites containing over 1 million files. About once a month, the archie software checks in with each site and revises its database to account for newly added, deleted, or moved files. In addition to its database of sites, directories, and filenames, archie also compiles "whatis" databases. These databases contain brief descriptions of resources—descriptions that you can search by keyword as you would search for books in a library catalog. The first whatis database to be implemented deals with descriptions of software packages and data sets, but new databases are being implemented that will help you find the location of other kinds of resources as well, such as library catalogs, mailing lists, and FAQ (Frequently Asked Questions) files. Figure 11-1 shows the components of the archie system and ways that you can access archie.

Ways to Use archie

As shown on the right side of Figure 11-1, you can access archie in three different ways. The preferred way in most cases is to run the archie client at your local Internet site. This program (simply called archie), automatically connects to an archie server and processes your search, using option switches and text that you supply on the command line.

If an archie client isn't available at your site, or if you need to perform a search that isn't supported by the client (such as a search of a whatis database), you can run archie interactively. You do this by using telnet (see Chapter 10) to connect to an archie server. The server gives you a prompt and you type commands that specify how you want archie to search and what you want it to find.

Finally, for people whose only access to the Internet is by electronic mail, there are archie servers that accept and process archie search requests by e-mail. Since ftp is also accessible by e-mail, this means that if you have only e-mail access to the Internet (perhaps through CompuServe, GEnie, or another commercial service), you can still find and obtain whatever you want from the thousands of files available.

Related Topics

To Learn How to...	See Chapter
Download files to your PC	9
Get files by ftp	7
Search for resources using hypertext	14

11 🌐 FINDING SOFTWARE WITH ARCHIE

Search for resources using menus	12
Send a mail message	3
Use telnet to connect to a server	10
Use Unix commands	6

How-Tos in this Chapter

11.1 Use an archie client
You run an archie client by typing a command line at the system prompt at your local site. The command line begins with the word archie, followed by a string to search for, and optional command switches that control how the search is performed.

11.2 Use an interactive archie server
You can use telnet to connect to an archie server. The server gives you an archie> prompt at which you type commands interactively to specify settings or to perform a search.

11.3 Get help with archie
When you telnet to an archie server, you can use the help command to get information about commands and settings. For an archie client, you have to resort to the online manual (and this book, of course).

11.4 Select archie features
Whichever way you use archie, there are a number of settings that can be important for getting the results you want. For example, settings can control whether archie will

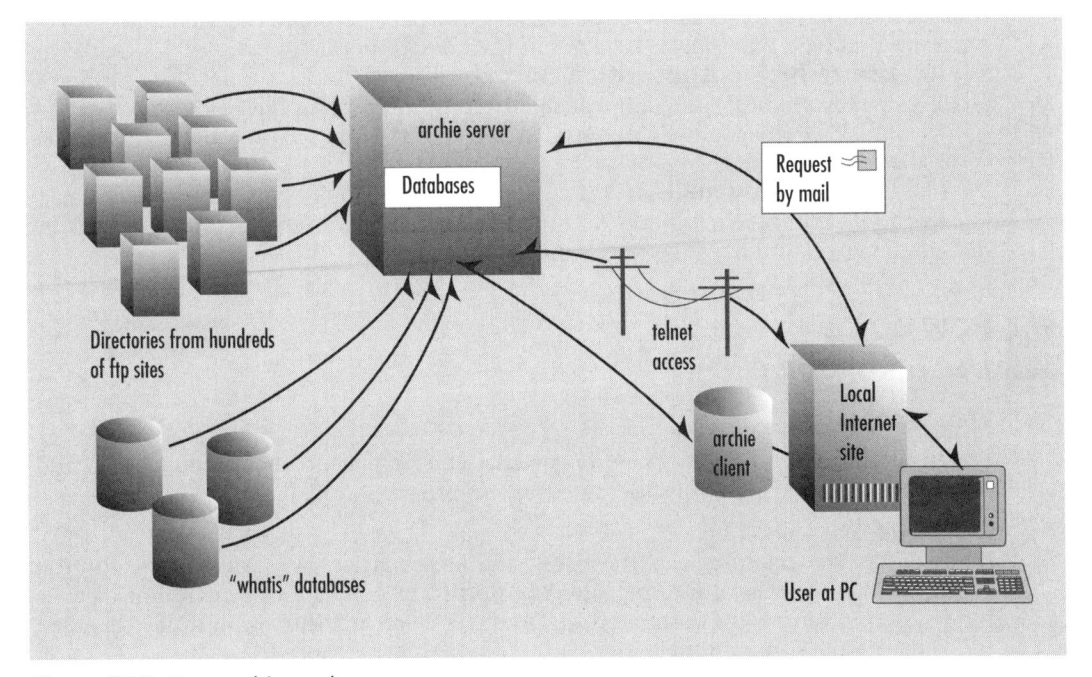

Figure 11-1 How archie works

327

INTERNET HOW-TO

search for an exact or partial match. You use command switches to make settings when you run an archie client. When you telnet to an archie server (or use archie by mail), you use the set command to set variables that control settings. A table presented in this how-to makes it easy for you to find the right switch or setting.

11.5   Specify the type of search
When you perform an archie search, you give archie a word (string) to match against the names of all the directories and files in the database. You can specify whether to return only exact matches, partial matches (substrings), or regular expressions that include wildcards. This gives you flexibility: you can use a more precise search if you know what the filename should look like, or a more general search if all you know is the name of the program itself.

11.6   Control how archie displays information
When you set up your archie search, you can specify how the results will be shown to you. You can limit how many hits will be shown, let the results scroll up the screen continually, or specify the use of a pager program to present data one screen at a time.

11.7   Sort the search results
You can also decide how the search results will be sorted: by filename, site name, date, or size—and in a forward or reverse direction.

11.8   Have archie mail me the results
A convenient way to use an interactive archie session is to give archie your e-mail address and ask it to mail the search results to you for later perusal.

11.9   Search by keyword
The growing whatis database provides brief descriptions of resources (software packages, data sets, and so on). You can use the interactive whatis command to search for files or programs that have a particular keyword in their description.

11.10 Use archie's output with a Unix command
archie provides a handy "program readable" output format that puts each search hit on a single line. This lets you use Unix utilities such as grep and sort to process and format your search results.

11.11 Use archie by mail
Finally, if you don't have full access to the Internet, you can send an archie request by mail to the server and have the results mailed back to you.

11.1 HOW DO I...
Use an archie client?

COMPLEXITY: EASY

Problem
You would like to find a copy of a program that you have heard about. You need to find the names of one or more ftp sites that have this program available.

Technique
If you're looking for a program, the fastest and most efficient way is usually to run the archie client at your local Internet site. You do this by typing a command line at your local system prompt. The command includes the word archie, a string to be searched for, and optional command switches.

Steps

1. At the system prompt, type `archie`. Add whatever command switches you need to specify the type of search and form of output you want. Type a string that should match the file you want to find and press ENTER.

   archie connects to the server, which processes your request and displays the results. Depending on how busy the server is, the search may take from a few seconds to several minutes.

2. For example, suppose you want to find the MS-DOS compression program pkzip.exe. In this case you know the complete filename, so you can use the default exact string search. Since you suspect that many sites have this file, you add the switch -m5 to limit the results to five sites:

```
% archie -m5 pkzip.exe

Host ajpo.sei.cmu.edu

    Location: /public/piwg/piwg_11_92/piwg
         FILE -rw-r--r--      31342  Jan 21 1991   pkzip.exe

Host ftp.bio.indiana.edu

    Location: /util/ibmpc
         FILE -rw-r--r--     136192  May 13 1991   pkzip.exe

Host ftp.cs.odu.edu

    Location: /incoming
         FILE -rw-------      42163  Feb 19 15:55  pkzip.exe

Host ftp.ucdavis.edu

    Location: /trash
         FILE -r--r--r--      31408  Sep 24 1990   pkzip.exe

Host math.sunysb.edu

    Location: /programs/dos-tools
         FILE -rw-r--r--      34296  Nov 16 1992   pkzip.exe
```

   Notice that each of the five hits consists of a site name, directory path, and a listing of the actual file showing its permissions, size, date, and name (similar to the output of the Unix command ls -l).

3. View the search results and pick a site that is near you (to minimize use of Internet resources).

4. Use the ftp program to get the file. If you don't know how to use ftp, see Chapter 7 for a complete discussion.

INTERNET HOW-TO

How It Works
When you type your archie command, the archie client connects to an archie server. The server used is determined by the administrators of your local Internet site. It will normally be a server that is nearby and that has a good, reliable connection to your site.

The switches and filenames you specify are translated into a search that is submitted to the archie server. The server looks through its massive database of site names, directories, and filenames, and returns the entries for the sites that have directories or files that match your search criteria.

The most useful command switches are summarized in the table in How-To 11.4. See How-To 11.5 for a discussion of search switches, 11.6 for display switches, and 11.7 for sorting switches.

If you know the exact filename, type it. Otherwise, you may want to use a *portion* of the filename or a regular expression with wildcards.

Comment
Using a client is the preferred way to access archie because it minimizes the use of resources. However, some kinds of searches (such as whatis searches) and some other features (such as getting results by mail) require the use of an interactive connection to the archie server, which is discussed in How-To 11.2.

Since an archie command may take several minutes to process, you may wish to run your command in background so you can continue to do other work at your local Internet site. To run the command in background, add & (ampersand) to the end of the command. Note that this works only if you're running a shell that has job control (nowadays, most do).

archie returns directories as well as files. Many programs consist of a whole set of files (this is particularly true of source code). The files will normally be found in a directory named for the program. Thus, a search for the name "nethack" will probably return *directories* containing the files for the nethack game.

11.2 HOW DO I...
Use an interactive archie server?

COMPLEXITY | **INTERMEDIATE**

Problem
You may need features that are available only with the interactive form of archie, such as the whatis database search (see How-To 11.9). Also, you may wish to use archie interactively so you can more easily experiment with options and searching techniques.

Technique
You get a list of archie servers and use telnet to connect to one near your local Internet site. You then enter commands at the archie prompt, setting various options and specifying your search.

Steps
1. Find a list of archie servers. One way to do this is to run the archie client with the -L (list servers) switch:

```
% archie -L
Known archie servers:
        archie.ans.net (USA [NY])
```

```
       archie.rutgers.edu (USA [NJ])
       archie.sura.net (USA [MD])
       archie.mcgill.ca (Canada)
       archie.funet.fi (Finland/Mainland Europe)
       archie.au (Australia)
       archie.doc.ic.ac.uk (Great Britain/Ireland)
archie.rutgers.edu is the default Archie server.
For the most up-to-date list, log into an Archie server & type `servers'.
```

As the listing suggests, once you telnet to one of the servers, you can enter the "servers" command to get a more up-to-date list.

2. Pick a server to connect to. You might start with the default server for your site (archie.rutgers.edu in the preceding listing). Later, you can try other servers (perhaps those that are closer or less frequently used, thus providing quicker response time).

3. At your local system prompt, type `telnet` followed by the address of the server to which you wish to connect:

```
% telnet archie.rutgers.edu
Trying 128.6.18.15 ...
Connected to archie.rutgers.edu.
Escape character is '^]'.
```

Assuming the server is up and running, a telnet connection will be established. (See Chapter 10 for more information on telnet.)

4. You will be prompted for a login ID. Type `archie` and press (ENTER). If you're prompted for a password, just press (ENTER) again. (If this procedure doesn't log you in, you've probably reached something other than an archie server. Perhaps you need to put "archie." in front of the site name.)

```
SunOS UNIX (dorm.rutgers.edu) (ttys8)

login: archie
Last login: Thu Feb 24 03:01:02 from armelle.cma.fr
SunOS Release 4.1.3 (TDSERVER-SUN4C) #2: Mon Jul 19 18:37:02 EDT 1993

# Bunyip Information Systems, 1993

# Terminal type set to `vt100 24 80'.
# `erase' character is `^?'.
# `search' (type string) has the value `sub'.
archie>
```

The archie server will greet you. As in the above listing, it may display some information about default settings, such as your terminal type, the character to use for backspacing and correcting a command ((CTRL)-(?) in this case), and the default search type, which in this case is a "sub" (substring search, which matches if your string is anywhere in the filename).

5. You will be presented with an archie prompt where you enter commands to specify settings and perform searches. To do a search, type `find` and the string to search for in the filename database.

INTERNET HOW-TO

For example, let's suppose you want to find a copy of the StuffIt file compression program for the Macintosh. You might enter the following commands to establish the search settings:

```
archie> set maxhits 10
archie> set search sub
```

These commands tell archie to limit the display of results to 10 hits and to treat your search string as a substring, matching any filename that contains it. See How-To 11.5 for search switches, 11.6 for display switches, and 11.7 for sorting switches. Note that the substring type search is the default with most servers, so you may not have to enter the "set search" command.

6. Now that you've specified settings, you enter the actual search command:

```
archie> find stuffit
```

archie will find any program or directory names that match the substring "stuffit".

The archie server will work on your request. First it will tell you where your search is in the queue (list of previously entered searches), and give you an estimated time of completion:

```
# Search type: sub.
# Your queue position: 10
# Estimated time for completion: 02:30
working... |
```

When archie is finished, the results (if any) will be displayed. Here are the results from our example search:

```
Host ftp.apple.com    (130.43.2.3)
Last updated 07:22 23 Feb 1994

     Location: /dts/utils
        FILE    -rw-r-xr-x  117661 bytes  00:00 25 Nov 1992  stuffit-expander-3-0.
hqx


Host ccu.umanitoba.ca    (130.179.16.8)
Last updated 05:45 30 Jul 1993

     Location: /Mac-Develop/Apps
        FILE    -rw-r--r--  117661 bytes  01:00 26 Nov 1992  stuffit-expander-3-0.
hqx


Host sumex-aim.stanford.edu    (36.44.0.6)
Last updated 07:57 22 Feb 1994

     Location: /info-mac/util
        FILE    -rw-r--r--   23854 bytes  23:00  3 Oct 1992  stuffit-converter-302
.hqx
```

332

11 ⊕ FINDING SOFTWARE WITH ARCHIE

```
Host plaza.aarnet.edu.au    (139.130.4.6)
Last updated 11:23   5 Feb 1994

    Location: /micros/mac/info-mac/util
        FILE     -r--r--r--    23854 bytes  01:00  4 Oct 1992  stuffit-converter-302
.hqx


Host lth.se    (130.235.20.3)
Last updated 10:16   5 Feb 1994

    Location: /mac/info-mac/util
        FILE     -rw-r--r--    23854 bytes  01:00  5 Oct 1992  stuffit-converter-302
.hqx


Host ftp.sunet.se    (130.238.127.3)
Last updated 07:48   5 Feb 1994

    Location: /pub/mac/info-mac/util
        FILE     -r--r--r--    23854 bytes  23:00  3 Oct 1992  stuffit-converter-302
.hqx


Host sics.se    (192.16.123.90)
Last updated 07:43   5 Feb 1994

    Location: /pub/info-mac/util
        FILE     -rw-rw-r--    23854 bytes  14:11  7 Nov 1993  stuffit-converter-302
.hqx


Host wuarchive.wustl.edu    (128.252.135.4)
Last updated 07:22 23 Dec 1993

    Location: /systems/mac/info-mac/util
        FILE     -r--r--r--    23854 bytes  23:00  2 Oct 1992  stuffit-converter-302
.hqx


Host uhunix2.uhcc.hawaii.edu    (128.171.44.7)
Last updated 07:21   1 Oct 1993

    Location: /mirrors/info-mac/util
        FILE     -rw-r--r--    23854 bytes  00:00  4 Oct 1992  stuffit-converter-302
.hqx
```

In this case, archie found some directories containing (apparently) a conversion program for use with StuffIt. If we want the actual StuffIt program, we'll probably need to refine our search. (We could try just the substring "stuf", or ask a Mac-using friend for a more exact filename.)

INTERNET HOW-TO

Note that the entry for each match includes the address of the host, the time the archie database for that location was last updated, the path location of the matching directory or file, and a listing for the directory or file in a format similar to that used by the Unix list command.

7. To end your archie session, type `quit` and press (ENTER). You always press (ENTER) after typing a command at the archie prompt.

How It Works
The telnet program at your local Internet site connects to the archie server at the remote site. The server provides a command prompt. When you enter commands, it parses them and makes appropriate settings or takes appropriate actions.

archie matches your search string to the directory and file names in the database using the rules you've specified in your client option switches or server commands. By default, the results are scrolled continuously on the screen (see How-To 11.6 for alternative ways to display output).

Comment
An easy way to capture the scrolling output of your archie command is to set your PC's communications software so that it will "capture to screen" or "log to file" the contents of the screen display. Do this before you enter the command that performs the search.

If the server you connected to is busy (has many searches queued ahead of yours), response to your commands (particularly searches) may be quite slow. If this is the case, try to find a server that is closer and/or less frequently used. You can also try connecting at off-peak hours.

When possible, use a client (archie command) rather than a server (telnet command).

11.3 HOW DO I...
Get help with archie?

COMPLEXITY: EASY

Problem
archie has a number of option switches (for the client version) or commands (for the interactive server version). You may need some help in remembering their names and how they work.

Technique
For the archie client, the online Unix manual entry provides a summary of archie's option switches. For the interactive server, you can use the "help" and "manpage" commands to get online help.

Steps
1. To get a quick summary of option switches for the archie client, just type `archie` at the system prompt and press (ENTER):

```
% archie
Usage: archie [-[cers][l][t][m#][h host][L][N#]] string
       -c : case sensitive substring search
       -e : exact string match (default)
       -r : regular expression search
```

334

```
    -s : case insensitive substring search
    -l : list one match per line
    -t : sort inverted by date
   -m# : specifies maximum number of hits to return (default 95)
-h host : specifies server host
    -L : list known servers and current default
   -N# : specifies query niceness level (0-35765)
```

2. To get more help, enter the usual Unix manual command:

```
%man archie
```

Or, to save the manual to a file:

```
%man archie > archie.man
```

3. To get help with the interactive archie server, type `help` at the archie prompt:

```
archie> help
  These are the commands you can use in help:

                  .        drop down one level in the hierarchy

                  ?        display a list of valid subtopics at the current level

      done, ^D, ^C         quit from help entirely

          <string>         help on a topic or subtopic
```

4. The prompt will change to the word help, indicating that you are now in the help system. Press ⑦ to get a list of topics at the highest level:

```
help> ?
# Subtopics:
#
#         about
#         autologout
#         bugs
#         bye
#         done
#         e-mail
#         exit
#         find
#         general
#         help
#         list
#         mail
#         motd
#         nopager
#         pager
#         prog
#         quit
#         regex
#         servers
#         set
```

Continued on next page

INTERNET HOW-TO

Continued from previous page

```
#       show
#       site
#       term
#       unset
#       version
#       whatis
#       whats_new
```

5. To get help on a topic, type the name of the topic:

```
help> set
```

The 'set' command allows you to set one of archie's variables. Their values affect how archie interacts with the user. archie distinguishes between three types of variable: "boolean", which may be either set or unset, "numeric", representing an integer within a pre- determined range, and "string", whose value is a string of characters (which may or may not be restricted).

Currently, the variables that may be set are:

```
autologout  - numeric.   Number of minutes before automatic log out
mailto      - string.    Address that output is to be mailed to
maxhits     - numeric.   'prog' stops after this many matches
pager       - boolean.   If set use the pager, otherwise don't
search      - string.    How 'prog' is to search the database
sortby      - string.    How 'prog' output is to be sorted
status      - boolean.   Report how the search is progressing
term        - string.    Describes your terminal
```

Each variable has a corresponding subtopic entry under 'set'. See them for more details. Also, see help on 'unset' and 'show'.

Note that the list of settings you see will vary depending on the configuration used at your site.

6. Once you ask for help on a topic, you automatically move down a level and can get help on the subtopics. (The prompt changes to "help set" to show that you've gone down a level.) You can press ⑦ again to get a list of subtopics under "set." Type the name of the subtopic to get help on it. For example, to find out about the maxhits setting, type `maxhits`:

```
help set> maxhits
```

'maxhits' is a numeric variable whose value is the maximum number of matches you want the 'prog' command to generate.

If archie seems to be slow, or you don't want a lot of output this can be set to a small value. "maxhits" must be within the range 0 to 1000. The default value is 1000.

Example:

```
set maxhits 100
```

'prog' will now stop after 100 matches have been found

7. As the instructions when you enter the help system indicate, you type `done`, or press CTRL-D, or CTRL-C to exit the help system and return to the archie prompt.

8. To get a complete listing of the online manual for the archie server, type `manpage` at the archie prompt. Note that it will scroll continually unless you have issued the "set pager" command. You can turn on the "capture to file" feature of your communications software to get a copy of the manual on your PC.

How It Works
The minimal help features for the client command are the standard ones used for Unix commands and programs. The help for the interactive server uses a standard hierarchical (topic and subtopic) approach common to many mainframe programs. None of these help features are as easy to use as the help for your typical Windows or Macintosh program, but you can probably find out what you need to know without too much fuss.

Comment
You can find additional help for archie in the form of documents available from ftp sites. Peter Deutsch at McGill University has written "archie—An Electronic Directory Service for the Internet," a brief guide to the problem of access to Internet resources and how archie meets this need. Another useful document is "A SURAnet guide to the archie service (v1.0.1)," by Eric Anderson.

11.4 HOW DO I...
Select archie features?

COMPLEXITY: INTERMEDIATE

Problem
You may need to specify how your search request should be handled. For example, you can specify an exact, substring, or regular expression search. You may also want to specify how the results should be displayed (limited number, continuous, or paged).

Technique
With an archie client, you use command line switches to specify features. When you connect to an archie server, you type commands at the archie prompt.

Steps
1. Look up the feature you need in Table 11-1. For each of the major features, the table gives the command option switch (if available), the interactive command, and the how-to that discusses the feature in more detail. Note that an item in italic (such as *number*) means that you have to use that type of item (number, string, and so on) with the option or command. Where there is more than one applicable interactive command they are separated by commas.

2. If you are using an archie client, add the appropriate command switch to the command line. Thus if you want archie to find a regular expression, you would type

INTERNET HOW-TO

FEATURE	SWITCH FOR CLIENT	COMMAND FOR SERVER	HOW-TO
Address to mail results		mailto *address*	11.8
End archie session		quit	11.2
Help		help, manpage	11.3
List known servers	-L		11.2
Mail results		mail	11.8
Maximum results to display	-m *number*	maxhits *number*	11.6
Output details shown		output_format terse, verbose	11.6
Output one screen at a time	l *pagername*	pager *pagername*	11.6
Output so programs can read	-l	output_format machine	11.10
Search		find, prog	11.1, 11.2
Search whatis database		whatis	11.9
Search exact string	-e	search exact	11.5
Search regular expression	-r	search regex, exact_regex	11.5
Search substring (case-sensitive)	-c	search subcase, exact_subcase	11.5
Search substring (not case-sensitive)	-s	search sub, exact_sub	11.5
Set variable (feature)		set	11.4
Show setting		show, show *setting*	11.4
Sort by file date	-t	sortby time, rtime	11.7
Sort by filename		sortby filename, rfilename	11.7
Sort by host name		sortby hostname, rhostname	11.7
Sort by size		sortby size, rsize	11.7

Table 11-1 Commands and switches for useful archie features

```
%archie -r
```

If you want archie to display only the first 10 hits, you would specify

```
%archie -m10
```

And of course you may wish to combine options, as in:

```
%archie -r -m10
```

3. If you are using an archie server interactively, type the appropriate command at the archie prompt. Commands that set a specification begin with "set." For example, to have archie search for a regular expression, you type

```
archie>set regex
```

If you want to limit the result to the first 10 hits, you type

```
archie>set maxhits 10
```

Unlike option switches, you can't combine interactive commands on the same line. Also note that interactive settings stay in effect until the end of your session (unless you change them). Thus if you set maxhits to 10, all subsequent searches during that session will have their results limited to the first 10 hits.

How It Works
For the archie client, the option switches are parsed by the system, as with other Unix commands, and are passed to the client for processing. The client in turn passes the settings to the server to perform the search.

For an interactive archie server, the commands you type change the settings used by the server.

Comment
Unfortunately there is no "settings file" that you can use to store frequently used settings for the archie client or server. You could use the Unix alias facility (discussed in many Unix books) to set up some common archie client commands, or put the commands in a shell script so that all you'd have to supply is the filename. For the interactive archie server, you could (if you have a program that supports it) set up keyboard macros that would enter the appropriate commands to the server. These techniques are beyond the scope of this book.

11.5 HOW DO I...
Specify the type of search?

COMPLEXITY: EASY

Problem
If you know the full name of the file you seek, you can specify an exact search for faster results. But filenames tend to change as software versions are upgraded, and the same program file may have a variety of different extensions due to the different file compression schemes in use. This means that you may need to control how exact your archie search will be.

Technique
You use option switches for the client, or commands for the server, to specify what kind of matching will be done on your search request. The kinds of searches you can specify are as follows:

➤ Exact Search
➤ Subcase search
➤ Substring search
➤ Regular expression search

As its name implies, an *exact* search means that only names that are exactly the same will be matched. The search string pkzip.exe will match pkzip.exe, but not pkzip or pkzip2.exe or pkzip.zip. Further, matching is case-sensitive, so stuffit won't match StuffIt. The exact search option is the default when using most archie clients.

A *subcase* search means that your search string will be matched if it appears anywhere in the filename. Like the exact search, the subcase search is case-sensitive. Thus the string pkzip will match pkzip.exe and pkzip2.exe, since the substring "pkzip" appears in both filenames. (It will also match the name pkzip, which is probably a

INTERNET HOW-TO

directory containing files for this program.) It won't match PKZIP however, because the latter is uppercase and the search string is lowercase.

A *substring* search is like a subcase search except that it is not case-sensitive. Thus a substring search on pkzip will match everything mentioned above, including PKZIP. Most servers default to a substring search.

A *regular expression* search lets you specify a string with wildcards following rules used by the Unix system. For example, ? matches any single character and * matches any number of characters up to the next character specified. DOS users can begin by using their usual wildcard rules and then learn more about regular expressions from any general book on Unix, or by reading Appendix A of "A SURAnet Guide to the archie Server."

Steps

1. Consult the features that begin with "Search" in Table 11-1 and find the kind of search you want to use.

2. If you are using a client, add the appropriate option switch to the command line. For example,

%archie -s

specifies a noncase-sensitive substring. (You then have to add the string and press ENTER.)

3. If you are using an interactive server, type s e t at the archie prompt. Follow it with the appropriate word from Table 11-1. For example, to set a noncase-sensitive substring search, enter

archie> set search sub

Note that the server version of archie provides the additional specifications of exact_subcase, exact_sub, and exact_regex. These specifications tell archie to try an exact search first and then, if no results are found, to try an alternative search (case-sensitive substring, noncase-sensitive substring, and regular expression, respectively).

4. Enter your search string and perform your search (see How-To 11.6).

How It Works

The option switch or command you specify determines how archie will match your string against the directory and file names in its database. An exact search is the fastest, but it fails if even one letter doesn't match (or is a different case). Use an exact search when you are sure you know the filename (including the extension), and want only a particular version of a program.

Substring searches are medium in speed. Use a substring when you know how the filename probably begins, but you aren't sure what versions are available or what extensions the files might have. Case-sensitive substring searches are a bit faster and are good for names of DOS and Windows files, since those are usually stored in all lowercase.

Regular expression searches are slowest and most difficult to formulate. They can be handy when you're looking for a particular version of a program that has many versions available.

11 FINDING SOFTWARE WITH ARCHIE

Comment
To get faster results (and to conserve Internet resources), use the fastest type of search that you are confident will work. (If you don't get satisfactory results, you can repeat the search using a more flexible but slower method.)

11.6 HOW DO I...
Control how archie displays information?

COMPLEXITY INTERMEDIATE

Problem
archie can produce a lot of output, particularly if you don't limit the number of hits to be displayed. This can make the results awkward to use.

Technique
There are several ways to make archie's output more manageable. One is to limit the number of matches that will be displayed. Another is to have archie's output sent through a paging program so you will see it one screen at a time. You can also save output from an archie client to a file.

Steps
1. To limit the number of hits from an archie client, add the `-m` option to your command line. Follow it with the maximum number of hits to be shown. For example, to limit the search results to 50, you would include the option `-m50` in your command line.

2. If you are using an interactive server, type `set maxhits` followed by the maximum number of hits. Thus to limit your next (and subsequent) searches to a maximum of 50 hits, you would type

```
archie>set maxhits 50
```

3. You can also have output sent through a pager so you see it one screen at a time. For a client, type your complete archie command and then type `| more`. (The |, vertical bar or pipe symbol, passes the output of the archie command to the more program, which is a pager.) For example:

```
% archie -s stuf | more
```

4. With a server, you can get screen-paged output by typing the command `set pager` followed by the name of the pager (such as `more`):

```
archie>set pager more
```

5. Whichever method you use, you then use the regular commands for the paging program. Usually you can get along fine by pressing SPACEBAR to see each screen, or Q to quit the pager. For more information on pagers, see the manual entry for the pager program ("more" and "less" are the two most common pagers on Unix systems).

6. Another alternative is to save archie's output to a file. With an interactive server there is no command to do this, but you can set your PC's communications program to capture the output. With a client, you can use the > redirection symbol to send output to a file. For example,

341

INTERNET HOW-TO

```
% archie -e pkzip.exe -m25 > results
```

does an exact search for up to 25 instances of the name pkzip.exe and saves them to a file called results for later use.

How It Works

Limiting the maximum number of hits can keep the volume of output down to a manageable size (as well as conserve resources).

A pager takes the output of the archie client or server and presents it one screen at a time. This makes it easier to read the output.

Since the archie client is a regular Unix program, you can use the Unix pipe (|) symbol to send its input to another program for processing (see also How-To 11.10), or use the redirection symbol (>) to save archie's output in a file.

Comment

Since an archie client command can take a while to run, piping its output to a pager can lock up your session at your local Internet site for a while. Redirecting to a file is better, because you can put the command in the background (by adding the & symbol to the end) and go on about your business.

11.7 HOW DO I... Sort the search results?

COMPLEXITY: EASY

Problem

By default, archie's output is more or less random (matches in the order encountered in the database). Sometimes it's useful to be able to sort archie's output. For example, you might want to sort by host (ftp site) so you can find a favorite site quickly. In some cases you might want to sort by date to help you find the newest versions of a file.

Technique

Most clients have very limited searching capabilities. With an interactive server, however, you can use several commands to specify how you want the output sorted.

Steps

1. With a client, you can add the -t switch to have your output sorted by date. For example,

```
% archie -m25 -t pkzip*
```

tells archie to display up to 25 hits on the string pkzip* and to sort the results with the oldest dated file first. (By default, archie displays files from newest to oldest, and that's what you would usually want.)

2. With a server, you have a greater variety of options. You enter the command `set sortby`, and follow it with one of these options:

filename	Sort by actual name of file or directory found
time	Sort by date and time from file directory
hostname	Sort by name of host (site) that has the file
size	Sort by size of file

You can precede each of these with r to sort in reverse order. Thus,

```
archie> sortby time
```

sorts by date and time from newest to oldest, while

```
archie>sortby rdate
```

sorts by date and time from oldest to newest.

Sorting by host (site) can be useful if you have a preferred site for obtaining your files. The following search lists sites having some version of the file pkzip with the sites in alphabetical order:

```
archie> find pkzip
# Search type: exact.
# Your queue position: 1
# Estimated time for completion: 00:11
working... -
Host csc.canberra.edu.au    (137.92.1.1)
Last updated 11:37  8 Feb 1994

    Location: /pub/msdos
      DIRECTORY     drwxr-xr-x     512 bytes  01:00 12 Jul 1993  pkzip


Host sunsite.unc.edu   (152.2.22.81)
Last updated 11:07 22 Dec 1993

    Location: /pub/packages/TeX/archive-tools
      DIRECTORY     drwxr-xr-x     512 bytes  01:14  2 Sep 1993  pkzip

    Location: /pub/packages/TeX/tools
      DIRECTORY     drwxr-xr-x     512 bytes  02:09 29 Oct 1993  pkzip


Host syr.edu    (128.230.1.49)
Last updated 11:09  5 Feb 1994

    Location: /novell
      DIRECTORY     drwxrwxr-x     512 bytes  23:00 22 Jul 1991  pkzip


Host wuarchive.wustl.edu   (128.252.135.4)
Last updated 11:27 22 Dec 1993

    Location: /packages/TeX/tools
      DIRECTORY     drwxr-xr-x    8192 bytes  11:57  1 Nov 1993  pkzip
```

How It Works

The archie database actually considers each entry to be made up of several fields, including host name, file date/time, filename, and so on. The sorting options find the

INTERNET HOW-TO

specified field and sort the search results so that records are displayed sorted in order by that field.

Comment
You can't combine sorts. The last type of sort you specify takes effect.

11.8 HOW DO I...
Have archie mail me the results?

COMPLEXITY: EASY

Problem
It's often useful to save the results of an archie search in some more tangible form. Having the results sent to you by electronic mail is a good way to do this.

Technique
The option to get your results by mail is available with an interactive server or by the use of an archie mail server (see How-To 11.11). It is not available with current archie clients.

With a server, you make your search. You then tell archie to mail you the results of the *last* search by issuing the mail command.

Steps
1. telnet to an archie server and perform the search whose results you want to see by mail.

2. Type `mail` followed by your Internet address at the archie prompt. For example:

`archie>mail jeanj@BigU.edu`

3. Alternatively, specify the `mailto` setting with your address:

`archie>set mailto jeanj@BigU.edu`

Once you've set this, you can type

`archie>mail`

to send the last result to the address you've specified.

How It Works
archie keeps its last search result in a buffer for you after displaying it. When you give the mail command, archie puts the buffer contents in a file and mails them to the address you specified.

Comment
Unfortunately there's no way to have the output mailed to you without it first being shown on the screen.

344

11.9 HOW DO I...
Search by keyword?

COMPLEXITY: INTERMEDIATE

Problem
Sometimes you are looking not for a particular program or file, but for programs or files that relate to a particular subject. The whatis command for archie servers lets you search a database of file descriptions.

Technique
You specify a word that is likely to be found in descriptions of the files you seek. For example, you might use the word "weather" to find files relating to weather data or weather forecasting.

Steps
1. Connect to an archie server as shown in How-To 11.2.
2. At the archie prompt, type `whatis`, followed by a keyword, and press (ENTER). For example, let's search the whatis database with the keyword "macintosh":

```
archie> whatis macintosh
macgetput               The "macget" and "macput" programs for transferring fi
les between a Macintosh and a UNIX system
macsend                 Send groups of files to a Macintosh using "macput"

mactermcap              Termcap(5) entry for a Macintosh running MacTerminal

multivariate            MacMul & GraphMu : Macintosh programs for multivariate
 analysis
psfig-tex               Including PostScript/Macintosh figures in TeX document
 s
sit                     produce StuffIt archives for downloading to the MacInt
osh
undos                   Convert between ASCII file format and CP/M, DOS, or Ma
cintosh file formats
uw42                    The "uw" multi-window terminal program for the Macinto
sh
archie>
```

As you can see, we found a small but interesting collection of files. (Unfortunately, the lines break in awkward places.) As the whatis databases grow, results should become lengthier and more interesting.

How It Works
The whatis facility uses a separate kind of database that includes descriptions of software packages and other resources. The size and variety of these databases is gradually growing.

Comment
Watch for news of additional whatis databases and new facilities for dealing with them. Upcoming versions of archie will probably have powerful resource-searching methods

INTERNET HOW-TO

that complement (or provide an alternative to) the Gopher facilities discussed in Chapter 12.

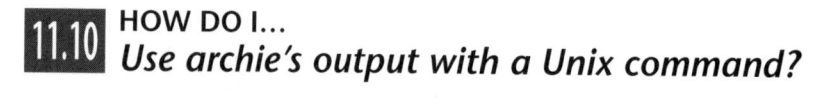

11.10 HOW DO I...
Use archie's output with a Unix command?

COMPLEXITY: ADVANCED

Problem
Sometimes you may want to process archie's output with your own program (Unix command or shell script) so you can format the information in more useful ways.

Technique
You tell the archie client or server to output its results so that each entry (host and file information) takes up only one line.

Steps
1. If you are using a client, add the -l option switch to your archie command.

2. If you are using an interactive server, type

```
set output_format machine
```

Here's an example archie search showing the "machine" output format:

```
archie> set search sub
archie> find compr
# Search type: sub.
# Your queue position: 1
# Estimated time for completion: 00:10
working... -

19920413230000Z archive.afit.af.mil 512 bytes drwxr-xr-x /pub/compress
19920310000000Z ccsun.unicamp.br 24576 bytes -rwxr-xr-x /bin/compress
19940113161700Z ccsun.unicamp.br 1024 bytes drwxrwxr-x /pub3/simtel20/compress
19930909133600Z fpspux.fapesp.br 32768 bytes -rwxr-xr-x /bin/compress
19920207000000Z ftp.3com.com 106496 bytes --x--x--x /bin/compress
19920722230000Z ftp.cc.mcgill.ca 24576 bytes --x--x--x /bin/compress
19920824230000Z ftp.cc.mcgill.ca 2048 bytes dr-xr-xr-x /pub/ftp_inc/dos/compress

19930326000000Z ftp.gsfc.nasa.gov 24576 bytes -rwxr-xr-x /bin/compress
19930409230000Z ftp.halcyon.com 17408 bytes -rwxr-xr-x /bin/compress
19930601230000Z ftp.halcyon.com 512 bytes drwxr-xr-x /pub/waffle/compress
19931108190600Z ftp.uwo.ca 512 bytes drwxrwxr-x /pub/unix/X-windows/X.V11R5/contrib/lib/andrew/contrib/compress
19931108180400Z ftp.uwo.ca 512 bytes drwxrwxr-x /pub/unix/X-windows/X.V11R5/mit/util/compress
19931206141400Z ftp.uwo.ca 512 bytes drwxr-xr-x /pub/unix/X-windows/XR5-mips/mit/util/compress
19931206134800Z ftp.uwo.ca 512 bytes drwxr-xr-x /pub/unix/X-windows/XR5-solaris/mit/util/compress
19931206144100Z ftp.uwo.ca 512 bytes drwxr-xr-x /pub/unix/X-windows/XR5-sun3/mit/util/compress
19931206130300Z ftp.uwo.ca 512 bytes drwxr-xr-x /pub/unix/X-windows/XR5-sun4/mit
```

```
/util/compress
19930502230000Z  ftp.wang.com 25684 bytes  ——x—x—x  /usr/bin/compress
19930112000000Z  lotos.csi.uottawa.ca 24576 bytes  ——x—x—x  /bin/compress
19910527230000Z  pineapple.bbn.com 15360 bytes  -rwxr-xr-x  /bin/compress
19930518230000Z  roxette.mty.itesm.mx 4096 bytes  drwxr-xr-x  /pub/X11R5/mit/util/c
ompress
```

Each result is actually a single line, though long lines break on the screen.

3. Arrange to have the output saved in a file. You can use the > symbol with an archie client command, or capture the output of an archie server to your PC's hard disk.

4. Use the appropriate program to further process the results. For example, on a Unix system, you can use the grep command to find text (such as a host name). You can also use a more elaborate program such as awk or a database to read, store, format, or retrieve the archie records.

How It Works
The "machine format" or "line format" puts each complete archie hit on a single line (it separates them with linefeeds). Since many Unix programs (such as grep and awk) are designed to read and process lines of text, this means that the archie output can be processed with such programs, usually with the aid of a shell script.

Comment
This feature is mainly for advanced users, but it illustrates the potential power of Unix for transmitting data between programs and for building customized processing options.

11.11 HOW DO I...
Use archie by mail?

COMPLEXITY INTERMEDIATE

Problem
If your only access to the Internet is by e-mail, you can't use an archie client or server directly. But you *can* mail your request to a server and get the results mailed back to you.

Technique
You send a mail message to the archie server. The mail message contains the commands you want the server to process.

Steps
1. To get a summary of how to use archie by mail, send mail to an archie server, prefixing its name with `archie@`. For example, you can send the mail to archie@archie.rutgers.edu. Put the word "help" in the subject or body of the message. You will receive an introduction and list of commands.

2. To send an archie request by mail, send a message to one of the server addresses as given in step 1. Leave the subject blank.

3. In the body of the message, put your archie commands, one per line. It's a good idea to make your first command `set mailto` followed by your e-mail address (so archie

INTERNET HOW-TO

knows where to mail the results of the search). You can then set the search type, display and sorting criteria, and so on, as you would for an interactive archie session. Your last commands should be the find command and the quit command (to end the archie session).

4. End the mail message as usual and send it to the server.

5. You will receive the results back by mail. Be patient...this is a rather inefficient process and has a low priority.

Here is an example message asking for a search for the name pkzip.exe:

```
mail archie@archie.rutgers.edu
Subject: press <Enter> to leave subject blank
set mailto hrh@well.com
set search exact
set maxhits 10
find pkzip.exe
quit
```

Here the plain old Unix mail program is used, with CTRL-D to send the message; but of course you can use any mail program. (If you're doing it from CompuServe, you'd use CompuServe mail and an address such as >INTERNET:archie@archie.rutgers.edu.)

How It Works

The archie server receives your mail, reads and executes the commands, and mails the output back to you. As in the old days of punched cards, it's easy to make a mistake (such as setting the wrong search type) and get less than useful results.

Comment

If you have access to an archie client or telnet access to an archie server, don't use mail access. It is slow and ties up valuable resources.

Finding Resources with Gopher

How do I....

12.1 Connect to a Gopher server
12.2 Navigate the Gopher menus
12.3 Get help while using Gopher
12.4 Connect to other Gopher servers
12.5 Use bookmarks to create my own menu
12.6 Identify Gopher item types
12.7 Read a text file
12.8 Get a file by mail
12.9 Save a file
12.10 Download a file
12.11 Access ftp sites from Gopher
12.12 Use a subject tree
12.13 Use telnet from Gopher
12.14 Find a person in an online directory
12.15 Search a database
12.16 Use Veronica to find Gopher items
12.17 Combine keywords to refine a search
12.18 Use Jughead to search a particular Gopher

As the Internet proliferates, more and more services are being offered through local Internet sites, such as universities, businesses, and local conferencing systems. There is

INTERNET HOW-TO

no end to the variety of services available: documents, executable programs, graphics, directories, indexes, databases, library catalogs, and many others.

A number of specialized tools covered earlier in this book enable you to find out about software (archie), get files (ftp), and access services (telnet). You can get a lot of information using these basic tools. However, their one drawback is that they are command-driven: you have to first get enough information to be able to enter the right command, and then you have to type in various requests.

This chapter introduces Gopher, a menu-driven tool for presenting and accessing documents and services throughout the Internet. With Gopher, you select the file or service you want from a series of menus. You can read text files or have copies of all sorts of files mailed to you, saved to your home directory, or even downloaded directly to your PC. You can connect to a variety of services (including databases, indexes, and catalogs), simply by selecting them from a menu...no address necessary.

If Gopher merely presented the files and services that are available at a particular site, it would still be useful. But Gopher does much more than that. Most Gopher servers have options to connect to other servers, so you can cruise around on the information highway. You can stop at a favorite university site and pick up a bibliography on networking. You can then take the next off-ramp and find yourself looking at the eclectic selection of documents offered by The WELL. Go to the train station, hop aboard the Ftp Unlimited, and get a ton of software just by selecting files from menus. You can end your trip by getting a real-world weather forecast for the weekend.

What's more, Gopher comes with Veronica, a searching mechanism that maintains a database of the titles of tens of thousands of menu items offered by several thousand Gophers around the world. With Veronica, you can specify a word, phrase, or other search specification and create your very own menu of items from around the Internet that deal with networking, or geology, or women's studies...or just about any other subject you can imagine.

How did Gopher get its name? Well, there are two possibilities. One is that the gopher is the state animal of Minnesota, and Gopher was originally developed at the University of Minnesota. The other is that you can think of the many connections between Gopher servers as tunnels through cyberspace. The Gopher can navigate these tunnels for you and retrieve items without your having to worry about (or even know) their precise location. Whatever you want, it's ready to go-fer it!

How Gopher Works

Like archie, Gopher is a client-server system. You run a Gopher client that connects to a Gopher server. The server sends its menu information to the client. The client presents the menu and lets you navigate around it and choose items. Figures 12-1 and 12-2 show two sample Gopher main menus.

Some of the items offered in a Gopher menu will be particular to the Gopher site. For example, a university menu might offer a calendar of campus events, new titles available at the bookstore, or class schedules. The WELL's Gopher, on the other hand, offers items that reflect the diverse interests of members of this conferencing system.

Most Gophers also offer links to items outside the local site. Typically these include a list of "all the Gophers Servers of the World" from which you can select other servers. Another popular facility is called "Gopher Jewels," and consists of a variety of ways to access information by topic, as shown in Figure 12-3.

12 FINDING RESOURCES WITH GOPHER

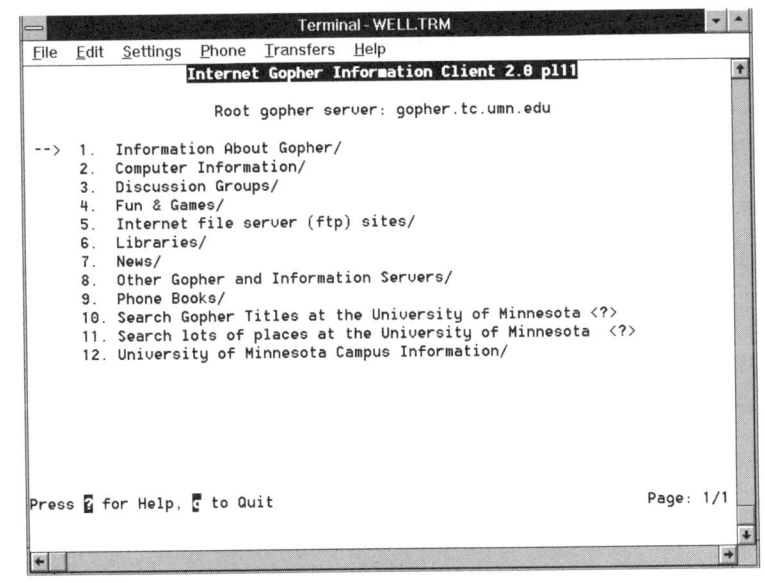

```
                    Terminal - WELL.TRM
 File  Edit  Settings  Phone  Transfers  Help
         Internet Gopher Information Client 2.0 pl11

              Root gopher server: gopher.tc.umn.edu

 -->  1. Information About Gopher/
      2. Computer Information/
      3. Discussion Groups/
      4. Fun & Games/
      5. Internet file server (ftp) sites/
      6. Libraries/
      7. News/
      8. Other Gopher and Information Servers/
      9. Phone Books/
     10. Search Gopher Titles at the University of Minnesota <?>
     11. Search lots of places at the University of Minnesota  <?>
     12. University of Minnesota Campus Information/




 Press ? for Help, q to Quit                              Page: 1/1
```

Figure 12-1 Main menu at the University of Minnesota's Gopher

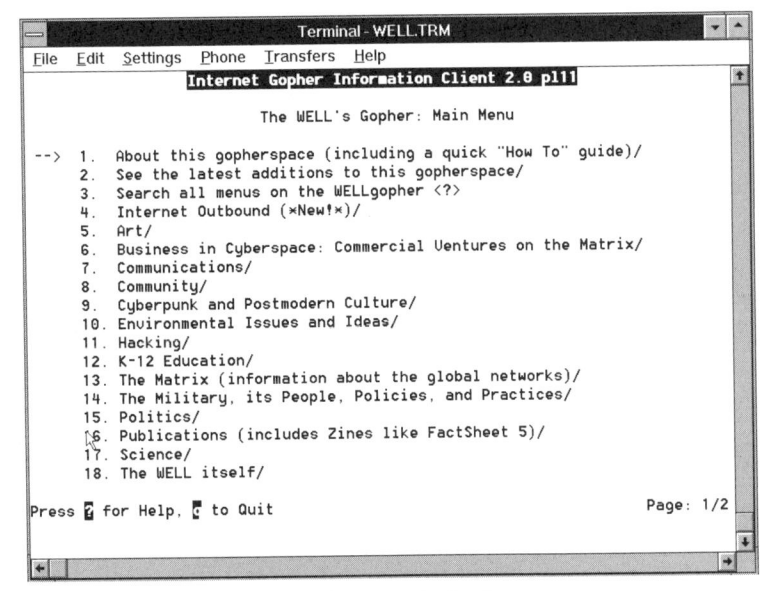

```
                    Terminal - WELL.TRM
 File  Edit  Settings  Phone  Transfers  Help
         Internet Gopher Information Client 2.0 pl11

                    The WELL's Gopher: Main Menu

 -->  1. About this gopherspace (including a quick "How To" guide)/
      2. See the latest additions to this gopherspace/
      3. Search all menus on the WELLgopher <?>
      4. Internet Outbound (*New!*)/
      5. Art/
      6. Business in Cyberspace: Commercial Ventures on the Matrix/
      7. Communications/
      8. Community/
      9. Cyberpunk and Postmodern Culture/
     10. Environmental Issues and Ideas/
     11. Hacking/
     12. K-12 Education/
     13. The Matrix (information about the global networks)/
     14. The Military, its People, Policies, and Practices/
     15. Politics/
     16. Publications (includes Zines like FactSheet 5)/
     17. Science/
     18. The WELL itself/

 Press ? for Help, q to Quit                              Page: 1/2
```

Figure 12-2 Main menu at The WELL's Gopher

INTERNET HOW-TO

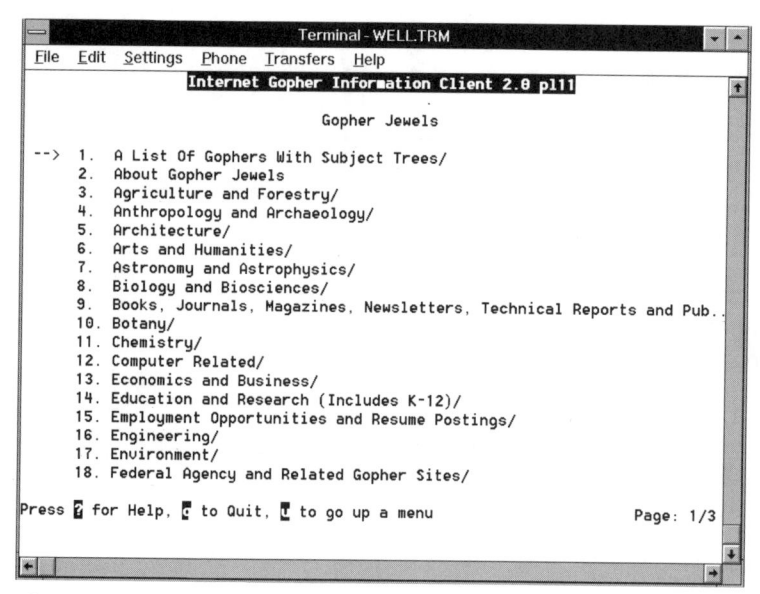

```
┌─                    Terminal - WELL.TRM                  ▼ ▲ ┐
 File  Edit  Settings  Phone  Transfers  Help
       ┌─Internet Gopher Information Client 2.0 p111──────┐↑
       │                 Gopher Jewels                    │
       │                                                  │
  -->  1.  A List Of Gophers With Subject Trees/
       2.  About Gopher Jewels
       3.  Agriculture and Forestry/
       4.  Anthropology and Archaeology/
       5.  Architecture/
       6.  Arts and Humanities/
       7.  Astronomy and Astrophysics/
       8.  Biology and Biosciences/
       9.  Books, Journals, Magazines, Newsletters, Technical Reports and Pub..
       10. Botany/
       11. Chemistry/
       12. Computer Related/
       13. Economics and Business/
       14. Education and Research (Includes K-12)/
       15. Employment Opportunities and Resume Postings/
       16. Engineering/
       17. Environment/
       18. Federal Agency and Related Gopher Sites/

  Press ? for Help, Q to Quit, U to go up a menu          Page: 1/3
```

Figure 12-3 Gopher Jewels menu

As you select menu items, the client makes the appropriate requests to the server. The details of the request depend on the kind of menu item you select. For example, if you select a file, the file will be fetched and presented to you for action. You can then choose to read the file (if it's a text file), have the file sent to you by mail, save the file to disk (at your Internet site), or download the file to your PC.

If you select a submenu (sometimes called a directory), you'll be shown a new menu with more choices on it. Menu choices can also connect you to another Gopher server, connect to a service by telnet, or search an index or database. Figure 12-4 summarizes how Gopher works and illustrates some of the things you can do with Gopher.

Searching Gopherspace

Just as archie regularly scans ftp sites and makes a database of their directory and file names, Veronica scans Gopher sites and creates a database of all the titles of the items on their menus. (Veronica is named after another character in the "Archie" comics, though the name has been given a "reverse-acronym": Very Easy Rodent-Oriented Netwide Index to Computerized Archives.)

To use Veronica, you simply choose it from your Gopher server menu and supply a word or phrase (you can also use Boolean searches, as explained in How-To 12.17). Veronica returns a menu consisting of all matching items (by default, up to 200 matches are displayed). You can then browse these items and choose the ones you want to explore further.

A similar program called Jughead (named for another "Archie" comic character), works much like Veronica, but searches only the local environs of a particular site. This gives you a faster method of retrieving information that is likely to be of local interest (such as job openings).

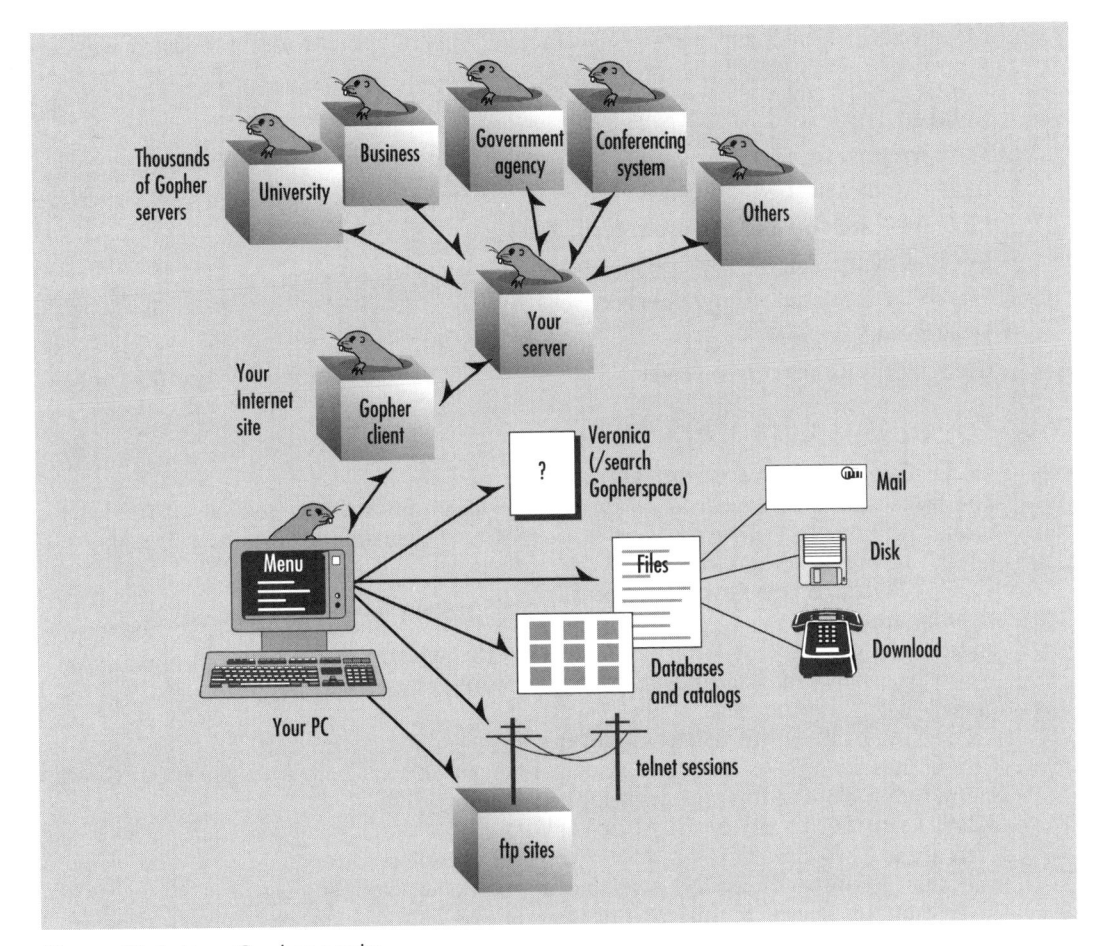

Figure 12-4 How Gopher works

Exploring Gopher

As you work through this chapter, you will find that the world of Gopher is vast, and the techniques you use to unlock it are simple. As you start to use Gopher, you will get a feeling for which services are most useful and/or reliable. When you find something that you will likely be returning to again and again (such as a weekly news report), you can use a *bookmark* to create a menu that you can use to jump directly to that item (see How-To 12.5).

The very utility and popularity of Gopher have led to its major drawback. Many Gopher servers (and the sites they connect to for various services) are often overwhelmed with traffic. As a result, you will frequently find that a particular server or service is unavailable. (You will be informed of this by a message like "Connection refused" or "Unable to connect to...".) The only thing you can do is try again, preferably during off-peak hours. We can only hope that the expanding capacity of the emerging information highway will eventually outpace the growth in users. It is likely

INTERNET HOW-TO

to get worse before it gets better. Nevertheless, when Gopher works, it is a truly wonderful thing.

Related Topics

To Learn How to...	See Chapter
Deal with files in special formats	8
Evaluate searching and browsing techniques	15
Get files by ftp	7
Search for resources using hypertext	14
Search WAIS databases	13
Use telnet to connect to a server	10

How-Tos in this Chapter

12.1 Connect to a Gopher server
The usual (and preferred) way to run Gopher is simply to type gopher at the system prompt at your local Internet site. If a client isn't available locally, however, you can telnet to a public access Gopher site.

12.2 Navigate the Gopher menus
Moving around in the Gopher menus is very easy. On most terminals, you have your choice of arrow keys or letter keys to move the selection cursor within and between menu pages. When you find an item you want, you just move the cursor to it and press (ENTER).

12.3 Get help while using Gopher
Gopher has a simple online help screen. You can also get help from an About Gopher menu that includes links to newsgroups and mailing lists.

12.4 Connect to other Gopher servers
Your local Gopher server is a doorway to thousands of other servers. If you want to check out resources or services available at a particular company, agency, or educational institution, its Gopher menus are only a couple of keystrokes away.

12.5 Use bookmarks to create my own menu
Bookmarks are a handy Gopher feature. Once you've navigated through several menus to find a service, you can add that service to your bookmark list. Next time, all you have to do is call up your list and select the service directly, bypassing all the intermediate menus.

12.6 Identify Gopher item types
Gopher usually knows how to "do the right thing" when you ask for a file. For example, it will show you a text file, but offer to save a binary file to disk. However, it's sometimes useful to ask Gopher for more information about the type of file or service you are dealing with. You'll learn how to recognize and deal with the most common Gopher item types.

12.7 Read a text file
This one's easy. You select a text file item from the Gopher menu, and the contents of the file are displayed for you through a pager program.

12.8 Get a file by mail
You can ask Gopher to e-mail the selected file to you. This can be handy if you want the file to end up somewhere other than your local Internet site or PC.

12.9 Save a file
Naturally, you can also have Gopher save a file to the home directory at your local Internet site.

12.10 Download a file
When you use ftp directly, you have to copy the file to your Internet site, and then use a separate program to download the file to your PC. With Gopher, you can just ask to download the file, and Gopher will send it directly to your PC, using the protocol of your choice.

12.11 Access ftp sites from Gopher
Combining the ability to download files directly to your PC with the ability to access many popular ftp sites from Gopher means that you have the easiest way yet to get software from the Internet. You'll learn how to navigate ftp directories, choose a file, and download it to your PC.

12.12 Use a subject tree
Some Gophers are organized by subject so that you can start with general fields of knowledge and narrow your focus until you reach the area you need. It's something like using a library catalog; but there aren't many library catalogs that can not only point you to a book about weather, but get you current satellite photos and weather forecasts as well!

12.13 Use telnet from Gopher
Gopher provides links to many services through telnet. You choose the Gopher item, and Gopher uses telnet to connect you to the service. You then use the telnet commands and techniques discussed in Chapter 10 to manage your session. When you're done, you go back to Gopher.

12.14 Find a person in an online directory
Gopher is good for finding people as well as things. There are a number of institutional "electronic yellow pages" available through Gopher. To use one popular type, the CSO directory, you fill out a form onscreen and get back a list of people with matching names and numbers.

12.15 Search a database
A wide variety of database systems are also linked to Gopher. You'll learn some simple search techniques for querying these databases through Gopher.

12.16 Use Veronica to find Gopher items
Veronica is an always-current master index to worldwide Gophers. You can search with a keyword or phrase and get matching menu items from thousands of Gophers. What's more, you can use this menu to go directly to files or services that interest you.

12.17 Combine keywords to refine a search
With Veronica (and some other databases on Gopher), you can use the Boolean terms *and, or*, and *not* to create searches that zero in on what you're looking for. This how-to shows you some simple examples and invites you to experiment further.

12.18 Use Jughead to search a particular Gopher
The last how-to looks at Jughead, a tool for searching the menus of a particular Gopher (or group of Gophers). When you're looking for material specific to a particular institution or locality, this can be faster and more efficient than a general Veronica search.

INTERNET HOW-TO

12.1 HOW DO I...
Connect to a Gopher server?

COMPLEXITY: EASY

Problem
Before you can use Gopher, you need to run a Gopher client.

Technique
You run the Gopher program at your local Internet site. If they don't have a Gopher client, you use telnet to connect to a public access client.

Steps
1. Log on your local Internet site. At the system prompt, type `gopher` and press ENTER.

2. You will probably see a screen like the one in Figure 12-1. If so, you are connected to a Gopher and you can browse the menus and select choices (see How-Tos 12.2 and 12.3). The screen you see will vary with the default Gopher server used by your client.

3. If instead of a screen you get a "Command not found" error message, this probably means that your Internet site doesn't have a Gopher client. In that case, type `telnet` followed by the name of a public access Gopher site. (If you live in North America, you can try consultant.micro.umn.edu, gopher.uiuc.edu, or gopher.uiowa.edu.)

4. Assuming the site is available, telnet will connect to it. If you get a login prompt, type `gopher` and press ENTER. You should now see a screen similar to Figure 12-1. For more information on running a telnet session, see Chapter 10.

5. When you are finished using Gopher, press q or Q. (Lowercase q prompts you for whether you really want to quit, Q simply quits immediately.)

6. If Gopher appears to be "stuck" (perhaps due to a bad connection), you can press CTRL-C to break out. Note that this will lose the results of any operation in progress.

How It Works
You run a Gopher client, either directly or through telnet. The Gopher client connects to a default Gopher server. The client requests and obtains the main menu from the server and shows it to you. The client is responsible for accepting your command input and making appropriate requests of the server.

Comment
If possible, run a Gopher client at your local Internet site rather than using telnet. The latter is inefficient and wasteful of network resources.

When you run a Gopher client you may find that it is unable to connect to the server (sometimes it just appears to freeze after a few minutes). This may mean that the server is down, but it may mean that too many people are connected (many servers impose a quota on the number of users who can be connected). If this happens, try again later (preferably during off-peak hours).

As an alternative, you can try to connect to a different server. To do this, simply add the name of the server to your gopher command. For example,

```
% gopher gopher.uiuc.edu
```

12 FINDING RESOURCES WITH GOPHER

tells the Gopher client to try to connect to that particular Gopher. (If you're using telnet, simply do another telnet command with the name of the specified Gopher.) You can find lists of Gophers from the All the Gopher Servers of the World menu on Gopher, and jot down some alternates for times when connection is difficult.

12.2 HOW DO I...
Navigate the Gopher menus?

COMPLEXITY: EASY

Problem
Now that you're looking at a Gopher menu, how do you find and select something?

Technique
You use arrow or letter keys to move a selection cursor up and down the menu (or back and forth between pages of longer menus). You press (ENTER) to select the item next to the cursor.

Steps
1. A selection cursor that looks like —> appears next to the first item when a menu is first displayed. You can move the cursor down by pressing the (↓) or (j) key. You can move the cursor up by pressing (↑) or (k).

2. You can also select any item by typing its item number and pressing (ENTER).

3. Some menus have more than one page. This is indicated by a pair of numbers in the lower right corner of the menu. For example, `Page: 2/3` means that there are three pages in this menu and that page two is currently being displayed. You can move to the next page by pressing (.) or (>), and move to the previous page with (-) or (<). (Moving the selection cursor past the first or last item will also move you to the adjacent page.)

4. Some menu items are themselves submenus (sometimes called directories). While viewing a submenu, you can return to its parent menu by pressing (u) or (←). If an item has a submenu, you can also press (m) at any time to jump directly to the main menu.

   Figure 12-5 summarizes the key portions of the Gopher menu screen and the navigation commands discussed so far.

5. You can search for a menu item containing particular text. To do this, press (/), type the text, and press (ENTER). This can be useful for going through long menus (such as a list of Gopher servers).

How It Works
The Gopher menu is a simple form of menu found in many text-oriented applications on mainframe systems. The arrow keys will work with most terminals. If they don't work for you, use (j) and (k) (which come from the vi editor).

Comment
If you are using a system with windowing facilities, such as a Unix X-Windows system or a PC or Macintosh that is *directly* connected to the Internet, you may be able to run a client that has GUI features. With such a client you'll be able to point and click on menu items, icons, and so forth to make selections.

INTERNET HOW-TO

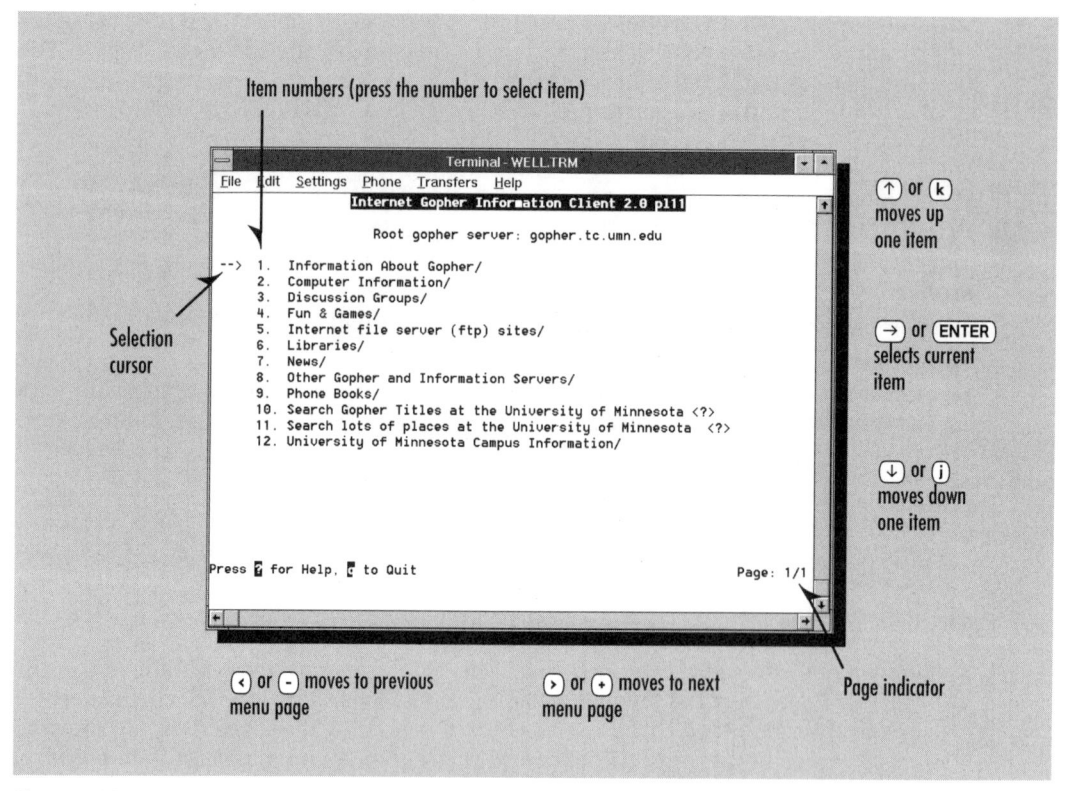

```
                    Item numbers (press the number to select item)
                                Terminal - WELL.TRM
                    File  Edit  Settings  Phone  Transfers  Help
                        Internet Gopher Information Client 2.0 p11              ↑ or k
                                                                                moves up
                            Root gopher server: gopher.tc.umn.edu               one item

                    --> 1.  Information About Gopher/
                        2.  Computer Information/
                        3.  Discussion Groups/
                        4.  Fun & Games/
      Selection       5.  Internet file server (ftp) sites/                   → or ENTER
      cursor          6.  Libraries/                                            selects current
                        7.  News/                                               item
                        8.  Other Gopher and Information Servers/
                        9.  Phone Books/
                        10. Search Gopher Titles at the University of Minnesota <?>
                        11. Search lots of places at the University of Minnesota  <?>
                        12. University of Minnesota Campus Information/           ↓ or j
                                                                                moves down
                                                                                one item

                    Press ? for Help, ? to Quit              Page: 1/1


              < or - moves to previous      > or + moves to next       Page indicator
              menu page                     menu page
```

Figure 12-5 Navigating Gopher menus

12.3 HOW DO I... Get help while using Gopher?

COMPLEXITY: EASY

Problem
Using Gopher is quite easy. Nevertheless, you may occasionally need to be reminded about the keys and commands available.

Technique
You can get a basic help screen (list of keys and their functions) at any time. You can also get more extensive help through About Gopher menu items, newsgroups, and mailing lists.

Steps
1. To get basic help for Gopher, press ? at any time while you're looking at a Gopher menu. You'll see a list like this:

358

```
                    Quick Gopher Help
                    -----------------

Moving around Gopherspace
-------------------------
Press return to view a document

Use the Arrow Keys or vi/emacs equivalent to move around

Up ..................: Move to previous line.
Down ................: Move to next line.
Right Return ........: "Enter"/Display current item.
Left, u  ............: "Exit" current item/Go up a level.

>, +, Pgdwn, space ..: View next page.
<, -, Pgup, b .......: View previous page.

0-9 .................: Go to a specific line.
m   .................: Go back to the main menu.   Bookmarks
---------
a : Add current item to the bookmark list.
A : Add current directory/search to bookmark list.
v : View bookmark list.
d : Delete a bookmark/directory entry.

Other commands
--------------
s : Save current item to a file.
D : Download a file.
q : Quit with prompt.
Q : Quit unconditionally.
= : Display Technical information about current item.
o : Open a new gopher server
O : Change Options
/ : Search for an item in the menu.
n : Find next search item.
!, $ : Shell Escape (Unix) or Spawn subprocess (VMS)
```

2. You can get more extensive help by selecting an About Gopher menu from your Gopher server. (The exact wording and location of the menu may vary.) Figure 12-6 shows a typical About Gopher menu. Note especially the following items:

```
1. About Gopher
2. Search Gopher News
3. Gopher News Archive
9. Frequently Asked Questions about Gopher
11. comp.infosystems.gopher (USENET newsgroup)
17. Reporting Problems or Feedback
```

3. Choose the appropriate item for your needs. Items 1 and 9 are good places to start.

INTERNET HOW-TO

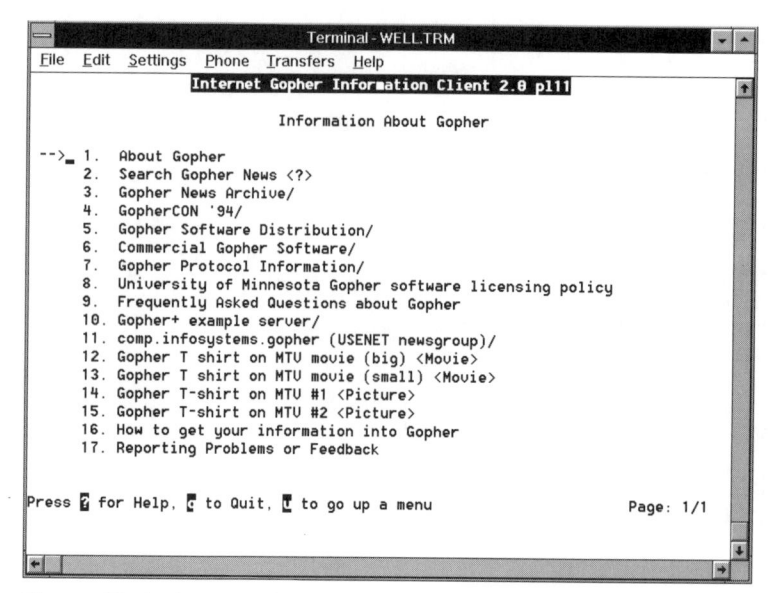

```
┌─────────────────────── Terminal - WELL.TRM ────────────────┬─┬─┐
│ File  Edit  Settings  Phone  Transfers  Help               │ │ │
│          ┌─────Internet Gopher Information Client 2.0 pl11─────┐ │▲│
│                         Information About Gopher               │ │
│                                                                │ │
│ -->_ 1.  About Gopher                                          │ │
│      2.  Search Gopher News <?>                                │ │
│      3.  Gopher News Archive/                                  │ │
│      4.  GopherCON '94/                                        │ │
│      5.  Gopher Software Distribution/                         │ │
│      6.  Commercial Gopher Software/                           │ │
│      7.  Gopher Protocol Information/                          │ │
│      8.  University of Minnesota Gopher software licensing policy│ │
│      9.  Frequently Asked Questions about Gopher               │ │
│     10.  Gopher+ example server/                               │ │
│     11.  comp.infosystems.gopher (USENET newsgroup)/           │ │
│     12.  Gopher T shirt on MTV movie (big) <Movie>             │ │
│     13.  Gopher T shirt on MTV movie (small) <Movie>           │ │
│     14.  Gopher T-shirt on MTV #1 <Picture>                    │ │
│     15.  Gopher T-shirt on MTV #2 <Picture>                    │ │
│     16.  How to get your information into Gopher               │ │
│     17.  Reporting Problems or Feedback                        │ │
│                                                                │ │
│ Press ? for Help, Q to Quit, U to go up a menu      Page: 1/1  │ │
│                                                                │▼│
└────────────────────────────────────────────────────────────────┴─┘
```

Figure 12-6 About Gopher menu

How It Works
Gopher's built-in help screen is rudimentary, but as you might expect, Gopher uses its menu system to link you to a variety of other sources of information about Gopher.

Comment
You can also get the usual Unix manual for the gopher command at your local Internet site by typing `man gopher`. This manual entry is for the Gopher client only, however, and isn't particularly useful for learning how to use the menus from the server.

12.4 HOW DO I...
Connect to other Gopher servers?

COMPLEXITY: EASY

Problem
You may be interested in focusing on services provided by a particular Gopher server (for example, the one at your school or the one at a government agency involved with your research needs).

Technique
You connect to your default Gopher server. From there, you go to a menu that lists other Gopher servers. Or, you can connect directly to the server you want.

Steps
1. If you're not sure what server you want, run Gopher to connect to your default server.

2. Look for a main menu item entitled "Other Gopher and Information Servers," or something similar. Select that item and you'll see a screen that lists items like these:

1. All the Gopher Servers in the World/
2. Search titles in Gopherspace using veronica/
3. Africa/
4. Asia/
5. Europe/
6. International Organizations/
7. Middle East/
8. North America/
9. Pacific/
10. South America/
11. Terminal Based Information/
12. WAIS Based Information/

   3. Choose a geographical area, or just choose item 1 (All the Gopher Servers in the World). You'll see a list of servers like that in Figure 12-7. Browse the list and select a server just as you would any other menu item.

   4. Once you've found some servers of interest, you can use bookmarks (How-To 12.5) to put them on your bookmark menu. Once you've done that, you can jump directly to a server by selecting it from your list of bookmarks.

How It Works

There are more than a thousand Gopher servers. Each server has a set of instructions that it can use to link to virtually any other server. (There *are* some private or restricted servers that don't allow connection from other servers.)

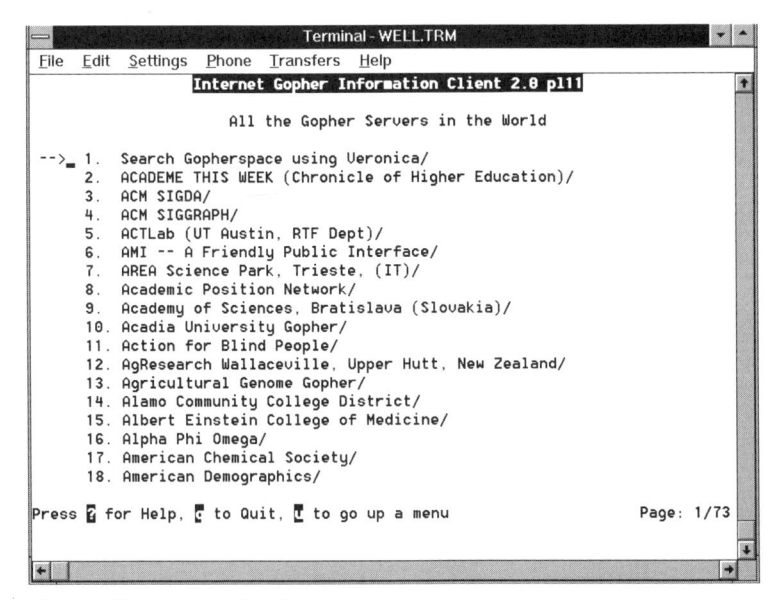

Figure 12-7 List of Gopher servers

INTERNET HOW-TO

Comment
Browsing the server list is a good way to find interesting places. For example, someone working with disabled people might want to check out item 11, Action for Blind People, in Figure 12-7.

Remember that when you choose a server to connect to, the connection may be refused due to excessive traffic. If so, "bookmark" the server and try it again later.

12.5 HOW DO I... *Use bookmarks to create my own menu?*

COMPLEXITY EASY

Problem
Reaching a particular service through Gopher can involve navigating through many layers of menus. It can be tedious to do this repeatedly for services you use often.

Technique
Once you've moved the cursor to a service that you think you're going to use again, you can put a bookmark at that location.

Steps
1. Select the service you want to bookmark by moving the selection cursor to it with the navigation commands discussed in How-To 12.2.

2. Press (a) to add the menu item to your bookmark list. You will see a dialog box like that in Figure 12-8. Gopher will suggest a name (based on the menu item name). Accept that name by pressing (ENTER), or press (CTRL)-(U) to erase the suggested name

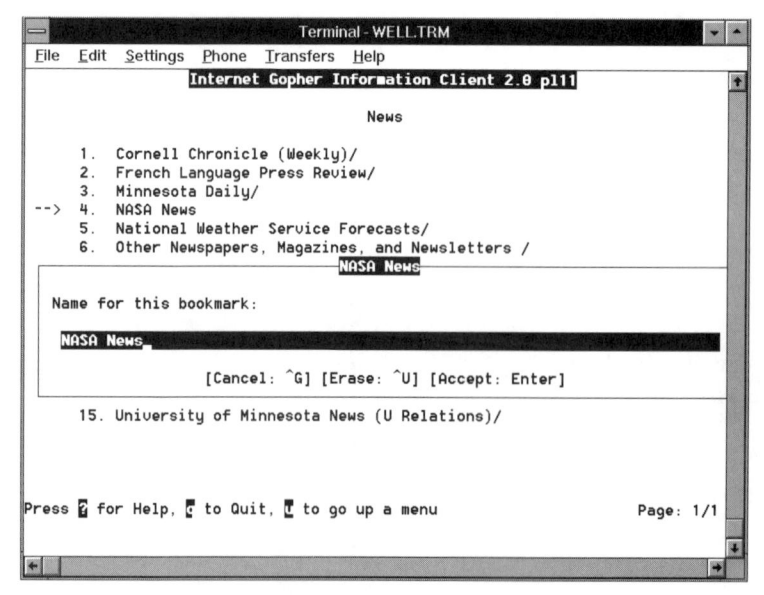

Figure 12-8 Adding a bookmark

12 🌐 **FINDING RESOURCES WITH GOPHER**

and type in your own. Press `CTRL`-`G` if you want to cancel creation of the bookmark. (This type of dialog box is found in a number of places in Gopher.)

The bookmark will be added to your list. (If you want to add the whole current menu to your bookmark list, rather than just the highlighted item, press `A` instead of `a`. You also use `A` when you want to add a database search you have made to your bookmarks so that the search will be performed each time you select the bookmark. (See How-To 12.15 for more on searching databases.)

3. To go to a place you have bookmarked, press `v` at any prompt to display the bookmark list. The list is just like a regular Gopher menu. Select the bookmark you want from the list, and you will go directly to that place in the menu system and select that item. (This means you will be connected to the service, the search will be performed, the submenu displayed, or whatever is appropriate.)

4. To delete a bookmark, press `v` for the bookmark menu, highlight the bookmark you want to delete, and press `d`.

How It Works
For each bookmark, Gopher creates a "path" that tells it how to navigate to that particular place. When you select the bookmark, Gopher takes you to that place and performs the indicated action, just as though you had gone there yourself, selected the item, and pressed `ENTER`.

Comment
Bookmarks are an extremely versatile and useful tool. In effect, you can create your own custom Gopher menu. Such a menu might include news that you check regularly (such as NASA News in Figure 12-8). It could also include favorite Gopher servers, Veronica searches, or ftp sites.

12.6 HOW DO I...
Identify Gopher item types?

COMPLEXITY | **INTERMEDIATE**

Problem
Gopher menu items actually represent a variety of objects, such as text files, submenus, or databases. Usually, Gopher knows what to do with the item you have selected. Sometimes, however, it may be useful to find out exactly what kind of file or service you are dealing with before you go farther into it.

Technique
You can have Gopher give you a report about the location and type of the currently selected menu item.

Steps
1. Select the menu item you want to inquire about.

2. Press `=`.

3. Gopher will display a report about the item. For example:

363

INTERNET HOW-TO

```
#
Type=1
Name=About this gopherspace (including a quick "How To" guide)
Path=1/about
Host=gopher.well.sf.ca.us
Port=70
URL: gopher://gopher.well.sf.ca.us:70/11/about
```

This shows that the item is type 1 (a directory or submenu). It gives the path (how to get there through the menu system) and the host (the Gopher containing this item: The WELL's Gopher in this case).

Table 12-1 summarizes the most common item types found in Gopher. Some item types are indicated by a special symbol at the end of the menu item. For example, in this listing,

1. Journal abstracts <?>
2. Economic databases/
3. Current forecast.
4. Price trends reports <Telnet>

menu item 1 is an indexed database or document that you can search, item 2 gets you a submenu, item 3 is a text document, and item 4 is a server that you can connect to by telnet.

Note that the symbols used in the menus to denote the item types may vary with the kind of client you use.

How It Works

Gopher uses item types to keep track of how a given item should be handled. For example, types 1, 4, 5, and 6 are different types of files that may need to be handled in

TYPE	DESCRIPTION OF CONTENTS	SYMBOL IN MENU
0	Text file	Period at end of name
1	Directory (submenu)	/ at end of name
2	CSO phone-book server	<CSO>
3	Error	
4	BinHexed Macintosh file	
5	DOS archive (.zip, .arc, and so on)	
6	Unix uuencoded file	
7	Index-search database	<?>
8	telnet to service	<telnet>
9	Binary file (client must read until collection closes) may cause problems	;
T	TN3270 connection (telnet to IBM mainframes, for example)	<TN3270>

Table 12-1 Gopher item types

12 ⊕ **FINDING RESOURCES WITH GOPHER**

different ways (for example, a text file can be displayed on your screen, but a binary file must be copied or downloaded).

Comment
There are two situations where you might want to check on an item's type. One is with files, if you're not sure what format the file is in (DOS binary, Mac binary, Unix, and so on) and you want to determine whether you can use the file in that form. The other situation is when an item is a database search and you want to determine what kind of database it is. In such cases the item report may describe the database type, (for example, WAIS). If you know the type, you may be better able to formulate searches for that database.

12.7 HOW DO I... Read a text file?

COMPLEXITY: EASY

Problem
Some Gopher items are ordinary text files. If the file is short, you might want to read it while using Gopher.

Technique
You select the item using standard navigation techniques (How-To 12.2). The item is displayed using a built-in pager.

Steps
1. Navigate to the item and press (ENTER) (or type the item's number and press (ENTER)).

2. The file will be shown to you in a pager, as in Figure 12-9. Note that you press (SPACEBAR) to see the next screen (page) or (b) to go back to the previous screen.

3. You can press (?) to get help with the pager commands, as shown in Figure 12-10. (Some servers may show a more extensive help display.) Note that you can search for text by pressing (/), typing the text you want to find, and pressing (ENTER). The mail and save commands are discussed in How-Tos 12.8 and 12.9, respectively. The print command is generally useless unless the machine running the Gopher client is physically accessible to you.

4. After you have read the last page of the file and pressed (SPACEBAR), you will be returned to the menu. You can also go back to the menu at any time by pressing (u).

How It Works
Gopher fetches the selected text file for you and displays it through the pager. The pager is rudimentary but serviceable and provides a subset of commands available through Unix pagers, such as "more" or "less." If you wish, you can set the PAGER variable in your environment to override the default pager. For example,

```
setenv PAGER more
```

sets the "more" pager for C-shell users in the .login file. The following commands,

```
PAGER = more
export PAGER
```

365

INTERNET HOW-TO

set the "more" pager for Bourne or Korn shell users in the .profile file.

Comment
You can only display and read text files. Fortunately, Gopher usually won't let you display a binary file, but offers to save it to disk.

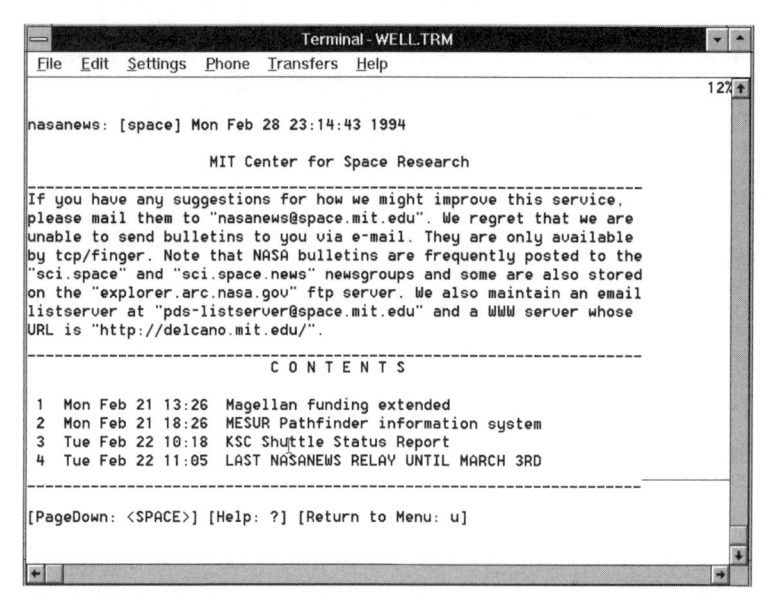

Figure 12-9 Reading a text file

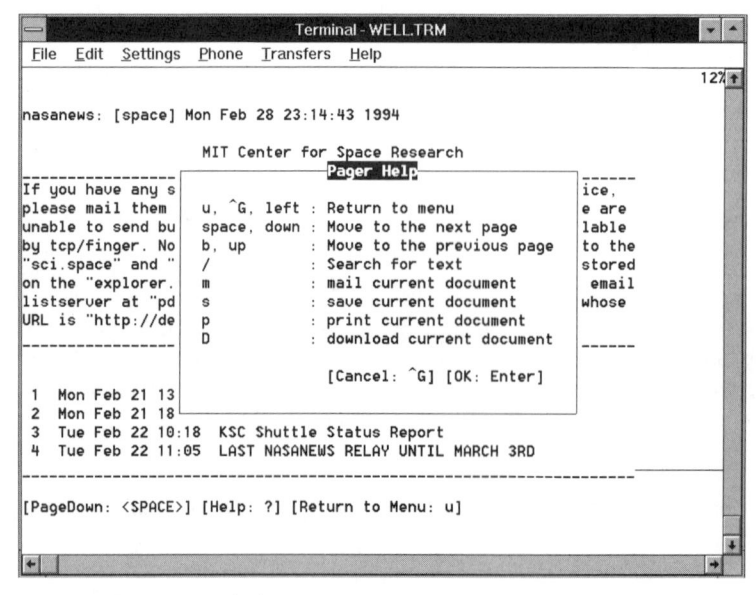

Figure 12-10 Pager help

12.8 HOW DO I... Get a file by mail?

COMPLEXITY: EASY

Problem
You may find it convenient to have a file mailed to you for later use. Also, if you are connected to a Gopher client that isn't on your machine (or another machine on which you have an account), you can't save a file to disk, but you can have the file mailed to a place where you have an account.

Technique
You select the appropriate menu item and have Gopher mail its contents to you.

Steps
1. Navigate to the menu item for the file you want to receive.

2. Press `m` and `ENTER`.

    You will see a dialog box that prompts you with:

```
Mail current document to:
```

   By default, the address from which you connected to Gopher will be displayed.

3. Press `ENTER` to have the file mailed to you at this address. Alternatively, press `CTRL`-`U`, type in a different address, and press `ENTER` to mail the file to that address.

How It Works
Gopher sets up a mail command and mails the file to the address you specify.

Comment
You can also press `m` from the pager display to mail a copy of the file you're currently viewing.

The mail command works best with text files. Some binary files may be corrupted when mailed. You may have to use ftp (with file type "binary") to get such files. Mailers *are* getting smarter about handling binary files, though.

12.9 HOW DO I... Save a file?

COMPLEXITY: EASY

Problem
If you are running a Gopher client on a machine where you have an account, you may find it convenient to save a copy of a Gopher file item to your home directory for later use.

Technique
You navigate to the menu item and then tell Gopher to save it in a file.

Steps
1. Navigate to the menu item for the file you want (see How-To 12.2).

2. Press `s`. You will see a dialog box with the prompt:

INTERNET HOW-TO

```
Save in file:
```

3. Press `ENTER` to accept the suggested filename. You can also press `CTRL`-`U`, type in a different name, and press `ENTER`.

   The file will be saved to the current directory at the site where the Gopher client is running. (This will probably be your home directory.)

How It Works
Gopher fetches a copy of the file and saves it to your directory on the machine where the Gopher client is running.

Comment
In order to save a file, you must be running the Gopher client on a machine for which you have an account (for example, your local dial-up Internet access site). If you're connecting to a public access Gopher client by telnet, you can't save files there because you don't have an account on that machine. You can, however, mail the file to yourself (How-To 12.8) or download the file to your PC (How-To 12.10).

12.10 HOW DO I...
Download a file?

COMPLEXITY INTERMEDIATE

Problem
It is often convenient to get a copy of a file from somewhere on the Internet to your PC. (For example, it may be a program designed for DOS, Windows, or Macintosh, or simply a long text file that is more convenient to read on your own machine.) With ftp, you have a two-step process: first copy the file from the remote site to your local site, and then download the file from your local site to your PC. Gopher lets you do it all in a single step.

Technique
You select the menu item for the file and tell Gopher to download the file to your PC.

Steps
1. Navigate to the menu item for the file you want and press `D`.

   You will see a dialog box that lists various file transfer protocols (Zmodem, several types of Xmodem, or plain text).

2. Choose a file transfer protocol that is supported by your PC's communications software. Type the number for the protocol and press `ENTER`.

3. Gopher will begin to download the file. Set your communications software to receive the file. Be sure to set the same protocol as you specified in the Gopher dialog box. If your software distinguishes between binary and text files, specify the appropriate type.

   The file will be downloaded to your PC and you will be returned to the Gopher menu.

12 🌐 FINDING RESOURCES WITH GOPHER

How It Works
Gopher knows about several of the popular file transfer protocols and uses the protocol you choose to send a file to your PC. This works even though you are probably not connected directly to the Gopher client, but are using the client through a dial-up connection to your local Internet site.

Comment
Zmodem is the best choice for a file protocol if your PC's software supports it. See Chapter 9 for more information about downloading and file protocols.

12.11 HOW DO I...
Access ftp sites from Gopher?

COMPLEXITY: INTERMEDIATE

Problem
ftp sites contain thousands of files grouped into hundreds of directories, often nested several layers deep. Browsing these directories using regular ftp directory-change and listing commands can be quite tedious. Gopher provides an alternative menu-driven way to browse files at many popular ftp sites.

Technique
You find a menu of ftp sites, choose a site, and browse its directories via the regular Gopher menu system.

Steps
1. Look for a menu that says "Internet File Server (ftp) sites" or something similar. A typical ftp main menu might look like this:

```
1. About FTP Searches
2. InterNIC: Internet Network Information Center/
3. Popular FTP sites via Gopher/
4. Query a specific ftp host <?>
5. Search FTP sites (Archie)/
```

2. Read the main ftp menu. You may want to select the "About" and "InterNIC" items to learn more about what is available. (InterNIC contains many useful directories of services.) "Query a specific ftp host" lets you look for directories and files. We'll try that in a minute. Archie lets you search for files at hundreds of ftp sites. (For more about archie, see Chapter 11.)

3. To search a particular ftp site, choose the "Query a specific ftp host" item. Choose the name of the host you want from the list provided.

4. You will see a menu that represents the list of archives (or main directories) available at that site, as in Figure 12-11.

5. Choose an archive (or main directory) and you'll get a submenu. This menu will probably contain subdirectories of the main directory, as in Figure 12-12, which shows the MSDOS Archive.

6. Finally, you'll get to a list of actual files, as in Figure 12-13. Move the pointer to the file you want and press (ENTER) to have the file sent to your local Internet site via ftp.

INTERNET HOW-TO

```
                    Terminal - WELL.TRM
 File  Edit  Settings  Phone  Transfers  Help
             Internet Gopher Information Client 2.0 p111

         Software Archives at MERIT (University of Michigan)

  --> 1.  Archive Introduction
      2.  Apollo       Archive (Merit Network, USA)/
      3.  Apple2       Archive (Merit Network, USA)/
      4.  Atari        Archive (Merit Network, USA)/
      5.  Economics    Archive (Merit Network, USA)/
      6.  Linguistics Archive (Merit Network, USA)/
      7.  Macintosh    Archive (Merit Network, USA)/
      8.  MSDOS        Archive (Merit Network, USA)/
      9.  Internet Tools Archive (Merit Network, USA)/
     10.  CELIA (Language Instruction) Archive (Merit Network, USA)/
     11.  ------- Mirrors --------------------------
     12.  Merit Apple2    Archive (mirror in USA, archive.orst.edu)/
     13.  Merit Apple2    Archive (mirror in USA, wuarchive.wustl.edu)/
     14.  Merit Atari     Archive (mirror in England, src.doc.ic.ac.uk)/
     15.  Merit Atari     Archive (mirror in USA, archive.orst.edu)/
     16.  Merit Atari     Archive (mirror in USA, wuarchive.wustl.edu)/
     17.  Merit Macintosh Archive (mirror in Australia, archie.au)/
     18.  Merit Macintosh Archive (mirror in England, src.doc.ic.ac.uk)/

 Press ? for Help, Q to Quit, U to go up a menu            Page: 1/2
```

Figure 12-11 List of archives at an ftp site

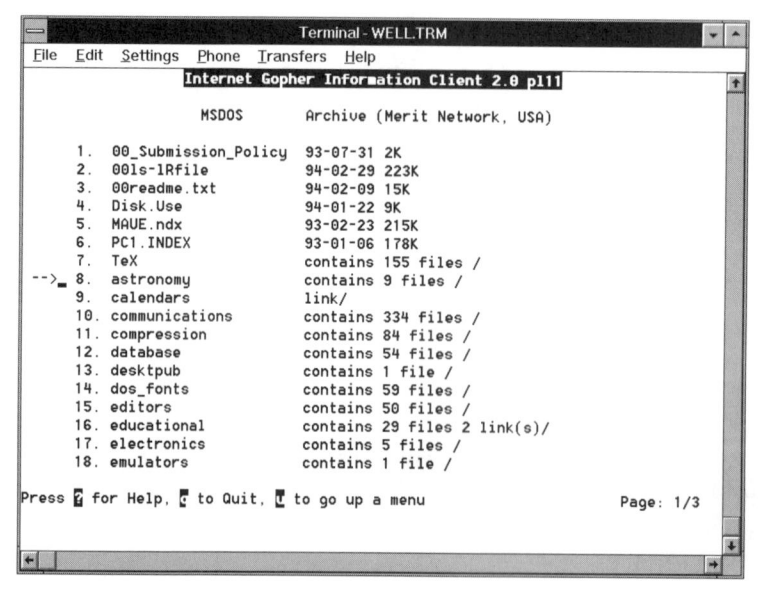

```
                    Terminal - WELL.TRM
 File  Edit  Settings  Phone  Transfers  Help
             Internet Gopher Information Client 2.0 p111

            MSDOS          Archive (Merit Network, USA)

      1.  00_Submission_Policy  93-07-31  2K
      2.  00ls-1Rfile           94-02-29  223K
      3.  00readme.txt          94-02-09  15K
      4.  Disk.Use              94-01-22  9K
      5.  MAUE.ndx              93-02-23  215K
      6.  PC1.INDEX             93-01-06  178K
      7.  TeX                   contains 155 files /
  --> 8.  astronomy             contains 9 files /
      9.  calendars             link/
     10.  communications        contains 334 files /
     11.  compression           contains 84 files /
     12.  database              contains 54 files /
     13.  desktpub              contains 1 file /
     14.  dos_fonts             contains 59 files /
     15.  editors               contains 50 files /
     16.  educational           contains 29 files 2 link(s)/
     17.  electronics           contains 5 files /
     18.  emulators             contains 1 file /

 Press ? for Help, Q to Quit, U to go up a menu            Page: 1/3
```

Figure 12-12 Looking at subdirectories

Or you may prefer to press `d` and have the file downloaded to your PC, as shown in the dialog box in Figure 12-13. See How-To 12.10 for steps involved in downloading.

12 FINDING RESOURCES WITH GOPHER

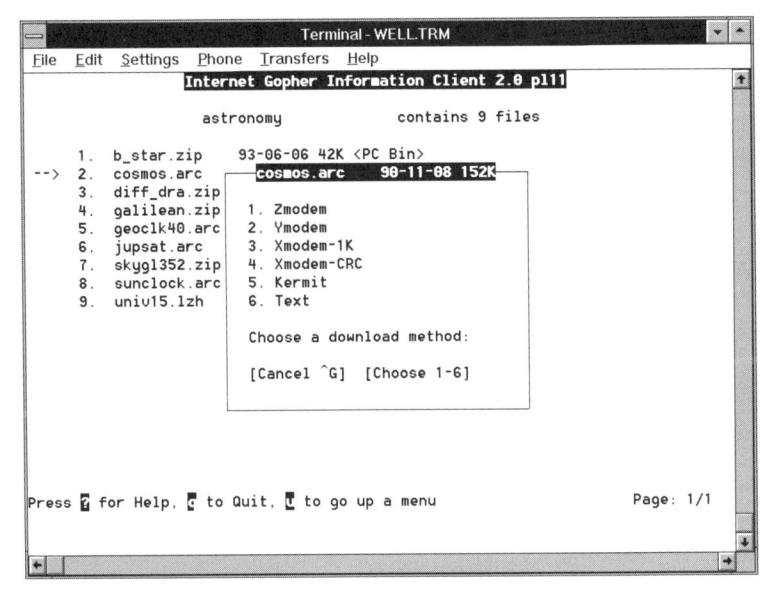

Figure 12-13 Downloading a file from an ftp site

How It Works
The directories and files listed in ftp sites can be arranged as Gopher menus and menu items. By storing the appropriate links, Gopher can get the files and either ftp them to you or let you download them directly.

Comment
Only a subset of ftp sites are available through Gopher, but the list includes some of the largest and most popular sites.
  Again, heavy traffic may make a particular site unavailable at peak times.

12.12 HOW DO I...
Use a subject tree?

COMPLEXITY: INTERMEDIATE

Problem
Since the first libraries were created several thousand years ago, people have used subject arrangements to organize knowledge so that it is accessible to the inquirer. Some Gophers provide menus arranged by subject to make it easier to access information, documents, and services.

Technique
You find a menu that is arranged by subject (perhaps through a Veronica search, as discussed in How-To 12.16). You then navigate from general subjects to more specific subjects until you find the precise item you need.

371

INTERNET HOW-TO

Steps

1. Find a subject-oriented Gopher menu. One good way to find a list of such menus is to do a Veronica search on the words "subject trees." (This is covered in more detail in How-To 12.16.) For our sample search, we'll look for items pertaining to environmental studies.

2. Choose a subject menu that looks appropriate. A typical top-level subject menu might look like this:

```
              Subject tree (based on UDC)

       1.  General, Bibliography, Library science/
       2.  Philosophy, Psychology, Ethics/
       3.  Religion, Theology/
       4.  Social sciences/
  -->  5.  Mathematics, Natural sciences/
       6.  Applied sciences, Medicine, Technology/
       7.  Art, Architecture, Music, Sports/
       8.  Linguistics, Philology, Literature/
       9.  Geography, Biography, History/
```

3. Choose the general subject that is likely to lead to your area of interest. Note that each item has a slash (/) after it, indicating that it has submenus. Let's choose number 5, Mathematics, Natural sciences, since natural sciences include biology, zoology, and so on.

```
                Mathematics, Natural sciences

  -->  1.  Generalities about the pure Sciences/
       2.  Mathematics. Computing/
       3.  Astronomy. Astrophysics. Space Research. Geodesy/
       4.  Physics/
       5.  Chemistry. Mineralogical Sciences/
       6.  Environmental Studies/
       7.  Earth Sciences. Geology. Meteorology etc./
       8.  Palaeontology/
       9.  Biological Sciences/
       10. Botany/
       11. Zoology/
```

4. Continue to navigate toward more specific subjects. Here we choose item 6, Environmental Studies:

```
                   Environmental Studies

  -->  1.  ANU–Australian–Economics:       <?>
       2.  ANU–CAUT–Academics:             <?>
       3.  ANU–CAUT–Projects:              <?>
       4.  ANU–Pacific–Archaeology:        <?>
       5.  ANU–Pacific–Relations:          <?>
       6.  ANU–Radiocarbon–Abstracts:      <?>
       7.  ANU–SSDA–Australian–Census:     <?>
       8.  ANU–SSDA–Australian–Opinion:    <?>
```

12 ⊕ FINDING RESOURCES WITH GOPHER

```
 9. ANU-SSDA-Australian-Studies:  <?>
10. ANU-Tropical-Archaeobotany:  <?>
11. DOE_Climate_Data: US Department of Energy Climate Data <?>
12. EIA-Petroleum-Supply-Monthly: US EIA's "Petroleum Supply Monthl.. <?>
13. FIS-UnitedNations-environment:  <?>
14. Global_Change_Data_Directory: Global Climatic Change Data Direc.. <?>
15. Miljo_bibliografier:  <?>
16. NOAA_Environmental_Services_Data_Directory:  <?>
17. NOAA_National_Environmental_Referral_Service: US National Envir.. <?>
18. UNEP-GRID:  <?>
```

As you can see, you've now reached some pretty specific areas—mainly databases on various subjects, such as item 14, which has data on global climate change.

5. Browse the list of specific resources and explore those that look like they might be useful.

How It Works
The subject organization works somewhat like a card catalog in a library. The difference is that the "cards" point not just to documents but to services (such as databases and news services) as well.

Comment
Coverage of subjects varies widely with the institution running the Gopher server. Use common sense: a physics department is not likely to have much under the subject "Art and literature."

12.13 HOW DO I...
Use telnet from Gopher?

COMPLEXITY: INTERMEDIATE

Problem
Gopher menu items often connect to services that are provided by remote programs at various sites. Gopher can't directly access these services, but it can use telnet to connect you to them.

Technique
You choose a menu item that indicates that it is a telnet session. Gopher runs telnet. You log into the service using telnet, as described in Chapter 10. When you're finished with the service, you exit telnet, and return to Gopher.

Steps
1. If the Gopher menu item you choose has <Telnet> or <TEL> after it, it is implemented as a telnet session.

2. Choose the menu item. You will see a warning box like the one in Figure 12-14. This box is warning you that past this point you will be using telnet, and Gopher can't be responsible for your connection or ability to use the remote service.

3. Press (CTRL)-(g) if you decide not to use telnet. Otherwise, press (ENTER) to make the telnet connection.

373

INTERNET HOW-TO

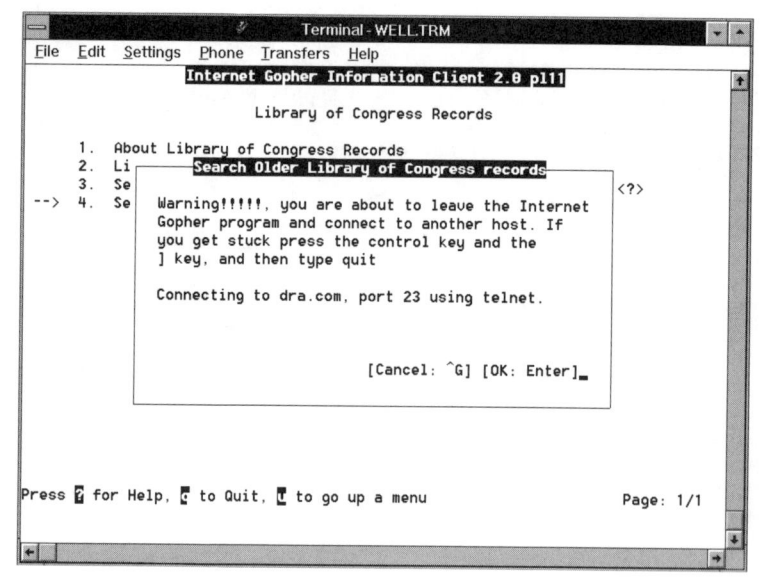

Figure 12-14 Preparing to use telnet

4. If telnet is successful, you will be connected to the remote service. You use the service exactly as you would if you had telneted to it directly. If you have trouble using telnet, see Chapter 10.

5. When you are finished, exit the remote service using its menu or command. You will be returned to Gopher at the point where you left.

How It Works
Gopher issues a telnet command with the name of the remote site. The rest is up to telnet (and you).

Comment
Sometimes the remote service may not be available, or may get "stuck." In the latter case, press (CTRL)-(]) to get back to a telnet prompt and type `close` and then `quit` to end the telnet session.

12.14 HOW DO I...
Find a person in an online directory?

COMPLEXITY: INTERMEDIATE

Problem
There isn't (yet) any single electronic phone book that lists everyone who has ever had any contact with the Internet. There are, however, a variety of phone directory services available on the Internet, and Gopher can connect you to many of them.

374

12 FINDING RESOURCES WITH GOPHER

Technique
You look for a general menu item such as "Phone Books" or "Directory Services," and then choose the phone book or service for the institution that is likely to be keeping track of the person you seek (for example, the person's school or employer).

Steps
1. Look for a Gopher menu that mentions phone books, directory services, or something similar.

2. From the submenu, choose the directory service for the institution that is likely to list the person you seek.

3. Choose the search option for the directory. You will be prompted for the person's name and perhaps other information. The type of information used in the search (and the format displayed) will vary with the type of software used in the directory. One common type is called CSO (named for the Computing Services Office at the University of Illinois, where it was developed). A CSO search is illustrated in Figure 12-15. With a CSO, you use the (TAB) key to move between fields, type in the information you know, and press (ENTER).

The search results, if any, will be displayed. Again, the format used will vary with the software.

How It Works
Phone directories are simple databases with fields describing contact information for a person. As you can see from the example in Figure 12-15, people can have lots of addresses and "phone numbers" of various sorts these days!

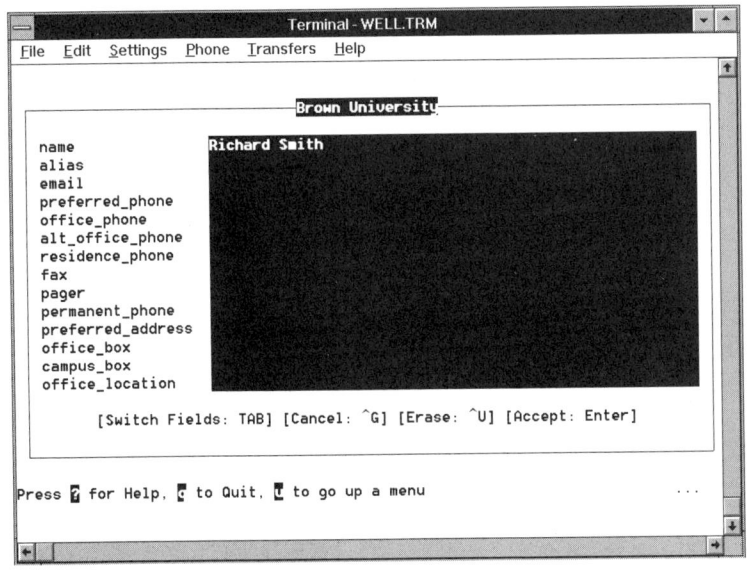

Figure 12-15 Searching for a someone in a CSO directory

INTERNET HOW-TO

Comment
The rules for performing a search vary with the type of software. Look for a "How to Search" option and read it to familiarize yourself with how a particular kind of directory works.

12.15 HOW DO I... Search a database?

COMPLEXITY: INTERMEDIATE

Problem
There are many different kinds of databases that you can access through Gopher. Each has its own rules about how searches are done and how results will be displayed.

Technique
You choose the database, try to get help, and try out some simple searches.

Steps
1. Gopher menu items that end in <?> are databases or indexes of some sort. When you choose such an item, you have access to the search mechanism for the index or database.

2. Once you are in the search menu, look for a way to get help. Often pressing ⟨?⟩ will get you a summary of commands. Also look for menu items such as "About this database" or "How to search this database" and read them.

3. Try a few sample searches. Start with simple keywords or phrases.

4. If the particular database supports it, you can try wildcard searches (such as "comput*") or Boolean searches (such as "internet and business"). Boolean searches are discussed in connection with Veronica in How-To 12.17.

How It Works
Gopher connects you to the database or index. You submit your search and view the results, then return to Gopher.

Comment
There are many different types of indexes or databases. One type, WAIS, is discussed in Chapter 13. Read the instructions carefully and don't be afraid to experiment.

12.16 HOW DO I... Use Veronica to find Gopher items?

COMPLEXITY: INTERMEDIATE

Problem
With thousands of Gophers, each with hundreds of menu items, how can you find the ones you need? Veronica to the rescue! Veronica builds a huge database out of all the menu items on all the Gophers and lets you search for them by keyword, phrase, or Boolean search logic.

12 ⊕ FINDING RESOURCES WITH GOPHER

Technique
You choose a Veronica menu item from a Gopher menu, formulate a search, view the results, and choose items for further exploration.

Steps
1. Find and choose a Gopher menu item that mentions Veronica. Such items are often titled "Search Gopherspace with Veronica."

2. View the submenu. It will probably list two kinds of Veronica searches: searches just by directory titles, and searches of "all of Gopherspace" (a broader search that includes filenames, and so on).

3. Choose the kind of search you want to do. The example here searches the Gopherspace (the Veronica database) at PSINet, as shown in Figure 12-16.

4. Type a word or phrase that describes what you are searching for. The example specifies `subject trees`. Press (ENTER).

5. Veronica will display a menu of matching items, as shown in Figure 12-17.

How It Works
Veronica matches your search specification against the database and fetches the matching menu items. These items work just like regular Gopher menu items: you can select them or mark them with bookmarks for later use.

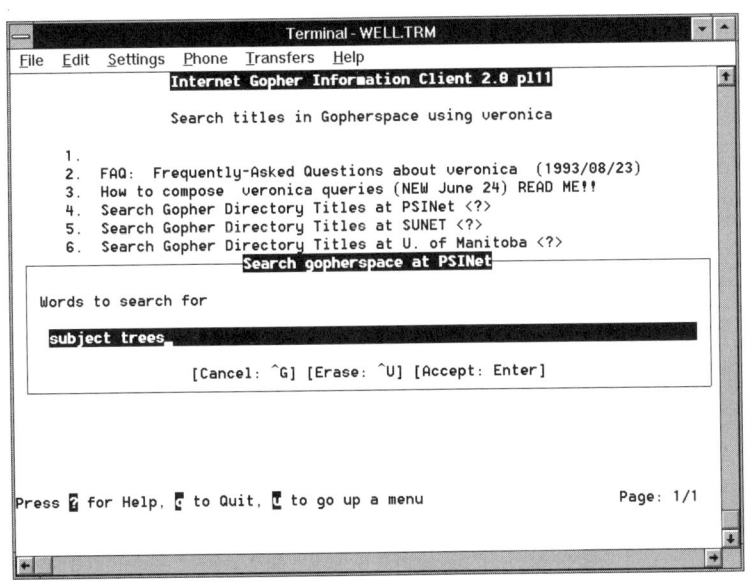

Figure 12-16 Searching with Veronica

INTERNET HOW-TO

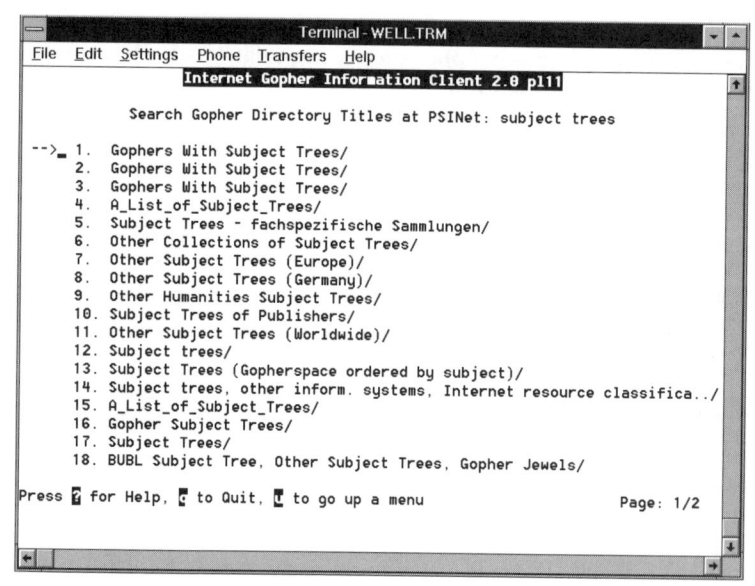

```
┌─────────────────────────── Terminal - WELL.TRM ───────────────── ▼ ▲ ┐
│ File  Edit  Settings  Phone  Transfers  Help                         │
│     ┌─────────── Internet Gopher Information Client 2.0 p111 ──────┐ │
│     │                                                              ↑│
│     │     Search Gopher Directory Titles at PSINet: subject trees  ││
│     │                                                               │
│     │ -->_ 1.  Gophers With Subject Trees/                          │
│     │     2.  Gophers With Subject Trees/                           │
│     │     3.  Gophers With Subject Trees/                           │
│     │     4.  A_List_of_Subject_Trees/                              │
│     │     5.  Subject Trees - fachspezifische Sammlungen/           │
│     │     6.  Other Collections of Subject Trees/                   │
│     │     7.  Other Subject Trees (Europe)/                         │
│     │     8.  Other Subject Trees (Germany)/                        │
│     │     9.  Other Humanities Subject Trees/                      │
│     │    10.  Subject Trees of Publishers/                          │
│     │    11.  Other Subject Trees (Worldwide)/                      │
│     │    12.  Subject trees/                                        │
│     │    13.  Subject Trees (Gopherspace ordered by subject)/       │
│     │    14.  Subject trees, other inform. systems, Internet resource classifica../│
│     │    15.  A_List_of_Subject_Trees/                              │
│     │    16.  Gopher Subject Trees/                                 │
│     │    17.  Subject Trees/                                        │
│     │    18.  BUBL Subject Tree, Other Subject Trees, Gopher Jewels/│
│     │                                                               │
│     │ Press ? for Help, Q to Quit, U to go up a menu    Page: 1/2   │
│     │                                                              ↓│
│     └───────────────────────────────────────────────────────────────┘
│ ←                                                                  → │
└──────────────────────────────────────────────────────────────────────┘
```

Figure 12-17 Results of Veronica search

Comment

By default, Veronica displays up to 200 matching items. You can specify a different maximum by adding *−mnumber* to your Veronica search string, where *number* is the maximum. For example, the search

    internet −m400

finds up to 400 items about the Internet, while the search

    Macintosh −m50

finds only the first 50 items about Macintosh.

You can also limit a search to particular *types* of Gopher items, as given in Table 12-1. For example, the search

    windows −t1

finds only *directories* (menus) with the word "windows" in them. You can combine the -m and -t options.

12.17 HOW DO I...
Combine keywords to refine a search?

COMPLEXITY: INTERMEDIATE

Problem

Searches using just a single word can be too broad or too narrow. In the first case, you may get many results that are irrelevant to your interests. In the latter case, you may get nothing at all. You can use logical combinations of keywords with Veronica (and some other databases) to fine-tune your request so you get the items you need.

Technique

You specify a combination of keywords that describes what you are interested in. These words are connected with the logical words *and*, *or*, or *not*.

Connecting two words with *and* means that matching records must have both of them: for example, "computers and arts" is matched by items having both words ("computers" and "arts") in them.

Connecting two words with *or* means that an item will match if it has *either* word in it. Thus "business or commerce" will match items with either "business" or "commerce" (or both) in them.

Putting the word *not* before another word *excludes* items that have that word in them. For example, the search "computers not mainframes" will return all items that have the word "computers" provided that they don't also have the word "mainframes" in them.

Steps

1. Think of single words that are relevant to your search. For example, suppose you want to find material on business use of the Internet. Two reasonable keywords here are "business" and "Internet."

2. Use a logical connector that expresses the relationship between the keywords you will be using. In our current example, the word *and* is appropriate, since you want material that pertains to *both* business and the Internet, not just one or the other.

3. Formulate your search phrase and submit it to the database program (such as Veronica). As an example, here is the result of a Veronica search of Gopher (directories only) on the specification "internet and business":

    ```
    Search Gopher Directory Titles at PSINet: internet and business
    ```

    --> 1. Business Information via Internet/
        2. Other Business Resources on the Internet/
        3. Internet Business Journal/
        4. Internet-Business-Journal/
        5. Internet-business-report/
        6. Internet Business Pages/
        7. internet-business-journal/

4. View your results and see whether you need to broaden or narrow your search. If necessary, search again with your new specification.

5. Some databases also let you use wildcards with keywords. For example, the search phrase "comput*" would match computers, computing, and computation. Remember that wildcards, like the use of *or*, expand a search.

How It Works

The database uses logical rules first formulated by mathematician George Boole in the nineteenth century to determine which items match your search.

Comment

Not all databases support Boolean logic. If a Boolean search doesn't work, try a simpler search using just a single keyword or phrase.

379

12.18 HOW DO I...
Use Jughead to search a particular Gopher?

COMPLEXITY: EASY

Problem
Searching all of Gopherspace may yield a result that is too large and unwieldy. Narrowing a search to a particular Gopher (or group of related Gophers) can make the results more manageable. Also, you may be interested in items that relate directly to a particular institution or location. Jughead provides a tool for searching particular Gophers for items of interest.

Technique
You select a Jughead search for a particular Gopher and specify what you want to search for.

Steps
1. Find a Gopher menu item that lets you conduct a Jughead search of that server. In Figure 12-18 we will look for job listings at the University of Texas at Austin.

2. Choose the Jughead search option. You will see a dialog box that asks you for keywords. Type in the word or phrase that describes what you would like to find. Here we simply type `jobs`.

3. Jughead displays a menu of matching Gopher items, as in Figure 12-18. Note that items relating to "jobs" in the computing sense were also retrieved. Although this was a fairly broad search, we nevertheless found some items worth further investigation (for example, items 5 through 7 and 12 through 18).

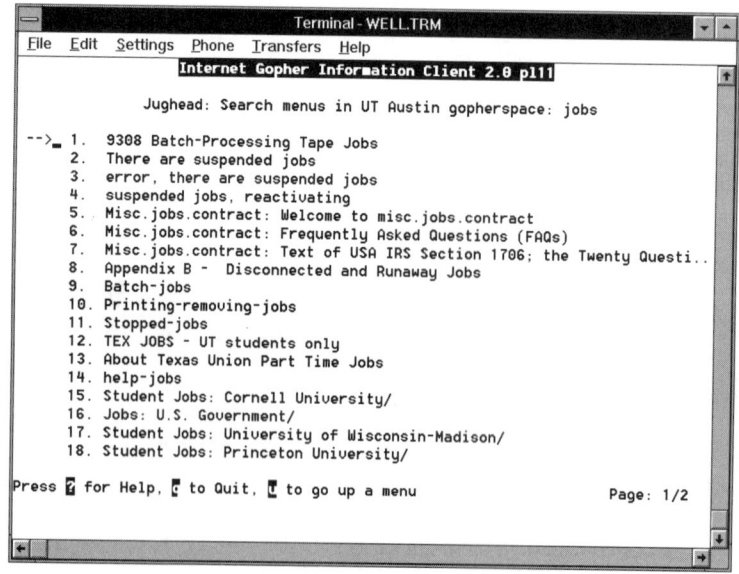

```
                    Terminal - WELL.TRM
 File   Edit   Settings   Phone   Transfers   Help
              Internet Gopher Information Client 2.0 p111

         Jughead: Search menus in UT Austin gopherspace: jobs

-->  1.  9308 Batch-Processing Tape Jobs
     2.  There are suspended jobs
     3.  error, there are suspended jobs
     4.  suspended jobs, reactivating
     5.  Misc.jobs.contract: Welcome to misc.jobs.contract
     6.  Misc.jobs.contract: Frequently Asked Questions (FAQs)
     7.  Misc.jobs.contract: Text of USA IRS Section 1706; the Twenty Questi..
     8.  Appendix B - Disconnected and Runaway Jobs
     9.  Batch-jobs
    10.  Printing-removing-jobs
    11.  Stopped-jobs
    12.  TEX JOBS - UT students only
    13.  About Texas Union Part Time Jobs
    14.  help-jobs
    15.  Student Jobs: Cornell University/
    16.  Jobs: U.S. Government/
    17.  Student Jobs: University of Wisconsin-Madison/
    18.  Student Jobs: Princeton University/

Press ? for Help, Q to Quit, U to go up a menu       Page: 1/2
```

Figure 12-18 Results of Jughead search

4. Choose any items of interest. Don't forget you can use bookmarks to make it easy to find items without having to conduct another search, or you can set a bookmark at the beginning of the search so you can repeat the search periodically. (See How-To 12.5 for more on bookmarks.)

How It Works
Jughead works much like Veronica except it restricts its searching to the Gopher on which it is running.

Comment
Jughead is particularly useful when you only want items that are available locally.

13

Looking Up Information with WAIS

How do I...

- 13.1 Use a WAIS Client
- 13.2 Select a database
- 13.3 Use the list of servers
- 13.4 Get help with WAIS
- 13.5 Perform a WAIS search
- 13.6 Set WAIS options
- 13.7 Look at a retrieved document
- 13.8 Get a copy of a WAIS document
- 13.9 Refine my search
- 13.10 Use WAIS through Gopher
- 13.11 Do a streamlined WAIS search
- 13.12 Learn more about WAIS

WAIS, pronounced "ways," stands for Wide Area Information Service. WAIS lets you access a great variety of documents from hundreds of databases using a simple searching technique. This chapter introduces you to the basic commands and techniques used to access WAIS databases on the Internet.

Solving Database Problems

There are two fundamental problems with using traditional databases. The first is selecting an appropriate database to search. With thousands of databases, reference works, and other documents now available through the Internet, this is no small problem.

INTERNET HOW-TO

Often you have to make a preliminary general search to find out where to begin to look for the specific information you seek.

The second problem has to do with the procedure for specifying your database search. Typically each database has its own rules and its own user interface. For example, some databases might let you search for only single keywords. Others will allow phrases, such as "information highway." Others might let you specify wildcards, as in "comput*", which would match computer, computers, computing, computation, and so on. Still others let you use Boolean searches, which among other things can specify whether both of two keywords must be present for a match, or whether just one or the other is sufficient. (Compare "weather or climate" with "weather and climate"—the former matches records that have at least one of the two words, while the latter matches only records that have both words.) If you regularly use several dozen different databases, how do you remember what you can do with each one, and which keywords and/or searching techniques are valid?

WAIS largely solves both database problems. First, WAIS makes it relatively easy to do the "search before the search" and find the databases that are most likely to have the information you need.

You connect to WAIS by running a client program (such as xwais or swais) or by using telnet to connect to a host that is running a client program. The client program connects to a server that has a list describing the nature and location of each available database (called a *source*). In turn, each of the more than 500 sources provides access to its database by means of a server. Figure 13-1 shows the relationship between client, server, sources, and databases.

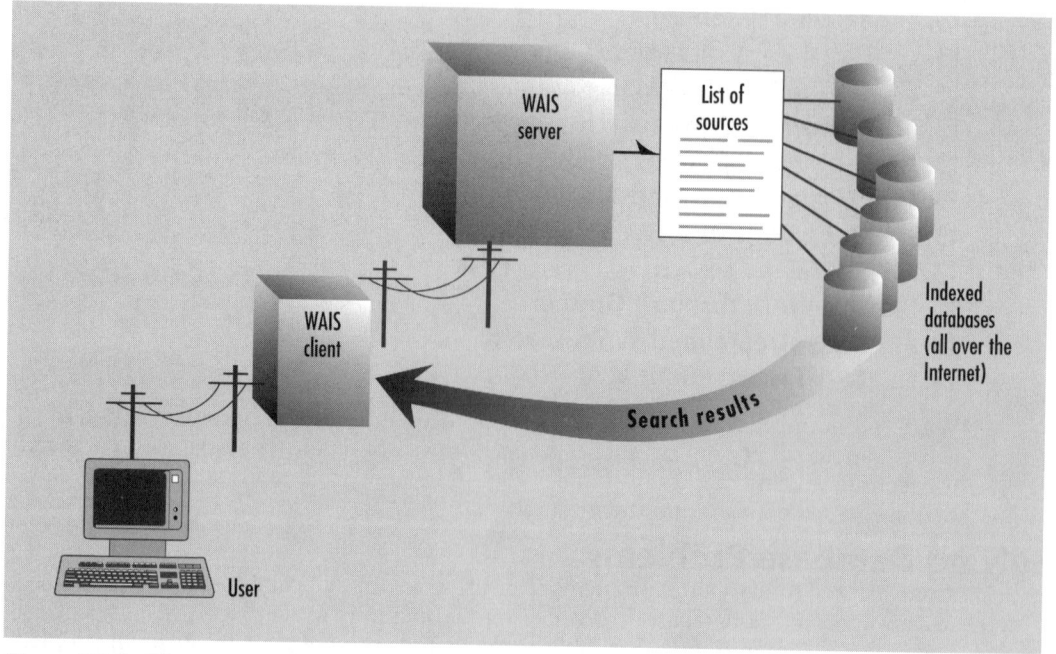

Figure 13-1 Clients, servers, sources, and databases

Overview of the Searching Process

You begin your search by selecting one or more databases from the list of sources—usually by searching the list itself. Once you've selected your sources, you specify a word or phrase that WAIS will try to find in the databases you have selected.

WAIS addresses the problem of keywords and searching rules by making things very simple. All databases on WAIS are fully indexed. This means that every word in every document in the database is included in an index, not just selected keywords. The advantage of full-text indexing is that you don't have to try to guess which keywords are recognized by the database software, or determine which searching techniques (such as wildcards or Boolean expressions) are allowed.

Indeed, while some WAIS sources do support these advanced search features, the full indexing guarantees a basic access method that can be used for every WAIS database. Thanks to the full-text index, your word or phrase is looked up in the index for each of the databases you have selected (you can search more than one database at a time).

It's true that this simplistic approach has its disadvantages. For one thing, you can't control the specificity of your search very well, since you can't use wildcards to capture variations of a word or use Boolean logic to focus on a subject that includes two different concepts, such as "medicine and computers."

However, you will see in How-To 13.9 that WAIS does provide a mechanism for refining a search through what is called *relevance feedback*. Basically, you do this by finding one or more documents in the search result that you feel are a good example of the kind of thing you want, and then you tell WAIS to find more documents that have similar words in them. Figure 13-2 is a schematic of the searching process in WAIS.

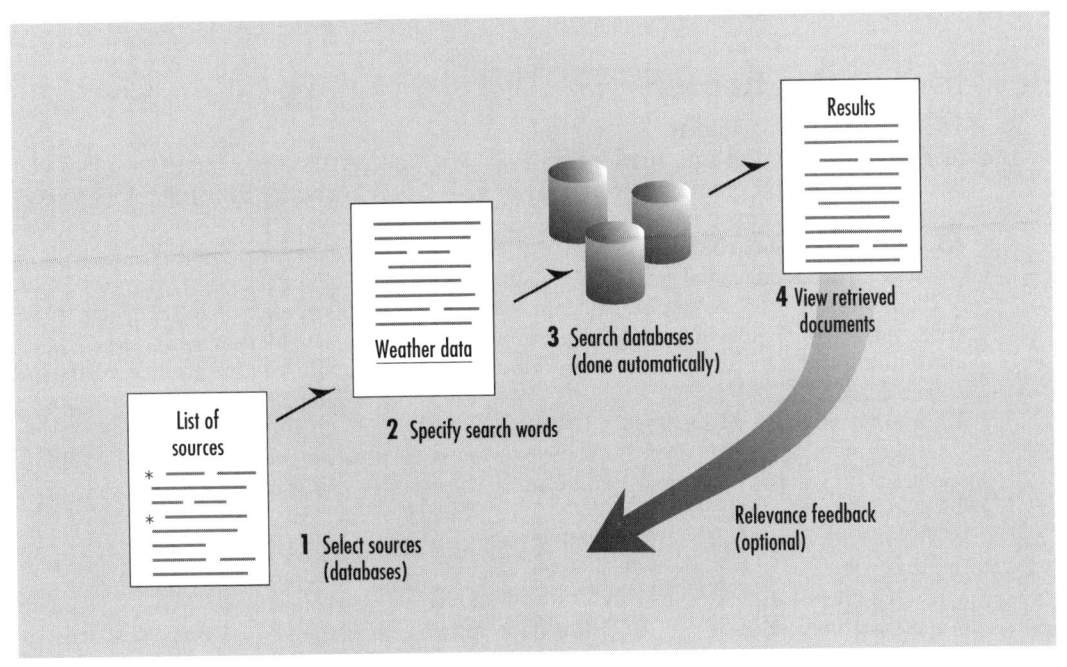

Figure 13-2 WAIS search procedure

INTERNET HOW-TO

What Can You Find with WAIS?
WAIS is a relatively new addition to the Internet. Nevertheless, a variety of useful databases are already available. Here are some examples:

- Contents of some scientific journals
- Archives of Usenet newsgroups
- Frequently Asked Questions (FAQ) files
- Full text of books such as the Bible and the Hacker's Dictionary
- A poetry database
- Lists of online library catalogs
- The *CIA World Factbook*, containing basic geopolitical data on the nations of the world

While WAIS is provided as a free service to the Internet, there are also commercial (fee-based) WAIS services provided by companies such as Dow Jones.

Related Topics

To Learn How to...	See Chapter
Choose the right data retrieval tool	15
Connect to remote services with telnet	10
Find information and services through Gopher menus	12
Find software with archie	11
Use hypertext to browse documents on the Internet	14

How-Tos in this Chapter

13.1 Use a WAIS client
As with most Internet information retrieval programs, WAIS uses a client-server model. You run a client program, either directly at your Internet site, or by using telnet to connect to a public access client.

13.2 Select a database
Once you have connected to the WAIS server with your client program, you have a list of databases, or sources, to choose from. Due to the large number of sources now available, most WAIS servers set things up so you search the list of sources using an appropriate word or phrase, and then choose the sources you wish to use for your actual data search.

13.3 Use the list of servers
An alternative approach used by some servers is to present the whole list of available sources. You can browse this list and choose the sources you want to use.

13.4 Get help with WAIS
WAIS provides a simple online help display that summarizes the various key commands.

13.5 Perform a WAIS search
Once you have chosen one or more data sources, you specify a word (or words) to search for in those sources. Since the data sources are fully indexed, there are no keywords or special search rules to worry about. WAIS presents a list of documents that

13 🌐 LOOKING UP INFORMATION WITH WAIS

best match the words you specified. WAIS ranks the documents in order of how completely they match your search request. You must then evaluate the documents to determine which ones are most relevant and useful.

13.6 Set WAIS options
WAIS has a few options you can set. For example, you can specify whether you want to see more than the default maximum of 40 items if available.

13.7 Look at a retrieved document
You can read any document on your results list using a simple pager.

13.8 Get a copy of a WAIS document
You can also save a copy of the current document to disk (if you have an account on the machine that is running the WAIS client). Alternatively, you can have a copy of the document sent to you by electronic mail.

13.9 Refine my search
Sometimes the results of a WAIS search may include a number of documents that more or less match your search words, but use the words in a different way than you expected. You can use relevance feedback by picking a document that *is* relevant to your needs, and asking WAIS to search again based on the words in that document. The result is usually a more useful set of search results.

13.10 Use WAIS through Gopher
You can access WAIS through a menu on Gopher. This is convenient if you are already running Gopher and would like to use WAIS, or if you don't have access to a WAIS client but do have access to a Gopher site.

13.11 Do a streamlined WAIS search
The "waissearch" utility lets you specify a WAIS search without going through the usual menus.

13.12 Learn more about WAIS
There are a number of sources available that provide further information about WAIS and techniques for using it.

13.1 HOW DO I... *Use a WAIS client?*

COMPLEXITY: EASY

Problem
In order to use WAIS you must be able to run a WAIS client program that will provide your interface to the WAIS server.

Technique
You can either run a WAIS client on your own machine (or your local dial-up Internet site), if available, or connect to a public access WAIS client using telnet.

Steps
1. Determine if there is a WAIS client available on the machine with which you connect to the Internet. (If you are a dial-up user, this will be the Internet site that you dial up and on which you have an account.)

2. If you are using a dial-up connection, you will probably want to use the swais ("simple WAIS") client. Try typing `swais` at your local system prompt. If you get a "command not found" message, try typing

```
% whereis swais
```

If a location is listed for swais, try adding that directory to your PATH variable (see Chapter 6) and try again.

3. If swais (or another WAIS client) is not found on your system, you will have to access a public WAIS client. You can do this with a command such as:

```
% telnet quake.think.com
Trying 192.31.181.1 ...
Connected to quake.think.com.
Escape character is '^]'.
```

4. Once connected to most servers, you type **wais** at the login prompt, and then type your Internet address:

```
SunOS UNIX (quake.think.com)

login: wais
Last login: Mon Mar 14 17:21:11 from 192.70.203.2
SunOS Release 4.1.3 (SUN4C-STANDARD) #9: Wed Oct 27 18:18:30 EDT 1993
Welcome to swais.
Please type user identifier (optional, i.e user@host): hrh@well.com
```

(Note that the actual login messages and prompts will vary with the site, and may be changed from time to time.)

5. You will be asked for your terminal type. (Often vt100 will be listed in parentheses as the default, in which case you just press (ENTER).)

```
TERM = (vt100) vt100
```

Here we are connected to the swais client at Thinking Machines, Inc., a major developer of WAIS software.

Once you are running a WAIS client, you will see a Source Selection screen like the one in Figure 13-3. Note that the server at think.com has been set up so that only one source, the "directory-of-servers" is initially presented. How-To 13.2 explains how to search the list of servers for the databases you need.

6. With some servers you may instead see a screen like Figure 13-4. This screen gives the first page of a complete list of sources. See How-To 13.3 for an explanation of how to use this list.

How It Works
Whether run directly or accessed through telnet, the WAIS client connects to a WAIS server. The server presents the list of sources (databases) known to it, and you select and search the databases.

Comment
An alternate to quake.think.com is sunsite.unc.edu. After you connect, log in as swais and specify your terminal at the terminal prompt (vt100 is the usual choice).

At the time of writing, this site presents a complete source list, while quake.think.com has you search the list of sources using a preliminary WAIS search.

Another public client can be found at wais.com.

13 LOOKING UP INFORMATION WITH WAIS

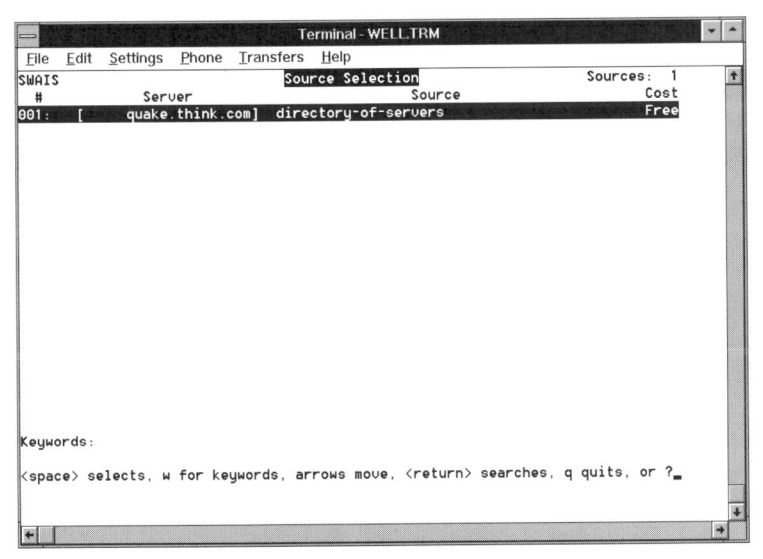

Figure 13-3 Connecting to the WAIS server

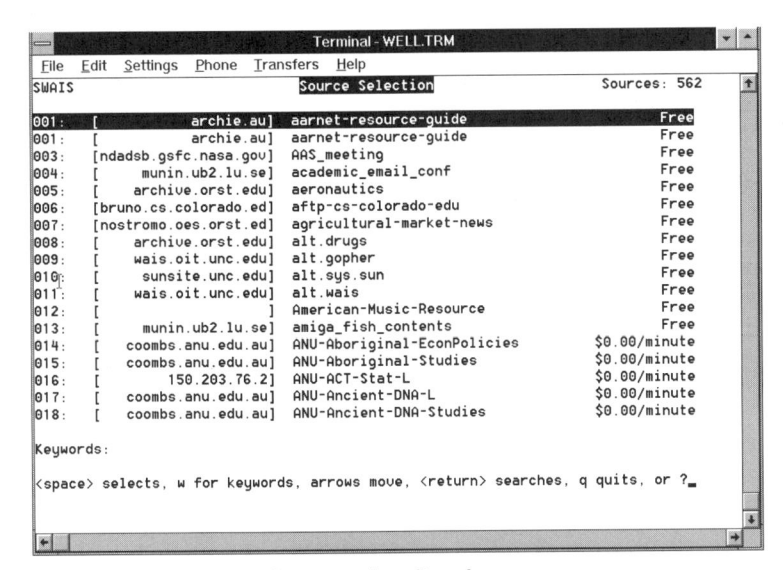

Figure 13-4 Server with a complete list of sources

INTERNET HOW-TO

13.2 HOW DO I...
Select a database?

COMPLEXITY: INTERMEDIATE

Problem
There are over 500 WAIS sources (servers) available, reflecting databases devoted to numerous subjects. You have to find the databases that are most likely to have the information you need.

Technique
You search the directory-of-servers source presented on the source screen when you first connect to WAIS.

Once you have completed the search, you browse the resulting list and choose the sources you want to use for your data search.

Steps
1. Log on WAIS as described in How-To 13.1. You should see a screen like the one in Figure 13-3. (Note: If you see the complete list of servers instead, as in Figure 13-4, see How-To 13.3.)

2. Press (SPACEBAR) to select the directory-of-servers source. It will be highlighted with an asterisk (*) before the name. (Note: Some sites are changing this so the directory-of-servers source is automatically selected for you. In that case, you don't have to press (SPACEBAR).)

3. Press (w) (word) to specify keywords. The cursor will move to the Keywords: prompt near the bottom of the screen.

4. Type the word(s) that best describe the *general* kind of information you are looking for and press (ENTER). For example, you might make a survey of available sources in biology by typing biology at the Keywords: prompt. On the other hand, you might use a more specific topic if you have it in mind (for example, genetic engineering). It's best at this stage not to be *too* specific, however, to avoid missing some relevant sources.

5. In the main example in this chapter we will take the role of an educator who is looking for reviews of software for the elementary to high school (el-hi) level.

    In Figure 13-5 we typed `software reviews`. This is a fairly general search, but it minimizes the possibility of missing sources by being too specific (for example, by specifying "educational").

    Figure 13-6 shows the result of our search. Note that WAIS has switched from the Source Selection screen (which you use for choosing databases) to the Search Results screen (which lists the items found by your latest search).

    Forty sources are shown for this search. This number is quite typical, because it is the default maximum number of hits shown after a search. This also means that if you don't see what you want in a "40 hits" search result, you may want to either attempt a more specific search or set a higher maximum (see How-To 13.6) and try again.

13 LOOKING UP INFORMATION WITH WAIS

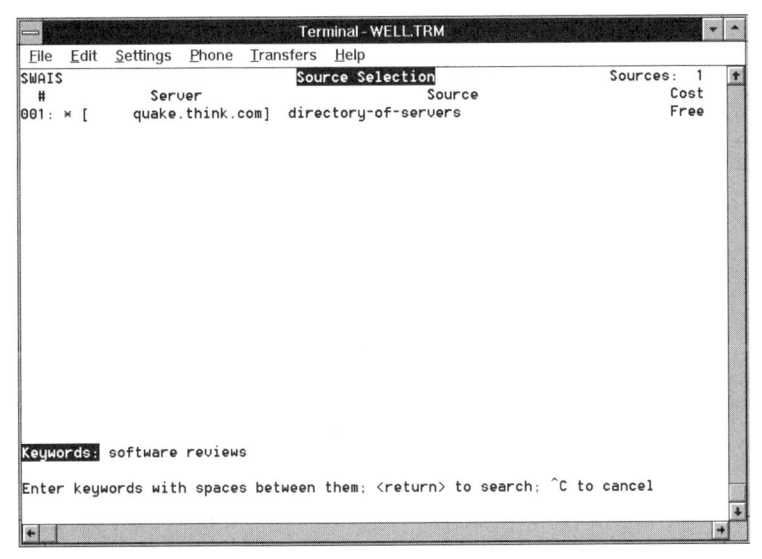

```
┌─────────────────────── Terminal - WELL.TRM ───────────────────────┐
 File  Edit  Settings  Phone  Transfers  Help
 SWAIS                      Source Selection           Sources:    1
    #           Server                  Source                   Cost
 001: * [   quake.think.com] directory-of-servers               Free











 Keywords: software reviews
 Enter keywords with spaces between them; <return> to search; ^C to cancel
```

Figure 13-5 Searching for sources

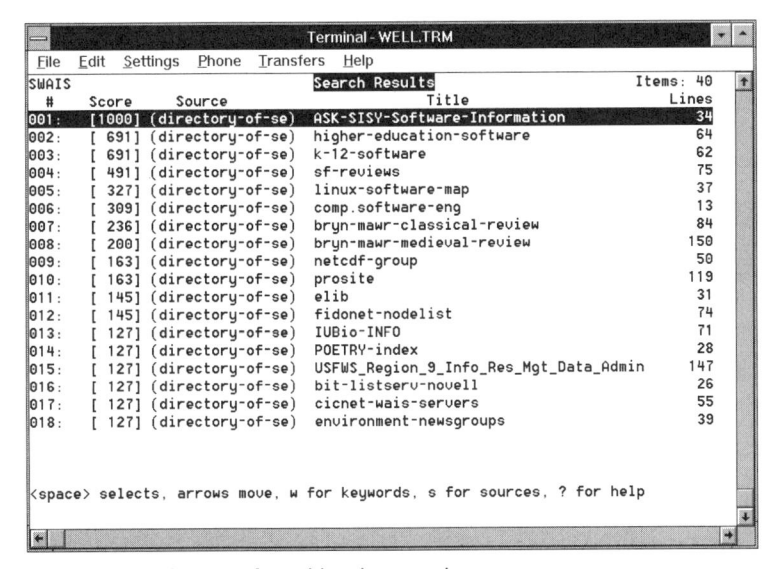

```
┌─────────────────────── Terminal - WELL.TRM ───────────────────────┐
 File  Edit  Settings  Phone  Transfers  Help
 SWAIS                       Search Results            Items:   40
    #    Score    Source              Title                     Lines
 001:   [1000] (directory-of-se)  ASK-SISY-Software-Information    34
 002:   [ 691] (directory-of-se)  higher-education-software        64
 003:   [ 691] (directory-of-se)  k-12-software                    62
 004:   [ 491] (directory-of-se)  sf-reviews                       75
 005:   [ 327] (directory-of-se)  linux-software-map               37
 006:   [ 309] (directory-of-se)  comp.software-eng                13
 007:   [ 236] (directory-of-se)  bryn-mawr-classical-review       84
 008:   [ 200] (directory-of-se)  bryn-mawr-medieval-review       150
 009:   [ 163] (directory-of-se)  netcdf-group                     50
 010:   [ 163] (directory-of-se)  prosite                         119
 011:   [ 145] (directory-of-se)  elib                             31
 012:   [ 145] (directory-of-se)  fidonet-nodelist                 74
 013:   [ 127] (directory-of-se)  IUBio-INFO                       71
 014:   [ 127] (directory-of-se)  POETRY-index                     28
 015:   [ 127] (directory-of-se)  USFWS_Region_9_Info_Res_Mgt_Data_Admin  147
 016:   [ 127] (directory-of-se)  bit-listserv-novell              26
 017:   [ 127] (directory-of-se)  cicnet-wais-servers              55
 018:   [ 127] (directory-of-se)  environment-newsgroups           39

 <space> selects, arrows move, w for keywords, s for sources, ? for help
```

Figure 13-6 Sources found by the search

6. To move around in the list of sources, use the ↑ and ↓ keys (the j and k keys used by the vi editor also work). You can press J (note the capital) to move to the next screen if there are too many items to fit on one screen. Press K to move back up one screen. You can also move to a specific source by typing its number.

INTERNET HOW-TO

7. Read the list and try to identify those sources that are actually relevant to your needs. One useful technique is to select a source and press (v) to view information about it. Since the source "k-12-software" looks like what we had in mind, we highlight it, press (v), and see the screen shown in Figure 13-7.

8. When you find a source that you want to use for your data search, select (highlight) it and press (u) ("use"). The source will be added to the list of available sources on the Source Selection screen (you will still be looking at the Search Results screen, however).

You are now ready to begin your data search. See How-To 13.5.

How It Works

Because there are so many sources available, many WAIS servers now provide the directory-of-sources as a starting point. You search this source with keywords just as you search other data sources. From the list of matching sources, you select the ones that you will be using for subsequent searches.

When you tell WAIS you want to use a source, the server loads information that it needs to connect to that source. Remember that the actual database sources are not located in the same place as the WAIS client you are running or the WAIS server that the client is connected to. Rather, the databases are provided by servers around the world.

Comment

It's usually best not to select more than a few sources at a time. This will help keep the number of hits down to a manageable level when you do your data search. It can also take some time for WAIS to connect to and search a lengthy list of sources.

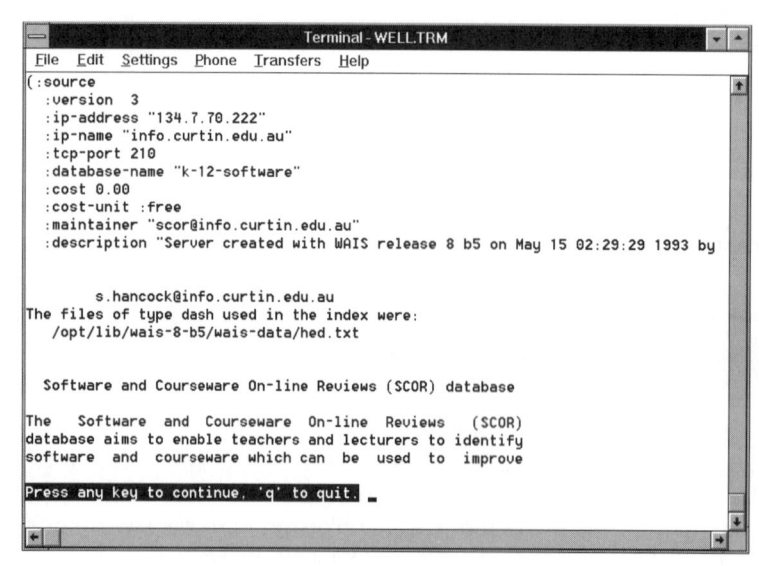

Figure 13-7 Information about the K-12-software source

13 🌐 **LOOKING UP INFORMATION WITH WAIS**

13.3 HOW DO I...
Use the list of servers?

COMPLEXITY | INTERMEDIATE

Problem
Some WAIS servers present the complete list of sources rather than having you search the directory-of-servers to find sources.

Technique
There are two approaches you can take here. You can either browse the whole list of sources and select those that seem relevant to your needs, or you can select just the directory-of-servers source and search it, as in How-To 13.2.

Steps
1. Connect to WAIS as described in How-To 13.1. You will be looking at the Source Selection screen. If you see only one source, the directory-of-servers, follow the procedure in How-To 13.2 to select appropriate sources.

2. Browse the complete list of sources. (The beginning of the list is shown in Figure 13-4.)

3. To move around in the list of sources, use the ⊤ and ⊥ keys (the ⒥ and ⓚ keys used by the vi editor also work). You can press ⒿⒿ (note the capital) to move to the next screen if there are too many items to fit on one screen. Press ⓚ to move back up one screen.

   You can also move to a specific source by typing its number, or select a specific source by pressing ⒮ and typing the source name (or part of the beginning of the name) and pressing ENTER.

4. Try to identify those sources that are relevant to your needs. One useful technique is to select a source and press ⓥ to view information about it. After moving down the list that begins in Figure 13-4, you'll come to a source called "k-12-software." Since this looks like what we had in mind, we highlight it, press ⓥ, and see the screen shown in Figure 13-7. This gives some descriptive information about the "k-12" source.

5. When you find a source that you want to use for your data search, select (highlight) it and press ⓤ. The source will be added to the list of available sources on the Source Selection screen.

6. Alternatively, press ⒮ and type `directory-of-servers` to go to that source. Press ⓤ to use that source. You can now use the procedure in How-To 13.5 to search the directory and obtain the names of sources for further research.

   You can also use this technique to go to and select a particular source whose name you know. (You must know the exact name, however; WAIS won't search for partial matches on the source list.)

   You are now ready to begin your data search. See How-To 13.5.

How It Works

Some WAIS servers start by showing you the complete list of available sources. Browsing this list takes time, but will give you a better idea of the scope and diversity of information available through WAIS.

As you find sources that appear to be relevant to your current search, you select them for later use. Then, when you go back to the Source Selection screen, you choose which of your selected sources will actually be used in your data search.

Comment

Most sites have discontinued showing the complete list of services, since it has grown to more than 500 items. A useful resource for more information about WAIS sources is a document called src-list.txt. This is a list of WAIS sources organized by broad subject categories. The current version of the list has the following table of contents:

```
Aeronautics  1
Archaeology  1
Astronomy  1
Biology  1
Chemical Engineering  2
Computer Platforms  2
Macintosh  2
PC  3
Sun Microsystems  3
Unix  3
Computer Science  3
Languages  4
Computer Software  4
Connection Machine (CM) information  5
CWIS  5
Gopher  5
WAIS  5
Education  6
Engineering  6
Environment  6
Finance  6
Graphics  7
Humanities  7
Journalism  8
Religion  8
Information Sources  8
Law  9
Libraries and Catalogues  9
Mathematics  10
Miscellaneous  10
Multimedia  10
Networks  10
Documentation and Standards  11
Security  11
Using the Internet  11
Phonebooks, Mail and Computer Lists  11
Recreation  12
```

13 LOOKING UP INFORMATION WITH WAIS

```
Music  12
Food  13
Robotics  13
Research (Miscellaneous)  13
Science (general)  13
US Government Departments  13
```

By looking for the appropriate category you can quickly zero in on the sources most likely to be useful for your research. This file can be obtained by ftp. One host that has it at the time of writing is archive.orst.edu, where it is found in the directory /pub/doc/wais. Most other sites that have WAIS program files should also have the sources file.

13.4 HOW DO I...
Get help with WAIS?

COMPLEXITY: EASY

Problem
Sometimes you will want to be reminded of the basic key commands for using the WAIS client.

Technique
You simply press ? or h and view the help screen.

Steps
1. At either WAIS screen (Source Selection or Search Results), press ? or h. You will see a help screen like the one in Figure 13-8.

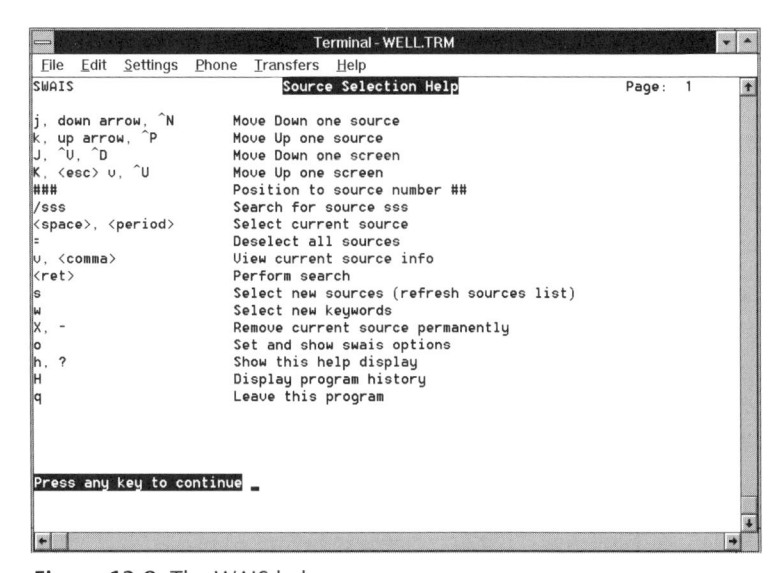

```
SWAIS                         Source Selection Help              Page:   1

j, down arrow, ^N     Move Down one source
k, up arrow, ^P       Move Up one source
J, ^V, ^D             Move Down one screen
K, <esc> v, ^U        Move Up one screen
###                   Position to source number ##
/sss                  Search for source sss
<space>, <period>     Select current source
=                     Deselect all sources
v, <comma>            View current source info
<ret>                 Perform search
s                     Select new sources (refresh sources list)
w                     Select new keywords
X, -                  Remove current source permanently
o                     Set and show swais options
h, ?                  Show this help display
H                     Display program history
q                     Leave this program

Press any key to continue _
```

Figure 13-8 The WAIS help screen

INTERNET HOW-TO

2. After you have looked at the help screen, press any key to return to the WAIS prompt.

How It Works
The help screen simply lists the command keys used by the client. As you can see, they are quite simple. Note that there are separate help displays for the Source Selection and Search Results screens, since the applicable commands are somewhat different in these two modes.

Comment
The screen shown here is for swais; more elaborate clients will have more commands and options.

13.5 HOW DO I...
Perform a WAIS search?

COMPLEXITY   EASY

Problem
Once you have selected data sources, you need to tell WAIS what kinds of documents to look for in the databases represented by the sources.

Technique
You select one or more sources and then specify words to be matched against the indexes for the databases.

Steps
1. If you are looking at the Search Results screen, press (S) to switch to the Source Selection screen.

2. You will see a list of all the sources you selected while viewing the results of your search of the directory-of-servers (How-To 13.2) or that you selected from the complete list of sources (How-To 13.3).

3. You move around in this list just as you do on the results list (using the arrow or (j) and (k) keys). To mark a source for use in your database search, move the highlight to the source and press (SPACEBAR). (You can press (SPACEBAR) again to clear a selection, or press (=) to clear all selections.)

4. Once you have marked the sources, press (w) to get to the Keywords: prompt, as shown in Figure 13-5. Type the word(s) that best describe what you are looking for. (At this point you should try to be reasonably specific so as to reduce the number of irrelevant documents retrieved.)

   For example, suppose we have marked the k-12-software source described in Figure 13-7. We decide we want to find software to help with reading, so we simply enter the word `reading` at the Keywords: prompt, and press (ENTER).

5. WAIS will connect to each of the databases you have marked and search its index using the keywords you specified. In this case, we are searching just one database (k-12-software.src), and the results of the search are shown in Figure 13-9.

13 LOOKING UP INFORMATION WITH WAIS

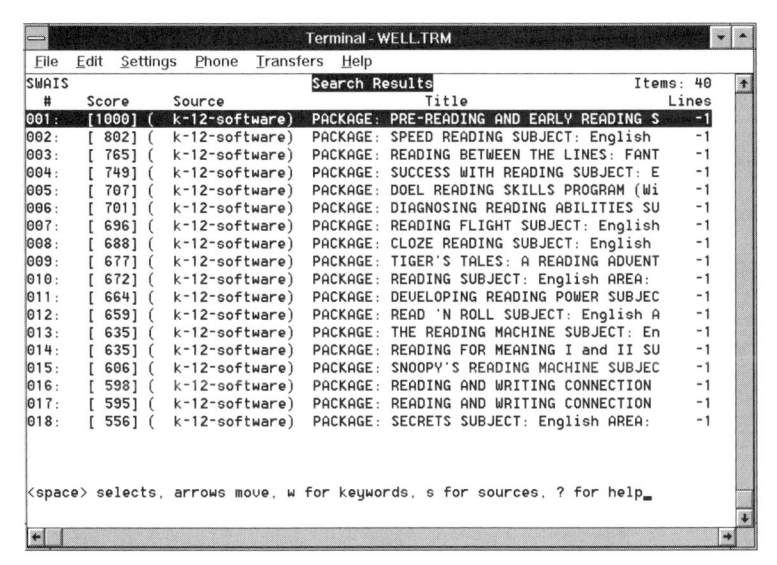

```
┌─────────────────── Terminal - WELL.TRM ───────────────────┐
File  Edit  Settings  Phone  Transfers  Help
SWAIS                          Search Results         Items: 40
  #    Score      Source                Title               Lines
001:   [1000] (  k-12-software)   PACKAGE: PRE-READING AND EARLY READING S   -1
002:   [ 802] (  k-12-software)   PACKAGE: SPEED READING SUBJECT: English    -1
003:   [ 765] (  k-12-software)   PACKAGE: READING BETWEEN THE LINES: FANT   -1
004:   [ 749] (  k-12-software)   PACKAGE: SUCCESS WITH READING SUBJECT: E   -1
005:   [ 707] (  k-12-software)   PACKAGE: DOEL READING SKILLS PROGRAM (Wi   -1
006:   [ 701] (  k-12-software)   PACKAGE: DIAGNOSING READING ABILITIES SU   -1
007:   [ 696] (  k-12-software)   PACKAGE: READING FLIGHT SUBJECT: English   -1
008:   [ 688] (  k-12-software)   PACKAGE: CLOZE READING SUBJECT: English    -1
009:   [ 677] (  k-12-software)   PACKAGE: TIGER'S TALES: A READING ADVENT   -1
010:   [ 672] (  k-12-software)   PACKAGE: READING SUBJECT: English AREA:    -1
011:   [ 664] (  k-12-software)   PACKAGE: DEVELOPING READING POWER SUBJEC   -1
012:   [ 659] (  k-12-software)   PACKAGE: READ 'N ROLL SUBJECT: English A   -1
013:   [ 635] (  k-12-software)   PACKAGE: THE READING MACHINE SUBJECT: En   -1
014:   [ 635] (  k-12-software)   PACKAGE: READING FOR MEANING I and II SU   -1
015:   [ 606] (  k-12-software)   PACKAGE: SNOOPY'S READING MACHINE SUBJEC   -1
016:   [ 598] (  k-12-software)   PACKAGE: READING AND WRITING CONNECTION    -1
017:   [ 595] (  k-12-software)   PACKAGE: READING AND WRITING CONNECTION    -1
018:   [ 556] (  k-12-software)   PACKAGE: SECRETS SUBJECT: English AREA:    -1

<space> selects, arrows move, w for keywords, s for sources, ? for help_
```

Figure 13-9 Search results

6. Look at the list of results and see if they reflect the kind of material you are looking for. If not, you may want to use relevance feedback to better focus your search (see How-To 13.9). The number shown before each retrieved document reflects the degree to which it matched your search criteria. (Note that a score of 1000 doesn't mean that the document will necessarily be relevant to your needs—it only means that all the words you specified were found, probably several times in the document.)

We seem to have found a variety of interesting-looking titles of software reviews dealing with various aspects of reading. How-To 13.7 shows you how to look at these documents.

How It Works

WAIS makes a network connection to the server representing each database you have marked. Your search words are submitted to the database. Any hits (matching documents) are displayed on the Search Results screen for you to browse, view, or save.

Note that some WAIS sources support more advanced searching techniques than the simple index search described here. Such sources have notes on searching features that you will see when you press $\boxed{v}$ to view information on that source. For example, the following source from the biology department at the University of Indiana includes detailed information on searching:

```
(:source
  :version  3
  :ip-address "129.79.224.25"
  :ip-name "ftp.bio.indiana.edu"
  :tcp-port 210
  :database-name "INFO"
  :cost 0.00
```

Continued on next page

INTERNET HOW-TO

Continued from previous page

```
:cost-unit :free
:maintainer "archive@bio.indiana.edu"
:description "
This WAIS service includes several indexed Biology information sources,
including Genbank nucleic acid gene sequence databank, Drosophila genetics
BioSci/Bionet network news, and others.

= = = = = = = = = = = = = = = = = = = = = = =

This WAIS service sports several zippy modifications.  These include
boolean operators 'and' and 'not', partial word matches,
literal phrase matches, and extended number of results.

Boolean searches: The terms 'and' and 'not' are effective
in modifying the query.    For example,

   Query: red and green not blue
   Result: just those records with both the words 'red' and 'green',
           excluding all records with the word 'blue'.

Partial words:  The asterisk (*) applied at the end of
   a partial word will match all documents with words that
   start with the partial word.  For example,

   Query: hum*
   Result: all records with 'hum', 'hummingbird', 'human',
           'humbug', etc.

Literal phrases:  If quotes (') or double quotes (\") surrounding
   a phrase, it will match that phrase exactly.  For example,

   Query: 'red rooster-39'
   Result:  only those records with the the full string
           'red rooster-39' will be matched.

   There are some practical limits on this.  The first part
   of a literal must be a word that is otherwise indexed.
   Thus your literal cannot start with a symbol or other
   word delimiter.  Within quotes, the boolean operators
   and the partial word key are not active.

These features can generally be mixed in a query, for example:
   Query:   'Df(32)-[34]red' and hum* not Brown
```

That's quite a tutorial in itself! You may need to practice a bit to get the most out of such advanced searching features.

Comment

Unfortunately one or more of the servers for the sources you have selected may be unavailable for some reason. If this is the case, you will see a cryptic error message

13 LOOKING UP INFORMATION WITH WAIS

(often something about broken sockets), and a "connection failed" notice will be added to the Search Results list. Your only options are to try alternate sources or to repeat the search at a later time when (perhaps) the affected server will be available.

13.6 HOW DO I...
Set WAIS options?

COMPLEXITY: EASY

Problem
WAIS has a few options that you can use to control searching and the display of results.

Technique
You go to the Option Settings screen and make whatever settings you wish.

Steps
1. Press (O) from the source or results screen to go to the Option Settings screen, shown in Figure 13-10.

   See Table 13-1 for a brief description of the options and their meaning.

2. Use the arrow keys to move the highlight to the option you want to set or change.

3. Press (SPACEBAR) to toggle an on/off option.

4. For options that require a directory path or a number, press (ENTER), and you will be prompted for the required information.

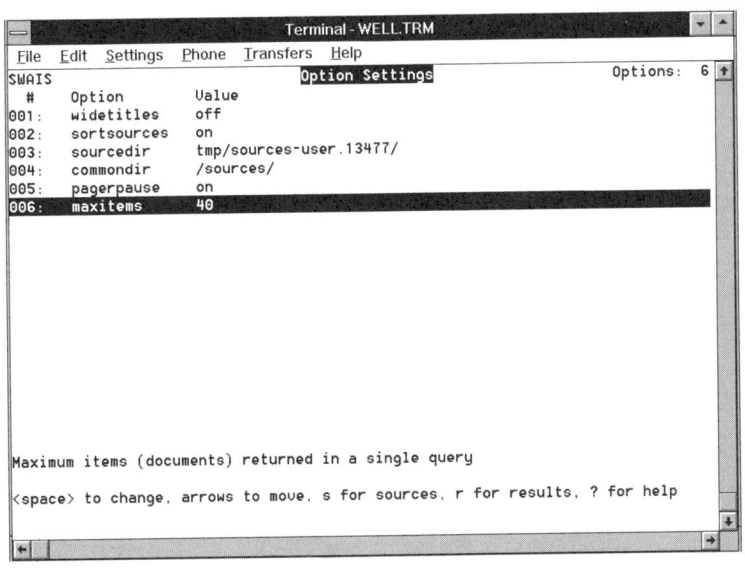

```
                    Terminal - WELL.TRM
 File  Edit  Settings  Phone  Transfers  Help
SWAIS                      Option Settings            Options:   6
   #     Option         Value
 001:   widetitles      off
 002:   sortsources     on
 003:   sourcedir       tmp/sources-user.13477/
 004:   commondir       /sources/
 005:   pagerpause      on
 006:   maxitems        40




















Maximum items (documents) returned in a single query
<space> to change, arrows to move, s for sources, r for results, ? for help
```

Figure 13-10 WAIS options screen

INTERNET HOW-TO

OPTION	MEANING	VALUES
widetitles	Amount of source or document title to show	On/off; when on, source name is omitted to allow for more of document title; default is off
sortsources	Sort sources in list alphabetically	On/off; default is on
sourcedir	Location of custom source description directory	Pathname (only useful if you run client on your own machine)
commondir	Location of general source description directory	Pathname (only useful if you run client on your own machine)
pagerpause	Whether to show documents a screen at a time or continuously	On/off; set off to use your text capture facility; default is on
maxitems	Maximum number of hits to show on Search Results screen	Numeric; default is 40

Table 13-1 WAIS options

How It Works
These simple options give you control over how large a search result WAIS will display, how document titles and sources will be displayed, and whether paging will be on or off. The sourcedir and commondir options are for advanced users.

Comment
These options are for swais. Other clients may have additional options, and may allow you to save options for future use.

13.7 HOW DO I...
Look at a retrieved document?

COMPLEXITY: EASY

Problem
Once you have a list of retrieved documents, you'll probably want to look at one or more of them.

Technique
You highlight the document you want to see in the list and press (ENTER)

Steps
1. Make sure you are in the Search Results screen. (If not, press (r) to go there.)

2. Use the arrow keys, (J) and (K) keys, or document number to move the highlight to the document you want to read. For this example we'll use item 1 from Figure 13-9, "Pre-reading and Early Reading."

3. Press (ENTER). The document will be displayed using a simple pager. In Figure 13-11, we are viewing the beginning of the review of a pre-reading software package. (Upon close inspection, you see that it is British.)

4. If the document is longer than one screen page, press any key to continue to the next page. Press (q) to quit the display and return to the Search Results screen.

13 LOOKING UP INFORMATION WITH WAIS

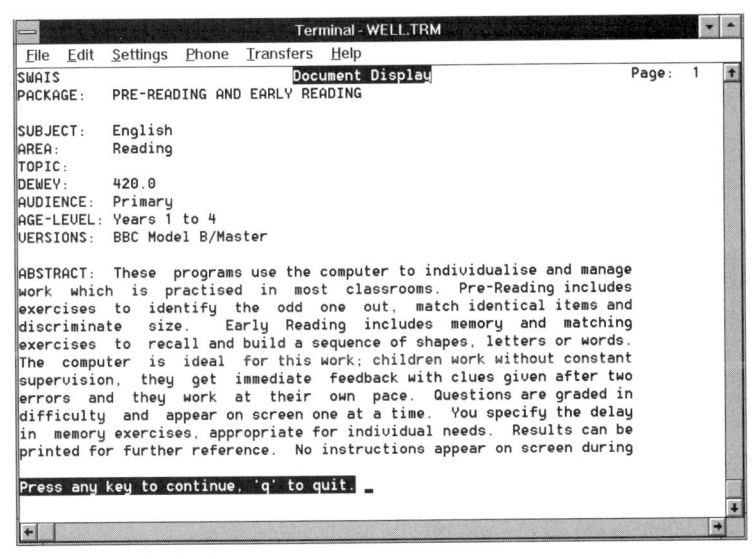

```
┌─────────────────── Terminal - WELL.TRM ───────────────────┐
│ File  Edit  Settings  Phone  Transfers  Help              │
│ SWAIS                   Document Display        Page:  1  │
│ PACKAGE:   PRE-READING AND EARLY READING                  │
│                                                            │
│ SUBJECT:   English                                         │
│ AREA:      Reading                                         │
│ TOPIC:                                                     │
│ DEWEY:     420.0                                           │
│ AUDIENCE:  Primary                                         │
│ AGE-LEVEL: Years 1 to 4                                    │
│ VERSIONS:  BBC Model B/Master                              │
│                                                            │
│ ABSTRACT:  These  programs use the computer to individualise and manage │
│ work  which  is  practised  in  most  classrooms.  Pre-Reading includes │
│ exercises  to  identify  the  odd  one  out,  match identical items and │
│ discriminate  size.   Early  Reading  includes  memory  and  matching   │
│ exercises  to  recall and build a sequence of shapes, letters or words. │
│ The  computer  is  ideal  for this work; children work without constant │
│ supervision,  they  get  immediate  feedback with clues given after two │
│ errors  and  they  work  at  their  own  pace.  Questions are graded in │
│ difficulty  and  appear on screen one at a time.  You specify the delay │
│ in  memory exercises, appropriate for individual needs.  Results can be │
│ printed for further reference.  No instructions appear on screen during │
│ Press any key to continue, 'q' to quit. _                 │
└────────────────────────────────────────────────────────────┘
```

Figure 13-11 Viewing a document

How It Works
WAIS uses an extremely simple pager to display the document. You may find it more convenient to get a copy of the document (see How-To 13.8) and use your own editor to view the document.

Comment
Not all WAIS documents are text—they can be graphics, such as maps or data sets. When you view such a document, you will actually be viewing the descriptive header information. You'll need to get a copy of the document before you can really use it (see How-To 13.8), and have a program that can display it for you. (Programs to view common graphics file formats on your PC are available at many ftp sites, bulletin boards, or services like CompuServe.)

13.8 HOW DO I...
Get a copy of a WAIS document?

COMPLEXITY EASY

Problem
You will probably want to get your own copy of a retrieved document so you can print it or read it at your leisure. (You may also want a copy of a graphic image so you can view it, since the text-based swais can't show you graphic images directly from within WAIS.)

Technique
You highlight the document and then tell WAIS to either mail you a copy or save a copy to a file.

401

INTERNET HOW-TO

Steps

1. Make sure you are on the Search Results screen. (If not, press (r) to go there.)

2. Highlight the document you want to receive. For example, we'll choose item 1 from Figure 13-9.

3. If you want to save the document to a file, press (S) (note the capital; lowercase (s) means "go to the Select Sources screen").

4. You will be prompted for a filename:

```
File: preread.txt
```
```
Enter the filename into which to save this item; ^C to cancel
```

   Here, since the document was about pre-reading software, you type `preread.txt` at the file prompt.

   The document will be saved to the file you specified (in the current working directory if no other directory was specified). Note: You can only use this command if you are running a WAIS client on a machine on which you have an account. If you try it while using telnet to connect to a public access client, you will get a "permission denied" message. In this case, ask to get the document by mail instead.

5. If you want to receive the document by mail, highlight it and press (m).

6. You will be prompted for your mail address. Supply your Internet address and press (ENTER). The document will be mailed to you:

```
Address: hrh@well.com
```
```
Enter your e-mail address; ^C to cancel
```

How It Works

Since each document in the database is a separate file, it is easy for WAIS to either save the document to disk or mail you a copy.

Comment

Saving to disk is better if that option is available to you, since it avoids adding mail headers to the document. For binary files, either run a local client or run the "wais-search" client (see How-To 13.11) so you can save the file.

13.9 HOW DO I... *Refine my search?*

COMPLEXITY: INTERMEDIATE

Problem

Sometimes only a few of the documents you retrieve will appear to be meaningful for your research. This is because WAIS doesn't know what words "mean," it only knows whether a document contains those words, in no particular order.

Technique

You mark one or more documents as "relevant" and then redo the search. WAIS will use the words in the relevant documents to refine the search.

Steps

1. Look at the Search Results screen and choose a document or two that has the kind of information you are actually seeking. Back at the results in Figure 13-9, we decide that we want to focus on software that uses the Cloze reading method.

2. Highlight and mark each document as relevant by pressing ⓡ. In Figure 13-9, we marked document 8, which mentions "Cloze."

3. If you want to review the documents you have marked as relevant, press ⓡ to go to the Relevant Documents screen, as shown in Figure 13-12. Press ⓘ to get help in working with this screen:

```
SWAIS                   Relevant Doc. Help                Page:  1

j, ^N         Move Down one item
k, ^P         Move Up one item
J             Move Down one screen
K             Move Up one screen
D             Delete All Relevant Docs
X             Delete Current Relevant Doc
<space>       Display current item
<return>          Display current item
v             View current item information
```

As you can see, you can select, delete, or examine your relevant documents.

4. Press ⓢ to go back to the Source Selection screen. Press ⓦ and (ENTER) to rerun the search using the relevant documents.

5. WAIS will perform the search again, but this time it will rank the results in a different order, giving extra weight to the words in the documents that had been marked as relevant. Figure 13-13 shows the results. If you compare it with Figure 13-9, you will see that the reviews involving the Cloze method have been scored higher (and moved up on the screen).

How It Works

WAIS uses the documents you marked as relevant as a kind of template against which to check the documents in the database. The documents that most closely match (that is, have the most words in common with the relevant document) are displayed first in the Search Results list when you rerun the search.

Comment

Relevance feedback may not be available with all clients, and the results are sometimes subtle and hard to evaluate.

INTERNET HOW-TO

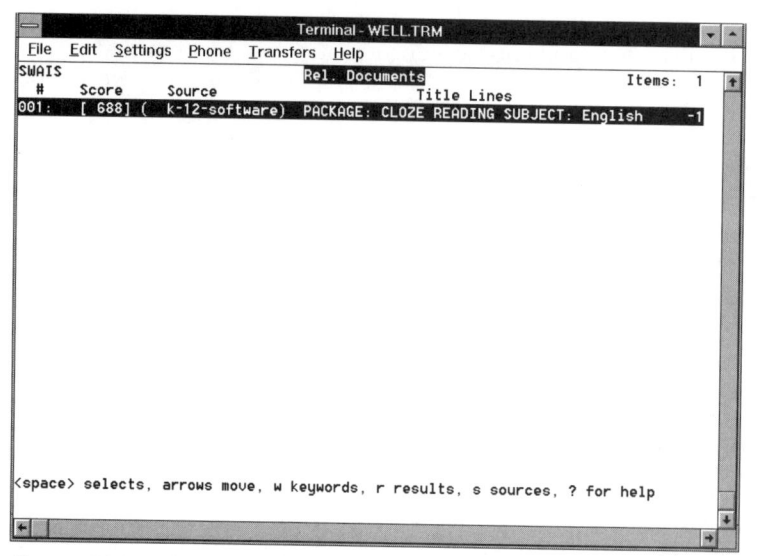

Figure 13-12 Relevant Documents screen

Figure 13-13 Results of relevance feedback

13.10 HOW DO I...
Use WAIS through Gopher?

COMPLEXITY INTERMEDIATE

Problem
You may find it convenient to do a WAIS search on a source found while using the Gopher program. This may also be useful if you don't have a WAIS client at your site, but you do have Gopher.

Technique
You run Gopher, choose an appropriate menu item, and perform the WAIS search. Depending on the menu item, you may either be connected to a general WAIS server by telnet, or be given a specific data source to search.

Steps
1. Run your Gopher client. (See Chapter 12 for complete information on using Gopher.)

2. At the main Gopher menu, look for an item with the title "Other Gopher and Info Servers."

3. Choose this menu item and you will see a submenu. Look for an item with a title like "WAIS-based information."

4. Select this item by highlighting it with ↓ and then pressing → or ENTER. You will see a listing of WAIS sources like that in Figure 13-14.

5. Select a source to search. You can do this either by browsing the list, highlighting the source, and pressing →, or by pressing / and typing in the name of the source. Here

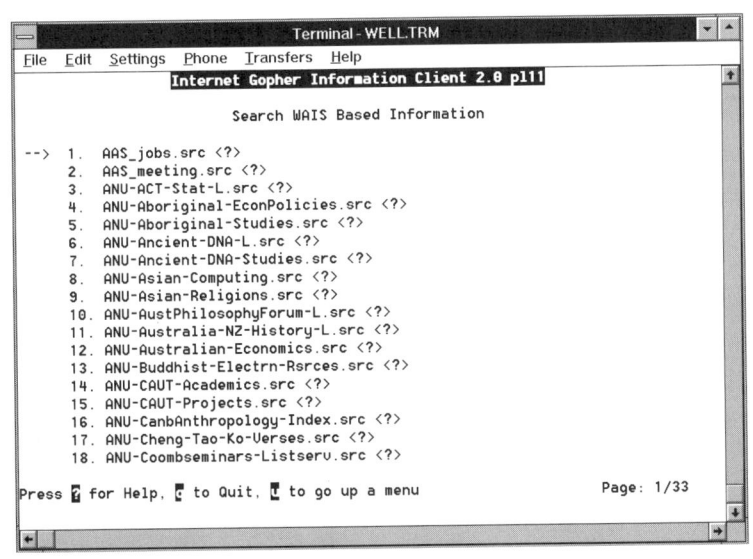

```
                    Terminal - WELL.TRM
 File  Edit  Settings  Phone  Transfers  Help
            Internet Gopher Information Client 2.0 p111

                      Search WAIS Based Information

 -->  1.  AAS_jobs.src <?>
      2.  AAS_meeting.src <?>
      3.  ANU-ACT-Stat-L.src <?>
      4.  ANU-Aboriginal-EconPolicies.src <?>
      5.  ANU-Aboriginal-Studies.src <?>
      6.  ANU-Ancient-DNA-L.src <?>
      7.  ANU-Ancient-DNA-Studies.src <?>
      8.  ANU-Asian-Computing.src <?>
      9.  ANU-Asian-Religions.src <?>
     10.  ANU-AustPhilosophyForum-L.src <?>
     11.  ANU-Australia-NZ-History-L.src <?>
     12.  ANU-Australian-Economics.src <?>
     13.  ANU-Buddhist-Electrn-Rsrces.src <?>
     14.  ANU-CAUT-Academics.src <?>
     15.  ANU-CAUT-Projects.src <?>
     16.  ANU-CanbAnthropology-Index.src <?>
     17.  ANU-Cheng-Tao-Ko-Verses.src <?>
     18.  ANU-Coombseminars-Listserv.src <?>

 Press ? for Help, ? to Quit, ? to go up a menu       Page: 1/33
```

Figure 13-14 WAIS sources in Gopher menu

INTERNET HOW-TO

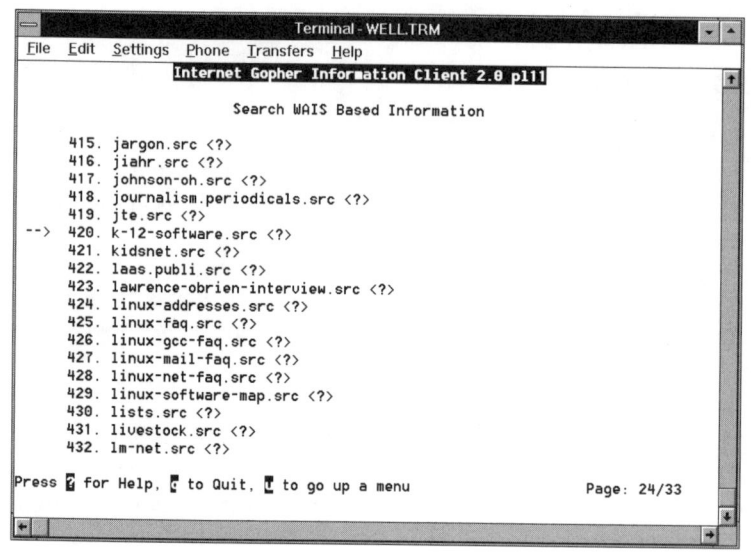

```
┌─────────────────────────────────────────────────────┐
│                  Terminal - WELL.TRM          ▼ ▲   │
│ File  Edit  Settings  Phone  Transfers  Help        │
│         Internet Gopher Information Client 2.0 pl11 │
│                                                     │
│              Search WAIS Based Information          │
│                                                     │
│       415. jargon.src <?>                           │
│       416. jiahr.src <?>                            │
│       417. johnson-oh.src <?>                       │
│       418. journalism.periodicals.src <?>           │
│       419. jte.src <?>                              │
│  -->  420. k-12-software.src <?>                    │
│       421. kidsnet.src <?>                          │
│       422. laas.publi.src <?>                       │
│       423. lawrence-obrien-interview.src <?>        │
│       424. linux-addresses.src <?>                  │
│       425. linux-faq.src <?>                        │
│       426. linux-gcc-faq.src <?>                    │
│       427. linux-mail-faq.src <?>                   │
│       428. linux-net-faq.src <?>                    │
│       429. linux-software-map.src <?>               │
│       430. lists.src <?>                            │
│       431. livestock.src <?>                        │
│       432. lm-net.src <?>                           │
│                                                     │
│ Press ? for Help, q to Quit, u to go up a menu      │
│                                        Page: 24/33  │
└─────────────────────────────────────────────────────┘
```

Figure 13-15 Selecting a source

we will press <kbd>/</kbd> and type `k-12-software` to get to the school software source we have used in the other examples in this chapter. The menu repositions to that source, which we can now select (see Figure 13-15).

6. Press <kbd>→</kbd> to select the highlighted source for searching.

7. You will be prompted for words to search for (see Figure 13-16). Here, we decide that we want to look for arithmetic software, so we type `arithmetic` and press <kbd>ENTER</kbd>.

The results of the search are shown in Figure 13-17. Since the results are a Gopher menu, you can view, save, or mail them just as you can other Gopher items.

How It Works

Gopher provides access to WAIS in two ways. One is simply a telnet connection to a public access WAIS client that you use, as in How-To 13.1. The other, shown in this how-to, is a specific data source. In that case, Gopher prompts you for the search words and then connects to WAIS to perform the search. The search results are displayed as items in a Gopher menu rather than on a WAIS Search Results list.

Comment

Searches by WAIS through Gopher may not support the advanced searching features (such as Boolean searches) allowed by some WAIS servers. On the other hand, you may find it easier to find and navigate through sources in Gopher than with a WAIS client. Also, if you have a Gopher client at your local site but no WAIS client, using Gopher gives you an opportunity to save files rather than having to mail them—this is particularly useful for binary files.

13 LOOKING UP INFORMATION WITH WAIS

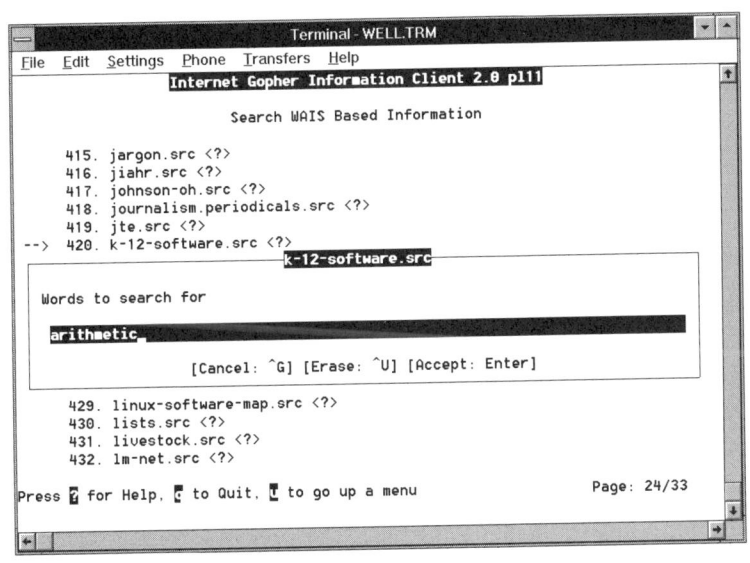

Figure 13-16 Performing the search

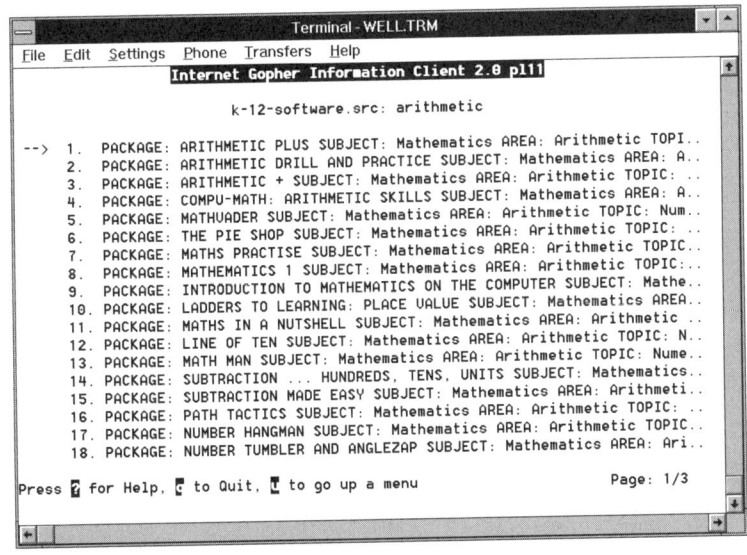

Figure 13-17 Search results in Gopher menu

INTERNET HOW-TO

13.11 HOW DO I...
Do a streamlined WAIS search?

COMPLEXITY: INTERMEDIATE

Problem
You may want to do a quick WAIS search without having to go through menus, or you may not have a full-fledged client available.

Technique
You use a utility called waissearch to perform a simple WAIS search without having to run a WAIS client, or telnet to a remote client.

Steps
1. Check to see whether your system has the waissearch utility. As usual, you can try the command `man waissearch` or `whereis waissearch` to search for it.

2. Type `waissearch` at your system prompt. Normally waissearch is set to use a default server. If you want to use a specific server, type `-h` followed by the server name (for example, `quake.think.com`). Next, type `-d` followed by the name of the source (database) to be used. Note that you must specify the exact database name (you may find the src-list.txt file mentioned in How-To 13.3 to be helpful in this regard). Finally, type the word or words you want to be searched for in the database and press (ENTER). Here is an example of a complete waissearch command:

```
% waissearch -h quake.think.com -d directory-of-servers factbook
```

This command says to connect to quake.think.com and search the directory-of-servers source for sources that contain the word "factbook" (we have the *CIA World Factbook* in mind).

If any documents are found, they will be listed by number:

```
Search Response:
  NumberOfRecordsReturned: 3
  1: Score: 1000, lines:   21 'world-factbook.src'
  2: Score:  333, lines:   25 'Connection-Machine.src'
  3: Score:  333, lines:   30 'world-factbook93.src'
View document number [type 0 or q to quit]: 1
```

3. To view a document, press its number and then (ENTER). Here we choose to look at document 1:

```
Headline: world-factbook.src
(:source
  :version  3
  :ip-address "131.239.2.100"
  :ip-name "cmns-moon.think.com"
  :tcp-port 210
  :database-name "CIA"
  :cost 0.00
  :cost-unit :free
  :maintainer "bug-public@think.com"
```

13 LOOKING UP INFORMATION WITH WAIS

```
    :subjects "social sciences demographics politics CIA world factbook   population economics
imports exports business"
    :description "Connection Machine WAIS server.  The 1990 World Factbook
by the CIA which contains a good description of every country.  The entry
for WORLD is also particularly good."
```

4. To make another search of the same database, press (q), and then press (y) when asked for new search words. Type in the words and press (ENTER).

How It Works
waissearch connects to the WAIS server you specify (or a default server if none is specified). It then submits the name of the database and your search words to the server. The server performs the search and passes the document list to waissearch, which lets you choose and read the documents you are interested in.

Comment
Note that waissearch lacks much of the functionality of a full WAIS client. For example, you can't search more than one database or have a document mailed to you. (You can save a document by displaying it and using your text capture facility, however.)

Another problem is that many sources that seem to be available using a telnet or wais/swais client don't seem to be available through waissearch. To get a list of sources that are supported for waissearch by a given site, the following command might be helpful:

```
% waissearch -h quake.think.com -d INFO -p 210 tcp
```

This command asks for a list of sources at quake.think.com that are in the INFO database and are available through a tcp connection (that is, through waissearch). You may have to add the -m option with a number higher than 100 to get the complete list.

13.12 HOW DO I...
Learn more about WAIS?

COMPLEXITY EASY

Problem
WAIS is already a significant resource on the Internet, but detailed documentation on its use is lacking. Nevertheless, there are several sources for further information about WAIS.

Technique
You can find newsgroups, files, and other sources that will help you learn more about WAIS.

Steps
1. Subscribe to the newsgroups comp.infosystems.wais and alt.wais. These are good places to find out about new servers, sources, and software, and to ask for help in using WAIS.

2. Get a bibliography of current resources on WAIS. You can ftp to quake.think.com and look for the file bibliography.txt in the /pub/wais.wais-discussion directory. (See Chapter 7 for instructions on using ftp.)

INTERNET HOW-TO

3. Use ftp to get the file src-list.txt that categorizes WAIS data sources by subject. See How-To 13.3 for more about this list.

4. Use ftp to check the WAIS directories at a WAIS server (such as quake.think.com). Look for text documents that describe various aspects of WAIS, such as an overview and discussion of concepts.

How It Works

At the time of writing there is no comprehensive tutorial or user reference to WAIS, although there are some brief introductions and overviews. The material in this chapter should be quite adequate to get started using WAIS successfully. As WAIS becomes more popular, more resources are likely to become available.

Comment

Fire up a WAIS client and experiment with a variety of searches to get a feel for how WAIS works.

Navigating the Information Highway with the World Wide Web

How do I...

14.1 Connect to the World Wide Web with Lynx
14.2 View a document
14.3 Follow a hypertext link
14.4 Get help with Lynx
14.5 Search for text in a document
14.6 Get a copy of a document
14.7 Send a comment to a document's author
14.8 Recall a previously seen document
14.9 Use bookmarks for fast navigation
14.10 Use URLs for direct access to services
14.11 Perform a database or index search
14.12 Read Usenet news from the Web
14.13 Look at an ftp site through the Web
14.14 Search Gopher menus from the Web

Hypertext is an increasingly common way of organizing documents through their conceptual connections. If you've used Windows Help or Hypercard on a Mac, you've used a simple form of hypertext.

INTERNET HOW-TO

The basic idea of hypertext is to mark the key words or phrases in a document so that they can be selected by the reader. When the reader selects such a highlighted link, the hypertext software displays a related document that serves to provide more information and in turn open up new possibilities for exploration. Indeed, a "document" in hypertext need not be simple text: hypertext links can point to graphic images, searchable databases and indexes, or even sound files.

For example, suppose you are reading about a country in an online atlas. There are many aspects of that country that might interest you: geographical features, history, economics, population, and so on. As you read about the country, you may come to references to any of these matters and want to learn more.

Navigating Hypertext

Figure 14-1 shows a set of simple hypertext connections. The main document is an atlas entry for the mythical country of Slobbobia. Note the highlighted (boldface) words in the document. Selecting any of the highlighted items will take you to a related document, index search, graphic, or other service.

For example, suppose you are studying the Slobbobian economy. You come to a reference to **rubber bands**, and select it. You now read a document that describes the origins of these useful devices. In turn, the document on rubber bands has a reference to their inventor.

By following the "web" linking the documents, you can let your own interests and curiosity guide you in your search for knowledge. And because there can be more than one link to a document, many paths through the information web are possible. For example, you could go from the reference to **paper clips** in the Slobbobia document to an entry that in turn can link you to entries for **safety pins**, **rubber bands**, and **modern bureaucracy**.

Web Browsers

The service that provides hypertext access to the resources of the Internet is called the World Wide Web, or WWW or the Web for short. As you will see, the Web is in many ways the easiest and at the same time one of the most powerful ways to navigate the information highway.

When you use WWW, you run a program called a browser. This is a client program that connects to a Web server. The starting point for a session with the Web is an introductory, general document that in turn provides links to more specific documents. You pursue your inquiry or exploration by following the links that are likely to bring you to subjects of interest. Along the way, you can read the current document, search for specific text in the document, or obtain a copy of the document for later reference.

There are a variety of browsers available for the Web. Some of them, such as Mosaic, provide a graphical user interface and multimedia capabilities. Unfortunately, as you might expect, such browsers require that you have a direct TCP/IP connection to the Internet, and they tend to run quite slowly even on "high-speed" phone lines (see Chapter 2 for information on types of Internet connections).

The browser used in this chapter is called Lynx. While it is limited to text documents, Lynx is fast, easy to use, and available to anyone who can emulate a full-screen terminal (such as VT-100). Lynx thus provides a good introduction to the Web's capabilities for the dial-up user.

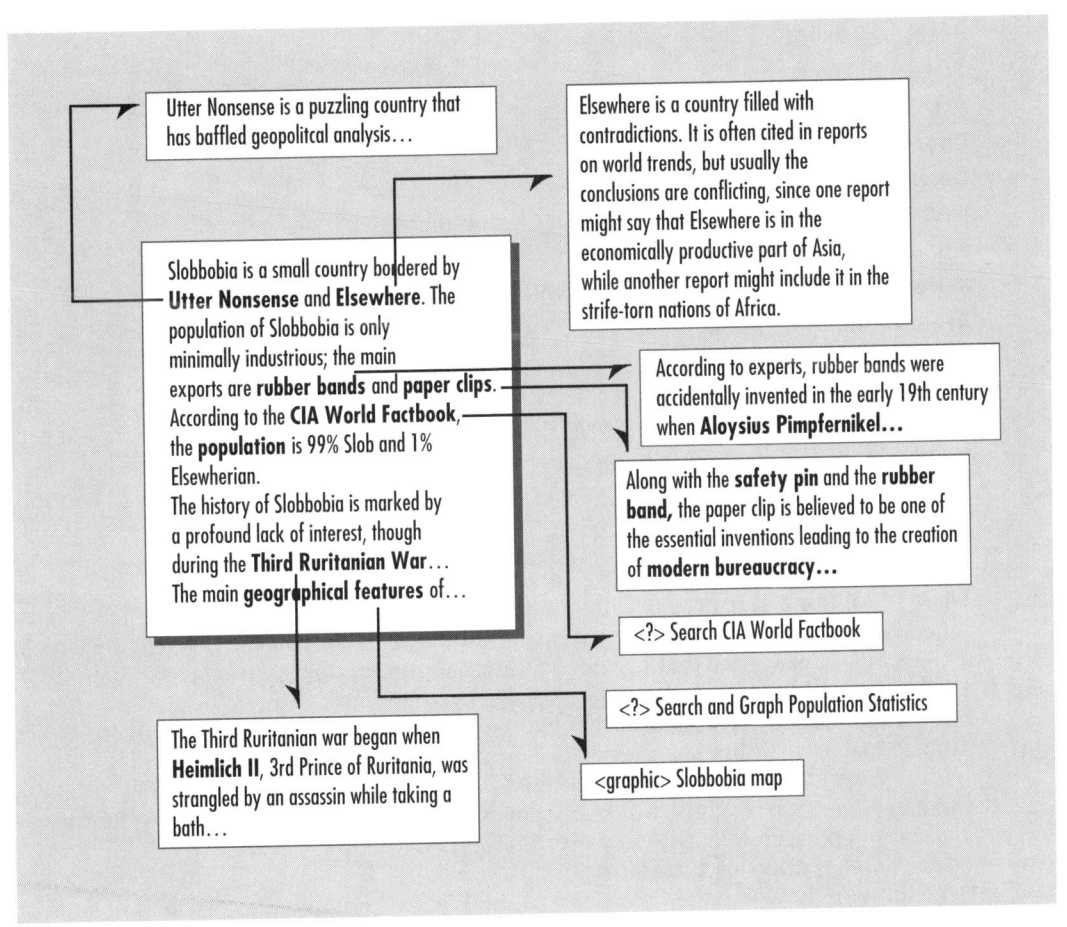

[Figure shows boxes with text connected by arrows:]

- Utter Nonsense is a puzzling country that has baffled geopolitcal analysis...

- Elsewhere is a country filled with contradictions. It is often cited in reports on world trends, but usually the conclusions are conflicting, since one report might say that Elsewhere is in the economically productive part of Asia, while another report might include it in the strife-torn nations of Africa.

- Slobbobia is a small country bordered by **Utter Nonsense** and **Elsewhere**. The population of Slobbobia is only minimally industrious; the main exports are **rubber bands** and **paper clips**. According to the **CIA World Factbook**, the **population** is 99% Slob and 1% Elsewherian.
The history of Slobbobia is marked by a profound lack of interest, though during the **Third Ruritanian War**... The main **geographical features** of...

- According to experts, rubber bands were accidentally invented in the early 19th century when **Aloysius Pimpfernikel**...

- Along with the **safety pin** and the **rubber band**, the paper clip is believed to be one of the essential inventions leading to the creation of **modern bureaucracy**...

- <?> Search CIA World Factbook

- <?> Search and Graph Population Statistics

- <graphic> Slobbobia map

- The Third Ruritanian war began when **Heimlich II**, 3rd Prince of Ruritania, was strangled by an assassin while taking a bath...

Figure 14-1 Following hypertext links

Even if you don't have Lynx (or choose to use a different browser), the basic techniques used in this chapter will still be useful to you. The actual way you browse documents and select links will differ, of course—some text browsers have you select links by number, while browsers with a graphical user interface let you use the mouse to click on them.

Gateways to Other Services

Lynx and the Web would be useful enough if they just let you read through text documents. The web concept is much more powerful than that, however. By following hypertext links you can access not only documents but indexes, databases, Gopher menus, archie searches, directories of ftp sites, and much more. The Web and your browser are thus a powerful way to access most of the important Internet tools discussed in this book.

INTERNET HOW-TO

Related Topics

To Learn How to...	See Chapter
Access remote services with telnet	10
Choose the right data retrieval tool	15
Download a file	9
Find information and services through Gopher menus	12
Find software with archie	11
Perform standard database searches with WAIS	13
Read Usenet newsgroups	4

How-Tos in this Chapter

14.1 Connect to the World Wide Web with Lynx
If Lynx is available at your Internet site, you can use it to connect to a Web server and view hypertext documents. If you don't have a browser, you can use telnet to connect to a public access Web browser.

14.2 View a document
You can move through a document from link to link or from page to page.

14.3 Follow a hypertext link
When one of the highlighted hypertext links interests you, you can select it and move to a document or service that provides additional information.

14.4 Get help with Lynx
Not surprisingly, Lynx provides help in a hypertext format that lets you choose topics from an extensive online manual.

14.5 Search for text in a document
Some documents may consist of many pages. You can use a string search to find items in a document, such as entries in a list of resources.

14.6 Get a copy of a document
Depending on how you are connected to the Web, you can save a copy of a document to your home directory, have a copy mailed to you, or even download a copy directly to your PC.

14.7 Send a comment to a document's author
Some documents identify their author or "owner." With such documents you can send a comment to that person, perhaps contributing to future versions of the document.

14.8 Recall a previously seen document
Lynx automatically keeps a list of documents that you have recently visited. You can use this "history list" to quickly return to a document and explore an alternative hypertext path from there.

14.9 Use bookmarks for fast navigation
Another way to get to particular documents quickly is to add them to your "bookmark page" the first time you visit them. Unlike the history list, the bookmark list is permanent until you delete or change it. You can thus build a custom menu of frequently used parts of the Web.

14.10 Use URLs for direct access to services
Each document or service accessible through the Web has a unique address called a URL (Uniform Resource Locator). The URL tells the browser how to get to the document. If

14 NAVIGATING THE INFORMATION HIGHWAY WITH THE WORLD WIDE WEB

you know the URL for a document or service, you can use it to jump there directly rather than having to go through the intermediate links.

14.11 Perform a database or index search
Some documents on the Web are "searchable" indexes or databases. When you access such documents you can enter some search words and get a list of matching records, which you can then access in the same way as you would other hypertext links.

14.12 Read Usenet news from the Web
By accessing a newsgroup through the Web you can get a listing of currently available articles in the form of links.

14.13 Look at an ftp site through the Web
The directories at an ftp site can be accessed as a set of links that in turn connect you to subdirectories and files.

14.14 Search Gopher menus from the Web
When accessed through the Web, a Gopher menu also becomes a series of links that in turn connect to submenus, documents, and services.

14.1 HOW DO I... Connect to the World Wide Web with Lynx?

COMPLEXITY: EASY

Problem
In order to explore the web of connected documents and resources, you must run a program called a browser that lets you display documents and move between them.

Technique
If you are a dial-up user with a text-based terminal, your best bet is to run Lynx, an increasingly available hypertext browser.

Steps
1. At the system prompt at your local Internet site, type

```
% lynx
```

   If Lynx is available at your site, you will see a screen like Figure 14-2. Note that the actual document you see will depend on what has been set up at your site; the figure shows the current Lynx default document.

2. If you get a "command not found" message, Lynx is probably not installed at your Internet site (though you can type the command `whereis lynx` to see if it exists somewhere, add it to your path if found (see Chapter 6), and then try the Lynx command again).

3. If Lynx is not available, you can telnet to a site that makes Lynx or another hypertext browser available for anonymous use. For example, the command,

```
% telnet ukanaix.cc.ukans.edu
```

   should connect you to Lynx at the University of Kansas. Type `www` at the login prompt.

4. To exit Lynx, press [q] and [y], or just press [Q].

INTERNET HOW-TO

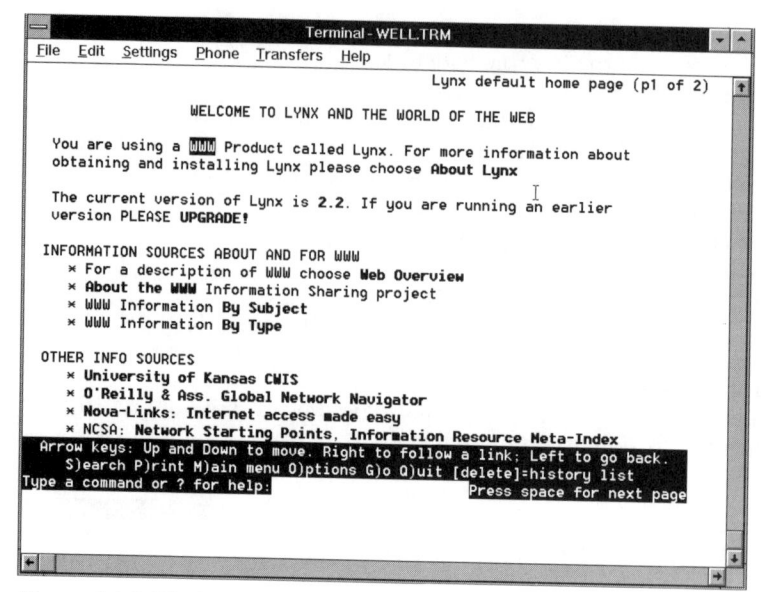

```
┌─────────────────────── Terminal - WELL.TRM ──────────────── ▼ ▲ ┐
 File  Edit  Settings  Phone  Transfers  Help
                                      Lynx default home page (p1 of 2)
              WELCOME TO LYNX AND THE WORLD OF THE WEB

   You are using a WWW Product called Lynx. For more information about
   obtaining and installing Lynx please choose About Lynx

   The current version of Lynx is 2.2. If you are running an earlier
   version PLEASE UPGRADE!

   INFORMATION SOURCES ABOUT AND FOR WWW
      * For a description of WWW choose Web Overview
      * About the WWW Information Sharing project
      * WWW Information By Subject
      * WWW Information By Type

   OTHER INFO SOURCES
      * University of Kansas CWIS
      * O'Reilly & Ass. Global Network Navigator
      * Nova-Links: Internet access made easy
      * NCSA: Network Starting Points, Information Resource Meta-Index
   Arrow keys: Up and Down to move. Right to follow a link; Left to go back.
       S)earch P)rint M)ain menu O)ptions G)o Q)uit [delete]=history list
   Type a command or ? for help:           Press space for next page
```

Figure 14-2 The home document on Lynx

How It Works

Lynx and other Web browsers use documents formatted in HTML (Hypertext Markup Language). These documents are formatted with links that in turn point to other resources, which can be text documents, multimedia (graphics or sound), or services such as indexes and databases. (Note that Lynx cannot display graphics or sound. A graphic will be indicated in the document by the symbol [Image]. Selecting the image will usually give you an opportunity to save it to disk so that you can display it later with an appropriate program.)

By default, Lynx starts with the "home document" set up when it was configured at your site. You can navigate to other documents by using the highlighted links (see How-To 14.3).

Comment

You can start Lynx so that it shows a document other than the default, by specifying the URL (Uniform Resource Locator) of the desired document. See How-To 14.10.

14.2 HOW DO I...
View a document?

COMPLEXITY: EASY

Problem

Many hypertext documents will be longer than a single page. The document in Figure 14-2, for example, has two pages, as indicated in the upper-right corner of the screen.

14 NAVIGATING THE INFORMATION HIGHWAY WITH THE WORLD WIDE WEB

Technique
You can use one of several pairs of keys to page forward or backward through the document.

Steps
1. To display the next page of the current document press (SPACEBAR) or (+). ((PGDN) on the keypad will also work on PC keyboards, if you have turned (NUM LOCK) on.)

   For example, if you press (SPACEBAR) at the screen in Figure 14-2, you will see the screen in Figure 14-3.

2. To display the previous page, press (b), (-), or (PGUP).

3. If you are browsing through the highlighted links (How-To 14.3), moving up past the first link on the page displays the previous page. Moving past the last link displays the next page.

How It Works
These simple paging keys let you examine a complete document. As you read the document, take note of the highlighted links and decide whether you would like to explore one or more of them (see How-To 14.3).

Comment
Most documents that are longer than two pages are lists of some kind (for example, lists of services or directories). It is sometimes more efficient to search such lists rather than page all the way through them (see How-To 14.5).

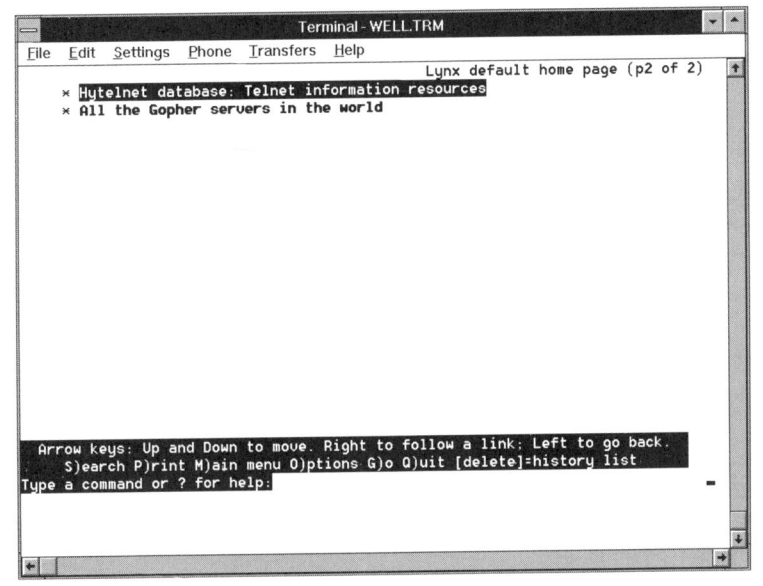

Figure 14-3 Moving to the next page in Lynx

INTERNET HOW-TO

14.3 HOW DO I...
Follow a hypertext link?

COMPLEXITY: EASY

Problem
When you see a highlighted link that interests you, you may want to select it to see what additional information will be provided.

Technique
In addition to simply reading a document (as in How-To 14.2), you can move between the various hypertext links embedded in the document. You navigate to the desired link using keys such as ↑ and ↓, and then select the link.

Steps
1. If you look closely at Figure 14-2, you see the hypertext links shown in boldface. For example, on page 1 of the home page, the words or phrases **WWW**, **About Lynx**, **UPGRADE**, **Web Overview**, **About the WWW**, **By Subject**, and **By Type** are examples of links.

   When you first arrive at a page of a document, the first link on the page is shown in reverse video (the link **WWW** in this case). This is the *current link*—the one that is ready to be selected.

2. To select a link, position the reverse video highlight by pressing the ↓ or ↑ key. As you might expect, the former takes you to the next link down the page, while the latter takes you to the previous link (toward the top of the page). Note: The TAB key also moves you to the next link down the page (but the SHIFT-TAB key will also move you forward, not back).

3. Once the link you want to follow is highlighted in reverse video, press → or ENTER to select it. The display will change to the document pointed to by the link. For example, pressing → at the link marked **By Subject** in Figure 14-2 takes you to the display shown in Figure 14-4.

4. If you want to move back to the *previous* document or level, press ←. For example, pressing ← in Figure 14-4 takes you back to Figure 14-2, with the reverse video highlight on the **By Subject** link.

5. You can press m at any time to return directly to the home document. You will be asked to confirm your intention. Press y.

How It Works
By navigating to and selecting a link you tell Lynx to go to the document "pointed to" by that link. The links and their pointers were set up by the creator of the document using the HTML format.

Comment
There are two other sets of navigation keys available. If you are accustomed to using the vi editor, you might want to press o to go to the Options screen, then press v and ENTER to turn on "vi mode." You can now use the h, j, k, and l keys to correspond to ←, ↓, ↑, and →, respectively.

418

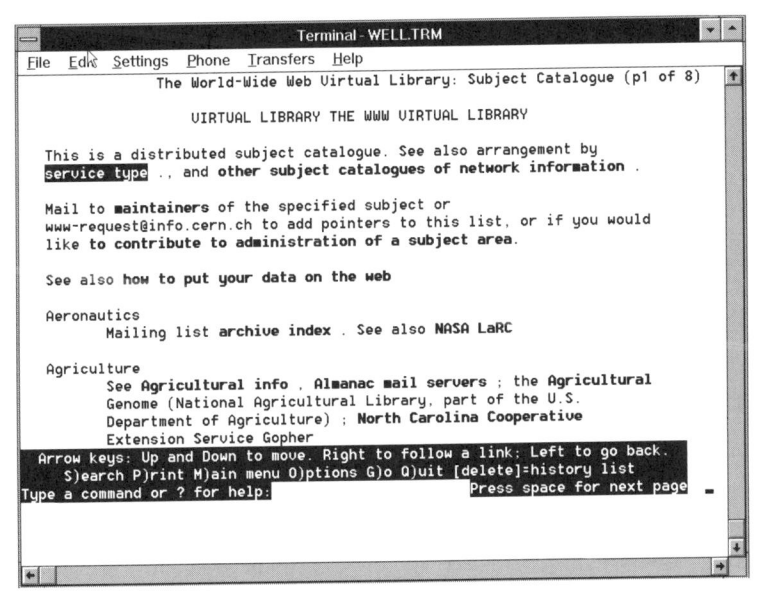

14 🌐 **NAVIGATING THE INFORMATION HIGHWAY WITH THE WORLD WIDE WEB**

```
                    Terminal - WELL.TRM
 File  Edit  Settings  Phone  Transfers  Help
             The World-Wide Web Virtual Library: Subject Catalogue (p1 of 8)

                     VIRTUAL LIBRARY THE WWW VIRTUAL LIBRARY

 This is a distributed subject catalogue. See also arrangement by
 service type .., and other subject catalogues of network information .

 Mail to maintainers of the specified subject or
 www-request@info.cern.ch to add pointers to this list, or if you would
 like to contribute to administration of a subject area.

 See also how to put your data on the web

 Aeronautics
          Mailing list archive index . See also NASA LaRC

 Agriculture
          See Agricultural info , Almanac mail servers ; the Agricultural
          Genome (National Agricultural Library, part of the U.S.
          Department of Agriculture) ; North Carolina Cooperative
          Extension Service Gopher
 Arrow keys: Up and Down to move. Right to follow a link; Left to go back.
    S)earch P)rint M)ain menu O)ptions G)o Q)uit [delete]=history list
 Type a command or ? for help:                         Press space for next page
```

Figure 14-4 Selecting the "By Subject" link

Emacs users can press (O), (M), and (ENTER) to activate the (CTRL)-(P), (CTRL)-(N), (CTRL)-(F), and (CTRL)-(B) keys that correspond to (↑), (↓), (→), and (←), respectively.

Note that there can be more than one link on the same line in a document. In this case you still use the (↑) or (↓) (or equivalent) key to move to the next link. If you use (←) or (→), you will jump to another page (and probably swear under your breath, at least until you get used to it).

Using a standard 101-key PC keyboard, you may find it convenient to leave (NUM-LOCK) on. In that configuration you can use the regular numeric keypad to browse between pages ((PGUP) and (PGDN)) and use the extra cursor keypad for browsing and selecting links with the arrow keys.

You can also select links by number rather than moving the highlight to them. To do this, press (O) to go to the Options screen, then press (K) and (ENTER). Links will now be displayed using numbers, and you can select them by pressing the number and pressing (ENTER). To return to the default display, repeat the (O), (K), and (ENTER) commands.

Unfortunately many links turn out to be unavailable for various reasons: either because they aren't configured properly or the server that provides them is down or busy. If you get a "this hypertext resource is not available at this time" message, try again during an off-peak time and you may get lucky.

INTERNET HOW-TO

14.4 HOW DO I...
Get help with Lynx?

COMPLEXITY: EASY

Problem
Although Lynx is an easy-to-use program, you may need to review command keys or get an explanation of certain features.

Technique
Lynx implements its online help using the same system of hypertext links used in the regular document display. Once you activate help, you navigate the help displays just as you would follow the links in a document.

Steps
1. Press (H) or (?). You will see the help document, as shown in Figure 14-5.

2. As you can see in the figure, there are several links in this document, each preceded by a bullet (*). Highlight the item you want by using (↑), (↓), or equivalent navigation keys, as described in How-To 14.3.

   For example, selecting the first link (which is in reverse video when you enter the help screen) gives you a list of the key commands used by Lynx:

```
HELP! — Press the left arrow key to exit help (p1 of 2)

      MOVEMENT:   Down arrow        - Highlight next topic
                  Up arrow          - Highlight previous topic
                  Right arrow,      - Jump to highlighted topic
                  Return, Enter
                  Left arrow        - Return to previous topic

      SCROLLING:  + (or space)      - Scroll down to next page
                  - (or b)          - Scroll up to previous page

      OTHER:      ? (or H)          - Help (this screen)
                  a                 - Add the current link to your bookmark file
                  c                 - Send a comment to the document owner
                  d                 - Download the current link
                  e                 - Edit the current file
                  g                 - Goto a user specified URL or file.
                  i                 - Show an index of documents
                  m                 - Return to main screen
                  o                 - Set your options
                  p                 - Print to a file, mail, printers, or other
Arrow keys: Up and Down to move. Right to follow a link; Left to go back.
```

3. Press (SPACEBAR) to see the second page of the keystroke help document:

```
HELP! — Press the left arrow key to exit help (p2 of 2)
                  q                 - Quit (Capital 'Q' for quick quit)
                  /                 - Search for a string within the current document
                  s                 - Enter a search string for an external search.
                  n                 - Go to the next search string
```

14 ⊕ NAVIGATING THE INFORMATION HIGHWAY WITH THE WORLD WIDE WEB

v	– View your bookmark file
z	– Cancel transfer in progress
[backspace]	– Go to the history page
=	– Show file and link info
\	– Toggle document source/rendered view
!	– Spawn your default shell
CTRL–R	– Reload current file and refresh the screen
CTRL–W	– Refresh the screen
CTRL–U	– Erase input line
CTRL–G	– Cancel input or transfer

You might want to skim through these listings to familiarize yourself with the commands available. The most important and useful ones are covered in how-tos later in this chapter.

4. If you select the **Lynx users guide version 2.2** link in Figure 14-5, you enter a document that organizes the complete online Lynx user's manual by topic link. Figure 14-6 shows the first (top-level) screen of the manual.

5. Navigate this screen as you would a regular document, using ↑ or ↓ to highlight a topic, → or ENTER to follow a link to more detailed information, or ← key to move back to the previous document (back up one level).

6. To exit the help system simply press ← until you are at the main screen in Figure 14-5, and then press ← again to return to the document you were viewing when you asked for help.

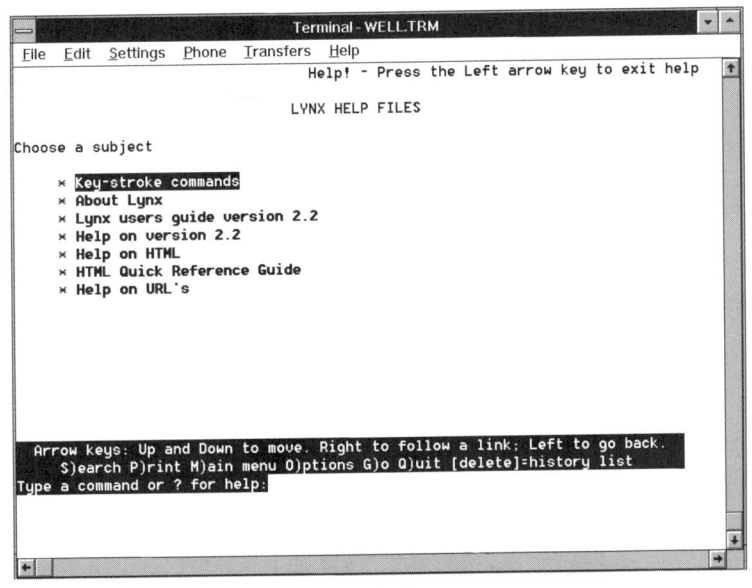

Figure 14-5 Main help document in Lynx

INTERNET HOW-TO

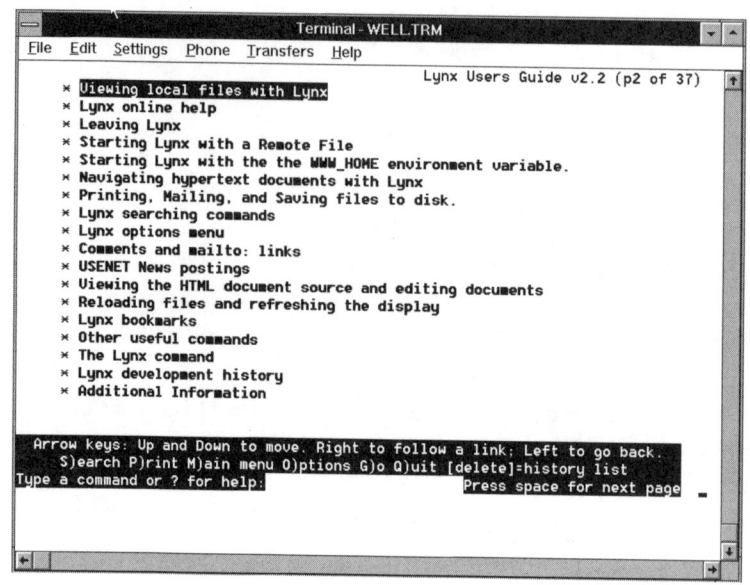

```
┌─                    Terminal - WELL.TRM                    ▼ ▲ ┐
 File  Edit  Settings  Phone  Transfers  Help
                                   Lynx Users Guide v2.2 (p2 of 37) ↑
      * Viewing local files with Lynx
      * Lynx online help
      * Leaving Lynx
      * Starting Lynx with a Remote File
      * Starting Lynx with the the WWW_HOME environment variable.
      * Navigating hypertext documents with Lynx
      * Printing, Mailing, and Saving files to disk.
      * Lynx searching commands
      * Lynx options menu
      * Comments and mailto: links
      * USENET News postings
      * Viewing the HTML document source and editing documents
      * Reloading files and refreshing the display
      * Lynx bookmarks
      * Other useful commands
      * The Lynx command
      * Lynx development history
      * Additional Information


  Arrow keys: Up and Down to move. Right to follow a link; Left to go back.
    S)earch P)rint M)ain menu O)ptions G)o Q)uit [delete]=history list
 Type a command or ? for help:                    Press space for next page
                                                                            ↓
 ←                                                                        → 
```

Figure 14-6 Online Lynx user's guide

How It Works
Lynx takes the logical and elegant approach of making its help screens regular hypertext documents, so that help is structured by topic and is accessed using the standard navigation keys.

Comment
You probably won't need to use the help facility very much, but you may want to look over the help screens once to note features you might have missed.

14.5 HOW DO I...
Search for text in a document?

COMPLEXITY EASY

Problem
Some documents (such as lists of resources) are long and can include many pages. You need a fast way to find the link you want.

Technique
You tell Lynx to search for a string in the document. If it finds the string and it is part of a link, you are then in position to follow the link.

Steps
1. Press ⟨/⟩. Lynx will ask you to specify the word you are searching for:

```
Enter a search string: history
```

Here, we are in the Subject Catalog document shown in Figure 14-4. After Lynx processes the search, it positions to a link that reads:

14 NAVIGATING THE INFORMATION HIGHWAY WITH THE WORLD WIDE WEB

History (separate list)

2. Choose this link to see the document shown in Figure 14-7. Here you can see various links to resources dealing with history.

3. Once you are positioned at the desired part of the catalog or list, you can select any link of interest using the link-following keys described in How-To 14.3. For example, you might select "Alphabetical list of history resources" and see a document whose first page looks like this:

```
FULL INDEX OF AVAILABLE RESOURCES

This is a full index of all available resources on HNSource

  * 1492 The Library of Congress exhibit on Columbus, composed of text
    and graphics files.
  * armadillo The Texas Studies Gopher at Rice University. Sources for
    K-12 teachers of Texas history and Government.
  * aarhms Newsletter of the American Academy of Research Historians
    of Medieval Spain.
  * adfa Australian Defense Force Academy Military history Files
  * absees American Bibliography of Slavic and East European Studies
    (login=absees;pw=slavbib)
  * biron The Essex Social Research Council searchable Archive.
    (Login: biron password: norib)
  * Black/African/Development Related Information Electronic sources
    on Black/African, indigenous peoples, sustainable development, and
    social activism.
  * byrd The Marshall University historical archives [ftp
```

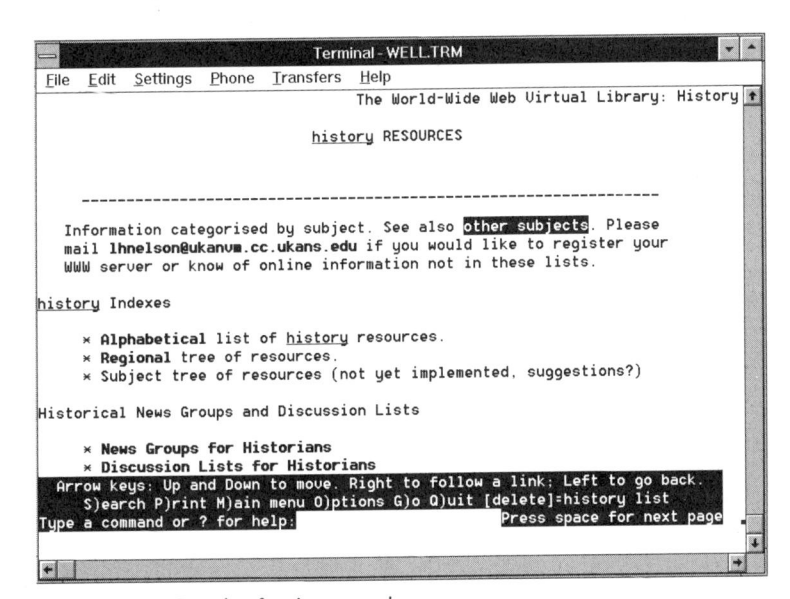

Figure 14-7 Result of string search

INTERNET HOW-TO

4. You then navigate this list (or perhaps search in it again), until you find a document or service of interest. (See How-To 14.6 for information about obtaining a copy of a file.)

How It Works
Lynx performs a simple string search for the word you specify. By default, the search is not case-sensitive.

Comment
You may need to repeat the search if you find a hit that doesn't show you the information you seek. Unfortunately you can't just press (/) and (ENTER) to repeat the search; you have to retype the string.

14.6 HOW DO I...
Get a copy of a document?

COMPLEXITY: INTERMEDIATE

Problem
Many Lynx documents may have extensive text (or other resources such as graphics or program files). You will probably want to get a copy of some documents or files for your own use.

Technique
Depending on how you are connected to the Web, you tell Lynx either to save a copy to disk or to mail the file to you.

Steps
1. Follow the appropriate link until you are looking at the document you wish to save.

2. Lynx manages file operations through its Printing Options menu. Press (p) to get to this menu. You will see a screen like the one in Figure 14-8.

3. If you are running a Lynx client on a machine with which you have an account (such as your local dial-up site), press (s) to save a copy of the document to disk. You will be prompted for a filename:

```
Please enter a file name: news:comp.binaries.ibm.pc
```

4. The default name given will be the file's name on its home system. You can accept this name by pressing (ENTER), or press (CTRL)-(U) to erase it, type your own filename, and press (ENTER). The file will be saved to your current working directory (usually your home directory at your Internet site). You can now download the file to your PC if you wish (see Chapter 9).

5. If you don't have an account on the machine that is running Lynx (for example, you used telnet and an anonymous login), the "save to disk" option won't be available (and won't be shown on the Printing Options screen). In this case, press (m). You will be prompted for an address to which the file is to be mailed:

```
Please enter a valid internet mail address: hrh@well.com
```

If you have an account, Lynx will know your address and supply it as the default. Otherwise, type your Internet address and press (ENTER). The document will be mailed to you.

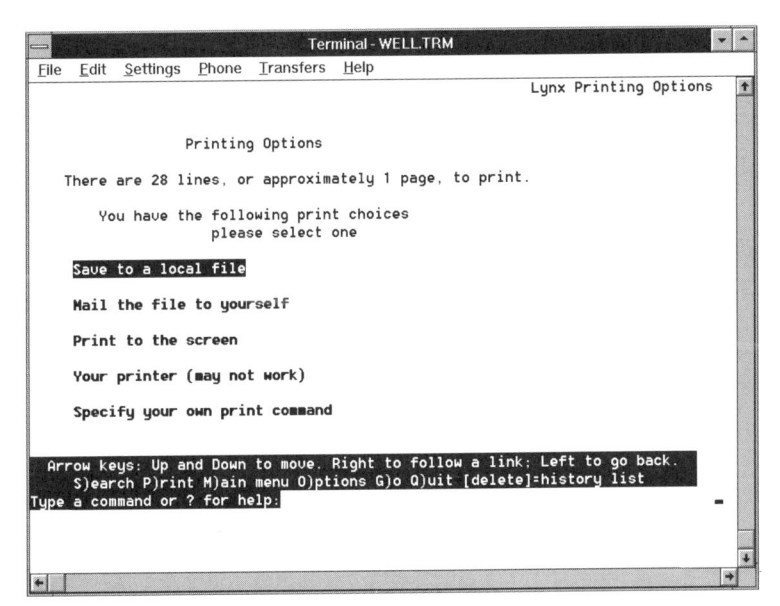

14 🌐 **NAVIGATING THE INFORMATION HIGHWAY WITH THE WORLD WIDE WEB**

```
┌─────────────────────── Terminal - WELL.TRM ──────────────── ▼ ▲ ┐
 File  Edit  Settings  Phone  Transfers  Help
                                              Lynx Printing Options

          Printing Options

 There are 28 lines, or approximately 1 page, to print.

     You have the following print choices
              please select one

 Save to a local file

 Mail the file to yourself

 Print to the screen

 Your printer (may not work)

 Specify your own print command


 Arrow keys: Up and Down to move. Right to follow a link; Left to go back.
    S)earch P)rint M)ain menu O)ptions G)o Q)uit [delete]=history list
 Type a command or ? for help:
```

Figure 14-8 The Lynx Printing Options screen

How It Works
Lynx provides two basic facilities for supplying a copy of a document: save to disk and mail. Since you can't save something to disk on a machine on which you don't have an account, anonymous users must use the mail option.

Comment
The save to disk option, if available, is preferable to mail, since you don't have to worry about binary files being mangled in transmission. Also, mail may take some time to arrive at your home site. Note that forthcoming versions of Lynx may support direct downloading of files to your PC.

Many Unix filenames are quite long. It is better to specify a shorter name if you are going to be downloading the file to your PC. If the file has several extensions reflecting archiving or compression steps, such as .gz, .tar, or .zip, however, you will have to resolve these first (see Chapter 8).

The other items on the Printing Options screen aren't generally useful. They involve printing, and usually won't work because they require that you have access to the remote printer or that the remote site has drivers that will work with *your* printer.

14.7 HOW DO I...
Send a comment to a document's author?

COMPLEXITY | INTERMEDIATE

Problem
You may have comments or suggestions about a resource offered through the Web, and you may wish to send them to the document's author.

425

INTERNET HOW-TO

Technique
If the document has a listed "owner" you can send that person a comment using a simple command.

Steps
1. Follow the appropriate link until you are viewing the document about which you wish to comment.

2. Press (c). If the document has an owner, you will be prompted for a comment:

```
Do you wish to send a comment? [N]
```

3. Press (y) if you want to write a comment. You'll be asked for your name. This is optional: you can type your name and press (ENTER), or just press (ENTER) if you want to comment anonymously.

```
You are now sending a comment to:
      montulli@ukanaix.cc.ukans.edu
 Please enter your name, or leave it blank if you wish to remain anonymous
Personal_Name: Harry Henderson
```

4. You'll be asked for an (optional) e-mail address that can be used for replies to your comment. You'll also be asked to specify the subject of your comment:

```
Please enter a mail address or some other
 means to contact you, if you desire a response.

From: hrh@well.com
Please enter a subject line
Subject: A source you might want to add to the History resources list
```

5. You're ready to enter the text of your comment. Press (ENTER) after each line. When you're done, type a period (.) on its own line and press (ENTER):

```
Please enter your message below.
 When you are done, press enter and put a single period (.)
 on a line and press enter again.

The Institute of Slobbobian History now has a gopher site. It specializes
in Slobbobian economic and social statistics and also provides a current
Outer Slobbobian weather report.
.
```

6. Finally, you'll be asked to confirm that you want to send the comment:

```
Send this comment? (y/n)y
```

Press (y) to send the comment, or (n) to cancel the procedure.

How It Works
Lynx leads you through the creation of a mail message to the person listed as the document's author.

Note that many documents don't have listed authors. If you press (c) for such a document, you'll be given a message that the document has no owner and thus you can't send a comment. If you wish, you can get more information about a document (including the name of its owner, if any) before making your comment. See How-To 14.10.

14 🌐 NAVIGATING THE INFORMATION HIGHWAY WITH THE WORLD WIDE WEB

Comment
Many documents don't have listed owners. No text editor is invoked when you write a comment, so it is best to keep comments brief. However, you can create your comment in an "offline" editor using Windows or a Mac, and then paste the text into the communications window.

14.8 HOW DO I... *Recall a previously seen document?*

COMPLEXITY: EASY

Problem
Navigating the Web is a matter of choosing and exploring alternative paths as you pursue a subject of interest. Sometimes you'll find it useful to be able to backtrack to an earlier point and take a different path.

Technique
You can use the history list to return to a recently visited document.

Steps
1. Press BACKSPACE or DEL. You will see a History Page screen like the one in Figure 14-9.

   Your history page shows documents you have visited recently, starting with the most recent one.

2. Use the ↑, ↓, or equivalent navigation keys to highlight the document you want.

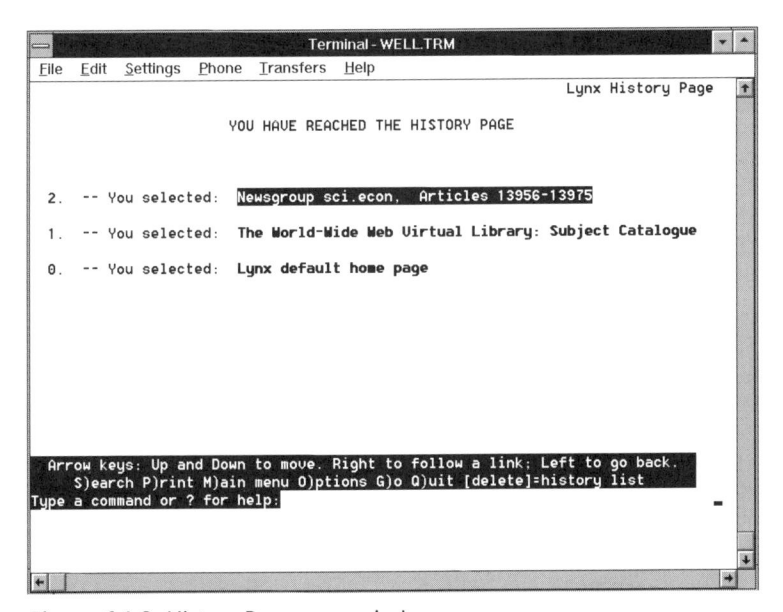

Figure 14-9 History Page screen in Lynx

427

INTERNET HOW-TO

3. Use ⟶ or ENTER to select the document. The document will be displayed and become the new current document.

How It Works
Lynx makes a note of documents you visit during the session and records their location (URL). This enables Lynx to send you back to a previously visited document without your having to go through the intermediate links.

Comment
The history feature can be very useful. You can explore several levels of links from a main document and then quickly return to that document to pursue a different path.

14.9 HOW DO I...
Use bookmarks for fast navigation?

COMPLEXITY: EASY

Problem
Once you have used the Web for a while, you will probably find that you are revisiting particularly useful documents or services. A quick way to jump directly to a favorite area would be helpful.

Technique
You can add bookmarks to your bookmark page and then use that page as a kind of menu from which you can jump to frequently used services.

Steps
1. When you are viewing a document or service that you want to add to your bookmarks, press (a).

2. To go to your bookmark page, press (v). You will see a screen like Figure 14-10.

3. Use the arrow keys as usual to highlight the document or service you want. Press ENTER or ⟶ to go directly to that location.

How It Works
When you ask Lynx to make a bookmark, it records the URL of that document and creates a link to it. In essence, the bookmark page is simply a hypertext document that Lynx writes for you, embedding the links you have created.

Comment
As noted on the bookmark page, you can use any plain text editor to remove bookmarks that are no longer wanted. Simply delete the line containing the bookmark and resave the file. Note that Lynx saves your bookmarks in a file called lynx.bookmarks.html in your current working directory.

If you are using Lynx anonymously, you can't have permanent bookmarks since there is no place to save them.

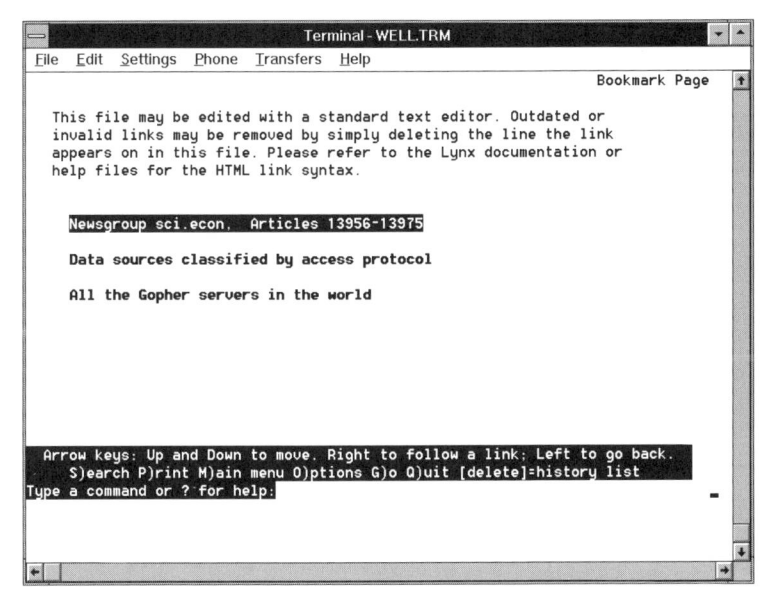

14 NAVIGATING THE INFORMATION HIGHWAY WITH THE WORLD WIDE WEB

Figure 14-10 Bookmark Page screen in Lynx

14.10 HOW DO I... Use URLs for direct access to services?

COMPLEXITY: INTERMEDIATE

Problem
Sometimes people publicize various documents or resources that are available on the Web. It would be very difficult to have to specify the whole series of links leading from the home page to the document, and besides, people can use different home pages. An "absolute" way of locating documents is necessary.

Technique
A specification called a URL (Uniform Resource Locator) is used to describe the nature and location of a document or resource. A URL consists of the following parts:

protocol://server/path

➤ *Protocol* refers to the kind of resource this item is and the way it is accessed. Examples of protocols include "file" (for an ordinary file or ftp resource), Gopher, WAIS, and news.
➤ *Server* refers to the site where the document or resource is made available. This is usually the regular Internet address for the site.
➤ *Path* refers to the location of the document at that site, for example, the directory and/or subdirectory and the filename.

For example, a file might have a URL like this:

```
file://ftp.apple.com/pub/mac/utils.htq
```

INTERNET HOW-TO

This means that this is a regular file obtainable by ftp from the site ftp.apple.com, in the directory /pub/mac, and having the filename utils.htq.

A Gopher server might have a URL like this:

```
gopher://gopher.well.com
```

This specifies the Gopher at The WELL.
A WAIS database source might have a URL like this:

```
wais://quake.think.com/directory-of-servers
```

And a newsgroup uses a simplified URL that looks like this:

```
news:rec.games.ibm.pc
```

Note that no server is currently specified for a newsgroup. Usually the local news server is specified when the browser is configured.

Steps

1. To have Lynx jump directly to a document by URL, press (g). Lynx will ask you for the URL to use:

```
Filename or URL to open:
```

2. Type in the URL and press (ENTER). You will go directly to that document or server.

3. To find the URL and other information about a document you are currently viewing, press (=). You will see a display like this:

```
YOU HAVE REACHED THE INFORMATION PAGE

File that you are currently viewing

    Linkname:  Index: Full Index of Resources
         URL:  http://history.cc.ukans.edu/history/index.html
    Owner(s):  mailto:lhnelson@ukanvm.cc.ukans.edu
        size:  106 lines
   Lynx mode:  normal

Link that you currently have selected

    Linkname:  adfa
    Filename:  gopher://ccadfa.cc.adfa.oz.au/Library/mihilist
```

How It Works

The URL tells Lynx (and other browsers) both *how* and *where* to accesses the document. The "how" is an access method such as ftp, Gopher, WAIS, or news. The "where" is specified by the address of the server and also (in the case of files) the path and filename.

Comment

URLs can be tedious to type. Once you've accessed a document by URL, however, you can press (a) and add it to your bookmark page (see How-To 14.9). You can then access the document without worrying about the URL.

14   NAVIGATING THE INFORMATION HIGHWAY WITH THE WORLD WIDE WEB

Unfortunately, URLs can become obsolete if a server is no longer available or a file is moved to a different location.

14.11 HOW DO I...
Perform a database or index search?

COMPLEXITY: INTERMEDIATE

Problem
Some resources available through the Web are actually indexes or databases. You may want to search these for specified information.

Technique
You select the index or database and then ask Lynx to submit a search request for you.

Steps
1. Follow the appropriate link and select the service you want. You can usually identify an index or database because a note like this will be displayed at the bottom of the screen:

```
This is a searchable index.  Use 's' to search
```

2. Press `s` to search the index or database. You will be prompted for the word(s) to search for:

```
Specify search words. DOS 6.0
```

Here we happen to be searching a database of README files relating to PC software. We specified the phrase DOS 6.0.

3. The results of our search are displayed as a series of links. You navigate through the links as usual, viewing and/or saving the documents you want:

```
Select one of:
   (FILE) /users/cwis/databases/ibm.pc.alt.FAQ 9) Why does DOS use the \
      instead of a / as a directory name separator?
   (FILE) /users/cwis/databases/ibm.pc.alt.FAQ 5.4) How do I turn the
      ECHO off from a batch file?
   (FILE) /users/cwis/databases/ibm.pc.alt.FAQ 5.2) Where can I get
      UNIX-like utilities? How do I remove a TSR from memory?
   (FILE) /users/cwis/databases/ibm.pc.alt.FAQ 1.4) The unpacking program
      said that the archive was corrupted.
   (FILE) /users/cwis/databases/ibm.pc.alt.FAQ 2.2) How do I do direct
      video access from C? Read/write an arbitrary byte?
   (FILE) /users/cwis/databases/ibm.pc.alt.FAQ 2.4) What is the
      difference between extended/expanded memory, and
   (FILE) /users/cwis/databases/ibm.pc.alt.FAQ 3.3) What is the file
      format that application X uses? What are the GIF,
```

How It Works
Lynx submits your search words to the index or database. When the results are returned, Lynx uses their URLs to build a set of links that you use to choose the document you want.

Comment

Searchable indexes can often be found through documents that contain reference resources. For example, here is one from the University of Kansas:

```
REFERENCE SHELF

    Directory services
            Phonebooks, e-mail addresses, and directory information.

    Guides and tutorials
            Guides to the Internet, UNIX, KU computers, and more.

    Internet resources
            Archie, Gopher, WAIS, World-Wide Web, et al.

    Library resources
            Access to the KU library and libraries around the world.

    Miscellaneous resources
            INK, Periodic Table of the Elements, Weather, History
```

Here there are several sources of indexes or databases: Directory services, Internet resources, Library resources (catalogs), and Miscellaneous resources.

Note that WAIS sources are searched in the same way as other searchable indexes. See Chapter 13 for more information on doing WAIS searches.

14.12 HOW DO I... Read Usenet news from the Web?

COMPLEXITY: INTERMEDIATE

Problem

Usenet newsgroups can be valuable resources for current information, particularly on technical matters. Unfortunately, there are hundreds of newsgroups to choose from, and it's hard to find the ones that fit a given context.

Technique

The Web can present newsgroups in two different ways: through the regular newsgroup hierarchy or as resources in particular subject areas. You can thus browse the newsgroup structure directly, or you can find newsgroups as an incidental part of searching the Subject Catalog document or other resources.

Steps

1. To browse the newsgroup hierarchy, choose the "WWW Information **By Type**" link in the home document in Figure 14-2. You will see a document like the one shown in Figure 14-11.

2. Choose the **Network News** link from this document. You will see a display of the newsgroup hierarchy, as in Figure 14-12.

3. Choose the general category of newsgroups you want to see (for example, **sci** for science). Follow this link to the subcategory (for example, sci.econ for economics).

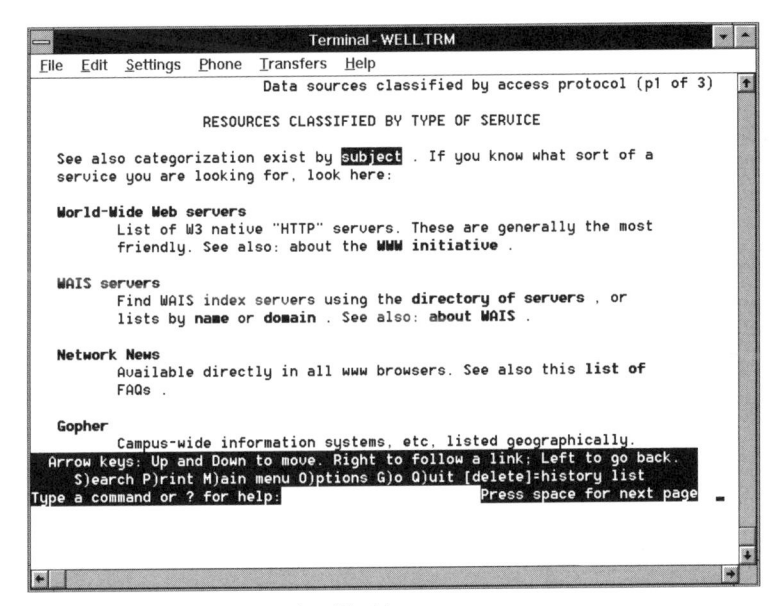

14 NAVIGATING THE INFORMATION HIGHWAY WITH THE WORLD WIDE WEB

Figure 14-11 Resources classified by type

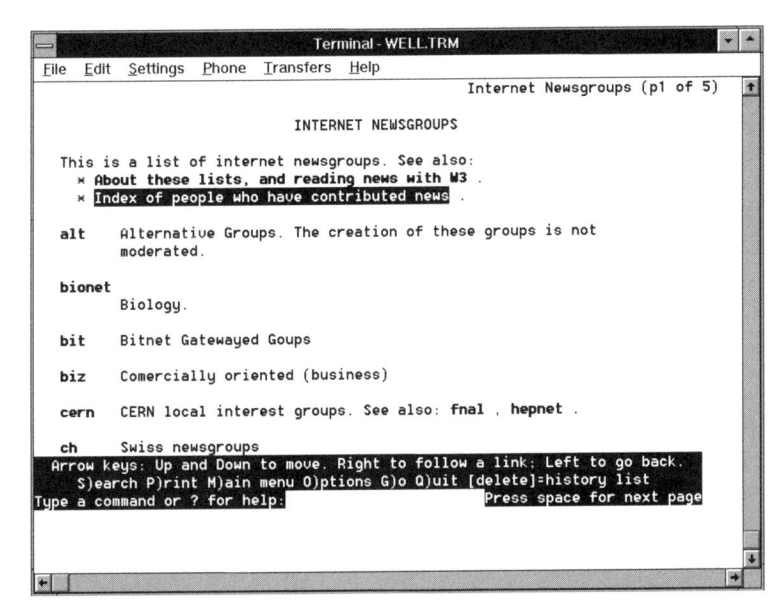

Figure 14-12 Browsing the news hierarchy

(Sometimes there can be several intermediate categories, as in the "comp" groups. See Chapter 4 for more information about how newsgroups are organized.)

INTERNET HOW-TO

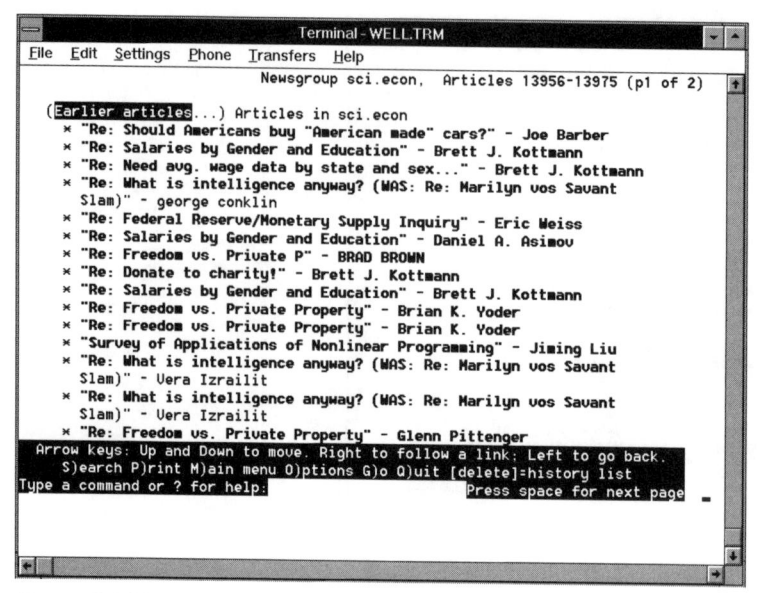

```
┌─────────────────────── Terminal - WELL.TRM ───────────────────┬─┐
│ File  Edit  Settings  Phone  Transfers  Help                  │ │
│              Newsgroup sci.econ,  Articles 13956-13975 (p1 of 2) │↑│
│ (Earlier articles...) Articles in sci.econ                    │ │
│   * "Re: Should Americans buy "American made" cars?" - Joe Barber │ │
│   * "Re: Salaries by Gender and Education" - Brett J. Kottmann │ │
│   * "Re: Need avg. wage data by state and sex..." - Brett J. Kottmann │ │
│   * "Re: What is intelligence anyway? (WAS: Re: Marilyn vos Savant │ │
│     Slam)" - george conklin                                   │ │
│   * "Re: Federal Reserve/Monetary Supply Inquiry" - Eric Weiss │ │
│   * "Re: Salaries by Gender and Education" - Daniel A. Asimov │ │
│   * "Re: Freedom vs. Private P" - BRAD BROWN                  │ │
│   * "Re: Donate to charity!" - Brett J. Kottmann               │ │
│   * "Re: Salaries by Gender and Education" - Brett J. Kottmann │ │
│   * "Re: Freedom vs. Private Property" - Brian K. Yoder       │ │
│   * "Re: Freedom vs. Private Property" - Brian K. Yoder       │ │
│   * "Survey of Applications of Nonlinear Programming" - Jiming Liu │ │
│   * "Re: What is intelligence anyway? (WAS: Re: Marilyn vos Savant │ │
│     Slam)" - Vera Izrailit                                    │ │
│   * "Re: What is intelligence anyway? (WAS: Re: Marilyn vos Savant │ │
│     Slam)" - Vera Izrailit                                    │ │
│   * "Re: Freedom vs. Private Property" - Glenn Pittenger      │ │
│ Arrow keys: Up and Down to move. Right to follow a link; Left to go back. │ │
│ S)earch P)rint M)ain menu O)ptions G)o Q)uit [delete]=history list │ │
│ Type a command or ? for help:              Press space for next page │↓│
└───────────────────────────────────────────────────────────────┴─┘
```

Figure 14-13 Newsgroup listing from the Web

4. Now try the **By Subject** link from the home document and find the subject that interests you. (You can use the (/) key to search for a string, as described in How-To 14.5.) Look for newsgroups as part of the subject area resource listings you find. For example, the sci.econ newsgroup is listed as a resource in the Economics resource list that you can reach by searching the Subject Catalog.

Select the link for the newsgroup you want.

5. Whether you select the newsgroup from the hierarchy or from a resource list, you will be presented with a list of articles from the newsgroup, as shown in Figure 14-13. Simply follow the links and read and/or save the articles you want.

How It Works
Lynx uses a URL and a link to the local news server to obtain the newsgroup you want and display its articles as a series of links.

Comment
Some newsgroups can be very large. If you will be reading a group on a regular basis, it is probably best to use a news reader such as nn (see Chapter 4), which has more powerful facilities for managing news articles.

14 ⊕ NAVIGATING THE INFORMATION HIGHWAY WITH THE WORLD WIDE WEB

14.13 HOW DO I...
Look at an ftp site through the Web?

COMPLEXITY: INTERMEDIATE

Problem
While pursuing a subject of interest you may want to browse and select files at an ftp site that you have located through a resource listing.

Technique
You browse the directories and files at the ftp site as a series of links. You can also access archie through the Web and use it to find sites that have a specific file.

Steps
1. Select the **By Type** link on the main document in Figure 14-2. You will see the screen shown in Figure 14-11. Press (SPACEBAR) to go to the next page, and select the link to ftp.

2. Follow the link to a list of ftp sites and select one to browse. Alternatively, if you know the location of an ftp site, you can type (g) and construct a URL with its name. For example, to go to ftp.apple.com, press (g), type `file://ftp.apple.com`, and press (ENTER).

3. Once you link to an ftp site you will see its root directory, with a series of links representing subdirectories, as in Figure 14-14. Select a link to view a list of subdirectories; repeat until you see the names of actual files. (Don't forget that you can use (←) to move back up a level.)

4. When you see the link for a file you want, press (p) and save or mail yourself a copy (see How-To 14.6).

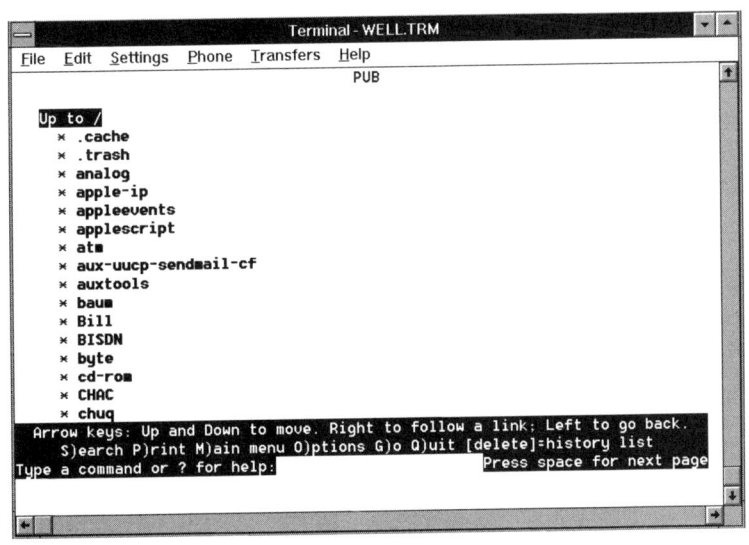

Figure 14-14 ftp directory hierarchy as links

435

INTERNET HOW-TO

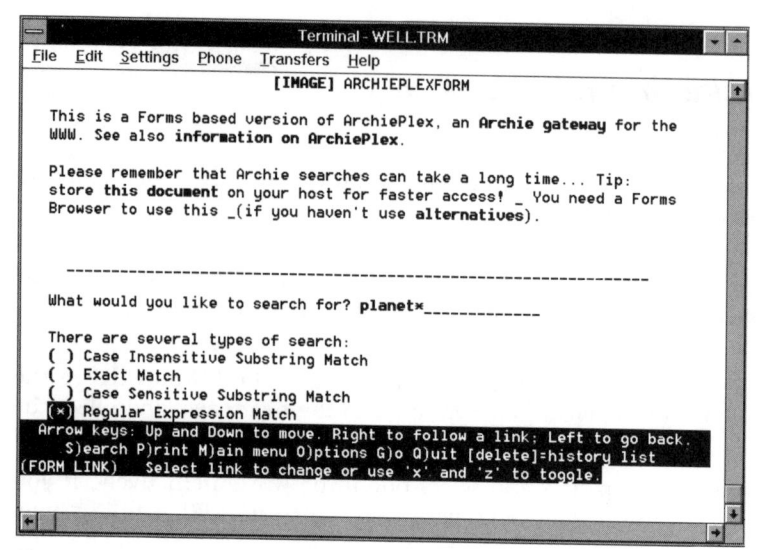

```
┌─                       Terminal - WELL.TRM                    ▼ ▲
 File  Edit  Settings  Phone  Transfers  Help
                      [IMAGE] ARCHIEPLEXFORM                       ↑
 This is a Forms based version of ArchiePlex, an Archie gateway for the
 WWW. See also information on ArchiePlex.

 Please remember that Archie searches can take a long time... Tip:
 store this document on your host for faster access! _ You need a Forms
 Browser to use this _(if you haven't use alternatives).

 ----------------------------------------------------------------
 What would you like to search for? planet×_____

 There are several types of search:
 ( ) Case Insensitive Substring Match
 ( ) Exact Match
 ( ) Case Sensitive Substring Match
 (×) Regular Expression Match
 Arrow keys: Up and Down to move. Right to follow a link; Left to go back.
   S)earch P)rint M)ain menu O)ptions G)o Q)uit [delete]=history list
 (FORM LINK)   Select link to change or use 'x' and 'z' to toggle.
```

Figure 14-15 Archie search form

    5. When you are finished browsing the site, you may find it easiest to press (m) to go back to the main document, or use the history list to backtrack to where you started the search (see How-To 14.8).

How It Works
Lynx assembles the directory and file information from the ftp site and uses the URL for each item to create a link that you can browse or select. When you select something, Lynx uses ftp to obtain it for you.

Comment
You can also use archie from the Web to find files by ftp. Follow the link from **By Type** to "search with archie" (or something similar). You will be connected to a service that submits archie searches. Most of these services use a form like the one shown in Figure 14-15.

    Fill out the form (use the arrow keys to move from one place to another), and press (ENTER) to enter text or toggle a setting. Press (SPACEBAR) to go to the next page of the form. To submit the search, select the Submit button and press (ENTER).

    The results of your search will be presented as a list of links. Highlight the desired link and press (p) to obtain a copy of the file (see How-To 14.6).

14.14 HOW DO I...
Search Gopher menus from the Web?

COMPLEXITY: INTERMEDIATE

Problem
Gopher and the Web are both powerful ways of organizing information and resources on the Internet. It can be convenient to explore the menus of a Gopher server from the Web.

Technique
You select a Gopher server or Gopher resource and then browse its menus, which appear as links.

Steps

1. Select the **By Type** link on the main document in Figure 14-2. You will see the screen shown in Figure 14-11. Select the link to Gopher.

2. Follow the link to a list of Gopher sites and select one to browse. If you know the location of a Gopher site, you can press `g` and construct a URL with its name. For example, to go to The WELL's Gopher, press `g`, type `gopher://well.com`, and press `ENTER`.

3. Once you link to a Gopher site you will see its main menu, with a series of links representing submenus and/or individual menu items, as in Figure 14-16. Select a link to view a submenu or menu item. (Don't forget that you can use `←` to move back up a level.)

4. When you see the link for a file you want, press `p` and save or mail yourself a copy (see How-To 14.6).

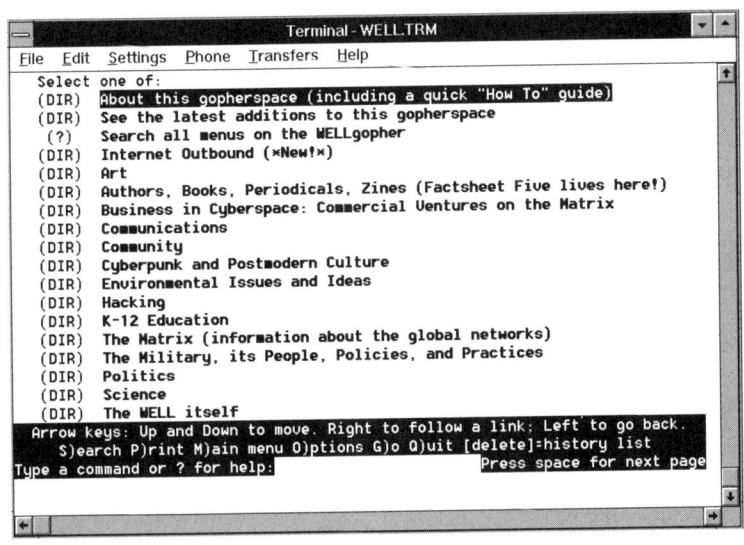

```
                    Terminal - WELL.TRM
File  Edit  Settings  Phone  Transfers  Help
   Select one of:
   (DIR)   About this gopherspace (including a quick "How To" guide)
   (DIR)   See the latest additions to this gopherspace
    (?)    Search all menus on the WELLgopher
   (DIR)   Internet Outbound (*New!*)
   (DIR)   Art
   (DIR)   Authors, Books, Periodicals, Zines (Factsheet Five lives here!)
   (DIR)   Business in Cyberspace: Commercial Ventures on the Matrix
   (DIR)   Communications
   (DIR)   Community
   (DIR)   Cyberpunk and Postmodern Culture
   (DIR)   Environmental Issues and Ideas
   (DIR)   Hacking
   (DIR)   K-12 Education
   (DIR)   The Matrix (information about the global networks)
   (DIR)   The Military, its People, Policies, and Practices
   (DIR)   Politics
   (DIR)   Science
   (DIR)   The WELL itself
   Arrow keys: Up and Down to move. Right to follow a link; Left to go back.
       S)earch P)rint M)ain menu O)ptions G)o Q)uit [delete]=history list
   Type a command or ? for help:            Press space for next page
```

Figure 14-16 Gopher menu as Web links

INTERNET HOW-TO

5. When you are finished browsing the site, you may find it easiest to press Ⓜ to go back to the main document, or use the history list to backtrack to where you started the search (see How-To 14.8).

How It Works

Lynx assembles the menu and file information from the Gopher site and uses the URL for each item to create a link that you can browse or select. When you select something, Lynx uses Gopher to obtain it for you.

Comment

Gopher resources on the Web typically also offer the ability to do Veronica searches to find menu items from all of Gopherspace. See Chapter 12 for more information on Gopher and Veronica.

15

Choosing Tools and Using Resources

How do I....

15.1   Approach the Internet with a question or problem
15.2   Choose the right communication tool
15.3   Choose the right data retrieval tool
15.4   Choose the right navigation tool
15.5   Use The Desktop Internet Reference
15.6   Find services with Hytelnet
15.7   Create my own resource guide
15.8   Find out more about the Internet

If you have worked through the preceding chapters of this book, you have seen that the Internet offers a great variety of tools for communicating with other users (mail, talk, and news programs), accessing files and services (ftp and telnet), retrieving data from many sources (archie, Veronica, WAIS, and other searchable indexes), and navigating the information highway (Gopher and World Wide Web). These tools vary considerably in sophistication, ease of use, breadth of coverage, and reliability.

Often you can use more than one vehicle to get to the same destination. For example, you can telnet to a server directly, discover the service in a Gopher menu, or find it through a hypertext link in a Web document. The method you choose depends on many factors: how much you already know about what you're looking for, the *kind* of information you seek (how specific or general), and even pure chance (part of the fun of browsing in Gopher or WWW is to explore whatever strikes your fancy).

This final chapter looks at broad strategies for choosing tools and accessing resources on the network. Unlike earlier chapters, which provided exact and detailed recipes, this

INTERNET HOW-TO

chapter offers offer guidelines, illustrations, and examples of methods that you can try out as you craft your own style of working with the Internet.

Choosing the Right Tool

Just as tools such as screwdrivers and wrenches are better suited for some jobs than for others, information tools also have their particular strengths and weaknesses. For example, one tool may be set up for browsing, while another is geared for answering specific queries in a database. Trying to use a tool for a purpose for which it wasn't designed is likely to be frustrating and unrewarding.

The approach in the first set of how-tos in this chapter will be to place tools in three broad categories: communications, data retrieval, and navigation. Within each group you will look at the tools available, the strengths and weaknesses of each, and the circumstances under which a given tool is likely to be most useful.

Using Resource Guides

Besides mastering the appropriate use of information tools, using the Internet effectively also requires your gradually developing a repertoire of services that you can easily find and connect to for a variety of needs. Therefore the second part of this chapter deals with the use of resource guides for finding services on the Internet. You will look at examples of resource guides that you can run on your PC while connected to the Internet, and even look at a way that you can "roll your own" resource guide as you explore the net.

Keeping Up with the Info Wave

The Internet is like a rapidly growing boomtown. The streets are filled with activity, there are traffic jams now and then, and the maps given out by the Chamber of Commerce are always a bit out of date. This chapter closes with a few tips for keeping in touch with trends and changes on the net, and some suggestions for further reading.

Related Topics

To Learn How to...	See Chapter
Access remote services with telnet	10
Browse the World Wide Web	14
Find information and services through Gopher menus	12
Find software with archie	11
Get files with ftp	7
Perform standard database searches with WAIS	13
Read Usenet newsgroups	4

How-Tos in this Chapter

15.1 Approach the Internet with a question or problem

Before you start running programs and issuing commands, it's good to take a moment to think about what you want to accomplish with the Internet during the coming session. Getting a clear picture of what you want to do or know is the first step in planning your approach.

15 CHOOSING TOOLS AND USING RESOURCES

15.2 Choose the right communication tool
How do you want to talk? One to one? One to many? A small group? Is immediate response essential, or can people respond at leisure? The answers to questions like these will help you pick the right communication tool.

15.3 Choose the right data retrieval tool
The Internet offers a bewildering variety of databases and indexes of various sorts. You need to think about what *kind* of database you might want to use, as well as which *particular* database is most likely to have the kind of information you seek. Thinking about what you want to know (and *how much* you want to know) can help you find the right one.

15.4 Choose the right navigation tool
Gopher and World Wide Web offer different kinds of "maps" of the information and services available on the Internet. By understanding how these approaches differ and looking at your particular needs, you can decide how best to navigate the information highway.

15.5 Use The Desktop Internet Reference
The Desktop Internet Reference is a free Windows Help file that brings together a cornucopia of guides to services and a selection of interesting readings about the net. You'll try out this resource guide by finding and connecting to a library database.

15.6 Find services with Hytelnet
Hytelnet is another form of hypertext resource guide that you can pop up in DOS or use in Windows or other platforms. It specializes in quick access to the command you need in order to connect to a particular service.

15.7 Create your own resource guide
Just as people keep a file of useful phone contacts and addresses, you can use tools available in your Windows or Mac environment to compile your own guidebook to favorite Internet services.

15.8 Find out more about the Internet
Finally, this how-to offers some suggestions on readings and online sources that you can use both to learn more about the Internet and to keep up with new developments.

15.1 HOW DO I...
Approach the Internet with a question or problem?

COMPLEXITY | INTERMEDIATE

Problem
It's always a temptation to jump right in and then think about what you want to do. Indeed, spontaneous interactive exploration is one of the Internet's main attractions. Nevertheless, when you are looking for specific kinds of information or services, a more methodical approach can be helpful.

Technique
Think about what you want to know or do, characterize your goal, and then think about approaches that are likely to be helpful.

INTERNET HOW-TO

Steps
1. Categorize your general goal. If your task primarily involves the need to *communicate* with people or express yourself in some way, turn to How-To 15.2.
2. If you mainly need to *find* some kind of information that is likely to be available in a database or index, turn to How-To 15.3.
3. If you don't have a very specific idea of the information you want, or you want to *explore* a general area of interest, turn to How-To 15.4.

How It Works
The kinds of tools you will use depend on many factors. Broadly speaking, Internet tools can be categorized by their purpose: communication, retrieval, or navigation.

The communication category is pretty obvious. The choice between data retrieval and general navigation is more subtle, however. Generally speaking, you should look for a retrieval tool (How-To 15.3) if:

➤ You already know the name of an index or database that is likely to have the information you need

➤ The information is fairly specific (for example, rainfall records for California is specific, but weather is general)

➤ The information is highly structured such that it is likely to be found in a database (for example, climate or economic statistics or lists of names and addresses)

➤ You don't have much time to find the information (and thus a browsing tool like the Web may take too long to use)

On the other hand, you should consider a navigation or browsing tool (How-To 15.4) if:

➤ You're not sure what you're looking for, or you have only a vague idea (for example "stuff about computer games")

➤ You want to make a general survey of a topic (for example, mathematics)

➤ You have time to explore the byways of the information highway with a browsing or navigation tool

Comment
The Internet communication tools are analogous to the telephone, newspapers, and TV. The data retrieval tools are like an airline or railroad that runs in a structured way, serving designated destinations. The navigation tools are more like renting a car and driving about on your own.

Note that you may often want to use two or even three kinds of tools for the same project. For example, suppose you are interested in writing a report for your geology class on current developments in earthquake research. You might devise a three-step strategy:

1. Use navigation tools (Gopher or the Web) to find documents and services dealing with seismology, earthquake statistics, and fault maps.

15 CHOOSING TOOLS AND USING RESOURCES

2. Look for newsgroups involved with seismology and/or earthquakes, read the regularly updated postings (such as Frequently Asked Questions), and ask for help in finding further information on or off the net.
3. Search specific databases using a retrieval tool, such as WAIS.

15.2 HOW DO I... Choose the right communication tool?

COMPLEXITY | INTERMEDIATE

Problem
Once you decide you have something to say and someone to say it to, you need to pick the right electronic medium for your communications on the Internet.

Technique
Identify your communications needs and goals and compare them to the information in Table 15-1.

Steps
1. Decide whether the communication must be interactive (real time), or can involve responses made over a period of hours or days.

TOOL	PURPOSE	STRENGTHS	WEAKNESSES
Internet Relay Chat (Chapter 5)	Interactive conversation with a group of people	Allows for spontaneous discussion and self-expression	Many channels may be full of immature or inconsiderate users
Mail (Elm) (Chapter 3)	Send individual messages to one or more people	Private, focused, easy to use	Not interactive; responses may be delayed
Mailing lists (Chapter 3)	Regular discussion by people interested in a topic or activity	Has people who share your interests; anyone can set up; can control membership; can be private	Takes work to administer; not as easy for reader to navigate as newsgroup
News (Chapter 4)	Disseminate and discuss information on a topic over a long term	Allows for sustained discussion and sharing of information with a large audience	Large volume of news may make navigation difficult; delay in response
Send/reply (Chapter 5)	Exchange messages with someone who is online	Interactive, immediate	Other person must be online; messages may be distracting or interrupt work
Talk (Chapter 5)	"Party line" conversation with several people	Private, focused, good for online meetings	Requires scheduling so everyone will be available at the same time

Table 15-1 Communication tools

INTERNET HOW-TO

2. Decide whether you want to communicate with a single person, a few individuals, or a larger audience.

3. Look at the communication tools summarized in Table 15-1. Read the descriptions and decide which tool is most likely to meet your needs.

How It Works

The Purpose column in Table 15-1 tells you what kind of communication a particular tool is designed to facilitate. Considering the last two columns (Strengths and Weaknesses) can further help you judge whether you want to use a particular tool for a given purpose.

For example, suppose you want to have a weekly online meeting to discuss the progress of a book project with authors and editors. A look at the Purpose and Strengths columns suggests that the talk program is your most useful tool in this situation.

Comment

There are of course a variety of non-Internet systems (other e-mail services, conference calls, voice conferencing systems, and so on) that you should also consider for your communications needs.

15.3 HOW DO I... Choose the right data retrieval tool?

COMPLEXITY: INTERMEDIATE

Problem

Once you've decided that you will be looking for data in a list, index, or database, you must decide how to go about retrieving the information.

Technique

You determine the kind of data you will be looking for, choose a tool, and connect to the database.

Steps

1. If you already know the name of the data source you will be using, access it and determine what data retrieval system it uses. With Gopher or the Web, for example, you can press = (equal sign) to get a summary description that should include the type of data retrieval used (WAIS, a library catalog system, a general index search, keywords, and so on).

2. If you don't know which data source you will be using, use the techniques described in How-To 15.2 and the navigation tools discussed in How-To 15.4 to research the topic. Note the names, types, and locations of likely data sources as you browse.

3. Once you have a list of one or more sources, check Table 15-2 and note which of the types of data retrieval are available for the particular source. Compare the purpose, strengths, and weaknesses of the retrieval methods and choose the one you think is most likely to be successful.

4. After you've completed a search, evaluate the results. If you're not satisfied, try another available search method, or possibly take another session to browse for additional data sources.

15 CHOOSING TOOLS AND USING RESOURCES

TOOL	PURPOSE	STRENGTHS	WEAKNESSES
Full text index (WAIS, for example)	Retrieve data from databases of text documents	Doesn't require knowledge of keywords or complex searching rules	May retrieve much irrelevant material
Keyword search	Retrieve data records containing specific topics	Easier to control the precise data retrieved	Requires skill and knowledge of valid keywords; may miss records that lack the precise words used
Bibliographical search (library catalogs, for example)	Find books or periodicals	Can search on a variety of fields (author, title, subject); familiar to most people from school days	Only tells you what books or periodicals exist; you still have to physically obtain them
Boolean search (*and, or, not*)	Refine full text or keyword search using relationships between topics	Allows more control over how general or specific a search will be	Requires knowledge of topic relationships; may not be available for many databases

Table 15-2 Data retrieval tools

How It Works

Each database (or list or index) supports certain searching methods. The most common methods are listed in Table 15-2. (Note that Boolean searching or wildcards/regular expressions often can be combined with either a keyword or full-text search.)

From the methods available for a given database, try to choose the one that is most likely to give you useful results. Where applicable, make the search general enough to have a reasonable chance of retrieving all the relevant records, but specific enough not to retrieve a large number of irrelevant hits.

For example, in a bibliographic search by book title, if you are looking for books about air pollution, a search for the word "air" would retrieve far too many irrelevant records. The words "air pollution" should get some specific hits, but you might find that a more general search on "pollution" would also retrieve useful titles, at the cost of having to spend more time browsing the results.

Comment

Database searching is an art. As you become more experienced using a particular database, your searches will become more precise. It is also important to determine the scope and depth of the database. *Scope* means the range of topics covered, and *depth* means the amount and level of detail provided. For example, a consumer health database is going to have a scope and depth different from a medical journal database: the latter will have more highly specialized information.

INTERNET HOW-TO

15.4 HOW DO I...
Choose the right navigation tool?

COMPLEXITY: INTERMEDIATE

Problem
Navigation or browsing tools let you explore the Internet and its resources in an interactive, free-form way. Each browsing tool has its own conceptual "map" or way of looking at the Internet. Tools such as Gopher and the Web are powerful and useful, and the one you choose will depend mainly on the kind of map you are most comfortable with.

Technique
You try out Gopher, the Web, and a variety of offline resource guides. Gradually, you decide which ones you like the best and want to use most frequently.

Steps
1. Familiarize yourself with the operation of Gopher (Chapter 12) and the Web (Chapter 14). Ideally you should devote several sessions to exploring each tool.

2. Try out offline hyptertext resource guides such as The Desktop Internet Reference (How-To 15.5) and Hytelnet (How-To 15.6).

3. Compare the ways each of these tools represents information about resources on the net.

4. Use Table 15-3 as an aid in choosing browsing tools for different purposes.

How It Works
Each browsing or navigation tool has its own way of looking at things. Gopher sees the Internet as a collection of menus that can lead to submenus, individual services, or

TOOL	PURPOSE	STRENGTHS	WEAKNESSES
Gopher	Access menus of services offered by hundreds of servers	Takes advantage of menu hierarchies set up by each institution; grows and changes automatically as new services are offered	No single master hierarchy for all services (though you can gather relevant menu items with Veronica)
World Wide Web	Provide hypertext access to services by subject or server	Easy hypertext access encourages browsing; information well-organized conceptually	Requires true hypertext documents for best use; may be slow, and many items may not actually be available
Offline browser (Desktop Internet Reference, Hytelnet)	Read useful documents about the Internet and find services	Used offline on your own PC; fast; some use Windows or Mac help with mouse	Gets out of date; you must obtain and install new versions; needs a separate step to actually access a service

Table 15-3 Navigation and browsing tools

other Gopher servers. The Web sees the Internet as a web of interlinked hypertext documents. Ideally this results in a kind of "living document" that unfolds as you read, and that can include a variety of services as well as multimedia information (if your browser supports it).

The offline guides are simpler but quite useful. (They are called offline because they aren't directly connected to the Internet, but rather are stand-alone programs on your PC.) These guides are essentially collections of documents and lists organized by topic. You use a simple hypertext system (Hytelnet) or Windows Help (The Desktop Internet Reference) to browse and choose what you want to read. When you find a service, you read the information on how to access it (usually through a telnet command) and enter the appropriate command through your communications software.

Comment
The choices among browsers are often less clear-cut than those among other kinds of tools. You may just happen to be a "Gopher person," while your housemate or partner is a "Web person."

See How-Tos 15.5, 15.6, and 15.7 for more information about offline resource guides.

15.5 HOW DO I... *Use The Desktop Internet Reference?*

COMPLEXITY: INTERMEDIATE

Problem
It is convenient to have a large number of interesting documents and lists about the Internet in one easy-to-access place.

Technique
You use standard Windows Help techniques to browse and access the information contained in The Desktop Internet Reference.

Steps
1. Obtain the latest copy of The Desktop Internet Reference. (Currently the filename is dir10.zip, but a new version might well be out by the time you read this.) You can ftp to ftp.uwp.edu to get the latest version, or consult archie (Chapter 11) for other possible locations.

2. Create a directory for Internet Reference files, copy the .zip file to that directory, and use the pkunzip utility to unpack the files. Use the instructions in the file INSTALL.TXT to finish installing and setting up the software to work with Windows.

3. Use the Windows File/Run menu to run Internet Reference, or double-click on its icon in a program group. You should see a screen like the one in Figure 15-1. This is a standard Windows Help file. (For more information on using Windows Help, see your Windows manual or choose Help from the Program Manager menu.)

4. Click to choose any topic that interests you. (By default, Windows Help puts selectable text in green type.) For example, if you are looking for sources for bibliographic information, click on the item "Databases and Bibliographies" indented under "Libraries on the Internet." You'll see a screen like Figure 15-2.

INTERNET HOW-TO

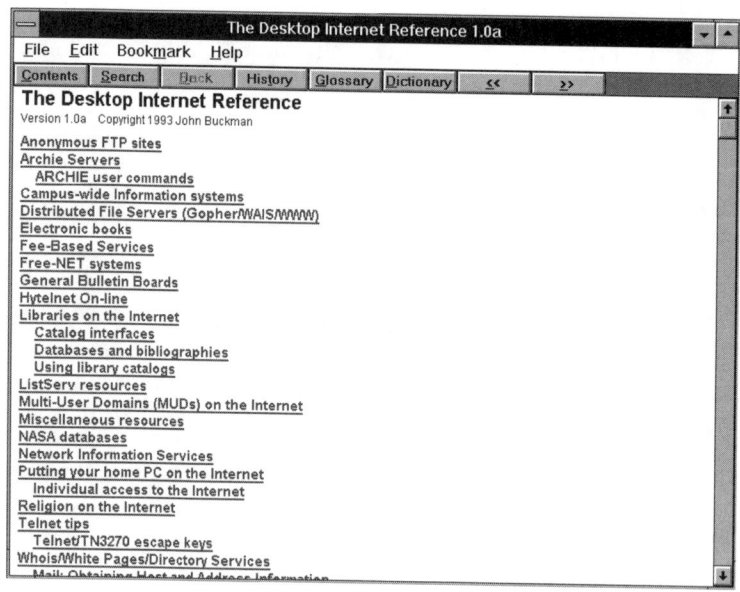

Figure 15-1 Main screen of The Desktop Internet Reference

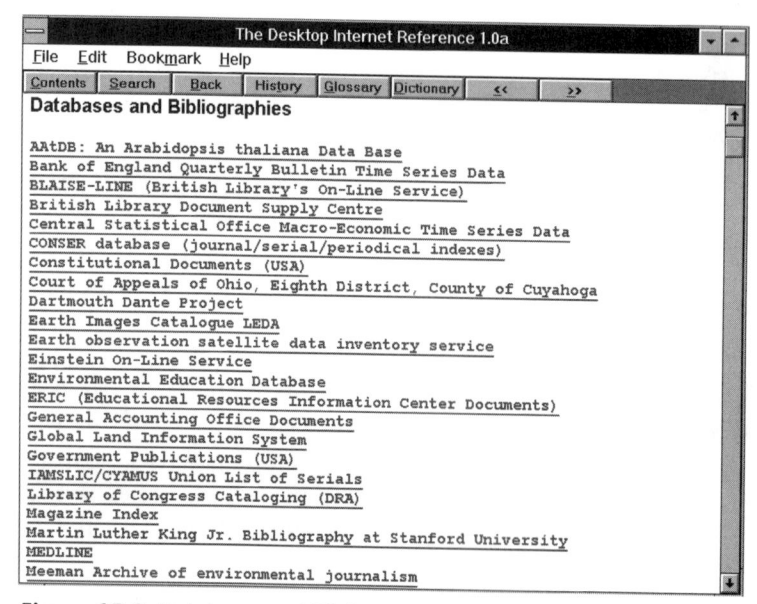

Figure 15-2 Databases and Bibliographies list

5. Choose a source from the list. For example, if you're looking for databases that list periodical titles, you can click on "CONSER database (journal/serial/periodical

15 CHOOSING TOOLS AND USING RESOURCES

```
┌─────────────────────────────────────────────────────────┐
│              The Desktop Internet Reference 1.0a     ▼ ▲│
│ File  Edit  Bookmark  Help                              │
│ ┌────────┬──────┬──────┬───────┬────────┬──────────┬──┬──┐
│ │Contents│Search│ Back │History│Glossary│Dictionary│<<│>>│
│ └────────┴──────┴──────┴───────┴────────┴──────────┴──┴──┘
│ CONSER database                                         │
│                                                         │
│ This database is available at CARL                      │
│ Select menu item 55                                     │
│                                                         │
│              SELECTED DATABASE:   CONSER                │
│                                                         │
│ The CONSER file is a subset of the authenticated MARC CONSER file. It│
│ contains approximately 220,000 bibliographic records for serials that│
│ were coded  c  (current) in byte 6 of the 008 field. Update tapes│
│ containing new records and changes are processed monthly. The records│
│ are cataloged using the same indexing rules that are applied to the CARL│
│ bibliographic files. Libraries may access this file for downloading│
│ bibliographic records through CARL Serials Control.     │
│                                                         │
└─────────────────────────────────────────────────────────┘
```

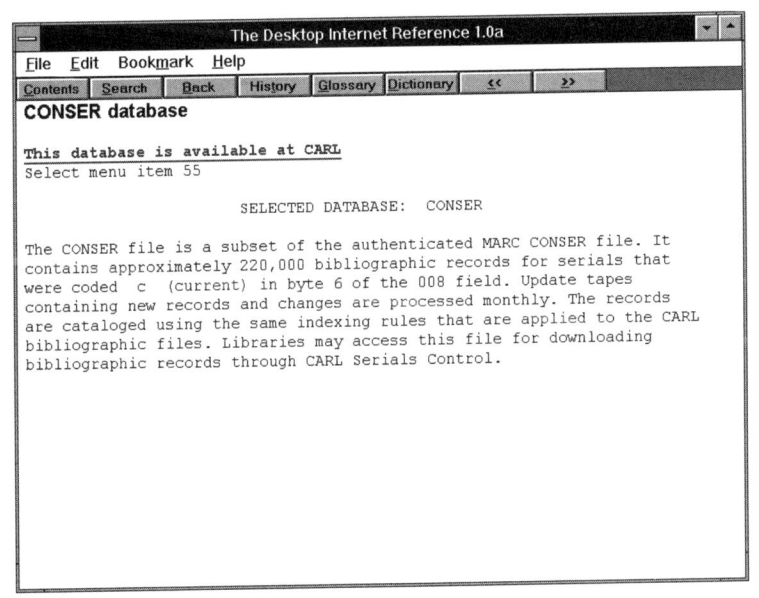

Figure 15-3 Information about the CONSER database

indexes)." You will see a screen that describes this database in more detail (Figure 15-3).

6. Notice that the screen in Figure 15-3 has an underlined link that says "This database is available at CARL." This means that you need to access the entry for CARL (Colorado Alliance of Research Libraries) to find out how to actually telnet to the CONSER database. Click on this link and you'll see the screen in Figure 15-4.

7. To access the service, go to your communications software and type in the appropriate telnet command as shown in the Internet Reference screen. (Note: Unfortunately, Internet Reference gives these commands in all capital letters, and you need to type them in lowercase online. This precludes a simple copy/paste, but they may fix this in a later version.)

```
well% telnet pac.carl.org
Trying 192.54.81.128 ...
Connected to pac.carl.org.
Escape character is '^]'.
```

If the connection is successful, you see CARL's opening messages:

```
WELCOME TO CSI.CARL.ORG [WINDOW $ZT2.#PTY11]
T9553C21 TELNET SERVER 18SEP92 VERSION AAR



Available Services:

EXIT     PAC
Enter Choice>
```

Continued on next page

449

INTERNET HOW-TO

Continued from previous page

```
>>>>

Welcome to the CARL system
Please identify your terminal. Choices are:
1.ADM (all)
2.APPLE,IBM
3.TANDEM
4.TELE-914
5.VT100
6.WYSE 50
7.ZENTEC
8.HARDCOPY
9.IBM 316x
Use HARDCOPY if your terminal type isn't listed
SELECT LINE #:
```

8. Type the number of your terminal and you'll be prompted for the particular CARL service you want:

```
CARL Corporation offers access to the following
                    groups of databases:

              1. Library Catalogs
                     (including Government Publications)

              2. Current Article Indexes and Access
                     (including UnCover and ERIC)
```

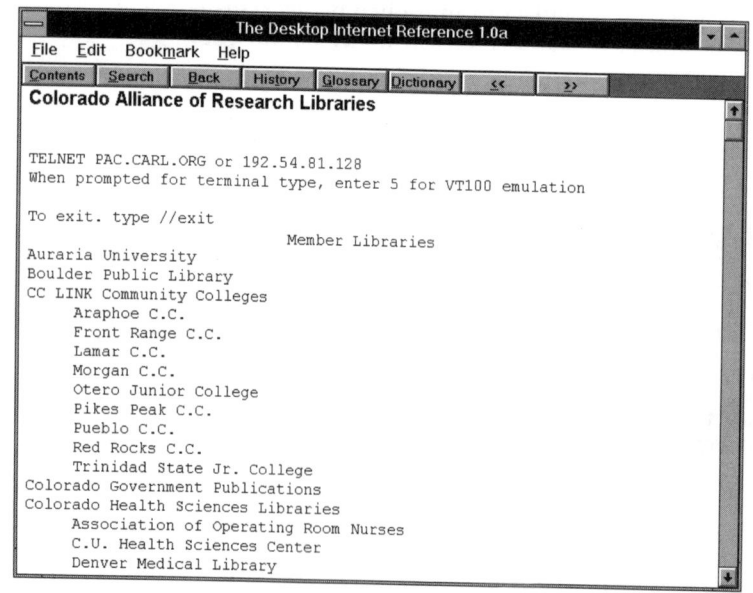

```
┌─────────────── The Desktop Internet Reference 1.0a ───────────┐
│ File  Edit  Bookmark  Help                                    │
│ Contents │ Search │ Back │ History │ Glossary │ Dictionary │ << │ >> │
│ Colorado Alliance of Research Libraries                       │
│                                                               │
│ TELNET PAC.CARL.ORG or 192.54.81.128                          │
│ When prompted for terminal type, enter 5 for VT100 emulation  │
│                                                               │
│ To exit. type //exit                                          │
│                     Member Libraries                          │
│ Auraria University                                            │
│ Boulder Public Library                                        │
│ CC LINK Community Colleges                                    │
│     Araphoe C.C.                                              │
│     Front Range C.C.                                          │
│     Lamar C.C.                                                │
│     Morgan C.C.                                               │
│     Otero Junior College                                      │
│     Pikes Peak C.C.                                           │
│     Pueblo C.C.                                               │
│     Red Rocks C.C.                                            │
│     Trinidad State Jr. College                                │
│ Colorado Government Publications                              │
│ Colorado Health Sciences Libraries                            │
│     Association of Operating Room Nurses                      │
│     C.U. Health Sciences Center                               │
│     Denver Medical Library                                    │
└───────────────────────────────────────────────────────────────┘
```

Figure 15-4 Telnet access information for CARL

15 CHOOSING TOOLS AND USING RESOURCES

```
        3. Information Databases
              (including Encyclopedia)

        4. Other Library Systems

        5. Library and System News

Enter the NUMBER of your choice, and press the <RETURN> key >>
```

Recall that The Desktop Internet Reference screen in Figure 15-3 said that CONSER is service 55. You can type 55 and press (ENTER), thus bypassing the submenu. You'll now see the CONSER search screen in Figure 15-5.

You're ready to complete your database search. (Note that menus and interfaces are constantly changing, as do references from one service to another.)

How It Works

The Desktop Internet Reference contains the necessary telnet commands for accessing hundreds of services. The services are organized by topics using the Windows Help file format. The help screens include opening screens and explanatory text captured from an online session with the service. Once you read the screens, you issue the necessary telnet (or Gopher or WAIS) command to access the service through the Internet.

The Internet Reference contains service information that includes information adapted from the Hytelnet database (see How-To 15.6). In addition to service contact information, the Internet Reference includes a selection of interesting documents about the Internet itself. Some of these are shown at the end of the opening screen in Figure 15-6.

You can also use the Windows Help program's Search facility to find specific items in an Internet Reference screen. Figure 15-7 shows the Search window for the item

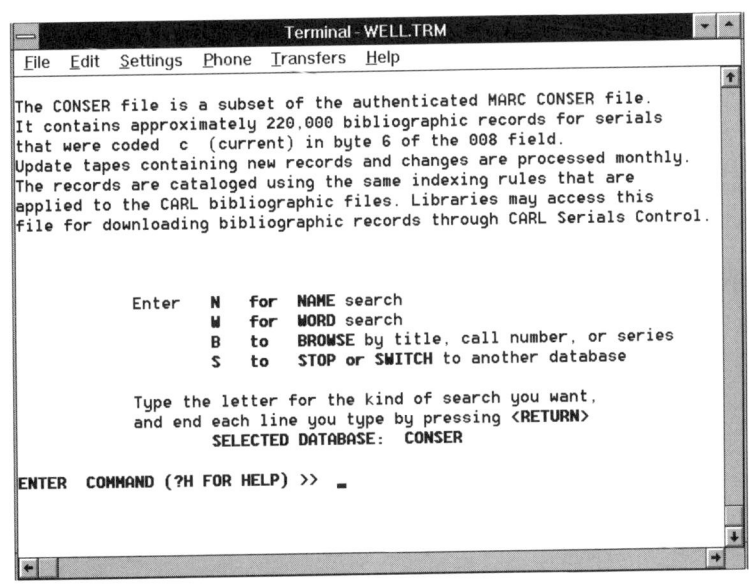

```
┌─────────────────── Terminal - WELL.TRM ──────────────────┐
│ File  Edit  Settings  Phone  Transfers  Help             │
├──────────────────────────────────────────────────────────┤
│ The CONSER file is a subset of the authenticated MARC CONSER file. │
│ It contains approximately 220,000 bibliographic records for serials │
│ that were coded  c  (current) in byte 6 of the 008 field. │
│ Update tapes containing new records and changes are processed monthly. │
│ The records are cataloged using the same indexing rules that are │
│ applied to the CARL bibliographic files. Libraries may access this │
│ file for downloading bibliographic records through CARL Serials Control. │
│                                                          │
│                                                          │
│            Enter  N   for  NAME search                   │
│                   W   for  WORD search                   │
│                   B   to   BROWSE by title, call number, or series │
│                   S   to   STOP or SWITCH to another database │
│                                                          │
│            Type the letter for the kind of search you want, │
│            and end each line you type by pressing <RETURN> │
│                   SELECTED DATABASE:  CONSER             │
│                                                          │
│ ENTER COMMAND (?H FOR HELP) >> _                         │
│                                                          │
└──────────────────────────────────────────────────────────┘
```

Figure 15-5 CONSER search screen

INTERNET HOW-TO

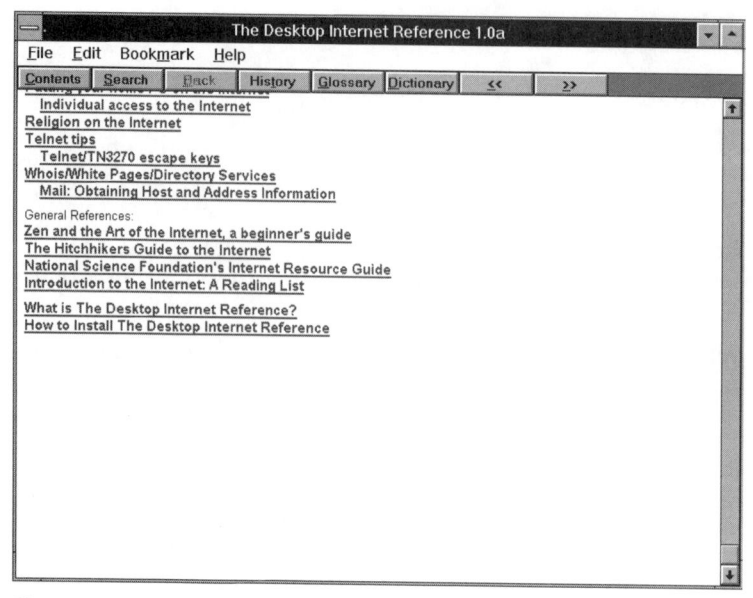

Figure 15-6 General references about the Internet

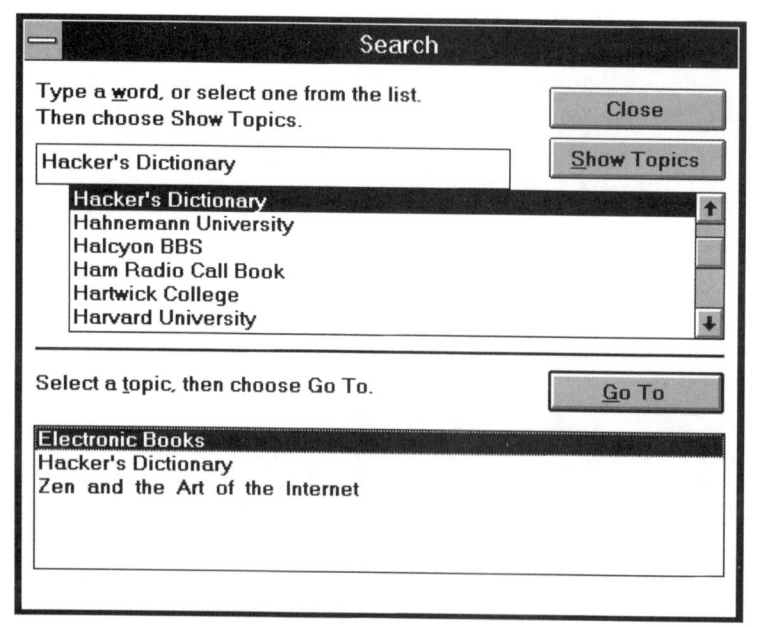

Figure 15-7 Searching for an item in The Desktop Internet Reference

15 CHOOSING TOOLS AND USING RESOURCES

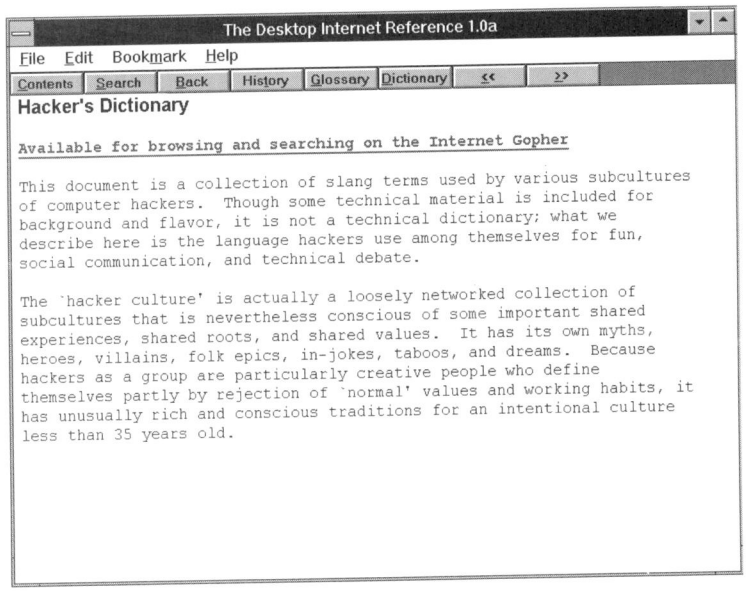

Figure 15-8 Information about the Hacker's Dictionary

"Hacker's Dictionary." (Note Search lets you type the first few letters you want, and it searches as you type, presenting you with lists of matching topics.)

The screen in Figure 15-8 gives more information about the Hacker's Dictionary. Note that this document (unlike, for example, the "Hitchhiker's Guide to the Internet") isn't actually part of the Internet Reference. Rather, you are informed that it is available from Gopher. To access it, you run your Gopher client and browse (or do a Veronica search) to find the particular item (see Chapter 12).

Comment
As you can see, The Desktop Internet Reference is easy to use and takes advantage of Windows features. Its main drawback is that it isn't directly connected to the Internet, so you have to "manually" access the service you want using the commands given.

COMPLEXITY INTERMEDIATE

15.6 HOW DO I...
Find services with Hytelnet?

Problem
A pop-up reference to Internet services can be handy for users of DOS and other systems. Hytelnet (Hypertext TELnet) is an example of such a reference.

Technique
You can install Hytelnet as a resident pop-up program with your DOS communications software, and refer to it before and during your sessions on the Internet.

453

INTERNET HOW-TO

Steps

1. Obtain a copy of the Hytelnet .zip file. This file can be found on CompuServe and other online services, as well as ftp sites.

2. Create a directory for the Hytelnet files and copy the .zip file to it. Use pkunzip to unzip the file. Read the README files for instructions on how to complete the installation.

3. Run Hytelnet at the DOS prompt by typing `hr` and pressing (ENTER). This will install the Hytelnet program in memory.

4. At any time, access Hytelnet from your DOS session by pressing (CTRL)-(BACKSPACE). When you do this, you'll see a main screen like this:

```
Welcome to HYTELNET
                        version 6.3
                        ...................

What is HYTELNET?          <WHATIS>      .    Up/Down arrows MOVE
Library catalogs           <SITES1>      .    Left/Right arrows SELECT
Other resources            <SITES2>      .    F1 for HELP anytime
Help files for catalogs    <OP000>       .
Catalog interfaces         <SYS000>      .    CONTROL/HOME returns here
Internet Glossary          <GLOSSARY>    .    ALT-T quits
Telnet tips                <TELNET>      .
Telnet/TN3270 escape keys  <ESCAPE.KEY>  .
Key-stroke commands        <HELP.TXT>    .


                        ......................
              HYTELNET 6.3 was written by Peter Scott,
      U of Saskatchewan Libraries, Saskatoon, Sask, Canada.  1992




    Screen 1 of 1  FILE: START.TXT                        F1=HELP
```

5. Press (F1) to get help and to learn the navigation keys. You'll see a list like this:

```
                      HELP!

    KEY commands:     Down arrow     Select next Topic
                      Up arrow       Select previous Topic
                      Right arrow    Jump to next Topic
                      Left arrow     Return to previous Topic

    SCREEN commands:  Page control   PgUp/PgDn/Home/End
                      Scroll Up      - (minus key)
                      Scroll Down    + (plus key)
```

15 CHOOSING TOOLS AND USING RESOURCES

```
OTHER commands:  F1           Help (this screen)
                 Esc          Leave (program stays in memory)
                 Control Home Main menu
                 Alt-T        Remove from memory
```

6. Navigate to the topic you're interested in. For example, you can use the ↓ key on the first screen to highlight "Other Resources" and then press → to jump to a list of services:

```
Other Telnet-accessible resources

         <ARC000>  Archie: Archive Server Listing Service
         <CWI000>  Campus-wide Information systems
         <FUL000>  Databases and bibliographies

         <DIS000>  Distributed File Servers (Gopher/WAIS/WWW)
         <ELB000>  Electronic books
         <FEE000>  Fee-Based Services

         <FRE000>  FREE-NET systems
         <BBS000>  General Bulletin Boards
         <HYT000>  HYTELNET On-line versions

         <NAS000>  NASA databases
         <NET000>  Network Information Services
         <DIR000>  Whois/White Pages/Directory Services

         <OTH000>  Miscellaneous resources

Screen 1 of 1   FILE: SITES2                              F1=HELP
```

7. Choosing "NASA databases" gets you the following:

```
NASA Databases

<NAS013> Astronomical Data Center
<NAS015> Coastal Zone Color Scanner Browse Facility
<NAS010> COSMIC Online Information Services
<NAS006> ENVIROnet (The Space Environment Information Service)
<NAS014> International CEDAR Data Base
<NAS001> NASA/IPAC Extragalactic Database
<NAS011> NASA Mid-continent regional technology transfer center BBS
<NAS002> NSSDC Online Data and Information Service (NODIS)
<NAS005> NASA Science Internet (NSI) Online Network Data
<NAS003> NASA Spacelink
<NAS008> NSSDC-National Space Science Data Center
<NAS009> Pilot land data system
<NAS007> PDS (Planetary Data System)
<NAS017> Space Data and Computing Division Information Service
<NAS004> Space Physics Analysis Network Information Center SPAN_NIC
<NAS016> Standards and Technology Information System

       Screen 1 of 1   FILE: NAS000                       F1=HELP
```

INTERNET HOW-TO

8. Finally, choose a specific service to get a description and instructions for telnet access:

```
Astronomical Data Center

Telnet NSSDCA.GSFC.NASA.GOV or 128.183.10.4
At username type NODIS
Select from NODIS main menu

              Welcome to the Astronomical Data Center (ADC)
              Online Information System for Astronomical Catalogs

This is a system for obtaining information about, and interactively
requesting, any of the ADC's more than 600 astronomical catalogs.
Catalogs are available on: the NASA Science Internet and NSI/DECnet
computer networks;  9-track magnetic tape; microfiche and/or microfilm
and CD-ROM.  Not all catalogs are available in all forms. The Online
System will tell you what is available and how it can be sent to you.

           Please forward any questions, comments, or suggestions to:
                       Astronomical Data Center, Code 933
                       NASA Goddard Space Flight Center
                       Greenbelt, MD 20771 U.S.A.
                       TEL: (301) 286-8310, FTS 888-8310

        For Catalog and Request Inquiries :
                   Ms. Gail L. Schneider
   Screen 1 of 2   FILE: NAS013                                 F1=HELP
```

How It Works

Hytelnet uses a simple hypertext system to provide access to lists of servers along with descriptions and contact information. The DOS version's "terminate and stay resident" (TSR) programming enables you to access the information with your communications program while online.

Comment

Hytelnet is most useful for DOS and Unix users (there is a Unix version). Windows users will probably find the Windows Help-based Desktop Internet Reference (How-To 15.5) easier to use.

15.7 HOW DO I...
Create my own resource guide?

COMPLEXITY: INTERMEDIATE

Problem

Prepackaged resource guides can be very useful, but information does change or go out of date. It's also useful to have your own personal database of notes and contact information for Internet resources.

Technique

The basic approach is to combine a simple Windows-based notecard or database program with your communications program. The example here uses a shareware program called WhizNotes.

Steps

1. Set up your Windows database program. (Although it is limited in functionality, the built-in Windows Cardfile program is quite adequate for a simple resource list.) The shareware program WhizNotes, which has more powerful organizational and retrieval facilities, is used here. This program is available on CompuServe and PC-oriented ftp sites.

2. Run your communications program as usual (Windows Terminal, for example).

3. When you find and connect to an interesting Internet service, click on your database program and create an entry for it. (With Cardfile there will be just one card entry per resource. WhizNotes lends itself to a more hierarchical organization by general topics under which specific resources can be organized.)

4. Type a brief description of the resource in your database entry. If you wish, you can copy/paste information from the opening screen in your communications window into the database. Be sure to include the appropriate connection command (telnet, or Gopher, for example). Figure 15-9 shows an example of a WhizNote for the Library of Congress catalog records service at dra.com.

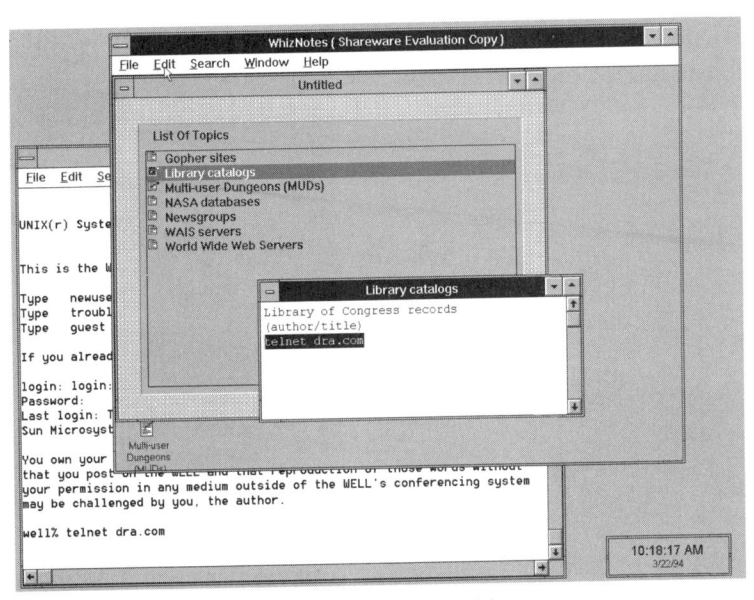

Figure 15-9 Creating your own resource guide

INTERNET HOW-TO

5. The next time you want to access the service, look it up in your database, run your communications program, and copy/paste the telnet or other connection command directly to the system prompt at your local Internet site.

How It Works
This procedure illustrates the power of Windows-type systems to let you combine various tools into customized systems. You can mix and match your choice of communications programs and index or database programs to build a resource guide that will be available whenever you connect to the Internet.

Comment
You can of course add whatever notes you want to your database, including hours of operation, a summary of the strengths and weaknesses of each resource, and so on.

15.8 HOW DO I...
Find out more about the Internet?

COMPLEXITY: EASY

Problem
The Internet is always growing and changing, and there is so much to explore.

Technique
Use a variety of approaches to explore the existing capabilities of the Internet and to keep up with future developments.

Steps
1. Familiarize yourself with Usenet newsgroups that deal with Internet tools and with the net in general. The nngrep program (Chapter 4) can help you find appropriate newsgroup names. Here are some to start with:

```
alt.bbs.internet
alt.best.of.internet
alt.culture.internet
alt.internet.access.wanted
alt.internet.services
comp.infosystems
comp.infosystems.announce
comp.infosystems.gis
comp.infosystems.gopher
comp.infosystems.interpedia
comp.infosystems.wais
comp.infosystems.www
comp.internet.library
vmsnet.infosystems.gopher
vmsnet.infosystems.misc
```

2. Search the news.answers newsgroup for FAQ (Frequently Asked Questions) files about Internet-related topics such as WAIS and Gopher.

3. Search for Gopher items with Veronica, using words such as "Internet" or "networking" as well as the names of specific tools (Gopher, WAIS, WWW, and so on). Also look for Gopher menus with titles such as "About the Internet." These

15 CHOOSING TOOLS AND USING RESOURCES

items will take you to "A Hitchhiker's Guide to the Internet" and other documents about the net.

4. Browse the World Wide Web using topics related to the Internet.
5. Obtain copies of interesting online documents such as the introductory readings found in the newsgroup news.announce.newusers.
6. Check out your local bookstore for detailed tutorials, references, and resource guides for the Internet. You may wish to supplement this book with a detailed reference. Two books that the author has found useful are

> *The Whole Internet User's Guide and Catalog,* Second Edition, by Ed Krol (Sebastopol: O'Reilly and Associates, 1994)

> *The Internet Complete Reference,* by Harley Hahn & Rick Stout (Berkeley: Osborne McGraw-Hill, 1994)

You can also find reviews of books on the Internet and other technical subjects in the newsgroups alt.books.technical and misc.books.technical.

How It Works
There are many sources of information about the Internet. There are many books on the Internet, and even a magazine called "Internet World." While you can expect the variety of printed materials to grow, many of the best documents are available on the Internet itself.

Comment
Generally speaking, online sources are likely to be more up to date about resources. Books are more useful for general philosophy and strategy and for detailed tutorials on particular programs.

Index

$ prompt, 21, 69, 191, 207, 244
% prompt, 21, 69, 191, 207, 244
< character in Unix, 56
> character in Unix, 194
@ in addresses, 59
@ in IRC, 174

A

A (ASCII/text) type, 240
acceptable use, 32-35
access tools, 439
addresses
    address book, 42, 69-72
    deciphering, 41, 58-60
    domain name system, 58
    finding, 41, 60-65
    other networks, 92
    president, 70
    vice-president, 70
alias files, 56, 72
alias/nickname, 42, 158, 173-174, 178, 243-244
alias system, 40, 97
aliases, 44, 66, 69-72. *See also* alias/nickname
America Online, 1, 92
anonymous ftp sites, 223, 227-229
anonymous as username, 227
antivirus, 35-37
Apple II, xv
Applelink, 92
apropos program, 284-285
arc file extension, 257, 264
arc program, 253, 264-266
archie program, 6, 229, 326
    clients, 327, 328-330
    command switches, 327-328, 337-339
    data displays, 328, 341-342
    data by mail, 328, 344
    data sorting, 328, 342-344
    features, 327-328, 337-339
    help, 327, 334-337
    by mail, 328, 347-348
    option switches, 334-337
    search by keyword, 328, 345
    search types, 328, 339-341
    servers, 327, 330-334
    and Unix commands, 328, 346-347
    and WWW, 435-436
archive files, 269-273
    shar files, 107, 140-141, 253, 256, 271-273
    tar files, 255-256, 269-271

archive programs, 253-254
archive sites, xiv
arj file extension, 257
awk program, 347

B

backbone (distribution site), 32, 125
bar (pipe), 77, 258, 260, 264, 271, 341-342
BBS (bulletin board system), xiv
binary files, 107, 138-140, 250
    archive, 250, 253
    btoa (binary to ASCII), 251, 255, 259-260
    capture of, 282, 287
    compressed, 250, 251-254
    encode/decode, 250-251, 255, 257-260
    executable, 250
    ftp, 226, 234, 236-237, 247
    graphics, 250
    mailing, 255, 257-258
    PostScript, 250
    sound, 250
    WAIS, 406
BinHex program, 267
Bitnet, 92
blocks (packets), 276, 289
bookmarks (Gopher), 353-354, 361-363, 381
bookmarks (Lynx), 414, 428
Boolean operators, 355, 379, 398, 445
Boolean options, 80, 145, 184
bots, 156, 169
bounce command, 68
"broken sockets" message, 399
browser programs, 8-9, 412-413, 415
browsing tools, 439, 442, 446-447
btoa (binary to ASCII), 251, 255, 259-260
buffers, 202, 206, 344

C

Caesar cipher (rot 13), 137-138
"cannot open <filename>" message, 193
carbon copies of mail, 89
case-sensitivity, 35, 53, 80, 143-144, 151, 195
    in archie, 338-340
    in Lynx, 424
charges for use, 13-15, 311, 316
CIA World Factbook, 386, 408
client, 11
"command not found" message, 356, 387, 415
commas, use of, 49, 56, 89, 178, 337

INTERNET HOW-TO

Commodore 64, xv
communication in real time, 155-156
communication tools, 439, 441, 443-444
communications protocol, 276
compare files, 190, 211-212
compress/uncompress, 255, 264-268
compressed files, 237, 255, 260-268, 271
Compression (reference), 254, 261, 266
CompuServe, 1, 92
conferencing, 22. *See also* newsgroups
connect charges, 14-15, 311, 316
connecting to Internet, 16, 17-20
connecting to programs, 307, 308-310
connecting to services, 307, 308-310
"connection failed" message, 399
"connection refused" message, 229, 353
connections, changing (telnet), 307, 313-314
conversation (real-time), 158, 163-167
    carrying on, 158, 175-177
    finding, 158, 174-175
    invitation to join, 159, 181
    multiparty, 158, 165-167
copy files, 189, 209-210
    in Lynx, 414, 424-425
    in WAIS, 387, 401-402
courtesy. *See* etiquette
cracking programs, 36
crash recovery, 288-289
"Csh: permission denied" message (ftp), 242
CSO directory, 355, 375
customizing Elm, 42, 80-85
customizing nn, 108, 145-147, 149-151
cyberspace, xiii

D

daemon, 65, 160
data retrieval tools, 439, 441, 444-445
database searches
    Gopher, 355, 376, 378-379
    Lynx, 414, 422-424
    WAIS, 383-387, 396-399
        refined, 387, 402-404
        streamlined, 387, 408-409
    World Wide Web, 415, 431-432
databases, 8
decode/encode, 251, 257-260
decryption/encryption, 37, 43, 91, 137-138
delete files, 190, 212-213
Delphi, 92
Desktop Internet Reference, 306, 441, 446-453
dial-up connection, 11-13
directory
    current, 189, 199-200
    list, 189, 195-199, 226, 231-233
    make, 190, 213-214
    online, 355, 374-376
    remove, 190, 213-214

"directory not empty" message, 193
discussion groups, 22. *See also* newsgroups
disk space, 35, 190, 218-219
disk usage charges, 96, 212, 260
download files (Gopher), 355, 368-369
downloading, 277

E

e-mail. *See* mail
edit files, 189, 200-202
electronic mail. *See* mail
Elm mail program, 2, 40
    Alias Mode, 44, 69-72, 100-101
    customizing, 42, 80-85
    defaults, changing, 42, 80-85
    error messages, 65
    Filter System Guide, 78
    help system, 41, 48-49, 97-101
    Index, 44, 47, 97-98
    key command help screens, 97-101
    Message Header Edit, 88-89
    learn more about, 43, 96-101
    Options Editor, 44, 80-85, 98-99
    print command, 54
    system commands and, 42, 89-90
encode/decode, 251, 257-260
encryption/decryption, 37, 43, 91, 137-138
error-correcting protocol, 276
error messages
    Elm, 65
    ftp, 229, 240, 242
    Gopher, 353, 356
    Lynx, 415, 419
    mail, 65
    telnet, 309
    Unix commands, 192-193
    WAIS, 387, 398-399, 402
error in syntax, 192
escape character, 308, 311-312, 315, 317
etiquette on the Internet, 32-35
    conversations, 167, 169, 183, 185
    flames, 34, 124, 141
    harassment, 159, 183
    nicknames, 173
    Usenet, 119, 124, 125
exe file extension, 257
extensions, 237, 255, 256-257, 264

F

FAQ (Frequently Asked Questions) files, 17, 29-32
    on compression, 254
    with ftp, 223
    in Usenet newsgroups, 109, 458
    with WAIS, 386
Fidonet, 92
file access permissions, 219-221

INDEX

file capture, 234-235, 280, 281-282, 287
file compression, 237, 255, 260-268, 271
file extensions, 237, 255, 256-257, 264
file group, get, 226, 237-239
file list, 226, 231-233
file transfer failures, 276-277
file transfer protocols, 276-280, 283-286. *See also* ftp
file transfer with rcp, 308, 322-323
files. *See* archive files *and* binary files *and* text files
filter program, 76, 97
filters for mail, 42
find files, 190, 215-216
find text in a file, 190, 216-217
finger command, 42, 60, 65, 86
    for online status, 159, 163, 165
flames, 34, 124, 141
folders for mail, 42
forums, 22. *See also* newsgroups
forward command, 67-68
Freenets, 14
ftp (file transfer protocol) program, 22, 222-226
    anonymous ftp sites, 223, 227-229
    client, 224
    commands
        !, 225, 242
        ?, 225, 229
        ascii, 225, 240
        binary, 225, 236-237, 240, 247
        cd, 225, 231, 233
        cdup, 225, 231
        close, 225
        dir, 225, 231
        get, 225, 233, 235
        hash, 225, 241
        help, 225, 229
        lcd, 225, 234
        ls, 225, 231-233, 243
        mget, 225, 237-239
        open, 225, 228
        prompt, 225, 241
        put, 225, 239-240
        pwd, 225, 231
        quit, 225, 245-246
        send, 225, 239-240
        status, 225, 241
        user, 225, 227-229
        verbose, 241
    commands, help for, 229-231
    commands, lists, 224-225, 230
    error messages, 229, 240, 242
    exit (bye), 228, 234
    get files, 254
    help, 27-28, 226, 229-231
    -l option, 232
    by mail, 227, 245-247
    navigating, 231
    options, 227, 240-242
    public directory, 223

    server, 224, 227
    server connections, 226, 227-229, 243-244
    tutorials, 223
ftp sites through WWW, 415, 435-436
full-text indexing, 385, 445

G

gateways, 43, 92-93
GEnie, 1, 92
get file (ftp), 226, 233-234
get file group (ftp), 226, 237-239
get files by mail (Gopher), 354, 367
GIF files, 140
Gopher, 6-7, 350-353
    All the Gopher Servers of the World, 350, 357, 361
    bookmarks, 353-354, 361-363, 381
    client, 7
    connections, 354, 360-362
    database search, 355, 376, 378-379
    directory, 355, 374-376
    download files, 355, 368-369
    error messages, 353, 356
    and ftp sites, 355, 369-371
    get files by mail, 354, 367
    Gopher Jewels, 350
    help, 354, 358-360
    item types, 354, 363-365
    Jughead, 352, 355, 380-381
    keyword combining, 355, 378-379
    menus, 354, 357-358
    navigating, 354, 357-358
    online directory, 355, 374-376
    read files, 354, 365-366
    save files, 355, 367-368
    servers, 7, 354, 356-357, 361
    subject tree, 355, 371-373
    and telnet, 355, 373-374
    Veronica, 8, 350, 352, 355, 376-379, 438, 458
    and World Wide Web, 415, 437-438
goto command, 126-128, 132-133, 137
graphical user interface (GUI), 12-13, 17, 188, 412-413
grep utility, 217, 347
gz file extension, 257
gzcat, 262
gzip/gunzip, 253, 260-262

H

harassment, 159, 183
hardware requirements, xv
help keys, 26
help systems
    archie, 327, 334-337
    Elm, 41, 48-49, 97-101
    ftp, 27-28, 225, 226, 229-231
    Gopher, 354, 358-360
    Internet, 16, 17, 22-24, 26-29

INTERNET HOW-TO

help systems *(continued)*
    Internet Relay Chat, 158, 171-172
    Lynx, 414, 420-422
    nn, 106, 112-115, 152-153
    telnet, 307, 311-313
    Unix, 188, 193-195
    WAIS, 386, 395-396
Hitchhiker's Guide to the Internet, 233, 246-247, 459
hits (matching documents), 397
host, xiv
"host inaccessible" message, 65
"host not found" message, 229
"host unavailable" message, 229
"host unknown" message, 65, 309
HTML (Hypertext Markup Language) format, 416, 418
huh utility, 157, 162
hqx file extension, 257
hypertext, 8, 411-412
hypertext links, 412, 416, 418-419
"hypertext resource not available" message, 419
Hytelnet (Hypertext TELnet), 441, 446-447, 453-456

I

I (image/binary) type, 236
"illegal option" message, 193
Inter-Network Mail Guide, 93
interactive communication, 155-156
Internet
    access, 13-15
    connections, 11-13
    host, 276
    planning approach, 440-443
    providers, 15-16
    reference file, 306, 441, 446-453
    reference guides, 223, 441, 458-459
    responsible use, 17, 32-35
    site, xiv
Internet Relay Chat. *See* IRC
Internet Starter Kit, 15
InterNIC, 15-16
IP (Internet Protocol), 12
IRC (Internet Relay Chat), 4, 156, 158, 169-172
    channel, start your own, 159, 181-182
    channels, 174-176
    commands, 158, 170-171
    help, 158, 171-172
    primer, 185
    reference guides, 159, 185
    settings, 159, 184-185
    tracking users, 158, 180-181
    tutorials, 185
    user identification, 158, 178-179

J

job control feature, 320, 330
Jughead, 352, 355, 380-381

jump command, 126-128, 132-133, 137

K

Kermit, 6, 54, 225, 276
    using, 280-281, 283-286, 291-298

L

lharc program, 264-266
lhz file extension, 257, 264
Library of Congress records, 314, 318-319
line kill character, 49, 73, 82
line noise, 276
links, 412, 416, 418-419
Listserv program, 93-94
local area network (LAN), 17
local system, 224, 227, 242
log out, 20
login names/IDs, 20, 56, 58, 92
login script, 281, 299-301
lurking, 3
Lynx program, 9, 412-413, 415-416
    bookmarks, 414, 428
    connection, 414-416
    copy document, 414, 424-425
    error messages, 415, 419
    follow hypertext link, 414, 418-419
    help, 414, 420-422
    history page, 427
    navigating, 417-419, 428
    online manual, 421
    read document, 414, 416-417
    recall document, 414, 427-428
    save document, 414, 424-425
    send comment to author, 414, 425-427
    text search, 414, 422-424

M

macros, 108, 150-151
mail on the Internet
    address book, 42, 69-72
    address deciphering, 41, 58-60
    address finding, 41, 60-65
    e-mail (electronic mail), 1, 40
    encryption/decryption, 43, 91
    exchange between networks, 43, 92-93
    filing mail folders, 42, 43, 73-74
    filter automatically, 42, 76-78
    forward, 42, 66-68
    forward automatically, 42, 78
    grouping mail, 42, 79-80
    header editing, 42, 88-89
    headers, 47
    inbox folder, 54
    information about, 42, 68-69
    mail folders, 73-78

INDEX

mail programs, 1-2, 40
mailing lists, 43, 93-96
message status, 44
printing mail, 41, 53-54
reading mail, 41, 43-48
reading mail folders, 42, 74-76
replying to mail, 41, 49-51
returned mail, 41, 65-66
search by sender/subject, 41, 52-53
sending file with mail, 41, 57
sending mail, 41, 54-56
transport agent, 55
user ID (finger), 42, 85-86
user ID (signature), 42, 87
managing sessions with windows, 16-17, 25-26
manual, online (Gopher), 360
manual, online (Lynx), 421
manual, online (nn), 27, 106, 113-115
manual, online (Unix), 28, 193-195, 229-231, 334
MCI Mail, 92
messages
   error. *See* error messages
   headers, edit, 88-89
   private, 177-178
   recall, 157, 162-163
   reply, 157, 161-162
   screening, 158, 167-169
   send, 157-161, 177-178
   status, 44
   unwanted, 158, 167-169
move files, 190, 210-211

N

name server program, 59-60
navigating
   in ftp, 231
   in Gopher, 354, 357-358
   in Lynx, 417-419, 428
   in newsgroups, 107, 129-130
   in mail programs, 46
   in Usenet, 107, 129-130
navigation tools, 439, 411, 446-447
netfind program, 62
newmail program, 68-69
news on the Internet
   article distribution, 123-124
   article posting, 107, 122-125
   collect by subject, 108, 148-149
   excluding unwanted articles, 108, 141-143
   follow-up, 106, 107, 121-122
   grouping articles, 106, 115-116, 117-119
   hierarchy, 104
   mail reply to article, 107, 119-121
   read articles, 106, 108-111
   read encrypted articles, 107, 137-138
   read folder, 107, 136-137
   save to a file, 107, 134-135
   save to a folder, 107, 135-136
   saving articles with binary files, 107, 138-140
   select articles, 106, 108-111, 115-117
   select articles automatically, 108, 143-144
   unread news, catching up, 108, 144-145
newsgroups, xiv, 30, 104
   jumping to, 107, 126-128
   moderated, 122, 125
   navigating, 107, 129-130
   presentation sequence, 107, 130-132
   search, 107, 132-134
nickname/alias, 42, 158, 173-174, 178, 243-244
NixPub (Unix public access), 15
nn news program, 3, 105
   article reading commands, 110-111, 153
   article reading mode, 105
   article selection commands, 109-110, 153
   article selection mode, 105
   consolidated-menu option, 117-119
   customization, 108, 145-147, 149-151
   encryption/decryption, 137-138
   features, 152-153
   greeting screen, 105-106
   help system, 106, 112-115, 152-153
   init file, 127, 129-132, 149-151
   key command changes, 108, 149-150
   key map entries, 149
   learn more about, 108, 152
   newsgroup navigation, 105
   online manual, 106, 113-115
   options, 145-147
   settings, 108, 145-147, 149-151
   shortcuts (macros), 108, 150-151
   system commands and, 108, 147-148
   variables, 145-147
nngrab utility, 108, 148-149
nngrep program, 30, 107, 132-134, 458
"no such directory" message, 193
"no such file" message, 193
NSFNET Backbone, 32-33

O

online directory, 355, 374-376
online manual (Gopher), 360
online manual (Lynx), 421
online manual (nn), 27, 106, 113-115
online manual (Unix), 28, 193-195, 229-231, 334

P

packets, 276, 289
pager program, 24
parsing commands, 192
passwords, 20, 35-37, 91, 227, 243-244
pathname, 195
pattern matching, 79-80
PDIAL list, 15

"permission denied" message, 193, 240, 242, 402
permissions, file access, 219-221
permissions, shell access, 242
pipe, 77, 258, 260, 264, 271, 341-342
pkzip/pkunzip, 236, 252-253, 261, 264-266, 329
port number, 308, 314
PostScript, 97, 250
PPP (Point-to-Point Protocol), 13
printmail program, 53
privacy. *See* security issues
private files, 190, 219-221
private messages, 177-178
Prodigy, 1, 92
public access site (Gopher), 356
public data network, 14-15
public directory (ftp), 231

Q

quit command (ftp), 225, 245-246

R

rcp (remote copy) command, 307, 308, 322-323
reading files, 189, 200-202
    in ftp text file, 226, 234-236
    in Gopher, 354, 365-366
    in Lynx, 414, 416-417
    in WAIS, 387, 400-401
reading news, 107, 136-138
recall messages, 157, 162-163
regular expressions, 128, 217, 340
relevance feedback, 385, 397, 403-404
remote program, control of, 307, 314-316
remote system, 20, 224
remote system, log on, 307, 310-311
rename files, 190, 210-211
reply program, 3, 156
replying to messages, 157, 161-162
requirements, xv
resource guides, 440, 441, 456-458
retries, 276
Return=Enter, 19
rlogin, 303-308, 320-323
rm (remove/delete) command, 74
rot 13 (Caesar cipher), 137-138

S

safety tips, 17, 35-37
saving files
    in Gopher, 355, 367-368
    in Lynx, 414, 424-425
    shar, 107, 140-141
saving news, 107, 135-136, 138-140
saving settings, 281, 298-299
screening messages, 158, 167-169
sea file extension, 257

search tools, 439, 441, 444-445
security issues
    encryption, 37, 43, 91, 137-138
    login ID, 244, 300
    mail, 55, 91
    private files, 190, 219-221
    private messages, 177-178
    rlogin connection, 307, 321-322
    safety tips, 17, 35-37
    shell access, 90, 242
send file (ftp), 226, 239-240
send private messages, 158, 177-178
send program, 3, 156
send real-time messages, 157, 159-161
sendmail program, 40
server, 11
session file, 281, 298-299
shar file extension, 257
shar (shell archive) files, 253, 256, 271-273
    saving, 107, 140-141
shareware, 4, 457
shell archives. *See* shar
shell escape, 161, 242
shell out, 42
shell script, 56, 253, 346-347
shell variables, 184
shells (Bourne, Korn, C)
    access, 90
    terminal emulation, 21-22
    user settings, 68-69, 173, 191, 207, 244
sit file extension, 257
SLIP (Serial Line Internet Protocol), 13
software requirements, xv
string search, 328, 331-332, 340, 422-424
StuffIt program, 252, 254, 257, 267-268, 332-333
subscribe/unsubscribe to lists, 94
subscribe/unsubscribe to newsgroup, 107, 126-127
swais (simple WAIS) program, 384, 387, 401
syntax error, 192
sysop (system operator), 34, 36, 78

T

tagging, 42, 79-80
talk program, 4, 156, 158
tar file extension, 257
tar files, 255-256, 269-271
tar (tape archive) program, 253-254
"target temp must be a directory" message, 193
tarmail program, 271
TCP (Transmission Control Protocol), 12
telecommunications, 281
telnet program, 6, 62, 303-320
    commands list, 312
    connections, changing, 307, 313-314
    error messages, 309
    help, 307, 311-313
    settings, 308, 316-317

INDEX

suspend, 308, 318-320
terminal emulation, xv, 16, 18, 20-22, 204, 208
Terminal program, xv, 17
text (ASCII) files, 189, 200-207, 250
text transfer, 280, 282-283
"this hypertext resource..." message, 419
toggle, 80, 111, 146, 240-241
tools, 439-440
TRS-80, xv

U

"unable to connect to..." message, 353
unacceptable uses, 33-34
Unix operating system, 187-188
    commands
        cat, 189, 201-202
        cd, 189, 199
        chmod, 189, 221, 243
        cmp, 189, 211-212
        cp, 189, 209-210
        du, 189, 218-219
        find, 216
        head, 189, 202
        learn, 222
        ls, 189, 195-199, 219
        man, 189, 193-195
        mesg y, 208
        mkdir, 189, 213-214
        more, 189, 200-202
        mv, 189, 210-211
        pwd, 199, 218
        rm, 189, 212-213
        rmdir, 189, 213-214
        stty, 208
        umask, 208, 220-221
        vi, 189, 202-207
        whereis, 215-216
    commands, entering, 188, 190-192
    commands, help for, 188, 193-195
    error messages, 192-193
    learn more about, 190, 222
    manual, online, 28, 193-195, 229-231, 334, 360
    options
        -a, 198, 214
        -i, 209
        -k, 218
        -l, 197, 212, 219
        -n, 217
        -r, 210
    pipe, 77, 258, 260, 264, 271, 341-342
    tutorials, 222
"unknown host" message, 309
unsubscribe to lists, 94
unsubscribe to newsgroup, 107, 126-127
uploading, 277
URL (Uniform Resource Locator), 414-415, 416, 429-430
use standards, 32-35

Usenet, 30, 104, 108, 415, 432-434, 458.
    See also news and newsgroups
user agent, 40
user settings, 189, 207-208
    and shells, 68-69, 173, 191, 207, 244
"user unknown" message, 65
usernames, 20, 56, 58, 92
usernames (anonymous), 227
uudecode, 139, 251, 257-260
uue file extension, 257
uuencode, 251, 257-260

V

Veronica, 8, 350, 352, 355, 376-379, 438, 458
vertical bar. See pipe
vi text editor, 49-51, 189, 202-207
virus, 35-37
VT-100 terminal, xv, 18, 20, 22, 388

W

WAIS (Wide Area Information Service), 8, 383-386
    clients, 386, 387-390
    copy document, 387, 401-402
    database selection, 386, 390-395
    error messages, 387, 398-399, 402
    and Gopher, 387, 405-408
    help, 386, 395-396
    learn more about, 387, 409-410
    options, 387, 399-400
    permission denied message, 402
    read document, 387, 400-401
    search, 386-387, 396-399
        refined, 387, 402-404
        streamlined, 387, 408-409
    sources, 384, 386, 390-395
    and telnet, 387
Weather Underground, 304-305, 308-309
whatis database, 326, 345
WhizNotes program, 457
whois command, 60
whois server, 61
wildcards
    and directories, 199, 210, 213
    and file groups, 190, 212, 214, 237
    with keyword search, 379
    and mail, 75
    with regular expressions, 128, 132
windowing environment, 25, 282, 357
windows (managing sessions), 16-17, 25-26
World Wide Web (WWW), 8, 412-413
    and archie, 435-436
    and ftp sites, 415, 435-436
    and Gopher, 415, 437-438
    search, 415, 431-432
    Uniform Resource Locator, 414-415, 416, 429-430
    and Usenet news, 415, 432-434

INTERNET HOW-TO

and Veronica, 438

X
Xmodem, 6, 54, 139, 148, 225, 280, 283-291
xwais program, 384

Y
yellow pages, electronic, 6-7, 374-376
Ymodem, 6, 280, 283-291

Z
Z file extension, 257
zcat, 261-264
zip file extension, 257, 264
Zmodem, 6, 280, 283-291, 369
zoo file extension, 257

ENVIRONMENTAL AWARENESS

Books have a substantial influence on the destruction of the forests of the Earth. For example, it takes 17 trees to produce one ton of paper. A first printing of 30,000 copies of a typical 480-page book consumes 108,000 pounds of paper which will require 918 trees!

Waite Group Press™ is against the clear-cutting of forests and supports reforestation of the Pacific Northwest of the United States and Canada, where most of this paper comes from. As a publisher with several hundred thousand books sold each year, we feel an obligation to give back to the planet. We will therefore support and contribute a percentage of our proceeds to organizations which seek to preserve the forests of planet Earth.

WAITE GROUP PRESS™

CREATE STEREOGRAMS ON YOUR PC
Dan Richardson

Stereograms are an astonishing new art form. At first glance, it appears to be a collection of random speckles, but when your eyes are focused on the image in a certain way, a full depth 3D picture appears. This book/disk combination provides step-by-step instructions for creating your own stereograms, suitable for printing and framing, on any IBM PC. The disk contains a complete set of graphics software tools to create 3D illusions on your PC.

September 1994 • 200 pages
ISBN: 1-878739-75-1
U.S. $26.95 Can. $37.95
Disk 1 - 3.5"

THE ROAD TO 2015
PROFILES OF THE FUTURE
John L. Petersen

This is an extraordinary time in history—dozens of "nologies" from nanotech to biotech are colliding in ways that promise to alter the very fabric of our daily lives. This book holds the key to unraveling these "threads of the future" for understanding and prospering in this coming age of flux. It provides an easy to read road map of the next 20 years in our planet's history—a bold projection of all that is possible in our lifetimes.

September 1994 • 300 pages
ISBN: 1-878739-85-9
U.S. $18.95 Can. $37.95
Level: Beginner-Intermediate
Category: Current Events

SIMPLE INTERNET
Jeffrey M. Cogswell

Simple Internet is an unique approach to learning the Internet: a detective story parody that actually leads you through the Internet. Assuming the identity of Archie Finger, a normal, bagel-eating, technophobic private eye, you'll unravel a mystery embedded in the Net. Once you've solved the mystery, you'll have a solid understanding of what the Net is all about.

September 1994 • 175 pages
ISBN: 1878739-79-4
U.S. $16.95 Canada $23.95

EROTIC CONNECTIONS
LOVE AND LUST ON THE INFORMATION HIGHWAY
Billy Wildhack

Cold silicone and hot blood? Whatever you're looking for, there's a real possibility of finding it electronically. You can meet people "on-line" and get to know them, without surrendering your privacy. This book gives you step-by-step instructions on how to enter and use the adult-oriented bulletin board systems (BBS).

November 1994 • 300 pages
Level: Beginning
ISBN: 1-878739-78-6
platform: DOS
U.S. $24.95 Can. $37.95
Category: Cybersex/Telecomm

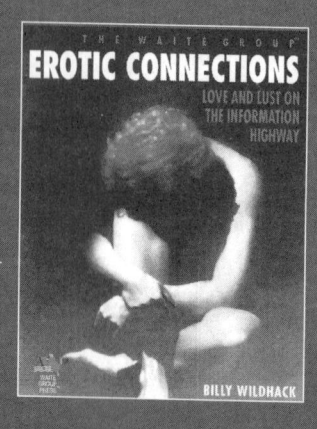

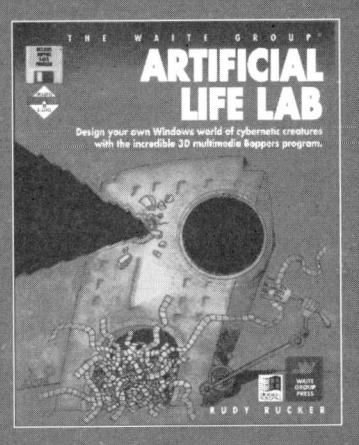

WAITE GROUP PRESS™

SIMPLE C++
Jeffrey Cogswell

Use POOP (Profound Object-Oriented Programming) to learn C++! Write simple programs to control ROBODOG in this entertaining, beginner-level programming book.

Available Now • 240 pages
ISBN:1-878739-44-1
U.S. $16.95 Can. $23.95

ARTIFICIAL LIFE LAB
Rudy Rucker

Run a bug society as you see fit. This book and colorful Windows application explain the rules of life and show how to program Turmites and Boppers to sound off, die off, or live off of each other. See the bugs in depth with 3D glasses.

Available now • 250 pages
ISBN: 1-878739-48-4
U.S. $34.95 Can. $48.95
(1 - 3.5" disk and 3D glasses)

USING COMPUSERVE TO MAKE YOU RICH
Terry R. Dettmann and
Susan Futterman

Manage your investments on-line. Novices will appreciate the introduction to stocks, mutual funds, bonds, and securities, and pros will find useful tips and valuable sources of information.

Available Now • 160 pages
ISBN: 1-878739-63-8
U.S. $26.95 Can. $37.95
(2 - 3.5" disks)

TO ORDER TOLL FREE CALL 1-800-368-9369
TELEPHONE 415-924-2575 • FAX 415-924-2576
OR SEND ORDER FORM TO: WAITE GROUP PRESS, 200 TAMAL PLAZA, CORTE MADERA, CA 94925

Qty	Book	US/Can Price	Total
___	Artificial Life Lab	$34.95/48.95	___
___	Create Stereograms	$26.95/37.95	___
___	Erotic Connections	$24.95/37.95	___
___	Road to 2015	$18.95/37.95	___
___	Simple C++	$16.95/23.95	___
___	Simple Internet	$16.95/23.95	___
___	Using CompuServe to Make You Rich	$26.95/37.95	___

Calif. residents add 7.25% Sales Tax   ___

Shipping
USPS ($5 first book/$1 each add'l)   ___
UPS Two Day ($10/$2)
Canada ($10/$4)
TOTAL

Ship to
Name _____
Company _____
Address _____
City, State, Zip _____
Phone _____

Payment Method
☐ Check Enclosed   ☐ VISA   ☐ MasterCard

Card#_____ Exp. Date _____
Signature _____

SATISFACTION GUARANTEED OR YOUR MONEY BACK.

SATISFACTION REPORT CARD

Please fill out this card if you wish to know of future updates to
Internet How-To, or to receive our catalog.

Company Name: _____

Division/Department: _____ Mail Stop: _____

Last Name: _____ First Name: _____ Middle Initial: _____

Street Address: _____

City: _____ State: _____ Zip: _____

Daytime telephone: ( ) _____

Date product was acquired: Month _____ Day _____ Year _____ Your Occupation: _____

Overall, how would you rate *Internet How-To*?
☐ Excellent ☐ Very Good ☐ Good
☐ Fair ☐ Below Average ☐ Poor

What did you like MOST about this book? _____

What did you like LEAST about this book? _____

How did you use this book (problem-solver, tutorial, reference...)? _____

What is your level of computer expertise?
☐ New ☐ Dabbler ☐ Hacker
☐ Power User ☐ Programmer ☐ Experienced Professional

What computer languages are you familiar with? _____

Please describe your computer hardware:
Computer _____ Hard disk _____
5.25" disk drives _____ 3.5" disk drives _____
Video card _____ Monitor _____
Printer _____ Peripherals _____
Sound Board _____ CD ROM _____

Where did you buy this book?
☐ Bookstore (name): _____
☐ Discount store (name): _____
☐ Computer store (name): _____
☐ Catalog (name): _____
☐ Direct from WGP ☐ Other _____

What price did you pay for this book? _____

What influenced your purchase of this book?
☐ Recommendation ☐ Advertisement
☐ Magazine review ☐ Store display
☐ Mailing ☐ Book's format
☐ Reputation of Waite Group Press ☐ Other

How many computer books do you buy each year? _____

How many other Waite Group books do you own? _____

What is your favorite Waite Group book? _____

Is there any program or subject you would like to see Waite Group Press cover in a similar approach? _____

Additional comments? _____

Please send to: Waite Group Press
                  Attn: *Internet How-To*
                  200 Tamal Plaza
                  Corte Madera, CA 94925

☐ Check here for a free Waite Group catalog